CAMBRIDGE STUDIES IN
NORTH AMERICAN INDIAN HISTORY

Editors
Frederick Hoxie, The Newberry Library
Neal Salisbury, Smith College

The middle ground

This book steps outside the simple stories of Indian-white relations – stories of conquest and assimilation and stories of cultural persistence. It is, instead, about a search for accommodation and common meaning. It tells how Europeans and Indians met, regarding each other as alien, as other, as virtually nonhuman, and how between 1650 and 1815 they constructed a common, mutually comprehensible world in the region around the Great Lakes that the French called the *pays d'en haut*. Here the older worlds of the Algonquians and of various Europeans overlapped, and their mixture created new systems of meaning and of exchange. Finally, the book tells of the breakdown of accommodation and common meanings and the re-creation of the Indians as alien and exotic.

The middle ground

Indians, empires, and republics in the Great Lakes region, 1650–1815

RICHARD WHITE

CAMBRIDGE
UNIVERSITY PRESS

Published by the Press Syndicate of the University of Cambridge
The Pitt Building, Trumpington Street, Cambridge CB2 1RP
40 West 20th Street, New York, NY 10011-4211, USA
10 Stamford Road, Oakleigh, Melbourne 3166, Australia

© Cambridge University Press 1991

First published 1991
Reprinted 1992, 1993, 1994, 1995

Printed in the United States of America

Library of Congress Cataloging-in-Publication Data is available.

British Library Cataloging in Publication applied for.

ISBN 0-521-37104-X hardback
ISBN 0-521-42460-7 paperback

Contents

Abbreviations

DHNY *Documentary History of the State of New York*, edited by E. B. O'Callaghan (Albany, N.Y.: Weed, Parsons, 1850–51)

HBNI *Handbook of North American Indians*, edited by William C. Sturtevant (Washington, D.C.: Smithsonian Institution, 1978–   )

IHC *Collections of the Illinois Historical Library* (Springfield, Ill.: The Trustees of the Illinois State Historical Library, 1915–40)

JP *The Papers of Sir William Johnson*, edited by James Sullivan et al. (Albany: University of the State of New York, 1921–65)

JR *The Jesuit Relations and Allied Documents*, edited by Reuben Gold Thwaites (Cleveland, Ohio: Burrows Brothers, 1898)

MPA *Mississippi Provincial Archives, French Dominion* (Jackson: Press of the Mississippi Department of Archives and History, 1927–84)

MPHC *Michigan Pioneer Historical Society: Collections and Researches* (Lansing, Mich.: The Society, 1877–1929)

NYCD *Documents Relative to the Colonial History of the State of New York; Procured in Holland, England and France, by John R. Brodhead*, edited by E. B. O'Callaghan (Albany, N.Y.: Parsons, Weed, 1853–87)

PA *Pennsylvania Archives* (Philadelphia, Pa.: Joseph Severns; Harrisburg: Commonwealth of Pennsylvania, 1852–1949)

PCR *Minutes of the Provincial Council of Pennsylvania from the Organization to the Termination of Proprietary Government*, edited by Samuel Hazard (Harrisburg, Pa.: Theophilus Fenn, 1838–53)

RAPQ *Rapport de l'Archiviste de la Province de Québec* (Quebec: Ls-A. Proulx, 1921–28; Redempti Paradis, 1929–44)

WHC *Collections of the State Historical Society of Wisconsin*, edited by Lyman C. Draper and Reuben G. Thwaites (Madison, Wis.: The Society, 1855–1911)

Introduction

Stories of cultural contact and change have been structured by a pervasive dichotomy: absorption by the other or resistance to the other. A fear of lost identity, a Puritan taboo on mixing beliefs and bodies, hangs over the process. Yet what if identity is conceived not as [a] boundary to be maintained but as a nexus of relations and transactions actively engaging a subject? The story or stories of interaction must then be more complex, less linear and teleological.

James Clifford, *The Predicament of Culture*

The history of Indian-white relations has not usually produced complex stories. Indians are the rock, European peoples are the sea, and history seems a constant storm. There have been but two outcomes: The sea wears down and dissolves the rock; or the sea erodes the rock but cannot finally absorb its battered remnant, which endures. The first outcome produces stories of conquest and assimilation; the second produces stories of cultural persistence. The tellers of such stories do not lie. Some Indian groups did disappear; others did persist. But the tellers of such stories miss a larger process and a larger truth. The meeting of sea and continent, like the meeting of whites and Indians, creates as well as destroys. Contact was not a battle of primal forces in which only one could survive. Something new could appear.

As many scholars have noted, American myth, in a sense, retained the wider possibilities that historians have denied American history. Myths have depicted contact as a process of creation and invention. With Daniel Boone and his successors, a "new man" appeared, created by the meeting of whites and Indians, a product of the violent absorption of the Indians by the whites. Myth, however, only partially transcended the stories of conquest and resistance. Only whites changed. Indians disappeared. Whites conquered Indians and made them a sacrifice in what Richard Slotkin called a "regeneration through violence."

The story told in this book steps outside these simpler stories and incorporates them in a more complex and less linear narrative. The book is about a search for accommodation and common meaning. It is almost circular in form. It tells how Europeans and Indians met and regarded each other as alien, as other, as virtually nonhuman. It tells how, over the next two centuries, they constructed a common, mutually comprehensible world in the region around the Great Lakes the French called the *pays d'en haut*. This world was not an Eden, and it should not be romanticized. Indeed, it could be a violent and sometimes horrifying place. But in this world the older worlds of the Algonquians and of various Europeans overlapped, and their mixture created new systems of meaning and of exchange. But finally, the narrative tells of the breakdown of accommodation and common meanings and the re-creation of the Indians as alien, as exotic, as other.

In this story, the accommodation I speak of is not acculturation under a new name. As commonly used, *acculturation* describes a process in which one group becomes more like another by borrowing discrete cultural traits. Acculturation proceeds under conditions in which a dominant group is largely able to dictate correct behavior to a subordinate group. The process of accommodation described in this book certainly involves cultural change, but it takes place on what I call the middle ground. The middle ground is the place in between: in between cultures, peoples, and in between empires and the nonstate world of villages. It is a place where many of the North American subjects and allies of empires lived. It is the area between the historical foreground of European invasion and occupation and the background of Indian defeat and retreat.

On the middle ground diverse peoples adjust their differences through what amounts to a process of creative, and often expedient, misunderstandings. People try to persuade others who are different from themselves by appealing to what they perceive to be the values and practices of those others. They often misinterpret and distort both the values and the practices of those they deal with, but from these misunderstandings arise new meanings and through them new practices – the shared meanings and practices of the middle ground.

This accommodation took place because for long periods of time in large parts of the colonial world whites could neither dictate to Indians nor ignore them. Whites needed Indians as allies, as partners in exchange, as sexual partners, as friendly neighbors. The processes of the middle ground were not confined to the groups under discussion here. Indeed, a middle ground undoubtedly began among the Iroquois and the Hurons during a period earlier than the one this book examines. The middle ground was not simply a phenomenon of the *pays d'en haut*, but this mutual accommodation had a long and full existence there. The *pays d'en haut*, or upper country, was the land upriver from Montreal, but strictly speaking it did not begin until the point where voyageurs passed beyond Huronia on the eastern shore of Lake Huron. The *pays d'en haut* included the lands around Lake Erie but not those near southern Lake Ontario, which fell within Iroquoia. It took in all the Great Lakes and stretched beyond them to the Mississippi. In the seventeenth century, the *pays d'en haut* included the lands bordering the rivers flowing into the northern Great Lakes and the lands south of the lakes to the Ohio. As the French fur trade expanded, the *pays d'en haut* expanded with it, but in the frame of this book, the *pays d'en haut* retains its original boundaries.

I have, with some reluctance, referred to the people living within the *pays d'en haut* as Algonquians. The term is admittedly problematic. *Algonquian* refers to a language group the domain of whose speakers stretched far beyond the *pays d'en haut*. And not all the peoples of the *pays d'en haut* were Algonquian speakers. The Huron-Petuns were Iroquoian as, later, were the offshoots of the Iroquois – the Mingos. The Winnebagos were Siouan. I have, however, taken the term as a collective name for the inhabitants of the *pays d'en haut* because Algonquian speakers were the dominant group, and because with the onslaught of the Iroquois, the Algonquians forged a collective sense of themselves as people distinct from, and opposed to, the Five Nations, or the Iroquois proper. Most, and often all, of these villagers of the *pays d'en haut* were also enemies of the Sioux and of the peoples south of the Ohio. A collection of individually weak groups – originally refugees – these villagers created a common identity as children of Onontio, that is, of the French governor. I have imposed the name "Algonquian" on them to distinguish them from Onontio's other children, with whom they often had little contact.

In writing this history of the *pays d'en haut*, I am practicing the "new Indian history." But as new histories age, they become, in part, new orthodoxies while surreptitiously taking on elements of the older history they sought to displace. This book is "new Indian history" because it places Indian peoples at the center of the scene and seeks to understand the reasons for their actions. It is only incidentally a study of the staple of the "old history" – white policy toward Indians. But this book is also, and indeed primarily, a study of Indian-white relations, for I found that no sharp distinctions between Indian and white worlds could be drawn. Different peoples, to be sure, remained identifiable, but they shaded into each other.

For the purposes of this book, many of the conventions of both the new history and the old are of dubious utility for understanding the world I seek to explain. I am, for example, describing imperialism, and I am describing aspects of a world system. But this is an imperialism that weakens at its periphery. At the center are hands on the levers of power, but the cables have, in a sense, been badly frayed or even cut. It is a world system in which minor agents, allies, and even subjects at the periphery often guide the course of empires. This is an odd imperialism and a complicated world system. Similarly, the European writings of the period on Indians – the endless dissertations on the *sauvage* (savage) – become of marginal utility for understanding a world where Europeans living alongside Indians of

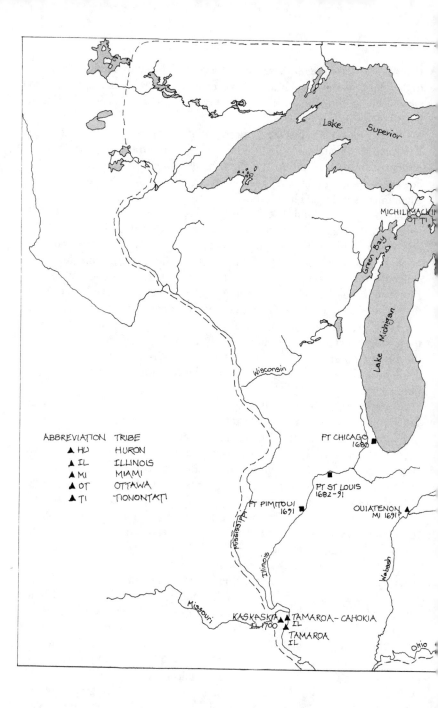

ABBREVIATION   TRIBE

▲ HU   HURON
▲ IL   ILLINOIS
▲ MI   MIAMI
▲ OT   OTTAWA
▲ TI   TIONONTATI

Lake Superior

MICHILIMACKIN
OT TI

Green Bay

Lake Michigan

Wisconsin

FT CHICAGO
1680

FT ST LOUIS
1682-91

FT PIMITOUI
1671

OUIATENON
MI 1691

Mississippi

Illinois

Wabash

Missouri

KASKASKIA
IL 1700

TAMAROA - CAHOKIA
IL

TAMAROA
IL

Ohio

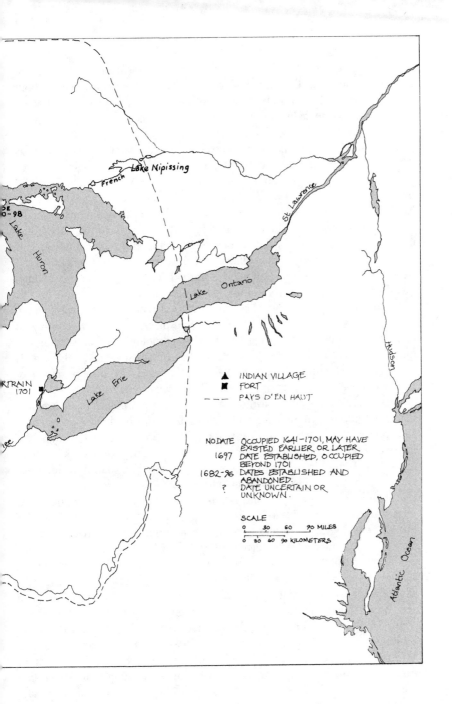

Lake Nipissing

French

Lake Huron

-98

Lake Ontario

St. Lawrence

Hudson

RTRAIN
1701

Lake Erie

ee

Atlantic Ocean

▲ INDIAN VILLAGE
■ FORT
— — — PAYS D'EN HAUT

NO DATE OCCUPIED 1641–1701, MAY HAVE
         EXISTED EARLIER OR LATER
  1697   DATE ESTABLISHED, OCCUPIED
         BEYOND 1701
1682–96 DATES ESTABLISHED AND
         ABANDONED.
    ?   DATE UNCERTAIN OR
         UNKNOWN.

SCALE
0   30   60   90 MILES
0   30 60 90 KILOMETERS

necessity developed a far more intimate and sophisticated knowledge of Indian peoples than did European savants. What Rousseau thought about Indians matters, but to understand the *pays d'en haut*, it does not matter as much as what the habitants of Vincennes or Kaskaskia thought, or what Onontio, the French governor at Quebec, thought.

The usual conventions of writing about Indians were as unhelpful as unmodified ideas about imperialism, world systems, or savagery. Ethno-historians have increasingly come to distrust the tribe as a meaningful historical unit, and the *pays d'en haut* was certainly not a place where tribal loyalties controlled human actions. I have used tribal designations through-out this book, but they should be understood largely as ethnic rather than political or even cultural designations. The meaningful political unit in this study is the village, and Indian villages usually contained members of several tribes, just as Anglo-American villages in the backcountry usually contained members of several different ethnic groups.

I have also tried to avoid the ethnohistorical technique of upstreaming, although diligent readers will, I am sure, find places where I have indulged in it. Upstreaming is a technique of using ethnologies of present-day or nineteenth-century Indian groups to interpret Indian societies of the past. If assimilationist studies have a built-in bias toward the disappearance of earlier culture, then upstreaming has a bias toward continuity.

I have similarly tried to avoid using the term *traditional* to convey any meaning but old. The Indian people I describe in this book have no essential Indianness. They are people who for a long time resolutely fought the European tendency to create them as the other. They asserted a separate identity, but they also claimed a common humanity in a shared world. They lost the fight to establish that claim, and this book is in part the story of that loss. Just as anthropologists and ethnologists have come to recognize how they, through their research, create the other as object, it is time for historians and ethnohistorians to pay more attention to such creations in the past and their own roles in perpetuating and adding to them.

The world of the *pays d'en haut*, then, is not a traditional world either seeking to maintain itself unchanged or eroding under the pressure of whites. It is a joint Indian-white creation. Within it well-known European and Anglo-American names appear: the Comte de Frontenac, Sir Jeffrey Amherst, William Johnson, Daniel Boone, George Washington, Benjamin Franklin, and Thomas Jefferson. So, too, do well-known Indian names such as Pontiac and Tecumseh. That so many names significant in the larger American history occur in this story without dominating it indicates that the parameters of American history need readjusting. Colonial and early-American historians have made Indians marginal to the periods they de-scribe. They have treated them as curiosities in a world that Indians also helped create.

This was a world created in the midst of great and far-reaching changes. To readers it may seem a world in perpetual crisis, but this is partially an artifact of the way I tell the story and of the nature of the records. I open with the onslaught of the Iroquois, who may appear initially as a deus ex machina. The wars of the Iroquois proper, or the Five (later Six) Nations, were, however, a result of changes as complicated as any I present here. The reader should not mistake their warfare for "normal" Indian warfare in North America. It, too, was a complex product of European expansion. By devoting a key part of the first portion of the book to the Fox, and by focusing a middle portion of the book on the confrontation along the Ohio, I emphasize the major crises of the alliance. This tactic is necessary because in crises the relations among these people emerged most clearly and also because the crises generated the most records. It should be remembered, however, that during most of the time between 1680 and 1763, the vast majority of Algonquians remained Onontio's loyal children.

The real crisis and the final dissolution of this world came when Indians ceased to have the power to force whites onto the middle ground. Then the desire of whites to dictate the terms of accommodation could be given its head. As a consequence, the middle ground eroded. The American Republic succeeded in doing what the French and English empires could not do. Americans invented Indians and forced Indians to live with the consequences of this invention. It is the Americans' success that gives the book its circularity. Europeans met the other, invented a long-lasting and significant common world, but in the end reinvented the Indian as other. Ever since, we have seen the history of the colonial and early republican period through that prism of otherness.

I would not have undertaken the research for, and writing of, this book if I had recognized the amount of labor it would involve. Indeed, this volume, which I originally envisioned as centering on Tecumseh, has become a *Tristram Shandy* of Indian history. It ends with what was once to be its beginning. Tecumseh becomes the product of an older history, not the creator of a new one.

The book is the result of extensive research in French, Canadian, British, and American archives. I decided to use the most accessible source whenever possible in citing the result of my labors in footnotes. Hence I cite published documents when they are available and manuscript documents only when there is no reliable published version. When a translation seems unreliable or incomplete, I say so in the footnote and use the manuscript document.

Because I found so much that surprised me and found my perspective on the period changing as the research for this book proceeded, I have, with one minor exception, refrained from publishing any of this material in an earlier form for fear I would only have to repudiate it later. I have, however, presented parts of this research as papers at various forums at the University of Chicago, the University of Arizona, Michigan State University, the University of Utah, the University of California at San Diego, and the D'Arcy McNickle Center of the Newberry Library. I would like to thank those who read all or parts of the manuscript. First, of course, are the editors of the series in which this volume appears, Fred Hoxie and Neal Salisbury, and Frank Smith of Cambridge University Press, but also Bill Cronon, James Clifton – who, luckily, demolished some of my earlier formulations – Marty Zanger, Ramon Gutierrez, Pat Albers, and Beverly Purrington. I would also like to thank Dean Anderson, whose excellent dissertation at Michigan State University, fortunately, coincided with my own examination of the fur trade. Dean's work on the material exchange involved in the trade is far more detailed and comprehensive than the small parts I have cited here, and interested readers should consult his dissertation. Helen Tanner's *Atlas of Great Lakes Indian History* served as the basis for the maps in this book, and I owe her a scholarly debt.

I would also like to thank for their financial assistance the Rockefeller Foundation, the Guggenheim Foundation, and the University of Utah, where I taught most of the time while this book was being prepared. The Rockefeller and Guggenheim foundations, in particular, were both generous and patient, and I am grateful for their aid. At Utah, Larry Gerlach, who chaired the History Department, made the department both a pleasant and a stimulating place to work. This is an achievement that only those who have had experience with the higher administration at the University of Utah, and the constraints on education in Utah, can appreciate.

1

Refugees: a world made of fragments

Human populations construct their cultures in interaction with one another, and
not in isolation.

Eric Wolf, *Europe and the People Without History*

I

The Frenchmen who traveled into the *pays d'en haut*, as they called the lands
beyond Huronia, thought they were discovering new worlds. They were,
however, doing something more interesting. They were becoming cocreators
of a world in the making. The world that had existed before they arrived was
no more. It had been shattered. Only fragments remained. Like a knife
scoring a pane of glass, warfare apparently far more brutal than any known
previously among these peoples had etched the first fine dangerous lines
across the region in the 1640s. Broad cracks had appeared, as epidemics of
diseases unknown before in these lands carried off tens of thousands of
people. And then, between 1649 and the mid-1660s, Iroquois attacks had
fallen like hammer blows across the length and breadth of the lands
bordering the Great Lakes and descended down into the Ohio Valley.

The Iroquois desired beaver and the hunting lands that yielded them, and
they wanted captives to replace their dead or to atone at the torture stake
for their loss. The coupling of the demands of the fur trade with Iroquois
cultural imperatives for prisoners and victims created an engine of destruction
that broke up the region's peoples. Never again in North America would
Indians fight each other on this scale or with this ferocity. Amid the slaughter
people fled west. The largely Algonquian-speaking world west of Iroquoia
broke up, and the Iroquois pushed the fragments west.[1]

Shattered peoples usually vanish from history, and many of the Iroquoian
peoples – the Eries, the Neutrals – who fell before the epidemics and the

---

[1] For recent accounts of the Iroquois wars, see Francis Jennings, *The Ambiguous Iroquois Empire*
(New York: W. W. Norton, 1984), 84–113; Daniel Richter, "War and Culture: The Iroquois
Experience," *William and Mary Quarterly* 40 (1983): 528–59; and Bruce Trigger, *The
Children of Aataentsic: A History of the Huron People to 1660*, 2 vols. (Montreal: McGill-Queens
University Press, 1972), 2:767–97, 820–21.

warfare, disappeared as organized groups. But most Algonquians did not disappear. Instead, together with Frenchmen, they pieced together a new world from shattered pieces. They used what amounted to an imported imperial glue to reconstruct a village world. This village world sustained, and was in turn sustained by, the French empire.

The story of the creation of this world forms the beginning of this book, and it must begin with the often horrific fragments left by the shattering of the old. To write a coherent story of the Iroquois hammer striking Algonquian glass, historians have traced the blows of the hammer. When they have featured the victims of the Iroquois, they have written about other Iroquoians – the Hurons, Petuns, Neutrals, and Eries – because these groups either had Jesuit missionaries among them or lived beside neighbors that did. They have not concentrated on the shattering Algonquian world, because it is hard to tell a story of fragmentation. And in any case, the very events grew vague as the Iroquois blows fell farther and farther west among peoples the French barely knew. When the French did come to know these peoples, the blows were still falling and the story seemed only chaos.

The result is a historical landscape that consists largely of dim shadows. There are tribal traditions collected a century and a half or more after the fact. There are the memories of French traders – their recollections in old age of a youth among strangers. There are contemporary accounts, vivid renderings of events in which details are unfamiliar and without apparent meaning. Thus a fractured society has been preserved in fractured memory. To pretend this world exists otherwise is to deceive. And in any case, this fragmentary, distorted world is, for the historian, good enough. For the history in question during the horrible years of the mid and late seventeenth century is a history of perceptions, of attempts to make sense, of attempts to create coherence from shattered parts. For the French and the refugees alike, older patterns and older routines were in collapse. For all concerned this was a world where dreams and nightmares happened. It was a desperate world where accidental congruences and temporary interests became the stuff from which to forge meaning and structure. The fragments are the history. It is, therefore, a world best initially perceived in fragments, as both Algonquians and Frenchmen perceived it and tried to make sense of its danger, strangeness, and horror.

The horror that the Iroquois would bring to the *pays d'en haut* was first prefigured by another confederation of Iroquoian-speaking peoples. The Neutrals, soon themselves to become Iroquois victims, obtained iron weapons from Europeans when their enemies to the west still relied on stone. In the mid-1640s a large Neutral war party "to the number of 2,000" attacked a stockaded Algonquian village in Michigan. These Algonquians were a people the Neutrals called the Nation of Fire. Most likely, they were Fox or Mascoutens. After a siege of ten days, the Neutrals captured the fort. They killed many on the spot, but they retained eight hundred captives – men, women, and children. Of these, they burned seventy warriors. The old men had a crueler fate. The Neutrals put out their eyes and girdled their mouths, leaving them to starve in a land they could no longer see.[2]

As Iroquois attacks depopulated the lands around Lake Ontario, refugees fled west and the Iroquois followed. Refugee Ottawas and remnants of the Hurons and Petuns fled in stages as pressure from the Iroquois increased. In 1653 eight hundred Iroquois cornered their prey at Green Bay, one of the stops on this staggered flight west. Many of the besiegers were, it turned out, "the offspring of the people whom they had come to attack." Far from their original home, Hurons adopted by the Iroquois attacked refugee Hurons. For a long time, the Iroquois besieged the fort and villages. But in this siege it was the attackers rather than the besieged who grew hungry, and so eventually the two sides negotiated a truce. In exchange for food and a safe withdrawal, the Iroquois agreed to surrender the Hurons who were among them.

Some of these Hurons, however, had developed ties to their captors. On the eve of the departure of the Iroquois, the Ottawas at Green Bay gave each Iroquois warrior a loaf of poisoned corn bread. A Huron woman, who had married an Iroquois man but had fled west with the refugees, knew the secret. She told her son, who, apparently, had come with the Iroquois, not to eat the bread. The son informed the Iroquois of the plot, and they escaped.

The salvation of the Iroquois proved temporary. They divided into two parties. The smaller party went north, where warriors from the bands of the people who were to become the Chippewas and the Mississaugas attacked and defeated them. Few escaped. The main force pushed south into the prairie country. They reached a small Illinois village. The men fled, and the Iroquois killed the women and children. But other Illinois were nearby, and the warriors surprised and overwhelmed the Iroquois. In this warfare their deaths only became the seeds for new attacks.[3]

The Iroquois onslaught did not halt other wars in the *pays d'en haut*, and sometime during the Iroquois wars, four or five hundred Miami warriors marched against their southern enemies. In their absence, a band of Senecas destroyed their village. Only one old woman, left for dead, survived. She told

---

[2] *JR* 27:25–27.
[3] Nicolas Perrot, *Memoir on the Manners, Customs, and Religion of the Savages of North America*, in Emma Helen Blair (ed.), *The Indian Tribes of the Upper Mississippi Valley and Region of the Great Lakes*, 2 vols. (Cleveland: Arthur H. Clark, 1911), 1:151–56.

Habit of an Ottawa Indian.

Although such portraits emphasized the exoticism of Indians, the trade blanket, the trade beads, and the breech cloth all testify to the mixing of European and Indian worlds. (Mackinac State Historic Parks)

the returning Miamis that the Senecas had marched the women and children east.

Every night as the Senecas traveled home, they killed and ate a Miami child. And every morning, they took a small child, thrust a stick through its head and sat it up on the path with its face toward the Miami town they had left. Behind the Senecas came the pursuing Miamis, and at every Seneca campsite, brokenhearted parents recognized their child.

When the Senecas were within a day's march of their own village, they sent their people a message telling them to prepare a great kettle and spoon to enjoy the good broth they were bringing them. It was at this last campsite that the pursuing Miami warriors at last caught the Senecas. But the Senecas had guns and the Miamis did not, and so the Miamis decided to set an ambush rather than attack the camp directly.

Two Miami spies watched the Seneca camp. And that night, as usual, for the evening meal one of the Senecas decapitated a child and prepared its body for the kettle. Hearing a noise outside the camp, the cook tossed the head into the bushes and told the wolf he imagined lurking there that he was giving it the head of a Miami for its supper. The Miami spies carried the head back to their companions who sorrowfully recognized it.

When the heavily laden Senecas reached the Miami ambuscade, they were overwhelmed. The Miamis killed all but six. Two escaped. Four were taken prisoners. The Miamis killed two of their captives and beheaded them. They ran a string through the ears of the heads and hung the heads around the necks of the remaining two prisoners whose hands, noses, and lips they cut off. They then sent them home to tell of the vengeance of the Miamis. At the Seneca village all was horror and confusion. The Miamis returned home with those of their relatives whom the Senecas had spared.[4]

Pierre Esprit Radisson and his brother-in-law Médard Chouart, better known as Des Groseilliers, were the bravest and most experienced of the French who followed the refugees west. In the late 1650s and early 1660s when Iroquois war parties haunted the rivers and portages, they made several voyages, going as far as the Mississippi in search of furs. Sometimes they traveled with Jesuits in search of souls; always they traveled with Huron-Petuns, Ottawas, and other refugees who had come to Montreal for guns and other goods. Their travels took them into a world of horrors. They recorded events that they could not fully decipher.

In 1658 Radisson and Des Groseilliers departed on the voyage which eventually took them to the Mississippi. Their own party contained twenty-nine Frenchmen, who desired "but to do well" for themselves, and six Indians, all or mostly Hurons. As was customary, they formed a convoy, with others going west. Of the French, only Radisson and Des Groseilliers had experience in the western woods. The novice voyageurs advanced carelessly

---

[4] C. C. Trowbridge, *Meearmeear Traditions: Occasional Contributions from the Museum of Anthropology of the University of Michigan*, no. 7, ed. Vernon Kinietz (Ann Arbor: University of Michigan Press, 1938): 75–76.

upriver, laughing at the caution of Radisson and Des Groseilliers and calling them women. After three days' travel, a single Iroquois appeared on shore with a hatchet in his hand, signaling the French to land. Even after the Iroquois threw his hatchet away and sat on the ground, the novices feared to approach him. The Iroquois finally rose, advanced into the water, and said (in the fractured English of the Radisson manuscript): "I might have escaped your sight, but that I would have saved you. I fear not death." When the canoes finally closed on him, and their occupants, binding him, took him on board, he began to sing his death song.

When he had finished singing, he made a speech. "Brethren," he began, "the day the sun is favorable to me [it] appointed me to tell you that you are witless, before I die." The enemy, he told them, was all around. The enemy watched the French; it listened to them. It regarded them as easy prey. "Therefore I was willing to die to give you notice.... I would put myself in death's hands to save your lives." He instructed them on how to proceed if they were to save themselves. The "poor wretch," wrote Radisson, "spoke the truth and gave good instructions." The next day, the party met Iroquois warriors on the river. After initial panic, the French and Hurons forted up. They then brought in the prisoner "who soon was dispatched, burned and roasted, and eaten. The Iroquois had so served them." Why the Iroquois warrior had surrendered to save the French, the French never knew. In the end, all the French but Radisson and Des Groseilliers decided to return to the French settlements. The two brothers-in-law, endangered and saved by events they did not understand, continued in company with the Indians. They could explain cruelty; they could not make sense of kindness, if that is what the Iroquois by the river had intended.[5]

The refugee villages in the West welcomed Radisson and Des Groseilliers and those who followed. Those who had no traders eagerly sought them. In the 1660s, the Miami and Mascouten refugees who had settled inland from Green Bay invited Nicolas Perrot and a companion to visit them. When the French landed at the Mascouten village, an old man carrying a red stone calumet – a long-stemmed pipe decorated with feathers – and a woman with a bag containing a pot of cornmeal met them. Behind the old man and the woman came two hundred young men with "headresses of various sort, and their bodies ... covered with tattooing in black, representing many kinds of figures." The young men carried weapons. The old man first presented the calumet to the French on the side next to the sun. He then presented the calumet to the sun, the earth, and all the directions. He rubbed Perrot's head, back, legs, and feet.

---

[5] Arthur Adams (ed.), *The Explorations of Pierre Esprit Radisson* (Minneapolis: Ross & Haines, 1967), 80–84; also see Introduction.

The old man spread a painted buffalo skin and sat Perrot and his companion upon it, but when he tried to kindle a fire with flint, he failed. Perrot drew forth his fire steel and immediately made fire. "The old man uttered long exclamations about the iron, which seemed to him a spirit." He lighted the calumet and they smoked. They ate porridge and dried meat and sucked the juice of green corn. They refilled the calumet, and the Mascouten blew smoke into Perrot's face. Perrot felt himself being smoked like drying meat, but he uttered no complaint. When the Mascoutens tried to carry the Frenchmen into the village, however, Perrot stopped them. Men who could shape iron, Perrot said, had the strength to walk.

At the village the ceremonies were renewed. The Miami chiefs, entirely naked except for embroidered moccasins, met them at its edge. They came singing and holding their calumets. A war chief raised Perrot to his shoulders and carried him into the village where he was housed and feasted.

The next day the French gave a gun and a kettle as presents, and Perrot told the Miamis and Mascoutens that acquaintance with the French would transform their lives. "I am the dawn of that light, which is beginning to appear in your lands, as it were, that which precedes the sun, who will soon shine brightly and will cause you to be born again, as if in another land, where you will find more easily and in greater abundance, all that can be necessary to man." The gun, he said, was for the young men, the kettle was for the old; and he tossed a dozen awls and knives to the women, adding some cloth for their children. The French expected gifts of beaver in return, but it turned out that the Miamis singed their beaver in the fire, burning off their fur, before eating them. They had no beaver skins.

A week later a leading chief of the Miamis gave a feast to thank the sun for having brought Perrot to them. He made the feast in honor of a medicine bundle which contained "all that inspires their dreams." Perrot did not approve of the altar. He told the chief that he adored a God who would not let him eat food sacrificed to evil spirits or the skins of animals. The Miamis were greatly surprised. They asked Perrot if he would eat if they closed the bundles. He agreed. The chief then asked to be consecrated to Perrot's spirit "whom he would … prefer to his own who had not taught them to make hatchets, kettles, and all else that men needed." Perrot departed leaving the Miamis and Mascoutens to make sense of him while he tried to make sense of them. Neither Perrot nor the Indians were sure of the intentions of the other. Both sides, however, knew what they wanted from each other.[6]

Refugees were never quite sure what to make of Catholic priests. On August 8, 1665, Father Claude-Jean Allouez embarked from Three Rivers with six

---

[6] Claude Charles Le Roy, Sieur de Bacqueville de La Potherie, *History of the Savage Peoples Who Are the Allies of New France*, in Blair (ed.), *Indian Tribes*, 1:322–32. Hereafter cited as La Potherie, *History*.

other Frenchmen and four hundred Indians who had come to Three Rivers to trade. The Indians objected to taking Allouez. They thought he was a witch. They thought the baptism that he administered caused children to die. A headman threatened to abandon the Jesuit on an island if he persisted in following them. When Allouez's canoe broke, the Hurons reluctantly agreed to carry him. They changed their minds the next day, however, and Allouez and his companions had to repair the broken canoe and follow as best they could.

Eventually the Indians relented again and agreed to take all the French except for Allouez. He, they said, did not have the skill to paddle nor the strength to carry loads on a portage. Only after Allouez prayed for divine assistance did the Indians consent to take him, but he became the butt of their jokes, and they stole every item of his wardrobe that they could lay hands on.

Allouez endured the usual hardships of the dangerous passage to the lakes, and he created other hardships for himself. The Indians ate lichen soup; they once ate a rancid deer that had been dead for five days. When the Indians were careless with the powder they were transporting, it blew up and badly burned four warriors. Allouez interfered with the shaman's attempt to cure a burned man. Furious, the shaman smashed the canoe that carried Allouez.

In September Allouez reached the mission of Saint Espirit at Chequamegon. He discovered that the Indians there had abandoned their belief that baptism brought death. They now thought the rite essential for a long life. Not all Indians proved to be so taken with Christian ceremonies. Allouez preached to more than ten visiting nations only to be often greeted with contempt, mockery, scorn, and importunity.[7]

Allouez only tasted the hardships the northern Great Lakes offered; Radisson and Des Groseilliers drank more deeply of them. In 1661–62 they wintered with a band of Huron-Petuns, a farming people driven to the inhospitable shores of Lake Superior. The Huron-Petun men were not as skilled hunters as the surrounding Crees, Ojibwas, or even the Ottawas. They had few food reserves. Snow usually aided hunters, but this winter the snow fell in such quantities and was of such a lightness that the hunters could not go forth. Even though they made snowshoes six feet long and a foot and a half wide, the snow would not support them. Those who did struggle out made such noise floundering in the snow that the animals heard them at a distance and fled. Famine overtook the Huron-Petuns.

Apparently (the broken English of Radisson's manuscript is unclear), the

[7] *JR*, 1666–67, 50:249–99.

already hungry Huron-Petuns were joined by 150 Ottawa families who had even less food than the Hurons. They, too, had to have their share, although Radisson regarded them as the "cursedest, unablest, the unfamous, and cowardliest people I have ever seen amongst four score nations." The Indians ate their dogs. They retraced their steps to earlier kills to eat the bones and entrails that they had discarded. The men ate their bowstrings, lacking strength to draw the bow. Starving, the women became barren. The famished died with a noise that made the survivors' hair stand on end. The living scraped bark from trees, dried it over fires, and made it into a meal. They ate skins; they boiled and ate skin clothing. They ate the beaver skins their children had used as diapers, although the children had "beshit them above a hundred times." Five hundred died before the weather changed. Then the snow crusted, and the deer, breaking through the crust, became trapped. Hunters could walk up to them and cut their throats with knives.[8]

Four years after his difficult passage into the *pays d'en haut*, the Fox greeted Father Allouez as a manitou, or an other-than-human person. The previous winter, Senecas had attacked a Fox village while the warriors were away hunting. The Senecas had slaughtered seventy women and children and the few men in the village. They had led thirty more women into captivity. Allouez gave the Fox presents to dry the tears caused by the Iroquois attack. He then explained to them "the principal Articles of our Faith, and made known the Law and the Commandments of God."

Later, in private, a Fox told Allouez that his ancestor had come from heaven, and that "he had preached the unity and Sovereignty of a God who had made all the other Gods; that he had assured them that he would go to Heaven after his death, where he should die no more; and that his body would not be found in the place where it had been buried." And this, indeed, the Fox said, had happened. The man informed Allouez that he was dismissing all his wives but one and was resolved to pray and obey God.

As for the other Fox, Allouez wrote his superior, "Oh, my God! What ideas and ways contrary to the Gospel these poor people have, and how much need there is of very powerful grace to conquer their hearts." They accepted the unity and sovereignty of God, but "for the rest, they have not a word to say." Allouez credited their resistance to an earlier visit by "two traders in Beaver-skins." If these French "had behaved as they ought, I would have had less trouble giving these poor people other ideas of the whole French nation." The Fox asked Allouez to stay near them, to teach them to pray to "the great Manitou." Allouez could protect them from their enemies and intercede with the Iroquois to restore their relatives. Allouez

[8] Adams (ed.), *Radisson*, 131–33.

postponed his answer, telling them in the meantime to obey the true God, "who alone could procure them what they asked for and more." That evening four Miami warriors brought more immediate consolation. They gave three Iroquois scalps and a half-smoked arm to the relatives of the dead.[9]

A few days later, entering the village of the Mascoutens, Allouez received the same treatment earlier accorded Perrot. They summarized in their requests to him the horrors of the period:

> This is well, black Gown, that thou comest to visit us. Take pity on us; thou art a Manitou; we give thee tobacco to smoke. The Nadouessious and the Iroquois are eating us; take pity on us. We are often ill, our children are dying, we are hungry. Hear me, Manitou; I give thee tobacco to smoke. Let the earth give us corn, and the rivers yield us fish; let not disease kill us any more, or famine treat us any longer so harshly!

Toward evening, Allouez gathered the Mascoutens together. He was not, he told them, the manitou who was master of their lives. He was the manitou's creature. The Mascoutens, he reported, only "half understood" him, but they "showed themselves well satisfied to have a knowledge of the true God."[10]

On his way to the Illinois country in the late winter of 1677, Father Allouez passed near the Potawatomi villages around Green Bay. He learned that a young man whom he had baptized had been killed by a bear in a particularly gruesome manner. The bear had "torn off his scalp, disembowled him, and dismembered his entire body." The bear had, in short, treated the young man as a warrior treated the body of an enemy. Allouez, being acquainted with the hunter's parents, detoured to console them. He prayed with the parents, comforting the distressed mother as best he could.

Afterward, "by way of avenging . . . this death," the relatives and friends of the dead man declared war on the bears. They killed more than five hundred of them, giving the Jesuits a share of the meat and skins because, they said, "God delivered the bears into their hands as satisfaction for the death of the Young man who had been so cruelly treated by one of their nation."[11]

II

In these fragments of contact and change are glimpses of both a world in disorder and the attempts of people to reorder it through an amalgam of

[9] *JR* 54:219–27.
[10] *Ibid.*, 229–31.
[11] *JR* 60:151–53.

old and new logics. The very nature of the Iroquois assault shaped the
Algonquian response. Because distance from Iroquoia created some measure of safety, the Algonquians and the remnants of other Iroquoian peoples
– for the Iroquois were just one of many Iroquoian-speaking groups – fled
west. Because the Iroquois had guns and their opponents initially did not,
the refugees clustered together hoping to counter Iroquois firepower with
their own numbers.[12]

This clustering produced refugee centers that occupied a strip running
north–south between the western Great Lakes and the Mississippi. As
refugees moved west to avoid the Iroquois hammer, they encountered an
anvil formed by the Sioux, a people whom the Jesuits called the Iroquois of
the West. Antagonized by refugee aggression, the Sioux proved more than
capable of holding their own against the Hurons, Petuns, and the various
Algonquian groups who opposed them.[13]

The refugees recoiled and concentrated themselves within an inverted
triangle whose point rested on Starved Rock in the Illinois country and
whose base ran between Sault Sainte Marie and Michilimackinac in the east
and Chequamegon in the west. Green Bay was approximately at its center.
Inhabiting this triangle were Iroquoian-speaking groups (Huron-Petuns)
and Siouan speakers (Winnebagos), but, for convenience, its peoples can be
referred to as Algonquians, since Algonquian-speaking groups – Ottawas,
Potawatomis, Fox, Sauks, Kickapoos, Miamis, Illinois, and many others –
dominated these settlements. To the east and south of this core of village
clusters was a huge area between the Ohio River and the northern shores of
the Great Lakes emptied of inhabitants by the Iroquois. Geographically
bifurcated into two sections – refugee and emptied lands – and peopled by
inhabitants whose original coherence came largely from the homes they had
lost and the enemies they shared, the *pays d'en haut* thus had meaning not
because of its isolation from outside forces, but because of the very impact of
those forces.

This clustering of diverse peoples had its own social and environmental consequences. It disrupted older notions of territory; geographical
boundaries between refugees became difficult to maintain. Ethnic or local
distinctions remained, but now villages of different groups bordered on each

---

[12] For these attacks, see Trigger, *Children of Aataentisic*, 2:767–97, 820–21; *JR* 47:145–49;
62:209; 53:245–47, 255; 54:115–17; Lettre du découvreur à un de ses associes, 1679, 29
sept. 1680, in Pierre Margry, *Découvertes et établissements des Français... de l'Amerique
Septentrionale, 1614–1698*, 6 vols. (Paris: Maisonneuve et Cie, 1879, repr., New York,
AMS, 1974), 2:33. Hereafter cited as Margry, *Découvertes*. For the wars around Green Bay,
see La Potherie, *History*, 1:293–94, 310.

[13] For the flight of some of the Ottawas and Petuns to the Mississippi and subsequent war with
the Sioux, see Perrot, *Memoir* 1:159–65; Adams (ed.), *Radisson*, 95–96; *JR* 49:249; *JR*
50:279; *JR* 51:53; *JR* 54:115.

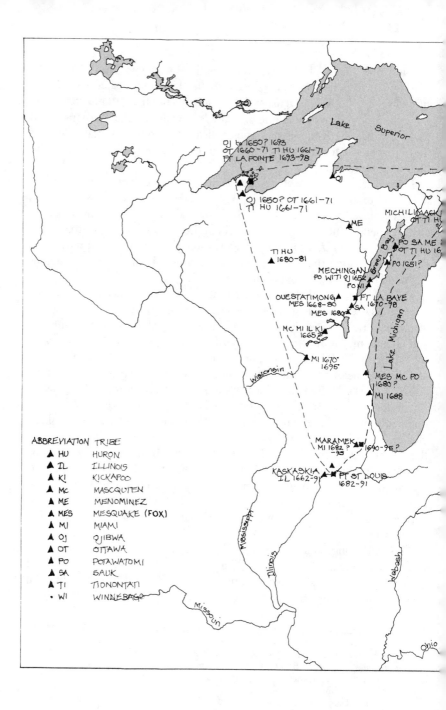

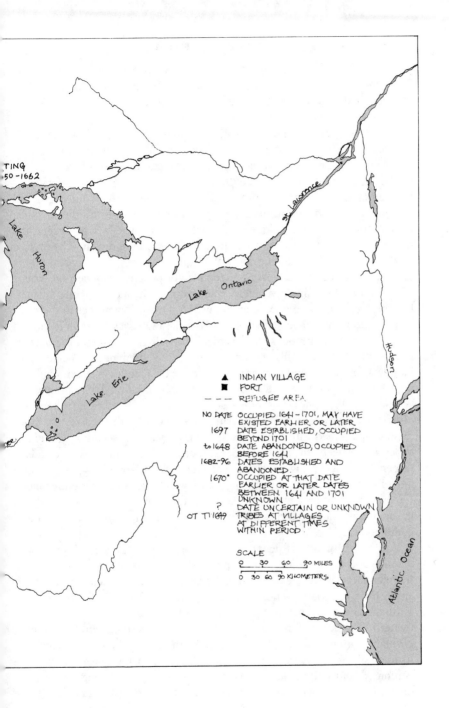

TING
50-1662

Lake Huron

St. Lawrence

Lake Ontario

Lake Erie

Hudson

Atlantic Ocean

▲ INDIAN VILLAGE
■ FORT
- - - REFUGEE AREA

NO DATE   OCCUPIED 1641-1701, MAY HAVE
          EXISTED EARLIER OR LATER
1697   DATE ESTABLISHED, OCCUPIED
          BEYOND 1701
to 1648   DATE ABANDONED, OCCUPIED
          BEFORE 1641
1682-96   DATES ESTABLISHED AND
          ABANDONED.
1670*   OCCUPIED AT THAT DATE,
          EARLIER OR LATER DATES
          BETWEEN 1641 AND 1701
          UNKNOWN
?   DATE UNCERTAIN OR UNKNOWN
OT TI 1649   TRIBES AT VILLAGES
          AT DIFFERENT TIMES
          WITHIN PERIOD.

SCALE
0   30   60   90 MILES
0   30   60   90 KILOMETERS

other, or previously separate groups mingled in a single village. These survivors of the Iroquois shatter zone and of the epidemics that preceded, accompanied, and immediately followed the Iroquois attacks came to be intimate neighbors and kinspeople.

During the 1650s and 1660s, for example, the Fox, the Sauks, the Mascoutens, the Potawatomis, the Kickapoos, the Noquets, the Atchatchakangouens (or Miamis proper), some Weas and members of other groups of the Miami confederation, the Ottawas, and refugee Petuns and Hurons invaded lands at Green Bay previously held by the native Winnebagos and Menominees. Reduced in numbers by disease and war with other nations, the Menominees and Winnebagos had little choice but to accept the newcomers. Eventually even a few Illinois settled in the region. The precise mix of the area changed constantly as some groups moved away and others entered. The region became a hodgepodge of peoples, with several groups often occupying a single village. Other groups inhabited separate villages, but these villages were often contiguous. On Green Bay proper in the mid-1650s, for example, a mixed village of Kiskakon Ottawas, a group identified as the Negaouichiriniouek, and some Petuns lived together near a large Potawatomi village, with a third village of Menominees, Winnebagos, Noquets, and, apparently, other Ottawas close by. Conditions were similar in 1670 when the Jesuits found a mixed village of Sauks, Fox, Potawatomis, and Winnebagos living near two other, separate villages. Further inland groups of Miamis and Mascoutens lived within a single palisade, and several other nations had joined with the Fox to make their village a seeming Babylon of tribes and dialects. In such conditions, there were no separate homelands at Green Bay. According to Jesuit estimates of the 1670s, 15,000–20,000 persons lived in these settlements, all of which were initially either along Green Bay or within a two- or three-day journey of it. Around Starved Rock in the Illinois country during the 1680s even greater numbers lived in a more confined area.[14]

Within this mixing of peoples lay the elements of the *pays d'en haut* as a distinct social formation, but a political glue was needed to hold the fragments together. A common residence and a common enemy could not alone produce social bonds among the refugees; indeed, proximity and tension more often than not produced conflict. In the seventeenth century, western Algonquians repeatedly murdered one another in the hunting grounds. On occasion, different nations thought it better to divert the Iroquois threat by betraying other peoples than to unite against the Five Nations. Mourning the loss of relatives to disease and seeking a reason for their loss, the refugees often accused each other of witchcraft. For these

---

[14] For mixed and contiguous villages, see *JR* 44:245–49; *JR* 54:197; *JR* 55:199, 219.

Algonquians, there were few accidents; most causes were personal and they traced them either to other humans or to manitous – the other-than-human persons with whom they shared the land. Blame had to be assigned. If the perpetrators were human, then deaths and insults were remembered, awaiting either revenge or compensation.[15]

Nicolas Perrot, a French trader who lived much of his life among the Algonquians, knew firsthand the strength of the hatred between different groups and the bitterness of their quarrels. He came to think of the refugees as uniformly treacherous, busily plotting one another's destruction when they were not contemplating killing the French. This assessment, overstated as it might be, is based on the observations of a man who lived among the western Algonquians for more than forty years, knew them well, and was respected by them. It also reflects his understandable frustration. Perrot spent much of the period resolving countless quarrels and thwarting many plots, and he nearly ended his days in the midst of the slow torture fire of the same Mascoutens who had first welcomed him as a manitou. His outbursts are exaggerations, but they are exaggerations that underline the reality of the deep animosities smoldering among these peoples. It was precisely because the divisions, suspicions, dangers, and rivalries inherent in the refugee centers were so intense that Algonquians worked so purposefully to overcome them.[16]

Each group of refugees sought ties with strangers precisely because they feared outsiders. The whole logic of Algonquian actions was that dangerous strangers had to be turned into either actual or symbolic kinspeople if the refugees were to survive hunger, disease, and Iroquois attack. The creation of such ties had also been possible in the older Algonquian world, but the need for them had seemed less pressing in that roomier and more secure past. Then a people could attack strangers or withdraw from them, but in the refugee centers both violence and withdrawal were far more difficult.

To create real or metaphorical kinspeople, the Algonquians turned to familiar cultural forms and borrowed new ones. Gift exchanges, through the conventions of reciprocity, created channels of mutual aid. Intermarriage created bonds of kinship and obligation. The Algonquians eagerly adopted the calumet ceremony, a political ritual of reconciliation. It stayed vengeful hands, brought reflection, and established ties of symbolic kinship. A dense

---

[15] For murders, see La Potherie, *History*, 1:310–11; *JR* 58:49, 55; James Clifton, *The Prairie People: Continuity and Change in Potawatomi Indian Culture* (Lawrence: Regents Press, 1977): 62–63; Perrot, *Memoir*, 163, 182. For personal causes, see Irving Hallowell, "Ojibwa Ontology, Behavior, and Worldview," in A. Irving Hallowell, *Contribution to Anthropology: Selected Papers of A. Irving Hallowell* (Chicago: University of Chicago Press, 1976), 381–83; *JR* 57:233; *JR* 61:149. La Potherie, *History*, 2:83. For manitous as cause, see *JR* 56:125–27.

[16] Perrot, *Memoir*, 252, 258, 260; La Potherie, *History*, 2:83.

network of mutual obligation gradually developed in each refugee center. Cumulatively, each person marrying outside his or her group, each calumet smoked, each gift offered and accepted tied these disparate peoples closer together than before. War, famine, and disease, which had been the executioners of the older, familiar world of the Algonquians, were also the gruesome midwives attending the birth of the new world of the *pays d'en haut*.

In our attempts to understand these bonds, the conventional units of discourse about Indians – tribes with their distinct territories and their chiefs – are misleading. These peoples are almost classic examples of the composite groups described by Elman Service as the product of "rapid depopulation by disease which, when combined with the ending of hostilities among the aborigines themselves under the dominance of the common enemy, resulted in the merging of previously unrelated peoples." At their most enduring, the connections between groups were not so much diplomatic ties between clear political entities as social bonds between much smaller social units.[17]

The ethnological details concerning these peoples have to be examined with care. The refugees ranged from hunting bands such as the various Ojibwa groups to the Miamis, who initially may have verged on being a chiefdom. Structurally, they ran the gamut from remnants of eastern confederations like the Hurons and Petuns to relatively intact western tribes like the Fox. Except for the Huron-Petuns, who were matrilineal, and the Ojibwas and Ottawas, who seem to have originally lacked clans, they were all patrilineal village peoples who were organized into exogamous clans which often had ritual functions. Such clans were sometimes grouped into paired moieties and sometimes organized into many phratries. The accounts of early ethnologists who studied these tribes and codified them are full of internal contradictions because they sought to freeze and codify what was, in fact, a world in flux.[18]

What is clear is that, socially and politically, this was a village world. The units called tribes, nations, and confederacies were only loose leagues of villages. The nature of authority within a Potawatomi village and that within a Miami village might, at least initially, differ significantly, but in neither case did authority extend beyond the village. Nothing resembling a state existed in the *pays d'en haut*. The entities that the French called nations, and which were later called tribes, thus had only the most circumscribed political

---

[17] Elman Service, *Primitive Social Organization: An Evolutionary Perspective* (New York: Random House, 1972), 97.

[18] Charles Callender, *Social Organization of the Central Algonkian Indians*, Milwaukee Public Museum, Publications in Anthropology 7 (Milwaukee: Milwaukee Public Museum, 1962): 19–28, 34–35, 38–41, 65, 70, 82–83.

standing. Nations shared a common language, culture, and ethnic identity, but the various villages of a nation did not necessarily share a common homeland. Whatever distinct homelands these villagers had once possessed, the diaspora provoked by the Iroquois had made irrelevant. The refugee nations now lived in contiguous villages or even in mixed villages. To decide, for example, what was Huron or Petun or Ottawa or Ojibwa territory at Chequamegon was both impossible and meaningless. Without a clear national territory and lacking even the most rudimentary national government, villages of the same nation, often located in separate refugee centers, could and did pursue independent policies. The Ottawas of Green Bay at a given moment might have closer relations to, and a greater community of interest with, their Potawatomi neighbors than they did with Ottawas at Chequamegon.[19]

Lacking political coherence beyond the village, groups had to forge connections at the village level. By standard ethnological reckoning, descent from male ancestors formed the key element in conceptualizing a person's place in this village world. The structural principle behind the Fox, Sauk, Potawatomi, and Kickapoo kinship systems, for example, has been described as "the unity and solidarity of the patrilineal lineage," and these same tribes had exogamous patrilineal clans "composed of either actual kin or conceptually related lineages," as did the Menominee and Shawnee. Most likely all the other people of the *pays d'en haut*, except the Iroquoian, matrilineal Huron-Petuns, shared in this system, but not enough information is available to be sure.[20]

This strong conceptual patrilineal emphasis is not, however, much of a guide to practice. These people reckoned descent patrilineally, but they were not patrilocal; that is, when a man married, he did not necessarily live with his own lineage. He often moved in with his wife's lineage; in practice, these peoples were bilocal. This bilocality takes on great significance given the prevalence of intertribal marriages. Intertribal marriages, as Frenchmen such as Perrot correctly perceived, created a larger community of interest among the refugees. Intermarriage solidified ties with outsiders who could assist a people in times of war and hunger, but the price paid was a weakening of the patrilineages – adult men left their own patrilineages and their own villages to reside in villages where they had only affinal relatives. Such bilocality mattered less in the mixed villages of the refugee centers, where a man residing with his wife's people initially remained in close touch with his own lineage, than it did later when villages dispersed. As villages

[19] Patricia Albers and Jeanne Kay, "Sharing the Land: A Reevaluation of Native American Territoriality," unpublished paper.
[20] Callender, *Social Organization*, 25–27, 35.

separated, the social unit with which a man lived was made up of his wife's relatives rather than his own.

There were other surprising twists in this patrilineal society. When a man married out of his own group, his children did not necessarily take his clan identity. Unless, as sometimes happened, their father began a new clan, the children of intermarried fathers belonged to the clan of their mother. Her clan adopted them. Among the Winnebagos, Sauks, Menominees, Fox, and Potawatomis, where a nephew was under strong obligations to assist his maternal uncle in war, this combination of clan adoption and obligation to maternal uncles linked the children of intermarried men to their mother's village despite patrilineal descent.[21]

Tribal identity and the technicalities of kinship reckoning thus did not dictate political behavior in this world of refugees. All kinship obligations were in a sense contingent, since they had to be activated and maintained by the person who embodied them. At birth every Algonquian, by virtue of his or her descent, clearly belonged to a patrilineage and patrilineal clan, but in daily life, that clan or lineage was not effectively composed simply of those genealogically assigned to it. A person's obligations to patrilineal relatives were necessarily inoperative on a daily basis if he or she lived far away in a different refugee concentration. But in an emergency, such ties beckoned and kinspeople might very well attempt to aid each other. Loss of population, loss of territoriality, extensive intermarriage, and the creation of multiple ties of actual and symbolic kinship between neighboring peoples heavily modified actual patrilineal organization.

In practice, kinship as an organizing principle moved far away from actual descent. The widespread custom of adoption forged social ties that had nothing to do with birth. If one person adopted an unrelated person as a relative, the adoptee acquired subsidiary kinship relations – a new mother, father, sisters, and brothers – while maintaining his or her old ones. In the case of a captive, adoption supposedly erased the social identity of the captive and replaced it with the preexisting social identity of a dead person. This process, while often effective, was apparently rarely complete. Many captives, though integrated into a new group, retained lingering ties of affection to their old ones. On a different level, sodalities or pan-tribal organizations formed other units that transcended kinship. The Catholic Church took on aspects of an intertribal sodality during this period, but the

---

[21] For intermarriage, customs, and ties, see Perrot, *Memoir*, 69, 188, 270; Callender, *Social Organization*, 23, 26; La Potherie, *History*, 1:277, 301. Conference between Frontenac and the Ottawas, 15 Aug. 1682, *NYCD* 9:176. For nephew, see *HBNI* 15:612. For clans, see *ibid.*, 614, 694–95. Also see Marshall Sahlins, *Tribesmen* (Englewood Cliffs, N.J.: Prentice Hall, 1968), 54.

most famous pan-tribal organization was the midewiwin society. Its lodges and curing rituals could be found in most of the villages of the *pays d'en haut*.[22]

As the French came to realize, the boundaries between the various tribes were not always clear. Perrot, in a proposed speech to the western Algonquians of Green Bay, emphasized the consequences of the refugee experience and widespread intermarriages at that refugee center: "Thou Pouteouatimais, thy tribe is half Sakis; thou Sakis are part Renards; thy cousins and thy brother-in-law are Renards and Sakis." Similarly, the Winnebagos, according to La Potherie, were composed largely of adoptees and intermarried peoples.[23]

The extreme political result of these denser connections between refugee groups was the dissolution of old groups and the creation of new ones. Various patrilineal bands – the Amikwas, Maramegs, and others – coalesced to form the two large divisions of the Ojibwas – the Chippewas, or the Southwestern Ojibwas, and the Mississaugas, or the Southeastern Ojibwas. The earlier bands apparently became clans within the new aggregate villages. This process was not complete until after the end of the refugee period, but its beginnings are apparent in the merging of several proto-Ojibwa groups with the Saulteurs at Sault Sainte Marie.[24]

Fragments of larger groups also merged. The remnants of the Petuns or Tionontati (the Tobacco Nation) and smaller numbers of Hurons who had fled west merged to form the Huron-Petuns, whom the French called the Hurons. Iroquoian in language and matrilineal in social organization, these refugees retained a sense of their separateness from the patrilineal Algonquian speakers who surrounded them. Their union was in this sense natural. In the collapse of remnants of two large leagues into a single village much disappeared. The Huron-Petuns organized themselves into three phratries, two of which, the Deer and the Wolf, clearly came from the Petuns. The Hurons proper formed a lineage, the Hatinnionen (Those of the Bear), within the Deer phratry. The origin of the third phratry, the Turtle, remains unclear and is a matter of controversy, but it probably

[22] For adoption, see Callender, *Social Organization*, 64. For connections between behavior and formal relations, see Ladslav Holy, "Kin Groups: Structural Analysis and the Study of Behavior," *Annual Review of Anthropology* (1976): 107–31. For midewiwin, see Harold Hickerson, "The Sociohistorical Significance of Two Chippewa Ceremonials," *American Anthropologist* 65 (1963): 67–85.

[23] For quotation, see Perrot, *Memoir*, 270. For intermarriage as bond, see La Potherie, *History*, 1:277. For Winnebagos, see La Potherie, *History*, 1:301. French sources, using the original French sense of the word *alliance*, often identify intermarriage with political alliances.

[24] Harold Hickerson, "The Feast of the Dead among the Seventeenth-Century Algonkians of the Upper Great Lakes," *American Anthropologist* 62 (1960): 81–107.

comprised outsiders who affiliated with the Huron-Petuns. Sastaretsy, the ritual name for the leader of the senior lineage of the Deer phratry, was always the titular head of the Huron-Petuns.[25]

Multiple ties, the dissolution of some social units, and the creation of others – all made the network of social and political loyalties within the refugee centers extremely complicated. In a given situation, people might very well have had to choose between several competing social groups that had claims on their loyalty. As a result, in the historical record the simple categories of tribe, village, and clan sometimes hold and sometimes break down as people consciously evaluated their conflicting loyalties.

The French chronicler La Potherie recorded a dispute among the Potawatomis at Green Bay that illustrates the complexity of these connections. A French trader assaulted a leader of the Red Carp clan of the Potawatomis, which led to a brawl in which Red Carp warriors knocked another Frenchman unconscious. The unconscious Frenchman was, however, a great friend of the "head of the Bear family" (or clan). The leader of the Bear clan seized a hatchet and declared that he would perish with the Frenchman. The daughter of the head of the Bear clan had married a Sauk headman and he, on hearing the brawl, gathered his Sauk followers and came to join his father-in-law and the Potawatomi Bear clan warriors. Only the recovery of the Frenchman prevented bloodletting between two groups for whom clan membership and relations through marriage overrode tribal affiliation. Tribal affiliation was always an unreliable predictor of social or political action in the *pays d'en haut*. There were too many other potential loyalties.[26]

Intermarriage and adoption formed one path to peace and solidarity, but the calumet was part of a more overtly political and ceremonial way of achieving peace. The calumet was the great token of peace. The name referred to the decorated stem of a pipe such as the one offered to Perrot and to Allouez when they appeared as strangers in the villages of the

---

[25] The organization of the Huron-Petuns is a matter of some controversy. See Lucien Campeau, *La Mission des Jesuites chez les Hurons, 1639–50* (Montreal: Editions Bellarmin, 1987), 362–67. See also *HBNI* 15:404–05, and James Clifton, "The Re-emergent Wyandot: A Study in Ethnogenesis on the Detroit River Borderland, 1747," *The Western District: Papers from the Western District Conference*, ed. K. G. Pryke and L. L. Kulisek (Essex County Historical Society and Western District Council, 1983): 7–8, 12–13. Also see Raudot lettres, AN, C11A, v. 122 (carton 64), f. 200f. Parolles, 14 juillet 1703, AN, C11A, v. 21. Part of this document appears in *NYCD* 9:752–53. Claude Charles Le Roy, Sieur de Bacqueville de la Potherie, *Histoire de l'Amerique septentrionale...* (Paris: J-L Nion & F. Didot, 1722, microcard, Lost Cause Press, Louisville, 1967), 3:298–99. Where the full French text is referred to instead of the abbreviated English text, the reference will hereafter be La Potherie, *Histoire*.

[26] La Potherie, *History*, 1:319–21.

Mascoutens and Miamis. Father Hennepin described the calumet itself in
1679 as

> a large Tobacco-pipe made of red, black or white marble [catalanite]:
> the head is finely polished, and the quill, which is commonly two foot
> and a half long, is made of a pretty strong reed or cane, adorned with
> feathers of all colors, interlaced with locks of women's hair. They tie to
> it two wings of the most curious birds they find which makes their
> calumet not much unlike Mercury's wand or that staff ambassadors did
> formerly carry when they went they went to treat of peace. The sheath
> that reed into the neck of birds they call huars [loons] . . . or else of a
> sort of ducks who make their nests upon trees. . . . However, every
> nation adorns the calumet as they think fit according to their own genius
> and the birds they have in their country.[27]

There was a pipe for peace, one for war, and others for other purposes, each
distinguished by the color of its feathers. The calumet, according to Father
Gravier, an early missionary, was "the God of peace and of war, the arbiter
of life and of death. It suffices for one to carry and show it to walk in safety
in the midst of enemies who in the hottest fight lay down their weapons
when it is displayed." Similarly, Hennepin called it a "pass and safe conduct
amongst the allies of the nation who has given it." Perrot, who used the
calumet often, wrote that it compelled obedience from those who conducted
the ceremony to the person in whose honor it was "sung." It halted the
warriors of those who sang it and arrested their vengeance. When offered to
another people and accepted, it stopped hostilities so that negotiations could
take place.[28]

The calumet had originated beyond the Mississippi among the Pawnees
who claimed to have received it from the sun. It had spread to the Sioux and
to the Illinois and was, during the mid and late seventeenth century, adopted
by the nations of the Great Lakes. The French, too, would use it, and,
eventually, in the form of the Eagle Dance, so would the Iroquois.[29]

The importance of the calumet ceremony can hardly be overstated. It
formed a part of a conscious framework for peace, alliance, exchange, and
free movement among peoples in the region. By arresting warriors, the
calumet produced a truce during which negotiations took place; when

[27] Reuben Gold Thwaites (ed.), *Father Louis Hennepin's A New Discovery of a Vast Country in America* (facsimile ed., Toronto: Coles, 1974 repr. of 1903 ed.), 125.

[28] For Gravier quote, see *JR* 63:123. See also Perrot, *Memoir*, 185; *JR* 65:123–25; Reuben Gold Thwaites (ed.), *New Voyage to North America by the Baron de Lahontan*, 2 vols. (Chicago: A. C. McClurg, 1905), 1:75–76.

[29] Perrot, *Memoir*, 186; Clifton, *Prairie People*, 124; William Fenton, *The Iroquois Eagle Dance: An Offshoot of the Calumet Dance* (Bureau of American Ethnology Bulletin 56, Washington D.C.: Government Printing Office, 1953).

negotiations were successful, the full calumet ceremony ratified the peace and created a fictive kinship relation between the person offering the pipe and the person specifically honored by the calumet. These people became responsible for maintaining that peace.[30]

According to Perrot, violation of the calumet was a crime that could not be pardoned. Yet, as Perrot admitted and witnessed, the calumet was violated. It appears that in practice the calumet was far more effective in settling disputes among peoples already allied – in this case allied against the Sioux and Iroquois – than between those allies and their enemies. This was not the fault of the Sioux, who apparently honored the calumet far more diligently than any other group, but who found their faith betrayed by the Algonquians. Sometime about 1669, the Sinago Ottawas killed and ate the ambassadors that the Sioux had sent them. This attack was countenanced by their headman, Sinago, to whom the Sioux had sung the calumet. He violated the calumet at the urging of the Huron-Petuns, the longtime allies of the Ottawas. Here alliance triumphed over the calumet, but to the Sioux the power of the pipe was vindicated when they defeated the Ottawas, captured Sinago, and subjected him to a grisly death.[31]

In their relations with the Iroquois, however, it was the western Algonquians who paid the greater honor to the calumet. René-Robert Cavelier, Sieur de La Salle, reported that the calumet was by 1680 the ordinary means of terminating wars in the Illinois country. The weaker party brought the calumet and bestowed presents on the "conquerors," thus preventing vengeance killings from escalating into prolonged wars. Such methods, however, did not work with the Iroquois who continued their attacks even after accepting the pipe.[32]

Intermarriage, gift exchanges, and ceremonies such as the calumet exerted their greatest force among peoples living in a single refugee center; their strength diminished with distance. They did, nonetheless, link one refugee center with another. The Ottawas of Chequamegon, for example, depended on kinship to obtain aid from the peoples of Green Bay against the Sioux, and the Illinois intermarried as far away as Michilimackinac. In the end, however, it would not be Algonquians who would bear primary

---

[30] Perrot, *Memoir*, 186; Donald Blakeslee, "The Calumet Ceremony and the Origin of Fur Trade Rituals," *Western Canadian Journal of Anthropology* 7 (1977): 81–82. Also see Alice C. Fletcher, "The Hako: A Pawnee Ceremony," *Twenty-Second Annual Report of the Bureau of American Ethnology to the Secretary of the Smithsonian Institution, 1900–1901* (Washington, D.C.: Government Printing Office, 1904), pt. 2.

[31] Perrot, *Memoir*, 186–90.

[32] Lettre du découvreur à un de ses associes, 29 sept. 1680, and Lettre de Cavelier de La Salle, automne de 1681, in Margry, *Découvertes*, 2:33, 141–42, 145; Narrative of... Occurrences... 1695, 1696, in *NYCD* 9:644.

responsibility for creating a larger alliance of all the refugee centers. It would be the French.[33]

III

The first Frenchmen who appeared in the West in the footsteps of fleeing Hurons and Ottawas did not come with any conscious desire to unite the refugees. Jesuits came in search of earlier converts dispersed by the Iroquois and for new souls to save. Traders came for furs. The traders obtained their furs and the Jesuits their converts, but they also became the mediators of a regional Algonquian alliance.

The fur trade and the missions enhanced the appeal of existing refuge centers. Frenchmen with their small but dazzling supplies of goods, their crude forts, their guns, and their powerful shamans – the Black Robes (the Jesuits) – became powerful figures within the clusters of refugee villages. But the French presence must be kept in context. Missions and forts were not magnets that pulled the Indians together. Missions did not attract Indians; Indians attracted missionaries who usually came to existing settlements. When missions did precede Indians, the missionaries were clearly anticipating movements by the Indians. A Jesuit mission, for example, preceded the Indian resettlement at Sault Sainte Marie in the late 1660s, but the Jesuits knew that this was an old village site whose primary attraction was the fisheries. Renewed war with the Sioux and temporary peace with the Iroquois made its resettlement attractive because it was farther away from the Sioux country than either Keweenaw or Chequamegon. The Jesuit mission was, at best, a secondary attraction. To argue that either this mission or the later fort and mission at Michilimackinac led the Indians to settle the area is like arguing that people go to airports to be solicited by religious zealots and only incidentally to catch airplanes.[34]

Missions and forts could buttress but not sustain population concen-

---

[33] Perrot, *Memoir*, 188, 270; La Potherie, *History*, 1:277, 301; Conference between Frontenac and the Ottawas, Aug. 15, 1682, *NYCD* 9:176.

[34] The classic statement of European dominance is in Louise Kellogg, *The French Regime in Wisconsin and the Northwest* (Madison: State Historical Society of Wisconsin, 1935), 137–38. Other, more recent scholars have taken roughly similar positions; see *HBNI* 603–04; Harold Hickerson, "Fur Trade Colonialism and the North American Indians," *Journal of Ethnic Studies* 1 (1973): 21–31.

For Sault Ste. Marie as a summer fishing ground in the 1660s, see *JR* 50:266. By 1669 there were 2,000 people at the Sault and a Jesuit mission had been established there, but whether this was a permanent population or only a summer fishing population is not clear, *JR* 52:213. For overstatement of French role, see *HBNI* 603. For Jesuit recognition that the mission was not the reason for settlement, see *JR* 55:161; *JR* 56:115–17.

trations. Certainly the strenuous attempts of the Jesuits to hold the Indians at Michilimackinac later failed. Similarly, at Starved Rock, in the Illinois country, La Salle did help create the large refugee concentration that numbered 18,000–20,000 persons by the mid to late 1680s, but this represented only the resettlement of the earlier refugee center of the Great Village of the Kaskaskias which had been destroyed by the Iroquois. As Iroquois pressure lessened, La Salle was unable to hold the settlement together. Internal tensions split the community, it disbanded, and the French abandoned their fort and followed the Illinois to Lake Peoria.[35]

Similarly, the ability to obtain valued French goods certainly increased the attraction of refugee centers for the Algonquians, but such goods did not reorient Algonquian life around the fur trade. As the French repeatedly discovered, no matter how much the refugees desired their goods, the Algonquians' most pressing needs remained food and defense. When French goods helped fill those needs, the refugees would go to great ends to obtain them; when they did not, the refugees did without them. Hunting beaver for exchange and undertaking the long and arduous journey to transport the beaver to Montreal could be justified only in years free from the threat of Iroquois attack, when ample food supplies were available. The priority Algonquians gave safety and security repeatedly overrode the French desire to increase the scale of exchange in the 1650s and 1660s. As La Potherie complained of those nations living around Green Bay in the late 1660s: "As the savages give everything to their mouths, they preferred to devote themselves to hunting such wild beasts as could furnish subsistence for their families rather than seek beavers of which there were not enough."

The French urged the Indians to come to Montreal to trade for iron weapons and guns to defeat their enemies. Indians balanced the admitted advantages of the weapons against the virtual certainty of combat with the Iroquois who awaited them along the Ottawa River. In the 1650s and 1660s, as often as not, they preferred to stay home. Even after the fur trade was firmly established during a period of peace with the Iroquois in the late 1660s and early 1670s, defense often came first. In 1675 Potawatomi elders

[35] For Starved Rock, see Le Clercq Memoir in Isaac J. Cox, *The Journeys of Robert Cavelier de La Salle*, 2 vols. (New York: A. S. Barnes, 1905), 2:155; Recit de Nicolas de La Salle, 1682, Margry, *Découvertes*, 1:570; De La Salle arrive aux Illinois, c. 1682, Margry, *Découvertes*, 2:175–76; Lettre de Cavelier de La Salle, 22 aout a l'automne de 1681, Margry, *Découvertes*, 2:149–58; Feuille détaché, n.d., *ibid.*, 2:201–02. La Salle à M. de la Barre, nov. 1683, *ibid.*, 2:314, 317–18. Tonty à M. Cabart de Villermont, 24 aoust 1686, *ibid.*, 3:559; "Voyage of St. Cosme" in Kellogg (ed.), *Narratives*, 350. For movements in the Illinois country in the 1680s and 1690s, see Emily J. Blasingham, "The Depopulation of the Illinois Indians," *Ethnohistory* 3 (Summer 1986): 198–201. For later French attempts at relocation, see Narrative of . . . Occurrences, 1694, 1695, *NYCD* 9:623.

blocked trading and trapping expeditions among the young men because they needed them at home for defense against the Sioux.[36]

In countering such concerns individual French traders quickly discovered that their most effective tactic was to claim that trade alone made victory in the war against the Iroquois and Sioux possible. The failure of any nation to sustain the trade would lead the French to look for other allies and customers. Such a threat certainly gave the Algonquians greater incentive to hunt and trade beaver, but it also clearly committed the French to helping defend them. The trade voyages of the 1670s also became diplomatic missions cementing the alliance between the trading Indians and the French. For both the French and the Indians trade and alliance thus became inseparable.[37]

Yet in the 1660s and 1670s it was still too early for a pan-Algonquian alliance under the leadership of the French. Instead, there were in practice only a series of individual alliances. The idea of a larger regional alliance was at least present by 1671, when the Intendant Talon wanted to establish the French as the mediators of all Indian quarrels, but neither agreement on such an ambition nor the means to fulfill it were yet apparent. The French were a formidable people in the West, but their early status depended as much on Algonquian misperceptions of them as on their real material advantages.[38]

The Algonquians received the first Frenchmen who arrived in the lands between Lake Michigan and the Mississippi during the 1650s and 1660s as *manidowek*, or manitous. As a noun, *manitou* meant an other-than-human person, a spiritual being capable of taking manifold physical forms. In greeting Perrot or Allouez, however, the Algonquians seem to have used the word more tentatively, as an adjective: These were strange and powerful men whose real significance was not yet apparent. The Ottawas, Hurons, and Petuns, who knew all too well the limits of Frenchmen, were initially apt

---

[36] For quotation, see La Potherie, *History*, 336–37. For fears of trade voyage, see La Potherie, *History*, 371–72, and Adams (ed.), *Radisson*, 99–100. For Potawatomi elders restraining young men, see *JR* 59:165. For Mascouten concern with subsistence hunting, see La Potherie, *History*, 372.

[37] For French arguments, see Adams (ed.), *Radisson*, 98–100; La Potherie, *History*, 337; Lettre du decouvreur à un de ses associes, 1679–29 septembre 1680, Margry, *Découvertes*, 2:39; W. J. Eccles, "The Fur Trade and Eighteenth-Century Imperialism," *William and Mary Quarterly* 40 (July 1983): 341–62. This linkage of trade and alliance has inspired some controversy. For major statements of two positions, see Abraham Rotstein, "Trade and Politics: An Institutional Approach," *Western Canadian Journal of Anthropology* 8 (1972): 1–28. Arthur Ray and Donald Freeman failed to find any such linkage in the Hudson's Bay region, but this settles little since the groups in this area were hunting and gathering bands, not the settled agricultural peoples farther south. Arthur J. Ray and Donald Freeman, *Give Us Good Measure: An Economic Analysis of Relations Between the Indians and the Hudson's Bay Company Before 1763* (Toronto: University of Toronto Press, 1978), 6, 232.

[38] Talon au roi, 2 nov. 1671, AN, C11A, v. 3, f. 159–60.

to treat the first missionaries harshly. They scorned Allouez for being unable to row or do his share on a portage. But the more westerly peoples regarded the Jesuits as men of power and treated them and the early traders with courtesy. As the Potawatomis told Perrot when he came among them: "Thou are one of the chief spirits, since thou usest iron, it is for thee to rule and protect all men. Praised be the Sun, who has instructed thee and sent thee to our country."[39]

The Algonquians expected benefits from these men of power, but the possibilities they envisioned clearly went beyond the acquisition of trade goods. The Jesuits recognized, for instance, that they were invited to many feasts "not so much for the sake of eating as of obtaining through us, either recovery from their ailments, or good success in their hunting and war." The Algonquians expected protection, aid against their enemies, cures, and a secure subsistence. They expected, in short, far more than the French missionaries or traders could ever deliver.[40]

To escape this dilemma, the priests denied that they were manitous and presented themselves only as ambassadors of Christ, the Master of Life. They sought to emphasize the transformative aspects of Christianity, but in seeking to convert Algonquians by attacking native beliefs, they, for tactical reasons, often themselves accepted native premises. The Jesuits ridiculed the manitous, but they did so in Algonquian terms. They often did not challenge the Algonquian logic of why fish or game appeared or did not appear. Instead, they denied credit to the manitous and gave it to Christ. Success in war, success in the hunt, survival after falling through the ice, all were evidence of the power of Christ. Victory in such debates over the causes of events in the Algonquian world only meant that heads of animals once offered to the manitous at feasts were now offered to Christ. Public offerings went to the cross and to the Christian God, the "Great Manitou." Indians were not so much being converted to Christianity as Christ was being converted into a manitou. As a Sauk headman told Father Allouez: "We care very little whether it be the devil or God who gives us food. We dream sometimes of one thing, sometimes of another; and whatever may appear to us in our sleep, we believe that it is the manitou in whose honor the feast must be given, for he gives us food, he makes us successful in fishing, hunting and all our undertakings."[41]

---

[39] La Potherie, *History* 1:309. *JR* 54:219, 229; Perrot, *Memoir*, 37, 332; Adams (ed.), *Radisson*, 128, 130; *JR* 55:203–05, 217. *JR* 50:255–57, 303–05.

[40] *JR* 55:203.

[41] The newer literature on missions stresses the ways in which missionaries transformed Indian cultures, but these authors emphasize that these people's lives had to be already severely disrupted and that for success, domination by whites was a prerequisite, not a result. See Neil Salisbury, "Red Puritans: The Praying Indians of Massachusetts Bay and John Eliot," *William and Mary Quarterly* 31 (1974): 27–54; Robert Conkling, "Legitimacy

The initial Indian assessment of Frenchmen and their God was quite pragmatic. And the predictable result of a French failure to deliver all that they had promised was an Algonquian reassessment of French capabilities. The Jesuits, for instance, claimed that Christ, rather than either the manitou Mitsipe (the Great Water Spirit) or the sun, brought the sturgeon in the spring. And for a season or more prayer might yield fish, but linking Christ's influence to the mating habits of a large fish did not contribute greatly to lasting Jesuit success in the region. When the fish failed, Christ failed. He was and remained a potent manitou, but Indians sought his aid so long as he delivered it reliably. Similarly, the Jesuits declined from spirits to, at best, powerful shamans. At worst, Indians regarded them as dangerous witches. In time the Jesuits would profoundly alter the way some Algonquians viewed the world, but for very many others these priests and their God could fit easily into the existing religion.[42]

The status of other Frenchmen declined more precipitously than did that of the Jesuits, since traders failed far more rapidly and seriously to fulfill Algonquian expectations. In 1686 Nicolas Perrot gave the mission of Saint François-Xavier at Green Bay a silver soleil whose brilliant sun with a cross above it was meant to evoke the glory of the Sun King, Louis XIV. For the Algonquians, however, the ornament probably recalled Perrot's original reception, as an emissary not of the Sun King but of the sun itself. By the 1680s such a status was largely a memory. The French had not acted as manitous. They were not, after all, powerful and wealthy beings who had come to grant the Algonquians protection and aid. The French were greedy and often quite vulnerable men with an insatiable desire for old, greasy beaver robes. According to Perrot, Indians who had initially welcomed the French as powerful benefactors came to "regard those of the French nation as wretched menials and the most miserable people in the world."[43]

and Conversion in Social Change: The Case of French Missionaries and the Northeastern Algonkian," *Ethnohistory* 21 (1974): 1–24, James P. Ronda, "We are Well as We Are: An Indian Critique of Seventeenth-Century Christian Missions," *William and Mary Quarterly* 34 (1977): 66–82. For missionaries as emissaries of Master of Life, see *JR* 55:201. For denials of mantiou status, see La Potherie, *History* 309–10, *JR* 54:231. For claims of efficacy of Christ's aid, see *JR* 57:209, 223, 231–33, 261, 289; *JR* 55:123–31; *JR* 60:151; *JR* 58:61; *JR* 61:149; *JR* 56:145. For feasts and offerings to Christ instead of manitous, see *JR* 57:23, 287–91; *JR* 58:63; "Jolliet and Marquette," 233–34. For the Sauk quotation, see *JR* 57:283.

[42] For sturgeons, see *JR* 57:287–89, 293; *JR* 58:275. For Jesuit claims of conversions, see *JR* 61:69, 71, 103, 153–54, 131; *JR* 57:233. For doubts about how Catholic such converts were, see "Journey of Dollier and Galinee," in Milo Quaife (ed.), *The Western Country in the Seventeenth Century: The Memoirs of Lanothe Cadillac and Pierre Liette* (Chicago: Lakeside Press, 1917), 206. *JR* 59:229.

[43] For the soleil, see facing page, *JR* 65. For Perrot quotation, see Perrot, *Memoir*, 63–64. See also La Potherie, *History*, 319, 333; *JR* 54:225; *JR* 55:185–87; Thwaites (ed.), *Hennepin's A New Discovery*, 82; Duchesneau to de Seignelay, 10 Nov. 1679, *NYCD* 9:133, Duchesneau's

Once they ceased to be manitous, the French were in danger of becoming merely rich, powerful, arrogant, and quarrelsome strangers to be appeased when necessary and looted when possible. They were as yet in no position to unite the Algonquians. How could they be, when they themselves often seemed more diverse and fractious than any single Algonquian group? The French, after all, had conflicting purposes for coming west. Saving souls, gathering furs, and gathering allies against the Iroquois were endeavors that could not always be easily reconciled. For example, coureurs de bois – the illegal traders who despite French efforts could not be removed from the West – diverted Miami war parties against the Iroquois by falsely telling them Onontio, the French governor, wished them to hunt beaver instead.[44]

Even a cursory examination of the accusations of Jesuit missionaries against traders and coureurs de bois, of the governor against the Jesuits, of the Montreal traders against the governor, and of the various trading factions against each other reveals the depths of French suspicion. A man like La Salle, who sought to carve out his own fur trade empire in the *pays d'en haut*, might be more willing in theory than the Algonquians to admit the role of chance or accident in human affairs, but in practice he was apt to detect malevolent agents behind every misfortune. He suspected that the Jesuits had sent the Iroquois against the Illinois in order to ruin him. He thought that rival traders might have conspired to sink his ship, which had vanished without a trace in Lake Michigan, and that they worked actively to lure away his men, who seemed to desert him every time he turned his back. His supporters thought that the Iroquois had pillaged Frenchmen on the order of the governor of Canada, La Barre. The French, too, sometimes seemed far more ethnically diverse and culturally mismatched than the refugees. Father Hennepin wondered in 1678 how the mix of Italians, Normans, Flemings, and French (all of "different interests . . . and . . . humours") going west with La Salle could ever hope to cooperate. They couldn't. Most of them deserted and left La Salle in the lurch. Forging a coherent policy in such conditions was difficult and the inability of the French to discipline and control the coureurs de bois was only the most prominent sign of this.[45]

Memoir on the Western Indians, Sept. 13, 1681, *NYCD* 9:161–62; Perrot, *Memoir*, 263–64; Denonville à M. de Seignelay, aoust 1688, AN, C11A, v. 10.

[44] For diversion of war party, see La Potherie, *History*, 2:97.

[45] For Jesuit conflicts with Frontenac, see W. J. Eccles, *The Canadian Frontier* (Albuquerque: University of New Mexico Press, 1974), 126. For differences between civil officials, see Duchesneau to Seignelay, Nov. 10, 1679, *NYCD* 9:131. For accusations revolving around the La Salle expeditions, see "Le Clercq Memoir," Cox, *Journeys of La Salle*, 98, 109–110, 126–27. Lettre de La Salle au Ft. Frontenac, 22 aoust 1682, Margry, *Découvertes*, 2:214–20, Lettre de Cavelier de La Salle à un de ses amis, Oct. 1682, *ibid.*, 2:295–301 and Extrait du mémoire (1682), *ibid.*, 2:347–48; De la Barre à Colbert, 14 nov. 1682, Margry, *Découvertes*, 2:303–04. La Salle à M. de la Barre, 2 avril 1683, Margry, *Découvertes*, 2:320–31, Lettre de Cavelier de La Salle (1681), *ibid.*, 2:116, 121, and Lettre de Cavelier

The political coherence of Algonquian and French societies might never have extended beyond the individual refugee concentrations if the Iroquois had not once again forced the peoples of the *pays d'en haut*, both French and Algonquian, to move toward a larger unity. The French had made their own peace with the Iroquois as early as 1667, and this peace had been extended uneasily over much of the West in the late 1660s and the 1670s. At the time the Iroquois had other wars on their hands. The end of the fighting with the Susquehannas of Pennsylvania and the decision of that people to relocate in Iroquoia, however, both reinforced the Iroquois and allowed the Five Nations to turn once more toward the West. In 1680 they launched the second phase of the Iroquois wars by attacking the Illinois, destroying the Great Village of the Kaskaskias and threatening to embroil the entire upper country in renewed warfare.[46]

These attacks prompted a crisis both in the refugee centers and Quebec. During the years of dwindling Iroquois pressure, Algonquian rivalries had reemerged. The Fox had antagonized most of the nations at Green Bay. The Miamis, as it turned out, had conspired with the Iroquois to destroy the Illinois but had themselves been betrayed by the Iroquois, who, after their successful attack on the Great Village of the Kaskaskias, had fallen on the Miamis. The Ottawas and their allies at Michilimackinac, instead of aiding the victims of the Iroquois attacks, desperately sought to conciliate the Iroquois and escape renewed war following the murder of a Seneca chief, Annanhae, by an Illinois at the Kiskakon Ottawa village at Michilimackinac. Divided among themselves, the Algonquians were equally at odds with the French, whose traders had so deeply antagonized Algonquian hunters that murder had become a commonplace of the trade.[47]

The Ottawas and Illinois thus desperately needed French aid, but they deeply distrusted the French. In 1681 the Ottawas piteously appealed to the

---

de La Salle, 22 aoust 1680 – automne 1681, *ibid.*, 2:145–47. For Hennepin quotation, see Thwaites (ed.), *Hennepin's A New Discovery*, 73. Mémoire . . . 1687, Margry, Découvertes, 2:346–47; Relation des découvertes and des voyages, 1679–81, Margry, *ibid.*, 1:504–13.

[46] For Iroquois, see Jennings, *Ambiguous Empire*, 137–40, 155–56. Chrétien Le Clercq, *The First Establishment of the Faith in New France*, 2 vols. (New York: J. G. Shea, 1881), 139–45; Relation du voyage de Cavelier de La Salle, du 22 Aout 1680 a l'automne de 1681, Margry, *Découvertes*, 2:128–35. Duchesneau's Memoir on Western Indians, Sept. 13, 1681, *NYCD* 9:163–64. De la Barre au Ministre, n.d. (1682), AN, C11A, v. 6, f. 60–61; Enjairan to de la Barre, Aug. 26, 1683, *WHC* 16:110–13. The Iroquois, in an attempt to maintain peace with the French, argued that they did not wish war in the West but would defend themselves. Conference de M. de Frontenac avec un deputation des Iroquois, 11 sept. 1682, AN, C11A, v. 6, f. 14.

[47] For Miamis, see Le Clercq, *First Establishment of the Faith*, 139; La Salle, Relations des découvertes, Margry, *Découvertes*, 1:525–29. For La Salle's original wish for neutrality, see Relation des découvertes, Margry, *ibid.*, 1:502–03; for Ottawas, Duchesneau's Memoir on Western Indians, Sept. 13, 1681, *NYCD* 9:163–64; for Fox, La Durantaye, 22 avril 1684, AN, C11A, v. 6, f. 521; for murders, see next chapter.

French for protection. Without it they considered themselves, in their words, already dead, yet they were not sure that some Frenchmen were not plotting with the Iroquois to destroy them. Rumors, believed by both Frenchmen and Indians, were rampant in the upper country that various French factions had encouraged the Iroquois attacks. It was true that Henry de Tonti, La Salle's lieutenant, had been wounded by the Iroquois during the attack on the Illinois, but it was also widely believed, by La Salle among others, that the Jesuits had condoned the Iroquois assault. In Quebec Governor Frontenac equivocated; he attempted to secure peace with the Iroquois while promising the Algonquians new protection that he did nothing visible to provide.[48]

At Quebec and Montreal French officials received these pleas for aid from the West and considered their options. Slowly they came to recognize the need for unity among the Algonquians and a joint French-Indian alliance to defeat the Iroquois. If the Illinois were lost, French strategists reasoned, Green Bay and the Ottawas would follow. The fur trade would vanish. Canada would be isolated and vulnerable to Iroquois attacks, and England, whom the French regarded as the sponsor of the Iroquois, would control the continent.[49]

As these discussions proceeded, French divisions did not disappear, but among those active in the West, those debating policy in Quebec and Montreal, and those overseeing the policy in Paris a consensus on the need to unite the western tribes began to emerge. Such an alliance, they agreed, depended on the ability of the French to protect and supply their allies and,

---

[48] For Tonti's actions, see Tonty Memoir, in Cox, *Journeys of La Salle*, 1:8–13. For Frontenac's attempts to secure peace, see Discours de M. de Frontenac au deputé de Iroquois, 12 sept. 1682, AN, C11A, v. 6, f. 46. *JR* 62:151–55; lettre à M. de la Barre, 14 aoust 1684, AN, C11A, v. 6, f. 293–94, Enjairan à M. La Barre, 7 mai 1684, AN, C11A, v. 6; Presents Made by the Onnontagues to Onontio . . . 5 Sept. 1684, *DHNY* 1:119. For La Salle's accusations against Allouez and other Jesuits, see Lettre de La Salle au Ft. Frontenac, 22 aoust 1682, Margry, *Découvertes*, 2:214–20, Lettre de Cavelier de La Salle à un de ses amis, oct. 1682, *ibid.*, 2:295–301, and Extrait du mémoire (1682), *ibid.*, 2:347–48.

[49] La Salle's actions encouraged an alliance of western villagers, Le Clercq, *First Establishment of Faith*, 156; Relation des découvertes, Margry, *Découvertes*, 1:525–34. Other officials and La Salle, fearing for his trade, wanted peace with the Iroquois, Lettre de Cavelier de La Salle à un de ses amis, oct. 1682, *ibid.*, 2:294–96. Duchesneau's Memoir on Western Indians, Sept. 13, 1681, *NYCD* 9:164–65; Conference on Intelligence Received from Iroquois, Mar. 23, 1682, *NYCD* 9:171, also *JR* 62:157–65. For Frontenac's decision to accord "la nouvelle protection" against the Iroquois, see Mémoire . . . à l'egard des sauvages . . . ., 12 sept. 1682, *RAPQ*, 1948–49, 141–42. For king's orders to maintain peace among allies and defend them from Iroquois, see king to La Barre, May 10, 1682, in Theodore C. Pease and Raymond C. Werner (eds.), *The French Foundations, 1680–93, Collections of the Illinois Historical Library* (Springfield Ill.: Illinois State Historical Library, 1934), *IHC* 23:17. For La Barre's measures, Abstract of Letters Received from Canada, *NYCD* 9:196–97. He, like other French officials, thought the English were behind Iroquois attacks, De la Barre au ministre, n.d. (1682), AN, C11A, v. 6, f. 60–61; M. de la Barre au ministre, nov. 1683, Margry, *Découvertes*, 2:331.

above all, to mediate the differences between them. In 1681 the Intendant Duchesneau advised that it was in "our interest to keep these people united and to take cognizance of all their differences, however trifling these may be, to watch carefully that not one of them terminate without our mediation and to constitute ourselves in all things their arbiters and protectors." From the West, Father Le Clercq, who had accompanied La Salle, reached similar conclusions: "If we wish to settle in those countries and make any progress for the faith, it is absolutely necessary to keep all these tribes, as well as others more remote in peace and union against the common enemy – that is, the Iroquois." Finally, in 1684, an anonymous memorialist restated the policy while warning against the selfish interests that might undermine it:

> Take heed of their plans, of their disagreements, and do not allow any of
> them to terminate without the participation and without the orders of
> those who, representing the person of the king, ought not to be so mean
> as to sell them [the Indians] their mediation at so high a price that they
> [the Indians] are forced to disregard it and come to terms without
> having recourse [to us].[50]

Even as the French in Quebec debated unifying the western tribes, the French in the West, who were more immediately threatened by the Iroquois than officials at Quebec, took the first hesitant steps to secure such an alliance. In order to resist the Five Nations, they moved somewhat clumsily toward healing divisions both between themselves and the Algonquians and between the various Algonquian groups. As Iroquois warriors plundered Frenchmen in the West, La Salle fortified and garrisoned Starved Rock and gathered Miamis, Illinois, and Shawnees around him. Daniel Greysolon Dulhut acted forcefully to halt the murders that plagued the trade and to try to reconcile warring Algonquian groups. Governor La Barre, who had succeeded Frontenac, garrisoned and provisioned Michilimackinac. In 1684 Frenchmen and Algonquians in concert turned back an Iroquois attack on the Illinois, and Governor La Barre summoned western warriors for an assault on Iroquoia. Working deftly out of Michilimackinac, the first French commander in the West, Oliver Morel de la Durantaye, secured the warriors. The alliance seemed a reality.[51]

---

[50] For divisions, see Lettre de La Salle au Ft. Frontenac, 22 aoust 1682, Margry, *Découvertes*, 2:214–20, Lettre de Cavelier de La Salle à un de ses amis, oct. 1682, *ibid.*, 2:295–301 and Extrait du mémoire (1682), *ibid.*, 2:347–48; Lettre M. de la Barre à M. Colbert, 14 nov. 1682, *ibid.*, 2:303–04. For Duchesneau quotation, see Duchesneau's Memoir on Western Indians, Nov. 13, 1681, *NYCD* 9:162. For Le Clercq quotation, see *First Establishment of Faith*, 156. Mémoire sur quelques ... dans la ferme de Canada (1684), AN, C11A, v. 6, f. 480.

[51] Recit de Nicolas De La Salle, 1682, Margry, *Découvertes*, 1:570, Tonti Memoir in Cox, *Journeys of La Salle*, 1:31; M. de la Barre to M. de Seignelay, 4 Nov. 1683, *NYCD* 9:202; De Baugy, 24 mars 1684, AN, C11A, v. 6; Memoir of M. de la Barre, Oct. 1, 1684, *DHNY*

Unfortunately La Barre's attack failed miserably. The French militia fell sick, Governor La Barre panicked and signed an embarrassing treaty abandoning the Illinois to the Iroquois, and the worst Algonquian fears of French cravenness and untrustworthiness seemed true. To recoup, the French court removed Governor La Barre and renounced his treaty. His successor, Jacques-René de Brisay Denonville, attached great importance both to protecting the western allies and mobilizing them against the Iroquois. He gave gifts of guns to the Illinois and other allies, maintained fortified posts not only at Michilimackinac and Starved Rock, but also at Saint Joseph, Maramek (near present-day Kalamazoo) and eventually many other places, and summoned the Algonquians for a second joint attack on Iroquoia in 1687.[52]

All of this only partially reassured the allies. The Ottawas, in particular, never lost their fear that the French would abandon them. The Iroquois preyed on this fear and, with English encouragement, sought to transform it into temptation. The Iroquois assured the Ottawas and also the Huron-Petuns that if they deserted the French, the Five Nations would secure them a trade with the English that would provide better European goods at cheaper prices. Even as the French-Iroquois war resumed with Denonville's attack, even as it became subsumed in a larger imperial war between France and England in 1689, the mutual distrust of the French and the western Indians, particularly the Ottawas and Huron-Petuns, persisted. Both nations repeatedly seemed on the verge of deserting the French. The Indians were motivated sometimes by the lure of English goods, at other times by the reasonable fear that the French would betray them. Separate French peace negotiations with the Iroquois disposed the allies to make a separate peace of their own.[53]

The French-Algonquian alliance rested on a delicate balance of fear and temptation. Renewed Iroquois attacks created the impetus for the alliance,

1:109–16. For Dulhut, see Thwaites (ed.), *Lahontan's Voyages*, 1:73; Enjairan to M. de la Barre, 26 aug. 1683, Margry, *Découvertes*, 5:3–7. For Durantaye, see M. de la Barre to M. de Seignelay, 4 Nov. 1683, *NYCD* 9:202.
[52] For La Barre's failure, see Presents Made by the Ononotagues to Onontio, 5 Sept. 1684, *DHNY* 1:117–19; De Meulles to Minister, Oct. 10, 1684, *DHNY* 1:120–271. For crown's disavowal, see Instructions to M. de Denonville, Mar. 10, 1685, *IHC* 23:68–78; Mémoire: De Denonville, Sept. 8, 1686, AN, F3, Moreau-St. Mery, v.6, f.270–71; Mémoire instructif, AN, F3, Moreau-St. Mery, v.2, f.218.
[53] For discontent of allies, see Denonville Memoir Concerning Present State of Canada, Nov. 12, 1685, *DHNY* 1:199–200. Instruction to M. Denonville, Mar. 10, 1686, *IHC* 23:68–78. See also Denonville's letter to Seignelay and reply, Aug. 20, Sept. 3, Nov. 12, 1685, *NYCD* 9:274; For initial English threat and French response, see Thwaites (ed.), *Lahontan's Voyages*, 1:98–101; Denonville au Ministre, 13 nov. 1685, AN, C11A, v.7, f.105; Denonville to Seignelay, May 8, 1686, *NYCD* 9:287–92, and Oct. 9, 1686, *NYCD* 9:286–303; Denonville to Seignelay, June 8, 1687, *NYCD* 9:324–25; *ibid.*, Aug. 25, 1687, *NYCD* 9:336–37; Denonville au Ministre, 15 juillet 1687, AN, C11A, v.9, f.36. For Huron-Petun

but trade with the English allies of the Iroquois perpetually threatened its dissolution. French denunciations of their allies as unfaithful and treacherous were as self-serving as they were common, but they also contained significant elements of truth. Particularly for the Huron-Petuns and the Ottawas at Michilimackinac, alliance with the French always had to be weighed against its alternative: rapprochement with the Iroquois and trade with the English. The French could not assume loyalty or dictate to the Algonquians as long as that risky alternative remained.[54]

From its inception, then, the alliance was not simply the natural result of poor and shattered peoples' seeking to share French wealth and power but, rather, an initially precarious construction whose maintenance seemed as essential to Canadian as to Algonquian survival. The alliance endured not because of some mystical affinity between Frenchmen and Indians, nor because Algonquians had been reduced to dependency on the French, but rather because two peoples created an elaborate network of economic, political, cultural, and social ties to meet the demands of a particular historical situation. These ties knit the refugee centers to each other and each center to the French. Central to this whole process was the mediation of conflicts both between the French and their various allies and among the allies themselves. In the end the alliance that the French and Algonquians created in the last two decades of the seventeenth century rested on the willingness of the French to undertake such mediation and their ability to perform it effectively. As in an Indian confederacy, the mobilization of force against outsiders was only a secondary achievement of the alliance. Primarily, the alliance sought to insure peace among its members. Ideally, of course, all the allies would agree to fight a common enemy, but before that could happen, all had to agree not to fight each other. As Governor Denonville realized, it was "absolutely necessary to reconcile them before thinking of deriving any advantage from them." Because mediation secured peace, mediation was at the heart of the alliance.[55]

IV

It is hard, accustomed as we are to think of European dominance in terms of conquest and commercial advantage, to accept mediation as a source of

measures to disrupt French-Iroquois negotiations, see Thwaites (ed.), *Lahontan's Voyages*, 1:220–25; also Mémoire: Chevalier de Callières, 1689, AN, C11A, v. 10. For separate peace, see Relation de cequi s'est passé d l'anneé 1694 jusqu'au mois de nov. 1695, AN, F3, Moreau-St. Mery, v. 7, f. 341.

54 For both recognition of and frustration at this situation, see Mémoire instructif de l'estat des affaires de la Nouvelle France ... Denonville à M. de Seignelay, aoust 1688, AN, C11A, v. 10, f. 64–70.

55 Memoir of Denonville, Nov. 12, 1685, *DHNY* 1:198–99.

power, but power it was. Admittedly, without goods to give as presents or French troops to aid the Algonquians against the Iroquois, mediation would have been impossible. But it is equally true that neither trade nor military force alone could have held the alliance together. It was the ability of the French to mediate peace between contentious and vengeful allies that did that. Anyone who has attempted to follow in La Potherie's *History* the tangled and dangerous negotiations conducted by men such as Perrot or has looked at the career of Henry de Tonti or of Daniel Greysolon Dulhut has some sense of both the immensity of the task and the difficulty of the achievement. Even with new Iroquois attacks imminent, Tonti in 1685 had to make a present of a thousand ecus worth of merchandise to reconcile the Miamis and Illinois. In effecting such reconciliations the French found a niche in Algonquian political systems, whose organization, as the Intendant Raudot later noted, made it easier to declare war than to secure peace.[56]

The alliance that took shape following the Iroquois attacks of 1680 survived the seemingly endless string of internal crises that afflicted it during the 1680s and 1690s to become the vehicle for the defeat of the Iroquois. It transformed the Algonquians from a terrified people confined to a few crowded and impoverished settlements to a confident and expanding people reoccupying country long denied them by the Iroquois. Once armed and organized, the Algonquians themselves became the protectors of Canada. They carried the war home to the Five Nations. It was they, as Governor Philippe de Rigaud de Vaudreuil would stress in the early eighteenth century, who had defeated the Iroquois. It was they whom the Iroquois most feared. It was on them that French security came in large measure to depend. The refugees recognized full well the implications of their military victories and came to possess, as Perrot said, the "arrogant notion that the French cannot get along without them and that we could not maintain ourselves in the colony without the assistance that they give us."[57]

The alliance was based on mediation, but mediation was only possible because of what might be called the infrastructure that supported the alliance itself. In the late seventeenth century this infrastructure consisted of the refugee centers themselves, which concentrated Indians in large, easily accessible numbers; French missions and forts located in these refugee centers; and the *congé*, or permit, system of trading, which not only supplied

---

[56] For Perrot, see La Potherie, *History*, 1:309, 311, 2:61–78, 84–85, 111–13. For others, see Boisguillot à M. de la Barre, 7 mai 1684, AN, C11A, v. 6, f. 528; Tonti à M. de Villermont Margry, *Découvertes*, 3:559; Raudot lettres, AN, C11A, v. 122 (carton 64) f. 200ff.

[57] For examples of attacks, see Narrative . . . of Occurrences, 1697–98, *NYCD* 9:680–81; Narrative . . . of Occurrences, 1696–97, *ibid.*, 672; Vaudreuil & Raudot to Minister, Nov. 14, 1708, *MPHC* 33:402; Yves Zoltvany, "New France and the West, 1701–13," *Canadian Historical Review* 46 (1965): 304. See also Tonti à M. de Villermont, 28 mars 1689, Margry, *Découvertes*, 3:564; *JR* 64:37. For quotation, see Perrot, *Memoir*, 262.

goods to the West but, by giving officials some control over traders, made them potential French emissaries and diplomats. French wealth and Algonquian and French military strength sustained this infrastructure. And the combination of French literacy – at least among Jesuits, officers, and a few traders – and the presence of Frenchmen in all the major refugee centers bound it together. The French established a command of distant events that allowed them to intervene propitiously in Indian politics at critical moments and coordinate their own actions with a precision and secrecy Indians could not match. The many occasions on which Frenchmen disrupted Indian "plots" that threatened to destroy the alliance or gathered widely separated nations for common endeavors testify to the importance of this communication network.[58]

Looked at from this perspective, the alliance was a French construction, but other angles of examination yield other perspectives. The underlying premise of the alliance – mediation as a source of influence – was essentially Algonquian. The precursors of the alliance were the Potawatomis who, in effect, showed the French the possibilities of mediation. According to La Potherie, the Potawatomis' role as mediators had made them the most influential group at Green Bay.

> The old men are prudent, sensible, and deliberate; it is seldom that they undertake any unseasonable enterprise. As they receive strangers very kindly, they are delighted when reciprocal attentions are paid to them. They have so good an opinion of themselves that they regard other nations as inferior to them. They have made themselves arbiters for the tribes about the bay, and for all their neighbors; and they strive to preserve for themselves that reputation in every direction.[59]

In the early 1680s, the Potawatomis responded to Iroquois attacks and to their own conflicts with the French by attempting to expand their role as mediators to include both the Illinois and the Miamis, who had by then once more moved south of Lake Michigan. These attempts, however, exacerbated conflicts with the French – with both the Jesuits at Green Bay and La Salle, who was establishing the French as the dominant people at Starved Rock – and overtaxed Potawatomi resources. And when, in retaliation for epidemics they believed to have been caused by Jesuit witchcraft, the Potawatomis

---

[58] For examples, see Boisguillot à M. de la Barre, 7 mai 1684, AN, C11A, v. 6, f. 528; M. De la Barre au Ministre, 9 juillet 1684, AN, C11A, v. 6, f. 284; Denonville à M. de la Durantaye, 6 juin 1686, AN, C11A, v. 8, f. 51–56; Tonty Memoir in Cox, *Journeys of La Salle*, 1:37–38; Mémoire instructif des mesures que M. Denonville a prises pour la guerre…26 aoust 1686, AN, C11A, v. 8, f. 98. Thwaites (ed.), *Lahontan's Voyages*, 1:149–63. Denonville to Seignelay, Jan. 1690, *NYCD* 9:440.

[59] La Potherie, *History*, 1:302.

murdered Jesuit donnés, a display of French force at Green Bay led them to concede leadership to the French.[60]

The French, not the Potawatomis, would lead the alliance. The Algonquians acknowledged the French governor of Canada, who bore the title of Onontio, as the head of the alliance. *Onontio* was an Iroquois word meaning great mountain. It was the Mohawk rendering of the name of Charles Jacques de Huault de Montmagny, an early French governor. Both the Iroquois and the Algonquians applied the name to all later French governors. Onontio was a person of real power, but none of the French governors who led the alliance was regarded as a conquerer. Instead, western Indians regarded Onontio and the Frenchmen who followed him as their allies, protectors, suppliers, and as the mediators of their disputes. Or, in Algonquian terms, Onontio was their father and thus they addressed him in council. Becoming fathers was, in a sense, a demotion for the French. They originally had been manitous – that is, in metaphorical kinship reckoning, grandfathers. They had taken a step down the generational ladder.[61]

Onontio deployed his power by directing French resources along Algonquian channels. Or, rather, goods that originated in French society were distributed according to customs that originated in Algonquian society for, as we shall see, it increasingly became meaningless to speak of the alliance as French or Algonquian. It was both. As Perrot noted, liberality was highly regarded among the Algonquians; it was both a mark of and a route to status and power. No request had significance and no agreement was binding without an exchange of presents. In the words of Intendant Duchesneau, "These tribes never transact any business without making presents to illustrate and confirm their words." The importance of any agreement was measured in terms of the gifts which accompanied it. Goods, bestowed wisely, were the mark of leadership and the route to influence; it was the route the French took.[62]

French agents of the alliance – the priests, officers, and traders – could,

---

[60] Lettre du Pere Enjairan à M. de la Barre, 26 aoust 1683, Margry *Découvertes*, 5:3–7; Perrot, *Memoir*, 188.

[61] For origin of *Onontio*, see Eccles, *Canadian Frontier*, p. 201, n. 15. I'd like to thank Ray Fogelson for pointing out the generational progression here. There remains much interesting work to be done in sorting out the complex metaphorical network the Algonquians used to govern political and social relations. For an attempt to do this for the Iroquois, see Mary A. Druke, "Linking Arms: The Structure of Iroquois Intertribal Diplomacy," in *Beyond the Covenant Chain: The Iroquois and Their Neighbors in Indian North America, 1600–1800*, ed. Daniel K. Richter and James H. Merrell (Syracuse: Syracuse University Press, 1987).

[62] Perrot, *Memoir*, 291; for quotation, see Duchesneau's Memoir on the Western Indians, Nov. 13, 1681, *NYCD* 9:161. Frontenac to Duchesneau, July 28, 1682, *NYCD* 9:175, Lettre de Cavelier de La Salle, 22 aout à l'automne de 1681, Margry, *Découvertes*, 2:150. Callières au Ministre, 20 oct. 1699, AN, C11A, v. 17, f. 7.

however, only act with the cooperation of Algonquian leaders. The alliance essentially merged the French politics of empire with the kinship politics of the village. The men – French and Algonquian – who translated one politics into the other were the people the documents refer to as chiefs. Frenchmen so often used the term *chief* as a generic tag for any Indian who showed signs of having influence within his own society that trying to give the word an operational meaning is hopeless. There was no more an office of chief in Algonquian societies than there was in French society. The men, and sometimes women, of influence whom the French most often took for chiefs were *okamas*, or village civil leaders. In most of these groups, leadership was clan- and lineage-based, with separate leaders for war and for peace.[63]

Leaders in the alliance were thus often leaders in their own society as well. Just as Onontio was the governor of New France, with duties, obligations, and interests totally distinct from those of the alliance, so chiefs could hold positions both within their own society and within the alliance. But Algonquian village leaders, unlike Onontio and his French officials, were not rulers. The French equated leadership with political power, and power with coercion. Leaders commanded; followers obeyed. But what distinguished most Algonquian politics from European politics was the absence of coercion.

Only among the Miamis did the French recognize leaders who seemed to possess power in the French sense. The first Jesuit accounts thought the leading man of the Miamis was "the King of the nation." And Chichikatolo of the Miamis later seemed to the French a formidable leader of a hierarchial society. On seeing Chichikatolo at Montreal in 1701, La Potherie reported that he carried himself with the bearing of a Roman emperor. When Chichikatolo gave orders, his people obeyed them, or so, at least, the French thought. But Chichikatolo was an exceptional figure; no later Miami chief equaled him.[64]

The normal influence of an Algonquian *okama* was far different. As Chigabe, a Saulteur chief, and probably a lineage head of one of the proto-Ojibwa bands of Lake Superior told Governor Frontenac: "Father: It is not the same with us as with you. When you command, all the French obey and go to war. But I shall not be heeded and obeyed by my nation in a like manner. Therefore, I cannot answer except for myself and for those immediately allied or related to me."[65]

Except for war leaders during a war expedition, chiefs could command no other men. There were people of power and influence among the Algonquians, but their power was, as Pierre Clastres has argued, non-

---

[63] *HBNI* 15:649, 693, 712–13, 732.

[64] For Miami chiefs, see La Potherie, *History* 2:330–31. For talk at Detroit, July 30, 1704, see *MPHC* 33:192, *JR* 55:215. For Chichikatolo, see La Potherie, *Histoire*, 4:202, 207–8.

[65] For Chigabe quotation, see Narrative of . . . Occurrences, 1694–95, *NYCD* 9:612.

coercive; it was a type of power that Europeans failed to recognize. In Algonquian village societies, people conceived of power as arising from outside. Power came from manitous, who gave it to individuals or to ancestors of the group. The power of clans usually derived from an ancestral vision, and that power was actualized in a ritual bundle consisting of objects that symbolized the original vision. Each bundle had its attendant ceremonies. A clan chief was the person responsible for these ceremonies. A village chief often was the head of the senior lineage of the chiefly clan, but this was not always so. Often leadership was not hereditary, and, even when it was, the leading candidate might be unsuitable. In such cases a village council composed of the elders and leading men met to select and to ratify the occupant of the office.[66]

To be a chief within a village seemed to many French observers a thankless task. The chief was under an obligation to give to all who asked. Villages were not homogeneous; they contained members of different lineages, clans, and families. The chief intervened to mediate quarrels between them, but they were under no obligation to listen to him. Chiefs and elders deliberated on what course a village should pursue, but no one was obliged to obey them. Chiefs were men with large responsibilities and few resources. But chiefs were also widely acknowledged as men of influence; they were not the same as other men.[67]

The French desired to transform this noncoercive leadership into a coercive leadership. Like the manitous the Algonquians originally equated them with, the French brought power in from outside. To chiefs in need of goods to redistribute to followers and in need of help in protecting the village, an alliance with the French was natural. And as the French singled out certain leaders to be the channels by which French power entered the villages, they created a new kind of chief which can best be distinguished as an alliance chief.

As used within the French alliance in the seventeenth and eighteenth centuries, the word *chief* came to refer to both Algonquians and Frenchmen. Alliance chiefs were people who represented their society to outsiders. They mediated disputes among allies and acted to focus the military power of the alliance against outside enemies. Any man who performed such tasks, no

---

[66] The most intriguing and suggestive discussion of chieftanship and politics in North and South America is Pierre Clastres, *Society Against the State: Essays in Political Anthropology* (New York: Zone Books, 1987); see particularly 7–47.

   Clastres's argument that the chief was the speaker for the group does not always literally apply to Algonquians. Chiefs usually employed special speakers to speak for them in council. Similarly, polygamy, while important among Algonquians, did not seem to have the same political significance as it did for Clastres's South American villagers, but this is a matter for additional research. For Algonquians, see *HBNI* 15:617–18, 649–50, 661, 732.

[67] For a discussion of chiefs as mediators, see Clastres, *Society Against the State*, 59–60.

matter what political or social position he held within his own society, was an alliance chief. Both the Sieur de Louvigny, a military officer who commanded the French expedition sent against the Fox, and Nicolas Perrot, a trader, were French chiefs despite the sizeable differences of their status within French society. As alliance chiefs, however, they, in effect, lost their French attributes of power: the ability to command. They acquired the Algonquian obligations of power: the obligation to mediate and to give goods to those in need. Alliance chiefs among the Algonquians did not claim the power to command. They always needed the consent of their councils.[68]

The prototype of Algonquian alliance chiefs was Onanghisse of the Potawatomis. His exact social position among the Potawatomis is difficult to determine. Like his French equivalent, Perrot, Onanghisse, however, increased his influence among his people because of his success as an intermediary with foreigners. Onanghisse had led Potawatomi attempts to negotiate an anti-French axis with the Miamis and Illinois in the early 1680s, but with the birth of the French alliance, he had become one of its leading figures. His standing increased as he mediated among neighboring peoples and the French as well as among his own people. His activities at the great peace conference of 1701 which ended the Iroquois wars are typical. He spoke to the French for the Sauks in order to arrange compensation for a Frenchman the Sauks had killed among the Sioux. He spoke for the Mascoutens who wished to make retribution for pillaging Perrot's goods and attempting to burn him at the torture stake. On different occasions at the same conference, he spoke for the Potawatomis, Fox, and Winnebagos. He was, in short, a mediator for the alliance among all the peoples gathered about Green Bay, and his activities extended beyond it into the Illinois

---

[68] For Indian reference to French chiefs, see Marest to Vaudreuil, Aug. 14, 1706, *MPHC* 33:268; Marest to Vaudreuil, July 2, 1712, *MPHC* 33:557; Speech of Illinois, 1725, *WHC* 16:456–57; Narrative of de Boucherville, 1728–29, *WHC* 17:40. For the king as a great chief, see La Potherie, *History*, 1:347. For French use of the term, see Pontchartrain to Vaudreuil, June 9, 1706, *NYCD* 9:777; Parolles des Outtauois de Michilmakina . . . 23 juillet 1708; Reponse, AN, C11A, v. 28, f. 215; Beauharnois & D'Aigremont au Ministre, 1 oct. 1728, AN, C11A, v. 50, f. 32.

For examples of chiefs saying their authority was delegated by the council or by the elders, see Narrative of . . . Occurrences, 1694–95, *NYCD* 9:610; Conseil, 27 sept. 1703, AN, C11A, v. 21 (Niquimar); Words of Ottawas, Sept. 24, 1707, *MPHC* 33:346–47; Words of Ottawas, 23 June 1707, *MPHC* 33:327.

The Algonquian system of alliance chiefs and native *okamas* did not parallel the Pueblo system of an internal religious leadership and a separate set of leaders to deal with the Spanish. Algonquian alliance chiefs might or might not be *okamas*, shamans, or clan leaders. Nor does this Algonquian system parallel the absorption of native leaders as vassals by the Spanish in Florida; see Amy Turner Bushnell, "Ruling 'the Republic of Indians' in Seventeenth-Century Florida," in Peter Wood, Gregory A. Waselkov, and M. Thomas Hatley, *Powhatan's Mantle: Indians in the Colonial Southeast* (Lincoln: University of Nebraska Press, 1989), 134–50.

country. It was no wonder that he identified so strongly with French chiefs, telling Governor de Callières that Perrot was his "body," aiding him in all the lands of Algonquians to *autoriser* the *parole* of Onontio.[69]

The alliance grafted together imperial politics and the village politics of kinship; the two became branches of a single tree. The politics of kinship remained strongest within the villages and among contiguous peoples. This was not a harmonious politics. Factionalism divided the village councils; and because village boundaries themselves were permeable, factions formed links with outsiders. The chiefs struggled to mediate these quarrels, but the politics of kinship grew weaker with distance. Imperial politics thus grew more significant as geographical scale increased. Distant groups were united within the French alliance not so much by their real or metaphorical kinship relations with one another as by their common standing as children of Onontio, who was the representative of the French king. The alliance had a center, an imperial center, and from this center the French focused their efforts to influence peoples who were allies rather than subjects of the empire. Where the bonds of kinship failed, French and Algonquian alliance chiefs interceded. They came with their calumets, their presents to cover (that is, to offer compensation for) the dead, and their captives to replace or raise up the dead. Those who refused to accept the mediation of the alliance chiefs risked the threat of having the united force of the alliance brought against them.[70]

V

The social and political bonds forged by the refugees and the French, for all their strength, could not hold the refugee centers together. The centers were the creations of desperate people who in seeking to create political and military security created ecological and economic instability. The centers concentrated large numbers of people who were often hungry and often sick. They became easy targets for the virgin soil epidemics ravaging the Western Hemisphere.

Among American Indian peoples there had been no prior exposure to

[69] James Clifton, "Potawatomi Leadership Roles: On Okama and other Influential Personages," in William Cowan (ed.), *Papers of the Sixth Algonquian Conference, 1974*, National Museum of Man, Mercury Series, Canadian Ethnology Service Paper no. 23 (Ottawa: National Museum of Canada, 1975), 43–99, Onanghisse, 58, 63, 65–69. See also Lettre du Pere Enjalran à M. de la Barre, 26 aoust 1683, Margry, *Découvertes*, 5:3–7; La Potherie, *Histoire*, 4:208–11, 212–13, 224, 234; Le Clerq, Memoir from Membre Papers, in Cox, *Journeys of La Salle*, 125.

[70] As Marshall Sahlins observes, tribes overcome local cleavages only insofar as necessary to prevail militarily, Sahlins, *Tribesmen*, 45.

diseases long endemic to Europe. Indian populations had not been selected over time for resistance to such diseases, nor had individuals developed antibodies to these diseases from previous exposure during childhood. Smallpox and measles struck virgin populations in the Western Hemisphere, and these so-called virgin soil epidemics carried off huge numbers of people. No matter how well fed or secure the Indians might have been, a significant proportion of them were doomed to die in such epidemics, but when virgin soil epidemics hit hungry people forced into crowded and contiguous settlements by warfare, the toll became enormous. The Iroquois, in effect, pushed the Algonquians onto a killing ground where smallpox and measles took a far greater toll than Iroquois muskets or scalping knives during the late seventeenth century. There are no reliable estimates of how many died, but calculations on selected tribes indicate a decline of anywhere from 25 percent to over 90 percent in the late seventeenth and early eighteenth centuries.[71]

Hunger exacerbated disease, and the refugees were often hungry because, in seeking to create a safe and familiar world, they taxed the natural world to its limits. The predictability of the natural world became uncertain. The Algonquians had recognized and depended on seasons of plenty and seasons of scarcity that were determined by the great natural rhythms of the planet. There were seasons when fish spawned and deer rutted, and both could be taken more easily. There were seasons when game animals were fat, their coats sleek, their fur heavy, and seasons when they were weak and emaciated and provided little food. There was spring when women could plant and fall when they could harvest. The subsistence cycles of the refugees, with variations according to skills, technologies, and cultural tastes, moved to these rhythms. These larger patterns were recurrent and predictable. Indians noted them and provided against expected times of dearth.

In the Great Lakes settlements scarcity came in the late winter and early

---

[71] Disease was depopulating the Ottawas in the mid 1660s, (*JR* 50:287). A little later the Mascoutens prayed for relief from the diseases killing their children (*JR* 53:229); in 1670–71 "bloody flux" was among the Ottawas (*JR* 55:117–31). In 1672 the people at the Sault Sainte Marie had been reduced to extremity by disease (*JR* 57:223). In 1676 disease followed a poor harvest among the Fox (*JR* 60:199, 151). In 1677 many died of an unnamed sickness around Lake Huron (*JR* 61:69–70). In 1679–81 there was smallpox among the Iroquois and at Montreal (*NYCD* 9:129, 154). This probably spread west. There was an epidemic that killed many at Green Bay in 1683 (La Potherie, *History*, 1:354), and there was sickness among the Menominees in the early 1680s, but it is unclear if this was smallpox (*JR* 62:205).

For Winnebagos, see La Potherie, *History*, 293–300. For Sauks, Fox, Winnebagos, and Menominees, see Jeanne Kay, "The Fur Trade and Native American Population Growth," *Ethnohistory* 31 (1984): 265–87. For a discussion of Iroquois demography, see Ann F. Ramenofsky, *Vectors of Death: The Archaeology of European Contact* (Albuquerque: University of New Mexico Press, 1987), 71–102.

spring when game animals were emaciated and yielded little meat. Horticulturalists in this area depended on their cached corn to pull them through
until the sturgeon ran and plenty returned. In the Illinois country the season
of scarcity extended from late winter into early summer. This was the period
between buffalo hunts and before new crops could be harvested. Then the
Illinois depended on dried buffalo meat and stored corn. Indians could and
did meet predictable seasons of scarcity by storing a surplus from the
seasons of plenty.[72]

In the refugee centers this environmental stability failed. Well before the
Iroquois wars there had inevitably been bad game years due to drought or
bitter winters. Fish populations fluctuated naturally. Poor weather disrupted
spawning runs and Great Lakes storms prevented fishing in late fall. And
drought, pests, or early frosts could kill or limit corn crops. Any such failure
of one component of the system obviously increased reliance on the others.
In this sense, there had never been a single, "normal" subsistence cycle.
There were only series of contingencies as annual variations shaped food
procurement. The refugee centers suffered these normal fluctuations, but in
the centers, precisely because they were in marginal agricultural and overcrowded hunting areas, resource depletion compounded the usual seasons
of scarcity. From necessity, the Algonquians came to rely on a narrower
range of resources.

By virtually all French accounts, it was corn and fish that made the refugee
concentrations possible outside of the Illinois country. Along the Great
Lakes there was no concentration of refugees where the fisheries and the
potential for corn agriculture did not coincide. According to the Jesuits, the
people of Chequamegon lived only on corn and fish. At Green Bay corn was
the Potawatomi protection against the famine "that is only too common in
these regions." The land cleared for cornfields stretched for three leagues
around the French post at Michilimackinac, and at both Green Bay and
Michilimackinac the French relied on Indian surpluses for their own corn
supply.[73]

[72] For storage of food, see Lettre du découvreur à un de ses associes ... 29 sept. 1680,
Margry, *Découvertes*, 2:36–37. De Gannes (Deliette) Memoir, *IHC*, 23:310–14; Thwaites
(ed.), *Hennepin's A New Discovery*, 154; *JR* 54:223, *JR* 51:27; *JR* 57:265; *JR* 55:111;
Thwaites (ed.), *Lahontan's Voyages*, 1:143–48, 168. Sufficient corn was available at
Michilimackinac and Green Bay for sale to the French; see Le Clercq Memoir and Joutel's
Journal, both in Cox, *Journeys of La Salle*, 1:128, 2:228–29.
[73] Perrot, *Memoir*, 120; La Potherie, *History*, 305; *JR* 54:151, 166; Thwaites (ed.), *Hennepin's A
New Discovery*, 116; Thwaites (ed.), *Lahontan's Voyages*, 1:146–48. For Michilimackinac, see
"Journey of Dollier and Galinee," 207; and "The Memoir of Lamothe Cadillac" in Quaife
(ed.), *The Western Country*, 12–15; and Letter of Cadillac, Aug. 3, 1695, in E. M. Sheldon,
The Early History of Michigan from the First Settlement to 1815 (New York: A. S. Barnes,
1956), 74; Narrative of ... Occurrences in 1694, *NYCD* 9:587. For Green Bay, see *JR*

Culturally, the consumption of corn and the idea of security were closely intertwined. As Perrot noted:

> The kinds of food which the savages like best and which they make the most effort to obtain are the Indian corn, the kidney bean, and the squash. If they are without these, they think they are fasting, no matter what abundance of meat and fish they have in their stores, the Indian corn being to them what bread is to the French.[74]

This need for corn prompted these fleeing and desperate peoples to seek arable lands in unpromising regions where agriculture yielded only a tenuous subsistence. The skilled Huron and Petun horticulturalists who fled into the Lake Superior region went well beyond the climatic edge of the reliable 160-day growing season needed for corn agriculture. There were, however, pockets of land where microclimates suitable for agriculture existed. These areas offered 140-day growing seasons that made agriculture risky but possible. At each of these pockets along southern Lake Superior and northern Lake Michigan – Chequamegon, Keweenaw, Michilimackinac, and Sault Sainte Marie – refugees eventually settled. Farther south, at Green Bay, the line of refugee villages hugged almost exactly the edges of the 160-day growing season. Because the refugees lived along the margins of the lands where corn could be grown, however, crop failures were a constant possibility. Agriculture, particularly at Chequamegon and Michilimackinac, ran great risks of late-spring and early-fall frosts. Repeated losses of corn crops at Michilimackinac in the 1690s helped to prompt the eventual abandonment of that place by the Ottawas and the Huron-Petuns. At Green Bay harvests were more certain, but the harvest failed there in 1675. It appears, too, that the crop failures like those at Michilimackinac later in the century may also have occurred at Green Bay, where the French Intendant Raudot claimed that corn no longer provided much security to the Fox, Mascoutens, and Kickapoos.[75]

With the precariousness of corn growing and the large populations the

---

56:121; *JR* 57:265–67. For evidence that Indians regarded fish and corn as necessary staples, see Perrot, *Memoir*, 237, and Narrative of ... Occurrences, 1695, *NYCD* 9:606.

[74] Perrot, *Memoir*, 102.

[75] A vivid graphic representation of how village sites related to climatic zones is available in Helen Hornbeck Tanner (ed.), *Atlas of Great Lakes Indian History* (Norman: University of Oklahoma Press, 1987), 20–21. The climate appears to have grown colder and moister beginning about 1400 A.D.–David Baerreis, Reid Bryson, and John Kutzbach, "Climate and Culture in the Western Great Lakes Region," *Mid-Continental Journal of Archaeology* 1 (1976): 52. For crop losses, see Narrative of ... Occurrences ... 1695, *NYCD* 9:607; *JR* 60:199; Antoine Raudot, "Memoir Concerning the Different Indian Nations of North America," in W. Vernon Kinietz, *The Indians of the Western Great Lakes* (Ann Arbor: University of Michigan Press, 1965); Cadillac's Account of Detroit, Sept. 25, 1702, *MPHC*, 33:138.

fisheries became a critical resource. François Dollier de Casson and Renée de Bréhaut de Galinée claimed that the fisheries alone could support 10,000 persons at Michilimackinac. And Antoine Laumet de La Mothe, Sieur de Cadillac, was only slightly more conservative when he claimed that fish alone could support most of the 6,000–7,000 Indians there. At Green Bay, the French were more restrained in their claims. They thought the net fisheries, snagging as they did fish, diving birds, and waterfowl on their flyways, sufficed for three months' subsistence, and this apparently did not include the sturgeon taken in the spring at fishing weirs or the fall catch of herring, which, smoked and stored, fed people over the winter. Father André in November 1672 found the Potawatomi cabins at Chouskouabika so full of nets and herring that he could hardly enter them.[76]

The fisheries tended to be more reliable than agriculture because the Algonquians were not at the margins of the fisheries but at their centers. All the great concentrations of refugee population on the Great Lakes were located at the best fishing sites on Lake Superior and Lake Michigan. Michilimackinac, the longest lived of these seventeenth- and eighteenth-century settlements, was, in Algonquian terms, the "native country" of the fish themselves. Yet fishing also remained a precarious endeavor that demanded precise skills and a suitable technology that not all refugees possessed. Those tribes who did fish extensively were at the mercy of the weather. Storms during spawning season, or a warm winter and weak ice, could doom a fishery. Fisheries at their most successful could provide only seasonal abundance. Algonquian techniques of drying could preserve the fall catch of herring and whitefish through the winter, but the yields of the spring runs of sturgeon could not be preserved long during the warm and humid summers.[77]

The hunt, the last major element in the food cycle of the refugee centers, was the least important in terms of yield, but still a critical seasonal resource and the last defense against famine. In most years the largely hunting peoples regularly resorted to fishermen and horticulturalists for food, but in

[76] La Potherie, History, 305. JR 54:151, 167; Thwaites (ed.), Hennepin's A New Discovery, 116; Thwaites (ed.), Lahontan's Voyages, 1:146–48. For Michilimackinac, see "Journey of Dollier and Galinee," 207; and "The Memoir of Lamothe Cadillac" in Quaife (ed.), The Western Country, 12–15; and Letter of Cadillac, Aug. 3, 1695, in Sheldon, Early History of Michigan, 74; Narrative of . . . Occurrences in 1694, NYCD 9:587. For Green Bay, see JR 56:121; JR 57:265–67.

[77] Charles Cleland, "The Inland Shore Fishery of the Northern Great Lakes: Its Development and Importance in Prehistory," American Antiquity 47 (1982): 761–84, particularly map on 765; For quotation, see JR 55:159–61. The Bell site, an early historic Fox village, shows numerous fish remains, but most of those came from rivers and from smaller lakes near the Fox village. Paul W. Parmalee "Vertebrate Remains from the Bell Site, Winnebago County, Wisconsin," The Wisconsin Archeologist, NS 44 (March 1963): 62. For lack of ability to use canoes, see JR 58:63. La Potherie, History, 2:20.

This sketch by Decard de Granville shows Indian fishing techniques and equipment on the Great Lakes about 1700. (New York Public Library)

years when crops or fisheries failed only hunting and gathering stood between the Algonquians and starvation. The anomaly of hunters clustering on overcrowded lands, whose major attraction is fisheries that the hunters themselves do not efficiently exploit is explained as soon as the context is broadened. Corn and fish sustained large settlements, and around these settlements hunters came for trade and protection. Around the horticultural villagers who relied heavily on the fisheries, therefore, were other villagers, some horticultural, some not, who relied more heavily on the hunt. This pattern predated the fur trade, but the fur trade reinforced it.[78]

This combination of marginal agriculture, sometimes precarious fishing, and the clustering of hunters for defense and trade set the stage for environmental disaster. As hunters depleted game around the refugee centers, hunger and famine ensued when the fisheries or the corn harvest failed. Pierre Esprit Radisson and the Huron-Petuns endured such a famine. Five hundred died, and hunger continued into the summer of 1661, when Father Menard died trying to reach the Huron-Petuns. In 1670 the Jesuits found the Potawatomis and other tribes of Green Bay proper pinched with hunger. The Mascoutens, Fox, and other outlying villagers complained of hunger during the 1670s. Even in the best years, the surplus stored from horticulture was relatively small. In 1671, Father Allouez claimed that a family with ten or twelve bags of corn considered itself wealthy. The Potawatomis might strive to fill their cabins with herring, but by late winter the fish were gone and they anxiously awaited the coming of the sturgeon.[79]

Winter became a time of particular horror. Those groups that did not fish extensively regularly departed on winter hunts, but when corn and fish were abundant, the fishing peoples preferred to remain in their villages taking what game they could obtain nearby. By staying home they avoided the prolonged winter hunts that had become the most dangerous point in the refugee subsistence cycle. To embark on a winter hunt was to leave stored

---

[78] The tribes who did not fish have been cited previously. The Ojibwa groups around Chequamegon, Keweenaw, Green Bay, and Sault Sainte Marie usually did not plant crops. The Fox, who did plant crops, also relied heavily on hunting, Parmalee, "Vertebrate Remains," *Wisconsin Archeologist*, 65. For game animals at each location, see *ibid.*, 65, and James E. Fitting, "Patterns of Acculturation at the Straits of Mackinac," in Charles Cleland (ed.), *Cultural Change and Continuity: Essays in Honor of James B. Griffin* (New York: Academic Press, 1976).

[79] For the Radisson account, see Adams (ed.), *Radisson*, 131–34; and for death of Father Menard, *JR* 48:127–37. Exact dates are hard to determine from the Radisson manuscript; Adams dates the starving winter of 1661–62, but the *Jesuit Relations* clearly date it as 1660–61. That this was the same winter seems certain because both accounts have it followed by a Feast of the Dead with the Sioux. *JR* 46:143. For other accounts of famine diets, see Perrot, *Memoir*, 102–03; *JR* 48:119; *JR* 50:177; Adams (ed.), *Radisson*, 130–33; *JR* 46:139–43, *JR* 48:119, 261–65; *JR* 51:171. For Green Bay in 1670, see *JR* 54:203, 207, 213. For Mascoutens, Fox, etc., see *JR* 59:229. For Allouez's claim, see *JR* 55:111.

supplies behind; without pack animals and with canoes useless on frozen streams or lakes, only small amounts of corn and fish could be carried on the journey. Echoes of disasters on the winter hunt reverberate through *The Jesuit Relations* and other early French sources. Jacques Marquette, at the beginning of his Mississippi voyage of 1673, reported that late fall and winter, when they moved into their hunting camps, was when the Mascoutens, Miamis, and Kickapoos most feared famine, and he later described the fatigues of such hunts as being "almost impossible to Frenchmen." Father Allouez, however, did endure them. He accompanied eighty cabins of Miamis and some Shawnees who were reduced to a famine diet of such roots as the women could grub as they staggered through half-frozen marshlands. He claimed later that such experiences were the common expectation of hunters. The Miamis survived their ordeal. But other hunters starved when game failed them and they could not get back to the food caches they had made. Starvation and hunger on the hunt were never predictable. In the winter of 1675–76, during a lull in the Iroquois wars, sixty-five Mississaugas starved to death north of Lake Erie, while several days away the Ottawas enjoyed abundant game.[80]

Such disasters were not the simple exigencies of the hunting life; they were the special problems of refugees crowded into lands which could not sustain the hunting pressure put upon them. Hunters eventually eliminated large game from the vicinity of the refugee centers. According to the Baron de Lahontan, no large game existed within twenty leagues of Michilimackinac by 1688, and this is supported by archaeological excavations which show few remains of large mammals in village middens. By 1675 the French noted

---

[80] For hunting patterns, see Fox: *JR* 54:223; *JR* 58:47–49; Miamis: *JR* 54:23; *JR* 68:63; *JR* 59:225, 171; Perrot, *Memoir*, 109, 118–19. Le Clercq says the Illinois hunted in large village groups. LeClercq Memoir in Cox, *Journeys of La Salle*, 1:102. According to Margry (*Découvertes*, 1:460), La Salle said the Illinois hunted by families "ou par tribus" meaning, apparently, clans. Each party consisted of 200 to 300 persons. By 1699 hunting parties composed only of active men and women departed from the winter camps, *JR* 65:73, 83. For variable hunting patterns of fishing peoples, see *JR* 51:29; *JR* 54:203–05, 211, 213; *JR* 55:191; *JR* 57:265–67, 291–93; *JR* 58:39, 63, 289; *JR* 55:43; *JR* 59:165–67. *JR* 57:249–55, 261; *JR* 61:103–05. The demographic composition of these parties changed over time. The large hunting party reported by the Baron de Lahontan in 1688 probably included women and children, Thwaites (ed.), *Lahontan's Voyages*, 1:143. In the same area during 1685–86, the Iroquois had captured children as well as adults when they raided winter hunting camps. Denonville to Seignelay, June 12, 1686, *NYCD* 9:293–94. La Potherie, who wrote in the early eighteenth century, indicated largely all-male hunts occurred out of Michilimackinac in the 1690s, La Potherie, *History*, 1:281–82.

For Marquette's statements, see "Jolliet and Marquette" in Kellogg, (ed.), *Narratives*, 233–34, and *JR* 59:171. For Allouez, see *JR* 62:207, 208. For starvation of smaller hunting bands, see Perrot, *Memoir*, 103, and La Potherie, *History*, 1:280. For praise of Fox hunting grounds, see *JR* 54:219. For starvation and hunger among the Fox, see *JR* 59:229. For death of Mississaugas, see *JR* 60:215, 229. The Mississaugas died on lands apparently often hunted by the Iroquois.

that deer grew noticeably more abundant as one traveled away from the
Potawatomi villages on Green Bay. Buffalo had markedly diminished on the
lands near the Great Village of the Kaskaskias by 1680.[81]

Game remained most abundant in the lands the Iroquois had emptied.
These, as French accounts make clear, were war grounds where all who
entered were in danger. Hunting nations confined to relatively small areas
thus depleted game locally, even though abundance might exist just beyond
them. Normal cultural controls for conserving game seem to have failed
when several nations competed for, or were compressed into, the same
hunting area. Baron de Lahontan and French traders mention hunting
practices which took care to spare breeding stock during hunts, but such
methods proved inadequate in the 1670s and 1680s. One of the Iroquois
complaints against the Illinois was that they slaughtered all the beaver and
failed to leave any breeding stock.[82]

The refugee centers became barometers of Algonquian fortunes: They
swelled with defeat and shrank with victory. The requirements of defense
acted as a centripetal force, holding the refugees around the centers, while
hunger and disease, acting as centrifugal forces, pushed them out. The price
of such defensive concentrations was very often misery. Their residents
endured the centers only because the alternatives were worse. Those who
escaped them did not seek to return. Three Shawnees, probably from the
Great Village of the Kaskaskias, summarized the everyday horrors faced by
the refugees. Captured and adopted by the peoples of Saint Louis Bay on
the Gulf of Mexico during La Salle's 1682 foray down the Mississippi, they
showed no desire to return to the *pays d'en haut*. When the French offered
them a chance to return to their villages, the Shawnees replied:

> They were not unnatural enough to abandon their wives and
> children; ... moreover, being in the most fertile, healthy, and peaceful

---

[81] For initial hunting on Green Bay and for Summer Island as a summer hunting station, see
David S. Brose, "Summer Island III: An Early Historic Site in the Upper Great Lakes,"
Historical Archaeology 4 (1970): 24. Michilimackinac, Sault Sainte Marie and surrounding
regions were praised as good hunting areas in the late 1660s and early 1670s, Perrot,
Memoir, 221; *JR* 50:263. Compare this to Lahontan's statements in Thwaites (ed.),
Lahontan's Voyages, 1:148; Perrot, *Memoir*, 120, and Cadillac Memoir in Quaife, *The Western
Country*, 15, and Fitting, "Patterns of Acculturation," 325. For deer diminishing near
Potawatomis, see *JR* 59:173. By 1699 St. Cosme reported a dearth of meat in the area almost
all the time, "Voyage of St. Cosme" in Kellogg (ed.), *Narratives*, 343. For buffalo, see Voyage
de M. de La Salle à la riviere Mississippi, Margry, *Découvertes*, 2:95.

[82] For neutral grounds, see Lettre de Cavelier de la Salle, 11 aoust 1682, Margry, *Découvertes*,
2:236–37, and Lettre du Découvreur à un de ses associes, 1679 – 29 sept. 1680, Margry,
Découvertes, 2:59–60, and Thwaites (ed.), *Lahontan's Voyages*, 1:318–20. The area around
the Detroit River and Lake Erie that Father Henri Nouvel described in 1676 was an old
neutral ground that was now being hunted, *JR* 60:219–21, 227. For attempts to conserve
game, see Thwaites (ed.), *Lahontan's Voyages*, 1:82, 114; Mémoire que la direction ... 16
avril 1703, AN, C11A, v. 24. For Iroquois complaints of Illinois, see Du Chesneau's Memoir

country in the world, they would be devoid of sense to leave it and expose themselves to be tomahawked by the Illinois or burnt by the Iroquois on their way to another where the winter was insufferably cold, the summer without game, and ever in war.[83]

In the 1690s, the horrors of the *pays d'en haut* eased as the French and Algonquians put the Iroquois on the defensive. French and Algonquian invasions of Iroquoia burned villages, killed warriors, and disrupted subsistence cycles, leaving the Iroquois hungry and poor. As the losses of the Five Nations mounted, the Iroquois ineffectually sought English aid. The Iroquois wars, sometimes as part of larger imperial wars, sometimes as a separate struggle, continued until 1701, when the exhausted Iroquois sought peace with Canada and its allies. The result was the so-called Grand Settlement of 1701 which established a general peace. The Iroquois essentially abandoned hunting territories west of Detroit and agreed to allow Onontio to arbitrate their conflicts with his allies. The Iroquois promised to remain neutral in all future Anglo-French wars.[84]

The triumph of the alliance over the Iroquois during the 1690s meant the decline of the very communities that had produced the alliance. The refugee centers, protected from Iroquois attacks, disbanded; their inhabitants moved into the more fertile and temperate lands opened up by Iroquois decline. Neither the alliance nor the common European-Algonquian world forged in these centers died, however. They continued to grow.

---

on Western Indians, Nov. 13, 1681, *NYCD* 9:162–63; Thwaites (ed.), *Lahontan's Voyages*, 1:82.
[83] Cavelier's Account of La Salle's Voyage to the Mouth of the Mississippi . . . , Cox, *Journeys of La Salle*, 277, 283.
[84] For the end to these wars and the Grand Settlement, see Richter, "War and Culture," 546–53.

2

The middle ground

For every time we make others part of a "reality" that we alone invent, denying their creativity by usurping the right to create, we use those people and their way of life and make them subservient to ourselves.

Roy Wagner, *The Invention of Culture*

In action, people put their concepts and categories into ostensive relations to the world. Such referential uses bring into play other determinations of the signs, besides their received sense, namely the actual world and the people concerned.

Marshall Sahlins, *Islands of History*

I

Because the French and Algonquians were trading partners and allies, the boundaries of the Algonquian and French worlds melted at the edges and merged. Although identifiable Frenchmen and identifiable Indians obviously continued to exist, whether a particular practice or way of doing things was French or Indian was, after a time, not so clear. This was not because individual Indians became "Frenchified" or because individual Frenchmen went native, although both might occur. Rather, it was because Algonquians who were perfectly comfortable with their status and practices as Indians and Frenchmen, confident in the rightness of French ways, nonetheless had to deal with people who shared neither their values nor their assumptions about the appropriate way of accomplishing tasks. They had to arrive at some common conception of suitable ways of acting; they had to create what I have already referred to as a middle ground.[1]

The creation of the middle ground involved a process of mutual invention by both the French and the Algonquians. This process passed through various stages, of which the earliest is at once the most noticed and the least interesting. It was in this initial stage that the French, for example, simply

---

[1] The impossibility of considering any society in isolation is one of the major themes of Eric Wolf in *Europe and the People Without History* (Berkeley: University of California Press, 1982), 3–23, 385. It is also a position taken by Anthony Giddens, *A Contemporary Critique of Historical Materialism* (Berkeley: University of California Press, 1981), 23–24.

assimilated Indians into their own conceptual order. Indians became *sauvages*, and the French reduced Indian religion to devil worship and witchcraft. Algonquians, for their part, thought of the first Europeans as manitous. On both sides, new people were crammed into existing categories in a mechanical way.[2]

Literacy gave this initial stage a potency and a durability for Europeans it might otherwise have lacked. Because the French were literate, knowledge of Indians was diffused far from the site of actual contact. Such knowledge, unchallenged by actual experience with Indians, survived as a potent cultural relict. Long after it ceased to govern the actions of those who actually lived among Indians, the idea of Indians as literally *sauvages*, or wild men embodying either natural virtue or ferocity, persisted among intellectuals and statesmen in France. Assimilated into European controversies, these imaginary Indians became the Indians of Chateaubriand and Rousseau. They took on importance, but it was one detached from the continuing processes of contact between real Algonquians and real Europeans. In the *pays d'en haut*, actual Indians and whites of widely different social class and status had, for a variety of reasons, to rely on each other in order to achieve quite specific ends. It was these Frenchmen (for Frenchwomen would not appear until much later) and Algonquian men and women who created a common ground – the middle ground – on which to proceed.[3]

This process of creation resulted quite naturally from attempts to follow normal conventions of behavior in a new situation. Each side sought different goals in a different manner. French officials and merchants sought to rationalize and order what they saw as the unpredictable world of the *sauvage*; Algonquians sought, in a sense, the opposite. They wanted to change or readjust the given order by appeals for personal favor or exemption. In much the same way that they sought special power to readjust the order of the world of plants, animals, and spirits by appealing to the

---

[2] For concentration on European images, see Bernard Sheehan, *Savagism and Civility: Indians and Englishmen in Colonial America* (Cambridge: Cambridge University Press, 1980); Olive P. Dickason, *The Myth of the Savage and the Beginnings of French Colonialism in the Americas* (Edmonton: University of Alberta Press, 1984); Cornelius Jaenen is correct when he points out that the French lacked the power to force American Indians to acculturate. Cornelius Jaenen, *Friend and Foe: Aspects of French-Amerindian Cultural Contact in the Sixteenth and Seventeenth Centuries* (New York: Columbia University Press, 1976), 195. James Axtell's work is an exception to the usual tendency to impose static categories on Indians and whites, and Karen Kupperman disputes the extent to which cultural concepts derived from early accounts actually governed relations, Karen Ordahl Kupperman, *Settling with the Indians: The Meeting of English and Indian Cultures in America, 1580–1640* (Totowa, N.J.: Rowman & Littlefield, 1980).

[3] Cornelius J. Jaenen, "Les Sauvages Ameriquians: Persistence into the Eighteenth Century of Traditional French Concepts and Constructs for Comprehending AmerIndians," *Ethnohistory* 29 (1982): 43–56.

manitous, so they sought beneficial changes in the social world by appeals to the French. Often, in the examples that follow, when the French sought the imposition of hard-and-fast rules, the Algonquians sought the "power" that comes from knocking the order off balance, from asserting the personal, the human exception. The result of each side's attempts to apply its own cultural expectations in a new context was often change in culture itself. In trying to maintain the conventional order of its world, each group applied rules that gradually shifted to meet the exigencies of particular situations. The result of these efforts was a new set of common conventions, but these conventions served as a basis for further struggles to order or influence the world of action.[4]

The middle ground depended on the inability of both sides to gain their ends through force. The middle ground grew according to the need of people to find a means, other than force, to gain the cooperation or consent of foreigners. To succeed, those who operated on the middle ground had, of necessity, to attempt to understand the world and the reasoning of others and to assimilate enough of that reasoning to put it to their own purposes. Particularly in diplomatic councils, the middle ground was a realm of constant invention, which was just as constantly presented as convention. Under the new conventions, new purposes arose, and so the cycle continued.[5]

Perhaps the central and defining aspect of the middle ground was the willingness of those who created it to justify their own actions in terms of what they perceived to be their partner's cultural premises. Those operating in the middle ground acted for interests derived from their own culture, but they had to convince people of another culture that some mutual action was fair and legitimate. In attempting such persuasion people quite naturally sought out congruences, either perceived or actual, between the two cultures. The congruences arrived at often seemed – and, indeed, were – results of misunderstandings or accidents. Indeed, to later observers the interpretations offered by members of one society for the practices of another can appear ludicrous. This, however, does not matter. Any con-

---

[4] A useful discussion of these processes is found in Roy Wagner, *The Invention of Culture* (Chicago: University of Chicago Press, 1981), 1–70, particularly 46–52, 87–88. Many Frenchmen of peasant backgrounds were probably closer to what Wagner calls the differentiating mode of tribal peoples than to the systematizing mode of French officials.

Attempts to get around the confining model of a basically static structure which is combined with an ephemeral history has been most thoroughly developed by Anthony Giddens, *Central Problems in Social Theory: Action, Structure and Contradiction in Social Analysis* (Berkeley: University of California Press, 1979); *Critique of Historical Materialism*; and *The Constitution of Society* (Berkeley: University of California Press, 1984). It has simultaneously emerged in anthropology, see Marshall Sahlins, *Islands of History* (Chicago: University of Chicago Press, 1985).

[5] For this, see Wagner, *Invention of Culture*, 52–55.

gruence, no matter how tenuous, can be put to work and can take on a life of
its own if it is accepted by both sides. Cultural conventions do not have to be
true to be effective any more than legal precedents do. They have only to be
accepted.

The middle ground of the *pays d'en haut* existed on two distinct levels. It
was both a product of everyday life and a product of formal diplomatic
relations between distinct peoples. For historians, however, the middle
ground is initially easiest to perceive as it was articulated in formal settings.[6]

In June 1695 the alliance of the Huron-Petuns, Ottawas, and French was
in one of its recurrent crises. The Ottawas and Huron-Petuns, fearing that
the French would make a separate peace with the Iroquois, had undertaken
secret negotiations of their own with the Five Nations. These negotiations
had received added impetus from English promises of trade at rates considerably below those of the French. The French commander at Michilimackinac, Antoine Laumet de La Mothe, Sieur de Cadillac, suspecting the
existence of such talks but not knowing the details of them, attempted to halt
the negotiations by soliciting war parties led by French partisans among the
Ottawas. Though relatively few, the war parties threatened the Iroquois and
thus disrupted plans for peace. The leaders of those who favored peace,
particularly a Huron chief known as the Baron, sought to stop the war parties
without mentioning the Huron-Petuns' negotiations with the Iroquois. To
succeed, the Baron had to accomplish one of two things. He had to provide
reasons acceptable both to the French and to their partisans as to why the
war parties should not depart. Or, failing this, he had to alienate the pro-
French Ottawas from Cadillac and the Jesuits. To achieve these ends, he
convened a "grand and numerous" council of the nations of Michilimackinac
to meet with one another as well as with Cadillac, the Jesuits, and "the most
respectable Frenchmen of the post."[7]

The council convened to do little more than hear a story from the Baron.
He told his listeners that recently there had been discovered in the country
around Saginaw Bay an old man and his wife, each about a hundred years
old. They had resided there ever since the expulsion of the Hurons from
their own country. The old man knew and had related all that had passed in
the western wars since the destruction of the Hurons and had paid particular
attention to the embassies of the Iroquois to Onontio. He knew all these
things because of his communications with the Master of Life who spoke
directly to the old man and who sent him animals and made his fields abound
with corn and pumpkins. The old man, too, knew of the present de facto

---

[6] The creation of the middle ground might serve as an example of what Anthony Giddens calls
structuration. Giddens, *Central Problems in Social Theory*, 2–7, 69–73, 82.

[7] Callières au Ministre, 20 oct. 1696, AN, C11A, v.14, ff.216–17. Narrative of...
Occurrences... 1694, 1695, *NYCD*, 9:604–9.

truce with the Iroquois and insinuated that the first side to break it would inevitably be destroyed.[8]

The old man exhorted the Indians to be attentive to the Black Gowns and to apply themselves to prayer because, if the Master of Life "who is one in three persons, who form but one Spirit and one Will" was not obeyed, he would kill the corn as he had last year. Finally the old man had told them the eighth day should be observed by abstinence from work and should be sanctified by prayer. The dead, he said, should be given scaffold burials instead of being buried in the ground, so that they could more easily take the road to Heaven. Finally, the old man had urged that they all hearken to the voice of Onontio and follow his will. On concluding his recitation of the old man's message, the Baron offered Cadillac a present of beaver from the old man himself. Cadillac, who thought that of the whole story only the beaver was not imaginary, refused the present, "this voice being unknown to him."[9]

The Baron's story was an attempt to use and expand the middle ground so that his own interest – peace with the Iroquois – could be secured. Peace could not be protected through normal Huron cultural forms. If the matter had depended only on non-Christian Ottawas and Huron-Petuns, the Baron would not have had to resort to the story of the old man, with all its Christian and prophetic elements. If he had been addressing Indians only, the council could have been convened to consider a dream that contained the same message. Dreams, however, as the Baron realized quite well, had no legitimacy for the French who were urging their partisans to action. What did have legitimacy for them was divine revelation, and so the Baron gave them one. Baron's attempt failed because, as the chronicler of his speech huffily observed, the French only attached "belief to certain revelations and visions . . . because they are authorized." The old man was unauthorized and so proved an unsuccessful device for conveying a message in a manner that had legitimacy for Europeans.[10]

Nonetheless, the Baron's tactics were both clever and revealing. He had consciously tried to buttress the legitimacy of the old man's message by filling it with fragments of Christian doctrine (the Trinity, exhortations to prayer, attentiveness to the missionaries) and with the commands to follow the will of Onontio, the French governor. These were all items the French could hardly quarrel with. Yet the Baron also gave the message a definite Huron tinge. The prophet was an Indian who changed the Sabbath from the seventh day to the eighth. It is unlikely this was accidental. As early as 1679, the Jesuits had praised the Huron-Petuns for their particularly scrupulous

---

[8] Narrative of . . . Occurrences . . . 1694, 1695, *NYCD* 9:607.

[9] *Ibid.*; it is interesting to note here that some Ottawas eventually did adopt scaffold burials, *HBNI* 15:777.

[10] Narrative of . . . Occurrences . . . 1694, 1695, *NYCD* 9:607.

observance of Sundays and feast days. The Huron-Petuns even had a special officer of the faith who gave notice of the meeting days. It would be surprising if the Baron had forgotten all this. It seems more likely that the Baron's movement of the Sabbath was intentional and that he meant it, along with the command for scaffold burials, to set the old man apart as an Indian prophet with an Indian message from the Christian God. It is unclear if the Baron seriously believed the French would accept the legitimacy of an Indian prophet, but by framing the story as he did, he created a situation in which even their rejection of the old man might serve his purposes. When Cadillac and the Jesuits rejected the old man, they rejected, too, exhortation to prayer and obedience to missionaries and Onontio. More than that, by rejecting the story, the French seemed to insinuate that God spoke directly only to whites, and not to Indians.[11]

Cadillac denounced the story as ridiculous, mocked the Baron's apparent confusion about the Sabbath, and demanded that the Indians strike the Iroquois. He left behind a troubled council. To the gathered Ottawa and Huron-Petun elders it now seemed that "the French were unwilling to listen to the voice of their pretended man of God, alleging that the Black Gowns were very desirous of being heard when they recounted stories about Paul and the anchorites of olden times; wherefore then, they asked, shall not our old man possess the same light?"[12]

The council was merely a skirmish within the larger diplomatic battle being waged over participation by the Michilimackinac Indians in the Iroquois war, but it reveals the process that formed the middle ground and made the boundaries between French and Algonquian societies so porous. To further its interests, each side had to attain cultural legitimacy in terms of the other. The Baron and Cadillac, as much as each might mangle the subtleties of the other's cultural view, had created a forum in which they could speak and understand each other. They did so by using, for their own purposes and according to their own understanding, the cultural forms of the other. The Baron appealed to a Christian tradition of prophecy and put it to Indian purposes. He sought to validate it, in Indian terms, by a gift of beaver. Cadillac, appearing in an Indian council, followed Algonquian forms and, knowing what acceptance of the gift signified, refused it. To accept the gift was to acknowledge the old man, whom the Baron would then make "talk on every occasion that he would judge favorable for his pernicious designs." He rejected an Indian adaptation of a Christian device through his own use of Algonquian-Iroquoian diplomatic forms. Both used the cultural

---

[11] For Huron-Petuns and Sabbath, see *JR* 61:105.
[12] Narrative of . . . Occurrences . . . 1694, 1695, *NYCD* 9:608. For a similar instance, see *JR* 59:223.

forms of the other cleverly, if crudely. The crudeness of the Baron's Christianity or Cadillac's mastery of Indian diplomacy mattered less than the need for each to employ these foreign elements at all. They merged them into something quite different from the Algonquian, Iroquoian, and French cultures that gave them birth.

The Baron's encounter with Cadillac took place in a diplomatic forum where representatives of each culture dealt with a well-formulated body of ideas and practices. This was one aspect of the middle ground and the one in which its methods are best documented and exhibited. The middle ground itself, however, did not originate in councils and official encounters; instead, it resulted from the daily encounters of individual Indians and Frenchmen with problems and controversies that needed immediate solution. Many of these problems revolved around basic issues of sex, violence, and material exchange. The need to resolve these problems, perhaps even more than the problems of alliance, forced the middle ground into existence. But even this misstates the issue, for the distinction between official dealings and personal dealings was a hazy and confusing one in Algonquian society, where coercive mechanisms and hierarchical structures were notoriously weak.

Although French officials spoke of their relationship with the Algonquians in economic, political, and, less often, religious terms, paradoxically economic and political institutions could not control the context of contact. In the day-to-day relations of the western country, the relationships of Algonquians and Frenchmen as trading partners and allies were abstractions, pertinent, perhaps, to Indians and French as aggregates, but having little to do with actual people in face-to-face relationships. In another society, with more coercive mechanisms at an elite's disposal, personal relations between intruders such as the French and the members of the host society might be kept to a minimum and mattered little. Traders might be isolated in special quarters and granted special privileges; they might be governed by separate rules and taxed at stated rates. Isolation, however, was impossible among the Algonquians, who lacked a state with coercive institutions and in whose society obedience to authority was usually neither a social fact nor a social virtue.[13]

This weakness of political authority and lack of subordination in Algonquian society struck both the Algonquians and the French as a major difference between the two peoples. For the French this lack of subordination, not the Algonquians' state of material or technological development, was at the heart of Algonquian "savagery." The northern Indians, according

[13] Narrative of . . . Occurrences . . . 1694, 1695, *NYCD* 9:608. For the development of trading enclaves, see Philip D. Curtin, *Cross-cultural Trade in World History* (Cambridge: Cambridge University Press, 1984), 11–12, 38, 46–49, 111–15.

to the Sieur d'Aigremont, "possess no subordination among themselves . . . being opposed to all constraint. Moreover, these peoples [have] no idea of Royal grandeur nor Majesty, nor of the powers of Superiors over inferiors."[14]

Father Membre, traveling south along the Mississippi with La Salle in 1682, clearly regarded authority as being at the heart of not only society but humanity. The Natchez and the hierarchical societies of the Mississippi were technologically like the Algonquians. They were a Stone Age people, but they were "all different from our Canada Indians in their houses, dress, manners, inclinations and customs. . . . Their chiefs possess all the authority. . . . They have their valets and officers who follow them and serve them everywhere. They distribute their favors and presents at will. In a word we generally found men there."[15]

The French did not err in noting the absence of class divisions and state and religious institutions among northern Algonquians, but they were mistaken when they took this for an absence of social order. Tradition was the storehouse of a tribal people's knowledge of themselves as a people and a guide to how they should act. As war and disease reduced populations and forced the amalgamation of previously distinct peoples, the survivors seemed to cling to their traditions. But they were like infants sucking the breasts of their dead mothers; tradition could no longer sustain them.[16]

The weakness of coercive authority among the Algonquians would have mattered less if French authority had officially reached the West. With the decline of the trade fairs, however, official French supervision of exchange became a mirage. Indians no longer traveled long distances to fortified European towns or outposts to exchange furs. Some limited exchanges of this type took place at Fort Saint Louis, in the Illinois country, and at Michilimackinac and the posts Perrot erected among the Sioux, but most trade was the work of small groups of Frenchmen traveling to Indian villages and hunting camps. Once these traders had lost their status as manitous, they were strangers without social standing in Algonquian villages. They were also wealthy strangers, with goods far in excess of their own immediate needs, who stood virtually defenseless. If they were to succeed as traders, they had to find means to protect themselves either through force or by establishing personal ties within the communities in which they traded.[17]

[14] For Sieur d'Aigremont, see D'Aigremont to Pontchartrain, Nov. 14, 1708, *WHC* 16:250.

[15] Chrétien Le Clercq, *The First Establishment of the Faith in New France*, 2 vols. (New York: J. G. Shea, 1881), 192.

[16] See Giddens, *Critique of Historical Materialism*, 93–94, 160, for a general discussion of these issues.

[17] *JR* 65:239. W. J. Eccles, *The Canadian Frontier* (Albuquerque: University of New Mexico Press, 1974), 110; Champigny au Ministre, 4 nov. 1693, AN, C11A, v. 12; Memoire . . . Denonville, aoust 1688, AN, C11A, v. 10 (765–66); Callières au Ministre, 15 oct. 1694, AN, C11A, v. 15; Memoire sur le ferme . . . 10 fev. 1696, AN, C11A, v. 16; Commerce du

The French elite feared the consequences of such contact. French authorities thought that Frenchmen moving within Algonquian society would slip the net unless kept under tight control. What horrified French officials quite as much as the economic damage they believed the coureurs de bois did was the social threat they represented. According to officials, the coureurs de bois were metamorphosing into *sauvages*, that is, men beyond the control of legitimate authority. What was particularly horrifying about the "savagery" of the coureurs de bois was that they seemed to glory in it. They used their freedom to mock the men who never doubted that they were their betters. On his return to the Illinois in 1680, La Salle found that his men had not only deserted but had also demolished his fort, stolen his goods, and, in the hand of a man La Salle recognized as Le Parisien, had left scrawled on a board a parting epithet: *Nous sommes touts Sauvages* ("We are all savages").[18]

Le Parisien, of course, was no more a *sauvage* than La Salle. He merely shared with his superiors a common misunderstanding of Algonquian society as a place of license without order. It was this misperception that gave the word *sauvage* its power as a metaphor for what officials regarded as a danger and men like Le Parisien saw as an opportunity – the escape from subordination. That most coureurs de bois could fully escape the restraining hands of the state and the church was an exaggeration. Yet, in another sense, the fear of the authorities and the hope of Le Parisien were not fully misplaced. Frenchmen in the West could to a remarkable degree act independently, if only temporarily, in reaching accommodations with the Algonquians among whom they traveled and lived. They made contact a complex social process only partially under the control of church and state. In the West, this process centered on Frenchmen whom the authorities did not regard as legitimate representatives of their own society and who were actually seen as a danger to it. There was always a tension between these men and those other Frenchmen who possessed legitimate standing: men who like La Salle, came with grants from the Crown; or missionaries, like the Jesuits; or military commanders; or licensed traders. Frenchmen in the West often cooperated, but such cooperation could never be presumed. Indians thus had to establish appropriate social ties with a diverse and often quarreling group of Frenchmen.[19]

---

castor ... 1696, AN, CllA, v. 14; Milo Quaife (ed.),*The Western Country in the Seventeenth Century: The Memoirs of Lanothe Cadillac and Pierre Liette* (Chicago: Lakeside Press, 1917), 16–18. Unititled mémoire (Par tout ce qui ...) AN, CIIA, v. 17 (f. 193).

[18] Duchesneau to M. de Seignelay, 10 Nov. 1679, *NYCD* 9:133–34; Denonville à Seignelay, 13 nov. 1685, AN, CIIA, v.7; Champigny Memoir, 10 mai 1691, AN, CIIA, v.11; Denonville to Seignelay, Jan. 1690, *NYCD* 9:442–43. For quotation, see Relation du voyage de Cavelier de La Salle, du 22 Aout 1680 a l'automne de 1681, Margry, *Découvertes*, 2:133. On coureurs de bois, see Jaenen, *Friend and Foe*, 115; Eccles, *Canadian Frontier*, 90.

[19] Louise Dechene, in examining records of those going west between 1708 and 1717, found

Certain of these diverse Frenchmen, in turn, posed dangers to Algonquian social order because they struck at the heart of Algonquian identity by arguing that traditional practices were not innate, but transferable from one people to another. Missionaries and Christianity, in this sense, represented a potentially subversive force that, if not assimilated into Algonquian traditions, could destroy the very identity of those who accepted it. Only in the Illinois country was this threat soon realized, and there, where the dangers of Christianity were most fully faced, the arguments of the opponents of the missionaries are revealing. The adversaries of the church based their attack partially on the argument that prayer was ineffective and baptism brought death, but they also worked from the assumption that Christianity displaced traditions central to the identity of various Illinois groups and appropriate to them. In a style of argument that foreshadowed later appeals to an "Indian way," Illinois elders contended that since identity was innate, Christianity was proper for the French; Illinois beliefs were proper for the Illinois. As a leading Peoria chief, an opponent of Christianity's, phrased it:

> I shall hold a feast . . . and I shall invite all the old men and all the chiefs of bands. . . . After speaking of our medicines and of what our grandfathers and ancestors have taught us, has this man who has come from afar better medicines than we have, to make us adopt his customs? His fables are good only in his own country; we have ours, which do not make us die as his do.

Or, in the words of a Kaskaskia elder, "full of zeal for the ancient customs of the country and apprehending that his credit and that of his class [*son semblable*] would be diminished if their people embraced the faith":

> All ye who have hitherto hearkened to what the black gown has said to you come into my cabin. I shall likewise teach you what I learned from my grandfather, and what we should believe. Leave their myths to the people who come from afar, and let us cling to our own traditions.[20]

The operation of the middle ground must be understood within a dual context. First, there was the weakness of hierarchical controls within Algonquian villages and the frailty of any authority French officials exerted over Frenchmen in the West. Second, there was the cultural threat each society seemed to pose to the elite of the other. What this meant in practice was that both the extent and meaning of social relations between Frenchmen

---

that of a total of 373 different individuals, 179 made just one trip and 112 made three or more. These 112 formed "l'armature du commerce interieur." The others made such voyages "une activité temporaire ou occasionnelle"; De Chene, *Habitants et Marchands de Montréal au xvii siècle* (Paris: Libraire Plon, 1974), 219–220.

[20] *JR* 64:173, 183.

and Algonquians were often negotiated largely on a face-to-face level within the villages themselves, and that these relations were not what either French authorities or Algonquian elders might have preferred them to be. This does not mean that there was no official element involved, but rather that official decisions could not determine the course of actual relations.

II

The array of relations negotiated in the middle ground was quite large, but leaving aside for now the liquor trade, problems in two arenas of contact – sex and violence – seem to have been particularly acute. Sexual relations between Frenchmen and Indian women and violence between French and Indians, both men and women, accompanied trade throughout the West. One facilitated trade, and the other threatened to destroy it; both presented problems of cultural interaction that had to be negotiated. Sex and violence are thus important not only in their own right but also as avenues for understanding how cultural accommodation on the middle ground, in fact, worked.

What made sexual relations between Frenchmen and Indian women so central to contact in the West was that until the 1730s relatively few Frenchwomen ever came west. Frenchwomen were a curiosity in the upper country. The appearance of Madame Le Sueur at Fort Saint Louis in the 1690s created such an uproar that she, like Indians visiting Europe, had to consent to a public display so that the curious could see her. The absence of Frenchwomen meant that French males actively sought out Indian women as sexual partners. Not all French males did so, of course. The Jesuits and often their donnés were celibate. This was a condition which, if not unknown among the Algonquians, was regarded by them with the same combination of curiosity and revulsion with which the French regarded the berdaches of the Illinois and the acceptance of homosexual relations among many Algonquian peoples.[21]

Algonquians eventually accepted Jesuit celibacy, but the Jesuits never accepted Algonquian sexual mores, particularly when other Frenchmen proved so enthusiastic about them. Sex was hardly a personal affair; it was governed and regulated by the appropriate authorities. The supreme arbiters of sex among the French were precisely those who, theoretically, had the

---

[21] For Madame Le Sueur, see De Gannes (Deliette) Memoir, *IHC* 23:338. For berdaches and homosexuality, see De Gannes (Deliette) Memoir, *IHC* 23:329–30; Le Clercq, *First Establishment*, 135; Relations des découvertes, in Pierre Margry, *Découvertes et établissements des Français... de l'Amerique Septentrionale, 1614–1698*, 6 vols. (Paris: Maisonneuve et Cie, 1879, repr. New York, AMS, 1974), 1:488.

least practical experience, the priests. The Jesuits took a vocal and active interest in the sexual activities of both the French and the Indians.[22]

It was the interest of the Jesuits in other people's sexual conduct, along with the more immediate experience and observations of men like Perrot, Lahontan, and Deliette, that makes possible reconstruction of their contemporaries' sexual relations, but the very nature of these sources requires that they be used carefully. To understand sexual relations between Algonquians and Europeans, we must remove the combination of sexual fantasy, social criticism, and Jansenism with which the French often veiled their descriptions. A few relatively straightforward descriptions of sexual relations exist, but sources are often openly polemical. The Jesuits were interested in denouncing and restraining what they regarded as Algonquian and French sexual immorality – polygamy, adultery, and prostitution – whereas, at the other extreme, the Baron de Lahontan sometimes delighted in using Indians as weapons in assaulting European law, custom, and hypocrisy.[23]

Despite their differing purposes, nearly all French accounts were united, first, by their inability to understand the status of women vis-à-vis men except in terms of conjugal relations and, second, by their tendency to group actual sexual relations in terms of two opposite poles of conduct, with marriage at one extreme and prostitution and adultery at the other. In attempting to impose their own cultural categories on the actions of Algonquian women, the French tended to select material that made the women seem merely a disorderly and lewd set of Europeans, not people following an entirely different social logic. The immediate result was to define a woman in terms of a person – her actual or potential husband – who may not have been anywhere near being the most significant figure in the woman's life. Depending on her tribal identity, an Algonquian woman often had a more durable and significant relationship with her mother, father, brothers, sisters, or grandparents, or with other, unrelated women than with her husband or husbands. Nor was an Algonquian woman's status dependent solely on her husband. Her own membership in ritual organizations or, among some tribes such as the Shawnees, Huron-Petuns, and Miamis, her own political status in offices confined to women had more influence on her social position than the status of her husband did.[24]

---

[22] *JR* 54:179–83; *JR* 65:235–45; Cadillac, Account of Detroit, Sept. 25, 1702, *MPHC* 33:143. Ordonnance du M. le Comte de Frontenac pour la traite et commerce du outaouacs . . . 8 avril 1690 (avec remarques faites par l'intendant), AN, F3, v. 6, f. 366.

[23] *JR* 65:193–99, 229–43; Reuben Gold Thwaites (ed.), *New Voyage to North America by the Baron de Lahontan*, 2 vols. (Chicago: A. C. McClury, 1905), 2:455–56, 460–61, 605–18.

[24] For general difficulties with European observations on Indian women, see Katherine Weist, "Beasts of Burden and Menial Slaves: Nineteenth-Century Observations of Northern Plains Indian Women," and Alice Kehoe, "The Shackles of Tradition," both in Patricia Albers and

Even when the most careful and sensitive of the European observers talked about the status of women and sexual relations, therefore, they eliminated much of the actual social world that gave those relations their full meaning. Perrot and Father Lafitau, for example, wrote dispassionate accounts of Algonquian marriage customs. They recognized marriage as a social contract between families, as it was in Europe, even if gifts were given to the bride's family, in exchange for, as Perrot said, the bride's body, instead of to the groom as in Europe. In marriage coercive authority, elsewhere so weak in Algonquian society, stiffened. Once married, a woman was clearly subordinate to her husband. The French viewed the harsh punishments inflicted on women for adultery among the Illinois and the Miamis as the most graphic evidence of subordination. Deliette said that he had seen evidence that more than a hundred women had been executed for adultery during the seven years he had spent among the Illinois. Others emphasized the mutilation of adulterous women by husbands, who cut off a nose or an ear, and the gang rapes inflicted on unfaithful wives by men solicited for the purpose by the husband. There were no equivalent penalties for adultery by men. For Frenchmen, these property exchanges, the subordination of women, and the double sexual standard made this a harsh but recognizable and comprehensible world.[25]

The problem was that this portrait, as the French sources themselves make clear, was incomplete. A woman's subordination to her husband was not necessarily permanent. She could call on male relatives to protect and vindicate her. She could leave her husband and return to her own family whenever she chose. Among many groups adultery was not harshly punished. According to Cadillac, the sexual freedom of married Ottawa and Huron-Petun women was so great that it made adultery a meaningless category. And, indeed, it was the categories themselves that were the problem.

Beatrice Medicine, *The Hidden Half: Studies of Plains Indian Women* (Washington, D.C.: University Press of America, 1983), 29–52, 53–73. Women among the Illinois gained power from visions and could become shamans. The culturally very similar Miami had female chiefs whose duties paralleled the male chiefs'. They inherited their status from their fathers and did not obtain it through their husbands. See *HBNI* 15:675, 677, 684–85.

25 For Perrot and Lafitau on marriage, see Nicolas Perrot, *Memoir on the Manners, Customs, and Religion of the Savages of North America*, in Emma Helen Blair (ed.), *The Indian Tribes of the Upper Mississippi Valley and Region of the Great Lakes*, 2 vols. (Cleveland: Arthur H. Clark, 1912), 1:64–65; Joseph-François Lafitau, *Customs of the American Indians Compared with the Customs of Primitive Times* (Toronto: Champlain Society, 1924–77), 1:336–37, 339. For adultery among the Illinois, see De Gannes (Deliette) Memoir, *IHC* 23:327, 335–37; Reuben Gold Thwaites (ed.), *Father Louis Hennepin's A New Discovery of a Vast Country in America* (facsimile ed., Toronto: Coles, 1974, repr. ed. of 1903 ed.), 167–68; Jolliet and Marquette, in Louise P. Kellogg (ed.), *Early Narratives of the Northwest, 1634–1699* (New York: Charles Scribner's Sons, 1917), 243.

European conceptions of marriage, adultery, and prostitution just could not
encompass the actual variety of sexual relations in the *pays d'en haut*.[26]

Jesuits and other Europeans did not impose these cultural categories as an
ethnographic exercise; they did so in an attempt to understand and regulate
sexual activity. This was a task that missionaries saw as an essential part of
their purpose in the West. Adultery, prostitution, and marriage obviously
existed, but most sexual contact took place between Frenchmen and single
Indian women, who enjoyed considerable sexual freedom but were not
prostitutes. There was no appropriate French category for such free, unmarried Algonquian women.

Because of this lack of readily available parallels from French society, and
because of differences between the hierarchical Miamis and Illinois, on the
one hand, and the remaining Algonquians, on the other, French accounts of
the sexual standards expected of unmarried young women among the
Algonquians vary widely and are often internally contradictory. Deliette, for
example, says the Illinois valued chastity highly, but he then goes on to say
that virtually all women, even married women, took lovers.[27]

Lahontan credited unmarried Algonquian women with virtually complete
sexual freedom.

> A Young Woman is allow'd to do what she pleases; let her Conduct be
> what it will, neither Father nor Mother, Brother nor Sister can pretend
> to controul her. A Young Woman, say they, is Master of her own Body,
> and by her Natural Right of Liberty is free to do what she pleases.

The only social barrier to premarital intercourse was fear of pregnancy,
which would make it impossible to obtain a high-ranking husband, but
Lahontan said women knew how to abort unwanted pregnancies. Among
most groups such sexual freedom apparently ended with marriage. But some
women never did marry. There was, according to Lahontan, a class of
women called Ickoue ne Kioussa, or Hunting Women – "for they commonly
accompany the Huntsmen in their Diversions." Such women argued that
they could not endure "the conjugal yoak," that they were incapable of
bringing up children and were "too impatient to spend winters in the
village." Lahontan regarded all this as a "disguise for lewdness," but he
noted that these women were not censured by their parents or other

---

[26] For Cadillac, see Quaife (ed.), *The Western Country*, 63. For references to prostitution, see *JR*
65:241; Memoire touchant l'yvrognerie des sauvages, 1693, AN. C11A, v. 12, f. 384.

[27] De Gannes (Deliette) Memoir, *IHC* 23:328–37; Thwaites (ed.), *Lahontan's Voyages*, 2:453.
Joutel gives a contradictory account similar to Deliette's; see Joutel's Memoir, in Isaac J.
Cox, *The Journeys of Robert Cavelier de La Salle*, 2 vols. (New York: A. S. Barnes, 1905), 2:222.

relatives, who asserted, for instance, "that their daughters have the command of their own Bodies and may dispose of their persons as they think fit." The children these women bore were raised by their families and "accounted a Lawful issue"; they were entitled to all privileges except that they could not marry into families of noted warriors or councillors.[28]

Such quotations from Lahontan must be read with caution, since Indians often served him as mere vehicles for his own critique of French society, and his analysis often differed from those of more experienced observers of the Algonquian nations. Lahontan, for example, made divorce among the Algonquians a far more trivial event than did Perrot, who spent much of his life among the western Indians. And certainly among the Illinois, women were not totally free before marriage; brothers greatly influenced their sisters' sexual lives. Nevertheless, despite Lahontan's tendency to overgeneralize and his notorious inventions, his assertions cannot be dismissed as simply romantic fabrication. Other accounts corroborate his descriptions of young Algonquian women. Joutel's memoir about the Illinois, although it confuses cohabitation with hunting women and marriage, substantiates Lahontan's description. According to Joutel, the marriages of the Illinois lasted no longer than the parties desired to remain together, for they "freely part after a hunting bout, each going which way they please without any ceremony," and he notes, "There are women who make no secret of having had to do with Frenchmen." Cadillac, too, noted that girls "are allowed to enjoy themselves and to experiment with marriage as long as they like and with as many boys as they wish without reproach."[29]

Younger women and hunting women thus enjoyed substantial freedom in engaging in sexual relations with Frenchmen and played a major part in establishing the customary terms of sexual relationships between the Algonquians and the French. Initially, many Frenchmen, like the Jesuits, may have viewed this sort of relationship as simple prostitution or, like Joutel, as a loose, easily dissolved marriage, but by the 1690s they recognized it as a separate, customary form for sexual relationships in the fur trade. Basically, women adapted the relationship of hunting women to hunters to the new conditions of the fur trade. Such women not only had sexual intercourse with their French companions, they also cooked and washed for

---

[28] For quotation, see Thwaites (ed.), *Lahontan's Voyages*, 2:453; *ibid.*, 454, 463. For pregnancy, see *ibid.*, 454, 463; for hunting women, see *ibid.*, 463–64.

[29] On divorce, compare Lahontan to Perrot and Cadillac; Thwaites (ed.), *Lahontan's Voyage*, 2:453; Perrot, *Memoir*, 64–65; Quaife (ed.), *The Western Country*, 38–39. For brothers' control over sisters, see De Gannes (Deliette) Memoir, *IHC* 23:332, 337, and Raudot, "Memoir," in W. Vernon Kinietz, *The Indians of the Western Great Lakes* (Ann Arbor: University of Michigan Press, 1965), 389. For Joutel, see Joutel Memoir, in Cox (ed.), *Journeys of La Salle*, 2:222. For Cadillac quotation, see Quaife (ed.), *The Western Country*, 45.

them, made their clothes, and cut their wood. In denouncing these women, the Jesuit Father Carheil described them in terms similar to Lahontan's:

> The traders have become so accustomed to have women for their use in the trading-places, and these have become so necessary to them, that they cannot do without them even on their journeys. . . . I refer to single women, women without husbands, women who are mistresses of their own Bodies, women who can dispose of them to these men, and whom the latter know to be willing to do so – in a word, They are all the prostitutes of Montreal who are alternately brought here and taken back; and They are all the prostitutes of this place, who are carried in the same way from here to Montreal, and from Montreal to here. . . . The pretext that they usually allege for taking women in preference to men on these journeys is, that women cost them less than men, and are satisfied with lower wages. They speak the truth; but the very Fact of their being Satisfied with less wages is a Manifest proof of their dissoluteness. . . . The women, Being depraved, want them as men; and they, on their part, want them as women, on all their journeys – after which . . . they quit one another. They separate from these only to Seek others.[30]

What Father Carheil misunderstood and denounced as *prostitution* had little to do with that term as commonly understood. These women did not solicit customers, and they did not sell discrete sexual acts. Sex accompanied a general agreement to do the work commonly expected of women in Algonquian society. Nor was the relationship a temporary marriage. In marriage a wife received no payment from her husband, nor was she as free as a hunting woman to dissolve one relationship and begin another. Finally, these relationships were not contracts between families. They were, instead, a bridge to the middle ground, an adjustment to interracial sex in the fur trade where the initial conceptions of sexual conduct held by each side were reconciled in a new customary relation. The appeal of unions that offered both temporary labor and sexual companionship to the coureurs de bois is obvious, but these relationships also may have flourished because of the badly skewed sex ratios within Algonquian societies, apparently the result of warfare.

Many late seventeenth-century accounts of western Algonquian population stress both sexual imbalance and the presence of soral polygamy – the practice of a husband marrying two or more sisters. Sexual relations with the coureur de bois offered an alternative to polygamy. Polygamy was also a particular target of Jesuit missionaries, who were not reluctant to assert a connection among the famines, the epidemics sweeping the villages, and

---

[30] For customary relation, see *JR* 65:233. For quotation, see *ibid.*, 241.

plural marriages. Jesuit denunciations of polygamy appear to have achieved at least some temporary success in the Michilimackinac region. In 1670, in response to an epidemic, the men at Sault Sainte Marie took back their first wives and put away those wives they had taken since their first marriage. Subsequently, the Kiskakon Ottawas, the most Christianized of the Ottawas, were also the Ottawa group with the fewest polygamists, and, supposedly, the Kaskaskias abandoned polygamy entirely by the early eighteenth century. Elsewhere the Jesuits never succeeded in completely eradicating polygamy, but even partial success yielded ironic results. Given the population imbalance between men and women, any increase in the class of single women yielded more women who might be willing to attach themselves to the French.[31]

That Jesuit battles against polygamy may have increased the number of women who consorted with Frenchmen was only one of the ironies created by French and Algonquian attempts to arrive at mutually intelligible patterns of sexual conduct. Hunting women, as a group, carried and modified one Algonquian pattern of sexual relations into the fur trade in their liaisons with the coureurs de bois, but a smaller group of Christian Indian women were also influential in creating other patterns of sexual conduct through their own relationships with both Algonquian men and Frenchmen. The influence of these women was not felt everywhere; necessarily, it was confined to groups in which the Jesuits had succeeded in making a significant number of converts: the Huron-Petuns, the Kiskakon Ottawas, and above all the Kaskaskias of the Illinois confederation.[32]

The influence of Christian women emerged most clearly among the Illinois. In the late seventeenth and early eighteenth centuries, there were signs of sexual crisis among the Illinois. They had a badly skewed sex ratio, which Deliette, probably exaggerating, extimated at four women to each man. The Illinois themselves thought that their traditional marriage pattern was in decay, and in French accounts, they combined draconian punishments for adultery with widespread sexual liaisons between Frenchman and Indian women. By 1692 the Illinois had largely abandoned Starved Rock and had built villages at the southern end of Lake Peoria, thus creating a new

---

[31] For references to sexual imbalance and soral polygamy, see Relation du voyage de Cavelier de la Salle, du 11 aout 1680 à l'automne de 1681. Margry, *Découvertes*, 2:157; *JR* 54:219, 229; La Salle on the Illinois Country, 1680, *IHC* 23:10. De Gannes (Deliette) Memoir, *IHC* 23:329. *JR* 54:219. For Jesuit attacks on polygamy and connections between polygamy and disease, etc., see *JR* 57:215–19; *JR* 57:231; *JR* 56:113. For renunciation of wives, see *JR* 55:129–31. For decline of polygamy, see *JR* 61:1312; *JR* 57:231, 81. Emily J. Blasingham, "The Depopulation of the Illinois Indians," *Ethnohistory* 3 (Summer 1986): 386–87.

[32] *JR* 65:67, 79; De Gannes (Deliette) Memoir, *IHC* 23:361. For emphasis Jesuits placed on sexual conduct among Kiskakon Ottawas and Kaskaskias, see *JR* 54:179–83, and *JR* 65:67–69.

collection of villages at Pimitoui. The French who accompanied the Illinois had built the second Fort Saint Louis near these villages. Pimitoui also served as the headquarters for Jesuit mission activity among the Illinois and surrounding nations. Father Gravier, missionary to the Illinois since 1688 or 1689, established a permanent mission there in 1693. By 1696 the priest estimated that over the preceding six years he had baptized some two thousand persons. Even allowing for large numbers of deathbed baptisms and baptisms of infants who did not grow up to be practicing Catholics, this is a substantial figure. Much of Gravier's lasting success took place among the Illinois, particularly among the young women, who, according to Deliette, "often profit by their teaching and mock at the superstitions of their nation. This often greatly incenses the old men."[33]

By the 1690s the differential sexual appeal of Catholic teaching began to have significant repercussions among the Illinois. This, in turn, influenced the way the French and Illinois societies were linked. Jesuit teaching among the Illinois in the 1690s stressed the cult of the Virgin Mary, and with it came a heavy emphasis on chastity and virginity. This stress on a powerful female religious figure, whose power, like that of the Jesuits, was connected with sexual abstinence, attracted a congregation composed largely of women, particularly young women and older girls. How these young women understood Christianity and the cult of the Virgin is not entirely clear. They may have identified it in terms of women's ritual organizations, but given their tendency to mock Illinois traditions, they also clearly saw it in opposition to existing religious practices. During a period of warfare, direct cultural challenge by the Jesuits, population decline, and, if French accounts are correct, widespread violence of men against women, the actions of these women had direct social and cultural implications. Women took the common Algonquian dictum that unmarried women were "masters of their own body" and justified not sexual experimentation but sexual abstinence. They then assayed the religious powers they derived from prayer and Catholic doctrine against the powers the elders derived from visions and tradition.

---

[33] De Gannes (Deliette) Memoir, *IHC* 23:329–30, 335–37; Joutel Memoir, in Cox (ed.), *Journeys of La Salle*, 2:222. Emily Blasingham estimates the ratio of adult warriors to the rest of the population at 1:3.17 which obviously would not allow for Deliette's estimate, but her estimate is perhaps even more of a guess than his. Blasingham, "Depopulation of the Illinois," 364. For village sites, see J. Joe Bauxar, "The Historic Period," in Elaine Bluhm (ed.), *Illinois Archaeology Bulletin No. 1*, Illinois Archaeological Survey, Urbana (Carbondale, Ill.: Southern Illinois University Press, 1959), 49. For Gravier's mission, see Mary Borgian Palm, "The Jesuit Missions of the Illinois Country (1673–1763)," Ph.D. diss., St. Louis University, 1931 (Cleveland, privately printed, Sisters of Notre Dame, 1931), 22, 24–25. For Father Gravier's claim of baptism, see *JR* 65:33. For conflict, see *JR* 65:67, and Fr. Rale quoted in Mary Elizabeth Good, "The Guebert Site: An Eighteenth-Century Historic Kaskaskia Indian Village in Randolph County, Illinois," *Central States Archaeological Societies Memoir*, 2 (n.p., 1972), 14.

Their actions outraged both the young men, who found their own sexual opportunities diminished, and the elders and shamans who were directly challenged.[34]

In this dispute, Christianity and the Algonquians' social and cultural world were becoming part of a single field of action, and the outcome influenced not just Algonquian but also French society. Frenchmen in the West were no more enthusiastic about the new Christian influence among Illinois women than were Illinois men. Frenchmen, too, resented the new ability of Jesuits, through their influence over women, to control the sexual lives of the coureurs de bois and the voyageurs. Their resentment went beyond this.

Jesuit influence threatened not only sexual activity but also the ability of traders and coureurs de bois to create the ties to Algonquian society on which their trade, and perhaps their lives, depended. The critical issue here was not casual liaisons, but marriage. Formal marriages between Indian women and Frenchmen were quite rare during the seventeenth century. Marriage à la façon du pays, that is, according to local Algonquian custom, may have occurred, but there are few references to interracial marriage of any kind until the 1690s. In 1698 Father St. Cosme mentioned voyageurs with Illinois wives, and about the same time Father Carheil mentioned other voyageurs at Michilimackinac who had married among the Indians. In theory, the Jesuits and the colonial elite in general might have been expected to approve marriage between Frenchmen and Indian women as an alternative to the unregulated sexual relationships of the pays d'en haut. Along the same line, the French voyageurs, operating in a world of abundant sexual opportunities, might have been expected to be indifferent to formal conjugal ties. In fact, however, their positions were nearly the opposite during the 1690s. The seemingly sudden rise of interracial marriages in the 1690s may be connected with the increasingly serious attempts of the French to force the coureurs de bois out of the pays d'en haut. These culminated in the French abandonment of most western posts in the late 1690s. Through marriage, the coureurs de bois may have been attempting to establish the necessary kin connections with Indians that would be vital to the ability of any Frenchman to remain safely in the West.[35]

---

[34] For Virgin Mary, see JR 59:187; 193, 201, 207, JR 63:217–19. For opposition of young men, see JR 65:67.

[35] For marriages, see JR 65:241; JR 65:69; St. Cosme, in Kellogg (ed.), Narratives, 251. The best work on intermarriage on the Great Lakes is by Jacqueline Peterson, "Prelude to Red River: A Social Portrait of the Great Lakes Metis," Ethnohistory 25 (1978): 41–68. For intermarriage in the Northwest, see Olive Dickason, "From One Nation in the Northeast to New Nation in the Northwest: A Look at the Emergence of the Metis" in Jacqueline Peterson and Jennifer S. H. Brown, The New Peoples: Being and Becoming Metis in North America (Lincoln: University of Nebraska Press, 1985). Interracial marriage within the later

Such attempts met with considerable sympathy from French commanders, usually with trading interests of their own, who were responsible not for larger policies but for day-to-day relations with the Indians. Both Henry de Tonti and the Sieur de la Forest at Fort Saint Louis supported attempts to fortify ties with the Illinois through intermarriage. Cadillac's plan for Detroit in the early eighteenth century included the promotion of marriages between soldiers and Indian women. He explained: "Marriages of this kind will strengthen the friendship of these tribes, as the alliances of the Romans perpetuated peace with the Sabines through the intervention of the women whom the former had taken from the others."[36]

Indians, like the commanders, saw marriage as an integral part of their alliance with the French. Male heads of families, at least, greeted marriages enthusiastically. Marriage, far more than the prevailing French liaisons with hunting women, put sex firmly in the political arena. As both sides recognized, marriage was an alliance between families that concerned many more people than the marital partners. Not only did property move into the hands of the bride's family, but kinship relations were established that enabled both families to call on their relatives for aid and protection. Because of the wider social implications of marriage, as compared to relations with hunting women, a woman found her family much more interested in her choice of a permanent French partner than in her casual liaisons.[37]

Jesuits and higher French officials, however, were unenthusiastic about marriage both because it gave voyageurs and coureurs de bois an independent hold in the *pays d'en haut* and also for racist reasons. The Jesuits did not favor interracial marriage in the seventeenth century. Their preferred solution to the problems of sexual morality was to banish most Frenchmen from the upper country and to place those who remained under strict Jesuit supervision. Gradually, however, the Jesuits and other priests in upper

---

fur trade has been the subject of two recent books, but both studies look at situations significantly different from those of the late seventeenth-century West, where many of the earliest Catholic marriages were solemnized by priests. See Sylvia Van Kirk, *Many Tender Ties: Women in Fur-Trade Society, 1670–1870* (Norman: University of Oklahoma Press, 1980), and Jennifer S. Brown, *Strangers in the Blood: Fur Trade Company Families in Indian Country* (Vancouver: University of British Columbia Press, 1980).

[36] *JR* 64:201–03; Cadillac to Minister, 18 Oct. 1700, *MPHC1* 33:189. For Cadillac's later opposition, see Mariage des francais avec les sauvagesses, 1 sept. 1716, AN, C13A, v. 4, f. 255.

Who was commanding at Fort. St. Louis in the Illinois at the time is unclear. Tonti was there in April 1694, Declaration de Henri de Tonti, 11 avril 1694, AN, C13A, Louisiana, v. 1 (fol, 27), but in the fall of 1693 he was in Montreal. Engagement of Viau to La Forest and Tonti, Sept. 11, 1693, *IHC* 23:273–75. Given the absence of Tonti and La Forest, Deliette may have been in command.

[37] *JR* 64:195, 197, 207, 211. Quaife (ed.), *The Western Country*, 39, 45; Perrot, *Memoir*, 64–69; Lafitau, *Customs*, 1:336–37.

Louisiana came to condone interracial marriage if the wife was Catholic. Of twenty-one baptisms recorded at the French village of Kaskaskia between 1704 and 1713, the mother was Indian and the father was French in eighteen cases. In 1714, the Sieur de la Vente, the curé for Louisiana, praised intermarriage as a way to people the colony. He contended that the women of the Illinois and neighboring tribes were "whiter, more laborious, more adroit, better housekeepers, and more docile" than Indian women found elsewhere in the West and the South.[38]

Leading colonial officials were much more consistent in their opposition to intermarriage than the priests were. In Canada they preferred that Frenchmen marry and settle around Quebec or Montreal. As long as official policy involved the suppression of the coureurs de bois and their removal from the West, officials could not be openly enthusiastic about marriages there. They coupled such policy considerations with racist disgust at the results of French-Indian intermarriage. As Governor de Vaudreuil explained in opposing interracial marriage at Detroit in 1709: "Bad should never be mixed with good. Our experience of them in this country ought to prevent us from permitting marriages of this kind, for all the Frenchmen who have married savages have been licentious, lazy and intolerably independent; and their children have been characterized by as great a slothfulness as the savages themselves." By the time he was governor of Louisiana, Cadillac, who had once advocated intermarriage, and his intendant, Duclos, opposed intermarriage in the same terms. Indian women were, they said, licentious and would leave men who did not please them, and even if the marriage lasted, the result would be a population of "mulattos [*mulâtres*], idlers, libertines, and even more knaves than [there] are in the Spanish colonies."[39]

Given this range of social and cultural concerns, the divisions within each society, and the inevitability of members of both societies being integral figures in deciding outcomes, it is not surprising that the prospect of a marriage between a Christian Illinois woman and a Frenchman precipitated a crisis that was ultimately decided on the middle ground. In 1694 Michel Accault's attempt to wed Aramepinchieue brought to light both the full

---

[38] For official attitudes toward marriage, see Jaenen, *Friend and Foe*, 164. For Father de la Vente, see Mariage des francais avec les sauvagesses, 1 sept. 1716, AN, C13A, v. 4. For banishment and supervision, see *JR* 65:233–45. For baptism, see Palm, "Jesuit Missions," 43–45.

[39] For governor's opposition, see Vaudreuil and Raudot to Minister, Nov. 14, 1709, *MPHC* 33:454. For Duclos and Cadillac, see Mariage des francais avec les sauvagesses, 1 sept. 1716, AN, C13A, v. 4, f. 255. For renewed concern in 1730, see Bienville et Salmon au Ministre, 16 mai 1735, AN, C13A, v. 20, f. 85. Memoire concernant les Illinois, 1732 AN, F3, v. 24.

Roy de La grande Nation p. 8

des Nadouessiouek, jl est armé f. 12. de fa Maßue. de guerre quon nomme. pakamagan, jl Regne. dans un grand. Pais. au defja de la mes de meil.

This sketch of about 1700 by Decard de Granville shows a tatooed Sioux chief with a calumet. (New York Public Library)

complexity of the relations between the two societies and the processes by which the middle ground was emerging.

The controversy over the marriage of Accault and Aramepinchieue did not pit the Illinois against the French. Rather, it divided each group in a way that can only be grasped by looking at the social positions of the bride and the groom. Aramepinchieue was the daughter of Rouensa, a leading

Kaskaskia chief. She was a fervent Christian and the pride of the Illinois mission. Michel Accault was a Frenchman who had first come west with La Salle. He had later accompanied Father Hennepin on his voyage to the Sioux. Afterward, he had traded widely in the West and had established a reputation among the Jesuits as a libertine and an enemy of the faith. Aramepinchieue thus had links both with the Kaskaskia elite and Father Gravier. Accault was leagued with Henry de Tonti and the Frenchmen around him at Fort Saint Louis and was an enemy of Gravier's. His marriage with Aramepinchieue would strengthen the connections of a prominent Kaskaskia family with the French to the benefit of both. Rouensa announced the marriage in precisely those terms. He was strengthening his alliance with the French.[40]

The problem was that this proposed union, while it might link French and Algonquians, also emphasized the internal divisions within each group. Aramepinchieue refused to marry Accault. Father Gravier supported her decision. His immediate target was Accault. He would not sanction the influence within Indian society of a Frenchman he regarded as dissolute. He might grudgingly permit the marriage of Catholic Frenchmen with Christian Indian women, but he would do so only in circumstances that would advance the cause of the true faith. He told Aramepinchieue's parents and her suitor that "God did not command her not to marry, but also that she could not be forced to do so; that she alone was mistress to do the one or the other." Gravier's statement demonstrates that no matter how repressive Catholic morality may appear in retrospect, it could be used to buttress women's influence over their lives and their families. Women like Aramepinchieue had always had some control over their choice of marriage partners, but Christianity presented them with a new mechanism of control. What made this unique was not the woman's ability to reject unwanted suitors but, rather, the allies who could be mustered to maintain her decision against family pressures.[41]

In one sense, Aramepinchieue's decision represents a clear rejection of Algonquian norms and an appeal to an alien set of standards, but in another sense Aramepinchieue was appealing to such standards only to strengthen a very Algonquian sense of a woman's autonomy. Gravier's assertion that she was "mistress to do either the one or the other" did, after all, echo the Algonquian tenet that unmarried women were "masters" of their own bodies. Gravier, who sought to subvert traditional Illinois sexual practices

---

[40] For Accault, see *JR* 64:213, 180. For Aramepinchieue and Rouensa, see *JR* 64:179–81, 193–237. Aramepinchieue took the Christian name Mary or Marie; see Palm, "Jesuit Missions," 38.

[41] *JR* 64:205–07, 213, 280. *JR* 64:211, 195. For Aramepinchieue, see *JR* 64:193–95, 205–07, 213–29.

because they contradicted Catholicism, and Aramepinchieue, who used Catholicism to maintain the values that supported those same practices, thus found themselves allies. By definition, then – the involvement of both French and Indians, the need for members of each group to get assistance from members of the other to fulfill desires arising within their own society, and the inability of either French or Indian norms to govern the situation – this was a conflict of the middle ground.

The initial result of the bride's refusal was a standoff, which both Rouensa and the French commander tried to break with the limited coercive means available to them. Rouensa drove Aramepinchieue from his house, but she was protected by Father Gravier, who secured her shelter with a neophyte family. Her rejection of her parents' wishes pained her deeply, but she justified her actions by appeals to Catholic doctrine. The chiefs in council retaliated by attempting to halt Catholic services at the chapel. At least fifty persons, virtually all of them women and girls, persisted in going to church. The council then (although they denied it) appears to have dispatched a warrior armed with a club to disrupt the services. The women defied him. Among the Illinois, the opposing sides had clearly formed along gender lines. Not all of the women abandoned the chiefs, but Christianity was, for the moment, a women's religious society acting in defiance of a male council. Among the French, the division was necessarily among males. The French commander, far from stopping this interference with the mission, gloated over it and denounced Gravier publicly before both the French and the Indians. When these tactics failed to sway the priest, neither the commander nor Rouensa felt confident enough to escalate the level of violence, although the Kaskaskias left the option of further coercion open.[42]

Such a face-off did not serve the interests of either side. Aramepinchieue was in turmoil over her alienation from her parents, to whom she was closely attached. Gravier found further missionary activities virtually impossible in the face of council opposition, which threatened to confine his promising mission to a besieged group of young women and girls. On the other hand, Gravier and the bride together blocked a marriage that both the Kaskaskias and the French deeply wanted.

The situation, in the end, was solved by a series of trade-offs. Aramepinchieue, in effect, negotiated a compromise with her father. She told Gravier, "I think that if I consent to the marriage, he will listen to you in earnest, and will induce all to do so," and she consented to the marriage on the terms that her parents, in turn, "grant me what I ask." They agreed. Rouensa disavowed his opposition to Christianity in full council and urged those present to "obey now the black gown." His agreement was sincere,

[42] *JR* 64:195–205.

and he and his wife began instruction for baptism. Accault, too, became a practicing Catholic once more and an ally of the Jesuits'. In return, the Kaskaskia chief, as he informed the other headmen of the confederation with considerable presents, was "about to be allied to a Frenchman."[43]

The marriage, therefore, was a great coup for Gravier. It brought into the church the most prominent Kaskaskia civil leader and his brother, an equally prominent war leader, and opened the way for making the Kaskaskias the most Catholic of the western Algonquians. The main agent in these events was a seventeen-year-old woman who appealed to alien standards both to control her condition and, eventually, to alter the condition of her nation. By 1711 the Kaskaskias were supposedly virtually all Catholic, and missionaries had made significant inroads among other Illinois groups. Aramepinchieue had maintained and strengthened the relationships that mattered most to her – those with her parents and the Christian congregation of women. The price was marriage to Accault, but this may very well have remained for her a subsidiary social arrangement. Christianity did not immediately transform marriage. French officials would later claim that Christian Illinois women less devout than Aramepinchieue still felt free to leave their French husbands whenever they chose.[44]

Women like Aramepinchieue are rarely visible in the documents, but their traces appear everywhere. Diplomatic negotiations and warfare, the large trading expeditions, these were the work of men, but the Frenchmen who appeared in Algonquian villages either traveled with Algonquian women or had liaisons with them there. Much of their petty trading was probably with women. The labor they purchased was usually that of women. On a day-to-day basis, women did more than men to weave the French into the fabric of a common Algonquian-French life. Both in and out of marriage, these women bore children with the French, some of whom in time would come to form a separate people, the *métis*, who themselves mediated between French and Algonquians and became of critical importance to the area.

Gravier himself would continue to make his greatest gains among the women of the Illinois, but in other tribes of the confederation he would not acquire allies of the status of Aramepinchieue. In 1706 Gravier returned to Pimitoui. The Kaskaskias had by now left to resettle on the Mississippi, the French had abandoned Fort Saint Louis, and the Peorias who remained at the site resented Gravier's aggressive tactics enough to attack him physically.

---

[43] For Aramepinchieue quotations, see *JR* 64:207–9; otherwise, *JR* 64:179, 213, 211.
[44] *JR* 64:79–81, 231–35; Palm, "Jesuit Missions," 38; André Penicault, *Fleur de Lys and Calumet: Being the Penicault Narrative of French Adventure in Louisiana*, ed. Richebourg Gaillard McWilliams (Baton Rouge: Louisiana State University Press, 1953), 139–40. For claims of success among other Illinois nations, see Callières et de Champigny au Ministre, 18 oct. 1700, AN, C11A, v. 18.

They wounded him and, revealingly, left him in the care of "some praying women" until Kaskaskias sent by Rouensa rescued the priest. Father Gravier never fully recovered from his wounds, and eventually he died of complications. His death, a reminder of how tentative and tenuous the middle ground could be, also serves as a transition to the second issue demanding French-Algonquian cooperation – violence and interracial murder.[45]

III

Although not all murders, as the killing of Father Gravier demonstrates, grew out of the trade, violence and interracial murder as a whole were inextricably bound up with commerce. In 1684 alone, the only year for which a summary is given, thirty-nine Frenchmen trading in the West died at the hands of their Algonquian allies. Indians murdered Frenchmen during robberies, killed them in disputes over debt or gift exchanges, attacked them in attempts to stop weapons from going to their enemies, killed them to avenge killings by the French, and, as the liquor trade expanded, killed them in drunken quarrels. The French, in turn, used force against thieves, which did not prevent theft from becoming as established a part of the exchange as gifts or bargaining.[46]

Commerce, in short, was not a peaceful process; violence was an option both for acquiring goods and for protecting them. In part, violence was so prevalent in the early trade because common agreement on the nature of the exchange itself developed only gradually. Frenchmen did not always meet Indian demands for gifts; they did not act as generously as friends and allies should; they, as the Indians soon discovered, asked more for their goods than the English asked; and finally, Frenchmen supplied arms to their allies' enemies. The Indians, in turn, stole. French traders readily classified Algonquian nations by their propensity to steal. The Fox were thieving; the Illinois carried off everything they could lay their hands on; the Chippewas on the north shore of Lake Superior would pillage any French canoe they

---

[45] *JR* 65:101–03; Palm, "Jesuit Missions," 36, 47; Blasingham, "Depopulation of the Illinois," 201; Bauxar, "Historic Period," 49. For Gravier, see *JR* 66:51–63.

[46] Some historians continue to divide Indian-white relations between peaceful commerce and violent conflict. For such a position, see Francis Jennings, *The Ambiguous Iroquois Empire* (New York: W. W. Norton, 1984), 83. In fact, violence cannot be separated from the trade. The larger question of the role of violence in commerce has recently been raised by Curtin, *Cross-Cultural Trade*, 41–45. It is a question still illuminated by the work of Frederic Lane, *Venice and History* (Baltimore: Johns Hopkins University Press, 1966), 412–28; see, particularly, the "Economic Consequences of Organized Violence." For the number of murders, see Raisons qu'on a proposee a la Cour, 1687?, AN, C11A, v. 15, f. 271.

caught alone. The Sauks were also thieves, but they did not have the skill of the neighboring Fox. When the French were supplying the Sioux, small-scale theft gave way to organized plunder, so that Father Nouvel thought no Frenchman's life was safe journeying to or from the Sioux country. Eventually theft itself became institutionalized, as French traders learned to leave out small items to be pilfered, but a certain level of violence remained endemic to the trade.[47]

Perhaps the most perplexing intercultural concern of the French and the Algonquians was how to settle and limit the number of murders arising from the trade, when there was no authority in the West capable of creating a monopoly on violence and establishing order. Violence became one of the central concerns of the middle ground. When murders occurred between Algonquians and Frenchmen, each side brought quite different cultural formulas to bear on the situation. For northeastern Indians, both Algonquians and Iroquoians, those people killed by allies could be compensated for with gifts or by slaves or, failing these, by the killing of another member of the offending group. The decision about how to proceed was made by the dead person's kin, but extensive social pressure was usually exerted to accept compensation short of blood revenge, since killing a person of the offending group often only invited future retaliation. Among the French the matter was simpler. Society at large took the responsibility for punishing murder. Punishment was not left to the kin of the victim but rather to the state. The expected compensation for murder was the death of the murderer.[48]

Of the obvious differences here, two were particularly important. In the French scheme of things, exactly who committed the murder was of supreme importance, since the individual killer was held responsible for the crime. Only when a group refused to surrender a known murderer did collective responsibility arise. For the Indians, identifying the murderer was not as important as establishing the identity of the group to which the murderer

---

[47] For Fox, see *JR* 54:225; Illinois, see Joutel Memoir, in Cox (ed.), *Journeys of La Salle*, 2:212; Chippewas, see Raudot and De Gannes (Deliette) Memoir, *IHC* 23:328, Memoir in Kinietz, *Indians of the Western Great Lakes*, 374; Sauks, see *ibid.*, 381–82. For dangers of Sioux trade, see Pere Nouvel à M. de La Barre, 23 avril 1684, AN, C11A, v. 6, f. 523. For institutionalization of theft, see Gary C. Anderson, *Kinsmen of Another Kind: Dakota-White Relations in the Upper Mississippi Valley, 1680–1862* (Lincoln: University of Nebraska Press, 1984), 63.

[48] In the cases that follow both sides try to make these positions clear. See, e.g., extract from a letter by Dulhut, April 12, 1684, *WHC* 16:120, hereafter cited as Dulhut's letter. For Algonquian custom, see Jaenen, *Friend and Foe*, 123. For a discussion of murder, revenge, and compensation that stresses revenge rather than compensation among the Cherokee, see John Phillip Reid, *A Law of Blood: The Primitive Law of the Cherokee Nation* (New York: New York University Press, 1970), 73–112. Reid says that a retaliatory killing does not bring revenge (78). This does not appear to have been true among the Algonquians. Note how in the Dulhut case below Achiganaga is given presents to compensate for his son's death.

belonged, for it was the group – family, kin, village, or nation – that was held responsible for the act. Both sides established cultural measures of equivalence in compensating for the dead, but the French equivalence was invariably another death. As the French emphasized again and again in the cases that follow, death could only be compensated for by more death. Indians would, if necessary, also invoke a similar doctrine of revenge, but their preference was always either, in their words, "to raise up the dead," that is, to restore the dead person to life by providing a slave in the victim's place, or "to cover the dead," that is, present the relatives with goods that served as an equivalent.[49]

Most murders in the West left no trace in the documents, but an examination of those that are recorded can be rewarding. Three incidents in particular offer enough documentation for cultural analysis. The first occurred in 1682 or 1683, when two Frenchmen were waylaid on the Keweenaw Peninsula in Lake Superior and murdered by a Menominee and several Chippewas. These murders took place when the *pays d'en haut* was in a state of near chaos. Iroquois attacks, which had devastated the Illinois, had so far gone unavenged. Iroquois parties had recently struck the Illinois and the Mascoutens and were edging closer to Green Bay itself. Not only did the French seem unable to protect their allies, but an epidemic that the Potawatomis blamed on Jesuit witchcraft had recently ravaged the villages around the bay. The Potawatomis had murdered two French donnés in retaliation and had begun efforts to create a larger anti-French alliance. A recent alliance between the Saulteurs and the Sioux, which Daniel Greysolon Dulhut had helped orchestrate, had further inflamed the peoples of Green Bay against the French. They attempted to block French trade with the Sioux. The Fox had already fought and defeated a large Sioux-Chippewa force at a considerable loss to themselves, and a full-scale Chippewa-Fox war seemed imminent. But apparently not all the Chippewas relished the new alignment. Achiganaga, an important headman at Keweenaw, had attacked the Sioux and planned further attacks. His war parties, as well as those of the peoples at Green Bay, threatened the lives of French voyageurs.[50]

---

[49] Report of Boisbriant Diron Desursins Legardeur De L'isle Ste. Therese Langloisere, June 17, 1723, in J. H. Schlarman, *From Quebec to New Orleans: Fort De Chartres* (Belleville, Ill.: Beuchler, 1929), 226–31. See also Jaenen, *Friend and Foe*, 97. Jaenen makes the distinction between the French emphasis on punishment and the Indian emphasis on compensation.

[50] For conditions at Green Bay, see Enjalran à Lefevre de La Barre, 16 aoust 1683, Margry, *Découvertes*, 5:4–5. For Saulteur-Fox conflict, see *ibid.*, 5; Claude Charles Le Roy, Sieur de Bacqueville de la Potherie, *History of the Savage Peoples Who Are the Allies of New France*, in Emma Helen Blair (ed.), *The Indian Tribes of the Upper Mississippi Valley and Region of the Great Lakes*, 2 vols. (Cleveland: Arthur H. Clark, 1912), 1:358–63; Dulhut letter, *WHC* 16:114. Durantaye à A. de la Barre, 11 avril 1684, AN, C11A, v. 6, 1.521–22. For activities

In the midst of this turmoil a party led by Achiganaga's sons and including at least one Menominee, a member of a Green Bay tribe, murdered two Frenchmen. Their motive may have been robbery. Or Achiganaga may have sought to disrupt the Sioux trade, break the new alliance of other proto-Ojibwa bands with the Sioux, and join with the peoples of the bay in a larger anti-French movement. In any case, his sons murdered two Frenchmen and stole their goods. Dulhut, despite the powerful kin connections of the accused murderers, seized the Menominee at Sault Sainte Marie and sent out a party that successfully captured Achiganaga and all his children at Keweenaw. The local Algonquian peoples reacted to Dulhut's acts by resorting to customary procedures. The Saulteurs offered the French the calumet – the standard ceremony for establishing peace and amity – and then they offered slaves to resurrect the dead Frenchmen and end the matter. Dulhut's cmissary refused all such offers and denied the legitimacy of such cultural equivalence, telling them "that a hundred slaves and a hundred packages of beaver could not make him traffic in the blood of his brothers."[51]

Up to this point, all seems to be merely another example of something that appears in the literature many times: an ethnocentric European imposing by force proper cultural forms on a people he regards as savages. Savagism as a way of looking at Indians was, however, of limited utility in the woods. Dulhut was hardly in a position to act as if Indians were without culture. The French state did not command a monopoly of violence in the West and its authority was feeble. Dulhut did not have an established judicial system to appeal to, unless he wished to try to convey his prisoners to Quebec or Montreal. When the murderers had been disposed of, he and his men would remain to travel among the surrounding Indians who were not likely to forget whatever action he took. Their thoughts on the matter could not be safely ignored, and Dulhut having rejected Indian norms, relaxed his own considerably.

What followed at Michilimackinac was a series of rather extraordinary improvisations as Dulhut and various Ottawa, Huron-Petun, and Chippewa headmen and elders struggled to create a middle ground where the matter could be resolved. Dulhut's primary appeal throughout was to French law and custom, but he tried repeatedly, if necessarily somewhat ignorantly, to justify his recourse to law and custom by equating them with Indian practices. Having rejected the preferred means of settling killings among

---

of French traders and danger they were in, see Denonville au Ministre, aoust 1688, AN, C11A, v. 10, (f. 66); Nouvel à M. de la Barre, 23 avril 1684, AN, C11A, v. 6.

[51] The only detailed account of this murder is Dulhut's own, but since he was in a position to justify his actions, he provided considerable detail. See Dulhut letter, April 12, 1684, WHC 16:114–15, 123.

allies – the covering or raising up of the dead – he insisted on the penalty exacted from enemies: blood revenge. The Indians, for their part, paid little attention to what mattered most to the French, the proper way of establishing guilt and punishing the perpetrator. They only sought to offer suitable compensation to the living and reestablish social peace.[52]

The result was a series of bizarre cultural hybrids. The various Ottawa, Chippewa, and Huron-Petun bands convened in council with Dulhut only to find themselves transformed into a jury by the French for the trial of the Menominee, Achiganaga, and two of his sons. Kinsmen of the accused were drafted as lawyers, testimony was given and written down, and the murderers, with the exception of Achiganaga, freely admitted the crime. The elders cooperated with this French ritual, apparently believing that after it was performed the French would accept appropriate compensation. Instead, Dulhut demanded that the Indians themselves execute the murderers. To the Indians, Achiganaga's failure to confess constituted acquittal, and he was no longer part of the proceedings, but execution of the remaining three men, after compensation had been refused, would have been the equivalent of a declaration of war on the Saulteurs and Menominees by the executioners. The elders were so shocked and confused by this demand that they did not even make an answer.[53]

Dulhut, at this point, decided unilaterally to execute the Menominee and the two sons of Achiganaga as the admittedly guilty parties. This decision not only upset the Indians at Michilimackinac, it also appalled the French wintering at Keweenaw, who sent Dulhut a message warning that if he executed the murderers, the Indians' relatives would take revenge on the French. They begged him to act with restraint. French standards simply could not be imposed with impunity. Dulhut, after consulting with the Sieur de La Tour, the man longest among the lake tribes and most familiar with their customs, sought once more to appeal to Indian custom and return the matter to the middle ground. He again tried to find some connection between French law and what he regarded as Indian custom. Since two Frenchmen had died, Dulhut would execute only two Indians – the Menominee and the eldest of the two sons of Achiganaga – for "by killing man for man, the savages would have nothing to say, since that is their own practice." He announced this decision in the cabin of an Ottawa headman the French called Le Brochet, adding that although French law and custom demanded the execution of all the men involved in the robbery, he would be content with a life for a life.[54]

---

[52] Dulhut letter, April 12, 1684, *WHC* 16:119.
[53] *Ibid.*, 118–20.
[54] *Ibid.*, 119–21.

By his decision, Dulhut established a tenuous connection between Algonquian and French customs – a life for a life – but he also revealed the very different meanings such a dictum had in each culture. Only now, according to Dulhut, did the Ottawas believe that the French would actually execute two of the men. The headmen of the Sable Ottawas and the Sinago Ottawas, themselves uninvolved in the murder, begged Dulhut to spare the murderers. They, too, sought a middle ground and appealed to French precedent. At the request of Onontio, the Ottawas had spared an Iroquois prisoner. The French should now do the same for them. Dulhut denied the situations were equivalent. The Iroquois was a prisoner of war; these men were murderers. Here the glaring differences between Ottawa and French cultural categories emerged in action.[55]

Blood revenge was appropriate in each society but for different categories of killing. For the Algonquians there were two kinds of killings – deaths at the hands of enemies and deaths at the hands of allies. The appropriate response depended on the identity of the group to whom the killer belonged. If the killer belonged to an allied group, then the dead were raised or covered. If the murderers refused to do this, then the group became enemies and the price appropriate to enemies, blood revenge, was exacted. For the French also there were two kinds of killings – killings in war and murders. Killing enemies in war theoretically brought no retribution once the battle ended. For them, the battlefield was a cultural arena separate from the rest of life. Releasing the Iroquois was thus only appropriate; he was a soldier, not a murderer. Algonquians in practice recognized no such cultural arena as a battlefield; they killed their enemies when and where they found them unless they were ritually protected. For the French it was murder that demanded blood revenge; for the Algonquians, it was killings by enemies, killings which the French saw as warfare. The French insistence on blood revenge in an inappropriate category, therefore, created great confusion. To the Ottawas the logic of such a response – that enemies should be spared but that allies should be killed – was incomprehensible.[56]

The way out of this deadlock was created by a man named Oumamens, a headman of the Amikwas (a proto-Ojibwa group). He spoke for the Saulteurs in council and resorted to the kind of cultural fiction that often disguises the beginnings of cultural change. He got up and praised, of all things, Dulhut's mercy, because he had released Achiganaga and all but one of his children. In effect, Oumamens chose to emphasize those of Dulhut's actions which conformed to Algonquian custom. He announced that the Saulteurs were

---

[55] *Ibid.*, 120–21.

[56] *Ibid.*. See also Jaenen, *Friend and Foe*, 132–34. It should be noted that by 1690 the French had begun imitating the Iroquois and were torturing and killing prisoners of war, Narrative of . . . Occurrences 1690, 1691, *NYCD* 9:518.

satisfied. Dulhut, for his part, stressed not mercy but deterrence. If the elders "had from the beginning made known to the young men that in case they committed any evil deed the tribe would abandon them, they would have been better advised, and the Frenchmen would still be alive." Both sides thus tended to stress the aspect of the affair that made cultural sense to them. An hour later, at the head of forty-eight Frenchmen with four hundred warriors watching, Dulhut had the two Indians executed.[57]

The executions did not establish the legitimacy of French justice. Indeed, in the days that followed the executions, the Indians treated them as two more murders to be resolved, and Dulhut consented to their proceedings. Because Achiganaga's son and the Menominee had been executed in the territory of the Huron-Petuns and the Ottawas, these groups were implicated, and they took steps to settle the whole affair.[58]

Three Ottawa tribes – the Sables, Sinagos, and Kiskakons – gave two wampum belts to the French to cover their dead and two other belts to Achiganaga and to the Menominee's relatives. The next day the Huron-Petuns did the same. Dulhut, for his part, held a feast for Le Brochet, the Sable headman, to "take away the pain that I had caused him by pronouncing the death sentence of the two savages in his cabin, without speaking to him of it." Dulhut then loaded Achiganaga with presents, and the Saulteurs gave the French at Keweenaw additional belts "to take good care that no trouble be made over the death of their brother; and in order, should any have evil designs, to restrain them by these collars, of which they are bearers."[59]

The incident is revealing precisely because it was so indecisive, so improvised, precisely because neither French nor Algonquian cultural rules fully governed the situation. Both French and Algonquian customs were challenged, consciously explained, and modified in practice. Dulhut did not establish the primacy of French law, and he did not prevent further killings. What he did do was to shake, but not eliminate, the ability of Algonquian norms to govern murders of Frenchmen by Indians. Both sides now had to justify their own rules in terms of what they perceived to be the practices of the other. What happened in 1683 was, in the end, fully in accordance with neither French nor Indian conceptions of crime and punishment. Instead, it involved considerable improvisation and the creation of a middle ground at a point where the cultures seemed to intersect, so that the expectations of each side could find at least some satisfaction. At Green Bay the next spring, Father Nouvel thought that Dulhut's executions had produced a good effect,

---

[57] *Ibid.*, 120–21.
[58] *Ibid.*, 124.
[59] *Ibid.*, 124–25.

but at the same time he attributed the Potawatomi and Sauk desire for reconciliation with the French to their growing fear of the Iroquois, not their fear of French reprisals. Nouvel, for his part, demanded no further executions; he was willing to accept the Potawatomi and Sauk offer to cover the deaths of the two French donnés they had murdered.[60]

At Michilimackinac in 1683, Dulhut had operated without specific authority from the French government for his actions. He had improvised his solutions. The killings at Detroit, some twenty years later, in 1706, led to negotiations with the highest colonial officials, at a time when the French-Algonquian alliance had created a considerably more elaborate middle ground on which Indians and Frenchmen might work. Indeed, it was the alliance itself that both created the conditions that caused the murders and provided the ceremonial forms that compensated for them.

IV

In 1706, as Ottawa warriors departed to attack the Sioux, a Potawatomi warned them that in their absence the Huron-Petuns and the Miamis would fall on the Ottawa village and kill those who remained. The Ottawa war leaders consulted with the civil leaders and, although some wavered, the old and powerful Sable chief whom the French called Le Pesant convinced them to strike first. The Ottawas ambushed a party of Miami chiefs, killing five of them, and then attacked the Miami village, driving the inhabitants into the French fort. The French fired on the attacking Ottawas and killed a young Ottawa who had just been recognized as a war leader. Although the Ottawa leaders tried to prevent any attacks on the French, angry warriors killed a French Recollect priest outside the fort and a soldier who came out to rescue him.[61]

The Ottawas tried all the ceremonial means at their disposal to effect a reconciliation with the French, but they were rebuffed by the man com-

---

[60] Fr. Nouvel à M. de la Barre, 23 avril 1684, AN, C11A, v. 6, f. 523. Reconciliation was also forwarded by Governor de la Barre who approved of Dulhut's actions, but the French court, which often had only a shaky grasp of what was going on in the upper country, confused Dulhut's executions with the killing of an Iroquois at Michilimackinac and denounced Dulhut and his presence in the backcountry, De la Barre au Ministre, 5 juin 1684, AN, C11A, v. 6. Louis XIV to De La Barre, July 21, 1684, DHNY, 1:108–9.

[61] For the Ottawa version of these events, see Speech of Miscouaky, Sept. 26, 1706, MPHC 33:288–92. For the French investigation, see Report of D'Aigremont, MPHC 33:435. For Cadillac's account, see Cadillac to de Vaudreuil, Aug. 27, 1706; E. M. Sheldon, The Early History of Michigan from the First Settlement to 1815 (New York: A. S. Barnes, 1956), 219. For mention of a second French soldier killed later, see Instructions to D'Aigremont, June 30, 1707, WHC 16:243.

manding in Cadillac's absence. In subsequent fighting, the French sided with the Miamis, as did the Huron-Petuns (the nation the Ottawas claimed had actually organized the plot against them). Before the Ottawas withdrew to Michilimackinac, three Frenchmen, about thirty Ottawas, fifty Miamis, and an unknown number of Huron-Petuns were dead. The critical issue between the French and Ottawas, however, was the men killed during the first exchange: the young Ottawa leader, another Ottawa man with powerful kin connections at Michilimackinac, the Recollect, and the first French soldier killed.[62]

The fighting at Detroit in 1706 sprang from some basic breaches in the alliance the French had constructed and threatened to dissolve the alliance completely. In his zeal to promote Detroit, a post he had founded in 1701, Cadillac had recruited French allies to settle there without much thought for the outstanding disputes among them. In 1706, the residents included, among others, members of three Ottawa tribes – Sinagos, Kiskakons, and Sables – Huron-Petuns, and Miamis. Basic to the alliance and critical to such multitribal settlements was mediation. The French had to make sure that killings between the tribes were settled and the dead covered. Cadillac had promised to do this, but uncovered and unrevenged dead continued to poison the relations between the Miamis and the Huron-Petuns, on the one hand, and the Ottawas on the other. Le Pesant himself had presented a list of the dead left uncovered and unavenged before the departure of the fateful war party. The result of the French refusal to act was the fighting of 1706 and a threat to the entire alliance.[63]

The killings at Detroit produced a situation neither the French nor the Ottawa leaders desired. As Vaudreuil lamented in his report of the affair to

---

[62] For Ottawa attempts to negotiate, see Speech of Miscouaky, 26 Sept. 1706, *MPHC* 133:290–92; Report of D'Aigremont, *MPHC* 33:435–36. For various casualty figures in the fight, see "Council with Ottawas, June 18, 1707," in Sheldon, *Early History of Michigan*, 228, where Jean le Blanc puts the Ottawa dead at 30; Speech of Miscouaky, Sept. 26, 1706, *MPHC* 33:294, where the figure is 26 for the Ottawas and 50 dead and wounded for the Miamis. For the significant Ottawa dead, see Speech of Miscouaky, Sept. 26, 1706, *MPHC* 33:290, and Fr. Marest to Vaudreuil, Aug. 14, 1706, *MPHC* 33:262–69. For the French emphasis on the priest and the first soldier killed, see Council with the Ottawas, June 20, 1707, Speech of Vaudreuil, Sheldon, *Early History of Michigan*, 242; Speech of Vaudreuil, June 21, 1707, *ibid.*, 245.

[63] "Account of Detroit," Sept. 25, 1702, *MPHC* 33:137–38, 147; Cadillac to Pontchartrain, Aug. 31, 1703, in Sheldon, *Early History of Michigan*, 105–6. For mention of quarrels and unsettled killings, see Cadillac to Vaudreuil, Aug. 27, 1706, in Sheldon, *Early History of Michigan*, 218–19. For earlier attack, see Memorandum of . . . Cadillac, 19 Nov. 1704, *MPHC* 33:234; Report of D'Aigremont, Nov. 14, 1708, *MPHC* 33:432–37. For a Miami–Huron-Petun rapprochement as early as 1703, see Speeches of Ottawas . . . 24 Sept. 1703, *MPHC* 33:223–25. For Vaudreuil's orders to keep the peace, see Vaudreuil au Cadillac, 10 juin 1706, AN, Moreau St. Mery, F3, v. 7, f. 308. For Huron-Petun resentment, see Vaudreuil to Minister, May 5, 1705, *MPHC* 33:242.

Count de Pontchartrain, the fiasco at Detroit threatened to "begin a war which can cause us only considerable expense, the loss of a nation that has served us faithfully, and, in addition to that, a considerable trade, every year." For the Ottawas the outcome looked no more favorable. Cut off from trade goods, impoverished, and driven from their fields, they found that "all the land was stupefied, and want had taken possession of our bones." Settling such a conflict was, however, far from simple. The prominence of the dead on both sides intensified the difficulties of settling the killings. The dead Ottawas had powerful kinspeople; the French stressed the particular horror of killing a priest; and Cadillac promised the Miamis and Huron-Petuns the destruction of the Ottawas as revenge for their own dead. The negotiations to resolve these killings would be, according to Governor de Vaudreuil, one of the most important affairs in the history of the upper country.[64]

The ceremonial forms of the Ottawa-French alliance shaped the negotiations from the beginning. The alliance was centered on Quebec, the home of Onontio, and it was formulated in the language of kinship to which both the French and the Algonquians attached great significance. Leaders of both the French and the Algonquians negotiated according to ritual forms which placed the French governor, Onontio, in the position of father to the Indians, of whom the Ottawas were his eldest sons. The French were quite at home with such patriarchal formulations and attached quite specific meanings to them. For them all authority was patriarchal, from God the Father, to the king (the father of his people), to the father in his home. Fathers commanded; sons obeyed. The Ottawas understood the relationship somewhat differently. A father was kind, generous, and protecting. A child owed a father respect, but a father could not compel obedience. In establishing a middle ground, one took such congruences as one could find and sorted out their meanings later.[65]

---

[64] For Vaudreuil quote, see Vaudreuil to de Pontchartrain, Nov. 4, 1706, *WHC* 16:242. For Ottawas, see Words of Ottawas to Cadillac, Sept. 24, 1707, *MPHC* 33:349. For difficulties, see Father Marest to Vaudreuil, Aug. 14, 1706, *MPHC* 33:262–69; Council with the Ottawas, Speech of Vaudreuil, June 20, 1707, Sheldon, *Early History of Michigan*, 242. Cadillac to Vaudreuil, Aug. 27, 1706, *ibid.*, 228–29. For importance of negotiations, see Vaudreuil to Father Marest, n.d. (1707), Sheldon, *Early History of Michigan*, 273.

[65] Many examples of the French councils survive. For examples for the period under consideration here, see Parolles des sauvages . . . , Archives Nationales, Archives Coloniales, F3, v. 8, f. 136–41; Talk between Marquis de Vaudreuil and Onaskin . . . , Aug. 1, 1707, *MPHC* 33:258–62; Speech of Miscouaky . . . to Marquis de Vaudreuil, Sept. 26, 1706, *MPHC* 33:288–96; Conference with Ottawas, June 18, 1707, in Sheldon, *Early History of Michigan*, 232–50. For the differences in how the Great Lakes Indians and the French perceived the relationship between parents and children, see Father Gabriel Sagard, *The Long Journey to the Country of the Hurons* (Toronto: Champlain Society 1939, facsimile ed., Greenwood Press), 130–31; Pierre de Charlevoix, *Journal of a Voyage to North America* (London: R. & J. Dodsley, 1761, Readex microprint facsimile ed., 1966), 2:55, 89–90, 109,

Within the alliance, these ritual forms for father and son thus had a built-in ambiguity that would influence the course of the negotiations that followed the fighting at Detroit. Negotiations in the West (at Sault Sainte Marie and Michilimackinac) covered the Ottawa dead to that nation's satisfaction, but covering the French dead proved more difficult. Many of the matters at issue here revolved around questions of the proper way for a father to act toward his errant sons. At Quebec, Vaudreuil, in his negotiations with the Ottawas in the fall of 1706 and the spring of 1707, insisted on phrasing the alliance and Ottawa obligations in terms of Christian patriarchy. The governor demanded that the Ottawas appear before him as penitent sinners appear before the Christian God. The customary Ottawa compensation for the dead was inadequate and inappropriate.

> I am a good father and as long as my children listen to my voice, no evil ever befalls them.... It is not belts that I require, Miscouaky, nor presents when my children have disobeyed me and committed such a fault as yours; the blood of Frenchmen is not to be paid for by beaverskins. It is a great trust in my kindness that I demand; a real repentance for the fault that has been committed, and complete resignation to my will. When your people entertain those feelings, I will arrange everything.[66]

The Ottawa response to these demands, in the usual manner of the middle ground, was to seek cultural congruence. They, too, focused on patriarchy, but of a different kind. Otontagan (or Jean le Blanc), the Sable chief second in influence to Le Pesant, spoke for the Ottawas when they came to Quebec the next summer. He admitted his guilt (even though he had, in fact, tried to save the Recollect) but attempted to place the primary responsibility for the affair with Le Pesant. Otontagan's major concern, however, was to get Vaudreuil to act like an Ottawa, not a French, father. He stressed Vaudreuil's beneficence. Vaudreuil certainly had the power to kill him, but "I have nothing to fear because I have a good father." Since

---

114–15; Lafitau, *Customs of the American Indian* 1:362; Perrot, *Memoir* 1:67; Thwaites (ed.), *Lahontan's Voyages* 2:458. See also Jaenen, *Friend and Foe*, 94–97.

[66] Kischkouch, the young Sinago chief killed at Detroit, had a brother, Merasilla, who had actually gone among the Saulteurs and Amikwas to raise a party to avenge his brother "and restore the name of Kischkouch." In the end, Merasilla excused himself from the war party, despite reproaches that he showed "no love for his brother," and helped negotiate a peace. The war party went to Detroit, accompanied by other Ottawas, but did not attack. Another Ottawa killed at Detroit had as relatives two of the principal women at Michilimackinac, and they went from cabin to cabin, weeping and demanding the deaths of Frenchmen there until negotiations covered their loss. Marest to Vaudreuil, Aug. 14, 1706, *WHC* 16:232–34; Marest to Vaudreuil, Aug. 16, 1706, and Aug. 27, 1706, *MPHC* 33:262–71; Cadillac to Vaudreuil, Aug. 27, 1706, Sheldon, *Early History of Michigan*, 226–27. For quote, see Reply of Vaudreuil to Miscouaky, Nov. 4, 1706, *MPHC* 33:295.

Vaudreuil had specifically rejected covering the dead, Otontagan concluded that he must want the dead raised up. The delegation accordingly brought two adopted captives to give to Vaudreuil "to bring the gray coat again to life." Vaudreuil held out for a stricter patriarchy. He demanded vengeance; he demanded the head of Le Pesant because "the blood of French is usually repaid among us only by blood." But such a demand, Otontagan told Vaudreuil, was impossible. Le Pesant was allied to all the nations of the Great Lakes. They would prevent his delivery and execution.[67]

On the surface, the negotiations at Quebec appear to be another example of a stubborn French refusal to compromise. The situation was, in fact, much more complex. Vaudreuil knew that no Ottawa leader possessed sufficient authority to hand over anyone, let alone someone of Le Pesant's stature. His intention was not to secure Le Pesant's death, rather it was to cut him off from the French alliance, destroy his influence, and demonstrate that any chief held responsible for the death of a Frenchman would suffer the same fate. Since Vaudreuil did not expect Le Pesant to be surrendered, the actual restoration of the Ottawas to the alliance would involve a compromise of some sort. Since patriarchs do not compromise, he sent the Ottawas back to Detroit, telling them to negotiate a peace with Cadillac. He would approve such a peace as long as Le Pesant was not included in any pardon Cadillac granted. By this maneuver Vaudreuil could make an impossible demand, while leaving the responsibility of negotiating what might be an embarrassing compromise to his rival and subordinate, Cadillac.[68]

At Detroit the larger issue remained – how the alliance could be restored within the cultural parameters of the parties involved. Le Pesant was called "that great bear, that malicious bear," and Vaudreuil's demand for his execution loomed over the proceedings. The people struggling with this problem were themselves political actors who were not necessarily wedded to the welfare of either Le Pesant or Vaudreuil. The chief Ottawa negotiators, Otontagan and Onaske from Michilimackinac, were Le Pesant's political rivals. They protected him not out of love but because they had no means at their disposal to deliver him, and they feared the repercussions if they tried. Cadillac, for his part, was a long-standing opponent of Vaudreuil and only too glad to use the affair to benefit himself and embarrass the

---

[67] For Otontagan, see Vaudreuil to Minster, July 24, 1707; *MPHC* 33:328–29, Council with Ottawas, June 18, 1707, Speech of Jean le Blanc, Sheldon, *Early History of Michigan*, 233–39. For Vaudreuil's position, see Council with Ottawas, June 20, 1707, Reply of Vaudreuil, Sheldon, *Early History of Michigan*, 242; Reply of Jean le Blanc, June 21, 1707, *ibid.*, 243–44.

[68] See the speech of Vaudreuil to Jean le Blanc, June 22, 1707, Sheldon, *Early History of Michigan*, 245–47; Vaudreuil to Minster, July 24, 1707, *MPHC* 33:328–30. For the rivalry of Vaudreuil and Cadillac, see Vaudreuil to Minister, Nov. 12, 1707, *MPHC* 33:371–72.

governor. Both Cadillac and the Ottawa chiefs could conceivably use the cultural demands of outsiders to advance their interests within their own society while simultaneously renewing the alliance.[69]

The willingness of both Cadillac and the Ottawa negotiators to move from their initial positions reflects this sense of their own political advantage. They could also violate the usual norms of their own cultures because the alliance, itself the middle ground, created cultural demands of its own. Cadillac shifted his position first. He indicated that the surrender of Le Pesant was more important than his death. "I wish him to be in my power, either to grant him his life or put him to death," he told Otontagan. Cadillac was, in effect, putting Le Pesant in the place of the slaves or captives usually given to raise the dead. Such cultural logic was more comprehensible to the Ottawas than a demand for execution, even if the surrender of a chief was without precedent. These were unusual conditions; the alliance itself was at stake. Otontagan agreed to deliver Le Pesant: "He is my brother, my own brother, but what can we do?" Since Otontagan and Kinouge, another headman, were, like Le Pesant, Sable Ottawas, they agreed to take responsibility for his surrender, thus making the matter an internal Sable matter and limiting the repercussions. In effect, a cultural fiction was agreed on. Cadillac and the Ottawas agreed to act as if Le Pesant were a slave being offered to the French in compensation for their dead. Cadillac would then determine if he lived or died. This made cultural sense in a way that Le Pesant's execution did not; it preserved the alliance, and it served the personal interests of both French and Ottawa negotiators.[70]

[69] Otontagan (Jean le Blanc), Kinouge, Meatinan, and Menukoueak were joined partway through the proceedings by Kataolauibois (Koutaouileone) and Onaske, who was headman of the Kiskakon Ottawas at Michilimackinac. Council held at Detroit, Aug. 6, 1707, Aug. 8, 1707, *MPHC* 33:331, 334; Speeches of Three Indians from Michilmackina (*sic*) Oct. 7, 1707, *MPHC* 33:362–64.

From the beginning of these negotiations, Otontagan and his brother, Miscouaky, had tried to lay the blame for the incident on Le Pesant. Speech of Miscouaky, Sept. 26, 1706, *MPHC* 33:288–89; Council with Ottawas, Speech of Jean le Blanc, June 18, 1707, Sheldon, *Early History of Michigan*, 234–35. Onaske and Le Pesant were engaged in a rivalry over whether the Ottawas should concentrate their settlements at Michilimackinac or Detroit. Onaske accused Le Pesant of giving the Iroquois gifts to come and attack the Ottawas of Michilimackinac. Father Marest to Vaudreuil, Aug. 14, 1706, *WHC* 16:238. Cadillac had earlier accused the Michilimackinac Ottawas of soliciting other nations to attack Detroit to force the Ottawas there to withdraw to Michilimackinac, Sheldon, *Early History of Michigan*, 196–97. Koutaouileone was also involved in the attempt to reunite the Ottawas at Michilimackinac. Marest to Vaudreuil, Aug. 27, 1706, *MPHC* 33:271. Cadillac's maneuverings will be discussed below. The French, of course, tried to use Ottawa divisions to their advantage, see Vaudreuil's comments on Cadillac's letter of Aug. 27, 1706, *MPHC* 33:282.

[70] Council Held at Detroit, Aug. 6, 1707, Speech of Cadillac *MPHC* 33:332. Council Held at Detroit, Replies of Otontagan, Aug. 6, 1707, Seventh Council, Speech of Onaske, *MPHC* 33:332–33, 335–36. Speeches of Three Indians from Michilimakina (*sic*), Oct. 7, 1707, *MPHC* 33:363–64.

There were two formidable obstacles to this solution. The first was the Miamis and the Huron-Petuns, whom Cadillac had made simple observers of the whole affair. For their benefit, Cadillac treated the Ottawa delegation imperiously. He gave the Huron-Petuns – and tried to give the Miamis – the Ottawa captives intended for Vaudreuil in order "to revive your dead a little – I do not say altogether." He even, in council, made the Huron-Petuns the elder brothers of the French alliance in place of the Ottawas. But he denied them revenge. He warned both nations that with the delivery of Le Pesant, he would consider the matter closed. "There shall be no blood left to be seen."[71]

The second obstacle was a practical one: Who exactly would persuade or force Le Pesant to consent to serve as a slave to the French? Who provided the solution to this problem is not known, but how it was solved is clear enough. A proceeding that had been half theater and half negotiation now became fully theater. After considerable negotiations at Michilimackinac, Le Pesant agreed to come to Detroit and surrender himself as a slave to the French. According to Vaudreuil, all that followed was prearranged between Le Pesant and an emissary of Cadillac. How much the other Ottawas or other Frenchmen knew of these arrangements is not clear.[72]

Cadillac compared the astonishment provoked by the appearance of Le Pesant at Detroit to that produced by the arrival of the Doge of Genoa in France. To evoke such a response, to make the Indians marvel at the culturally unimaginable things Cadillac and the French could achieve, was, in fact, the sole point of the drama now enacted at Detroit. Cadillac's production of "The Surrender of Le Pesant," however, had to play to a suspicious and critical audience of Miamis, Huron-Petuns, and those French officials who watched from afar. All of them were concerned not so

---

[71] The Huron-Petuns and Miamis wondered out loud why Cadillac should bother to demand Le Pesant when there were so many Ottawa chiefs in Detroit upon whom they could take revenge. Council Held at Detroit, Aug. 7, 1707, Aug. 9, 1707, *MPHC* 33:333–35; Speeches of Three Indians from Michilimakina (*sic*), Oct. 7, 1707, *MPHC* 33:363–64.

[72] How Le Pesant was persuaded, or forced, to come was not clear. Kataolauibois told Vaudreuil that it was Onaske, Sakima, Meyavila, and himself, all of them Kiskakons and Sinago Ottawas from Michilimackinac, who compelled Le Pesant to embark. He minimized the role of Otontagan, even though Onaske had stressed at Detroit that the surrender of Le Pesant was Otontagan's responsibility. Kataolauibois's account of negotiations is, however, sketchy and he told Vaudreuil that he would leave it to the Sieur de St. Pierre, who had been present, to give a full account. It appears clear, however, that Le Pesant in reaching his decision to come had to deal with strong pressure from leading men that he go. The pressure was strong enough so that Kataloauibois feared Le Pesant's revenge if Cadillac did not execute him. Speeches of Three Indians from Michilimakina (*sic*), Oct. 7, 1707, *MPHC* 33:365. Vaudreuil, deriving his account from the Sieur de St. Pierre, says that Le Pesant made private arrangements with the Sieur d'Argenteuil, Cadillac's emissary, to come to Detroit. Vaudreuil to Minister, Oct. 1, 1707, *MPHC* 33:354.

much with the plot as with the culturally symbolic details that gave the drama its meaning. Vaudreuil delivered the most extended review of the performance, although, as shall be seen, the Miamis were the most critical.[73]

Le Pesant, until now the Godot of this drama, put in his appearance at Detroit on September 24, 1707. He delivered his only recorded lines while looking to shore from the canoe that brought him. He trembled, either from malaria or fear, and said, "I see I am a dead man." Yet what Vaudreuil noted was his escort. He came with ten warriors who were not Kiskakon or Sinago Ottawas, but Sable Ottawas from his own village. They were sent, Vaudreuil said, not to deliver him but to protect him from angry Huron-Petuns and Miamis. Cadillac verbally abused Le Pesant, referring to him as his slave, but Cadillac spoke to Le Pesant on a wampum belt. One did not speak to slaves on wampum. One spoke to representatives of nations in that manner. The Ottawas then asked for Le Pesant's life and, offering a young slave, asked that they be allowed to return to Detroit.[74]

With Le Pesant's ritual submission, the first act ended. Le Pesant, Vaudreuil pointed out, had served his purpose. His continued presence now became a problem for Cadillac. Vaudreuil had ordered his death and Cadillac had earlier promised the Miamis and Huron-Petuns that he would kill him. But if Cadillac actually killed Le Pesant, he risked conflict with the Sable Ottawas and their allies on the Great Lakes. Le Pesant's surrender was useful; his continued presence was not.[75]

Cadillac and the Ottawas solved the problem by writing Le Pesant out of the script. That night, leaving behind his shoes, his knife, and his shabby hat, Le Pesant escaped from the fort at Detroit. Cadillac, in retaliation, locked up his escorts for a day and then released them, contending that Le Pesant would perish in the woods, and, in any case, his influence was now gone. Vaudreuil was skeptical. Le Pesant – whose name translates from the French as the heavy one, or the fat one – was notoriously obese and nearly seventy years old. That a seventy-year-old fat man whose surrender had been the object of French policy in the upper country for more than a year could escape past sentinels from a French fort on the first night of his captivity strained credibility. Cadillac's only explanation was that Le Pesant had lost a lot of weight lately. With Le Pesant gone, Cadillac assured the Ottawas that

---

[73] Cadillac to Vaudreuil (copy made), Oct. 1, 1707, *MPHC* 33:352–52. Words of the Ottawas to Cadillac, Sept. 24, 1707, *MPHC* 33:346–50. Vaudreuil to Minister, Oct. 1, 1707, *MPHC* 33:350–53.
[74] Cadillac to Vaudreuil (copy made), Oct. 1, 1707, *MPHC* 33:351–52; Words of the Ottawas to Cadillac, Sept. 24, 1707, *MPHC* 33:346–48; Vaudreuil to Minister, Oct. 1, 1707, *MPHC* 33:354–57.
[75] Vaudreuil to Minister, Oct. 1, 1707, *MPHC* 33:355–58.

he had intended to pardon him anyway, thus freeing himself from complicity in his death if the Huron-Petuns or Miamis should catch him.[76]

Vaudreuil, skeptical and critical as he was, appreciated good acting and clever staging, even as he deciphered the drama and explained away the illusions it sought to create. With both the Ottawas and the French acting according to script, the cultural demands of each had been met by creating an artificial and controlled stage, a special kind of middle ground. Vaudreuil appreciated this.[77]

The Miamis and Huron-Petuns were less enthusiastic. Their response to the drama was so harsh that Cadillac did not choose to fully report it. Instead, he reported only the closing part of the council that followed Le Pesant's escape and was attended by the Miamis, the Huron-Petuns, the French, and the Ottawas. In council, following the usual ritual forms, he calmed the waters, removed the fallen trees, smoothed the land, and opened the way for peace and the return of the Ottawas to Detroit.[78]

Unfortunately for Cadillac, the audience in historical dramas of this sort must consent to the script, for they always have the option of adding a final act. Le Pesant returned to Michilimackinac in the same canoe and with the same warriors who had escorted him down to Detroit, but this did not close the play. Cadillac had gained the Ottawas but lost the Miamis, who soon killed not only Ottawas but also Frenchmen, and so began yet another round of negotiations. The resolution of the killings at Detroit was thus only partially successful, but the negotiations are, nevertheless, illuminating. They reveal the substantial and expanding middle ground the French-Algonquian alliance had created. Here common problems could be worked out and mutually comprehensible solutions arrived at. The negotiations also reveal the extent to which solutions could be elaborately scripted cultural fictions, political theater. Such fictions deeply influenced events in both societies.[79]

V

Once established, the middle ground was extended in surprising directions. Killings the French once considered solely their own concern became

[76] Cadillac to Vaudreuil (copy made), Oct. 1, 1707, *MPHC* 33:351; Vaudreuil to Minister, Oct. 1, 1707, *MPHC* 33:355; Words of Ottawas to Cadillac Sept. 25, 1707, *MPHC* 33:348–50.

[77] Vaudreuil to Minister, Oct. 1, 1707, *MPHC* 33:355.

[78] Words of Ottawas to Cadillac, Sept. 25, 1707, *MPHC* 33:348–50.

[79] For the retaliation of the Miamis and the events which followed, see Vaudreuil and Raudot to Minister, Nov. 14, 1708, *MPHC* 33:403–5, 408; Father Marest to De Vaudreuil, June 4, 1708, *MPHC* 33:383–87; De Vaudreuil to Minister, Nov. 5, 1708, *MPHC* 33:395–99;

issues to be settled on the middle ground. On April 25, 1723, a French soldier spoke "impertinently" to a warehouse keeper, a man named Perillaut, who responded by running his sword through the soldier's body. The French tried Perillaut and condemned him to death, but Perillaut, as warehouse keeper (or *maître de la marchandise*, as the Indians called him), had had many dealings with the Illinois, and his death sentence disturbed them deeply. On April 29 three chiefs of the Kaskaskias, accompanied by thirty warriors, appeared to plead for his life. They were followed in early May by a Cahokia delegation that included Marie Rompiechoue (or Rokipiekoue). This woman, who was "greatly respected in her village and among the French," was the wife of a Cahokia, Joseph Ouissakatchakoue. In all likelihood, Marie Rompiechoue was Aramepinchieue, the daughter of Rouensa who had married Michel Accault thirty years earlier. The actions and speeches of these delegations, particularly those of the Kaskaskia chiefs Kiraoueria and Michel, present a clear picture of eighteenth-century Algonquian views on murder and revenge, and of how such views could influence French actions.[80]

Kiraoueria, a Kaskasia chief who was "of the Prayer" (a Christian), held a particularly advantageous position for articulating Indian logic and extending it to French affairs. The Kaskaskias opened matters by presenting the calumet, a symbol of friendship and alliance. The French knew from a half century of experience that to accept the calumet was to grant the giver's request. Kiraoueria then tried to bring the French to their senses. "Would you," he asked, "spill the blood of a Frenchman to blot out the blood of another and would you add to the loss of one man the loss of another?" This was folly. If the French insisted on killing someone to cover the body of the soldier, then they should strike the Fox and Chickasaws, their enemies. These people would be full of joy when they heard that the French had, in

Report of D'Aigremont, Nov. 14, 1708, *MPHC* 33:937–40. For the reaction of the Ottawas to Le Pesant's surrender, see Speeches of Three Indians from Michilimakina (*sic*), Oct. 7, 1707, *MPHC* 33:365.

80 This account is partially drawn from the report of Boisbriant Diron Desurins Legardeur De L'isle Ste. Therese Langloisere of June 17, 1723, in Schlarman, *From Quebec to New Orleans*, 225–31. For original, see Chefs du villages . . . , 17 juin 1793, AN, F3, v. 24, f. 157 Moreau St. Mery. The account of the Cahokia delegation and Marie Rompiechoue is from a document of May 11, 1723, entitled Remis par M. Diron, AN, C13A, v. 7, f. 322. That Marie Rompiechoue was Aramepinchieue is made likely by (1) the similarity of their names, (2) the fact that Aramepinchieue's baptismal name was Marie (see Palm, "Jesuit Missions," p. 38), and (3) the high standing of both women among the Illinois and the French. Aramepinchieue was still alive in 1723 because four years later the French ransomed "the Illinois woman who passed as the wife of michelako" from the Fox who were about to burn her. Accault was by now presumably dead. Deliette to Lignery, Oct. 15, 1726, *WHC* 17:18. For an additional, briefer account of the murder, see "Journal of Diron D'Artaguiette . . . ," in Newton D. Mereness, *Travels in the American Colonies* (New York: Macmillan Company, 1916), 75–77.

effect, avenged the Chickasaws and Fox's dead by killing one another.[81]

Kiraoueria then went on to explain the Algonquian view of murder. Murderers were madmen, and no nation could glory in being free of them. But they were not permanently mad. They could be redeemed, and rather than their being killed, the relatives of their victims should be compensated and the blood of the victim covered. More blood should not be spilled on top of it. But Kiraoueria did not expect the French simply to accept Algonquian logic. In the usual manner of creating the middle ground, he connected what he was saying with French culture. He joined it with Christianity:

> I know that the Great Spirit, the Spirit Creator, God, forbids us, my father, to kill our children. . . . But does not God, who is Master of all, raise his eyes above our follies when we ask him to be no longer angry? He forgives; pardon as He does, my fathers, and for the love of Him.[82]

Finally, Kiraoueria and Michel, a war chief, appealed to the underlying basis of the middle ground, the alliance, and the symbol of peace and alliance, the calumet. Kiraoueria begged the French not to humiliate him and his chiefs by refusing their request. Michel cited times when Kaskaskias had lost their lives to avenge the French and how those warriors remained unavenged at the request of the French. Those men, warriors for whom revenge should be taken, lay uncovered, and now the Kaskaskias were being asked to watch the French take inappropriate vengeance on one another.[83]

The affair, so phrased, was, as the French commander Boisbriant realized, "a delicate matter." To send the Illinois away without a concession was dangerous, particularly when Michel had obliquely raised the matter of the uncovered Kaskaskia dead. Boisbriant, in delivering his response, insisted that the affair set no precedent, but he agreed to petition the king for Perillaut's pardon and release. Those Kaskaskias who "have died to avenge the Frenchman, cover the body of the one who has now been killed." So ended the first recorded criminal case tried by the French in Illinois. Perillaut was free that May. He owed his freedom, just as fifty years before the son of Achiganaga owed his death, to an evolving cultural logic that sprang from the convergences, some accidental, some quite close, of two different cultural systems faced with a common set of problems.[84]

Separately, the stories of Dulhut and Achiganaga's sons, of Le Pesant and Cadillac, and of Perillaut and Kiraoueria are incidents widely scattered over

[81] *Ibid.*, 226–27. Kiraoueria's position was not unusual; Joachim, a Michigame chief, was also of the prayer. He had married three of his daughters to Frenchmen. St. Ange au Ministre, n.d., (1733) AN, C13A, v. 17, f. 248. For an Illinois interpretation of patriarchal relations, see Parolles de Chachagouesse . . . chez Illinois du 20 aoust 1712, AN, C11A, v. 33.

[82] *Ibid.*, 227.

[83] *Ibid.*, 227–30.

[84] *Ibid.*, 228–31.

time and space, but together they form an evolving ritual of surrender and redemption that would be central to the French-Algonquian alliance. This ritual of the middle ground clearly drew elements from both cultures but fully corresponded to neither. The ritual operated by analogy. The murderer was to the governor as a sinner was to God. The governor was to the murderer as a stern but forgiving father was to an erring son. Such analogies were hooks, both attaching the new ritual to the purely Algonquian or French way of settling murders and pulling elements of the older process into the middle ground. As under the French system, Indian murderers would be imprisoned while their crimes were investigated; as under the Algonquian system, Indian and French dead would be covered or raised up.

Once formulated, this ritual of surrender and redemption became a centerpiece of the middle ground. Orders from Governor Duquesne to the Sieur de Pean in 1754 expressed its basic elements well: "He must manage to see that he obtains the murderers, to whom he will grant pardon in the customary manner." The ritual, however, was under constant pressure from Frenchmen who, having seen to it that murderers were surrendered, wished to see these murderers executed, and from Algonquians who hesitated to surrender kinspeople for even temporary imprisonment before their pardon "in the customary manner." Each murder, each surrender, and each pardon thus became a test of the health of the alliance. Onontio's failure to pardon and his children's failure to surrender signaled crises that only a renewal of the ritual could resolve. Like all structural elements of culture, the ritual remained meaningful only insofar as it was constantly replicated in action.[85]

What was being created in social action was a world very different from the one historians would expect to find if they relied on the older ethnographies. Nor does the evolution of this world conform to much acculturation literature with the gradual adoption by Indians of certain European values. Instead, members of two cultures established an alliance that they both thought furthered interests generated within their own societies. They maintained this alliance through rituals and ceremonials based on cultural parallels and congruences, inexact and artificial as they originally may have been. These rituals and ceremonials were not the decorative covering of the alliance; they were its sinews. They helped bind together a common world to solve problems, even killings, that threatened the alliance itself. These solutions might have been, as at Detroit, elaborate cultural fictions, but through them change occurred. Such changes, worked out on the middle ground, could be remarkably influential, bringing important modifications in each society and blurring the boundaries between them.

[85] Instruction de Duquesne à Pean, 9 may 1754, in Fernand Grenier (ed.), *Papiers Contrecoeur, et autres documents concernant le conflit anglo-français sur l'Ohio de 1745 à 1756* (Quebec: Les presses universitaires, Laval, 1952), 122.

3

The fur trade

You have forgotten that your ancestors in former days used earthen pots, stone
hatchets, and knives, and bows; and you will be obliged to use them again, if
Onontio abandons you. What will become of you, if he becomes angry?

Nicolas Perrot, *Memoir*

The universal modeler attributes to exotic economic practices a motivation and
intentionality which is our own.

Stephen Gudeman, *Economics as Culture*

I

Normally, any discussion of the fur trade is segregated from the wider
spectrum of social relations and exchanges between Indians and whites. Yet
the exchange of goods is not so easily fenced off into an economic realm
whose rules are at once distinct from other aspects of life and present in all
societies. After all, goods changed hands virtually every time Frenchmen and
Algonquians struggled to unite against common enemies; or met to resolve
the murders between them; or asked for aid in surviving hunger, disease,
droughts, and blizzards; or made love or married. Such exchanges normally
either are excluded from considerations of the fur trade or are reduced to a
purely economic relation. It is just as possible, however, to create a counterimage in which the fur trade proper is merely an arbitrary selection from a
fuller and quite coherent spectrum of exchange that was embedded in
particular social relations. The fur trade was a constantly changing compromise, a conduit, between two local models of the exchange – the French
and the Algonquian.

In part, the counterimage presented in this chapter reenters on the side of
the substantivists the old, and now tired, debate between substantivists and
formalists, between local formulations of "economy" and universal models.
In producing and exchanging goods, the Algonquians were not acting as
"rational" human beings would have acted in their place. A complicated set
of human activities can be reduced to mere business transactions. If everyone and everything is for sale, and buying and selling at once encompasses

and explains all, then the world is a relatively simple and coherent place. But the Algonquians acted for reasons that cannot be reduced to universal economic laws without creating a caricature of their society and their relationship to Europeans. In the seventeenth- and eighteenth-century *pays d'en haut*, gifts were not merely bribes or wages; allies were not simply mercenaries; women were not merely prostitutes; missionaries did not just buy their converts; murderers did not kill simply for gain and then buy off those who would avenge their victims. Life was not a business, and such simplifications only distort the past.[1]

Thus far, this is only a restatement of the substantivist position; what moves us beyond substantivism is the realization that, no matter how the Algonquians conceived of exchange, they had indeed become part of a world market that then stretched across the Atlantic to Europe. When they accepted European goods and gave furs in return, a still emerging market system in Europe impinged on their lives. Individual European traders sought profit; at least some Frenchmen had to derive more wealth from the trade than they invested in it. But precisely because the fur trade could not be completely separated from the relationship of French fathers to their Algonquian children, that is, from relations of political and military alliance, a straightforward domination of the local Algonquian village by the market never emerged. Instead, a system of exchange developed that was notably different from earlier Algonquian models; it was a system influenced by, and yet buffered from, the market. The French-Algonquian alliance was the buffer. To allow profit alone to govern the fur trade threatened the alliance, and, when necessary, French officials subordinated the fur trade to the demands of the alliance. They acted as "fathers."[2]

Tied to the world market and embedded in the larger world of the alliance, the fur trade became part of the middle ground. It was not a realm where the French dictated to the Indians. To assert, as one prominent scholar has, that by the end of the seventeenth century, resistance to French policies could "mean a cessation of trade and consequent famine" is to overestimate the actual presence of trade goods, and to ignore both chronic

---

[1] The literature on the formalist-substantivist debate is too extensive to cite here. The basic substantivist text I have relied on is Marshall Sahlins, *Stone Age Economics* (Chicago: Aldine, 1972).

Arthur J. Ray and Donald Freeman, *Give Us Good Measure: An Economic Analysis of Relations Between the Indians and the Hudson's Bay Company Before 1763* (Toronto: University of Toronto Press, 1978), contains by far the most reasoned discussion of a modified formalist position. Its authors admit that the trade was subject to much regional variation (8–9), that it was a political as well as economic system (20–23), and that it conformed to neither European nor Indian models (236).

[2] W. J. Eccles, "The Fur Trade and Eighteenth-Century Imperialism," *William and Mary Quarterly* 40 (July 1983): 341–62.

resistance and the alternatives to French dictation. In the final stages of the fur trade, Indians depended on European manufactures and food supplies to survive, and Europeans dictated the terms of an exchange that reduced them to poverty. But this was the result of a long process; it was not simply a fact the moment the first hatchet gleamed in the North American sun.[3]

In assuming that trade goods themselves created instant dependence, we only repeat the mistakes of early French traders. Nicolas Perrot once told the Ottawas: "You have forgotten that your ancestors in former days used earthen pots, stone hatchets, and knives, and bows; and you will be obliged to use them again, if Onontio abandons you. What will become of you, if he becomes angry?" But Perrot misinterpreted Algonquian enthusiasm for knives, guns, and cloth and the ritual Algonquian language designed to evoke pity and generosity. Theirs was not abject dependence. Perrot eventually learned that his assumption of dependency was premature. A few years after his first speech, he indulged in a revealing diatribe against French policy. Citing repeated Indian murders of Frenchmen, Indian trade with the English, and French concessions to Indian demands, Perrot claimed that the western Indians possessed the "arrogant notion that the French cannot get along without them and that we could not maintain ourselves in the colony without the assistance that they give us." Exactly who was capable of dictating the actions of whom apparently remained an open question for some time.[4]

Reconstructing the fur trade as part of the middle ground involves more than following the movement of goods. It necessitates discovering what meaning these goods and their exchange had for both the Algonquians and the French. During the seventeenth and eighteenth centuries, the Indians most commonly gave furs – but also bark canoes, corn, berries, meat, and fish – to the Europeans; the Europeans gave the Algonquians cloth and

---

[3] Quoted in Harold Hickerson, "The Feast of the Dead among the Seventeenth-Century Algonkians of the Upper Great Lakes," *American Anthropologist* 62 (1960): 99.

   For a revealing debate on similar issues in a Latin American context, see Steven J. Stern, "Feudalism, Capitalism, and the World System in the Perspective of Latin America and the Caribbean," *American Historical Review* 93 (Oct. 1988), and the following AHR Forum, 829–97.

[4] For the first quotation from Perrot, see Claude Charles Le Roy, Bacqueville de la Potherie, *History of the Savage Peoples Who Are the Allies of New France*, in Emma Helen Blair (ed.), *The Indian Tribes of the Upper Mississippi Valley and Region of the Great Lakes*, 2 vols. (Cleveland: Arthur H. Clark, 1911), 2:77. The second quotation is from Nicolas Perrot, *Memoir on the Manners, Customs, and Religion of the Savages of North America*, in Blair (ed.), *Indian Tribes*, 1:262.

   In 1667 the French took for granted the need of the western Indians to come down to Montreal for goods. Mémoire sur le Canada, 1667, AN, C11A, v. 2, f. 352. The French regarded guns, hatchets, etc., as absolutely necessary to the Iroquois and other nations and saw their control of supply as an effective coercive device. Description du Canada, 1671, AN, C11A, v. 3, f. 198.

clothing, alcohol, tobacco superior to native varieties, and metal tools which ranged from awls, knives, and hatchets to kettles and muskets. Both sides gave each other wampum – the shell beads made by eastern Indians from whelks (*Busycon carica, B. canaliculatum*) and hard-shell clams (*Mercenaria mercenaria*). In addition, when Indians provided their labor, their service as warriors, or sexual favors, goods changed hands.[5]

Both sides had models of equitable exchange. The French model had not yet fully detached itself from the older idea of a just price for commodities, and a whole series of regulations covered the trade. A *fermier*, usually a company of French merchants, held a monopoly on beaver exports for most of this period and set, with the advice of French officials, a fixed price for beaver. The government regulated the number of traders in the West by issuing *congés* (permits to trade) or, at various times, by leasing out the exclusive trade at western posts to officers, individual traders, or groups of traders. The various *fermiers*, however, regarded the European market as the ultimate determinant of the price they could pay for furs, and both they and the individual traders assumed that the ultimate point of exchange was to garner a profit from transactions with the Indians. What means were legitimate in accumulating this surplus were not fully agreed on. The French in the seventeenth century were in the process of divorcing buying and selling (outside the immediate family) from other social relations. Supply and demand, rather than a person's relation to the seller, for example, tended to determine the rate of exchange. The price for most, but not all, goods was a matter for negotiation.

The rule of the market, however, was not complete. In setting the price and in making the exchange, not everything was permissible. An honest trader did not steal, did not use false weights, did not knowingly sell damaged goods. For most of the period before the fall of Canada to the English in 1763, an honest trader also did not sell brandy or other liquor to Indians, except under certain special conditions. The seventeenth- and early eighteenth-century French had not yet made exchange a purely economic enterprise, but they had proceeded much farther in this direction than had the Algonquians.

The Algonquian model proceeded from a different logic and can be distinguished from the French on a series of important points. First of all,

---

[5] For wampum, see Lynn Ceci, "The Value of Wampum among the New York Iroquois: A Case Study in Artifact Analysis," *Journal of Anthropological Research* 38 (Spring 1982): 97–107; Michael Foster, "Another Look at the Function of Wampum in Iroquois-White Councils," in Francis Jennings, et. al (eds.), *The History and Culture of Iroquois Diplomacy* (Syracuse: Syracuse University Press, 1985), 99–144. There came to be a particular set of goods adopted to the trade, as Governor Kerlerec of Louisiana put it much later, "un gout particulier adopté par les sauvages," Kerlerec au ministre, 4 mai 1753, AN, C13A, v. 37.

the goal of the transaction was not necessarily profit – securing the maximum material advantage. It was, as will be explained below, to satisfy the *besoins*, or needs, of each party. Second, the relation of the buyer and the seller was not incidental to the transaction; it was critical. If none existed, one had to be established. Third, the need of the buyer was an important element in the logic of exchange, but it exerted an influence opposite to that it exerted in the French model. The greater the need – provided a social relationship had been established – the greater the claim of the buyer on the seller.

To understand this exchange system it is best to take a particular example of Algonquian exchange. Nicolas Perrot gives a good account of "trade" between the Ottawas and Crees in the 1660s:

> The Outaouas went away toward the north, and sought to carry on trade with those tribes, who gave them all their beaver robes for old knives, blunted awls, wretched nets, and kettles used until they were past service. For these they were most humbly thanked; and those people declared that they were under great obligation to the Outaouas for having had compassion upon them and having shared with them the merchandise which they had obtained from the French. In acknowledgment of this, they presented to them many packages of peltries, hoping that their visitors would not fail to come to them every year, and to bring them like aid in trade-goods.[6]

There are several significant aspects of this account. The first is that neither side produced goods simply for exchange. Both sides used what they traded fully before the trade took place. The Cree gave *castor gras* – old beaver robes, worn, dirty, and no longer of much use to them – for goods that to them seemed amazing – the iron tools that made their everyday lives substantially easier. The Ottawas surrendered European goods, which were not commodities that existed only as a medium of exchange; they were goods that had been nearly used up before they were passed on to others who lacked them.

A second significant feature here was that both sides framed the exchange in terms of gifts rather than trade. The Crees thanked the Ottawas for sharing with them and, in turn, made presents to the Ottawas of other peltries. They praised the Ottawas for the social virtue of "compassion"; the exchange constituted a social relationship of a kind that was very common. Gifts created "peace and a sort of conditional friendship between potentially hostile persons or groups." And precisely because "to break off the gift giving [was] to break off the peaceful relationships," the exchange was consciously and purposefully uneven. After giving the *castor gras* for the

---

[6] Perrot, *Memoir*, 173–74.

European goods, the Crees made a further gift of furs to induce or, perhaps, obligate the Ottawas to return.[7]

This elaborate arranging of a social space and the establishment of social relationships within it were inseparable from the trade. Friendship was essential for this kind of exchange. Other social relationships (and other kinds of goods) dictated other forms of exchange. Cadillac, for example, describes the exchange between a hunter and his kinspeople and fellow villagers. The "good hunters," he concluded, "profit the least from their hunting."

> They often make feasts for their friends or relatives, or distribute the animals they have killed among the cabins or the families of the village. One proof of the liberality or the vanity which they acquire from this occupation is that those who are present when they arrive at their village are permitted to appropriate all the meat in the canoe of the hunter who has killed it, and he merely laughs.[8]

This kind of redistribution between kinspeople and fellow villagers formed one pole of exchange. Strangers and enemies, who tended to exchange goods by theft, formed the other extreme. Both Iroquois and Algonquians readily plundered each other. In between these extremes lay the "trade" that Perrot described.

II

The Algonquian desire for trade goods and the European desire for fur forced an accommodation between these different modes of exchange, but the desire for goods was neither automatic nor simple. There is intriguing and suggestive evidence that Algonquian and Iroquoian Indians were first attracted to European goods not for their material utility but rather for their symbolic value. Northeastern Indians, for example, equated glass beads with native crystal and valued mirrors highly because they reflected images and thus, like water, became tools for divination. Native copper, crystals, and shells already had rich ritual significance for Algonquians, and the European

---

[7] See George Dalton, "The Impact of Colonization on Aboriginal Economies in Stateless Societies," *Research in Economic Anthropology* 1:113–84, quote, 138. For a fuller explanation of this kind of uneven exchange see Sahlins, *Stone Age Economics*, 302–03. Once the exchange stopped being one of preciosities and the Ottawas themselves lost their position to the French, this exchange relationship could turn to war as when the Ottawas and some coureurs de bois attacked and pillaged the Cree. Dulhut á M. de Frontenac, 5 avril 1679, Pierre Margry, *Découvertes et établissements des Français . . . de l'Amerique Septentrionale, 1614–1698*, 6 vols. (Paris: Maisouneuve et Cie, 1879, repr. New York, AMS, 1974), 6:30–31.

[8] For quotation, see Milo Quaife (ed.), *The Western Country in the Seventeenth Century: The Memoirs of Lamothe Cadillac and Pierre Liette* (Chicago: Lakeside Press, 1917), 21.

equivalents of glass and copper arrived endowed with ready-made symbolic value. Indeed, Europeans could initially be regarded as manitous because they arrived bearing otherworldly gifts. Indians thus at first were "trading in metaphor," and the value of trade goods was then "predominantly ceremonial and ideological."[9]

In another sense, too, European trade goods acted like existing goods. Like wampum, not only were these trade goods objects of everyday use, but they were also ritual objects which, when given as gifts, created special bonds between societies. With European commodities Algonquians could transform potential enemies into friends and prepare the way for intermarriage that would solidify this tentative connection into one of kinspeople and allies. Social groups might have many reasons for extending their network of peaceful contacts. They might need allies for defense or a place of refuge if forced to flee. They might want to create sources of aid in times of food shortage or famine. And all of these might be combined in an inclusive but more diffuse desire for political status. According to that most astute of early French observers, Father Lafitau, honor – the respect accorded by others – was the mainspring of individual Indian actions. People pursued these ends even when the exchanges they inspired, when calculated in terms of economic profit, brought only losses.[10]

By the late seventeenth and early eighteenth centuries, wampum (a trade item now acquired through Europeans) and European trade goods enjoyed primacy of place in gift exchanges between various Indian groups. For diplomatic exchanges they were essential. Gifts of Algonquians to Europeans usually consisted of wampum belts and beaver furs; affairs of great moment between Indians themselves were marked by gifts of trade goods and wampum belts. When Monso, a Mascouten chief, sought to have the Illinois expel La Salle, he gave them kettles, hatchets, and knives. In 1701 when Kondiaronk, or the Rat, sought to ensure the participation of the nations around Green Bay in the great peace conference with the Iroquois, he gave Onanghisse of the Potawatomis a kettle and a gun. When Michipichy, a Huron chief, tried to persuade the Miamis to resettle at Detroit, he gave gifts of wampum belts, kettles, hatchets, blankets, shirts, a capote, a gun, powder and ball. Gifts that brought influence, prestige, and honor were, by and

---

[9] For this argument see Christopher L. Miller and George R. Hamell, "A New Perspective on Indian-White Contact: Cultural Symbols and Colonial Trade," *Journal of American History* 73 (Sept. 1986): 311–28, for quotes, 326. Hamell has developed this argument in more detail in "Strawberries, Floating Islands, and Rabbit Captains: Mythical Realities and European Contact in the Northeast During the 16th and 17th Centuries," *Journal of Canadian Studies* 21 (Feb. 1987).

[10] For an excellent discussion of political motives for exchange, see Dalton, "Impact of Colonialization," 138–44. Joseph-François Lafitau, *Customs of the American Indians. Compared with the Customs of Primitive Times* (Toronto: Champlain Society, 1974–77), 2:61.

large, gifts of scarce European goods. They allowed the giver influence across significant social boundaries. Thus, long before they were a material necessity, European goods became a cultural necessity for those who sought to stabilize the refugee communities and for those who sought positions of influence and honor in this new, heterogeneous society.[11]

La Potherie's account of the Potawatomis presents, perhaps, the best illustration of the political disposal of trade goods. The Potawatomis gave away such goods in a conscious attempt to extend their political ties and establish influence in the villages surrounding Green Bay.

> They have made themselves arbiters for the tribes about the bay, and for all their neighbors; and they strive to preserve for themselves that reputation in every direction. Their ambition to please everybody has of course caused among them jealousy and divorce; for their families are scattered to the right and to the left along the mecheygan.... With a view of gaining for themselves special esteem, they make presents of all their possessions, stripping themslves of even necessary articles, in their eager desire to be accounted liberal. Most of the merchandise for which the Outaouas trade with the French is carried among these people.[12]

The distribution of goods created obligation and established status, but here, in extending alliances and social relationships, Potawatomi leaders neglected existing internal obligations and eventually fragmented their villages and clans. The political or religious benefits Algonquians obtained from European goods should not be confused with the prestige Europeans associated with wealth. Algonquians, as individuals, did not accumulate wealth. Goods in Algonquian society actually belonged to no single person, although they always rested with some person for a time. The Jesuits noted in 1675 that with the exception of rosaries, their catechists did not keep the gifts the priests gave them. They passed them on to others. Goods, in effect, only paused with a recipient and then flowed on through established social channels. This did not mean that any commodity belonged to everyone in common – for all these social streams were distinct, and people shared only in particular ones – but rather that those people within what might be called the social watershed of family, clan, or village might eventually come to claim the item for a time. Each recipient incurred a reciprocal obligation to the giver thus ensuring that goods were constantly in motion. Defining what were

[11] For examples of other gifts being necessary for social and political networks, see (Monso) Lettre du Découvreur ... 29 sept. 1680, Margry, Découvertes, 2:41; (Michipichy) Paroles des quatre Hurons, 17 fevrier 1701, ibid. 2:266–67; (Kondiaronk) Claude Charles Le Roy, Sieur de Bacqueville de la Potherie, Histoire de l'Amerique septentrionale... (Paris: J-L Nion & F., Didot, 1722, microcard, Lost Cause Press, Louisville), 4:224.

[12] Quotation is from La Potherie, History, 1:302–3; see also James Clifton, The Prairie People: Continuity and Change in Potawatomi Indian Culture (Lawrence: Regents Press, 1977), 67.

surplus goods in this situation – goods beyond the basic needs for subsistence and production – is difficult, since groups, not individuals, accumulated
goods, and possession was so fluid. The only dam that stopped the circulation of goods in these social streams was death. The dead acquired goods
through burial gifts, but they could no longer reciprocate.[13]

Perhaps the most striking warning against assessing the meaning of goods
simply in terms of material use and accumulation is the dramatic increase in
the amount of grave goods buried with the dead and given away to honor the
dead following the opening of the fur trade. In the Michilimackinac area, for
example, there were 130 times more burial goods for each burial at the
historic Lasanen site than at the prehistoric Juntunen site. And of these
goods, 99 percent were either of European origin or were manufactured with
introduced European technology.[14]

According to Perrot, when an Algonquian was at the point of death, "he
[was] decked with all the ornaments owned by the family – I mean, among
his kindred and his connections by marriage," who "clad him in the best
clothes, placed his weapons and articles of war beside him, and surrounded
him with necklaces of wampum and glass beads." These goods accompanied
him to the grave while his relatives gathered other items to distribute to the
mourners. Among the Algonquians of the northern Great Lakes such a

---

[13] Perrot, *Memoir*, 67–70; *JR* 59:231; La Potherie, *History*, 2:127–28. The key work on gifts
remains Marcel Mauss, *The Gift: Forms and Functions of Exchange in Archaic Societies* (New
York: W. W. Norton, 1967), see particularly 67. Stephen Gudeman, "Anthropological
Economics: The Question of Distribution," *Annual Review of Anthropology* (1978): 347–77,
raises suggestive questions about the creation and distribution of surpluses in societies such
as this, but data available for the Algonquians does not allow them to be pursued very far.

[14] For Lasanen and Juntunen, see James E. Fitting, "Patterns of Acculturation at the Straits of
Mackinac," in Charles Cleland, *Cultural Change and Continuity* (New York: Academic Press,
1976), 330–31. At the Lasanen site, male burial goods were heavily European in origin.
Decorative items in the graves tended to be imported. There were far more glass beads
(5,481) and wampum beads (13,298) than catilinite beads and pendants (131) or native shell
beads and pendants (25). Compared with decorative items, the iron artifacts were few (40)
but valuable. An important male, for example, had six clasp knives, ten sheath knives, three
iron awls, an iron harpoon, a pair of ember tongs, a copper saw, a bond hand saw, a gun flint,
a bone cup, a beaver jaw, a shell bead, a shell gorget, and a bear effigy pipe buried with him.
All except the saw, beaver mandible, and possibly the pipe were of European manufacture;
see Charles E. Cleland, *The Lasanen Site: An Historic Burial Locality in Mackinac County,
Michigan* (East Lansing: Publications of the Museum, Michigan State University, 1971),
90–91. For heavy use of European goods at Gros Cap burials, see Craign F. Nern and
Charles E. Cleland, "Gros Cap Cemetery Site: St. Ignace, Michigan," *Michigan Archaeologist*
(March 20, 1974): 1–56. Fitting, "Patterns of Acculturation," 331, points out that the
Lasanen site contains 130 times more artifacts per burial than the neighboring precontact
Juntunen site and that 99 percent of these burial goods were either trade goods or items
manufactured with introduced European technology. For burial goods at other sites, see
James E. Brown (ed.), "The Zimmerman Site: A Report on Excavations at the Grand Village
of the Kaskaskia, La Salle County, Illinois," *Illinois State Museum, Report of Investigations*, no.
9 (Springfield: Illinois State Museum, 1961), 60–67. Here 6 of the 20 burials contained
European trade goods, but in these virtually all of the grave goods mentioned are European.

distribution of surplus goods was but a preliminary to a larger redistribution at the Feast of the Dead, a ceremony that the French, with their ideas of personal accumulation, saw as mad. The Feast of the Dead was in Algonquian terms, however, only the logical conclusion of a distribution system in which the movement of both surplus goods and necessities validated social relationships, honored the recipient, and created prestige for and obligation to the giver.[15]

In preparation for the Feast of the Dead, which took place periodically in order to rebury the dead after a temporary interment, the host village amassed large amounts of European and native goods. These they gave as grave offerings and as gifts to allied groups invited to the feast. The hosts, who often devoted an entire year to gathering the necessary goods,

> lavish all that they possess in trade goods or other articles; and they reduce themselves to such an extreme of poverty that they do not reserve for themselves a single hatchet or knife. Very often they keep back for their own use only one old kettle; and the sole object for which they incur all the expenditure is, that they may render the souls of the departed more happy and more highly respected in the country of the dead.[16]

Events such as the Feast of the Dead are useful for decoding the meaning that European valuables took on in this society. The distribution of the surplus that they represented was of a social and political nature. Many of the goods given away in these ceremonies lost their utilitarian value. What went into the grave did not come back out. Other goods did not disappear forever. Mourners would reciprocate when death touched their families, but these gifts should not be considered some hidden form of investment. Their real significance was social. They bound people to each other. The village funerals and other occasions for exchanges strengthened and made manifest through the reallocation of goods a larger network of social relationships. The flow of goods within these relationships seemed backward to the French: Leaders did not amass wealth but, rather, gave it away; the dead did not leave property to the living; instead, the living bestowed scarce goods on the dead. Algonquians had put European goods to the service of an existing social reality.

European goods entered village societies to serve familiar practical and symbolic purposes, but they were, nonetheless, subversive. They gradually created new meanings and altered the meanings of old objects. Furs, for

---

[15] For quotation, see Perrot, *Memoir*, 78–83. For French objections to Feast of the Dead, see *ibid.*, 87–88.
[16] For quotation, see Perrot, *Memoir*, 88. For the standard treatment of the Feast of the Dead, see Hickerson, "The Feast of the Dead."

example, acquired a special social meaning because, more than any other
goods produced by the Algonquians, they could be transformed into
European goods. And the Algonquians, apparently for this reason, began to
treat furs differently from other products of the hunt. By the late seventeenth
century, for example, any hungry man was entitled to kill game even outside
his usual village or tribal hunting territory, but if a hunter did not have
hunting rights in a territory, he was obliged to give the furs of the animals he
killed to those who did. In other words, to obtain food, hunters could kill
animals wherever they found them; to obtain kettles or blankets, however,
they could kill only where they had certain rights.[17]

Similar small changes took place elsewhere as Algonquians fitted European
goods into existing social niches, for Algonquians increasingly relied on
Europeans for culturally required items. Acquiring sufficient European
goods became a requirement of Algonquian ceremonials and diplomacy. In
one sense, such goods became as "Indian" as moccasins, but in another,
complementary sense they remained exotic, for this is what gave them their
value. Indians now clearly desired goods they could not produce themselves,
but more than that, they had integrated these valued goods into a series of
social relationships on which the honor, power, and prestige of both
individuals and groups depended. Those who had access to goods had
access to influence totally out of proportion to the physical effects the goods
they gave away could achieve. In 1683–84, La Durantaye made a gift of two
guns. The guns had little material impact on the outcome of the Iroquois
wars, but as gifts, they helped hold the alliance together during a crisis and
placed hundreds of warriors in the field. Kondiaronk's gift of a gun,
similarly, won over the Potawatomi leader Onanghisse, who, in turn, brought
the wavering Green Bay peoples to Montreal to make peace with the
Iroquois in 1701. Symbol and utility merged here to give European trade
goods an influence far beyond their simple use value.[18]

III

The accommodation between French and Algonquian models of exchange
that became the French fur trade of the *pays d'en haut* was structured by the
overarching political relationship of French fathers to their Algonquian

---

[17] For hunting rights, see La Potherie, *Histoire*, 3:176–77; 4:179–81. By the early eighteenth
century disputes over hunting territories and the willingness of French traders to buy even
immature beaver had led to serious depletion, Mémoire que les Directeurs..., 26 avril
1703, AN, C11A, v. 21, f. 132–43.

[18] See, e.g., Perrot, *Memoir*, 67–70; La Potherie, *History*, WHC 16:3, 8. For these gifts, see
Expense Account of La Durantaye, 1683–84, *IHC* 23:60–67. For Kondiaronk, see La
Potherie, *Histoire*, 4:224.

children. This alliance provided the means for linking the Algonquian system of exchange, with its emphasis on the primacy of social relation, to a much larger world economy. Such a connection involved considerable cultural adjustment, but this adjustment cannot be understood separately from the whole range of other changes taking place on the middle ground. Its departure point was the alliance against the Iroquois.[19]

In the 1650s and 1660s, with the Iroquois threat dominant, exchange took place in an openly political forum – the Montreal trade fairs – whose rules initially conformed closely to Algonquian cultural forms. During the years when the Iroquois did not block the western trade routes, large convoys of Ottawas, Huron-Petuns, Saulteurs (and other proto-Ojibwa groups), Nippisings, and occasionally Potawatomis came to Montreal. Undeniably, a strong desire for European goods prompted these dangerous journeys, but this was not their sole motive. As early French traders in the West such as Radisson and Des Groseilliers discovered, the desire for allies against the Iroquois could stir western Indians to trade when purely commercial incentives could not. The Indians regarded these trade fairs both as annual renewals of the alliance and as commercial transactions. The Indians held ceremonies and formal councils with the French officials, were feasted, exchanged gifts, renewed the alliance, engaged in supervised exchange, and departed.[20]

The Indians who brought the furs down to Montreal were middlemen who gathered the furs of numerous groups for exchange at the trade fairs. The motives and identities of these middlemen are, however, easily confused. The "Ottawas" were perhaps the most famous middlemen of the late seventeenth century, but the name *Ottawas*, as used in the late seventeenth century, does not necessarily designate any specific tribal group. During much of the seventeenth century, *Ottawa* was the generic French name for any western Indian who traveled east to trade with the French. Ottawas seemed to monopolize the trade, but as the Jesuits explained, "all who go to

[19] For attachment to world economy, see Eric Wolf, *Europe and the People Without History* (Berkeley: University of California Press, 1982), 158–194.

[20] M. Duchesneau's Memoir on Western Indians, 13 Nov. 1681, *NYCD* 9:20–21. The Potawatomis appear on at least one occasion to have consented to accompany the French to Montreal as much from fear of losing the French as allies as from a desire for trade goods; Arthur Adams (ed.), *The Explorations of Pierre Esprit Radisson* (Minneapolis: Ross & Haines, 1967), 98–100; La Potherie, *History* 1:337.

For a discussion of the trade fairs and their forms, see Abraham Rotstein, "Trade and Politics: An Institutional Approach," *Western Canadian Journal of Anthropology* 8 (1972): 13–22. For Huron trade ceremonies, see Bruce Trigger, *The Children of Aataentsic: A History of the Huron People to 1660*, 2 vols. (Montreal: McGill-Queen's University Press, 1972). For a contemporary account, see *JR* 42:219–11. For Lahontan's description of fairs, see Reuben Gold Thwaites (ed.), *New Voyage to North America by the Baron de Lahontan*, 2 vols. (Chicago: A. C. McClurg, 1905), 1:92–95.

trade with the French, although of widely different nations, bear the general name of Outaouacs, under whose auspices they make the journey." When the sources are specific, it is clear that the Ojibwas (particularly the Saulteurs), the Nippisings, and less often the Potawatomis, as well as the Ottawas proper, all acted as middlemen in the Great Lakes trade.[21]

The French Intendant Duchesneau gave three reasons for the existence of middlemen in 1681: the distance of many Indians from the French, their inability to manufacture or maneuver the birchbark canoes needed for the trade, and intimidation by the Ottawas, who wished to monopolize direct exchange with the French. In fact, the first two reasons were far more important than the third. Indeed, the Ottawas proper do not seem to have tried to exclude other tribes from the early trade, on the contrary, they attempted to entice them to join the expeditions. Expeditions to Montreal during the 1650s and 1660s, when Iroquois war parties lay in wait, were a flirtation with death, and Ottawas, "very cowardly and little used to war," in the opinion of Nicolas Perrot, had no desire to face the danger alone. The problem was not excluding people from the flotillas; it was recruiting them and holding them together. Repeatedly the convoys dwindled or were abandoned before the Iroquois threat. Not only did Hurons, Saulteurs, and Nippisings all regularly journey to Montreal, but the Ottawas showed a remarkable willingness to help the people with whom they had once enjoyed exclusive exchange relations to establish contact with the French. They escorted Potawatomis to Montreal in the late 1660s, and in 1664 the Ottawas brought the Crees, their major suppliers of fur, to Montreal to trade directly with the French. The Ottawa claim to exclusive middleman status, insofar as it existed at all, was a narrow one. They claimed on exclusive right to the Ottawa River route to the French settlements and expected gifts from all who used it. Their purely economic interest, therefore, lay in increasing the trade, not limiting it.[22]

This general willingness of middlemen to share the carrying trade has an important exception, however, which is often misread as a desire to maintain

[21] For Jesuit quote on Ottawas, see *JR* 51:21; also see Mildred Mott Wedel, "Le Sueur and the Dakota Sioux," in Eldon Johnson (ed.), *Aspects of Upper Great Lakes Anthropology...*, Minnesota Prehistoric Archaeology Series, no. 11, Minnesota Historical Society (St. Paul: Minnesota Historical Society, 1974), 159. For groups acting as middlemen in the trade, see *JR* 45:105; Adams (ed.), *Radisson*, 112, 114–16; Letter of La Salle, 1682, *WHC* 16:107; Margry, *Découvertes* 2:252; *JR* 41:77–78; Perrot, *Memoir*, 157; Clifton, *Prairie People*, 64.

[22] For Duchesneau's analysis, see Duchesneau Memoir, 13 Nov. 1681, *NYCD* 9:161. For quotation, see Perrot, *Memoir*, 211. For desertion from convoys and fear of attack, see *JR* 42:219–33; *JR* 49:245; *JR* 50–117; *JR* 45:161–62; Perrot, *Memoir*, 175–76; Adams (ed.), *Radisson*, 96–99. For Ottawas bringing others to the French: Potawatomis, see La Potherie, *History*, 303, 313–14, 336–39; Clifton, *Prairie People*, 52–53; Crees, see *JR* 48:237. For Ottawa claim to the river, see *JR* 51:21.

an economic monopoly. Because exchange and alliances were so closely linked, no nation could countenance trade, particularly in weapons, with its enemies or its enemies' allies. In 1680 a Mascouten chief named Monso, acting as the agent for other French traders, tried to persuade the Illinois not to open alliance and exchange relations with La Salle because, Monso asserted, he was an ally of the Iroquois. As the French role in the carrying trade increased, nations repeatedly intervened to block their enemies' access to the French. The Ottawa, Fox, Huron-Petun, and Illinois attempts to cut off trade with the Sioux became particularly notorious. Outside the interlocking networks of family, clan, village, and nation there were for Algonquians only potential enemies. Enemies exchanged goods, but the means they used was force and the exchange itself was theft.[23]

For the Algonquians exchange and alliance at the trade fairs were necessarily mutually reinforcing. The exchange of goods itself established conditions of peace. Peace between strangers could be validated only by gifts and could be maintained only through the continuation of gifts. When the exchange of gifts ceased, the relationship terminated. At the Montreal trade fairs, however, Frenchmen, in the classic gambit of the middle ground, proved quite adept at using Algonquian cultural forms for their own ends. Instead of participating in an exchange of gifts, Indians found themselves subjected to a series of extortions by French officials and their subordinates. The soldiers sent to guard Indian peltries demanded large presents for their services. French officials refused the customary gifts of moose hides and wampum and demanded instead large quantities of beaver. The reciprocal presents given by the French were small and, to the Indians, demeaning. In Montreal Indian men were arrested and huge ransoms in beaver demanded for their release; brawls erupted and Indians were beaten. In such cases Indians returned home angry, bitter, and eager for revenge. The Potawatomis, mistreated in Montreal, retaliated by abusing the French "in

---

[23] For the monopoly interpretation, see Harold A. Innis, *The Fur Trade in Canada: An Introduction to Canadian Economic History* (Toronto: University of Toronto Press, 1956), 54–55. Louise De Chene, too, presents the traditional picture of Ottawa middlemen in *Habitants et marchands de Montréal au xvii siècle* (Paris: Librairie Plon, 1974), 173. La Salle thought that Monso was a Miami (Lettre du découvreur à un de ses associés, 29 sept. 1680, Margry *Découvertes* 2:41–42), but he was more likely, as Le Clercq said, a Mascouten (Le Clercq, "Narrative," in Isaac J. Cox, *The Journeys of Robert Cavelier de La Salle*, 2 vols. (New York: A. S. Barnes, 1905), 1:102–03 since the Miamis and the Illinois were then at odds. For blocking French trade to enemies, see "The Voyage of St. Cosme, 1698–99" in Louise P. Kellogg (ed.), *Early Narratives of the Northwest, 1634–1699* (New York: Charles Scribner's Sons, 1917), 344, 353; Thwaites (ed.), *Lahontan's Voyages*, 1:175–76. La Potherie, *History* 1:366; Licenses of Trade Revoked, De Champigny, 13 Oct. 1691, *MPHC* 33:75; Narrative . . . of Occurrences, 1692, 1693, *NYCD* 9:570; Parolles des sauvages . . . 12 juillet 1699, AN, F3, Moreau de St. Mery, v. 8, f. 136–41.

deed and word, pillaging and robbing them of their goods . . . and subjecting them to unbearable insolence and indignity." By the 1670s the fairs were clearly failing to fulfill Indian expectations.[24]

The fairs dwindled during the 1670s and 1680s. The abuses that had crept into the fairs and the increasing penetration of the West by both illegal coureurs de bois and legal voyageurs brought about their decline. During the decade and a half that followed the peace made with the Iroquois in 1666, French traders transferred the site of exchange to the forts, Indian villages, and hunting camps of the West. As early as 1671, French officials complained that because of the coureurs de bois, Indians were not coming to Montreal. Diplomatic and military missions continued to draw some western Indians down and these people usually conducted some trade, but the old fur convoys gradually vanished. Even the temporary resurgence of fur convoys in the late 1670s seems to have consisted in large part of Indians bringing down furs already owned by the French.[25]

As voyageurs outfitted by Montreal merchants resituated the trade in the *pays d'en haut* itself, the Crown attempted to reassert its control by allowing only a limited number of *congés*, or permits to trade, in the West. The sale of these *congés* provided Canada with revenue intended to support the poor and created, at least theoretically, a way to limit the supply of furs coming into Canada. The Crown did not reap this revenue directly. A *fermier*, usually a company of French merchants, leased the right to export beaver fur from Canada. In exchange for this monopoly, the *fermier* had the obligation to buy at a fixed price all the beaver skins that met certain standards. Other furs and animal skins remained outside this monopoly. If the *fermier* had to purchase too many furs or paid too high a price for them, it faced bankruptcy.[26]

The *congé* system of the late eighteenth century proved only partially successful, and there are many signs of a crisis in exchange in the 1670s and 1680s. Coureurs de bois who traveled throughout the *pays d'en haut* trading

[24] Mémoire sur le Canada, 1687, AN, C11A, v. 2; Mémoire sur quelques . . . dans la ferme de Canada, 1684, AN, C11A, v. 6; Duchesneau to Seignelay, 10 Nov. 1679, *NYCD* 9:134–35. King to Frontenac and Champigny, 1692 *IHC* 23:257. For Potawatomi anger over their mistreatment, see *JR* 55:185–87; La Potherie, *History* 333.

[25] Description du Canada, 1671 AN, C11A, v. 3. De Frontenac sometimes tried to pass such diplomatic and French convoys off as the old trade convoys. Frontenac au Ministre, 9 oct. 1679, AN, C11A, v. 5; Frontenac au Ministre, 12 nov. 1690, *RAPQ*, 1927–28, 38. Other sources make it clear that this was not the case; see Duchesneau to Seignelay, Nov. 13, 1681, *NYCD* 9:154–55; Champigny au Ministre, 16 nov. 1689, AN, C11A, v. 10; Narrative of . . . Occurrences . . . 1692, 1693, *NYCD* 9:562; Champigny au Ministre, 8 aout 1686, AN, C11A, v. 10.

[26] Alice Jean Elizabeth Lunn, "Economic Development in New France, 1713–60" (Ph.D. diss., McGill University, 1942), 112–13, 136–55. For nostalgia over trade fairs as late as 1715, see Mémoire sur ce qui concerne le commerce des castors . . . (1715), *RAPQ* 1947–48, 69–73.

without *congés* were a perennial threat to good order. Canadian officials manipulated *congés* and military expeditions for their own benefit. The system failed to prevent overproduction; it failed to stop the drain of manpower to the West; and it failed to prevent disorder. The disorder so often mentioned during the period was, in part, a result of the failure of the French and the Algonquians to agree on appropriate mechanisms of exchange.

In the West, individual French traders were no more ready to accede to the Algonquian logic of exchange than they had been at Montreal. They rejected Algonquian demands for generosity as excessive and sought to obtain what the market would bear. They saw the western country as, in La Potherie's apt phrase, a "Peru," for the "savages could not understand why these men came so far to search for their worn-out beaver robes; meanwhile they admired all the wares brought to them by the French which they regarded as extremely precious." The missionaries Dollier and Galinée were astonished in 1670 to find that at Sault Sainte Marie a fathom of tobacco, or six knives, or a quarter pound of powder could obtain a beaver robe. Eighteen years later, at Michilimackinac, Lahontan still found French prices "extravagant," but by then Frenchmen had pushed west where they hoped, as Hennepin said of La Salle in 1679, "to buy all the Furs and Skins of the remotest Savages, who, as they thought, did not know their Value; and so enrich themselves in one single voyage."[27]

French traders in search of their Peru so thoroughly managed to disabuse the Fox and Potawatomis of expectations of generosity that by 1670 Father Claude-Jean Allouez found them with "a poor opinion of the French." According to Perrot, Indians who had initially welcomed them as powerful benefactors came to be so disgusted by the French obsession with old beaver robes as to "regard those of the French nation as wretched menials and the most miserable people in the world." In 1670, from the Senecas west, the source of disdain was the same – cupidity. Frenchmen drawn west for wealth had a zeal for accumulation and an eye for the main chance that only drew scorn from the western villages. The Indians, the Intendant Duchesneau claimed, "despised us on account of the great cupidity we manifested."[28]

---

[27] Quote from La Potherie, *History*, 1:307; also "Journey of Dollier and Galinee," in Quaife (ed.), *The Western Country*, 207; Thwaites (ed.), *Lahontan's Voyages*, 1:148; Reuben Gold Thwaites (ed.), *Father Louis Hennepin's A New Discovery of a Vast Country in America* (facsimile ed., Toronto: Coles, 1974 repr. of 1903 ed.), 110. André Penicault, *Fleur de Lys and Calumet: Being the Penicault Narrative of French Adventure in Louisiana*, edited by Richebourg Gaillard McWilliams (Baton Rouge: Louisiana State University Press, 1953), 53.

[28] For Allouez quotation, see *JR* 54:225. For Perrot quotation, see Perrot, *Memoir*, 63–64. For Duchesneau quotation, see Duchesneau to de Seignelay, 10 Nov. 1679, *NYCD* 9:133. For similar assertions, see Duchesneau's Memoir on Western Indians, Sept. 13, 1681, *NYCD* 9:161–62; Perrot, *Memoir*, 263–64. De Dedonville à M. de Seignelay, aoust 1688, AN, C11A, v. 10.

Algonquians who came to despise and scorn greedy Frenchmen could hardly be expected to regard them as friends and allies. They could easily reclassify them as enemies, and the proper form of exchange with enemies was theft. When traders failed to fulfill Algonquian expectations of legitimate exchange, they became vulnerable to the kind of extortion and violence they themselves had used against the Algonquians in Montreal. The low opinion Algonquians came to hold of venal French traders threatened not only the livelihood but the lives of Frenchmen. Violence became rampant in the trade. In 1684 alone, the thirty-nine Frenchmen who died at the hands of western Algonquians were testimony on the dangers of not meeting Algonquian expectations. Dulhut's trial of the murderers at Michilimackinac and his subsequent show of force at Green Bay further demonstrated the breakdown of peaceful exchange and the drastic steps the French felt were necessary for their own safety.[29]

Scholars regularly misinterpret the violence surrounding the trade as an Algonquian political attempt to regain or retain middleman status. But such an argument is seriously flawed, for, in fact, French officials were much more eager for Indians to be middlemen than Indians were to retain the position for themselves. French authorities, with their mercantilist plans for the development of Canada, feared the departure of so much scarce French manpower to the West. They also believed that the Ottawas and other middlemen must have resented the usurpation of the carrying trade by the French. Their evidence, however, seems to have been that any rational person in pursuit of economic gain would have resented such a loss and not that the Indians actually resented it.[30]

Eventually, in 1698, officials in France acted on their belief that if the *congés* (the licenses to carry goods to the West) were eliminated or curtailed,

---

[29] Raisons qu'on proposee à la cour, 1697, AN, C11A, v. 15; f. 27.

[30] For assertions of Ottawa resentment of loss of middleman status and eagerness to resume it, see Commerce du Castor de Canada, 1699, AN, C11A, v. 17; Pontchartrain to Frontenac, May 21, 1698, *NYCD* 9:678; Mémoire du Roi, 17 avril 1697, *RAPQ* 1918–29, 329; Mémoire, 1699, AN, C11A, v. 17. f. 193–95. Historians picture the Fox as fighting to preserve middleman status at a time when they could hardly be middlemen since they themselves lacked access to European goods. Later, when the Fox regained access to French goods, they used them not for economic profit but to secure an alliance with and a potential haven among the Sioux. For Sioux refuge, see letter of Ramezay, Jan. 10, 1723, *WHC* 16:422–23; Memoir, 1726, *WHC* 16:464. This was common among tribal peoples. See Dalton, "Impact of Colonization," 154–55. The French attempted to cut off this haven by opening their own exchange relations with the Sioux; see Memoir, 1726, *WHC* 16:464; *WHC* 3:153–54. The Fox were worried about alienating the Sioux and did not try to completely sever that nation's contacts with the French. Extrait . . . Vaudreuil, 4 nov. 1720, Margry, *Découvertes*, 6:510; Charlevoix, *Journals*, 2:74–75. It is more likely that the goal of the Fox trade was political and not economic, as the Jesuit Father Chardon contended in 1725; see Longueuil & Begon au Ministre, 31 oct. 1725, AN, C11A, v. 47, f. 134. For the ease with which the French passed the supposed blockade, see Relation of Father Guignas, May 29, 1728, *WHC* 17:24.

Indians would gladly reassume the middleman role. The results are revealing. There was little enthusiasm on the part of the western nations for
carrying their furs to Montreal. The convoys did resume after 1701, but they
were tied rather closely with large diplomatic gatherings. The great Iroquois
peace conference of 1701, negotiations over various matters in 1702, and
condolences on the death of Callières in 1703 were as central to Indian
journeys to Montreal as was trade. Even during these years, convoys could
not be depended on. In 1703 few Indians came down during the summer
trading season because of fears of the epidemic then raging in Montreal, and
only the death of Callières attracted even a small delegation to offer
condolences in the fall. The general absence of Indians in 1703 does not,
however, seem to have interrupted the flow of furs, since the receipts of
castor sec, the major western trade item, were actually higher that year than
for any other year between 1701 and 1704. People other than western
Indians were obviously still transporting furs to Montreal and Quebec.[31]

After 1704, trade journeys to Montreal were, at best, sporadic.
D'Aigremont reported in 1710 that few western Indians had come to trade at
Montreal for eight or nine years, except in 1708, when sixty canoes had
descended, and these had come in large part for diplomatic reasons. If
D'Aigremont exaggerated, he did so only slightly. In 1706 Governor de
Vaudreuil had lamented the ruin of the Montreal trade, and later officials
reported in their *mémoires*, their reports to France, that low prices had
virtually ended the trade. French officials and later scholars, in their
common belief that the Indians ardently desired a middleman role, have
misinterpreted much of the history of exchange in the Great Lakes trade.
Whatever was driving Algonquian exchange, it was not a search for monopoly
profit.[32]

---

[31] Canadian officials, who admittedly often had a financial interest in the interior trade, tended
to be far more skeptical of the Indian desire to journey to Montreal. See Frontenac et
Champigny au Ministre, 9 nov. 1694, *RAPQ*, 1927–28, 199; Mémoire . . . de Frontenac and
de l'intendant Bochart de Champigny au Ministre, 26 oct. 1696, *PAPQ*, 1928–29, 322; De
Champigny to Pontchartrain, 13 oct. 1697, *MPHC* 33:76; Narrative of . . . Occurrences . . .
1694, by Lamothe Cadillac, *NYCD* 9:586–87; Narrative of . . . Occurrences . . . 1695, 1696,
NYCD 9:647. For revocation of *congés* and opinion of the court, see Proclamation, Jean . . . de
Champigny, 15 juin 1698, AN F3, Moreau St. Mery, v. 8, f. 85; Louix XIV to de Frontenac
and Champigny, May 26, 1696, *NYCD* 9:637–38; Mémoire du Roi pour le gouverneur de
Frontenac et l'intendant Bochart de Champigny, 27 avril 1697, *RAPQ*, 1928–1929,
328–35, Pontchartrain to Frontenac, May 21, 1698, *NYCD* 9:678.
   The convoys had not resumed by 1698, Mémoire sur la Ferme, 1698, AN C11A, v. 16,
f. 209–16, For 1701 conference, see La Potherie, *Histoire*, 4:203–65. For diplomatic
negotiations of 1702, see Parolles de Outauoiiaes, 5 juillet 1702, AN, F3, Moreau St. Mery,
v. 8, f. 310–11. For 1703 and fur receipts, see Etat . . . des castors, 1705 (mutilated copy,
title missing), AN C11A, v. 23; Vaudreuil et Beauharnois au Ministre, 15 nov. 1703, AN
C11A, v. 21; and Vaudreuil to Pontchartrain, Oct. 14, 1703, *NYCD* 9:743.
[32] For deterioration of trade fairs, see D'Aigremont Report, Nov. 18, 1710, *WHC* 16:
266; Parolles des Outtauois . . . 23 juillet 1708, AN C11A, v. 28, f. 205–11; letter of

Despite the violence, exchange never completely broke down because the large political relationship of which it was a part persisted. The French-Algonquian alliance and renewed war with the Iroquois gave both sides an incentive to control violence. They eventually reached a tacit compromise on exchange typical of the middle ground. The French accepted much of the old Algonquian structure of exchange, but within that structure significant changes in meaning took place. The Algonquians managed, despite sporadic French efforts to disengage the two, to keep exchange anchored within the alliance itself. Like the model for the alliance, the model for exchange was familial. The French were fathers and the Algonquians their children. From this central metaphor certain consequences flowed. Governor de Beauharnois and the Intendant Hocquart explained to the court in 1730, "You know, Monseigneur, that all the nations of Canada regard the governor as their father, which in consequence, following their ideas, he ought at all times to give them what they need to feed themselves, clothe themselves, and to hunt."[33] The obligation of Onontio to provide for the needs of his children became the basis for trade, and this in turn obligated the Algonquians, as good and satisfied children, to obey and aid him. As the speaker for the Saint Joseph Potawatomis put it in 1750: "Why not love the French, since you, my father, provide for all our needs and without the French we would lack knives and all the rest? We respect your commands and have nothing more at heart than to obey them." A half century after Onanghisse, the Potawatomis continued, at least rhetorically, to conceptualize exchange as the means by which their father provided for their needs.[34]

Onontio most obviously fulfilled his obligation to provide for his children's needs through gifts. He gave special gifts to those who visited him at Montreal, Quebec, or at his posts, and he gave annual presents to his children. The nature of gift exchanges had, however, altered during the seventeenth and eighteenth centuries in a compromise between French and Algonquian expectations. The French desired to attach the giving of gifts to services performed. They wanted to make them, in effect, payments for services rendered or bribes for future services. They wanted a direct connection between gifts and specific actions.[35]

D'Aigremont, Oct. 18, 1710, *MPHC* 33:488; Vaudreuil to Minister, 4 Nov. 1706, *MPHC* 33:311; Copies, Traittes des Sauvages, 1711, AN C11A, v. 32, f. 190. Even when the French returned west, the crown tried to reserve middleman roles for the Miamis and Illinois, who, as noncanoe Indians, had never had such a role, and the Ottawas, Mémoire du Roy, 10 juillet 1715, AN F3, Moreau St. Mery, v. 9, f. 306.

33 Beauharnois et Hocquart au Ministre, 15 oct. 1730, AN C11A, v. 51, f. 33–36.

34 Parolles des P8tet8atamis de la riviére St. Joseph, 29 juin 1750, AN C11A, v. 95, f. 249. The figure "8" in "P8tet8atamis" is pronounced "dh."

35 The French claimed the reciprocal gifts were always of lesser value, Beauharnois et

In 1683 and 1684, for example, while commanding at Michilimackinac, Oliver Morel, Sieur de la Durantaye, worked to maintain the western alliance against the Iroquois and to place Algonquian warriors in the field with the French. He later submitted an account of both the presents and payments he made to the nations at Michilimackinac and Green Bay between July 1683 and July 1684. In it gifts per se ("Gave to the Potawatomi...21b. of tobacco"), payments for services ("Gave to eight men...whom I was obliged to take to guide me to the Outagamie village"), and gifts to obtain larger ends ("Gave to the Outagamie in order to keep them in their village") are all mixed together. Taken together, however, these gifts are directed toward a quite specific end. La Durantaye used his expenditures to hold the alliance together and bring the western Indians into the field against the English.[36]

The French were not able, however, to keep their payments geared precisely to services rendered, to make them, in effect, wages and bribes. A large proportion of the gifts that the French gave were unconnected with any specific actions on the part of the Algonquians. As the Iroquois wars continued, gifts became an annual occurrence and grew in number. Gifts "aux Nations Sauvages eloignes" in 1693 amounted to 9,527 livres in value. It is useful to keep in mind what this meant in actual goods. Guns were the most valuable item distributed, although 1,935 livres worth of guns amounted to only 158 fusils. (There were also 83 pistolets at 249 livres.) In finished clothing, the Indians received 76 capots, 13 justaucorps, 228 shirts, and 216 blankets, plus cloth. In terms of numbers distributed rather than value, powder, ball, gun flints, and tobacco dominated the gift lists. Such items allowed small gifts to individual Indians: 930 pounds of tobacco could be distributed among many people. The amount spent on presents apparently continued to rise after 1693. By 1696 the Crown spent 25,000 livres a year on gifts to Indians (not all of them in the West). Various attempts to reduce gift giving followed, but by 1716 the French budgeted 20,000 livres a year for Indian presents. The actual amount spent on gifts often rose well beyond this figure. Presents had become, and would remain, a critical component of French attempts to hold Algonquian loyalty in the face of English trade advantages.[37]

Exchanges between individual Indians and traders became part of this

Hocquart au Ministre 25 oct. 1729, AN C11A, v. 51, for provisions for gifts at post, see Lease for Post at Green Bay, 1747, *WHC* 17:454.

[36] Expense Account of La Durantaye, 1683–84, *IHC* 23:60–67. I made no attempt to distinguish here between payments to those who rendered some service, such as guiding the French, and direct gifts.

[37] Etats des marchandises et munitions distributees en 1693, AN C11A, v. 12; for another estimate of presents necessary for a major expedition down the Mississippi, see Tonti, Mississippi Navigation, Sept. 12, 1693, *IHC* 23:280–82, and to secure peace among the

compromise. The Algonquians did not confine the familial metaphor of exchange to Onontio and his chiefs. Traders who came to their villages also had to give gifts which the Indians reciprocated. The gifts given by traders either established the symbolic ties of kinship or fortified the ties so that further exchange could proceed. In the turmoil of the 1680s, Frenchmen in the West learned that the absence of such ties could cost them their lives. To avoid being greedy strangers, traders gave gifts, but they did not abandon their overarching search for profit.

Because the middle ground consisted, in part, in the acceptance and transformation of another people's customs, French traders could at one and the same time accept the practice of giving gifts and begin to alter it. Gifts provided French traders with the opportunity to secure greater control over Indian fur production. Gifts of powder or blankets given in the fall before a hunt would be reciprocated in the spring with furs. The French gradually reinterpreted these gifts as loans to be paid back regularly, rather than to be reciprocated at a time when the giver needed aid and the recipient was able to give it. The French attempt to corrupt gifts into loans became such a cause of perennial conflict in the trade that many officials wished to ban the giving of credit. Credit remained central to the trade, but Indians never fully acknowledged advances as debts. When the amount of furs they were expected to give in return seemed exorbitant, especially during periods when goods were scarce, they refused to meet their obligations.[38]

Chippewas and Dakotas, see Wedel, "Le Sueur," 159–60. For 1696 estimate, see Mémoire sur les affaires du Canada, 1696, AN C11A, v. 14, f. 305.

Twenty thousand livres continued to be budgeted (Projet de la dépense . . . 1733, AN, C11A, v. 60, f. 191), but costs often exceeded this. In 1729, e.g., 24,662 livres were spent (Hocquart et Beauharnois au Ministre, 15 oct. 1730, AN, C11A, v. 51), and in 1736 24,436 livres (Presens fait aux sauvages en 1736, AN, C11A, v. 63, f. 87). In addition, officers were forced to expend other money on gifts, Statement of Boisbriant, Mar. 26, 1725, *MPA* 2:422–23; Dupuy to Minister, Oct. 20, 1727, *WHC* 16:470–71. Costs began to escalate precipitously in the 1740s and 1750s bringing complaints from the Minister and apologies and excuses from Canadian officials. For 1741 figures at Montreal, see Extrait des munitions . . . jusqu'au premier septembre, 1741, AN, C11A, v. 75, Beauharnois to Minister, Oct. 13, 1743, *NYCD* 9:1098–99; Bigot au Ministre, 2 nov. 1752, AN, C11A, v. 08, f. 308. The installation of new governors and the Indian visits this entailed proved particularly costly, Duquesne to Rouillé, Oct. 27, 1753, *IHC* 29:841–43. By the 1750s the annual expenditure on Indian presents had reached 150,000 francs (or livres) a year, Bougainville Memoir, *WHC* 18:195.

For an early recognition of the importance of presents in Indian diplomacy, see Wilbur R. Jacobs, *Diplomacy and Indian Gifts: Anglo-French Rivalry along the Ohio and Northwest Frontiers, 1748–63* (Stanford, Calif.: Stanford University Press, 1950). For English recognition, see Thomas Elliot Norton, *The Fur Trade in Colonial New York, 1686–1776* (Madison: University of Wisconsin Press, 1974), 41.

38 French commanders and governors were accused of extorting gifts and of not fulfilling the promises their acceptance entailed; Cadillac: Report of Sr. D'Aigremont, Nov. 14, 1708, *MPHC* 33:426; Vaudreuil: Raudot to Minister, *ibid.*, 33:465. For suggestion that credit be banned, see Louvigny to Council, Oct. 15, 1720, *WHC* 16:387–91. During the revolt of the

Both traders and officials often resented the necessity for gifts, but there were significant obstacles to their desires to reorient exchange away from the middle ground and toward the market. First of all, not all Frenchmen were willing to see exchange as something regulated by supply and demand. The most obvious example is the tenacious and often successful opposition of the Jesuits to the brandy trade, even when the English trade in rum cost the French furs. Second, the fur trade in its very organization could not be disentangled from political and imperial concerns. Because the French fur trade was a combination of entrepreneurial traders, merchant financiers, licensed monopolists, and government regulators, it was a hive of diverse interests which, while incorporating market concerns, tended to check their dominance. The crown derived revenues from its sale of the beaver monopoly to the *fermier* and thus depended on the health of the fur trade to help finance Canada. On the other hand, since the Indians had already established a clear connection between alliance and trade, any measures that increased revenues but alienated the Indians would rebound against French political and imperial interests. The Crown could not afford to ignore Algonquian discontent with the course of trade. Similarly, the *fermier* depended on royal assistance to suppress smuggling and enforce the monopoly, but the *fermier* could not afford to be insensitive to the demands of Indian policy. The traders certainly desired unlimited gain in the West, but they were constrained, at least theoretically, by the presence of French officers, the regulation of Canadian officials, and the power of the priests to grant absolution for their sins in regard to transgressions such as the sale of brandy to the Indians. In the eighteenth century, officials such as Governor de Beauharnois feared policies, such as leasing the posts, that would leave the traders free to seek profit and neglect French paternal obligations. A scathing *mémoire* written in 1758 indicated that Beauharnois's fears had come true: Greedy lessees had alienated the Indians and would bring about the fall of Canada.[39]

The Algonquians conjured up and fed the fears of the French Crown. Algonquians had been unable fully to impose their own logic of exchange on the French, but they had exacted a compromise that limited the range of French options in the trade. The concept *bon marché* embodied this compromise. What the Indians understood as a *bon marché* was close to the European conception of a just price. The Algonquians came to accept unit prices for items, but they did not accept market variations in price. Real

---

late 1740s, Indians refused to pay on goods advanced them by the traders, Bigot to Minister, Oct. 22, 1748, *WHC* 17:502.

[39] For leasing, Beauharnois et D'Aigremont au Ministre, 1 oct. 1728, AN, C11A, v. 59, f. 31–32. For *mémoire* complaining of results, see Mémoire, Canada, 1758, AN, C11A, v. 103, f. 511.

value did not change; it was customary. This did not mean that Algonquians expected exchange rates to be absolutely stable. Because Indians conceptualized exchange in terms of the generosity of a father to his children, they did not complain if he became more generous. They only complained when he became less so. Since Onontio and his chiefs were fathers, it was their obligation to make sure that their Algonquian children secured a *bon marché* from Onontio's French children, the traders. The Algonquians expected the governor to intercede with the traders when prices rose.

Given these Algonquian expectations, the beaver monopoly had unanticipated advantages for the French. Because prices were fixed, exchange often proceeded, at least at the posts, at predictable rates without extensive bargaining. As Governor de Beauharnois and Intendant Hocquart reported to the Crown, Indians normally received the same quantity of merchandise in exchange for their beaver. When, however, monopolists faced bankruptcy because of oversupply and falling prices in Europe or had to face intense English competition, or when the crown tried to cut costs by farming out posts to individual traders or raising the prices on goods that the king supplied, then the French ability to meet Algonquian expectations faltered and the whole structure of the alliance shuddered. It was during such periods of crisis that the Algonquian understanding of how trade should proceed was most clearly articulated.[40]

The first of these revealing crises occurred at the end of the Iroquois wars. With the French market for furs glutted, the value of beaver dropping, and *congés* for the West discontinued, Governor de Callières attempted to induce the western Indians coming to Montreal to accept a lower rate of exchange on their furs. He urged the chiefs not to ask him, as their father, to guarantee a *bon marché* but, rather, to go from merchant to merchant seeking the best bargain. Such a request apparently confused the Ottawas. In 1701 the Ottawa leader Otontagan, speaking for the Sable Ottawas and the Saulteurs on a gift of four packs of beaver, told Onontio: "It is useless to ask you for a *bon marché*, because we know that each person is master of his merchandise, nevertheless urge them to give the same price as last year." When Otontagan's negotiations with the merchants failed to obtain a *bon marché*, he returned much troubled to Callières to ask him to intercede. At Detroit two years later, Le Pesant of the Ottawas delivered a similar speech, but he was no more ready than Otontagan to detach the idea of a *bon marché* from the requirements of the alliance. Le Pesant did not ask for Onontio's intercession. He threatened to go to the English.[41]

Failure to secure a *bon marché* strained the alliance to the breaking point.

[40] Beauharnois et Hocquart au Ministre, 15 oct. 1744, AN, C11A, v. 81.
[41] La Potherie, *Histoire*, 4:203, 205, 212; for Le Pesant, see Conseil . . . 29 aoust 1703, Margry, *Découvertes*, 5:294–97.

Michipichy, speaking for all the Indians at Detroit, angrily denounced the governor as a liar. Although Cadillac cited previous warnings by the governor to the Indians that the merchants were "les maîtres de la marchandise" and thus could alter prices, Michipichy contended that the Indians had settled at Detroit only on the promise of getting goods at the same prices as at Montreal. "When we came here," Michipichy asserted, "the governor did not tell us that the merchants were masters of the merchandise. He has lied to us."[42]

Indians interpreted the failure to get customary prices within the familial logic of the alliance. It was proof that the French no longer "loved" them, that they had abandoned them and now "stole" their beaver. It was now the English who loved them. The French might denounce the Algonquians for "never having other friends than those who give them a good bargain," but to maintain the alliance they would have to give the Algonquians physical tokens of their paternal love. When, after the War of the Spanish Succession, the monopoly foundered in the face of an increasingly determined English attempt to win western trade, the Algonquians again phrased the problem in terms of paternal neglect. Shamgoueschi, an Ottawa chief from Saginaw, explained in 1717 that the Ottawas and Potawatomis had departed from Detroit to trade with the English because the commander at Detroit, Sabrevois, "whom we looked upon as our father at Detroit," had not, in turn, looked "upon us as his children." A failure to deliver a *bon marché* was part of a larger catalog of paternal neglect. His failure to feast the chiefs, to give the appropriate gifts, and "to give us suck" (that is, to give the Indians brandy to drink) had "offended our old men extremely, and ... driven us to adopt the course ... of going in the direction of Orange [Albany]." The removal of Sabrevois and, after him, Tonti testified to the French need to meet Algonquian objections to the commanders. Indeed, Algonquian expectations became a rationale for trying to ensure that commanders had no interest in the trade itself. Commanders with a stake in the trade, the Sieur de Noyan reported, could not act as fathers, and the Indians claimed that they had in such men tormentors instead of fathers.[43]

Not even war, with its concurrent shortage of goods due to English blockades, relieved the French of their paternal obligations. In 1744 and 1745 when increases in freight and insurance costs and the failure of French supplies to arrive drove up the price of goods, the Sieur de Chalet, who had

---

[42] Conseil tenu au fort Pontchartrain dans le Detroit...8 juin 1704, AN, F3, Moreau St. Mery, v. 2, f. 378.

[43] For argument that French no longer loved them, see Mémoire à M. le Comte de Pontchartrain, AN, C11A, v. 27, f. 135; it is also in Mémoire...les moyens de retablir le commerce...1707, AN, C11A, v. 27, f. 1124. For Sabrevois, see A Talk with the Ottawas and Their Reply, June 24, 1717, *MPHC* 33:584–85. For De Noyan, see De Noyan, State of Canada in 1730, *MPHC* 33:77.

purchased the *ferme* at Niagara and Frontenac, found that he could not pass
on the price hikes to the Indians without endangering the alliance. The
Algonquians, "accustomed as they are to sell their furs at a certain price, . . .
have trouble resolving to receive in exchange only a part of the merchandise
that they have traded at other times." When the Indians refused to accept
French difficulties as a legitimate cause for a change in price, the intendant
blamed the Sieur de Céloron, then in command, for failing to explain the
reasons properly out of hostility to the *fermier*. But in the end, Intendant
Hocquart went to the core of the difficulty. Since the problem was not the
price rise per se, but the change in the exchange rate of goods for beaver that
this involved, he persuaded the Compagnie des Indes to raise the monopoly
price on beaver thus restoring in effect the old exchange. This worked at
Niagara but did not alleviate the shortage of goods farther west.[44]

Threats to desert the alliance and appeals to Onontio's paternal duty to
guarantee a *bon marché*, like the older tactic of theft, buffered the impact of
the market on the Algonquian fur trade. Customary prices might date from
the years when the West was a Peru, but the growing burden of gifts, high
transportation costs, and English pressure on the definition of a *bon marché*
took their toll of French profits. In the late seventeenth and early eighteenth
centuries, certainly the *pays d'en haut* did not deliver the bonanzas early
writers had promised. La Salle had projected potential profits of from
150–200 percent on the trade at Fort Frontenac in the early 1680s, and the
Baron de Lahontan estimated in the mid 1680s that two canoe loads of
goods sent west yielded profits of 700 percent. Even in the 1720s the normal
markup of goods purchased in Montreal and transported west was apparently
100 percent. At the Illinois, the Compagnie des Indes sold to the traders at
50 percent above the purchase price in France, plus 200 livres per ton in
freight charges. Louise De Chêne, in evaluating such potential profits, has
cautioned that "although such calculations of profit are justifiable, they are
valid only if we split up the various transactions and exclude some from the
calculations." Her own breakdown of the various transactions and expenses
that went into the late seventeenth- and early eighteenth-century trade
indicates a profit of about 21 percent on a cargo, and she warns that this may
have been exceptional. Nonetheless, it was a profit healthy enough to sustain
the trade as long as the crown continued to cover the large and constantly
rising costs of presents and services necessary to keep the Indians loyal.[45]

[44] Beauharnois & Hocquart au Ministre, 23 oct. 1744, AN, C11A, v. 81, f. 72; for quotation,
see Beauharnois & Hocquart, 15 oct. 1744, AN, C11A, v. 81, f. 43. For continuing crisis and
need to hold Indians, see Beauharnois & Hocquart au Ministre, 23 oct. 1745, AN, C11A,
v. 83. For Céloron, see Hocquart au Ministre, 23 oct. 1744, AN, C11A, v. 81, f. 406. For
Hocquart's plan, see Hocquart au Controlleur General, 16 oct. 1744, AN, C11A, v. 81,
f. 350.
[45] Louis Armand de Lam d'Arc, Baron de Lahontan, *Collection Oakes. Nouveaux documents de*

The idea of *bon marché* was flexible enough to encompass both a French profit and the Algonquian notion of a father's generosity to his children, but the room to maneuver within it remained limited. To violate the compromise worked out for exchange on the middle ground and exact excessive prices threatened the entire structure of relations. When, in 1745, M. Lenormant, a "zealous servant of the King," attempted to correct the disastrous finances of Louisiana by doubling the profit of the king on the goods that he dispatched to the posts of that colony, Governor de Vaudreuil protested. Such things, he wrote, could not be easily changed.

> He [Lenormant] has never been near understanding the ways of the Indians and the manner in which one must conduct oneself with them, and in the time that he has been staying here he has been too much occupied with fulfilling his mission . . . to have been able to acquire a sufficiently perfect idea of the management of these nations . . . but because people sometimes wish to conserve the interests of the King overmuch they often incur greater expenses, as would be the result if the new practices continued longer.

Forcing changes on the Indians led not only to killings but also to the Indians' refusal to repay the traders for goods advanced them and, ultimately, to their resorting to the English. French governors and intendants came to see the search for large profits (although they exempted their own efforts) as a danger to the larger good of the colony.[46]

IV

It was the English, of course, who gave the Algonquians the freedom to extort this hybrid exchange system from the French. When the French tried to arrange the trade solely according to the supply of furs and the demand in Europe, the Algonquians went to the English, who virtually always offered them better terms than the French. Trade with the English first became a serious possibility for the Algonquians of the *pays d'en haut* in the 1690s. The Iroquois in making peace overtures to the Ottawas and Huron-Petuns

Lahontan sur le Canada et Terre-Meuve, édités avec introduction par Gustave Lanctôt (Ottawa: J. O. Patenaude, 1940), 27; De Chêne, *Habitants et Marchands*, 163 (quotation), 170; Representation of Sieur de la Salle, 1682, *NYCD* 9:220; Thwaites (ed.), *Lahontan's Voyages*, 1:53–54, 99–101, 146–47; Memorandum of Goods which M. de Boucherville Was Obliged to Give for the King's Service, Oct. 12, 1728–29, *WHC* 17:83–86. For Louisiana, see Mémoire, aoust 1724, AN, C13A, v. 8, f. 222.

46 La Galissonière to Minister, Oct. 23, 1748, *WHC* 17:503; Bigot to Minister, Oct. 22, 1748, *WHC* 17:502; Abstract of dispatches, La Galissonière and Bigot, April 30, 1749, *NYCD* 10:199–200. For Vaudreuil quotation, see Vaudreuil to Maurepas, Oct. 30, 1745, *MPA* 4:251.

offered access to such trade, and New York traders actually tried to penetrate the *pays d'en haut*. With the failure of these parties, attempts at direct trade lapsed, but by the early eighteenth century both Frenchmen and mission Indians from Montreal were actively engaged in smuggling furs to Albany. Attracted by higher English prices for furs and by better quality cloth, coureurs de bois and mission Indians, acting for French merchants, diverted so many beaver to England that the *fermier* received only 7,000 livres of beaver fur by weight in 1707. This represented a trickle compared to the flood of beaver that had reached nearly 300,000 livres in 1699.[47]

This illicit fur trade to Albany was the beginning of an English commercial assault. With the end of the War of the Spanish Succession, in 1713, the English capitalized on both clause 15 of the Treaty of Utrecht, which guaranteed equal French and English access to the Indian trade, and the beginning of a period of Anglo-French peace in Europe, which inhibited the use of force by the French against the English traders in North America, to attempt the capture of the western trade. Governor Robert Hunter of New York (1710–19) and then his successor, George Burnet, used an unrestricted trade in brandy, superior English woolen strouds, better kettles, lower prices, and a simple grading system for furs to expand what had previously been a very limited direct trade with the western Algonquians. The value of beaver exports from New York doubled in 1713 and nearly doubled again in 1714.[48]

By 1720 New York officials were confident enough of success in securing direct trade to outlaw the smuggling of furs between Montreal and Albany, thus striking at the French source for what had become the most important manufactured good in the western trade – English strouds. The high quality

---

[47] For smuggling, see Yves Zoltvany, *Philippe de Rigaud de Vaudreuil, Governor of New France, 1703–25* (Toronto: McClelland and Stewart, 1974), 75–76; Guy Fregault, "La Compagnie de la Colonie," *Revue de l'Universite d'Ottawa* 30 (1960): 7–13, 143–48; Innis, *The Fur Trade in Canada*, 71–81; Ramezay au Ministre, 1708 AN, C11A, v. 29. For cloth, see Lunn, "Economic Development," 157–61.

[48] In 1716 and 1717 Hunter granted licenses for traders to go to Irondequoit halfway between Niagara and Oswego on Lake Ontario, Norton, *The Fur Trade in Colonial New York*, 158–59. Using Indian emissaries, the English also sent wampum belts and gifts of liquor west to inform the Algonquians that the French robbed them and that the English would offer better prices. Vaudreuil au Conseil, 14 oct. 1716, AN, C11A, v. 37; Conseil...dec. 1717, AN, C11A, v. 37, f. 379–80; Sabrevois to Vaudreuil, Apr. 8, 1717, *MPHC* 33:582–85. For actual departures, see A Talk with the Ottawas, and A Talk of the Poutouatamis, both *MPHC* 33:584–86, and Vaudreuil to Council, 12 Oct. 1717, *MPHC* 33:591–92. For Ohio, see Outauacs et autres sauvages, 14 oct. 1716, AN, C11A, v. 36, f. 79.

For British plans, see Norton, *The Fur Trade in Colonial New York*, 134–35; State of British Plantation in America in 1721, Sept. 8, 1721, *DHNY* 5:621–25; Beauharnois au Ministre, 22 sept. 1726. AN, C11A, v. 48; 134–35. Figures from Stephen Cutcliffe, "Indian Policy and the Rise of Imperialism, New York and Pennsylvania, 1674–1755," unpublished paper in author's possession.

and low price of English blankets and strouds and the Indian demand for them gave the English perhaps their greatest advantage over the French. Red strouds – the *écarlatines* – became the preferred trade item in the *pays d'en haut*.[49]

Burnet believed the new laws would cause Montreal to "sink to nothing" and saw them as but the first step in a plan "to trade into all the Great Lakes of North America with all the Indians bordering on them, with whom we may have an immense trade never yet attempted by us, and now carried on by the French with goods brought from this Province." By 1720, Vaudreuil and his intendant, Michel Bégon, were reporting that the English were threatening to secure "the greater part of the peltries both of the French and Indians belonging to the Upper Country," and in July 1721 Burnet reported an "immense number of Indians of far Nations" flocking to Albany. Trade figures from Schenectady dramatically reflect the changes in western commerce. Between 1716 and 1720 only 30 canoes of "far" Indians came there; from 1720 to 1724, 323 canoes arrived – a tenfold increase in trade.[50]

By 1725 the French trade seemed to be hemorrhaging. An English estimate for that year put the western trade at twelve hundred packs of skins and furs. The combined trade of Fort Frontenac at the eastern end of Lake Ontario, and of Niagara at the western end, which was valued at 40,911 livres in 1723, and at 29,297 livres in 1724, plummeted to 9,151 livres in 1725. Cadwallader Colden, New York's surveyor, exuberantly predicted that such encroachments on the French trade would deprive France of her allies, render Canada useless to them, and oblige them to abandon the colony altogether.[51]

49 Representation of Lords of Trade, July 14, 1724, *NYCD* 5:707–8; Albany, Norton, *The Fur Trade in Colonial New York*, 137. For woolens and French efforts to match, see Raudot to Minister, 14 Nov. 1709, *MPHC* 33:460–61; Vaudreuil & Bégon au Ministre, 20 sept. 1714, *RAPQ*, 1947–48, 285; Minutes, Conseil, 19 jan. 1717, AN, C11A, v. 37, f. 35; Vaudreuil au Conseil 30 oct. 1717, AN, C11A, v.38; Bégon & Vaudreuil au Conseil, 17 oct. 1722, AN, C11A, v. 44; Vaudreuil & Bégon au Ministre, 14 oct. 1723, AN, C11A, v. 45. Also see Lunn "Economic Development," 157–60.
50 For Burnet quotation, see Burnet to Lords of Trade, Nov. 26, 1720, *NYCD* 5:577, 580. For Vaudreuil and Bégon quotation, see Abstract of Vaudreuil and Bégon, Oct. 20, 1720, *NYCD* 9:897; also see Vaudreuil & Bégon au Conseil, 26 oct. 1719, AN, C11A, v. 40. For number of Indians, see Burnet to Lords of Trade, 12 July 1721, *NYCD* 5:587. In June 1723 he reported that 20 men of the far nations had come in the spring, 80 more from Michilimackinac (and apparently Detroit) had arrived in June, and 40 or 50 more were en route from the *pays d'en haut*. All of these parties had also brought women and children. Burnet to Lords of Trade, 25 June 1723, *NYCD* 5:684–85; for origins, see Conference . . . Western Tribes, May 29, 1723, *NYCD* 5:693–97. For trade figures, see Governor Burnet to Lords of Trade, Nov. 21, 1724, *NYCD* 5:739.
51 For 1725 estimate, see Norton, *The Fur Trade in Colonial New York*, 164. In 1725 on a voyage to Iroquoia, Longueuil met more than 100 canoes of Indians from the upper country either coming to trade with the English or returning. The English, Longueuil complained, were trading at the Niagara portage, despite the blockhouse the French had built there, and were

In this context the English post established at Oswego in the Iroquois country in 1727 seemed to both sides a knife pointed at the heart of Canada. Located at one of the few sheltered harbors of Lake Ontario and with easy access to the *pays d'en haut*, the English at Oswego threatened, in combination with incursions by English traders on the Ohio, to detach the Algonquians from the French alliance and join them to the covenant chain of the Iroquois. The French feared Oswego, but by and large they managed to blunt the threat that it represented. As Chart 3.1 shows, the trade at French posts increased between 1730 and 1757.[52]

The French blunted the English challenge by expanding into new areas and by subsidizing the trade in old ones. This subsidy took several forms. The crown and private traders gave presents. The Crown also provided the services of blacksmiths and gunsmiths to the Indians at the French forts. As a final direct subsidy, the Crown took over for long periods of time the trade at Forts Niagara and Frontenac and eventually established a post at Toronto. Here Indians on their way to the English found French goods sold at or near English prices. The Crown took a loss on such sales in order to keep the trade from the English.[53]

These were only the direct subsidies. The French-Algonquian wars against the Fox and the Chickasaws in the 1730s and the imperial wars of the 1740s and 1750s tended, because of the distances involved, to divert warriors from the hunt. The French not only equipped the warriors and made them gifts for scalps and to redeem prisoners, but they also helped to support the wives and children of those absent on war parties. The amounts expended in these wars were considerable. The unsuccessful Fox campaign of 1728, for example, alone cost 28,401 livres and between 1732 and 1735, the expenditures made in the posts of the *pays d'en haut* alone were 33,833

selling rum within a day and a half of Fort Frontenac, Longueuil & Bégon au Ministre, 31 oct. 1725, AN, C11A, v. 47. For the trade of Fort Frontenac and of Niagara, see Bégon au Ministre, 30 oct. 1723, AN, C11A, v. 45; Estat des Pelleteries ... 1724–25, AN, C11A, v. 47; Estat de les ventes des Pelleteries ... 1726, AN, C11A, v. 49. For Colden, see Of the Trade of New York by C. Colden, *NYCD* 5:687.

[52] For Oswego established, see Burnet to Board of Trade, May 9, 1727, *DHNY* 1:447. For French fear of, see Beauharnois & D'Aigremont au Ministre, 1 oct. 1728, AN, C11A, v. 50, f. 27; Projet pour s'opposer à l'agrandissement des Anglais ... 15 oct. 1729, AN, C11A, v. 51, f. 467. Oswego always remained a thorn in the French side, Galissonière & Bigot au Ministre, 20 oct. 1748, AN, C11A, v. 91; Jonquière & Bigot au Ministre, 1 oct. 1749, AN, C11A, v. 93. Ohio, Mémoire concernant les Ilinois, 1732, AN, F3, v. 24, f. 138.

[53] For new posts, see Mémoire, Beauharnois & Hocquart au Ministre, 1737, AN, C11A, v. 67, f. 101; Réponse au Mémoire du Roy, 13 oct. 1745, AN, C11A, v. 63, f. 84. For problems faced, see Hocquart au Mss. Les Directeurs de la Compagnie des Indies, 1 nov. 1739, AN, C11A, v. 72, f. 167. For no hope for profit on royal posts, see Hocquart au Ministre, 10 oct. 1734, AN, C11A, v. 62, f. 37–40. For Toronto, see La Jonquière au Ministre, 20 aoust, 1750, AN, C11A, v. 95. The English recognized the French tactic, Colden to Clinton, Aug. 8, 1751, *NYCD* 6:743.

Chart 3.1: Total Packs

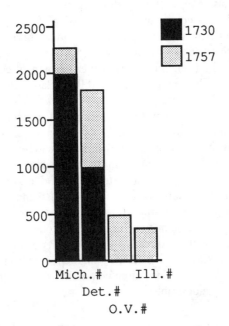

Mich. = Michilimackinac and dependencies; Det. = Detroit and dependencies; O.V. = Ohio Valley; Ill. = Illinois

Notes:
Michilimackinac total for 1730 included dependent forts: Saint Joseph, Nipigon, Green Bay, Gamasettigoya, and Michipicton; in 1757 it included dependent posts at Green Bay, Saint Joseph, Chequamegon, Kamanistigoya, Michipicton, and Sault Sainte Marie.
Detroit in 1730 included the posts at Miami and the Wea post (Ouiatenon); in 1757 it included the Miami, Wea, and Vincennes posts.
The Ohio Valley posts where trade was conducted were Fort Duquesne and the Rivière au Boeuf.
Illinois trade included the whole confederation.
Sources: Noyan, State of Canada in 1730, *MPHC* 34:73–85; Bougainville Memoir, *WHC* 18:167–195.

livres, most of which went to equipping Indian warriors. Outfitting additional large western expeditions incurred other substantial costs, at least part of which eventually found its way into the hands of Indian auxiliaries. The Noyan expedition of 1734, for example, cost 33,107 livres. Such payments lessened both the necessity and the opportunity for warriors to seek goods in trade from the English.[54]

The French also altered their trading practices to conform to Algonquian desires. They increased the number of *congés* so that by 1740, Noyan, the commander at Detroit, complained that the traders there were too numerous and the competition so ruinous that the traders sold at cost. Such conditions did not last, but the French did make other permanent changes in their fur trade procedures. They not only modified their elaborate system for grading beaver furs, but they also expanded the kinds of furs they would accept in trade. By the 1720s the Algonquian shift south away from the prime beaver country following the Iroquois wars, combined with the overhunting of beaver, had contributed to the decline of the trade in beaver fur over much of the *pays d'en haut*. Indian hunters shifted to seeking the so-called *menues pelleteries* and, more significantly, to trading deerskins and bearskins, although initially there was not much French demand for either. In 1726 Intendant DuPuy suggested importing leather workers or finding some way for the army to use the skins which otherwise would either be smuggled to New York or traded there directly by the Indians. Although the Louisiana posts sought deerskins, the Canadians took them only from necessity. As late as the 1750s, when deerskins dominated the English trade, the French regarded them as undesirable.[55]

[54] For war disrupting hunt, see Réponse au Mémoire du Roy, 1735, 13 oct. 1735, AN, C11A, v. 63, f. 84; Mémoire, Beauharnois & Hocquart au Ministre, 1737, AN, C11A, v. 67, f. 104–05; for general statement of costs, see Beauharnois and Hocquart to Minster, Oct. 9, 1732, *WHC* 17:163–64. For Fox campaign 1728, see Hocquart au Ministre, 4 oct. 1730, AN, C11A, v. 53. For example of families of warriors, see Estat general de la depense . . . 6 juillet 1739, AN, C11A, v. 71. For De Noyan, see Estat des cequi a eté a fourny . . . d'un party commandé par M. de Noyan, 6 sept. 1734, AN, C11A, v. 62, f. 156. For *pays d'en haut*, see Estat des payements faits . . . pour le prix des munitions de guerre et de bouche et autres marchandises et effets qu'ils on fourny dans les pais d'en haut . . . depuis les anneés 1732, 1733, 1734 . . . AN, C11A, v. 63, f. 132. In 1736 direct payments in the *pays d'en haut* for the Chickasaw war were 8,300 livres, Detroit, De Noyan to Minister, Aug. 6, 1740, *WHC* 17:326.

[55] The number of beaver declined over large portions of the Great Lakes, Mémoire, Beauharnois & Hocquart au Ministre, 1737, AN, C11A, v. 67, f. 100. For beaver depletion around Green Bay, see Jeanne Kay, "The Land of La Baye: The Ecological Impact of the Green Bay Fur Trade, 1634–1836" (Ph.D. diss., University of Wisconsin, 1977), 158. For deerskins, see DuPuy au Ministre 21 oct. 1726, AN, C11A, v. 48; Conseil, Louisiane, sept. 1725, AN, C13A, v. 9, f. 221. For English demand, see Clinton A. Weslager, *The Delaware Indians: A History* (New Brunswick, N. J.: Rutgers University Press, 1972), 173–74; Beauharnois et D'Aigremont, 1 oct. 1728, AN, C11A, v. 50; Mémoire, Duc de Mirepoix, 6 avril 1755, AN, C11A, v. 100; Bienville & Salmon to Maurepas, Apr. 3, 1734, *MPA* 3:645. For fur trade as small part of Canadian trade, see Mémoire, Duc de Mirapoix, 6 avril 1755, AN, C11A, v. 100.

For grading distinctions modified, see Marchands & negotiants, 1728, AN, C11A, v. 50, f. 270; Ordonnance, Du Puy, 21 juillet 1727, AN, C11A, v. 49, f. 481. See also Lunn, "Economic Development," 172.

This change in the trade is reflected in the receipts of Forts Frontenac and Niagara, forts that existed partially to intercept trade from the upper country destined for Oswego and Albany. (See Table 3.1.) The furs these posts received were largely raccoon, deerskins, and bearskins, along with a mix of the more valuable *menues pelleteries*. Of the posts in the upper country, only Michilimackinac, Green Bay, and Chequamegon retained a substantial beaver trade into the 1730s. Although less pronounced, this same trend away from beaver affected the trade as a whole. Of the furs exported from Canada and received at La Rochelle between 1728 and 1737, only 47.4 percent were beaver.[56]

Ironically, the French also succeeded in retaining the trade because of what they – and New York officials – were together unable to accomplish. The French never succeeded in halting smuggling with the English colonies. In 1725 two Albany traders estimated that 80 percent of the beaver shipped from New York to Europe was obtained from French smugglers. As a result, French traders retained access to red strouds, the *écarlatines*. Despite many attempts, the French never succeeded in manufacturing strouds that matched those of the English in either quality or price. Nor did they persuade those Indians who had a choice to accept French equivalents. French traders smuggled strouds from New York, carried these blankets west, and traded them for Algonquian furs. As French officials reiterated again and again, *écarlatines* had become the essential commodity in the trade. Caught between the *fermier*'s demand that smuggling be halted and the necessity for providing *écarlatines*, the French Crown sporadically gave royal permission to purchase strouds directly from England and market them in Canada, but the main source was usually smuggling.[57]

Taken as a whole, the French adjustment to the English challenge shows how much the relationship between commerce and empire had changed

---

[56] For decline of beaver, everywhere but Michilimackinac, Green Bay, and Chequamegon, see Mémoire, 1737, AN, C11A, v. 67, f. 100–1. For shipments between 1728 and 37, see E. R. Adair, "Anglo-French Rivalry," *Culture* 8 (1947): 435.

[57] For smuggling, see Statement of John Groesback and Dirk Schuyler on Indian Trade, Feb. 15, 1724/25, Shelbourne Papers, v. 45, Clements Library. For écarlatines, see Vaudreuil & Bégon au Conseil, 8 oct. 1721, AN, C11A, v. 44; Bégon & De Vaudreuil au Conseil, 17 oct. 1722, AN, C11A, v. 44; Hocquart à M. Controlleur general, 19 oct. 1738, AN, C11A, v. 70, f. 115; Lunn, "Economic Development," 157–63. Beauharnois & DePuy au Ministre, 26 oct. 1726, AN, C11A, v. 48; Abstract, 1 Oct. 1728, *NYCD* 9:1011; Hocquart à Mss. les fermiers generaux, 12–20 oct. 1729, AN, C11A, v. 51, f. 349; Beauharnois & Hocquart au Ministre, 12 oct. 1731, AN, C11A, v. 54; Hocquart à Mss. les directuers generaux de la Compagnie des Indies, 17 oct. 1737. AN, C11A, v. 69, f. 137–43; La Galissonière & Hocquart au Ministre, 26 sept. 1747, AN, C11A, v. 87, f. 116–17. This demand continued until the colony's last days, Mémoire, 1758, AN, C11A, v. 103, Le Comité à M. le Controlleur, juin 1758, AN, C11A, v. 103.

Smuggled strouds, which escaped English duties, may actually have been sold for less by the French than by the English in the 1750s, Colden to Clinton, Aug. 8, 1751, *NYCD* 6:741.

Table 3.1. *Fur trade at Forts Frontenac and Niagara (total fur receipts)*

	1726	1728	1730	1733	1734	1736	1738
Value (livres)	8,108	39,948	52,308	11,844	34,296	21,410	21,124
Beaver[a]	28%	—[b]	30.5%	23%	17.8%	24.3%	11.3%

[a] Beaver given as percentage of total value of furs traded.
[b] Figure not available.

Source: Estate de la vente des pelleteries, 1726, 1728, 1730, 1736, 1738; Estat des pelleteries, 1733, 1734; all in AN, C11A, vis. 48, 50, 52, 53, 62, 66, 70. The figures for 1735 are not given here, because the ships failed to arrive in time to supply the posts (Beautharnois & Hocquart to Minister, October 12, 1736, *NYCD* 9:1048–49).

from the earlier mercantilist origins of the colony. Earlier in Canadian history the fur trade had largely justified the existence of Canada. Furs had provided the lion's share of the colony's exports and revenues. But increasingly in the eighteenth century, the political benefits of the trade outweighed its revenues. The trade of the *pays d'en haut* supported Canada not through its profits, but because it was part of the glue holding the Algonquians to the alliance. Royal officials accepted Algonquian restrictions on the trade because the very survival of Canada seemed to depend on subordinating trade to the alliance. The aggressiveness of the English allowed the Algonquians to have significant and increasing influence on the terms and forms of exchange. The French raised prices for beaver, altered their grading of beaver, increased their sale of brandy, and accepted deerskins in trade because continued trade with the Algonquians, and thus the alliance itself, depended on such actions.[58]

The limited economic and considerable political importance of the trade was apparent to strategists by the end of the period. In 1755 one French strategist admitted that the fur trade of the Great Lakes and the Ohio Valley was not worth 1 percent of the expense that it had cost the Crown. He would have gladly allowed the entire trade to go to the English in exchange for English acknowledgment of French boundaries along the Ohio. Ceding the trade to the English would be less expensive than courting the Algonquians. Yet court the Algonquians the French did. The English were not ready to acknowledge French claims in the Ohio Valley, and if, because of lower prices, the English were able "to persuade the Indians that they have more regard for the interest of the nations than the French," then the French could lose not only their supply of furs, but the allied Indians. And the French well knew "what importance it is to the colony to maintain them in the alliance." If the French increased the prices they charged for goods and lowered those they gave for beaver, they threatened not just commerce but perhaps the "colony itself."[59]

French concessions proved enough, at least until the late 1740s, to satisfy Algonquian demands for generosity. The Indians recognized, and constantly reminded the French, that the English offered better bargains and better goods than the French. And, of course, there were always those whom rum or cheaper woolens lured to Oswego. But such straying could be easily

---

[58] For examples of Indian pressure, see Du Puy au Ministre, 20 oct. 1727, AN, C11A, v. 49, f. 207; Beauharnois & Hocquart, 8 oct. 1741, Postes des Pays d'en haut, AN, C11A, v. 78.
[59] For small value of trade, see Mémoire sur la depêché de M. Le Duc de Mirepoix du 6 avril 1755, AN, C11A, v. 100. For importance of alliance, see Observations sur les Réponses fournies par la Compagnie des Indes . . . (1749), AN, C11A, v. 93, f. 10–12. For rationale of setting prices so as not to alienate Indians, see Ordonnance de M. de Beauharnois et Hocquart . . . 6 juin 1746, AN, C11A, v. 85, f. 3.

enough incorporated into the logic of the alliance as a necessary rebuke to
their father's lack of generosity. If rum led to murders among the Indians,
the French, in turn, could argue that by regulating the sale of liquor, they
were, unlike the English, looking out for their children's welfare. The
alliance, in any case, remained more than exchange, and Algonquians often
did respond to French appeals to the other links beside trade that tied the
French and the Algonquians together and to reminders of past Iroquois
and English perfidy. And the English themselves often enough cooperated
by demonstrating the dangers of trade without alliance and a father to
whom one could appeal for justice. In the words of Lieutenant Governor
Montgomerie of New York, the traders, "greedy of gain, never considered
what was just, but sometimes with a high hand, sometimes with deceit and
Artifice, surreptitiously got from the Indians their Furrs and peltry, and
when they were thus posesst of them, obliged these poor wretches to take
what they would give them, whereby they were in a great measure deterred
from coming to Oswego, and compelled by this usage to seek another market
among the French." The Ottawas and Huron-Petuns drifted toward the
English in the 1720s, and the villagers south of the Great Lakes opened
extensive trade relations with the English in the 1740s and 1750s, but on the
whole the French alliance held, even though by the late 1740s it was in a
perpetual state of crisis.[60]

V

Trade goods served both symbolic and utilitarian purposes. The same kettle
that served to cement an alliance also cooked venison. I have thus far
stressed the symbolic and political aspects of exchange, neglecting the
utilitarian appeal of trade goods. Turning to trade goods as items of
everyday use draws attention to another facet of exchange: the possibility of
dependency. The question of dependency – the possibility that without
European goods and the fur trade the Algonquians would no longer be able
to feed, clothe, or house themselves – looms over recent studies of the trade.
To determine if this possibility became fact during the French fur trade, it is
necessary to assess the place and prevalence of trade goods in everyday
material life and the dependence of Algonquians upon them.

Superficially, Algonquian statements and actions regarding these matters

---

[60] For French appeal to other connections (French as father; gratitude toward priests; allies
against Iroquois; French who have died to defend them), see Parolles aux anciens chefs des
illinois, oyatanons, et miamis . . . 1736 (misdated, actual date c. 1715), AN, C11A, v. 65. For
quotation, see Montgomerie to Lords of Trade, Dec. 1, 1730, NYCD 5:907. For continued
complaints of frauds, see Colden to Clinton, Aug. 8, 1751, NYCD 6:744.

seem to mimic the terms of the marketplace and indicate a material dependence on the French. On closer examination, however, their views and actions make sense only in the context of the particular social relationships that the goods themselves helped to establish. In referring to exchange, Algonquians spoke in terms of their *besoins* – their needs or necessities – and they visualized exchange as a way of satisfying these needs. *Besoin*, as used by the Algonquians, was not simply a statement of desire; the term had a particular resonance in their society because, once an appropriate social relationship had been established, an assertion of need for something could become a special claim on the thing needed. To be needy is to excite pity and thus to deserve aid. Just as in addressing manitous Algonquians sought to portray themselves as weak and miserable, so in addressing Onontio, Jesuits, or traders, they usually stressed their own misery and need. The Algonquians' emphasis on exchange as a way of satisfying their *besoins*, therefore, had a meaning quite different from that expressed in the French view of commerce as a way of filling needs.[61]

In stressing their *besoins*, the Algonquians were actually making a claim on the French. Because they needed goods and were friends and allies of the French, they deserved to have those goods that the French possessed but did not themselves immediately require. Indians, like the Fox at their first contact, thought that "whatever their visitors possessed ought to be given to them gratis; everything aroused their desires, and yet they had few beavers to sell." Among the Potawatomis at initial contact, the French demand for payments for goods that Indians received led to violence. According to Algonquian cultural logic, the French, as allies, should act as if they were kinspeople of the Algonquians. Each side would supply the other's needs. Each side would graciously bestow what the other lacked.[62]

Such a conception of exchange makes it clearer why middleman status was a matter of relative indifference to the Algonquians. If the French chose to bring them goods at their villages, this was to be praised not opposed. These western Algonquians conceived of traders as men who came to supply their *besoins*, and they welcomed them for their presence which promised to enhance the prestige, wealth, and strength of their villages. What infuriated them was not the loss of the opportunity to make the long and arduous journeys to Montreal to obtain their *besoins*, but the French announcement in the late 1690s that they were withdrawing their traders from the *pays d'en haut* and that they expected the Algonquians to resume their trade journeys.

---

[61] *Besoins* may be taken as the language of dependency if the Algonquians either acted as if they were dependent or could be shown in these early years to have been dependent on European goods for survival, but this, as will be shown later, was not the case.

[62] For Fox quotation, see La Potherie, *History*, 319.

Onanghisse, the Potawatomi leader whose people the French presumed to be potential middlemen, was outraged:

> Father! Since we want powder, iron, and every other necessary which you were formerly in the habit of sending us, what do you expect us to do? Are the majority of our women who have but one or two beavers to send to Montreal to procure their little supplies, are they to intrust them to drunken fellows who will drink them and bring nothing back? Thus, having in our country none of the articles we require and which you, last year, promised we should be furnished with, and not want; and perceiving only this – that nothing whatsoever is yet brought to us, and that the French come to visit us no more – you shall never see us again, I promise you, if the French quit us; this Father, is the last time we shall come to talk with you.[63]

Significantly, Onanghisse said nothing about lower prices or potential profits; he spoke for the women, who, by implication, were a major force in exchange in the villages. They and the other Potawatomis relied on the French for their *besoins*, their "little supplies." Exchange in Montreal was the domain not of calculating middlemen out for profit but of "drunken fellows" who drank up their beaver and failed to bring home the *besoins* they had been sent to fetch. Although these *besoins* were highly valued goods, they were not yet essential to Potawatomi survival. For if they were, how could Onanghisse have spoken of never seeing the French again and thus, presumably, doing without them?

This orientation toward *besoins* rather than profits appears also in the reaction of the Ottawas and Huron-Petuns of Michilimackinac to the French domination of their old carrying trade to the western tribes. The Ottawas, Huron-Petuns, and various western Chippewa bands continued, as they had for years, to gather furs on the lakes, but they now operated on the margins rather than at the center of exchange. The Ottawas lost their old lucrative trade with the Crees, who had begun trading at Hudson's Bay. Only the Saulteurs, who as allies of the Sioux carried French goods to that people, continued to tap a major source of prime beaver. To obtain their *besoins*, the Huron-Petuns and Ottawas of Michilimackinac, as well as the Potawatomis of Green Bay, became provisioners of the trade. They sold corn and fish to the French who, according to Cadillac, reequipped themselves once on the outward journey from Montreal and again on their return. They compensated for the huge charges the French made for their goods by setting prices on their own commodities that made the French howl in protest. As La Potherie recognized, they now

---

[63] For quotation, see Narrative of ... Occurrences ... 1696, 1697, *NYCD* 9:673.

[do] not need to go hunting in order to obtain all the comforts of life. When they choose to work, they make canoes of birch-bark, which they sell two at three hundred livres each. They get a shirt for two sheets of bark for cabins. The sale of their French strawberries and other fruits produce means for procuring their ornaments, which consist of vermillion and glass and porcelain beads. They make a profit on everything.[64]

What La Potherie called their profit, however, was probably not understood by the Indians in these terms, for, as La Potherie also noted, all except the Huron-Petuns saved nothing and realized no lasting gain from such exchanges. "They would be exceedingly well-to-do if they were economical," but the social and cultural demands of their own society prevented such accumulation. They gave away their last food to a visiting stranger and then did not hesitate to beg for food from the French who came among them. The underlying logic of such exchange patterns was that *besoins* took precedence over profits. They had an obligation to visitors, and the French had an obligation to them.[65]

The actual demand for the goods that the Algonquians identified as their *besoins* was surprisingly limited during the century of the French fur trade that ended in 1760. Father Charlevoix observed in the 1720s that Indian wants were, by European standards, meager. When he asserted that the Indians were "true philosophers and the sight of all our conveniences, riches, and magnificence affects them so little that they have found out the art of easily dispensing with them," he was not simply indulging in the myth of the noble savage. Indian wants do appear to have remained limited even at the height of the trade and Indian demand remained relatively inelastic. Unless presented with brandy, Algonquians traded largely to clothe and ornament themselves, buy some metal tools, and acquire enough gunpowder for the next hunt. An analysis of French account books for Michilimackinac, Ouiatenon, Detroit, and Green Bay between 1715 and 1750 reveals that cloth, blankets, gunpowder, and shirts were the dominant trade goods at all the posts. These, along with capotes and, at Detroit, brandy, accounted for between 60 and 75 percent of the trade. The Indians did not trade for the guns they used in the hunt, for such guns rarely appear on the trade

---

[64] For intertribal exchange, see Mémoire que la direction ... 26 avril 1703, AN, C11A, v. 24, f. 142–44; Speech of Ottawas, July 23, 1708, *MPHC* 33:39. For loss of Cree trade by Ottawas and Sioux-Chippewa exchange, see Mémoire que la direction ..., *ibid.*, and Callières et Champigny au Ministre, 5 oct. 1701, AN, C11A, v. 19. For corn and fish, see Quaife, *The Western Country*, 17–18. For long-standing French protests over prices, see Declaration des marchands, 14 avril 1684, AN, C11A, v. 6; Narrative of ... Occurrences ... 1689, 90, *NYCD* 9:481. For quotation, see La Potherie, *History* 1:282.

[65] La Potherie, *History*, 28–82.

manifests. Guns seem to have come largely as presents from the Crown. The increase in the scale of trade apparent after 1720 resulted largely from the widespread adoption of woolens and other cloth to replace fur robes and leather garments.[66]

In local economies where trade goods satisfied limited *besoins*, the fur trade involved relatively little disruption of native subsistence systems. Production for the fur trade came from a hunt not yet separated from the larger subsistence cycle. Success in the hunt remained a function of the hunters' relations with the manitous who controlled the game. And a successful hunt yielded goods whose distribution proceeded according to the demands of the manitous and the *besoins* of kinspeople. This was not an economy in which the production or distribution of goods formed a separate sphere of practical activity. Nor was it an economy that had yet, in any meaningful sense, rendered the Algonquians politically dependent on the Europeans. All of these points obviously demand substantiation.[67]

Taken as a whole, the material day-to-day existence of Indian peoples showed remarkable continuity during the seventeenth and early eighteenth centuries. The fur trade barely altered Algonquian housing, transportation, and diet. The fur trade did initially put a greater emphasis on beaver hunting. And certain groups such as the Ottawas and Huron-Petuns increased the scale of their hunt. But for most groups, the fur trade did not immediately or drastically alter hunting or subsistence patterns. Furs were the products of hunts in which men, women, and children departed together and in which household units consumed the meat while processing and reserving the furs for market. The trade certainly increased the amount of labor women had to devote to preparing furs for exchange, but, on the other hand, the purchase of cloth and ready-made clothing lessened the labor involved in producing finished garments. How this balanced out in the end is impossible to determine from the existing evidence.[68]

[66] For quotation, see Pierre de Charlevoix, *Journal of a Voyage to North America* (London: R. and J. Dodsley, 1761, microprint facsimile ed., 1966), 2:107. For account books, see Dean Anderson, "Variability in Trade at Eighteenth-Century French Outposts," unpublished paper in author's possession.

[67] There were assertions as early as 1706 that without powder the Indians would starve, but such claims have to be put within the cultural context of Algonquian attempts to make themselves appear miserable when asking favors (e.g., Extraits, De Tonti, 15 oct., AN, C11A, v. 24, f. 203). In fact, a modified bow technology long remained in place, Charlevoix, *Journal*, 2:208; Sabrevois Memoir, 1718, *WHC* 16:373; La Potherie, *Histoire*, 4:216.

[68] In 1688 the Baron de Lahontan witnessed the return of 400 to 500 Ottawas to Michilimackinac after a winter hunt in the Saginaw Bay region, Thwaites (ed.), *Lahontan's Voyages*, 1:143. A party of this size certainly included women and children. In the same area during 1685–86 the Iroquois had captured children as well as adults when they raided winter hunting camps. Denonville to Seignelay, June 12, 1686, *NYCD* 9:293–94. La Potherie, who wrote in the early eighteenth century, indicated that largely all-male hunts occurred out of Michilimackinac in the 1690s (La Potherie, *History* 1:281–82), but during

Even when beaver failed and Indians turned to other game, the immediate consequences were not severe. Deer and bear, the staples of the fur trade of the Ohio Valley and lower Great Lakes, also yielded meat. Subsistence and the hunt for furs remained as closely linked as ever. When the distance of beaver from the villages and the scarcity of other game in the region did create a conflict, the demands of subsistence took priority. Even around Green Bay into the mid 1740s, Indians long involved in the trade still had to be actively recruited to hunt beaver in the Sioux borderlands instead of remaining nearer their villages to hunt deer and bear. The ties to the trade of tribes such as the Sioux, whose involvement in the trade was much more recent, were even weaker. The French feared that increases in prices for trade goods would cause the Sioux to "lose their ardor for coming to find the merchandise whose use they have known only for a little while." Only later in the eighteenth and nineteenth centuries, and even then only among some tribes, did production for market become a separate sphere in which men, leaving their families behind, departed on long hunts whose sole goal was the accumulation of furs for market.[69]

If production did not demand immediate alterations in the society, neither did the European goods that entered the society transform it. Indians acquired trade goods at a surprisingly gradual rate. A preexisting native technology survived for a remarkably long time alongside the new technology. Kettles boiled water, knives cut meat, and guns killed game, but they did not chain their users inevitably, inexorably, and immediately to the will of the suppliers. A far less efficient, but still serviceable, native technology remained available if trade goods were lacking.

Given existing interpretations of the scale and importance of the fur trade, the assertion that European goods remained relatively scarce in the *pays d'en haut* for generations and that a native technology remained available is bound to be controversial. Basically, there are three major problems with assuming that European goods rapidly and nearly completely replaced native manufactures in the *pays d'en haut*. First, according to the archaeological record, native technology persisted for a considerable time. Second, given the carrying capacity of French canoes and the limited number that departed annually for the West, there was simply no way to transport all the goods that

the eighteenth century virtually the whole village departed on the hunt from Detroit and Michilimackinac.
[69] In concentrating on the fur trade, as Charles Cleland has rightly emphasized, scholars have ignored the persistence of basic subsistence patterns during the seventeenth and eighteenth centuries; see Charles Cleland, "The Inland Shore Fishery of the Northern Great Lakes: Its Development and Importance in Prehistory," *American Antiquity* 47 (1982): 776. Surpluses from the existing native economy fed Europeans in the West during much of this period. For Sioux, see Copie de l'article de la lettre du S. Chalet à mes. les directeurs . . . 28 oct. 1746, AN, C11A, v. 85.

would have been necessary to supply the native population. Third, when read carefully, contemporary accounts make it clear that European goods remained relatively scarce over much of the *pays d'en haut* well into the eighteenth century.

It is necessary here to cite only a few examples of this evidence. Stone tools persisted alongside metal tools in the Ojibwa sites on the north shores of Lake Huron and Lake Superior that were occupied during the late seventeenth and early eighteenth centuries. Sites in the Michilimackinac region, the nexus of the trade, show the same pattern. At the Lasanen site, probably an Ottawa and Huron-Petun burial site used primarily between 1690 and 1700, "projectile points, scrapers and stone knives imply the maintenance of the prehistoric technological and economic patterns." Similarly, at the late seventeenth-century Summer Island site in Green Bay, stone tools persisted alongside European metal tools. Farther south, the Zimmerman site that the Kaskaskias occupied between 1683 and 1691 shows the same pattern of stone technology lingering alongside metal tools. Even at the eighteenth-century Guebert site occupied by the Kaskaskias after 1719, there are vestiges of stone technology. The Jesuits could collect stone daggers in everyday use as late as 1687, and, according to Father Sebastian Rale, arrows tipped with stone remained the principal weapon into the 1690s. Native pottery persisted even longer; it is readily available at all late seventeenth- and early eighteenth-century sites.[70]

Other goods penetrated the region even more slowly. By 1679 the Fox Indians, a tribe described only five years later as a major supplier of furs, had acquired firearms, but a 120-man war party encountered by the French that year possessed only eight muskets. Cloth remained so rare that when the Fox captured a coat from the French, they ripped off the buttons and cut up the material in order to divide the coat into the maximum number of pieces. If the Wisconsin Fox ever acquired large amounts of cloth, such supplies vanished after their estrangement from the French. In 1718 the men still wore "scarcely any garments made of cloth." Similarly, in the 1680s, members of the La Salle expedition reported that the Illinois, the best armed

---

[70] For persistence and only gradual replacement, see Warren L. Wittry, "The Bell Site, Wn9, An Early Historic Fox Village," *The Wisconsin Archeologist*, N. S., 44 (March 1963): 35; James Fitting, *The Archaeology of Michigan* (Bloomfield Hills, Michigan: Cranbrook Institute of Science, 1975), 210–11; Ronald J. Mason, *Great Lakes Archaeology* (New York: Academic Press, 1981): 404; Cleland, *Lasanen Site*, appendix A. Nern and Cleland, "The Gros Cap Cemetery Site," 9–16, 48; J. V. Wright, "A Regional Examination of Ojibwa Culture History," *Anthropoligica* 9 NS 7 (1965): 196, 202, 208; David S. Brose, "Summer Island III: An Early Historic Site in the Upper Great Lakes," *Historical Archaeology* 4 (1970), 5–6, 13–23; Brown (ed.), "The Zimmerman Site," 13, 72–73, 53–54; Mary Elizabeth Good, "The Guebert Site: An Eighteenth-Century Historic Kaskaskia Indian Village in Randolph County, Illinois," *Central States Archaeological Societies Memoir* 2 (n.p., 1972), 78–79. For stone daggers, see *JR* 63:291. For stone arrowheads, see Good, "Guebert Site," 12.

tribe south of Lake Michigan, had virtually no guns and that the peoples around them lacked metal knives and hatchets. In 1706, nearly half a century after the first guns appeared among them, the Peorias, one of the tribes of the Illinois confederation, attacked a Jesuit priest, Father Gravier. Not only did they shoot him with arrows, but the arrows were tipped with flint. It is equally notable that the French response was to cut off powder for such guns as the Illinois possessed. The incident is a clear example of the persistence of old technology alongside the new. When, toward the end of the French and Indian War, supplies of powder failed at Detroit, the Ottawas, Huron-Petuns, Potawatomis and Chippewas there resumed hunting with bows and arrows. They did it without enthusiasm, but they did it. When French traders during the same period failed to supply cloth to the Illinois, those Indians clothed themselves in skins.[71]

This failure of European goods rapidly to displace native manufactures is more understandable when we examine estimates of available cargo space during the late seventeenth and early eighteenth centuries. The French could not transport the amount of goods necessary to provide Algonquians with the tools and clothes they would need to abandon native manufactures. The intendant Jean Bochart de Champigny estimated that about seventy canoe loads of goods reached the West in the late 1680s (see Table 3.2), with this number increasing dramatically in the early 1690s, when Governor de Frontenac, on the pretext of supplying Michilimackinac and other posts, allowed large amounts of additional trade goods, including brandy, to be shipped west.[72]

When these cargoes are placed next to estimates of the population they were meant to supply, the reasons for the persistence of native technology become apparent. Until some time after 1700, this was a population in decline from disease, displacement, and war, but it was still sizable. Considering only the major population clusters, there were 15,000–20,000

---

[71] For Fox war party, see Thwaites (ed.), *Hennepin's A New Discovery*, 130–33. For their role in the fur trade, see La Durantaye au Gouverneur, 22 avril 1684, AN, C11A, v. 6. For the Fox in 1718, see Memoir on the Savages of Canada ... 1718, *WHC* 16:371. For the Illinois in 1680, see Chretien Le Clercq, "Narrative," Cox, *Journeys of La Salle*, 1:118. For La Salle on the Illinois country, see enclosed with letter of Frontenac, Nov. 9, 1680, *IHC* 23:12. Emily J. Blasingham, "The Depopulation of the Illinois Indians," *Ethnohistory* 3 (Summer 1986): 197, citing Margry's narrative account of La Salle, indicates the Illinois had several hundred guns in 1680, but I have been unable to find substantiation in the documents. For the Peorias, see *JR* 66:53–57, 265–67. The Kickapoos and Mascoutens still used the bow and arrow. The Illinois still used the bow and arrow a great deal and dressed in skins in 1718, "Memoir," *WHC* 16:373. For Detroit Indians, see Conseil tenu le 28 novembre 1760 au detroit, AN, C11A, v. 105, f.358, For resumption of use of skin garments, see Macarty à Kerlerec, 30 aoust 1759, AN, C13A, v.41. f. 103.

[72] W. J. Eccles, *Frontenac: The Courtier Governor* (Toronto: McClelland & Stewart, 1959), 275–78.

Table 3.2. *Estimates of annual canoe loads and goods reaching the West*

	1670s		1690	1680s–1690s		
	Low	High	Congés	Low	High	Extreme
Canoes (number)	40	55	70	85	100	130
Guns (number)	320	440	560	680	800	1,040
Blankets (number)	60	825	1,050	1,275	1,500	1,950
Tobacco (livres)	2,560	3,520	4,480	5,440	6,400	8,320
Cloth (ells)	3,160	4,345	5,530	6,715	7,900	10,270
Hatchets (number)	1,440	1,980	2,520	3,060	3,600	4,680
Knives (number)	16,320	22,240	28,560	34,680	40,800	53,040

Note: The canoe numbers above come from the following estimates: *40*: the minimal trade for the early 1670s; *55*: the capacity based on the high range of fur receipts for the 1670s; *70*: Champigny's 1690 figure, which, since it is close to the estimated figure for combined fur receipts and furs smuggled to the English, is the best official estimate; *85*: the high figure based on fur receipts for the 1680s and 1690s; *100*: Hennepin's estimate for 1679 and probably the high figure for the 1690s; *130*: the extreme 1684 estimate.

persons in the towns around Green Bay in the 1670s, nearly 20,000 in the Illinois, Miami, and Shawnee villages around Starved Rock during the 1680s, 3,200 in Chequamegon at its height in the mid 1660s, and an estimated 6,000–7,000 in Michilimackinac in 1695. Such estimates ignore the Sioux, Crees, Nippisings, Mississaugas, and other Ojibwa groups, except the Saulteurs, all of whom were served at least partially by the French fur trade. Knives and, perhaps, hatchets had probably begun to meet the demand by the end of the century, but other goods, even by the highest estimates, could not have replaced native manufactures.[73]

Conditions did change after 1720 when English and French competition

[73] The best discussion of the demography of the region is Jeanne Kay, "The Fur Trade and Native American Population Growth," *Ethnohistory* 31 (1984), 265–87. Kay effectively challenges the usual account of constant population decline after contact. For epidemics and initial decline, see Marest to Vaudreil, Aug. 14, 1706, *WHC* 16:237, and Marest to Vaudreuil, 4 June 1708, *MPHC* 33:386. For Ohio Valley, see discussion in Chapter 5.

For population, see Green Bay: *JR* 56:125 (1671–72); *JR* 61:149, 153–54 (1679); Starved Rock: Wayne C. Temple, *Indian Villages of the Illinois Country: Historic Tribes*, Scientific Papers, Illinois State Museum, vol. 2, pt. 2 (Springfield: Illinois State Museum, 1958), 27; Chequamegon: *JR* 50:273, 301. I translated warriors into total population by using a 4:1 ratio. For Michilimackinac, see *HBNI* 15:399, 773–74. For Cadillac, see letter of Lamothe Cadillac, Aug. 3, 1695, in E. M. Sheldon, *The Early History of Michigan from the First Settlement to 1815* (New York: A. S. Barnes, 1956), 74.

for the fur trade increased the number of goods moving west. By the 1720s the *canots de maître* had replaced the much smaller eighteenth-century canoes, and considering the number of *congés* for western posts, it appears that in a year such as 1739 the fifty-six canoes allowed under the *congés* could contain cargos of approximately 336,000 livres of goods by weight (56 @ 6,000 = 336,000) as against 175,000 transported west in the late 1690s (100 canoes @ 1,750 = 175,000). Since these cargo figures do not include that portion of the trade of the Illinois country that went down the Mississippi to New Orleans, the portion of trade at Forts Niagara and Frontenac that came from the West, the illegal trade of coureurs de bois operating without *congés*, or the trade at Oswego, even this substantial increase still obviously underestimates the total. A rough estimate would be that Niagara-Oswego-Frontenac normally supplied an additional ten canoe loads of goods to the *pays d'en haut* during the 1730s and 1740s.[74]

This rise in the scale of trade seems to have been largely a function of an increase in Indian consumption of cloth and woolen goods. Cloth had been a significant trade item since the late seventeenth century, but during the early eighteenth century European cloth had yet to replace native clothing. In 1718 the Indians around Detroit, and presumably the peoples who bordered them, wore a mixture of European clothing and native garments. The Potawatomi men, for example, wore "red or blue cloth" in the summer, but their winter clothing was buffalo robes. Farther west, the men of the Illinois, the Fox, and presumably the other peoples of the region mostly continued to wear clothing fashioned from animal skins.[75]

[74] For the Illinois trade, see Bienville, Memoir on Louisiana, 1725–26, *MPA* 3:533. French voyageurs in 1729 promised to ship 20,000 livres worth of beaver to New Orleans annually, Perier de la Chasse to Director, Jan. 30, 1729, *MPA* 2:619. Problems of storing furs in warm, humid New Orleans always hindered the fur trade there.

In 1750, 300 packs of fur went to Oswego from Lake Superior, Jonquière to Minister, Sept. 20, 1756, *WHC* 18:67. At 7.1 packs per canoe, this would represent more than forty canoes, but these were smaller Indian canoes and they carried more passengers and less cargo.

Louise De Chêne, *Habitants et Marchands*, 130, says the larger freight canoes carrying 3,000 livres of cargo were in use by 1714. For capacity of 5,000 livres, see De Noyan to Minister, Oct. 18, 1738, *WHC* 17:295. I have used a higher 6,000-livre estimate given in Beauharnois & Hocquart au Ministre, Mémoire, 1717, AN, C11A, v. 67, f. 104, in order to avoid the risk of underestimating shipments west. In addition, and for the same reason, I have calculated as if the entire cargo space were taken up by trade goods and furs, although it is estimated that up to one-third of the capacity was used for provisions for the journey itself. See Carolyn Gilman, *Where Two Worlds Meet: The Great Lakes Fur Trade* (St. Paul: Minnesota Historical Society, 1982), 36. Since the livre was a measure of both weight and money, many cargo references are unclear. I have cited only those in which the reference is clearly to the weight of the cargo.

[75] For the increased use of woolen clothing during the 1690s, see Frontenac au Ministre, 25 oct. 1696, *RAPQ*, 1928–29, 312–13. In 1685 the Chippewas of Chequamegon had only recently adopted woolen clothes, Narrative of . . . Occurrences, 1694–95, *NYCD* 9:611. For

Table 3.3. *Relative percentages of cargoes by category (in livres/value)*

	Textiles and clothing	Arms and ammunition	Metal implements	Alcohol
Detroit 1732	358/25%	509/36%	200/14%	178/13%
Detroit 1736	504/57%	68/8%	20/2%	167/19%
Green Bay 1740	4,545/53%	2,549/30%	541/6%	421/5%
Green Bay 1747	14,938/73%	3,049/15%	1,133/5%	628/4%

Source: Dean L. Anderson, "Merchandise for the Pays d'en Haut: Eighteenth Century Trade Goods and Indian Peoples of the Upper Great Lakes," paper presented at the Canadian Archaeological Association Annual Meeting, April 24–27, 1986, Toronto, Ontario.

By the 1720s and 1730s, cloth clearly dominated the trade. (See Table 3.3.) Whether smuggled English cloth or imported French cloth, it was cloth and clothing that filled the canoes going west. An examination of four surviving lists of cargoes shipped to Detroit and Green Bay between 1732 and 1747 reveals that cloth and clothing dominated every cargo except the one shipped to Detroit in 1732, when ammunition was being sent west in preparation for war against the Fox.

Yet even with the increase in cargo capacity and the rapid spread of European clothing, Indian consumption of trade goods remained relatively low. When the cargoes shipped to Green Bay during the 1740s are analyzed in the context of total population served by the traders, it becomes clear that the fur trade at Green Bay would not suffice to supply every Indian in the Green Bay trade area with a blanket. The trade would, however, certainly supply them all with knives, a cloth garment – a blanket, shirt, or capote – and powder. Farther east, where the abundance of imports was greater and sources of supply more varied, the trade probably did serve to

cloth and skin clothing in 1718, see Memoir on the Savages of Canada...1718, *WHC* 16:366–76. A proposal to ban the sale of woolen goods in order to increase the amount of *castor gras* – the greasy beaver obtained from beaver robes that the woolen cloth was replacing – brought an outraged Canadian response; see Mémoire sur l'etat de la ferme des castors, 10 oct. 1698, AN, C11A, v. 16, f. 231–34.

clothe the Indians and to provide basic metal technology. It did so, however, only in the peak years; in other years, Indians had to be prepared to supply their own clothing and to rely on old knives, hatchets, and so forth, repaired by French blacksmiths. Excavations at Fort Michilimackinac indicate that even as the number of trade goods increased after 1725, reflecting the growth of trade at the site, native technology persisted. Pottery and work in bone, antlers, and even stone hung on after imports had become part of everyday life.[76]

James Fitting has attempted to determine whether "the introduction of European trade goods, particularly axes, kettles, knives and guns, altered the subsistence patterns of the area to the point that social and ideological orientations changed as well." To do so, he compared the artifact connections from the two villages: the Juntunen site, a typical late prehistoric settlement on the straits of Mackinac, and Lasanen, an Ottawa and Huron-Petun burial and village site seven miles from Juntunen which was occupied approximately from 1671 to 1701. He concluded: "If the introduction of European trade goods had any effect at all on the subsistence base, it was to amplify the trends already present. . . . We must reject the hypothesis that European trade goods drastically altered the subsistence base of the peoples of the Straits of Mackinac."[77]

Apparently, this was true not only at Mackinac but also at the Bell site, a Fox village occupied well into the eighteenth century. Here, too, "contact with the Whites had not yet drastically altered their mode of life," and Fitting, in evaluating the same site, sees the way of life as "similar to that of peoples of the Late Woodland period." Farther north, at Lake Nipigon, K. C. A. Dawson concludes, with the introduction of European goods "no major discontinuity appears evident." And David Brose, while hypothesizing that the Summer Island site (1650–1700) in Green Bay was occupied as a direct result of the fur trade, also says that native manufactures remained more significant than European and that the native tools most closely associated with subsistence were the slowest to change.[78]

---

[76] Lyle M. Stone, "Archaeological Research at Fort Michilimackinac, An Eighteenth-Century Historic Site in Emmet County, Michigan, 1959–1966 Excavations" (Ph.D. diss., MSU, 1970), 1:60. Moreau S. Maxell, "Indian Artifacts at Fort Michilimackinac, Mackinaw City, Michigan," *Michigan Archaeologist* 10 (1964): 23–30.

[77] James Fitting, "Patterns of Acculturation at the Straits of Mackinac," in Charles Cleland (ed.), *Cultural Change and Continuity: Essays in Honor of James B. Griffin* (New York: Academic Press, 1976), 327.

[78] For the Bell site, see Paul W. Parmalee, "Vertebrate Remains from the Bell Site, Winnebago County, Wisconsin," *Wisconsin Archeologist*, NS 445 (Mar. 1963): 58, and Fitting, *Archaeology of Michigan*, 208. For Lake Nipigon, see K. C. A. Dawson, *Algonkians of Lake Nipigon: An Archaeological Survey*, National Museum of Man, Mercury Series, Archaeological Survey of Canada, Paper no. 48 (Ottawa: National Museums of Canada, 1976), 30. For Summer Island, see Brose, "Summer Island III," 23.

There is no denying that European goods had become an integral part of Algonquian life, but by the end of the French period there was not, as yet, material dependence. In an emergency Algonquians remained able to feed, clothe, and shelter themselves without European assistance, and more significantly they had more than one source for the manufactures they wanted. Politically powerful Algonquian groups could not only obtain such goods, they could have them bestowed as gifts. An understanding of regional relationships and of the emerging links between French and Indians during the French period cannot, therefore, be based on a simple model of early and decisive material dependence of Indians upon the French. Instead it is the relationships – political and social – through which goods moved and which, in part, gave the goods their meaning and influence that must be kept in mind.[79]

How intricate this network of exchange had become and how thoroughly it was integrated into the political and social relationships of the French and Algonquians is apparent in the journal of Joseph de la Malgue Marin for 1753–54. Marin was the commander at Green Bay and a member of the company that leased the post there. He thus acted both as an agent of the king and as a trader, and he had virtually no dealings with the Indians in which goods did not change hands. On his arrival, meeting the inhabitants of the first small Menominee village on his route, he gave them "the gifts for their village." He repeatedly made such gifts, "commensurate with their number," to the inhabitants of each village of Fox, Sauks, Menominees, Winnebagos, and Sioux he visited. When such villages had suffered the loss of prominent inhabitants, he frequently made additional gifts to cover the graves of the dead.[80]

Such gifts were the expected courtesies of allies, but Marin also had to disburse goods to achieve specific ends. He worked simultaneously, for example, to prevent wars between the Green Bay peoples and the Illinois, who had attacked a Sauk village in Illinois and killed a Frenchmen, and to keep the peace between the Sioux and Menominees and the western Chippewas. All these negotiations involved covering the dead, consoling the

---

[79] Those who thought that the Indians depended on Europeans to meet their basic needs tended to be those who were least familiar with them. In 1758, e.g., the French minister, Rouillé, objected to the introduction of the potato among the Indians because it would detach them from the French by allowing them to feed themselves without French aid. Governor Vaudreuil and Intendant Bigot had to point out that the Indians fed themselves, trading only for munitions and clothing. Vaudreuil & Bigot au Ministre, 8 aoust 1758, AN, C11A, v. 103, f. 04.

[80] Kenneth P. Bailey (ed. and trans.), *Journal of Joseph Marin, French Colonial Explorer and Military Commander in the Wisconsin Country, Aug. 7, 1753–June 20, 1754* (Los Angeles: printed for the author, 1975): gifts for village, 51; to inhabitants, 52–54, 57, 62; cover dead, 34, 52, 82, 91.

mourners with gifts of brandy, and rewarding Indian emissaries active in the negotiations. He also gave presents to turn back war parties and to reward those who had refused to organize war parties. Ultimately, to guarantee negotiations, he agreed to give the Sauks and Fox a large present to give to the Illinois so that they would consent to peace. When the peace was concluded, he clothed and provisioned the Illinois delegation and then made additional gifts to the Sauks and Fox. Marin estimated his cost in preventing the Illinois war alone at 10,000 livres.[81]

While all this was going on, other goods changed hands through trade. French traders granted goods to the Indians on credit with payment to come in the spring after the hunt. Other French traders departed with the Indians to their hunting camps. Despite all Marin's efforts, the returns of this trade were problematic. That winter the Lake Sioux, fearful of Chippewa attacks, did not hunt, thus depriving the French of a major source of furs.[82]

For both the Indians and the French all of these exchanges were of a piece; they bound the French and the Algonquians together. Conceptually trade and gift exchanges were different, but in actual social practice they could no longer be disentangled without the collapse of the entire exchange network. And when the network worked properly, the Algonquians could continue to conceive of it as a system designed to satisfy their *besoins* (just as the French traders thought of it as a source of profit). As a Sauk speaker, Weasel, told both the Sauks and the Fox, they must be obliged to the French

> for all they were doing to help them. They came from a long way off and endured many difficulties and much misery to bring them the things they needed. Not only that but they were good enough to take an interest in reconciling them with the people they warred against. And but for that their villages would soon be reduced to nothing. And if they would think about all that, they would be at a loss to how to show their gratitude to the French for all the trouble they take for them. They would all indeed be ungrateful if they didn't do as I wished, especially as I [i.e., Marin] only spoke for their own good.[83]

In the exchange network, commerce was obviously a part but hardly the whole of a larger structure. And to understand Algonquian actions within this structure, sentiments such as those of Weasel must be taken seriously for they represent not the illusions of duped primitives but a powerful formulation of a reality Algonquians and French had called into being. Without the middle ground, Weasel was a fool; with it, he was a wise and perceptive man.

---

[81] Bailey (ed.), *Journal of Joseph Marin*, for Sioux-Chippewa peace, 64; covering dead, 59–60, 69; rewards, 82; Fox-Illinois peace, 86, 99; cost, Marin to General, 1 June 1754, *ibid.*, 133.

[82] *Ibid.*, credit, 62; hunting camps, 93.

[83] *Ibid.*, quotation, 87; was speaker, 66.

4

The alliance

There is no king in the tribe, but a chief who is not a chief of state [and] has no
authority at his disposal, no power of coercion, no means of giving an order. The
chief is not a commander; the people of the tribe are under no obligation to obey.
The space of the chieftanship is not the locus of power, and the "profile" of the
primitive chief in no way foreshadows that of a future despot.

Pierre Clastres, *Society Against the State*

I

Out of the French and Algonquian triumph over the Iroquois there evolved
during the eighteenth century a Janus-faced alliance. Facing east, the
French appeared at the head of an Algonquian host. This was the alliance
armed and breathing fire in the service of imperial France, the alliance that
cowed the Iroquois and repeatedly fought the far more numerous British to a
standstill. This eastern face of the alliance is too often the only one that
appears in histories of the eighteenth century, but by itself it is incomplete
and inscrutable. To explain why Algonquian warriors responded when
Onontio summoned them, it is necessary to examine the other face of the
alliance. Facing west, Onontio and his chiefs – French and Algonquian –
ideally carried the calumet, not the hatchet. They sought to cover the dead,
not to avenge them. Onontio was a benefactor. He mediated the quarrels of
his Algonquian children. He supplied their needs with presents and trade.
Only when faced with disobedient children did Onontio appear armed and
angry. Accompanied by his other children, he came to scourge those who
embrouillent la terre (embroil the land); but even here his only goal was to
reimpose the peace that allowed his children to hunt, to farm, and, in the
ritual language of the councils, to smoke peaceably on their mats. In real
political terms, this peace initially eased the movement of the Algonquians
into lands emptied by the Iroquois wars of the seventeenth century.

These are, of course, theatrical images, simplifications of a more tangled
reality. Algonquians did not fight simply from loyalty to their father; the
French sought more in the West than an arena in which to exercise their
patriarchal benevolence. Moreover, the faces connected. Between them –
their common mind, in a sense – was the middle ground where the politics of

the village and of the empire met. To understand the alliance, its neglected, nearly invisible western face must be taken seriously; only then can a fuller sense of events on the continent in the imperial age emerge. Not surprisingly, this benevolent western face of the alliance was not so much a reflection of French beneficence as it was a product of a tangled and bloody history.

The alliance, because it was largely Algonquian in form and spirit, demanded a father who mediated more often then he commanded, who forgave more often than he punished, and who gave more than he received. These demands frustrated the French even as they preserved Canada, and they longed for – and sporadically tried to create – an alliance that was a simple extension of the French state.

Events in 1701 gave a particular urgency to such French attempts to recast the alliance in a more conventional and far less expensive imperial mold. France, despite its victory over the Iroquois – indeed, because of it – was losing control of the *pays d'en haut*. The Algonquian world was breaking up and its members were spreading out over previously empty lands. Migrants avoided the still formidable Sioux and began to settle the lands to the east and south of the refugee centers – lands that promised a more secure agriculture and abundant game. These were not the prime beaver lands, for the best beaver were found north of the Wisconsin River, but then these were not a people dependent on beaver for trade. These migrations, the product of peace, eventually brought conflict among the migrants themselves and between Algonquians and Iroquois. They also brought the Algonquians increasingly into proximity to the English. Thus, the French attempt to reshape the alliance in 1701 arose from a desire to secure the fragile Iroquois peace and to prevent the defection of their allies.[1]

The alliance that the French desired received symbolic expression at the great conference of 1701 that ratified peace with the Iroquois following their defeat by the alliance. The expression was somewhat macabre because, quite literally, the new version of the alliance and chieftainship that the French presented to the Algonquians sprang from the corpses of the old chiefs. As Kondiaronk had told Governor de Callières in his opening speech at the conference, the allies had found their brothers dead along the rivers as they journeyed to Montreal, but they had made a bridge of these bodies to reach the city. "La maladie" had ravaged the Indian camps at Montreal that summer. According to La Potherie, the French, looking for benefit in the midst of disaster, took the epidemic as a sign of God's mercy since he allowed Indians to die where they might be baptized. Kondiaronk died at

---

[1] For a similar reinterpretation of the French alliance, see W. J. Eccles, "The Fur Trade and Eighteenth-Century Imperialism," *William and Mary Quarterly* 40 (July 1983): 341–62.

Montreal; Chichikatolo of the Miamis died on the way home. Onanghisse of the Potawatomis died sometime in the next year on a journey to the Illinois.[2]

The French seized on Kondiaronk's death to try to retrieve advantage from a conference that was on the verge of disaster. Astute, eloquent, and brave, he was both "of the prayer" (Christian) and of high status in his own society (he was Sastaretsy of the Huron-Petuns). Kondiaronk was Adario in the Baron de Lahontan's *Voyages* (1703) and thus the model for all the noble savages who followed him in European literature. At the time he died he was furious with French conduct at the treaty council, but the French honored Kondiaronk in death as if he had been a trusted agent of the state. In doing so, they tried to use his death to transform the nature of chieftainship.[3]

The French buried Kondiaronk in an elaborate ceremony in which representatives of an institution of the French state were paired with delegations of Indians representing a roughly parallel segment of Huron-Petun society. A French officer and sixty soldiers marched in front of the coffin, and sixteen Huron warriors, dressed in beaver robes and carrying guns, followed. Then came the French clergy and behind them six war leaders carrying the coffin which was covered with flowers and upon which rested a plumed hat, a sword, and a gorget. Kondiaronk's relatives followed behind the coffin accompanied by the Ottawa and Huron-Petun chiefs. Finally, Mmme. de Champigny, who was the wife of the intendant; M. de Vaudreuil, then governor of Montreal; other French dignitaries; and the entire officer corps closed the procession. At the grave the soldiers and the war leaders fired a salute. The French marked Kondiaronk's resting place with an inscription that read: *Cy git le Rat, Chef des Hurons* ("Here lies the Muskrat, Chief of the Hurons").[4]

[2] Nicolas Perrot, *Memoir on the Manners, Customs, and Religion of the Savages of North America*, in Emma Helen Blair (ed.), *The Indian Tribes of the Upper Mississippi Valley and Region of the Great Lakes*, 2 vols. (Cleveland: Arthur H. Clark, 1912), 115.

[3] For sickness at Montreal, see Claude Charles Le Roy, Sieur de Bacqueville de la Potherie, *Histoire de l'Amerique septentrionale . . .* (Paris: J-L Nion & F. Didot, 1722, microcard, Lost Cause Press, Louisville, 1967), 4:202, 209, 232, 228–29, 239, 262. For Onanghisse, see Parolles des Kiskakons, Sakis, Poux, and Puants, 23 juillet 1702, AN, C11A, v. 8, f. 312.

Kondiaronk at the time of his death felt betrayed by the French failure to compel the Iroquois to return Algonquian prisoners, and he was threatening to disavow the peace. His death was thus tactically fortunate for the French, but his loss was nevertheless dismaying. For Kondiaronk's opposition to peace without the restoration of prisoners, see La Potherie, *Histoire*, 4:205–6, 221–26; for description, see *ibid.* 4:221, 228–29. The demands for the return of the prisoners made by Joncaire and Father Bruyas were apparently undercut by Callières and his emissary M. de Maricourt. See Le Roy de la Potherie à Comte de Pontchartrain, n.d. AN, F3, Moreau-St. Mery, v. 2, f. 378; see also Instruction pour le P. Bruyas . . . 15 juin 1701, AN, F3, Moreau-St. Mery, v. 8, f. 260.

For Adario, see Reuben Gold Thwaites (ed.), *New Voyage to North America by the Baron de Lahontan*, 2 vols. (Chicago: A. C. McClurg, 1905), 2:517–618.

[4] La Potherie, *Histoire*, 4:234–35. I would like to thank Jim Clifton, who may not agree with this particular interpretation, for pointing out to me the significance of Kondiaronk's funeral.

The French used the dead Kondiaronk to demonstrate what a chief should be. By equating Kondiaronk in death with French rulers and institutions, the French envisioned chiefs who would command and thus reject consensual politics and noncoercive power. The chiefs would become the governors of petty principalities and agents of the French state.

From the Grand Settlement of 1701 until the demise of French Canada there would persist an unresolved tension between the Algonquian ideal of alliance and mediation and the French dream of force and obedience. These dual agendas, which underlay the controversy that swirled around Le Pesant at Detroit in 1706, held the alliance in perpetual tension. The Algonquians had to compel Onontio to act as an Algonquian father or the *pays d'en haut* would be awash in blood as Onontio's children slaughtered each other. Onontio complied, for he needed to maintain Algonquian loyalty and at least the form of their participation in the defense of New France. The result was an odd imperialism where mediation succeeded and force failed, where colonizers gave gifts to the colonized and patriarchal metaphors were the heart of politics.

II

Algonquians clung stubbornly to their image of Onontio as a father mediating among his children, in large part because they needed his mediation badly. As the refugee centers dissolved, they were replaced in the early eighteenth century by a series of regional village blocs. In moving and scattering their settlements and in securing a more abundant subsistence base, most Algonquians had made their villages less vulnerable targets for disease. Epidemics continued to strike and losses were often heavy, but many of these peoples now recovered and replaced their dead. A population increase, albeit an uneven one, took place among virtually all the tribes who remained along the Great Lakes or west of them. For reasons that are not entirely clear, only the Illinois and the Miamis continued to decline. The Miamis fell dramatically in number; their total warrior strength dropped from 1,400 or 1,600 in 1718, to 600 or 700 in 1733, to about 550 in 1736. The once powerful Illinois confederation eventually courted oblivion. Whatever the cause of the different demographic patterns, the less highly organized peoples expanded in population while the more elaborate proto-chiefdoms of the large river valleys dwindled.[5]

---

[5] Jeanne Kay, "The Fur Trade and Native American Population Growth," *Ethnohistory* 31 (1984): 265–87; Emily J. Blasingham, "Depopulation of the Illinois Indians," *Ethnohistory* 3 (Summer 1986): 361–96. In 1718 the Miamis proper numbered about 400 warriors. Below them on the Wabash were five villages of people the French lumped under the name

These regional blocs, the subunits of the *pays d'en haut*, were flexible and shifting; they gained and lost members. Members of a single tribe were often scattered through several different blocs. In the early eighteenth century the first and most westerly bloc stretched from Saint Joseph and Chicago on lower Lake Michigan up through Milwaukee and Green Bay and then west to the Mississippi. Most of its members had once lived around Green Bay. The Sauks, Fox, Kickapoos, and Mascoutens maintained particularly close ties and intermarried extensively, but the bloc also encompassed the Winnebagos, Menominees, and the more westerly Potawatomi villages.

The second regional grouping centered on the Illinois country and was made up of the Illinois confederation. The abandonment of Starved Rock, the great refugee center of the Illinois country, proved temporary for some Peorias eventually returned to settle there, but the major Peoria settlement remained at Pimitoui. The Kaskaskias and other members of the confederation gradually concentrated in the area where the Kaskaskia River met the Mississippi. The Shawnees had by now left the Illinois country entirely to seek Iroquois and English protection east of the Appalachians, but for a brief period members of the Miami confederation maintained a marginal membership in this bloc. The Miamis, however, gradually moved east to Saint Joseph and Detroit before settling the Maumee and the Wabash region.[6]

The eastward movement of the Miamis brought some of them temporarily into the third, and most volatile, regional bloc – the one that centered on Detroit. In 1701, Antoine Laumet de La Mothe, Sieur de Cadillac, had induced part of the Ottawas and most of the Huron-Petuns to his new settlement at Detroit. Eventually some Potawatomis, Miamis, and other groups also congregated there. To the east of Detroit, and loosely associated with it, were villages formed by some of the proto-Ojibwa bands who now became the Mississaugas of northern Lake Erie and Lake Ontario.[7]

Ouiatenons and the English called the Weas, but who were actually the remaining tribes of the confederation: the Weas proper, the Piankashaws, Pepikokias, Kilatikas, and Megakonias. Together they mustered an additional 1,000 to 1,200 warriors. Because there had been a major smallpox epidemic in 1715 these figures were certainly larger before 1715. Sabrevois, Memoir on the Savages, 1718, *WHC* 16:375–76; Ramezay to Minister, Nov. 3, 1715, *WHC* 16:322–24. Smallpox struck again in 1732–1733. In 1733 the number of warriors belonging to the five tribes on the Wabash had declined to 600 to 700, and by 1736 was down to 350. For 1733 figures, see Vincennes à ?, mars 1733, AN, C13A, v. 17, f. 259. For 1736, see Census of Indian Tribes, *WHC* 17:250.

6 Blasingham, "Depopulation of the Illinois," 193–224, 361–413, and Wayne C. Temple, *Indian Villages of the Illinois Country: Historic Tribes*, Scientific Papers, Illinois State Museum, vol. 2, pt. 2 (Springfield, Ill.: Illinois State Museum, 1958).

7 For Ottawa movements and divisions, see Speech of Miscouaky, 26 Sept. 1706, *MPHC* 33:288; Report of Detroit in 1703, *MPHC* 33:162–63; Marest to Vaudreuil, 4 June 1708, *MPHC* 33:383–86; Marest to Vaudreuil, June 21, 1712, *WHC* 16:290–91. For general

The fourth regional grouping centered on Michilimackinac and included the Chippewa village at Sault Sainte Marie and the Ottawa village on Manitoulin Island. The Chippewas, like the Mississaugas, arose out of the proto-Ojibwa bands of whom the Saulteurs had been the most prominent. The French continued to refer to all the Chippewa bands of Lake Superior as Saulteurs, but by the early eighteenth century differences were forming between the Chippewas of Chequamegon and Keweenaw on western Lake Superior and the Saulteurs proper at Sault Sainte Marie. Increasingly the western Chippewas emerged as a separate group. The Saulteurs meanwhile became closely linked with the Ottawas of Michilimackinac. Together, the two groups eventually colonized Saginaw Bay and the Ottawas themselves gradually shifted west onto the shores and islands of northern Lake Michigan. By the 1740s the villages of the old Michilimackinac Ottawas centered on Arbre Croche on Little Traverse Bay.[8]

Increased intermarriage between the Ottawas and Chippewas around Michilimackinac and the movement west of the Chippewas of Chequamegon created a fifth regional grouping, composed of the Chippewa of western Lake Superior. First the alliance of these people with the Sioux against most other Algonquians, and, later, warfare between the Chippewas and the Sioux made the upper Mississippi an area of chronic conflict in the late seventeenth century and the eighteenth.

The final regional grouping, and the last to clearly emerge, was in the Ohio Valley. This region, which will be treated in much greater detail later, included the lands from Lake Erie south to the Ohio and the Appalachians and west to the Wabash. The members of this bloc eventually included migrants from virtually all the other blocs as well as new migrants from outside the *pays d'en haut*. Members of the Miami confederation moved into it from the north, as did, eventually, the Kickapoos and Mascoutens. A splinter group of Huron-Petuns who proclaimed themselves the Wyandots settled at Sandusky and a few Ottawas also moved south of Lake Erie. From the northeast came various Iroquois who became known as the Mingos. From Pennsylvania the Shawnees, the Delawares, and various smaller refugee groups moved first to the Allegheny and then deeper into the region.

Within a bloc, the normal mechanisms of village politics could often preserve the peace without recourse to Onontio. This was the realm of politics that Father Charlevoix later found so puzzling and impressive. It might, Charlevoix thought, seem that nations "who may be said to possess nothing, neither public nor private, and who have no ambition to extend their territory, should, in appearance, have few affairs to settle with one another."

---

account of movements, see *HBNI*, 15:772–74.

[8] For Chippewas, see Harold Hickerson, *The Chippewa and Their Neighbors: A Study in Ethnohistory* (New York: Holt, Rinehart and Winston, 1970).

Yet the Indians were "eternally negotiating." They always "had some affairs or other on the tapis such as the concluding or renewing of treaties, offers of service, mutual civilities, making alliances, invitations to become parties in a war, and lastly, compliments of condolence on the death of some chief or considerable person."[9]

But the politics that worked within a block weakened outside of it. As the migration continued and members of different blocs came into contact, disputes, hostility, and conflict arose. Without Onontio to mediate, the result was often war. The violence largely occurred along the borders of regional groupings: beside the upper Mississippi, at Detroit, and along the northern edges of the Illinois country. These were the fault lines of the *pays d'en haut*. Even before the end of the Iroquois wars, Algonquian-Sioux warfare had resumed along the Mississippi. In northern Illinois the Fox and their allies moving out of Green Bay came into conflict with members of the Illinois confederation. At Detroit Cadillac's attempts to attract disparate groups to the region led to constant friction.

French withdrawal from the *pays d'en haut* had created a vacuum that the Algonquians lacked the resources to fill. Mediation, given the nature of Algonquian politics, was expensive and time-consuming. Only the French possessed the wealth, the contacts across the entire *pays d'en haut*, and the incentive to undertake mediation on a large scale. No Algonquian group could take their place. Conflicts were well underway by the peace conference of 1701, and they made even that year's ceremonies of the alliance seem only gilding over a deep rot. The Sioux and their allies, the western Chippewas of Chequamegon, were at war with virtually all of the other tribes of the *pays d'en haut*. This fighting against the Sioux should not have directly affected the French since they had supposedly withdrawn from the region, but, in fact, coureurs de bois and others still moved over the western lakes, and many Frenchmen such as Pierre Charles Le Sueur sought the Sioux country where rich pelts could be obtained for few goods. These men brought arms to the Sioux. To stop this traffic, Algonquians once more murdered and pillaged Frenchmen in the upper country.[10]

The French governors condemned both the trade and the attacks, but they proved incapable of stopping either. Of the western villagers who arrived in Montreal that year, the Miamis, Fox, Illinois, Sauks, Potawatomis, and Mascoutens had recently either attempted or succeeded in murdering

---

[9] Pierre de Charlevoix, *Journal of a Voyage to North America* (London: R. & J. Dodsley, 1761), 2:27.

[10] For French worry over these wars, see Relation de cequi s'est passé en Canada . . . de l'anneé 1694 jusqu'au mois de nov. 1695, AN, F3, Moreau-St. Mery, v. 7, f. 342; Relation de cequi s'est passé en Canada . . . de l'anneé 1696 jusqu'au mois d'oct. 1697, AN, F3, v. 8, f. 1–5.

and pillaging Frenchmen. They expressed regret, and Governor de Callières negotiated a peace between the Fox and Saulteurs, but the peace was as fleeting as the regret. There were no more Perrots to work for *bonnes affaires*. The Algonquians lamented the absence of French chiefs over much of the *pays d'en haut* and the failure of those chiefs present at Detroit to mediate their quarrels. As one of the rare Menominee envoys from that region during these years told Vaudreuil, everyone disobeyed Onontio and waged war against each other. This isolation and warfare was a constant cause for distress among most of the Algonquians of the far west. The Potawatomis of Saint Joseph responded to the turmoil that followed the crisis of 1706 at Detroit by asking for a return of licensed traders, a garrison, and a French commander. By 1712 the Peorias recalled the days of Tonti and Fort Saint Louis as a golden age of peace and plenty and contrasted it with the violence and deprivation of their present condition. The Weas, too, asked for French officers and missionaries.[11]

In seeking to escape the burdens of village politics, the French found that refusing to mediate quarrels often meant participation in them. It was a hard lesson to accept, and the French had to learn it repeatedly at a great cost to both the Algonquians and themselves. Their teachers were often the Fox, and the first lesson the Fox administered took place at Detroit.

III

The Fox wars provided the basic primer for alliance politics. They told a cautionary tale to French and Algonquian alike. From them all involved could draw a catalog of mistakes and the failures of chieftainship that, if uncorrected, would destroy the alliance. Populated by fathers who failed in their patriarchal duties and chiefs who failed to mediate, the Fox wars demonstrated how fragile the whole structure of alliance was.

The Fox wars began in the lands around Detroit. During most of the first

---

[11] For attempts to negotiate peace in the upper country, see La Potherie, *Histoire*, 4:215–16, 255; Callières to Minister, 16 Oct. 1700, *NYCD* 9:713; Callières au Ministre, 4 oct. 1701, AN, C11A, v. 19; Aveneau to Cadillac, June 4, 1702, *MPHC* 33:123; Callières & Beauharnois au Ministre, 3 nov. 1702, AN, C11A, v. 20; Conferences of Indian Envoys, Sept. 27, 1703, *WHC* 16:221–27. For attacks on Frenchmen, see Report on Detroit in 1703, *MPHC* 33:173–76; Parolles, 5 juillet 1702, AN, Moreau St. Mery, F3, v. 8. For Vaudreuil's condoning the war, see 19 oct. 1705, *RAPQ*, 1938–39,92. For later conflicts, Vaudreuil & Raudot au Ministre, 2 nov. 1710, *RAPQ*, 1946–47, 390; Vaudreuil au Ministre, 3 nov. 1710, *ibid.*, 396; Memoir of De la Forest, July 14, 1711, *MPHC* 33:512. For the Menominee speech, see Parolles des folles avoines, 23 juillet 1708, AN, C11A, v. 28, f. 211. For Potawatomis, Chardon à M. de Vaudreuil, 6 mai 1708, AN, C11A, v. 28. For Peorias, see Parolles de Chachagouesse . . . 20 aoust 1712, AN, C11A, v. 33. For Weas, see Conseil, 11 jan. 1718; Vaudreuil, 12 Oct. 1717, AN, C11A, v. 124.

decade of the eighteenth century, Detroit was the only seat Onontio maintained in the West outside of the missions. Cadillac had persuaded Jerome Phelypeaux de Pontchartrain, the French minister of the marine, to allow him to occupy Detroit by arguing that the Algonquians he gathered there could intimidate the Iroquois into observing neutrality in case of future French wars with England. The settlement of Detroit in 1701, when coupled with the Sieur d'Iberville's newly founded colony of Louisiana in the south, would supposedly block English expansion.[12]

Detroit thus officially faced east toward the Iroquois and the English whom it was intended to confine. Cadillac at Detroit and Onontio at Quebec remained mediators, but they desired to mediate only disputes between their allies around Detroit and the Iroquois, not disputes among other Algonquian groups. During the War of the Spanish Succession, Governor de Vaudreuil repeatedly stressed that Iroquois neutrality was a sine qua non for the survival of Canada. Neutral, they blocked the invasion route from New York to New France. To keep the Five Nations neutral, Vaudreuil played on their fear of his western allies, while simultaneously defusing any actual violence that might drive the Iroquois into the arms of the English.[13]

This task demanded all of Vaudreuil's considerable talents. Although the peace of 1701 had ended open warfare, the failure of the Iroquois to return all their captives created a great deal of tension, and the Ottawas, Mississaugas, Nippisings, and Saulteurs increased the pressure by continuing to reoccupy lands north and south of Lake Erie and north of Lake Ontario from which they had previously been driven by the Iroquois. The issue in this region was not territory per se, but rather the right to trap beaver for trade. Virtually all Indians granted the right of hungry people to take game, including beaver, where they found it, but the furs became the property of those who had the primary hunting rights on the land. These rights the Iroquois claimed by conquest, but the Algonquians regarded the Iroquois as uninvited and unwelcome guests rather than as conquerors. As a

[12] Jean Delanglez summarized Cadillac's efforts at Detroit in a series of articles: "The Genesis and Building of Detroit," "Cadillac at Detroit," "Cadillac, Proprietor of Detroit," *Mid-America* 30 (1948): 75–104, 152–76, 233–56; 32 (1950): 155–88, 226–58. For plans of D'Iberville, see Mémoire de D'Iberville, 20 juin 1702, in Pierre Margry, *Découvertes et établissements des Français... de l'Amerique Septentrionale, 1614–1690*, 6 vols. (Paris: Maisonneuve et Cie, 1879, repr., New York, AMS, 1974), 4:593–607. For a critique by de Champigny, see Champigny Mémoire, 1702, AN, C13A, v. 1. For Detroit, see Mémoire adresse au Comte de Maurepas, Margry, *Découvertes*, 5:138–53; and Cadillac to Minister, Oct. 18, 1700, *MPHC* 33:96–101. For controversy over the wisdom of the Detroit settlement, see Louis XIV to Callières & Beauharnois, May 30, 1703, *NYCD* 9:742; and Vaudreuil to Pontchartrain, Nov. 14, 1703, *NYCD* 9:743–44.

[13] Yves Zoltvany, "The Problem of Western Policy under Philippe de Rigaud de Vaudreuil, 1703–25," *Rapport 1964 de la Société Historique du Canada*, 9–11, and Yves Zoltvany, *Philippe de Rigaud de Vaudreuil: Governor of New France, 1703–25* (Toronto: 1974), 46.

result, both groups murdered each other with alarming frequency and recklessly overhunted the beaver and other fur bearers in the contested area. Young beaver, which the French reported had earlier been routinely spared, now flooded the market. Apparently, Indian hunters acted on the theory that their rivals would take any animals that they left.[14]

Only Governor de Vaudreuil's repeated personal intervention prevented war. He covered the dead hunters and obtained compensation for Algonquian attacks. But his success was precarious. When the War of the Spanish Succession ended, the Iroquois were preparing to strike both Canada and the *pays d'en haut*. When, to counter this threat, Vaudreuil summoned his allies to Montreal to intimidate the Iroquois and, if necessary, to take up the hatchet, he discovered that years of neglect had reduced the western alliance to a shambles. The conference was an embarrassing failure. Only the fortuitous end of the war in Europe saved him. The French themselves would have to rediscover through experience that the alliance could not face east unless it simultaneously faced west.[15]

During the War of the Spanish Succession, Governor de Vaudreuil had allowed events in the West, even at Detroit itself, largely to take their own course, and the old alliance had predictably disintegrated. In 1706, just before fighting erupted between the Huron-Petuns, Miamis, and Ottawas, Le Pesant had confronted M. de Bourgmont, commanding at Detroit in Cadillac's absence, with a long list of dead. The French had promised mediation and had held back Ottawa war parties, but they had, in effect, done nothing. They were allowing the West to become the scene of bitter and festering conflicts.[16]

With Onontio failing to act as father, his chiefs – French and Algonquian – maneuvered for advantage. Only the Indians around Detroit and, to a lesser extent, those at Michilimackinac had reliable access to Onontio, and the French attempt to draw many different peoples to Detroit made it a

---

[14] For overhunting of beaver and nature of land dispute, see Mémoire que les Directeurs, 26 avril 1703, AN, C11A, v. 21, f. 132–43; La Potherie, *Historie*, 3:176–77, 4:179–81. For Iroquois position and tactic of ceding conquest to English, see Deed from the Five Nations, July 13, 1701, *NYCD* 4:908–09. For mediation, see Parolles . . . Teganisorenstles, 25 mai 1701, AN, Moreau St. Mery, F3, v. 8, f. 231–33; Paroles de Alleououye, 19 fev. 1702, Margry, *Découvertes*, 5:268–69; Vaudreuil to Pontchartrain, 16 Nov. 1704, *NYCD* 9:758–60; Vaudreuil & Beauharnois au Ministre, 17 nov. 1704, *RAPQ*, 1938–39, 54–55; Conference, Aug. 16, 1705, *NYCD* 9:767–69; Vaudreuil au Ministre, 19 oct. 1705, *RAPQ*, 1938–39, 93; Parolles des Outtauous de Michilmakina . . . 23 juillet 1708, AN, C11A, v. 28. For Seneca recognition of cost of war, see Peter Wraxall, *An Abridgment of the Indian Affairs* . . . , ed. Charles Howard McIlwain (Cambridge, Mass.: Harvard University Press, 1915), 73.

[15] For trouble at conference, see Vaudreuil to Pontchartrain, Nov. 6, 1712, *NYCD* 9:860. Zoltvany covers this in his first chapter of *Vaudreuil*.

[16] Conseil tenu au Fort Ponchartrain, 8 mars 1706, AN, F3, v. 2 Moreau-St. Mery, f. 378.

nexus of village and tribal rivalries, intrigues, and violence. With the French failure to mediate these disputes, the chiefs logically sought to use the French against their rivals. In this struggle, the Ottawas and Huron-Petuns, who were the first peoples to settle at Detroit, secured an initial advantage that they tried to maintain against later arrivals. The French were sucked into the maelstrom of rivalries both within villages and between villages. At Detroit by 1711 the conflicts of villages had begun to dominate the politics of empire.

The language of the alliance disguised artful manipulation. Cadillac had employed the Huron-Petun chief Michipichy (or Quarante Sols) as his prime agent in persuading Algonquian villagers to settle at Detroit. Cadillac assumed, of course, that he was controlling Michipichy, but by 1704, Governor de Vaudreuil was worried that their collaboration was "in contradiction with our invariable policy... of retaining the Indians in a sort of submission." Cadillac had placed negotiations critical to the entire imperial strategy in the hands of a leader of the Huron-Petuns, a nation that had for years maintained ties with the Iroquois, the very group the French had sought to intimidate in settling Detroit.[17]

Governor de Vaudreuil had good reason to worry. The interests Michipichy pursued were only incidentally French interests. Unknown to Cadillac, he carried on parallel negotiations with the Iroquois and, at one point, considered settling his people among them. By 1704 even his nominal submission was so slight that as speaker for the Detroit Indians, he called the governor a liar. He refused to allow Cadillac's wife to return to Montreal, fearing that it was a sign that the French were about to abandon the post. And in 1706 it was Michipichy who audaciously transformed Cadillac's request that the Miamis join a French-condoned attack on the Sioux into the message that gave French approval to the Huron-Petun–Miami attack on the Ottawas. These attacks began the negotiations over the fate of Le Pesant that forced the French back into operating on the actual middle ground instead of in a fantasy world of French domination.[18]

---

[17] For Vaudreuil's concerns, see Vaudreuil to Pontchartrain, 16 Nov. 1704, *NYCD* 9:760. For Michipichy's negotiations, see Parolles des sauvages, Hurons, 14 juillet 1703, AN, C11A, v. 21, f. 74; Mermet to Cadillac, Apr. 19, 1702, *MPHC* 33:118; Marest to Cadillac, 30 May 1702, *MPHC* 33:121–22; Vaudreuil to Pontchartrain, Oct. 14, 1703, *NYCD* 9:743–44. Mermet to Cadillac, Apr. 19, 1702, *MPHC* 33:118–19; Proposals Made by... Cornbury ... to Five Nations, July 15, 1702, *NYCD* 4:989; Proposals... by Farr Indians, July 10, 1702, *NYCD* 4:979. Many of Michipichy's actions sprang from Huron-Petun resentment of the Ottawas. The murder of Kondiaronk's son in 1696 had badly inflamed existing resentments. The French had anticipated trouble between the two groups. Champigny au Ministre, 18 aoust 1696, AN, C11A, v. 14, f. 182; Narrative of... Occurrences, 1695–96, *NYCD* 9:648; Vaudreuil to Minister, May 5, 1705, *MPHC* 33:242; Vaudreuil to Minister, 5 Nov. 1705, *MPHC* 33:242.

[18] For plans for movement to Iroquoia and problem of independence, see Vaudreuil to

Table 4.1. *Chiefs representing tribes at conferences with French or emissaries*

Group	1694–98	1699–1708	1701 conference
Fox	2	3	3
Huron-Petuns[a]	6	18	3
Illinois	—	4	4
Mascoutens	—	1	1
Menominees	1	2	1
Miamis (including Weas and Piankashaws)	3	13	3
Ottawas[a]	12	46	5
Potawatomis	3	5	2
Sauks	1	1	1
Chippewas (Amikwas, Saulteurs, and Mississaugas)	1	6	2
Winnebagos	—	1	1
Total:	29	100	26

[a] The Ottawas and Huron-Petuns combined made up 62 percent of the representatives during the period 1694–98 and 64 percent during 1699–1708. The figure rises to 76 percent during 1699–1708 if the 1701 conference is eliminated.
Sources: La Potherie, *Histoire*, and conferences recorded in AN, C11A, AN, F3, Moreau St. Mery, *MPHC*, *NYCD*, and Margry, *Découvertes*.

But the French movement was insufficient; indeed, the stronger the French made their connections with the Indians at Detroit, the weaker was their hold on other peoples of the *pays d'en haut*. While the old alliance had maintained its footing by incorporating a variety of Algonquian and French chiefs, during these critical early years of the century, relatively few Algonquian chiefs dominated the councils with Onontio and Cadillac. As Table 4.1 shows, the Ottawas and Huron-Petuns of Detroit and, to a lesser degree, of Michilimackinac monopolized contacts with the French. Even during the 1690s these two groups had been disproportionately represented

Minister, 5 May 1705, *MPHC* 33:242; D'Aigremont, Nov. 14, 1708, *MPHC* 33:447; Raudots au Minstre, 12 nov. 1708, AN, C11A, v. 28. For calling governor a liar, etc., see Conseil tenu au fort Pontchartrain ... 8 juin 1704, AN, F3, Moreau-St. Mery, v. 2, f. 378. For later Huron-Petun and Miami collaboration and plan for assault on Detroit, see Vaudreuil and Raudot to Pontchartrain, Nov. 14, 1708, *MPHC* 33:404; Report of D'Aigremont, Nov. 14, 1708, *MPHC* 33:436. Michipichy's solicitation of Miami aid against the Ottawas in 1706 was an attempt to get satisfaction from the Ottawas and probably to increase his own standing among the Petuns. Speech of Miscouaky, 26 Sept. 1706, *MPHC* 36:289; Report of D'Aigremont, Nov. 14, 1708, *MPHC* 33:433.

in the Montreal conferences, but then the Indians of the farther west had easy access to the French chiefs at the posts or to licensed traders in their villages. After 1700 the dominance of the Ottawas and Huron-Petuns was nearly total.

Quarrels between the Ottawas and the Huron-Petuns engulfed Detroit in 1706, but that fighting only foreshadowed a far greater cataclysm in 1712–13, when the French failed to defuse tensions resulting from the migration of more powerful outsiders – this time the Fox – to Detroit. The result was fighting on such a scale that the French mistook a clash between villagers for an imperial confrontation. As they had earlier in the controversy over Le Pesant, village politics overwhelmed imperial politics.[19]

The trouble began in 1710 when more than a thousand Fox along with their Kickapoo and Mascouten allies moved to Detroit at the invitation of Cadillac. From Detroit they hunted in southern Michigan, northern Indiana, and northern Illinois. They also opened, as had the Ottawas, Huron-Petuns, and Miamis before them, tentative diplomatic and trade negotiations with the Iroquois and the British. They did all this with an arrogance and ready violence that alarmed all the nations from Michilimackinac south to the Peorias. The Fox claimed (presumably on the basis of their residence in the area before the Iroquois wars) that they were the rightful masters of Detroit. Soon rival hunters were murdering each other in the woods.[20]

The situation, created by the French, demanded French mediation, but

[19] The Fox wars, which spanned a generation between 1710 and 1740, have long perplexed historians because they have insisted on seeing them as primarily wars between the French and the Fox rather than as intertribal wars that eventually became an imperial war by default. Having made these wars a conflict between the French and the Fox, historians have been forced to find a cause. So, despite Fox trade with the French since at least the 1660s, their voluntary movement to Detroit, and the willingness of their chiefs to have French posts among them, otherwise perceptive historians write of their "implacable resistance to French trading posts and military garrisons." Others talk of their fighting to protect "their trade monopoly," or their middleman role, when there is virtually no evidence for such a trade monopoly and not much more for an economic middleman role. Portraying the Fox as either premature Indian nationalists or as Indians with the mentality of French bourgeoisie eliminates the need to understand them in the more complicated context of alliance politics and Algonquian rivalries. In fact, peace, not war, with the Fox served French interests, and only when they despaired of their ability to mediate peace between the Fox and their neighbors did the French attempt a war of extermination. They would try to eliminate the Fox role in intertribal wars by eliminating the Fox. Here, too, they failed. For quotations, see James Axtell, *The Invasion Within: The Contest of Cultures in Colonial North America* (New York: Oxford University Press, 1985), 49, and Gary C. Anderson, *Kinsmen of Another Kind: Dakota-White Relations in the Upper Mississippi Valley, 1650–1862* (Lincoln: University of Nebraska Press, 1984), 40. The evidence against this view will be discussed below, but for Fox fighting with other tribes and their demands for renewal of later wars, see Canada, Guerre des Renards, AN, C11A, v. 50, f. 383.

[20] For invitation by Cadillac, see "Another Account," *WHC* 16:293. For Fox claims, see Dubuisson to Vaudreuil, 15 June 1712, *WHC* 16:268. The Wagenhaes, the generic Iroquois name for western Algonquians, who made an alliance with the Seneca in 1709 and who appeared at Onondaga to conclude an alliance with the Iroquois as a whole in 1710 were almost certainly Fox. In 1711 six "farr Indians from Tuchsakrondie" or Detroit appeared to

Governor de Vaudreuil was at the time understandably preoccupied with the danger of an Anglo-Iroquois invasion of Canada. Although he presciently warned the Fox not to provoke a conflict that might destroy them, he delegated the affair to the Detroit chiefs and to the temporary commander at Detroit, Joseph Guyon Dubuisson. Events rapidly escaped Dubuisson's control. The report this poor Frenchman submitted of what followed is full of mysterious comings and goings, British plots, fortuitous rescues, and the inexplicable failure of the Fox to undertake the attack about which they and the British had supposedly long conspired. It is a document written by a man who never understood what was going on around him.[21]

Dubuisson had gotten his conspirators wrong. The Fox were not conspiring to eliminate the French; instead, virtually all the Algonquians from the Peorias to the Ottawas of Michilimackinac had agreed to eliminate the Fox, Mascoutens, and Kickapoos from southern Michigan and surrounding areas. The other Detroit Indians and their allies not only refused to negotiate their differences with the Fox, but they prevented the French from doing so. It was they who managed to convince the French that the Fox were conspiring to destroy Detroit. The Algonquian roots of the fighting at Detroit are revealed in a remarkable speech delivered by Makisabe, a Potawatomi war leader and chief from Saint Joseph who, on the verge of death, spoke to Governor de Vaudreuil in Montreal in 1712. According to Makisabe, the originator of the plan to attack the Fox was Sakima, a much feared Michilimackinac Ottawa war leader and chief. He enlisted Makisabe who in turn enlisted his own people and the Miamis and the Peorias. During the fall and winter of 1711–12, the Potawatomis and Ottawas attacked the Mascoutens hunting along the headwaters of the Saint Joseph River, slaughtered the prisoners they took, and destroyed the village they found. In the early spring the Mascoutens fled toward Detroit pursued by a large force of Peorias, Potawatomis, Ottawas, and a scattering of other peoples.

The Mascoutens fled toward Detroit not only because their Fox allies

tell the English that they were mindful of their original agreement with the Iroquois in 1709. Since the Fox had settled at Detroit in 1710, it appears that all of the Wagenhaes negotiations were in fact with the Fox and their allies. For negotiations with the Iroquois and English, see Wraxall, *Indian Affairs*, 64, 70, 73, 74; Hunter to Lords of Trade, July 24, 1710, *NYCD* 5:168; Conference of Governor Hunter . . . Aug. 16, 1710, *NYCD* 5:221. Vaudreuil knew of these negotiations, Vaudreuil to Minister, 8 Sept. 1711, *MPHC* 33:532. For murders of and by Fox, see Words of De Vaudreuil, 1711, *MPHC* 33:504, 505. As the Potawatomi leader Makisabe said in 1712, excepting only himself, there had been a struggle of various peoples and their chiefs to be master at Detroit, Parolles de Makisabe, 17 aoust 1712, AN, C11A, v.33. For the Fox claim to be masters at Detroit, see Words of De Vaudreuil, 1711, *MPHC* 33:505.

21 Zoltvany, *Vaudreuil*, 108–9. Vaudreuil at this time had also to deal with the Chippewas, who were threatening to widen the fighting around Green Bay, and the Mississaugas and Potawatomis, who in separate incidents had murdered and cruelly mutilated Iroquois; see Vaudreuil & Raudot au Ministre, 2 nov. 1710, *RAPQ*, 1946–47, 391; Vaudreuil au Ministre, 3 nov. 1710, *RAPQ*, 1946–47, 397–98. For Vaudreuil's orders, see Memorandum of

were there but also because they expected the French to mediate the conflict. During the fighting that winter, they had already offered to submit the dispute to Dubuisson, but Makisabe and Sakima had refused. Sakima greatly feared that once the Mascoutens reached Detroit they would receive protection and mediation from the French. He said, according to Makisabe, that he would not hesitate to attack the French if they tried to protect the Mascoutens. He had no need to worry. At Detroit, Dubuisson had convinced himself that he was about to be attacked by the Fox whose behavior had grown increasingly more insulting and threatening as they suspected French complicity in the killing of their allies. If the Fox were, however, actually contemplating the attack on Detroit, they had a rather odd plan. The French numbered only thirty men and could not even man all the fortifications at a post whose palisades, in any case, were rotten and falling down. Nor could Dubuisson rely on the Ottawas and Huron-Petuns of Detroit for help. Most were still absent on their winter hunt. Instead of attacking, however, the Fox allowed Dubuisson to repair his fort and send desperate messages to the Huron-Petuns and Ottawas to come and rescue him. In the midst of all this, Makisabe arrived with the news that hundreds of Illinois, Ottawas, and Potawatomis, along with some Sauks, Menominees, and even a few Osages and Missouris, were on their way to "rescue" him from the Fox. Dubuisson regarded their arrival as "miraculous." Makisabe's and Sakima's warriors joined the returning Ottawas, Huron-Petuns, Saulteurs, and Mississaugas of Detroit in besieging the Fox and Mascoutens whom the bewildered Dubuisson was now convinced were the agents of a British plot.[22]

Vaudreuil for Sieur Dubuisson, Sept. 3, 1710, *MPHC* 33:485. De la Forest, an experienced officer, had been named as successor to Cadillac at Detroit, but quarrels with Cadillac over the terms of his possession of the post and business in Canada prevented his taking immediate command. Vaudreuil to Minister, 3 Sept. 1710, *MPHC* 33:480; Report from Vaudreuil, Nov. 7, 1711, *MPHC* 33:530–31, and Memorandum of De la Forest, July 14, 1711, *MPHC* 33:521. For warning to Fox and reliance on Ottawas and Huron-Petuns, see Words of Vaudreuil, 1711, *MPHC* 33:505–6. Vaudreuil considered the Iroquois more of a danger "than the whole of New England" and thus gave them the most attention, Vaudreuil to Minister, Sept. 8, 1711, *MPHC* 33:529–30, 535. The major French account of the fighting is the Report of Dubuisson, June 15, 1712, *WHC* 16:267–87. The most convincing account is Parolles de Makisabe, 17 aoust 1712, AN, C11A, v. 33; Francis Parkman noted long ago that the known events at Detroit are difficult to interpret as a Fox plot to attack the post. For his account, see Francis Parkman, *A Half Century of Conflict* (New York: Collier Books, 1962), 192–207.

22 Ironically, until Dubuisson's account arrived, the French seem to have made an accurate assessment of what was happening at Detroit. The first reports stressed fighting between the tribes, not an assault on the French; see Memorandum of M. De La Forest, July 14, 1711, *MPHC* 33:512 and Vaudreuil to Minister 7 Nov. 1711, *MPHC* 33:530. A later account, too, actually says that the Ottawas and Hurons conspired against the Fox. Account of Siege of Detroit, *WHC* 16:292–95. For presentation as Fox assault on Detroit, see Vaudreuil to Minister, 15 Oct. 1712, *MPHC* 33:570. After Makisabe's arrival, Vaudreuil seems to have

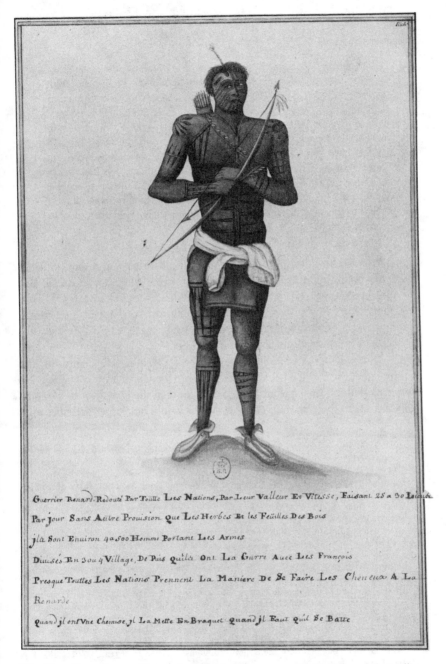

Guerrier Renard. Redouté Par Toutte Les Nations, Par Leur Valleur Et Vitesse, Faisant 25 a 30 lieües

Par Jour Sans Autre Prouision Que Les Herbes Et les Feüilles Des Bois

jlz Sont Enuiron 4 a 500 Homme Portant Les Armes

Diuisés En 3 ou 4 Village, De Puis Quilz Ont La Gurre Auec Les François

Presque Touttes Les Nations Prennent La Maniere De Se Faire Les Cheueux A La

Renarde

Quand jl ont Vne Chemise, jl La Mette En Braquet Quand jl Faut Quil Se Batte

The French caption testifies to the considerable respect the French and their allies
had for Fox military abilities. (Bibliothèque nationale, Paris)

During the bloody fighting that followed, the Fox repeatedly sought Dubuisson's intercession. Dubuisson himself described their attempts to gain mercy:

> Their messengers were their two great chiefs, one of peace, the other of war; the first named Allamima, and the other Pemoussa. With them were two great Mascouten chiefs, one Kuit, and the other Onabimaniston. Pemoussa was at the head of the three others, having a crown of wampum hung upon his head and many belts of wampum on his body, and hung over his shoulders. He was painted with green earth [a symbol of life], and supported by seven female slaves, who were also painted and covered with wampum. The three other chiefs had each a chichory [probably *chichikoué*, a small drum used by shamans] in their hands. All of them marched in order, singing and shouting with all their might to the song of the Chichories, calling all the devils [manitous] to their assistance, and to have pity on them.

They made Dubuisson the master of their lives. "Do not believe I am afraid to die," Pemoussa told him. "It is the life of our women, and our children, that I ask of you." Dubuisson, under pressure from Makisabe, Sakima, and the Huron-Petuns, refused them mercy. The French had passed from being mediators in the *pays d'en haut* to being a participant in internecine Algonquian warfare. When the carnage was over, nearly a thousand Fox and Mascoutens were dead or prisoners.[23]

In many ways, 1712 marked the nadir of the alliance. Confused and manipulated, the French became prisoners in a web of their own making. No longer mediators, they had become participants in the slaughter of a people who had asked their mediation. The victims would not forget their betrayal.

once more obtained some perspective on the affair, although he still also clung to the Fox conspiracy theory. For activities of Makisabe, see Parolles de Makisabe, 17 aoust 1712, AN, C11A, v. 33. Father Marest credited Sakima and Makisabe with planning the war while Vaudreuil made Sakima the leader. Marest to Vaudreuil, June 21, 1712, *WHC* 16:289 and Vaudreuil au Ministre, 6 nov. 1712, *RAPQ* 1948–49, 163. For Sakima, see Words of Ottawas, June 18, 1707, *MPHC* 33:320–21; Words of Ottawas, Sept. 24, 1707, *MPHC* 33:347; Marest to Vaudreuil, 4 June 1708, *MPHC* 33:384–85; Parolles des Outtauois ... 23 juillet 1708, AN, C11A, v. 28, f. 205–12; Parolles de Makisabe, 17 aoust 1712, AN, C11A, v. 33.; Report of Dubuisson, June 15, 1712, *WHC* 16:275. The Peorias were at this period eager to repair their relations with the French. They had been isolated since the shooting of Father Gravier, *JR* 66:265–95. The Osage and Missouris who were present must have come with the Illinois.

23 Another Account of the Siege of Detroit, *WHC* 16:293–95. Even in Dubuisson's account, it was the Indian leaders who controlled the fighting with the Fox and demanded their destruction. Father Marest said 800 Fox and Mascoutens died or were captured at Detroit and another 200 Mascoutens were killed in Sakima's and Makisabe's winter attack at the Grand River. See Marest to Vaudreuil, June 21, 1712, *WHC* 16:288–89. Dubuisson put the loss at Detroit alone at 1,000; see Report of Dubuisson, June 15, 1712, *WHC* 16:284. For speech, see *ibid.*, 281–82.

The surviving Fox, some of whom sought refuge among the Iroquois, and others who had remained at Green Bay along with their allies, took their vengeance across nearly the entire breadth of the *pays d'en haut*. Both Frenchmen and other Algonquians paid with their lives. The Fox attacks were only the most serious fissure in the alliance. The Miamis and Weas were at war with the Peorias, and the Saulteurs fought with the nations of Green Bay. The British granted themselves the most liberal possible interpretation of the Treaty of Utrecht, which, in ending the War of the Spanish Succession, had acknowledged British suzerainty over the Iroquois while opening the trade of the *pays d'en haut* to both Britain and France. The British used the disarray of the alliance to renew their attempts to lure western Indians out of the French orbit.[24]

IV

The disaster at Detroit in 1712 had a dual legacy. It made the surviving Fox and their allies a dangerous menace to the French, but it also spurred a French attempt to restore the old alliance to the *pays d'en haut*. It pushed the political pendulum back toward mediation. After 1713 Governor de Vaudreuil recognized that the alliance had to face west as well as east and it could not do so without the old forts, regulated trade, and regular gifts being restored. His old allies, he reported, "were destroying one another, having no person in the place [Michilimackinac] to prevent their doing so."[25]

Vaudreuil needed, of course, to provide the court with a convincing rationale for reconstructing the expensive French presence in the West. Fox connections with the Iroquois provided such a rationale. The governor argued that the Fox were agents of the Iroquois just as the Iroquois were spurred on by the British. To subdue the Fox was thus to counter the British. It is not clear whether Governor de Vaudreuil really believed that the British were responsible for Fox actions, but he did not hesitate to use the Fox as evidence of the danger the British posed to the *pays d'en haut* and of the necessity of reestablishing a French presence in the region. Gradually, between 1712 and 1720, the *congés* were restored and posts occupied at Michilimackinac, Green Bay, Ouiatenon, Chequamegon, Saint Joseph, and

---

[24] For Fox attacks, fear of English and intertribal war, see Extracts, Ramezay and Begon to Minister, Sept. 13 and 16, 1715, *WHC* 16:320. De Louvigny, 26 oct. 1715, AN, C11A, v. 35, f. 355. Proceedings of Council of Marine, Dec. 2, 1721, *WHC* 16:397. For attempts to restore peace, see Vaudreuil to Minister, Sept. 6, 1712, *MPHC* 33:561–64; Vaudreuil to Council, 12 Oct. 1717, *MPHC* 33:592–93; Vaudreuil au Conseil, 30 oct. 1718, AN, C11A, v. 39. Louvigny au Conseil, 21 sept. 1717, AN, C11A, v. 38, f. 196–99; Memorial of De Louvigny to Council, Oct. 15, 1720, *WHC* 16:387–91.

[25] For quotation, see Vaudreuil to Pontchartrain, Nov. 6, 1712, *NYCD* 9:863.

Pimitoui; a French officer was also stationed at the Miamis. The government of Louisiana, for its part, established Fort Chartres near the mouth of the Kaskaskia River in 1720 among the Kaskaskias, Michigameas, Tamaroas, and French and later established a post at Vincennes, on the lower Wabash.[26]

But blocking any restoration of the alliance was the blood of the hundreds of dead Fox and Mascoutens that stained Algonquian and French hands. With vengeful Fox warriors striking all along the lakes, the Ottawas, Huron-Petuns, and Saulteurs demanded French cooperation in renewed attacks on the Fox. Vaudreuil, who was absent in France in 1714, later asserted that his invariable policy was to avoid Indian wars. He had always sought, he said, to "reunite the divided nations to the end of maintaining these people in unity," and Claude de Ramezay, who governed in his absence, hoped to obtain peace with the Fox without fighting. But the first stage of French mediation was a preparation for war, not peace. They tried to soothe a new escalation in the tensions between the Ottawas and Huron-Petuns. The Sieur de Vincennes mediated between the Miamis and Weas and the Peorias. French allies resolved their differences only to demand French aid against the Fox. The French launched an initial expedition against the Fox in 1715. It was a fiasco. In 1716 the Sieur de Louvigny, after mediating differences between the Saulteurs and those nations of Green Bay not allied with the Fox themselves, undertook a second expedition.[27]

---

[26] For use of English threat, see Vaudreuil to Duke of Orleans, Feb. 1716, NYCD 9:868; Mémoire, 1713, AN, C11A, v. 3, f. 363–65. Zoltvany, Vaudreuil, 137, 143–51. For allocation of congés, see Etat des conges, 9 nov. 1718, AN, C11A, v. 38. The congés now operated alongside a continuing system of trade concessions such as the one at Detroit, Conseil, dec. 1717, AN, C11A, v. 37. By 1715, there were 20 soldiers at Michilimackinac, 10 more were ready to go to the Illinois country, and 10 others destined for Detroit. Ramezay to Minister, Nov. 7, 1715, WHC 16:336. For officers among Miamis and Illinois, see Vaudreuil to Minister, Sept. 6, 1712, MPHC 33:561. For court approval, see Ministre à M. de Vaudreuil, 4 juillet 1713, RAPQ, 1948–49, 221; Ramezay to Minister, Sept. 18, 1711, WHC 16:301; Vaudreuil au Ministre, 16 sept. 1714, RAPQ, 1947–48, 266. For overall plan on posts, see Conseil, jan. 1718: Vaudreuil, 12 oct. 1717, AN, C11A, v. 124; for withdrawal of commander, Deliettes, from the post among the Illinois at Pimitoui, see Conseil, mars 1720, AN, C11A, v. 41, f. 98. He also requested, but failed to receive, missionaries; see Conseil, jan. 1718: Demande de missionarie, AN, C11A, v. 124. In 1717 there were 3 Jesuits at Michilimackinac. There were also 2 missions among the Illinois, and at least plans for a mission on the Wabash. Conseil, 16 fev. 1717, AN, C11A, v. 123, f. 366. For Chequamegon, see Vaudreuil to Council, Oct. 28, 1719, WHC 16:380. For Fort Chartres, see Blasingham, "Depopulation of the Illinois," 261. For post on lower Wabash, see Frances Krauskopf (ed.), Ouiatanon Documents (Indianapolis: Indiana Historical Society, 1955), 145.

[27] For Vaudreuil's claim, see Vaudreuil au Ministre, 25 oct. 1724, AN, C11A, v. 46. For importance of mediation in his activities in the West, see Conseil, 11 jan. 1718: Vaudreuil, 12 oct. 1717, AN, C11A, v. 124, f. 46. Vaudreuil rejected war for, among other reasons, being too expensive, Conseil, 28 mars 1716, AN, C11A, v. 123, f. 144. For earlier mediation, see Ramezay to Minister, Sept. 18, 1714, WHC 16:307; Ramezay & Begon to Minister, Sept. 13, 1715, WHC 16:313; Ramezay and Begon to Minister, Nov. 7, 1715, WHC 16:333–34; Vaudreuil & Begon au Ministre, 20 sept. 1714, RAPQ 1947–48, 279; Conseil,

Although Louvigny commanded an army, his intention in 1716 was "to try to make peace with the Fox," not to conquer them. A year earlier, in a series of brilliant reports to the court, he had examined the limits of French power in the West and the dangers involved in the use of military force. Compelled to resort to arms, Louvigny had organized a peace mission disguised as an army. His own allies were outraged when, after briefly besieging the major Fox village, he quickly negotiated a settlement and opened trade. Mediation in this instance disappointed his allies, but it also established French primacy in a manner military victory never could. Peace, however, was never final; it had constantly to be renewed, and in this case it was not even complete.[28]

The immediate objects of mediation and the major obstacles to peace among the Algonquians were the dead, who had to be covered, buried, and forgotten, and the captives. Prisoners had to be returned or acknowledged as having assumed a new identity among their captors. The peace Louvigny had established had not clearly settled the status of prisoners taken away from Detroit by the Peorias in 1711. And because the French had not mediated this issue, fighting soon broke out along the Illinois border. First the Mascoutens and Kickapoos and then the Fox renewed their war with the Peorias who, they claimed, had never returned the prisoners taken at Detroit as they had promised. The Peorias retaliated by torturing all the Fox they captured. In 1721, when Father Charlevoix visited Pimitoui, he entered past

---

9 avril 1717, AN, C11A, v. 123, f. 372. For Louvigny's efforts, see Louvigny au Ministre, 30 oct. 1715, AN, C11A, v. 35. For success among Illinois, Miamis, and Weas, see Conseil, jan. 1718: Vaudreuil, 12 oct. 1717, AN, C11A, v. 124. For Ramezay and Algonquian pressure to pursue war and intertribal conflicts, see Conseil, mai 1713, AN, C11A, v. 123, f. 14–15; Ramezay and Bégon to Minister, Nov. 7, 1715, WHC 16:329, 333. For extracts, see Ramezay and Bégon to Minister, Sept. 16, 1715, WHC 16:321.

[28] For Louvigny's criticisms of wars in the West, which he had already, in part, made verbally while in France, see Louvigny au Ministre, 9 sept. 1715, 20 oct. 1715, 30 oct. 1715, all in AN, C11A, v. 35. Nicolas Perrot, by now largely ignored, shared these criticisms; see Perrot, Memoir, 266–68. For decision to go to war and lack of enthusiasm, see Vaudreuil & Bégon au Ministre, 20 sept. 1714, RAPQ 1947–48, 279–80; Louvigny au Ministre, 26 oct. 1715, AN, C11A, v. 35; Ministre à Vaudreuil & Bégon, 8 mai 1714, RAPQ 1947–48, 255. For plans, see Ramezay & Bégon to Minister, Sept. 13 and 16, 1715, WHC 16:311–22. For disaster, see Ramezay to Minister, Nov. 3, 1715, WHC 16:322, Ramezay & Bégon to Minister, Nov. 7, 1715, WHC 16:327–28, Louvigny au Ministre, 26 oct. 1715, AN, C11A, v. 35. See also Zoltvany, De Vaudreuil, 140–42. For Louvigny's determination to secure peace, see Ramezay & Bégon to Minister, Nov. 7, 1715, WHC 16:328. For Council's desire for peace, see To Be Laid Before the Council of the Regency, Apr. 28, 1716, MPHC 33:573. For authorization of campaign, see Mémoire du Roi, 15 juin 1716, RAPQ 1947–48, 296–99. For campaign, see Vaudreuil to Council of Marine, Oct. 14, 1716, WHC 16:341–44, Louvigny au Conseil, 14 oct. 1716, AN, C11A, v. 36; for location of Fox village, see Wittry, "Bell Site," 3. For terms, see Louvigny au Conseil, 14 oct. 1716, AN, C11A, v. 36. The expenses for the 1715 and 1716 expeditions were 27,563 livres; see Expenses, in Bégon to Council, Nov. 10, 1721, WHC 15:400–7. For complaints see Charlevoix, Journal, 2:10–11.

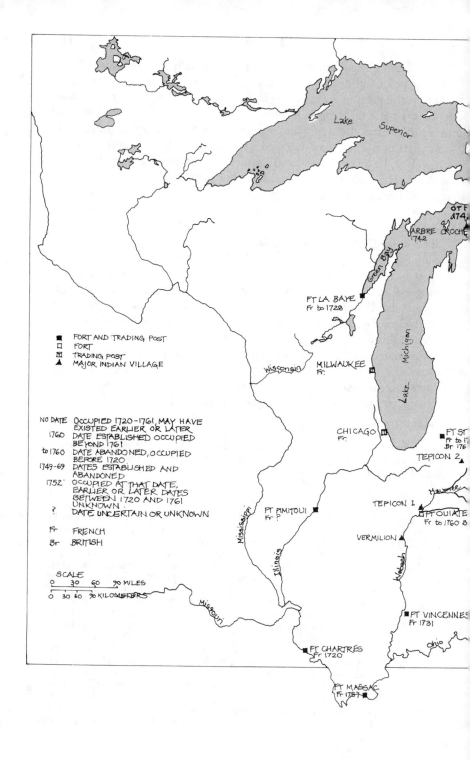

FORT AND TRADING POST
FORT
TRADING POST
MAJOR INDIAN VILLAGE

NO DATE OCCUPIED 1720-1761, MAY HAVE
    EXISTED EARLIER OR LATER
1760 DATE ESTABLISHED OCCUPIED
    BEYOND 1761
to 1760 DATE ABANDONED, OCCUPIED
    BEFORE 1720
1749-69 DATES ESTABLISHED AND
    ABANDONED
1752 OCCUPIED AT THAT DATE,
    EARLIER OR LATER DATES
    BETWEEN 1720 AND 1761
? UNKNOWN.
    DATE UNCERTAIN OR UNKNOWN

Fr FRENCH
Br BRITISH

SCALE
0 30 60 90 MILES
0 30 60 90 KILOMETERS

Lake Superior

OT F
474
ARBRE CROCHE
1742

FT LA BAYE
Fr to 1728

Green Bay

Lake Michigan

Wisconsin

MILWAUKEE
Fr.

CHICAGO
Fr.

FT ST
Fr to 17
Br 176

TEPICON 2

TEPICON 1

Maumee

FT OUIATE
Fr to 1760 B

VERMILION

Wabash

FT PIMITOUI
Fr ?

Mississippi

Illinois

Missouri

FT VINCENNES
Fr 1731

FT CHARTRES
Fr 1720

Ohio

FT MASSAC
Fr 1757

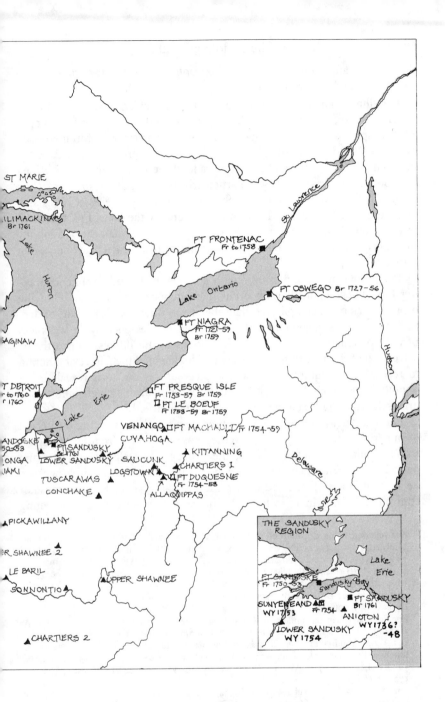

ST MARIE

ILIMACKINAC
Br 1761

Lake Huron

SAGINAW

FT DETROIT
r to 1760
r 1760

ANDOSKE
59-53
ONGA
IAMI

Lake Erie

FT SANDUSKY
Br 1761
LOWER SANDUSKY

TUSCARAWAS

CONCHAKE

PICKAWILLANY

R SHAWNEE 2

LE BARIL

SONNONTIO

CHARTIERS 2

FT FRONTENAC
Fr to 1758

Lake Ontario

FT OSWEGO Br 1727-56

FT NIAGRA
Fr 1721-59
Br 1759

Hudson

FT PRESQUE ISLE
Fr 1753-59 Br 1759

FT LE BOEUF
Fr 1753-59 Br 1759

VENANGO   FT MACHAULT Fr 1754-59
CUYAHOGA

KITTANNING

SAUCUNK   CHARTIERS 1
LOGSTOWN   FT DUQUESNE
                Fr 1754-58
ALLAQUIPPAS

UPPER SHAWNEE

Delaware

THE SANDUSKY REGION

Lake Erie

FT SANDOSKE
Fr 1750-63   Sandusky Bay

SUNYENEAND
WY 1753   FT 1754

FT SANDUSKY
Br 1761

ANIOTON
WY 1736?
-48

LOWER SANDUSKY
WY 1754

the charred and rotting bodies of Fox captives still hanging from the X-shaped scaffolds where they had died.[29]

The Illinois border became an open sore of the alliance because from the lower Wabash, north to the Illinois River, and then along the upper Mississippi hostile regional blocs of Algonquian villagers confronted each other while Louisiana and Canada competed for preeminence. At issue between the two colonies was the fur trade of the upper Mississippi. Along this border, it was no longer particularly meaningful to speak of "the French." There were Illinois French, who were now residents of Louisiana, and there were Canadians. Their interests were not the same. Fox attacks on traders from Illinois, far from hurting the Canadians, actually helped solidify their grasp on the beaver trade. Divisions among the French made mediation difficult.[30]

The French at the Illinois eventually accused the Canadians of encouraging Fox attacks upon them in order to monopolize the fur trade, but the problem was more complicated than this. Even when the Canadians undertook negotiations in good faith, their influence was lessened by the weakness of the Fox alliance chiefs and by the actions of the Illinois French themselves. The first stage of the Fox wars had highlighted the failure of Onontio to reconcile his children. The second stage of the Fox wars revealed that Onontio's mediation was useless without strong alliance chiefs, and this is precisely what the Fox and the Illinois French lacked.[31]

The slaughter at Detroit and isolation from the French during the period of imperial retrenchment had prevented any Fox leader from becoming an effective alliance chief. Ouachala, the principal Fox alliance chief of the period, was a man who by 1720 was ignored and distrusted precisely because he seemed "too well affected toward the French." He made no pretense of controlling events. In 1720 he told Governor de Vaudreuil that the young

[29] For renewed fighting, Vaudreuil to Council, Oct. 30, 1718, *WHC* 16:377; Vaudreuil au Ministre, 25 oct. 1724, AN, C11A, v. 46; Vaudreuil to Boisbriant, Aug. 17, 1724, *WHC* 16:442–44; Lignery to Boisbriant, Aug. 22, 1724, *WHC* 16:445; Villedoné to du Tisne, Oct. 4, 1724, *WHC* 16:448–49; Charlevoix, *Journal*, 2:198–202; Chassin to Father Bobé, 1 July 1722, *MPA* 2:276–77. For Sioux involvement, see Lettre de Bourgmont à MM. les Commissaires . . . 11 jan. 1724, Margry, *Découvertes*, 6:396–97.

[30] For Louisiana-Canada conflict, see Conseil, jan. 1718: Vaudreuil, 12 oct. 1717, AN, C11A, v. 124. W. J. Eccles, *Canadian Frontier* (Albuquerque: University of New Mexico Press, 1974), 148; Vaudreuil had to withdraw his commander, Deliettes, from the post among the Illinois at Pimitoui; Conseil, mars 1720, AN, C11A, v. 41, f. 98. For complaints, see Extrait, Vaudreuil, 4 nov. 1720, Margry, *Découvertes*, 6:510–11; Vaudreuil to Minister, Oct. 11, 1723, *WHC* 16:430.

[31] For charges against Canadians by Louisiana officials and denials, see Superior Council of Louisiana to General Directors of the Company of the Indies, Feb. 27, 1725, *MPA* 2:405–6; Vaudreuil to Minister, Oct. 11, 1723, *WHC* 16:433–37; Du Tisne to Vaudreuil, Jan. 14, 1725, *WHC* 16:451; Missionaries to Du Tisne, Jan. 10, 1725, *WHC* 16:456.

men had lost their senses, and he would be forced to abandon peace with the Illinois. He then participated in the great attack of the Fox and their allies that not only forced the Peorias to abandon the resettled village at Starved Rock but to leave Pimitoui as well. When, in 1722, he and other elders subsequently agreed not to permit further Fox attacks, he cautioned Vaudreuil that: "You know well that chiefs like us, although they may be well-disposed, are scarcely listened to." Later, in the mid 1720s, when the French renewed negotiations again, Ouachala privately told the French that without a missionary and an officer with a small garrison among the Fox – that is, French chiefs to assist him – he could not control the young men. Ultimately the Fox themselves split up into peace and war factions that by 1728 had physically separated from each other.[32]

The Peorias, too, were difficult to manage. They were in Louisiana and beyond Onontio's grasp. They considered themselves so completely removed from Canadian protection that in 1731 they petitioned the governor of New France to once more count them among his children. Necessarily the Peorias came to rely for protection on their ties with the other Illinois tribes and the French of the Illinois settlements. Their links with the French of Illinois were actual, not fictive, kinship ties. There was extensive intermarriage between the Christian Illinois and French voyageurs, soldiers, and habitants, particularly in the Kaskaskia region where French villages adjoined Illinois villages. Intermarriage involved the French in the quarrels of their kinspeople. This involvement might have provided an opportunity for mediation if the French, acting as fathers, reconciled their quarreling children. Instead the Illinois French, both military and civilian, sided with the Illinois against their enemies. They did not act as chiefs. When given Fox prisoners by the Illinois, the French did not send them back to their own villages as they should have if they wished to mediate a peace; instead they either burned the captives or broke their heads. They thus ensured Fox vengeance and reinforced the belief that the Louisiana French were a different people from the Canadian French who sought to end the war.[33]

[32] Vaudreuil to Council, Oct. 22, 1720, *WHC* 16:393. For quotation from Ouachala, see Speeches of Foxes, Sept. 6, 1722, *WHC* 16:420; Memoir, 1726, *WHC* 16:466; Memoir Concerning the Peace, *WHC* 3:148; Concerning the Foxes, 1727, *WHC* 17:4, 6. Du Tisne also contended that the chiefs were "not masters of their young men"; letter of Du Tisne, Jan. 14, 1725, *WHC* 16:450–51; and de Longueil complained of no authority in Fox villages, Reply of . . . De Longueil, 1726, *WHC* 3:166. Indeed, Ouachala could not stop the attacks; see Journal of D'Artaguiette, in Newton D. Mereness, *Travels, in the American Colonies* (New York: Macmillan, 1916), 77–82. For a speech by the Fox chief, 8ekina8e, disavowing the young men and stating his willingness to abandon the war faction, Parolle de 8ekina8e, n.d., AN, C11A, v. 49. The figure "8" in 8ekina8e is pronounced "dh." For Fox factions in 1728 and attacks by war faction, Extraits des lettres ecrites à Mons . . . Beauharnois, 1 & 14 juillet, AN, C11A, v. 50.

[33] For an otherwise excellent account of French villages in Louisiana that utterly ignores their

The inability of French and Algonquian chiefs to secure mediation meant that the chorus of ghosts demanding revenge, partially stilled by Louvigny, began to be heard once more. In 1724 a Michigamea chief named Jouachin delivered a long and moving recital of Illinois losses. The dead – French and Illinois; men, women, and children – were listed in almost Homeric cadences. Their names, the times and circumstances of their deaths, and the treachery of the Fox all remained fresh. New ghosts, too, called to the Fox. The chief among them was Minchilay, a nephew of Ouachala's and a relation of the Sauks'. His gruesome death at the torture stake had brought Fox, Sauks, Sioux, Winnebagos, Mascoutens, and Kickapoos into the field to avenge him.[34]

The French in Illinois accused Governor de Vaudreuil of doing nothing to stem this mounting toll of dead because the closing of the upper Mississippi to Illinois traders served Canadian interests. But Governor de Vaudreuil, in fact, attempted mediation until his death in 1725. He sincerely desired to avoid a war which would cause considerable expense and interrupt commerce. His successor, Governor de Beauharnois, persuaded that the British were at the root of the Fox attacks that had begun to take an increasing toll of Frenchmen, abandoned mediation and decided to launch an ultimately unsuccessful expedition under the Sieur de Lignery against the Fox in 1728. This attack marked a resort to force welcomed by the still numerous Algonquian enemies of the Fox. The Potawatomis, Illinois, Saulteurs, Huron-Petuns, and Ottawas eagerly cooperated with the French, and gradually virtually every other nation of the *pays d'en haut* enlisted in the war that would go on until 1739.[35]

connections with Indians, see Winstanley Briggs, "Le Pays des Illinois," *William and Mary Quarterly*, 3rd series, 47 (Jan. 1990): 30–56. Charlevoix, *Journal*, 2:221; Lignery to De Siette (*sic*), June 19, 1726, *WHC* 3:155–56. For Louisiana and Canadian French as different peoples, Chaumuer à M. Beauharnois, 17 juin 1730, AN, C11A, v. 52, f. 180–82; Letter of Dutisne, Jan. 14, 1725, *WHC* 16:451. For intermarriage, see discussion in Chapter 3 and also Mémoire concernant les Ilinois, 1732, AN, F3, v. 24, f. 235, which indicates the opportunities intermarriage created for conflict as well as cooperation. The Illinois apparently valued residence near the French because they realized that it would inevitably involve the French in their quarrels with their enemies; see Boullenger & Mercier au Ministre, 28 avril 1733, AN, C13A, v. 17. To be fair to the French, any failure to support the Illinois in these conflicts led to insults and attacks on the French; see Bienville au Ministre, 22 avril 1734, AN, C13A, v. 18, f. 142.

[34] Speech of Illinois, 1725, *WHC* 16:456–63. For Illinois position, see Missionaries to du Tisne, Jan. 10, 1725, *WHC* 16:453–55; Du Tisne to Vaudreuil, Jan. 14, 1725, *WHC* 16:450–51. For Minchilay's death, see Speeches of Fox, Sept. 6, 1722, *WHC* 16:418–22. For attacks, also see Vaudreuil to Minister Oct. 11, 1723, *WHC* 16:434; Journal of D'Artaguiette, in Mereness, *Travels in the American Colonies*, 71.

[35] The French believed they had secured peace with the Fox not only in 1716, but in 1719, Vaudreuil to Council, Oct. 28, 1719, *WHC* 16:380–81. In 1723 the Fox sought allies against the French, Fr. Aubrey to Vaudreuil, Oct. 3, 1723, *WHC* 16:431–32, but in 1724, the French were again confident of peace, De Lignery to Boisbriant, Aug. 23, 1724, *WHC*

Onontio depended on his "good children" to subdue the Fox, and his dependence increased when just to the south of Illinois, in Louisiana proper, the Natchez rose up and destroyed the French settled among them and then fled to the Chickasaws who were supported by British traders. The French now had a second conflict – the Chickasaw wars – on their hands, and this further increased their need for Algonquian warriors. And while these wars raged, the British overtures to the Algonquians – overtures the war was supposed to prevent – actually increased: first from Albany, then Oswego, and ultimately along the Ohio. French allies, and not the Fox, most actively pursued contacts with the British. By the 1720s Ottawas, Huron-Petuns, and Chippewas all had fairly regular contacts with the British at Albany and Oswego. The Miamis and Weas by the 1730s had diverted nearly all of their trade to Oswego or to British traders on the Ohio, and the Sieur de Vincennes feared that the French might lose their hold on the Wabash.[36]

Instead of overawing the loyal children of Onontio with French military

16:444–46. For Vaudreuil's position, see Vaudreuil au Ministre, 25 oct. 1724, AN, CiiA, v. 46; Memoir, 1726, WHC 16:463–68; Letter of Beauharnois, Oct. 1, 1726, WHC 3:159. As late as 1727, Beauharnois was confident of peace, Beauharnois to Minister, May 18, 1727, WHC 16:468–70. For continuing attacks, see Letter of Beauharnois, Oct. 1, 1726, WHC 3:160; Perier & De Chaise to the Directors, Apr. 22, 1727, MPA 2:539; letter of Du Tisne, Jan. 14, 1725, WHC 16:450–51; Beauharnois au Ministre, 25 sept. 1727, AN, CiiA, v. 49; Bearharnois (sic) to De Siette (sic), Aug. 20, 1727, WHC 3:163. The death of their chiefs in this letter apparently refers to Ouachala who had been seen as the leading advocate of peace and who does not appear in the records hereafter, Extrait d'une lettre de M. Mercie . . . 31 jan. 1728, AN, CiiA, v. 50, f. 308.

In opting for war, Beauharnois, as was customary, blamed the trouble on the English, but although by this time the Fox were, not surprisingly, negotiating with the Iroquois for refuge and an alliance, and anti-French belts may very well have been circulating, there is no evidence that the war, which followed years of tension, was due to English instigation. Beauharnois and DuPuy to Minister, Oct. 25, 1727, WHC 16:476–77; Guerre des Renards, 1728, AN, CiiA, v. 50, f. 383–86; Louis XV to Beauharnois and DuPuy, NYCD 9: 1004–5; Projet de Guerre (misdated 1737, actually, 1727), AN, CiiA, v. 67, f. 204–6; Reflexions sur la lettre de M. Perier . . . du 15 aoust 1729, Indian Documents, Chicago Historical Society. For de Lignery's attack, see Lignery to Beauharnois, Aug. 30, 1728, WHC 17:31–35. For report critical of de Lignery, Extraits, Beauharnois & D'Aigremont, 25 jan. 1729, AN, CiiA, v. 51, f. 446–49. For Algonquian support and solicitation of war, Guerre des Renards, 1728, AN, CiiA, v. 50, f. 383–86.

36 For the general background to the Chickasaw wars, see Richard White, *The Roots of Dependency: Subsistence, Environment, and Social Change among the Choctaws, Pawnees, and Navajos* (Lincoln: University of Nebraska Press, 1983), 52–61. For a brief summary, see Arrell Gibson, *The Chickasaws* (Norman: University of Oklahoma Press, 1971), 39–57. For war parties against Chickasaws and Fox, see Beauharnois and Hocquart to Minister, Oct. 1, 1732, WHC 17:161; Boishébert to Beauharnois, 24 July 1733, MPHC 34:108. For list of parties from one area, the Poste de Pianquichias, see AN, CiiA, v. 67, f. 212 ff.

For Oswego and trade with English, see Chapter 2; also Reponse au mémoire du Roy, 13 oct. 1735, AN, CiiA, v. 63. For fear of English capturing trade of *pays d'en haut*, Beauharnois and D'Aigremont au Ministre, 1 oct. 1728, AN, CiiA, v. 50, f. 27; also Projet pour s'opposer a l'agrandissement des Anglois en Canada . . . , 15 oct. 1729, AN, CiiA, v. 51.

power, the war with the Fox bred unrest. Although bitter enemies of the Fox and impatient at earlier restraint, the allies proved unpredictable once war with the Fox was declared. The greater the victories they and the French won, the more Algonquian enthusiasm dwindled. In 1730 the French and their allies trapped over a thousand Fox in the Illinois country. The Fox were attempting to flee to the Iroquois for refuge. In the ensuing slaughter somewhere between two hundred and three hundred Fox warriors died along with two hundred women and children. Another four hundred to five hundred women and children were taken prisoners and distributed among the victors. Governor de Beauharnois briefly thought he detected signs of a new order, "a submission and resignation to the will of the King" brought about by the fighting. He thought now that the absolute destruction of the Fox was possible, a destruction, he claimed, some of his allies desired. He had acceded to their demands; he would fight for genocide.[37]

Beauharnois should have looked more closely at the events surrounding the siege for they revealed the tangled demands of kinship politics and the difficulty of destroying the Fox. The French alliance had been restored in large part because the Fox posed a dual threat. Their attacks threatened other Algonquians, and their potential union with the British threatened the French. For years most Algonquians had urged forceful measures against the Fox while the French had pursued mediation. When the French finally undertook the forceful measures urged by their allies and embarked on a campaign of genocide against the Fox, however, the united front against that nation collapsed. The French now seemed a greater danger than the Fox.

[37] The French were not initially determined on genocide. They were still willing to make peace with the Fox following the failure of de Lignery, Guerre des Renards, 21 mars 1729, AN, C11A, v. 51. 405–7; Beauharnois to Minister, Aug. 17, 1729, WHC 17:65–66. The French apparently pressed the war from fear of appearing weak before allies who demanded that the Fox be subdued, Sauvages Renards, 1728, AN, C11A, v. 50, f. 402–3, De Noyan Memoir: War Against the Fox, 1731, WHC 17:121–22. Suggestions that the Renards be totally destroyed were made as early as 1727. The king, however, apparently did not approve the decision to destroy the Renards until 1732, Mémoire du Roy, 29 avril 1727, AN, C11A, v. 50, f. 368–70. King's Memoir, 1732, WHC 17:155. The French decision for extermination apparently arose from French successes in 1730 against the Fox. For new order, see Beauharnois & Hocquart au Ministre, 12 oct. 1731, AN, C11A, v. 54, f. 155. Orders "not to leave one of the race alive in the upper country," Beauharnois to Minister, July 1, 1733, WHC 17:183. For allies' desire to destroy Fox, see Canada, Guerre de Renards, AN, C11A, v. 50, f. 383. Beauharnois au Ministre, June 24, 1730, WHC 5:106–7; Beauharnois au Ministre, 23 mai 1731, AN, C11A, v. 54; Sur les sauvages, Renards, 1733, AN, C11A, v. 60, f. 436–38. Beauharnois to Minister, Oct. 10, 1731, WHC 17:148; (Detroit Indians) De Noyan Memoir, War against the Fox, 1731, WHC 17:121–22; (Michilimackinac Indians) Sauvages Renards, 1731, AN, C11A, v. 56. For disastrous defeat in Illinois of those Fox who sought refuge among the Iroquois, see Deschaillons to Beauharnois, Aug. 22, 1730, WHC 17:100–2; Beauharnois & Hocquart to Minister, Nov. 2, 1730, with Letter of De Villiers, WHC 17:109–18; Hocquart to Minister, Jan. 15, 1731, WHC 17:129–30 (best casualty figures); Illinois, Beauharnois to Minister, Oct. 10, 1731, WHC 17:148.

The Illinois, the Huron-Petuns, and the mission Indians continued to pursue the war, but the Illinois grew increasingly fearful of the French and hostile toward them. Rumors spread among the Cahokias, Kaskaskias, and Michigameas that they would be the next French victims. The French and their allies switched roles. Most Algonquians increasingly urged mediation while the French resorted to force. Faced with Onontio the avenger, the Algonquians demanded the return of Onontio the mediator.[38]

The Fox memory of this period, embodied in tales recorded more than a century later, captured a similar tension between the demands for mediation made by chiefs and the dangers presented by young men enamored of war, killing, and death. The tales about White-Robe, or Wâpasalya, a name that belongs to the Fox clan of the Fox, ascribe the disasters that befell the Fox to White-Robe's inability to curb his own taste for violence and death. Chiefs made distinctions between allies and enemies; for White-Robe all outsiders were enemies. Indeed, among other possible readings, the tales are texts on chieftainship and the consequences of its failure. White-Robe was a man who

---

[38] For sympathy of victorious Algonquians for Fox, see Sauvages Renards, 13 fev. 1731, AN, C11A, v. 56, f. 322; account of Sauks supplying them with food during the siege in Illinois, Victory over the Foxes, WHC 17:111–12. De Villiers reported that "our tribes were very anxious to spare the Renards lives," Letter of De Villiers, 1730, WHC 17:116. For redemption of captives, see Beauharnois to Minister, Oct. 15, 1732, WHC 17:167–68; Beauharnois to Minister, May 1, 1733, WHC 17:172. For belief that all French allies secretly wanted Fox to survive and aided them, see State of Canada in 1730, Noyan, MPHC 33:74, 82. For Sauks defending Fox, see Beauharnois & Hocquart to Minister, Nov. 11, 1733, WHC 17:188–91; Beauharnois to Minister, Oct. 5, 1734, WHC 17:200–4.
    The English encouraged the Senecas to grant the Fox refuge, but they did not instigate the request; see Minutes of Commissioners of Indian Affairs, Nov. 23, 1730, NYCD 5:912–13. The French by the early 1730s were seriously concerned with the loyalty of the Illinois, who had urged war on the Fox, and with that of the Wabash villagers. Mémoire concernant les Ilinois, AN, F3, v. 24, f. 235; Vincennes au Ministre, mars 1733, AN, C13A, v. 17, f. 259; Beauharnois au Maurepas, May 18, 1733, MPA 6:14–15; De Loubouey au Ministre, 20 mai 1733, AN, C13A, v. 17, f. 226; Bienville au Ministre, 22 avril 1734, AN, C13A, v. 18, f. 142. The French encouraged the Peorias to resettle Pimitoui in part to remove them from the French at the Illinois, king to Bienville, Feb. 2, 1732, MPA 3:555–56. For threat of revolt, see Les P. P. Boullenger and Mercier au Ministre, 25 aout, 1733, AN, C13A, v. 17. For fear of Illinois, see St. Ange à?, n.d. 1733, AN, C13A, v. 17, f. 248. Les Peres Boullenger & Mercier au Ministre, 25 avril 1733, AN, C13A, v. 17. The defeat of the Fox allowed the Peoria and Cahokia to reoccupy Starved Rock and Pimitoui in 1733, Les P. P. Boullenger and Mercier au Ministre, 28 avril 1733, AN, C13A, v. 17. This movement and mediation along with the arrival of a strong garrison quieted the Illinois, Beauharnois and Hocquart au Ministre, 7 oct. 1734, AN, C11A, v. 61, f. 97; Bienville au Ministre, 22 avril 1734, AN, C13 AN, v. 18, f. 142.
    Mission Indians and Hurons continued to strike the Fox in 1731–32, Boishébert to Beauharnois, Feb. 28, 1732, WHC 17:148–52; For mission Indians' determination to continue war, see Canada, Sauvages Renards, 9 janvier 1736, AN, C11A, v. 66. For Illinois attacks, see Extrait d'une lettre ecritte par le Sr. Douville, 5 juillet 1731, AN, C11A, v. 54, f. 426. A later attack by Detroit Hurons, Potawatomis, and Ottawas turned into peace negotiations, Extrait de la lettre du Sr. de Boishébert...à M. le Marquis de Beauharnois, 7 nov. 1732, AN, C11A, v. 57, f. 345.

failed to act as a chief; instead of mediating and avoiding disputes, he provoked them; instead of preserving peace, he sought perpetual war; instead of protecting his people from misfortune, he nearly destroyed them. In one version he was the son of a great manitou sent to protect a Fox town, but instead he went to war and slayed people. He no longer heeded "what he had been told by his father." In both versions of the tale he was a man who, despite his status as chief, continually killed strangers who came into Fox villages, an absolute violation of the chief's duty to extend hospitality and protection.

White-Robe even killed the French when they came among the Fox. When he spared them, he did so only to use them as bait for others seeking revenge. In one story he sliced off the ears, noses, and hands of two prisoners and sent them back to their comrades. "A few more of you should come," he said to them. And when the French came against the Fox with their soldiers and allies, the Fox killed more. This is why the "Red-Earths [that is, the Fox] were assailed and encompassed about by all the nations."

In another version, the Fox had a great conjurer able to put enemies to sleep, and he did this, allowing the Fox to flee their camps. When overtaken, one group built a stockaded fort. From that fort, first the old men and then the young went out, and fewer and fewer returned each time. Finally White-Robe was no longer willing to fight; unknown to him, a Peoria had dreamed of his capture. "Let us be taken captive," he said. White-Robe broke the bows of his friends, who protested, telling him that he had caused the war and now he refused to fight.

The Peoria captured White-Robe and bound him. "Are you hungry, White-Robe," he was asked. "Yes," said the captive. First they sliced away the flesh of his thigh, roasted it, and fed it to him; and then they sliced and roasted the flesh of his calves; and then, all his flesh. And they burned his bones. When they were all burned up, an old Peoria said, " 'White-Robe, you shall burn together with your town.' 'Oh, no it is with your town that I shall burn,' the bones of White-Robe replied." And the terrified Peorias nearly clubbed the old man to death.[39]

The virtues of a war leader were not the virtues of a chief. Without true chiefs, the war leader's courage and cruelty in destroying enemies would also destroy his own people. Fox legend and memory, and indeed the actual history of the period, reveal the repeated failure to find chiefs who could check the White-Robes, who could cover the dead and reconcile the living. The Algonquian division of leadership so obvious in the division between

[39] William Jones, *Fox Texts: Publications of the American Ethnological Society* (Leiden: The Netherlands, 1907), 9–31. This summary represents a combination of the two texts.

war chiefs and civil chiefs became, to a great degree, immanent in the alliance itself. For violence by the alliance to be legitimate, it had to be directed outside. When other Algonquians ceased to define the Fox as outside, then Onontio should have stayed the violence. When he did not, he was no different from White-Robe.

The French attempt to maintain a policy of force after many of their allies once more sought to number the Fox within the alliance, condemned French officials to nearly a decade of frustration following the victory of 1730. The Fox, unlike enemies of the alliance outside the *pays d'en haut*, had relatives and friends among the French allies. These people always formed a latent pro-Fox faction. When the Fox were strong and aggressive, these factions were too weak to dominate their villages. For example, Wilamek, a leading chief of the Potawatomis, was the offspring of a marriage between a Sauk and a Fox, and he had, in turn, married among the Potawatomis. In 1712, arguing against an Ottawa chief from Michilimackinac, K8ta8iliboe, he had tried unsuccessfully to restore peace between the Fox, on the one hand, and the Potawatomis and French, on the other. With the outbreak of war, however, ties such as those of Wilamek did not vanish. The prevailing sentiment among warriors in a village might be anti-Fox, but pro-Fox warriors might war against them in the hopes of saving their own relatives. In the fighting of 1711, for example, while some warriors besieged the Fox, others rescued their relatives from the Fox fort. During the siege of 1730, some of the attackers brought the Fox food and water during lulls in the fighting.[40]

When military disaster weakened the Fox, those people linked to them by marriage could push their case more effectively. The French should have paid more attention to the Illinois who complained that the other Algonquians, instead of killing their Fox prisoners as the Illinois did, were keeping them as slaves. It was from these slaves that the very tribes that defeated the Fox in 1730 helped to reconstitute that nation. The French

[40] The figure "8" in "K8ta8iliboe" is pronounced "dh." For factionalism of villages, see Vaudreuil to Minister, Oct. 11, 1723, *WHC* 16:433–34; 398; Vaudreuil to Council, Oct. 22, 1720, *WHC* 16:393–94. For earlier attempts to use kinship ties to procure peace, see Villedonné to commandant at Kaskaskia, Oct. 4, 1724, *WHC* 16:446–47; Speech of Illinois, 1725, *WHC* 16:456–63. Kinship ties could also help promote war. The same faction of Sauks active in negotiations between the Fox and Illinois, because of their ties with the Illinois, was also willing to wage active war against the Fox, Vaudreuil to Minister, Oct. 11, 1722, *WHC* 16:433. For Wilamek, see Vaudreuil au Ministre, 6 nov. 1712, *RAPQ* 1948–49, 163; Vaudreuil au Ministre, 8 sept. 1713, *RAPQ*, 1948–49, 228–30; Conseil, may 1713, AN, C11A, v. 123. For ancestry and Vaudreuil's rejection of peace efforts, see Vaudreuil to Minister, 6 Sept. 1712, *MPHC* 33:560. Vaudreuil au Ministre, 15 sept. 1714, *RAPQ*, 1947–48, 266. For aid to Fox, see Beauharnois & Hocquart to Minister, Nov. 2, 1730, *WHC* 17:111–12.

were appalled to find that many of their allies had released the Fox prisoners and that the weakened Fox had obtained protection in the Sauk villages where they had many relations.[41]

In 1733 it briefly appeared that the Sauk chiefs and the French chief, the Sieur de Villiers, would be able to restore the Fox to the alliance. The Sieur de Villiers, with the cooperation of the Sauks, persuaded four Fox chiefs to go to Montreal to beg Onontio for mercy. The Fox chiefs, however, panicked on reaching Montreal and fled. Governor de Beauharnois ordered the Sieur de Villiers to return west and compel the Sauks to destroy the Fox. When Sieur de Villiers tried to force the removal of Fox refugees from a Sauk village, he not only died for his pains but gave France yet another Algonquian enemy. The Sauks had maintained far stronger ties with other villages of the *pays d'en haut* than had the Fox, and they could rightfully argue that they had incurred French enmity only because they tried to defend their relatives. French efforts to gather warriors to go against them foundered. The Ottawas, after originally demanding French aid in avenging both their own people and the French who had died with the Sieur de Villiers, refused to join the ultimately unsuccessful expedition of the Sieur de Noyelle's against the Sauk and Fox in 1734–35. They claimed they had never wished to eat the Sauks and Onontio should pardon them. Other tribes were no more helpful. The Kickapoos apparently purposefully misguided Noyelles in his attempts to find the Sauk and Fox.[42]

By 1737 it was the Algonquians who played mediator between the French and the Sauks and Fox. Ottawas, Potawatomis, Menominees, and Winnebagos all asked that the French grant the Sauks and Fox peace. The

[41] For complaint of Illinois, see Périer to Maurepas, March 25, 1731, *MPA* 4:72. De Villiers reported that "our tribes were very anxious to spare the Renards' lives," Letter of De Villiers, 1730, *WHC* 17:116. For redemption of captives, Beauharnois to Minister, Oct. 15, 1732, *WHC* 17:167–68; Beauharnois to Minister, May 1, 1733, *WHC* 17:172. For belief that all French allies secretly wanted Fox to survive and aided them, see State of Canada in 1730, Noyan, *MPHC* 33:74, 82.

[42] For Sauks defend Fox, see Beauharnois & Hocquart to Minister, Nov. 11, 1733, *WHC* 17:188–91; Beauharnois to Minister, Oct. 5, 1734, *WHC* 17:200–4. For union of Sauk and Fox, their overtures to the Illinois, and account of Villier's expedition, see Bienville au Ministre, 22 avril 1734, AN, C13A, v. 18, f. 142. On Noyelles, see Canada, Sur les sauvages: Renards & Sakis, AN, C11A, v. 63, f. 246–48; Beauharnois and Hocquart to King, Oct. 7, 1734, *WHC* 17:206–12; Bienville and Salmon au Ministre, 16 mai 1735, AN, C13A, v. 20; Hocquart au Minister, 14 oct. 1735, AN, C11A, v. 63; Beauharnois and Hocquart to Minister, Oct. 16, 1736, *WHC* 17:254–59; and, particularly, Canada, Sauvages Renards, 9 jan. 1736, AN, C11A, v. 66, f. 143–54; Beauharnois to Minister, Oct. 9, 1735, *WHC* 17:216–20, and Relation of the Sieur de Noyelle, *WHC* 17:221–30. For Ottawas, see Beauharnois and Hocquart, Reply to King's Memorial, Oct. 7, 1734, *WHC* 17:206–13; Reponse au mémoire du roy, 1735, AN, C11A, v. 63 (f. 90); Beauharnois to Minister, Oct. 9, 1735, *WHC* 17:216–17; Sur les sauvages, Renards, janvier 1735, AN, C11A, v. 63, f. 03–06. For Kickapoos, see Relation of the Sieur de Noyelle, *WHC* 17:224.

French did so with reluctance and bitterness. As Governor de Beauharnois and Intendant Hocquart reported to the minister:

> You may imagine, Monseigneur, that the Savages have their policy as we have Ours, and that they are not greatly pleased at seeing a nation destroyed for Fear that their turn may come. They manifest Much ardor towards the French, and act quite differently. We have had Recent proof of this among the outawaois, who have begged for mercy for the Sakis, although they Had an interest in Avenging the death of their people and their great Chief.[43]

The alliance, with its mediation, its endless negotiations and ritual forms, and its need to recognize the policies of the villagers, was not an arrangement that the French had freely chosen. What Governor de Beauharnois called the "careful management" necessary to preserve the alliance was time-consuming, expensive, and frustrating for even experienced officials. It is no wonder that the French continued to yearn for a simpler world of force and dictation, a world where the French commanded and Indians obeyed. To officials or officers freshly arrived from France, the alliance seemed, as it did to Louis Antoine de Bougainville,

> an obligation . . . of being a slave to these Indians, of hearing them night and day in council and in private, when caprice takes hold of them, when a dream, or an excess of vapors and the constant objective of begging brandy or wine leads them on . . . an eternal little detail, petty and one of which Europe has no idea.[44]

The French always retained a hope of reducing their allies to subjects. Indulging in their own modification of the ritual language of that middle

[43] For Sauks desire rapprochement with the French, see Hocquart au Ministre, 8 oct. 1736, AN, C11A, v. 66; Beauharnois and Hocquart to Minister, Oct. 16, 1736, WHC 17:254–59. For peace, see Réponse au mémoire du Roy, 1737, AN, C11A, v. 67, f. 109; Beauharnois to Minister, Oct. 16, 1737, WHC 17:274–76 (here Beauharnois says the "position of Affairs did not permit me . . . to hesitate . . . to grant them what they Urgently asked" and tries to put the best face possible on it); see also Beauharnois au Ministre, 14 oct. 1738, AN, C11A, v. 69, f. 115; Canada: Sauvages, Renards & Sakis, 1738, AN, C11A, v. 70, f. 257; Canada: Sauvages, Renards & Sakis, 1739, AN, C11A, v. 72, f. 289. For quotation, see Beauharnois and Hocquart to Minister, Oct. 16, 1736, WHC 17:254–56; also Beauharnois au Ministre, 14 oct. 1738, AN, C11A, v. 69, f. 115. For other statements of Algonquian dissimulation and treachery, see Beauharnois au Ministre, 4 oct. 1738, AN, C11A, v. 69. It should be noted that the Fox, Winnebagos, and Sauks, despite their peace with the French, continued their war on the Illinois, Beauharnois to Minister, Oct. 12, 1739, WHC 17:317; Words of Puants to Sieur Marin, Nov. 17, 1738, WHC 17:318.

[44] For recognition of need for "menagement" but desire for force, see Beauharnois au Ministre, 17 sept. 1743, AN, C11A, v. 79, f. 113. For Bougainville, see Edward P. Hamilton (ed. and trans.), *Adventure in the Wilderness: The American Journals of Louis Antoine de Bougainville, 1756–60* (Norman: University of Oklahoma Press, 1964), 133. For example of longing to instill fear and respect, see Beauharnois and Hocquart to Maurepas, Oct. 1, 1731, NYCD 9:1030.

ground, Governor de Beauharnois and Intendant Hocquart complained in 1731 that Onontio's children were spoiled and would little by little have to be reduced to a proper obedience, inspired by fear and respect, rather than to a cooperation secured by negotiation and generosity. This, however, could be accomplished only temporarily or locally until the colony became more powerful or the king sent troops sufficient to overawe the Indians.[45]

Still officials sometimes tried. Beauharnois believed that the strong garrison dispatched to Fort Chartres in the Illinois country in the 1730s had made the Indians there "more submissive and docile." And in 1737 Intendant Hocquart urged a strong garrison at Detroit so that fear could supplement presents in controlling the Indians. The French desire to control the Algonquians by fear was, however, a chimera in the 1730s, 1740s, and 1750s. The French were formidable forest fighters, far more dangerous than the British, and the Algonquians certainly retained a healthy respect for French military prowess, but French soldiers did not cow them. In 1754 the Sieur de Lery, himself a proud and experienced soldier, watched as the Algonquians observed a large French force parade and maneuver at Detroit. Far from being impressed by the soldiers sent west to show the flag and intimidate Indians, the gathered Algonquians laughed at maneuvers they regarded as useless. As the Chickasaws – who defeated two armies sent against them by France – and Fox demonstrated, French armies did not always achieve victory. Defeated, the French lost status; victorious, they aroused Algonquian fears. As Governor de Beauharnois admitted, he lacked the necessary force to contain the Indians of the *pays d'en haut*, and he had to rely on foresight, good management, and dissimulation. Only in the 1750s did the French make a real attempt to fulfill their fantasies of domination, and the result was disaster.[46]

Over the course of their careers, most governors learned the paradox

[45] For an early complaint about presents, see Louis XIV to Frontenac, Mar. 25, 1699, *NYCD* 9:701. For later complaints and responses, see Maurepas à Hocquart, 8 may 1731, AN, C11A, v. 56; Beauharnois et Hocquart au Ministre, 15 oct. 1730, AN, C11A, v. 51, f. 33–36; Beahharnois & Hocquart au Ministre, 1 oct. 1731, AN, C11A, v. 54. Beauharnois reiterated the necessity to manage Indians since the French lacked the force to contain them in 1743, Beauharnois au Ministre, 17 sept. 1743, AN, C11A, v. 79.

[46] For quotation, see Beauharnois and Hocquart to Minister, Oct. 7, 1734, *WHC* 17:210–13; Hocquart to Minister, Oct. 7, 1737, *WHC* 17:265. Mediation and the old ritual forms still also covered murders between the French and the Algonquians, as when a Frenchman killed Corbeau, a Potawatomi chief, and the Saulteurs killed a Frenchman, Beauharnois au Ministre, 2 oct. 1740, AN, C11A, v. 74.

The Illinois were apparently not as overawed as Beauharnois thought since the Jesuits spread rumors of a conspiracy against the French involving the Sauks, Fox, Potawatomis, Miamis, Weas, Kickapoos, and some Illinois, Bienville au Minstere, 21 juin 1737, AN, C13A, v. 22. For the lack of necessary force, see Beauharnois au Ministre, 17 sept. 1743, AN, C11A, v. 79, f. 108. Journal de Joseph-Gaspard Chaussegros de Léry . . . 13 aoust 1754, *RAPQ* 1927–28, 400.

of power in the *pays d'en haut*. Beauharnois longed for a world in which French strength allowed him to dictate to his allies, but he increasingly realized that mediation and forgiveness were the best means for holding the alliance together. In 1734, after a fight between a Wea Indian and a young Frenchman had led to a brawl in which the Weas plundered the French traders at the Ouiatenon post, the French made what turned out to be an unnecessary show of force to settle the matter. Beauharnois thought the threat of force had a "very good Effect upon the nations which It has inspired with Dread." But Beauharnois's pleasure at intimidation did not blind him to the realities of alliance politics. He had pardoned the Weas because

> the peace we are since some time endeavoring to establish in the Upper countries, and the conditions of affairs required mild and moderate means to be preferred on an occasion involving neither the honor of the French nation nor the King's arms, and arising merely out of a simple fray between some drunken young Ouitanons and two or three Voyageurs, in an affair of trade.[47]

V

The Fox wars were the cautionary lesson; they showed what happened when chiefs failed and when Onontio used violence against his own children. The early eighteenth century, however, also produced more positive lessons. Unable to make force effective, the French and Algonquians gradually created a contested, but mutually intelligible, system of chieftainship and a structure to sustain the alliance.

The British provided the inducement for this reconstitution of the alliance and the eventual reabsorption of the Fox within it. The British had succeeded the Iroquois as the great danger for New France. The British came not in the guise of conquerors but as men bringing gifts and trade goods, giving a *bon marché* that the French could not match. The actual physical incursions of the British into the *pays d'en haut* after the Treaty of Utrecht, which ended the War of the Spanish Succession, were limited, but the French suspected the Iroquois of being their agents. And, by the mid 1720s, the British themselves were easily accessible at Oswego.[48]

---

[47] For first quotation, see Beauharnois and Hocquart to Minister, Oct. 7, 1734, *WHC* 17:210–13. For second quotation, see Beauharnois and Hocquart to Minister, 12 Oct. 1736, *NYCD* 9:1050–51.

[48] For English posts on the Ohio, see De Vaudreuil au Conseil, 14 oct. 1716, *RAPQ*, 1947–48, 330; Memoir on Louisiana, 1726, *MPA* 3:495–96. On Mississippi, see Ramezay & Bégon to Pontchartrain, Sept. 13, 1715, *NYCD* 9:931. For fear of English trade, see Ramezay and Begon, Nov. 7, 1715, *WHC* 16:331; Conseil, jan. 1718: De Vaudreuil, 12 oct. 1717, AN, C11A, v. 124.; Longueuil & Bégon au Ministre, 31 oct. 1725, AN, C11A, v. 47.

The French feared that the British would triumph by stripping Canada of its allies and leaving it defenseless. The survival of New France, therefore, made it necessary to accommodate allies who, if considerations of trade alone determined loyalty, would desert to the British. The French could not treat the Algonquians as subordinates; Onontio could not give them orders or ignore their wishes. The French often hoped that quarreling Algonquians could be separated and villagers quarantined from British influence by the simple expedient of moving Indians about the *pays d'en haut*. Such attempts rarely succeeded. Plans to move the Miamis and Weas out of the Wabash country and into Saint Joseph and Chicago between 1715 and 1722 failed. Nor could the French force the Saginaw Ottawas to return to Michilimackinac in 1717. In the late 1730s attempts to move the Huron-Petuns to Montreal, and the Shawnees to Detroit, collapsed. Unable to isolate Indians, the French had to mediate between them and keep them from the British by other methods. As Beauharnois argued in attempting to prevent the Crown from breaking promises he had made to the Weas and their neighbors: "The stratagems resorted to by the English to attract our Savages, compel me to use great circumspection toward them, and to Content them as much as I can." They "were kept in check solely by careful management, and . . . would seize the first pretext to break the word they have given me were I to fail to keep mine."[49]

---

[49] Even Vaudreuil succumbed to panic in the last years of his reign as governor. He saw the whole *pays d'en haut* as threatened and demanded extraordinary aid from France, Vaudreuil au Ministre, 22 mai 1725, AN, C11A, v. 47, f. 165–73. For French attempts to move the Weas to Chicago and, when that came to naught, to the Kankakee, see Ramezay to Minister, Nov. 3, 1715, *WHC* 16:326. For Miamis to St. Joseph, see Vaudreuil to Council, Oct. 28, 1719, *WHC* 16:383. By 1720 Vaudreuil, losing patience at their continued refusal, tried to coerce a relocation of the Miamis and Weas by threatening a trade embargo, Extrait du Mémoire de M . . . de Vaudreuil, 26 aout 1720, AN, C11A, v. 43, f. 158–60. The attempt blew up in his face. Forty or fifty Weas moved to the Kankakee, and about 100 Miami warriors and their families removed to St. Joseph. Most of the remaining Indians showed no sign of moving west. The Piankashaws, the single most numerous group on the Wabash, were determined to remain and French traders from the Illinois country had promised to supply them with goods. As for the Miamis, the large majority of that nation responded to the withdrawal of French traders by threatening to move east into Iroquoia where the English could easily supply them. By 1721, these Miamis were trading at Albany. In 1722, even the small group of Weas who had moved to the Kankakee returned to the Wabash. Vaudreuil abandoned further coercive measures against the various Miami villages. Vaudreuil to Boisbriant, Aug. 17, 1724, *WHC* 16:443; Vaudreuil to Council, Oct. 22, 1720 *WHC* 16:394–95; Vaudreuil au Conseil, 24 oct. 1722; AN, C11A, v. 44; Vaudreuil au Conseil, oct. 6, 1721, AN, C11A, v. 44. For Saginaw Ottawas, see A Talk with the Ottawas, June 24, 1717, *MPHC* 33:584–85. For French attempts to bring the Shawnees to Detroit and thus cut them off from the English, see Canada, Sauvages, 1733, AN, C11A, v. 60, f. 439; Beauharnois au Ministre, 18 oct. 1731, AN, C11A, v. 54; Paroles de . . . Beauharnois . . . aux Cha8anons, 1 aoust 1739, AN, C11A, v. 71, f. 54.; Canada sur les nations sauvages, 1741, AN, C11A, v. 76, f. 316–17. The figure "8" in Cha8anons is pronounced "dh."

For summary of attempt to move Huron-Petuns, see Canada, Sur les nations sauvages,

The careful management Beauharnois spoke of became institutionalized into a new system of alliance chiefs, medals, gifts, and mediation. Less a militant extension of French power than a forum for maintaining peace, the alliance blended Algonquian rituals, the kinship connections between villagers, and French goods into a potent force. The human center of this alliance were the chiefs, French and Algonquian; from them radiated the network of ties that bound Onontio to his children.

Creating alliance chiefs meant finding Algonquian leaders who could counter the rashness and violence of men like the Fox White-Robe or the Ottawa Sakima. It meant relying on French officers such as Louvigny and avoiding men like Dubuisson. Selecting such men became a complicated process that was neither fully French nor fully Algonquian. It was a process understandable only in terms of the middle ground. Each side had to understand what the other expected from an alliance chief. Unless both sides accepted a man as a chief, he could not act effectively or maintain his position. As a result, a French commander – that is, a French chief – and an Algonquian chief came to have similar profiles. The Sieur de Noyan's description of a successful commander as "always . . . true, pleasant, and firm, and above all generous" was essentially a description of an Algonquian chief. Like a chief, a commander ideally gave more than he received. At each post the commander saw to it that Indians regularly received small gifts of powder, ball, tobacco, and sometimes brandy. He had the post blacksmith repair their tools and weapons.[50]

If a French commander violated the standards of chieftainship, he risked the loss of his command. The Huron-Petuns and other villagers at Detroit, the Mississaugas along Lake Ontario, the Miamis, Weas, and Piankashaws all realized that both their position between the British and the French and the French need for assistance in the Fox wars gave them considerable

Hurons, 1742 AN, C11A, v. 78, f. 390. For mediation, reconciles Peorias and Saulteurs, Menominees, Nippisings, and Sauks after attack by former, see Beauharnois to Minister, Oct. 1, 1733, WHC 17:183–84; for mediates between mission Indians and Potawatomis, Ottawas of Saginaw, Peorias, Nippisings, Ottawas of Michilimackinac and Mississaugas, see Beauharnois au Minstre, 3 oct. 1737, AN, C11A, v. 67; for Potawatomis and Saginaw Ottawas, see Beauharnois to Minister, Oct. 9, 1735, WHC 17:221; Beauharnois au Ministre, 15 oct. 1736, AN, C11A, v. 65; for Saulteurs, Potawatomis, and Mascoutens, see Sauteux, Maskoutins, & Sonontoüans, Canada, Sauvages, 1738, AN, C11A, v. 70, f. 259. For between Illinois, Saulteurs, Menominees, Nippisings, and Sauks; Potawatomis and Ottawas, see Beauharnois au Minister, 11 oct. 1734, AN, C11A, v. 61, f. 314. For quotation, see Beauharnois to Minister, Sept. 5, 1742, WHC 17:410.

50 De Noyan's description did not mean he assented. He believed that Indians must learn to fear the French, and he yearned for French dictation; for quotation, see Noyan, State of Canada, 1730, MPHC 33:84; see also 77, 82. In contrast to the seventeenth century, the presents given officers were less than what they gave away, Beauharnois & Hocquart au Ministre, AN, C11A, v. 51. JR 65:207–09.

leverage within the alliance. The Detroit tribes had by the 1730s achieved what seemed a virtual veto over the appointment of the commander at Detroit. First Sabrevois in 1717 and then the aged and experienced Alphonse de Tonti in 1727 lost their positions at Detroit, in part because they had offended the resident Indians. In the case of Tonti, the Indians then conspired with other Frenchmen to remove him. Even a man as experienced as Tonti could not remain once he had ceased to please the nations among whom he had been sent. The most experienced officers agreed that "at the present juncture of affairs," a choice between a single officer and a nation as important as the Huron-Petuns was no choice at all. The Huron-Petuns and the Ottawas continued to exert such leverage throughout the 1730s.[51]

Onontio, of course, could exert similar veto power over Algonquian alliance chiefs, but like the Algonquians, he had to tread a fine line and use his power sparingly and adroitly. Even the domiciled Indians of the missions bridled at anything that smacked of French dictation to a free people. In 1757 the Indians at the mission of La Présentation were outraged that Onontio presumed to name a man unselected by themselves as a chief. And what outraged mission Indians could be an even more delicate subject among the allied peoples of the West. Although most western Algonquians eagerly sought medals, they believed Onontio only recognized chiefs; he did not make them. They, too, resisted any insinuation otherwise. There gradually developed an accepted procedure for guaranteeing the succession of alliance chiefs. In 1740, for example, the Ottawas de La Fourche relayed by their speaker the talk of Nagach8o, an alliance chief who had died while on an expedition against the Chickasaws. Nagach8o spoke from the grave:

> My father has always had pity on me during my life, and although I am
> dead, I am not entirely dead. I have left a second of myself at
> Michilimackinac before departing; he holds my place. This is my
> brother, Cabina. I hope that my father will have the same care of my
> younger brother that he had for me. I think that my brother will listen to
> the word of my father as I have always done.[52]

[51] For Mississauges, see Conseil, 30 mars 1716, AN, C11A, v. 123, f. 149. For complaints against Sabrevois, see A Talk with the Ottawas, and Talk of the Potawatomies, June 24, 1717, MPHC 33:584–86. For his removal, see Conseil, 28 avril 1716, AN, C11A, v. 123, f. 277/377. For leverage, see Vaudreuil to Council, 12 Oct. 1717, MPHC 33:590–93. For Tonti, see Letter of Tonti, Aug. 8, 1727, MPHC 34:46–48; Petition from Detroit Citizens, Oct. 21, 1726, MPHC 34:38–44; Beauharnois au Ministre, 25 sept. 1727, AN, C11A, v. 49; Ordre 1727, AN, C11A, v. 48, f. 122; Words of Huron, Aug. 9, 1727, MPHC 34:49–51. Intendant Du Puy protested the decision saying it was a serious matter to admit "the complaints of the savages against Frenchmen" and that Beauharnois had no authority to deprive Tonti of his post. Tonti's death rendered his position moot. Du Puy to Minister, Oct. 25, 1727, MPHC 34:59–61. On the Wabash by 1733, the Sr. de Vincennes reported that the members of the Miami confederation and the Illinois were more insolent than ever before, Vincennes à ?, mars 1733, AN, C13A, v. 17, f. 259.
[52] For naming of chiefs, see Hamilton (ed.), Adventure in the Wilderness, 102; Charlevoix,

The elders, in effect, were recognizing Cabina (who as the brother of Nagach8o was first in line to succeed him as head of his patrilineage) as the legitimate successor of Nagach8o. They used the dead Nagach8o to request a medal for Cabina. Leadership positions remained under Ottawa control. Just as La Fourche had named Nagach8o as his successor, so Nagach8o named Cabina and the elders recognized him. Beauharnois, too, however, had a role in legitimating this transfer of authority as was perfectly suitable when a chief was to act on the middle ground. Beauharnois followed the recommendation of the elders. He gave Cabina a medal.[53]

Medals were the visible mark of alliance chieftainship, and most Algonquian leaders welcomed the renewal in 1719 of the French practice of bestowing medals. When the French bestowed a medal on an Algonquian war leader, lineage head, or council chief, they agreed to recognize a man who had already attained status in his village as an intermediary between that village and the French. The French awarded such honors to men who "merit them by their essential services and their attachment to religion," but the French also recognized, in the words of Governor de Vaudreuil, that medals sometimes must go to "those I believe necessary to attach to our interest by this mark of honor." In other words, service to the French or the need of the French for one's services could both bring medals.[54]

The French intended the medal chiefs to render services to Onontio and to keep their villages out of the British orbit, but for the chiefs the appeal of medals was the influence they yielded within the villages. Medals were more than a mark of honor; their recipients acted as conduits of the presents given by the French to Algonquian villagers. Gifts gave the chiefs the ability to be liberal, and liberality was the great mark of chieftainship. The French recognized that they increased the limited power of these chiefs by giving them regular presents. But these medals did not create compliant puppets, and the gifts were not bribes. The alliance was more complex than that. As in the seventeenth century, the alliance chief joined two worlds, and his position in each proved mutually reinforcing. The standing a leader attained

Journal, 136 For eagerness for medals, see Beauharnois au Ministre, 25 sept. 1727, AN, C11A, v. 49; Beauharnois au Ministre, 19 oct. 1734, AN, C11A, v. 61, f. 325; Paroles des Outa8acs de Missilimakinac de la Bande de la fourche . . . , 6 juillet 1740, AN, C11A, v. 74, f. 16. The figure "8" in Outa8acs and in Nagach8o in the text is pronounced "dh." For example of medals to help secure warriors, see Réponse au Mémoire du Roi, 13 oct. 1735, AN, C11A, v. 63.

[53] Paroles des Outa8acs . . . 6 juillet 1740, AN, C11A, v. 74, f. 16.

[54] For importance of outward marks of honor to both groups, see Hocquart au Ministre, 10 oct. 1730, AN, C11A, v. 53. For granting of medals, see Vaudreuil & Bégon au Conseil, 26 oct. 1719, AN, C11A, v. 40. He apparently had received none since 1705. Beauharnois au Ministre, 25 sept. 1727, AN, C11A, v. 49. Beauharnois to Minister, Oct. 15, 1732, *WHC* 17:171. For second quotation, see Vaudreuil au Ministre, 21 oct. 1722, AN, C11A, v. 44, f. 364; for first quotation, see Beauharnois au Ministre, 1 oct. 1728, AN, C11A, v. 50.

among his own people could secure a French medal and presents, and these presents, when redistributed, could then further increase his standing within his village. Accumulating wealth meant little to Algonquians, but the status and influence that came from bestowing goods on others meant much. Obtaining French recognition as a chief thus became an important aspect of village politics.[55]

In one sense, presents bound the chiefs to Onontio, but in another sense, presents made Onontio but a large version of a chief. For the presents in question here were not the reciprocal presents that marked diplomatic agreements. These gifts instead were the fruits of the French acceptance of the Algonquian interpretation of patriarchy. Governor de Beauharnois and the Intendant Hocquart explained to the court in 1730: "You know, Monseigneur, that all the nations of Canada regard the governor as their father, which in consequence, following their ideas, he ought at all times to give them what they need to feed themselves, clothe themselves, and to hunt."[56]

The material basis of the alliance was thus embodied in a series of gifts from fathers to children. A definite protocol of distribution evolved at the posts of the upper country, at councils in Montreal, and in the villages. The major source of presents was the 20,000 livres granted annually by the king. From this fund powder, ball, guns, vermilion, knives, cloth, and other goods were sent to Canada. On special occasions, such as the appointment of a new governor or the return of a governor after a visit of France, Onontio gave larger gifts. The governor either distributed these goods to the chiefs of the nations who came to speak to him or sent the presents to the officers commanding near those nations. In either case, the Crown envisioned alliance chiefs controlling actual distributions to the Indians. As Governor de Vaudreuil put it in regard to the Miamis in 1717, presents should go to "this nation, or rather to some chiefs for the purpose of engaging them to work effectively."[57]

The logic of distribution remained constant, but the site and specific arrangements varied. At each post, the commander – acting as a father – saw to it that individual Indians regularly received small gifts of powder, ball, tobacco, and sometimes brandy. Similarly, at Montreal Onontio made sure

---

[55] For liberality as early mark of chiefs, see La Potherie, History, *WHC* 16:3. For generosity of chiefs, see Abstract of the Life and Customs of the Savages of Canada, 1723, *WHC* 3:146–47. For French recognition of weakness of chiefs, see Abstract, 1725, *WHC* 3:146; Vaudreuil au Conseil, 30 oct. 1718, AN, C11A, v. 39; *JR* 66:221; Proceedings of Council of Marine, Dec. 2, 1721, *WHC* 16:397. For need for presents, see Ramezay and Begon to Minister, Nov. 7, 1715, *WHC* 16:337.

[56] Beauharnois et Hocquart au Ministre, 15 oct. 1730, AN, C11A, v.51, f.33–36.

[57] For Vaudreuil, see Conseil, 11 Jan. 1718: Vaudreuil, 12 oct. 1717, sur les postes et conges, AN, C11A, v.124.

that visiting Indians received rations and that those who came as part of official delegations received special gifts. At forts such as Niagara and Frontenac, where the trade monopoly remained in the hands of the king, and at Montreal, the Crown bore the expense. At leased posts, the *fermier* or lessee bore the expense as part of the price of the lease, although the king might also subsidize gifts, such as powder, or make special presents. It appears that from the beginning the actual royal costs of such presents far exceeded the 20,000 livres allotted by the king. In 1740 presents to all the Indians of Canada totaled over 65,000 livres, and the Intendant, Hocquart, cited the constant augmentation of presents as a source of the excessive expense of New France.[58]

When Onontio or his officers gave presents to individual villagers, they acted directly as fathers, but in most distributions Algonquian chiefs acted as intermediaries. Some of these gifts were personal. The French usually clothed chiefs visiting Montreal by giving them shirts, capotes, and leggings, but such gifts were not necessarily exempt from further redistribution. In 1729, for example, a Huron chief received a second capote from the French because he had given the first to another chief. Years earlier, Sakima – again acting inappropriately for a chief – had asked that such a personal present be delivered to him in secret, since it would otherwise be taken by his warriors.

---

[58] For use of fund, see Zoltvany, *Vandreuil*, 149; Conseil, 1716; Sur les 20,000 . . . , AN, CiiA, v. 123, f. 235. For special occasions, see Conseil, Presens a faire aux sauvages, 30 mars 1716, AN, CiiA, v. 123. In 1716, when Vaudreuil returned to Canada, 40,000 livres were allotted for presents and this was in addition to guns, powder, and ball sent from France. For rise, see Hocquart au Ministre, 24 oct. 1741, AN, CiiA, v. 76, f. 14; Hocquart au Ministre, 31 oct. 1740, AN, CiiA, v. 73, f. 335. For additional expenditures, see Hocquart & Beauharnois au Ministre, 9 oct. 1732, AN, CiiA, v. 5. For lessee, see Dupuy to Minister, Oct. 20, 1727, *WHC* 16:470–71. When the commander had a share in the trade, he supplied presents, Mémoire of Vaudreuil & Bégon, June 19, 1722, *WHC* 3:167; Beauharnois & Hocquart au Ministre, 18 oct. 1731, AN, CiiA, v. 54. For cost of commanders' presents, see Noyan to Minister, Oct. 18, 1738, *WHC* 17:295. Beauharnois et Hocquart au Ministre, 25 oct. 1729, AN, CiiA, v. 51; Beauharnois au Ministre, 25 sept. 1727, AN, CiiA, v. 48; Beauharnois au Ministre, 1 oct. 1728, AN, CiiA, v. 50; Minutes of Council of Louisiana, Mar. 26, 1725, *MPA* 2:422–23; Lease for the Post at Green Bay, 10 Apr. 1747, *WHC* 17:451–55. For quotation, see Noyan, State of Canada, 1730, *MPHC* 33:84.

For distribution of presents by location, see Presens aux sauvages, 1732, AN, CiiA, v. 59, f. 130; Beauharnois & Hocquart au Ministre, 6 oct. 1733, AN, CiiA, V. 59, f. 121; Etat des vivres, munitions, et autres effets qui ont ete delivres des magazins du roy à Montreal aux sauvages . . . 1729, AN, CiiA, v. 53, f. 296, hereafter, Etat . . . 1729, AN, CiiA, v. 53, f. 296ff.

Wars and other emergencies necessitated additional presents, e.g., Memorial of Captain de Lignery to Council, 1720, *WHC* 16:386–87. Conseil, 9 avril 1717, AN, CiiA, v. 123, f. 372; Beauharnois et Du Puy au Ministre, 20 oct. 1726, AN, CiiA, v. 48, f. 97. Compte . . . de la campagne des Renards, AN, CiiA, v. 58, f. 25–26; Hocquart & Beauharnois au Ministre, 9 oct. 1732, AN, CiiA, v. 57. These costs had apparently been borne by the officers in the 1720s, Beauharnois au Ministre, 25 sept. 1727, AN, CiiA, v. 48, f. 125. For Louisiana, Statement of Boisbriant, Minutes of Council, March 26, 1725, *MPA* 2:422.

The French also gave the chiefs much larger presents of powder, ball, cloth, knives, tobacco, and sometimes a small amount of brandy – virtually all of these items were redistributed in their villages. Important chiefs who did not visit Montreal often had such presents forwarded to them.[59]

Somewhat more problematical than the gifts given to a specific chief were the presents designated for a village as a whole, such as those given "*pour distribuer aux Sauvages du Village etably au Sanguinan*," or "*aux Sauvages du Sault Ste. Marie pour present*," or "*pour le village des Miamis.*" In the distribution lists, the French often enumerated these gifts after the specific presents they gave to the medal chiefs, and it was presumably these chiefs who carried the presents west to redistribute in the name of the French. At other times the governor may have forwarded such gifts directly to a post commander for distribution, particularly when the gifts were earmarked for specific recipients such as the Miami warriors who received special presents from the French in July 1729.[60]

There was a final category of presents that straddled the line between a gift and a payment for services. Both mediating peace and recruiting and equipping war parties cost money. In 1741, for example, the Sieur de la Ronde charged 2,304 livres' worth of goods to the account of the king in order to make peace between the Saulteurs and the Sioux. Similarly, putting war parties in the field against the Fox or against the Chickasaws in order to aid Louisiana against that redoubtable people became a steady drain on French resources. Not only did the French supply the warriors, but on occasion they also had to feed their families in their absence since long war expeditions meant a precipitous decline in hunting.[61]

Mediation and compromise achieved stability and cooperation where force failed. Gifts countered the appeal of British trade. The French were at their strongest when they appeared, at least to themselves, the most weak. When they offered goods freely, when they mediated quarrels, when they stayed Algonquian hatchets and covered the dead, then they achieved a status that no other group could rival. They were, conversely, at their

---

[59] Etat... 1729, AN, C11A, v. 53, f. 296ff. For Sakima, see Marest to de Vaudreuil, June 21, 1712, *MPHC* 33:557. The Jesuits had reported in 1675 that the Indians commonly gave away all presents they were given with the exception of rosaries. *JR* 59:231. For Louisiana, see Minutes of the Council of Commerce, Sept. 13, 1719, *MPA* 3:260–61.

[60] Etat... 1729, AN, C11A, v. 53, f. 296ff.

[61] For Saulteur-Sioux peace, 1741, see Mémoire des marchandises, 1741, AN, C11A, v. 75. See also Depense faite dans le Poste de Chaouamigon, 1743, AN, C11A, v. 79, f. 230. For equipping war parties, see Estat des fournitures ... par ordre ... de St. Pierre, Commandant pour le roy au Poste Miamis, 18 juin 1742, AN, C11A, v. 76, f. 186. For supplying families, see Ramezay and Bégon to Minister, Nov. 7, 1715, *WHC* 16:329. Estat general de la depense ... 1739, AN, C11A, v. 71, f. 153; Mémoire de fournitures ... Missillimackinac pour les subsistence des femmes..., 12 oct. 1739, AN, C11A, v. 73, f. 273. Mémoire des fournitures ... Missillimackinac, 26 sept. 1739, AN, C11A, v. 73.

weakest when they appeared the most dangerous and powerful. When Onontio, either for his own reasons or at the urging of his allies, abandoned mediation and deployed force, then his special status began to dissipate. One welcomed a kind father; one sought protection against a vengeful father. The logic of the alliance could not easily encompass a father who participated in, rather than settled, the quarrels of his children.[62]

The Algonquians wrestled the French onto the middle ground, but for them, too, the alliance had its uncomfortable demands. The ritual subordination to Onontio did not always come easily in a society that knew little of subordination. "Born free and independent," Father Charlevoix wrote, "they are struck with horror at whatever has the shadow of despotic power." Onontio's children always remained prickly about their status; they accepted him as a father not as a master. But they, too, bent under the demands of the alliance and their own craving for respect. Father Charlevoix caught the cultural complexity on which the alliance was built. "On the other hand," he wrote, "these people, so haughty and so jealous of their liberty, are beyond imagination slaves of human respect." The alliance chiefs who mediated the quarrels of the *pays d'en haut* and ritually accepted Onontio's will, had once been, in the words of the councils, the rash and heedless young men who disturbed the land, but the standing and respect medals brought from both the French and their own people helped induce them to conform to a different standard.[63]

In July 1757, "Pennahouel" (Pendal8on), an Ottawa chief, spoke in council to General Montcalm on the eve of the French campaign against the British at Fort George. Louis Antoine de Bougainville, a French officer and aide-de-camp of the Marquis de Montcalm, recorded his speech. Bougainville, who would later become famous as an explorer and the first European to visit Tahiti, explained that Pennahouel was "celebrated for his spirit, his wisdom, and his conversations with M. de la Galissonière." It was a description that recalled Kondiaronk, now dead for more than half a century. He, too, had been a man celebrated for his spirit, wisdom, and conversations with Frenchmen.[64]

But Pennahouel, Bougainville also noted, had not always been on good terms with the French. He had "in the war with the Foxes carried the hatchet against us, but since then has always been devoted to Ononthio." Bougainville got the story wrong, but he grasped its essential theme: the transformation of an initially rebellious war leader into a devoted alliance chief. Pennahouel was the apotheosis of the transformation the alliance

[62] Beauharnois au Ministre, 17 sept. 1743, AN, C11A, v. 79. f. 108.
[63] For Charlevoix's quotation, see *Journal*, 2:87–88, 136.
[64] Hamilton (ed.), *Adventure in the Wilderness*, 145.

demanded of Algonquian warriors: rash and proud young men like White-Robe or Sakima must become the ritual, if not actual, subordinates of Onontio.

Young men who had gained their own status through war could be impatient with the tinge of subordination medals carried. In 1740 Governor de Beauharnois gave Pennahouel a medal for his services in the war against the Sauks and Fox, but Pennahouel, asserting that he had "no need of this mark of preference to distinguish him," gave it to a friend. Governor de Beauharnois was angered by his audacity but suppressed his desire to punish him. Instead, he had an interpreter inform Pennahouel that gifts from Onontio should be received with grave submission. Pennahouel apologized, excusing himself by saying that he had only wished his friend to be a chief also. Beauharnois concealed his anger, gave Pennahouel another medal, and continued to give him presents.[65]

The issue was not, however, settled. When, sometime later, Governor de Beauharnois summoned the chiefs then at Montreal to council, Pennahouel, who was drunk, refused to come. He was, he said, as great a chief as Governor de Beauharnois, and he would come at his own convenience. On saying this, he threw his medal into the mud. On receiving word of this, Governor de Beauharnois indulged himself in a rage more typical of a French officer than an Algonquian chief. He had Pennahouel seized, tied, and exhibited as an example to the others. The other Ottawa chiefs were not, it seems, unhappy to see Pennahouel reduced and humiliated, for there are signs in the incident of imperial politics serving the ends of village politics. In Ottawa society status was by and large achieved rather than ascribed, but leading civil chiefs do seem to have come from certain powerful lineages, and Pennahouel, the other chiefs informed Beauharnois, was not "of the family of chiefs." As they viewed the matter, Onontio had raised Pennahouel up and acknowledged his influence among the warriors. If Onontio now wished to cast him down and throw him back on his own resources, they would not object. Pennahouel had only his own stupidity to blame.[66]

Onontio's public humiliation of Pennahouel sobered him in a dual sense. He could blame his rash action on liquor, but he could not ignore the village leadership's consent to his humiliation. The chiefs acceded to Onontio's request that Pennahouel no longer be allowed to speak in council. Onontio, however, while he could demand ritual subordination in Montreal, could not, even with the chiefs' cooperation, break Pennahouel's influence at

[65] Beauharnois au Ministre, 3 oct. 1740, AN, C11A, v. 74, f. 21.
[66] For Pennahouel's not being "of the family of chiefs," see Paroles de M. de Beauharnois aux Outa8acs etc., 8 juillet 1740, AN, C11A, v. 74, f. 23. For punishment, etc., see Beauharnois au Ministre, 3 oct. 1740, AN, C11A, v. 74, f. 21.; Reponse des Outa8acs..., 7 aoust 1740, AN, C11A, v. 74, f. 25.

Michilimackinac. He remained a powerful voice among the young men, and
the French soon found that they needed him. In 1741 the Ottawas, whose
lands at Michilimackinac were exhausted, were in the midst of a search
for new village sites. They were planning to move from the post leaving
it weakened and relatively unprovisioned. The chiefs were unwilling to
consent to the French choices among possible village sites and had resolved
on either moving to the Grand River or Grand Traverse Bay, where some
had begun clearing land. The French turned to Pennahouel for help. Both
he and the French saw advantages in a rapprochement. He negotiated a
compromise satisfactory to the French, the maintenance of a village at
Michilimackinac and new settlements at Arbre Croche on Little Traverse
Bay. Governor de Beauharnois, in return, restored him to favor in 1742. By
1751 he was the leading alliance chief at Michilimackinac. That year at
Montreal he was central to the efforts to restore the Ottawas to an alliance
once more in crisis. He operated with skill and self-assurance, but he was
also fully aware of the ritual subordination to his father that the alliance
demanded.[67]

During the first half of the eighteenth century the resurrected alliance
created a complicated and precarious world of careful management and
constant compromise. Village and imperial politics merged and flowed into
each other. A creature of the middle ground, and perhaps its most imposing creation, the French-Algonquian alliance was, nonetheless, a fragile
structure threatened by French dreams of force and the rivalries of village
politics. Only through the blending of village and imperial politics had the
alliance taken on life, but the resulting mix was so volatile that it eventually
exploded in imperial confrontation and village rebellions in the 1750s.

[67] For French worries, see Beauharnois au Ministre, 18 oct. 1741, AN, C11A, v. 75, f. 226;
Address of . . . Beauharnois . . . to the Outaouacs of Missilimackinac 8 July 1741, *NYCD*
9:1072. For new villages, see Speech of Outaouacs of Missilmackinac of the band of la
Fourche, Sinagos, and Kiskakons, June 16, 1742, *WHC* 17:372. For Grand River, see
Beauharnois to Minister, Oct. 5, 1741, *WHC* 17:367. For Grand Traverse, see Beauharnois
to Outaouacs of Missilimakinac, July 8, 1741, *WHC* 17:351–52. Céloron to Beauharnois,
Sept. 2, 1741, *WHC* 17:60. For intervention with Pennahouel, Beauharnois to Minister,
Oct. 5, 1741, *WHC* 17:368. For restoration of Pennahouel, see Beauharnois to Min-
isters, Sept. 24, 1742, *WHC* 17:419–20. As a successful alliance chief, see Paroles de
Pennant8eunt, 7 juin 1751, AN, C11A, v. 97.

5

Republicans and rebels

> The *historical* reality of traditional societies is locked together for the rest of time with the historical reality of the intruders who saw them, changed them, destroyed them. There *is* no history beyond the frontier, free of the contact that makes it.
>
> Greg Dening, *Islands and Beaches*

I

The alliance, with its particular blending of material interests and cultural logics, always served political purposes. It excluded the British from the *pays d'en haut*; it protected Canada; ideally, it preserved peace among the villages and distributed goods to Onontio's children. At one end of the spectrum, the alliance served imperial politics; at the other end, village politics. But the converse was also true. The alliance was vulnerable to changes in imperial politics, and it was vulnerable to rivalries within the villages. In the 1740s and 1750s, the direct clash of empires, largely absent for a generation, exacerbated bitter political rivalries within villages. Rebellion racked the alliance, and the result was the rise of what the French called Indian republics.

For eighteenth-century French administrators, all the connotations of the word *republic* were pejorative. Republics destroyed hierarchy, order, and authority. The Indian republics shattered existing political arrangements, earning both British and French distrust. The republicans were a potentially volatile mix of the discontented from all over the *pays d'en haut* and the East. As Conrad Weiser noted of Logstown, one of the leading republican villages, the inhabitants were "very jealous at one another, they being of so many different nations. Each of them pretending to have as wise people as the rest." They lived together as much from fear as from friendship. No group, Indians believed, would attack a mixed village that contained some of their relatives. Or, as the Canadian officer Pierre-Joseph de Céloron de Blainville observed of the Senecas in a village of Miamis, "It is the policy of these nations always to have with them some other Indians who serve as shields [*boucliers*]." Richard Peters of Pennsylvania pithily summarized the British attitude toward the republicans: They were "ye Scum of the Earth . . . this mixed dirty sort of people."[1]

Migration produced this "mixed dirty sort of people," and the great destination of eighteenth-century Indian migration in the *pays d'en haut* was a broadly defined upper Ohio Valley – roughly the area between the Ohio River and the Great Lakes and between the Appalachians and the Wabash River. The migration came from every direction. Scattered Cherokees moved in from the south. The Mascoutens and Kickapoos came in from the Illinois country. But the two largest streams flowed from the north and east. Despite Canadian attempts to divert them, the Miami confederation moved down from Michigan into the Wabash River Valley, and later the Wyandots broke away from the Huron-Petuns and moved south to Sandusky. In the 1720s, 1730s, and 1740s, the Iroquois and their dependents, the Delawares and Shawnees, came from the east.[2]

Migrants came to the region for a variety of motives, but the lure of abundant game usually figured strongly in their decision. After the creation of forts at Oswego and Niagara, French and British competition in the fur trade caused game to decline precipitously in both Iroquoia proper and the lands bordering Lake Ontario. Iroquois hunters moved west along the southern shore of Lake Erie. There they encountered Ottawa hunters moving east from Detroit seeking easier access to Oswego. The Shawnee and Delaware migrants to the Ohio who came west in the 1720s also sought game. But poverty and social disruption brought on by the virtually unrestricted rum trade in Pennsylvania and by British pressure on their village sites and hunting lands created additional spurs for their migration. The addition of the Tuscaroras had increased the Iroquois confederation from

---

[1] Canada, Sauvages, 1739, AN, C11A, v. 72, f. 287; Paul A. W. Wallace, *Conrad Weiser, 1696–1760, Friend of Colonist and Mohawk* (Philadelphia: University of Pennsylvania Press, 1945), 269–70; Journal de la Campagne . . . Céloron, 28 aoust 1749, in Pierre Margry, *Découvertes et établissements des Français . . . de l'Amerique Septentrionale, 1614–1698*, 6 vols. (Paris: Maisonneuve et Cie, 1879; repr., New York: AMS, 1974), 6:715. For Peters quotation, see Wallace, *Weiser*, 269–70.

[2] The best maps of villages and posts in the *pays d'en haut* are in Helen Hornbeck Tanner (ed.), *Atlas of Great Lakes Indian History* (Norman: University of Oklahoma Press, 1987); see map 9. For plans for post on Wabash, see Postes dans la colonie de la Louisianne, 27 aoust 1716, AN, C13A, v. 4. For disputes over region, see Vaudreuil to Council, Oct. 22, 1720, *WHC* 16:394; Vaudreuil to Boisbriant, Aug. 17, 1724, *WHC* 16:442; J. H. Schlarman, *From Quebec to New Orleans: Ft. De Chartres* (Belleville, Ill.: Beuchler, 1929), 263–65; Frances Krauskopf (ed.), *Ouiatanon Documents* (Indianapolis: Indiana Historical Society, 1955), 145–46; Canada, fev. 1731, AN, C11A, v. 56 (f. 294); Beauharnois & Hocquart au Ministre, 15 oct. 1730, AN, C11A, v. 52, f. 29. For Piankashaws with Vincennes, see Boishébert to Beauharnois, July 24, 1733, *MPHC* 34:108. In 1737, the Piankashaws quit their village and moved farther up the Wabash, Bienville au Ministre, 21 juin 1737, AN, C13A, v. 22. At the same time, Louisiana and Canada quarreled over where the Kickapoos and Mascoutens, who were unhappy with the Miamis, should settle, *ibid.* For dispute between Miami and Wea chiefs which split the two tribes, see Vaudreuil to Council, Oct. 22, 1720, *WHC* 16:394.

five to six nations, but those groups that were dependents rather than members of the confederation did not fare well in the early eighteenth century. The Six Nations, which Pennsylvania regarded as the overlords of the Shawnees and Delawares, not only failed to intercede for their dependents but abetted Pennsylvania's abuses. For the Miamis, Kickapoos, and Mascoutens, access to Louisiana and British traders, as well as better conditions for agriculture, joined game as inducements to migrate.[3]

The movement of Shawnees, Delawares, and Iroquois from the east introduced into the upper country peoples who were not tied to the alliance, but it differed in another way from much of the migration within the *pays d'en haut* itself. The movement of the Miamis, Weas, Piankashaws, Kickapoos, and Mascoutens – but not the Wyandots – was a migration of relatively intact village and tribal groups. The movement from the east, like the Wyandot migration, was a migration of smaller social units – village fragments, families, even individual hunters. It created no single dominant tribal or ethnic group. The typical village between Lake Erie and the Ohio was multiethnic and without clear territorial claims.

These multiethnic villages were the first republics. They represented a mixture of peoples who established a political existence that was inside the *pays d'en haut* but outside the French alliance. They were also beyond the control of the British and their usual allies, the league of the Iroquois. East of the Wabash, the republicans fell into two large divisions: the Ohio River villages and the White River villages. The French called the more northerly migrants – the villagers who lived between Lake Erie and the upper Muskingum – the White River Indians. They were a mixture of all six Iroquois nations, particularly the Senecas and Onondagas, lesser numbers of Delawares and Mohicans, and members of French-allied groups such as the Ottawas, the Abenakis of Saint Francis, and the Chippewas. They numbered six hundred fighting men by 1743. The Ohio River Indians were a mixture of Iroquois – who became known as the Mingos – Delawares, Shawnees, Munsees, and various fragments of French-allied groups.[4]

---

[3] For migration by Delawares and Shawnees, see James Logan to Governor Clarke, Jan. 22, 1737, Logan Papers X, 58, Historical Society of Pennsylvania, copy in Ohio Valley–Great Lakes Ethnohistorical Archives, University of Indiana, Shawnee notebook, hereafter cited as GLEHA. For French negotiations and the attempt to detach them from the Iroquois, see Reponse au Mémoire du Roy, 13 oct. 1735, AN, C11A, v.63. The French feared the widening trade network created by English traders operating from these villages, Bienville au Ministre, 22 avril 1734, AN, C13A, v. 18, f. 142. For motives, also see Paroles des chefs de la riviere blanche, Canantechiareron et Araguindiaque à M. de Longueüil (1744), AN, C11A, v. 79, f. 44. For relationship of Shawnees and Delawares to Iroquois, see Francis Jennings, " 'Pennsylvania Indians' and the Iroquois," and Michael N. McConnell, "Peoples 'in Between': The Iroquois and the Ohio Indians, 1720–1768," both in Daniel K. Richter and James H. Merrell (eds.), *Beyond the Covenant Chain: The Iroquois and Their Neighbors in Indian North America, 1600–1800* (Syracuse: Syracuse University Press, 1987), 75–112.

[4] The name "White River" is a cause of some confusion because it does not refer to the

From the outset, the French were ambivalent about the repopulation of the lands between Lake Erie and the Ohio, largely empty since the Iroquois wars. During the 1730s, they nurtured high hopes that they could integrate the White River Indians, Mingos, Shawnees, and Delawares into the alliance. But they feared Iroquois attempts to link the migrants to the Iroquois council fire at Onondaga and British efforts to lure the migrants into the British chain of friendship. Despite temporary successes, the French, British, and Iroquois all failed to achieve their ends. But the very competition for the allegiance of these migrants shifted the critical area of European-Indian interaction south, away from the old centers and toward the borders of the *pays d'en haut*.

In the mid eighteenth century, imperial competition in North America focused to a surprising degree on the Ohio country, and this competition between empires was also a competition within the villages. The leaders who arose in the Ohio country were men and, indeed, sometimes women previously considered minor figures by the French, the Iroquois, the British, and the French alliance chiefs. The Ohio, a heaven to hunters, proved a purgatory to chiefs. A crisis for the French alliance became inextricably linked to a crisis for the chiefs.

II

The increasingly direct competition of the French and the British for influence in the Ohio country created new opportunities for previously marginal or subordinate figures in Algonquian societies. The prototype of the new political brokers was Peter Chartier, the son of a Shawnee mother and a French father. This man of ambiguous ethnicity and loyalty served as a mirror to reflect the possibilities of a new social order on the Ohio.[5]

Chartier was a trader who joined the Shawnee migration west of the Appalachians in the 1720s. Initially aligning himself with British traders who had followed the Shawnees, he resided by the Allegheny, below the mouth of the Kiskiminetas, at a place that became known as Chartier's Town.

present-day White River in Indiana. At this period, the White River country was the area between Lake Erie, the forks of the Beaver, and the Upper Muskingum. The "White River" itself was usually the Cuyahoga, but the name was applied, or misapplied, to many other streams. The White River Indians were ethnically overwhelmingly Iroquois, but they were increasingly only loosely bound by the Iroquois covenant chain. Like the Shawnees, they sought French sanction and protection for their migration. Navarre, Mémoire, 1743, AN, C11A, v. 79, f. 48–52. For discussion of White River, see Charles A. Hanna, *The Wilderness Trail, or The Ventures and Adventures of the Pennsylvania Traders on the Allegheny Path*, 2 vols. (repr. of 1911 ed., New York: AMS Press, 1971), 1:332–33. The Mingos were Iroquois, but their distance from their native villages had deprived them of an equal voice in the councils.

5 Jerry Eugene Clark, "Shawnee Indian Migrations: A Systems Analysis" (Ph.D. diss., University of Kentucky, 1974), 41.

Chartier also, however, participated in the Shawnee negotiations with the French, and this soured his relationship with both the British and the Iroquois since, as dependents of the Iroquois, the Shawnees were not supposed to undertake independent diplomatic ventures of their own.[6]

Because of his British associations, the French distrusted Chartier. Only when he led a large party of Shawnees who plundered several British traders in 1745 did the French become convinced of his loyalty. Chartier, however, proved to be no more reliable as a French partisan than he had been as a British agent. He successfully opposed French attempts to relocate the Shawnees at Detroit, and he did his father's will only when it coincided with his own.[7]

Chartier was a political chameleon whose changes in coloring reflected opportunities rather than convictions, but it is the scope of his transformation that it is most revealing. Chartier's switch from a British to a French partisan is perhaps less significant than his metamorphosis from *métis* trader to Shawnee factional leader. Originally he was an important but marginal political figure, a man who acted through the chiefs, tying them to him by debts or gifts. Eventually he became a man who challenged chiefs, and ultimately, he acted like a chief himself. This was not an easy transition, for

---

[6] The Shawnees and Iroquois offered different versions of their mutual alienation. The Shawnees claimed that in 1727, when the English were putting great pressure on the Iroquois to allow them to fortify Oswego, the Iroquois had demanded that the Shawnees and Delawares prepare to take up arms against the English. When the Shawnees refused, the angry Iroquois had reduced them to the status of women within the covenant chain and ordered them to look west "toward Ohioh, The place from whence you Came and Return thitherward," for the Iroquois planned to sell their Pennsylvania lands. Seeing no hope of aid from the Delawares, who also bid them depart since they "wanted to Drink ye land away," and being harrassed by the English, who insisted that they stop sheltering runaway slaves, the Shawnees decided to leave. The Iroquois denied the particulars of this account, but their version, too, stressed land disputes as a factor in the Shawnee migration. Most likely, loss of land, a desire to escape Iroquois domination, a decline in game, and the ravages of the rum trade were all ingredients in the Shawnee migration. Message Shawnee Chiefs to Gov. Gordon, June 7, 1732, *PA*, series 1, 1:329–30. The Iroquois said that they had sold only a small amount of land to Pennsylvania, not enough to threaten the Shawnees, but the Pennsylvanians had used the sale as a pretext for seizing more. For Iroquois denial, see Conference between Lieutenant Governor Clarke and the Indians, Albany, June 28, 1737, *NYCD* 6:105–6. Francis Jennings discusses this migration in both "'Pennsylvania Indians' and the Iroquois," 75–93, and Francis Jennings, *Empire of Fortune: Crowns, Colonies, and Tribes in the Seven Years' War in America* (New York: W. W. Norton, 1988), 25, 29–30.
  For Chartier's town, see Census, George Miranda, A true Acct. of all the men of the Shayners in the three Townes in Alegania, Sept. 27, 1737, Logan Papers IX, Historical Society of Pennsylvania, Philadelphia, copy GLEHA. For location, see Hanna, *Wilderness Trail*, 1:304. For the English and Chartier, see Edmd. Cartlidge to Gov. Gordon, May 14, 1732, *PA*, series 1, 1:327–28.

[7] For plunders English, see Hanna, *Wilderness Trail*, 1:311. For Chartier's influence in halting move to Detroit, see Canada, Sauvages, 1740, AN, C11A, v. 74, f. 236. Despite his visit to Montreal in 1740, Chartier was distrusted by the French who sought to isolate him, Beauharnois to Minister, Sept. 17, 1741, *MPHC* 34:207–8.

the Shawnees had originally not accepted Chartier as a Shawnee, let alone as a chief. Those Shawnees who opposed him vigorously emphasized his standing as a *françois métis*. They stressed to Governor de Beauharnois that he was of French flesh (*de votre viande*) and not their own. Unlike most contemporary *métis* who regarded themselves as French, Chartier claimed to be Shawnee. When he spoke to Governor de Beauharnois, he spoke as an Indian, calling the governor "my father."[8]

As a trader, Chartier had privileged access to goods, and he used this to recruit his own following in defiance of existing social and political arrangements. The eighteenth-century Shawnees were a confederation rather than a single tribe. The nation was divided into five more or less autonomous political units (the Chillicothe, Hathawekela, Kispoko, Mequachake, and Piqua), and each unit was further subdivided into bands, which often acted independently. Titular political leaders, or "kings," of the entire confederation were drawn from the Chillicothe (Calaka) and the Hathawekela (Øawikila). Nucheconer (or Neucheconno), one of these "kings" of the Shawnees, and probably a Chillicothe (Calaka) headman, had allied himself with the French. Friction quickly developed, however, when Nucheconer resisted the French attempt to settle the Shawnees near the Miamis. Instead he preferred settling at Sonnontio, on the lower Scioto River, near an existing Mingo and Shawnee village. Nucheconer's differences with the French gave Chartier a chance to move from being a counselor of the chiefs to their rival. Dramatically planting the French flag before one of Nucheconer's subordinate chiefs, he defied the putative leadership and demanded that the Shawnees follow their father's will and move near the Miamis. He made his appeal directly to the warriors to whom he gave a barrel of powder as a present.[9]

---

[8] The nature of Chartier's influence over the chiefs is unclear. The chiefs could have been in debt to him, or he might have had influence with them through presents. The document says "par son credit [?] empêcher quelques chefs accredités d'y consentir." He more clearly used gifts in 1745, Anonymous Diary of a Trip from Detroit to the Ohio River, Papiers Contrecoeur, 1–10, Archives of the Seminary of Quebec, V–V 17:1, June 16, 1745, copy in GLEHA, Shawnee file, p. 5. For Chartier as being "de votre viande," see Paroles des Cha8anons, 3 aoust 1742, AN, C11A, v.77. For Chartier's speech, see Paroles des Cha8anons, 25 juin 1740, AN, C11A, v.74, f.62. By 1750 Governor de Vaudreuil of Louisiana regarded him as a chief, Vaudreuil to Rouillé, June 24, 1750, MPA 5:48. The figure "8" in "Cha8anons" is pronounced "dh."

[9] The Shawnees are the most perplexing group in terms of hierarchy. In the 1720s and 1730s both the French and English recognized "grand chefs" and "kings." These leaders were members of the Hathawekelas (Øawikila) and Chillicothes (Calaka). Governor de Beauharnois, Reponse au memoire du roy, 1737, AN, C11A, v. 37, f. 139. For Nocheknonee (or Nucheconer) as "king" of French Town, see Census, George Miranda, A true Acct. of all the men of the Shayners in the three Townes in Alegania, Sept. 27, 1737, Logan Papers, IX, Historical Society of Pennsylvania, Philadelphia, copy GLEHA. For tribal chiefs, see HBNI 15:624, 627. The pro-French Shawnees in the early 1740s included both the king

Although most of the Shawnees settled in Sonnontio, Chartier led away a faction, which became his personal following. He, revealingly, did not lead his followers to the Miami post, his ostensible goal in breaking with Nucheconer. Instead, he settled temporarily in the vicinity of present-day Terre Haute, before moving south to the Creek country. Claims of loyalty to Onontio served largely to established him as an independent political leader. By 1750 Chartier had legitimized his position. The governor of Louisiana, at least, regarded him as one of the Shawnee chiefs.[10]

Understanding the creation of the republics and the political counterlife to the alliance that they created involves tracing the careers of other men like Chartier. Orontony (or Nicholas) of the Wyandots also thrived on the opportunities that migration into the lands between the Ohio and the Great Lakes presented. He represented a second stage in the development of the republics, for he rose to prominence not among migrants from the east but among a group central to the French alliance. He threatened not only the empire but the alliance chiefs as well; he became the steersman of a republic in actual rebellion against Onontio; and he floated on a social tide that we can best trace by following him. Initially content to maneuver in the coves of village politics, Orontony eventually became diverted into much wider and wilder waters. Understanding him involves a detour back into the maze of

---

Nocheknonee and Chartier, who challenged the chiefs. Nocheknonee remained at Sonnontio, and when that town rebelled and sought English aid, the English demanded his chastisement. He appears to have lost influence. The younger warriors seemed to have exerted great influence at Sonnontio when it became a "republic," but they did give great respect to an ancient chief who appears to have been nearly senile. This was Kekewatcheky who remained loyal to the English when the other Shawnees attacked the traders, and may have acted as a figurehead for the warriors who sought English aid. For Nocheknonee and Kekewatcheky, see Treaty at Lancaster, July 19, 1748, *PCR* 5:314. For old, feeble Shawnee chief, see Croghan Journal, May 21, 1751, in Reuben Gold Thwaites (ed.), *Early Western Travels 1748–1846...*, 38 vols. (Cleveland: Arthur H. Clark, 1904–07), 1:60; "Cochawitchiky", Gist Journal, 107; Logstown Conference, Lois Mulkearn (ed.), *George Mercer Papers Relating to the Ohio Company of Virginia* (Pittsburgh: University of Pittsburgh Press, 1954), 280, 500, n. 122, *ibid*; Wallace, *Weiser*, 267.

For Neucheconno (or Neuchenor) as a French partisan, see A Treaty... Lancaster, July 19, 1748, *PCR* 5:314–15. For Chartier's actions, see Anonymous Diary of a Trip from Detroit to the Ohio River, May 22 – Aug. 24, 1745, Papiers Contrecoeur, 1–10, Archives of the Seminary of Quebec, v. 17:1, p. 3–5, copy in GLEHA. It would be interesting to know the identity of Chartier's followers, but the documents do not make this clear.

10 For movement, see Anonymous Diary of a Trip from Detroit to the Ohio River, May 22 – August 24, 1745, Papiers Contrecoeur, 1–10, Archives of the Seminary of Quebec, v. 17:1, p. 3–9, copy in GLEHA. Clark, "Shawnee Migrations," 42, 45–48. Clark, however, had not seen Vaudreuil's letter of 1750 that gives Chartier's own accounts of his band's movements (Vaudreuil to Rouillé, June 24, 1750, *MPA* 5:48). Not all the Shawnees who moved south followed Chartier. Vaudreuil in 1744 mentioned 70 to 80 Shawnees who had come among the Alibamons when Chartier was still in the north, Vaudreuil to Maurepas, Feb. 12, 1744, Vaudreuil Letterbook 1, Loudoun Papers, (English translation), Huntington Library. As a chief, Vaudreuil to Rouillé, June 24, 1750, *MPA* 5:48.

village politics among the Huron-Petuns – from whom the Wyandots were an offshoot.

Orontony was a Huron-Petun who became a Wyandot because of yet another intervillage conflict at Detroit. In the 1730s the Huron-Petuns made peace with the Têtes-Plattes (a generic term for southern Indians but which in this case probably refers to the Catawbas). Tired of the wasting southern war they and other Algonquians had been waging in conjunction with the Iroquois, the Huron-Petuns acted without the consent or participation of either the French, or more critically – since this was an Indian war that did not involve fighting between members of the alliance – their Algonquian allies. When the Huron-Petuns attempted to include their neighbors at Detroit in the peace, not only did the Ottawas, Potawatomis, and Saulteurs refuse the wampum belts sent by the Huron-Petuns, they accused the Huron-Petuns of plotting to join the Catawbas in attacks against them. The other Detroit villagers immediately organized a small war party to continue the war. The Huron-Petuns, in turn, dispatched warriors to warn the Catawbas. As it turned out, these Huron-Petun warriors did more than warn the Catawbas; they joined them in ambushing the other Detroit Indians. In the fighting that followed, only three members of the seventeen-man Ottawa, Chippewa, and Potawatomi war party escaped.[11]

For both the Huron-Petuns and their Detroit allies, the incident seemed less an aberration in their friendship than a reaffirmation of the basic divisions between them that French mediation had heretofore bridged. The Huron-Petuns now recalled how years earlier at Michilimackinac, their relatives at the missions of Sault Sainte Louis and Lac des Deux Montagnes had invited them to settle near Montreal. The mission Indians had said: "My brothers, you are here, in the midst of a multitude of nations who do not love you, you do not understand their language. You are ignorant of their customs, and because of this, you are in a position each day to involve yourselves in evil affairs." Now, seemingly faced with a league of all the Algonquians against them, the Huron-Petuns recalled this message and saw it as a disturbingly accurate assessment of their current situation. They were, the commander at Detroit confirmed, universally hated.[12]

---

[11] It is unclear whether this was new peace or a renewal of an older one made in 1729; see Beauharnois to Minister, July 21, 1729, *WHC* 17:64–65. For basic account, see Canada, Sauvages, jan. 1739, AN, C11A, v. 72, f. 291–93. For the Catawba wars, see James Merrell, "'Their Very Bones Shall Fight': The Catawba-Iroquois Wars," in Richter and Merrell (eds.), *Beyond the Covenant Chain*, 115–34, and James Merrell, *The Indians' New World: Catawbas and Their Neighbors from European Contact Through the Era of Removal* (Chapel Hill: University of North Carolina Press, 1989), 135–40.

[12] For speech, see Paroles des Hurons du Detroit, 1738, AN, C11A, v. 74, f. 72–76 (a brief synopsis which does not contain this full quote is in *WHC* 17:282); Memorandum of what occurred in the Affair of the Hurons of Detroit . . . from the 12 of Aug. 1738 to 12 of June 1741, *WHC* 17:279; Noyelle to Beauharnois, 1 Feb. 1739, *MPHC* 34:163.

This village crisis at Detroit quickly became a crisis of the alliance with the Huron-Petuns at the center. The proper French role was clear: As fathers, they should mediate this dangerous dispute among their eldest children. They should cover the dead, and, it was eventually agreed, remove the Huron-Petuns to a site away from Detroit. But the French commander Noyan dawdled and did nothing to reconcile the nations. When Governor de Beauharnois acted, his emissaries neglected the proper ceremonies, and the French fell into factional disputes of their own over the proper course of action. For four years after the initial attack in the Catawba country, negotiations dragged on. Without adequate French support, and torn by divisions among their own people, the Huron-Petun chiefs lost their power. A major realignment in the politics of the nation began. In effect, the young men and the women vetoed the council decisions. The clan matrons took such a prominent role in opposing the French attempts to move the Huron-Petuns to Montreal that Governor de Beauharnois's nephew and agent, the Chevalier de Beauharnois, resorted to secret councils restricted to men in an unsuccessful attempt to break the influence of the women. With no consensus emerging, power began to shift away from the alliance chiefs – Sasteretsy, the titular head of the nation, and Tayatchatin, the head of the Turtle phratry – and toward two lesser chiefs, Angouriot and Orontony.[13]

From the beginning of the crisis, even when the Huron-Petuns appeared

---

[13] For example of negotiations over removal, see Parolles des Hurons, 1738, AN, C11A, v. 74, f. 72–76. For French recognition of significance, see Canada, Sauvages, 1739, AN, C11A, v. 72, f. 289. For French intervention, see Paroles de . . . Beauharnois aux hurons & Outa8as du Détroit, 1738, AN, C11A, v. 69; Canada, Sauvages, jan. 1739, AN, C11A, v. 72, f. 291–93. For requests for removal, see Noyelle to Beauharnois, 1 Feb. 1739, MPHC 34:163; Memorandum of what occurred in the Affair of the Hurons of Detroit . . . from the 12 Aug. 1738 to 12 of June 1741, WHC 17:281–84. Beauharnois agreed in 1740 to grant the Huron-Petuns lands near Montreal, and the next year sent his nephew to negotiate their removal and mission Indians to perform the necessary ceremonies and to escort them to Montreal. He thought by 1741 that the matter had been arranged. Beauharnois to Minister, Oct. 1, 1740, MPHC 34:184; Canada, Sauvages, 1740 AN, C11A, v. 74, f. 234–35. For invitation, see Secret Council . . . Message to the Hurons of Detroit, June 12, 1741, WHC 17:340–44. For Huron-Petun refusal, see Beauharnois to Minister, Oct. 1, 1740, WHC 17:329–35. For exclusion of women, see Conseil particulier aux huronnes, 2 aout 1741, AN, C11A, v. 54, f. 99.

Governor de Beauharnois eventually blamed Father de la Richardie, who had begun to urge a settlement at Grosse Isle at the mouth of the Detroit River, and de Noyan, who did nothing to reconcile the nations, for their failure; Richardie, in turn, blamed Beauharnois. Beauharnois to Richardie, June 14, 1741, WHC 17:349–50; Beauharnois to Minister, Oct. 8, 1741, WHC 17:369–70; Beauharnois à Richardie, 30 aout 1741, AN, C11A, v. 75, f. 105; Richardie to Fr. de Jaunay, Dec. 1741, WHC 17:370–71; Beauharnois to Minister Sept. 15, 1742, WHC 17:412–15; Chev. de Beauharnois to M. de Beauharnois, Aug. 2, 1741, WHC 17:354. For division of young men and elders, see Richarie (sic) to St. Pé, June 10, 1741, WHC 17:339. The chiefs became unwilling to act without first consulting the mass of the young men even when pressured by de Beauharnois at Montreal, Beauharnois to Minister, Oct. 8, 1741, MPHC 33:209–10. And it was apparently the young men who in 1742 made

to be acting with near unanimity, signs of division between the leading chiefs and minor Huron leaders were visible. In early negotiations with Governor de Beauharnois, Orontony acted as the emissary for Sastaretsy and Tayatchatin. Yet neither of these prominent chiefs trusted him. They secretly informed Beauharnois that if Orontony agreed to anything but a new village at Montreal, they would disavow him.[14]

Orontony himself eventually broke openly with the leading chiefs over the best course to pursue, and in doing so he joined Angouriot, a man he had earlier opposed. Angouriot was one of the three elders who had objected to removing to Montreal from the beginning. He was both a clan chief and a leader of the non-Christian Huron-Petuns. Father de la Richardie, the influential missionary at Detroit, hated him and referred to him as the "Drunkard Angouriot." Other Frenchmen, however, regarded him as a man who could control his drinking when the occasion demanded. They thought he joined to "a cunning and subtle mind, the ability of an accomplished politician." Angouriot gained support as the senior chiefs proved unable to forge a consensus on relocation. By the late summer of 1740, half the village followed him. While other Huron-Petuns planned a new village at Grosse Isle at the mouth of the Detroit River, Angouriot and his "brothers" had begun to clear fields at Sandusky near the southwestern shore of Lake Erie where the Huron-Petuns had wintered following the initial conflict over the Catawbas.[15]

Angouriot's move to Sandusky signaled a fundamental fracture in Huron-Petun society. Two minor chiefs, Angouriot and Orontony (who later joined Angouriot at Sandusky), had broken with the Huron-Petun hierarchy and led an exodus toward the margins of the Ohio country. The Ohio country was not unknown to the Huron-Petuns. They had hunted there and warred there, and some, like the forty Hurons who already lived among the Shawnees, had even settled there. But none of the established leadership of

---

the decision to settle at Grosse Isle and not to remove to Montreal, Beauharnois to 3 Huron chiefs of Detroit, June 28, 1742, *WHC* 17:377–80.

[14] James Clifton, in his article "The Re-emergent Wyandot: A Study in Ethnogenesis on the Detroit River Borderland, 1747" in *Papers from the Western District Conference*, ed. K. G. Pryke and L. L. Kulisek (Essex County Historical Society and Western District Council, 1983), 10–15, makes this division an ethnic split, but Lucien Campeau, *La Mission des Jesuites chez Les Hurons, 1639–50* (Montreal: Editions Bellarmin, 1987), 362–67, calls this into question. On this point, I have followed Campeau. For negotiations, see Memorandum . . . the Affair of the Hurons of Detroit . . . 12 of August 1738 to 12 of June 1741, *WHC* 17:280, 283–85; Secret Council, Message . . . to the Hurons of Detroit, June 12, 1741, *WHC* 17:340.

[15] For Angouriot, see Richardie to St. Pé, Aug. 26, 1740, *WHC* 17:328–29; Memorandum, *WHC* 17:286–87; Chevalier de Beauharnois to Marquis de Beauharnois, Aug. 2, 1741, *WHC* 17:353–54. For controls half a village, see Beauharnois to Richardie, June 14, 1741, *WHC* 17:349.

the Huron-Petuns joined the dissidents in their shift south. Neither the phratry leaders nor any of the *hondatorinke* (or Stay-at-Homes), the most senior male council chiefs, left Detroit. Those who did follow Angouriot and Orontony began to designate themselves as Wyandots, an older name for the Hurons that had gone largely unused for generations. This was a political rebellion against the village hierarchy, but it was also a rejection of the alliance. British traders apparently encouraged the Wyandots from the outset, and Orontony would in the 1740s confirm his break with the French by seeking British aid. When asked by the British their reason for deserting the French, the Wyandots denounced the French for the endless wars they demanded of their allies and the high price of their trading goods. In effect, Orontony and his followers challenged Onontio's patriarchal credentials. Onontio brought peace to the *pays d'en haut* only at the price of war outside it, and he failed to provide the *bon marché* that a good father should guarantee among his children.[16]

Where Chartier had indicated possibilities, Orontony and Angouriot indicated directions. Orontony, who emerged as the leader at Sandusky, served as a particularly important transitional figure. He stepped free of both the alliance and the old tribal hierarchy and entered the lands south of Lake Erie just as the first imperial storms in a generation were about to break over the region.

III

Without any clear plan, men like Chartier and Orontony began a political reorganization of the *pays d'en haut*. Their immediate goals centered on their villages, but at least hazily they began to envision a peace between villages that extended to all Indians, north and south. The troubles of the Huron-Petuns had begun, after all, in an attempt to end the chronic fighting between northern and southern Indians. In the Ohio Valley the Shawnees also made attempts to secure peace. The implications of a peace achieved without Onontio's mediation worried the French, for it threatened the

---

[16] Clifton, "Re-emergent Wyandot," 7–8, 14–15; Beauharnois to Minister, Sept. 15, 1742, *WHC*, 17:414–15. For reference to Hurons among English, see Beauharnois to Fr. de la Richardie, *WHC* 17:350. The other Huron-Petuns remained in a state of turmoil. They had supposedly decided to settle near Detroit at the Isle de Bois Blanc (Beauharnois au Ministre, 2 nov. 1742, AN, C11A, v. 75) and then at la Grande Terre on the mainland near Detroit (Beauharnois to Ministre, Nov. 12, 1742, *WHC* 17:431). More settled at Sandusky in the Ohio country, Beauharnois au Ministre, 17 sept. 1743, AN, C11A, v. 108. Paroles de Kinonsaki aux Hurons etablis à Sandoské . . . 5 mai 1743, AN, C11A, v. 79, f. 95. Some of those at Sandusky returned, at least temporarily, to La Grande Terre in 1744, Beauharnois to Minister, Oct. 9, 1744, *WHC* 17:440. For among Shawnees, see Reponse au mémoire du Roy, 13 oct. 1735, AN, C11A, v. 63; Canada, Sauvages, dec. 1735, AN, C11A, v. 63, f. 218. For denouncing French, see Journal of Conrad Weiser, Sept. 8, 1748, *PCR* 5:350.

Habit of a Wiendot Woman.

(Courtesy Mackinac State Historic Parks)

alliance itself. In 1747 Charles des Champs de Boishébert noted reports that "the Red skins made a treaty some years ago not to kill one another, and to let the whites act against each other." Refusing to fight other Indians, French allies "favored the parties of our enemies who attacked us, without putting themselves to the trouble of defending us."[17]

---

[17] For Shawnee efforts, see Beauharnois au Ministre, 3 nov. 1746, AN, CIIA, v. 85, f. 230. For Shawnee-Cherokee peace, see Beauchamp's Journal, (1746), *MPA* 4:289. For inter-

Boishébert wrote as a new round of imperial wars exploded in North America. King George's War and the Seven Years' War gave urgency to British and French attempts to win Indian allies while submerging the village struggle beneath the struggle for empire. Discovering the nature of the new "republican" political and social order that Boishébert and other officials feared and that Orontony sought therefore requires reading between the lines of accounts of the imperial wars of the period.

With the eruption of King George's War in 1744, the French moved quickly to attach the peoples of the Ohio country to the alliance. At first they seemed to succeed. The largely Iroquois migrants living by the Cuyahoga River (White River) declared for the French and promised to plunder British traders, and under the leadership of Chartier, the Shawnees did plunder the British. The Miamis declared for the French, as did the Weas. Even some Wyandots at Sandusky returned to Detroit, becoming once again Huron-Petuns. The Six Nations proper at their council fire at Onondaga announced their neutrality. Many western villagers – the Ottawas, Menominees, Winnebagos, Saulteurs, Mississaugas, Illinois, Huron-Petuns, Potawatomis, and others – sent warriors to Montreal to join the French in attacks on the British. Only the Mohawks, breaking away from the neutrality of the Iroquois confederation as a whole, declared war against the French. The French envisioned the Ohio country swept free of the British traders who had followed the Shawnees, Iroquois, and Delawares west.[18]

But after their initial success in mobilizing their allies, things went awry for the French. By 1747 the alliance was in disarray and so many villages were in open rebellion that Boishébert wrote, somewhat overdramatically, of a "general conspiracy of the redskins against the white." Ottawas and Chippewas murdered French traders on Lake Superior. The Miamis sacked the French post located among them. The Wyandots of Sandusky, some Ottawas, and the White River Indians of the Cuyahoga attacked a French

tribal peace, see Vaudreuil to Maurepas, Apr. 1, 1746, *MPA* 4:266–67; Vaudreuil to Maurepas, Nov. 20, 1746, Loudoun Papers, Extracts from Letterbooks, LO 9 vol. 1 (2), Huntington. Governor de Vaudreuil and his agents in Louisiana hoped the Shawnee attempts at peace would halt Choctaw attacks on the French, Beauchamp's Journal, (1746), *MPA* 4:289. Boishébert to Minister, Nov. 1747, *NYCD* 9:87. Boishébert says they made a concordat, Enterprises de guerre . . . , 1747, AN, C11A, v. 87, f. 20. There is, in addition, a mention as early as 1737 of a broad anti-French conspiracy, Bienville au Ministre, 21 juin 1737, AN, C13A, v. 22.

[18] For Indians accepting war belts, see Beauharnois to Maurepas, Oct. 8, 1744, *NYCD* 9:1105; *ibid.*, 7 Nov. 1744, *NYCD* 9:1111–12. For White River, see Conference between M. de Longueuil . . . and the Indians, 1700, (*sic*) *NYCD* 9:704–07. For movement of Shawnees, see Beauharnois to Minister, Oct. 28, 1745, *WHC* 17:448. For Wyandots' return, see Beauharnois to Minister, Oct. 9, 1744, *WHC* 17:440. For joining war parties and accepting hatchet against Mohawks, see Etrait des differens mouvements . . . de la guerre, Dec. 1745 – Aug. 1746, AN, C11A, v. 87.

party, killing five traders. The success of this attack, in turn, led the Ottawas who had participated to promise to attack Detroit, but an informant betrayed the plan and the Detroit attack never took place. The Illinois ceased all activity in favor of the French, and rumors had them conspiring to destroy the posts in Illinois country. Only the Potawatomis seemed loyal.[19]

The French blamed their problems on British machinations, and the British clearly encouraged the rebels in the Ohio region and beyond. But the causes of disruption went much deeper. The French themselves had planted the seeds of widespread revolt with the Crown's drive for economy in the years preceding the war. In 1744, after several years of increasing expenditures, the minister of the marine, the Comte de Maurepas, noted with pleasure that the intendant and the governor had managed to cut back significantly on the presents given to Indians in Canada. At the same time, in an attempt to reduce the expense of maintaining the posts, the king had farmed out many of them, including Niagara, Miami, Ouiatenon, and Green Bay, to lessees. To recover the cost of the lease and capitalize on their monopolies, these lessees had raised prices for goods and cut back on the presents they bestowed. One result of these measures was Indian discontent, which was further exacerbated as the inevitable British wartime blockade curtailed the supply of French trade goods.[20]

By 1745 there were serious shortages of trade goods in the West. The British told Indians visiting them at Oswego that the French would no longer be able to supply their allies. Governor de Beauharnois, for his part, rightly

---

[19] For French fears and countermeasures, La Galissonière to Maurepas, Oct. 22, 1747, *IHC* 29:38–39. For murders at Sandusky, planned attack on Detroit, and attacks of Chippewas and Ottawas of Michilimackinac, see Raymond to Maurepas, Nov. 2, 1747, *WHC* 17: 474–77; Galissonière to Minister, 23 Oct. 1748, *NYCD* 10:181–82. For Ottawa and Chippewa attacks, see Continuation du journal, 9 oct. 1747, AN, C11A, v. 87; Hanna, *Wilderness Trail* 1:323–32. For Wyandot belts seeking allies and aid, see Weiser to Peters, Oct. 15, 1747, *PCR* 5:136–37. For crediting Wyandots as well as Iroquois with spreading rebellion to Illinois and Wabash, Vaudreuil to Maurepas, Sept. 19, 1747, *IHC* 29:32–34. For blaming English, see Raymond to Maurepas, Nov. 2, 1747, *WHC* 17:474–77. For Potawatomis loyal, see Journal of Whatever Occurred of Interest at Quebec . . . since the sailing of the Ships in November 1747, *NYCD* 10:137–38, hereafter, *Journal*. For quotation and account of rebellion, see Report of M. Boisherbert, Nov. 1747, *NYCD* 10:83–88. For Miami post pillaged, see Bigot to Maurepas, Oct. 19, 1748, *IHC* 29:75.

[20] For cut back in presents, see Maurepas to Beauharnois, Mar. 24, 1744, *WHC* 18:5. For previous increase and complaints, see Beauharnois to Maurepas, Oct. 13, 1743, *NYCD* 9:1098–99. For leases, see Postes des pays d'en haut, Beauharnois & Hocquart, 8 oct. 1742, AN, C11A, v. 78, f. 378–85; Beauharnois au Ministre, 6 juin 1743, AN, C11A, v. 79, f. 97; Beauharnois to Minister, Oct. 9, 1744, *WHC* 17:442–43; Beauharnois to Minister, Oct. 25, 1744, *WHC* 17:445–46; Galissonière to Minister, Oct. 23, 1748, *WHC* 17:503. For Wea complaints about lessees and high prices, see Speeches of Ouyatanons, etc., July 8, 1742, *WHC* 17:381. For failure of supplies, high prices, and scarcity, see Beauharnois au Ministre, 19 juin 1745, AN, C11A, v. 83; La Galissonière & Hocquart to Minister, Oct. 7, 1747, *WHC* 17:470–72.

feared a "great change" in the upper country. In 1746 the French somewhat desperately granted *congés* gratis in an attempt to get goods and supplies to the posts. Some goods reached the upper country, but traders demanded far more than the customary prices for them. French attempts to explain market forces and to blame their lack of supplies on the war fell on deaf ears, as well they might since Algonquians had already seen prices rise with the leasing of the posts.[21]

Some Indians reacted to the changes in exchange rates by refusing to pay for goods advanced them for their hunts; others began to attack and plunder French trade canoes. In and of themselves, the attacks represented less an Algonquian repudiation of the alliance than an armed and angry protest against French violations of the principles of the alliance. Most warriors in the *pays d'en haut* resented the shortages and high prices of French trade goods, but killing Frenchmen instead of simply robbing them or, indeed, ignoring them and trading with the British at Oswego or in the Ohio country reflected a deeper anger at what these high prices represented. By demanding that their allies shed blood in an imperial war while giving them fewer and fewer goods, the French had ceased to act as fathers. For Algonquians each decrease in what the French traders offered for furs and skins was not a demonstration of economic necessity but an example of French greed that violated the concept of the alliance. The French, not they, had broken the alliance. The account of George Croghan, a Scots-Irish trader, of a sudden murder committed by a Wyandot captures the bitterness and anger of individual warriors. "Another French Trader has since been killed in a private quarrel with one of the Jonoontatichroanu [Wyandots], between the River Ohio and the Lake Erie – the Frenchman offering but one charge of powder and one bullet for a beaver skin to the Indian; the Indian took up hatchet and knocked him on the head."[22]

This wave of murders and attacks alarmed the French considerably, but as information filtered in from the West, it became apparent that the attacks did not, as yet, constitute a concerted attempt by the Indians to drive the French out of the *pays d'en haut*. There were, however, Indians who sought to turn anger against the French into a rearrangement of the political map of the region. The most prominent of these men were Orontony, his Wyandot

---

[21] For lease system, see Beauharnois to Minister, Oct. 28, 1745, *WHC* 17:449; La Galissonière to Minister, Oct. 23, 1748, *WHC* 17:503–4. For early warning of problems from cost of trade, see Bienville au Ministre, 21 juin 1737, AN, C13A, v. 22, f. 101. For *congés*, gratis, see Beauharnois and Hocquart to Minister, Sept. 22, 1746 *WHC* 17:450–51. For English claim to have cut off French supplies, see Longueuil to Beauharnois, July 28, 1745, *WHC* 17:446–47. For French lack supplies for posts, see Beauharnois au ministre, 3 nov. 1746, AN, C11A, v. 85, f. 230; Vaudreuil to Maurepas, March 22, 1747, *IHC* 29:15; Bigot to Minister, Oct. 22, 1748, *WHC* 17:509.

[22] Hanna, *Wilderness Trail*, 324–33; for quotation, see 325.

followers at Sandusky, and their Mingo and White River allies. Orontony
and the Wyandots attacked the alliance itself as exploitative. The French
"would always get their young men to go to war against their enemies, and
would use them as their own people; that is like slaves; and their goods were
so dear that they, the Indians, could not buy them."[23]

Their break with the French was only the first fracture that Orontony and
his Mingo and White River allies made in the political networks of the *pays
d'en haut*. Orontony used the Wyandots' attack on the French to underline
his own independence from the Huron-Petuns, while the Mingos and White
River Indians declared their independence of the Iroquois council at
Onondaga. Canachquasy, a speaker for the Mingos on the Ohio, rightly
attributed Mingo attacks not to decisions at Onondaga – which remained
neutral – but to the young warriors of the western villages.[24]

To sustain themselves against the French, Orontony and his allies needed
aid, and in seeking it, they complicated the politics of the Ohio Valley still
further. They appealed to Pennsylvania for help, and in doing so they
attached their rebellion against the French to the imperial war between
Great Britain and France. Pennsylvania's interest in the *pays d'en haut* had
until the late 1740s been represented largely by the Scots-Irish traders who
had followed the Shawnees and Delawares west. In September of 1747, the
most prominent of these traders, George Croghan, sent a desperate message
to Pennsylvania officials warning them that unless presents arrived quickly,
the rebelling Indians would return to the French. Only after some delay did
Croghan receive any goods. With his belated aid, the government of
Pennsylvania partially abandoned its own long-held fiction that the western
migrants were dependents of Onondaga, controlled by the Iroquois council
at Onondaga.[25]

Orontony sought to extend his alliance with the Pennsylvanians throughout the *pays d'en haut*. British belts and Orontony's appeals for revolt
following the Wyandot attacks apparently convinced many Chippewas and
Ottawas that merely plundering and murdering Frenchmen would bring

---

[23] For quotation, see Journal of Conrad Weiser in Thwaites (ed.), *Early Western Travels*,
1:24–25 (presents), 29 (Wyandot discontent); for Shawnees and Miamis, see Wallace,
Weiser, 259. For attacks, see Galissonière to Minister, 23 Oct. 1748, *NYCD* 10:183. For
Green Bay, see La Jonquiére to Minister, Aug. 18, 1750, *WHC* 18:63–64. For Miamis and
Shawnees to Pennsylvania, see A Treaty . . . Lancaster, July 19, 1748, *PCR* 5:307–19.

[24] For Wyandot belts, see Weiser to Peters, Oct. 15, 1747, *PCR* 5:136–37. The White River
Indians claimed they had accepted the English hatchet offered the Six Nations at Albany in
1746. But, in fact, the Iroquois had rejected the hatchet; only the Mohawks had accepted it.
The confederacy as a whole maintained its neutrality.

[25] Hanna, *Wilderness Trail*, 324–33, summarizes material on the conflict. For Pennsylvania, see
Wallace, *Weiser*, 260. For goods to Croghan, see Weiser Journal in Thwaites (ed.), *Early
Western Travels*, 1:39. For solicitation of goods, see Penn. Council, 25 Sept. 1747, *PCR*
5:119. For warriors on Ohio, see Penn. Council, 13 Nov. 1747, *PCR* 5:145–47.

British traders among them. Other belts carried by the Mississaugas, now allies of the British in New York, contained plans for a general slaughter of the "white dogs." But the result of these messages was only more scattered attacks on French traders. Discontent over trade goods had spawned attacks on the French and hopes for British trade, but only in the lower Ohio Valley and among the Mississaugas had it produced an actual alliance with the British.[26]

The end of King George's War in 1748 gave the French a chance to repair the damage, but instead they accelerated the deterioration of the alliance. In the language of the councils, young warriors were *étourdi*, thoughtless and heedless; inevitably they would in troubled times block the paths and darken the sky. The great achievement of the alliance was that Onontio and his chiefs – both French and Algonquian – had created the means to repair damage and restore tranquillity. But in the midst of this crisis, the French seemed determined to undercut the alliance chiefs and to abandon the well-tried customs of covering and raising the dead. Onontio neglected the rituals of surrender and forgiveness; instead, he humiliated his own chiefs and demanded the death of his errant children. The French governors seemed in the late 1740s and early 1750s ready to abandon all the compromises achieved on the middle ground during the last century. They seemed determined, as Orontony contended, to treat the Algonquians as subjects or, in Algonquian terms, as slaves.

It is doubtful that the officials who attempted to substitute force for mediation knew the significance of the changes they were demanding. Experience alone taught French governors the limits of their power and the necessity of the middle ground. The long terms of Governor de Vaudreuil and Governor de Beauharnois had educated them, but with the retirement of Governor de Beauharnois in 1747, no governor had time to be educated until Governor de Vaudreuil's son, Pierre Rigaud, Marquis de Vaudreuil-Cavagnal, assumed office in 1755. The appointed successor to Beauharnois, Pierre-Jacques de Tafanel, Marquis de La Jonquière, was captured on the high seas by the British. In his absence from September 1747 until 1749, the Marquis de La Galissonière served as governor. La Jonquière arrived in 1749, after the close of the war, but he died in 1752. Charles Le Moyne, Baron de Longueuil, served briefly as an interim governor until the Marquis Duquesne de Menneville took office in July 1752. Duquesne served for only three years. Meanwhile, in France, the long tenure of the Comte de Maurepas as minister of the marine and the colonies had ended in 1749, and

---

[26] For message carried by Mississaugas, see Parolles ... Missisague du village du fond du lac Ontario, AN, C11A, v. 91, f. 107. La Jonquière later dated this message as 1747, La Jonquière to Minister, Oct. 5, 1751, *WHC* 18:100–01.

Antoine Louis Rouillé had succeeded him in office. Neither continuity nor experience in the formulation of French policy existed during the period of revolts in the *pays d'en haut*. Threats of force replaced mediation.[27]

Under the new governors, the formal ritual language of Onontio to his children remained, but the logic of his actions increasingly belied his words. The new governors expected obedience, and they mistook the Algonquians' ritual demands for pity for admissions of dependence. French officers in the West knew better, but the governors subverted their efforts to end the crisis. The commanders at Michilimackinac and Detroit, working through loyal chiefs, used the convoys and reinforcements that reached the *pays d'en haut* in 1747 and 1748 to begin the restoration of the alliance. In January 1748, Paul Joseph Le Moyne, Chevalier de Longueuil, commanding at Detroit, attempted to reconcile the Indians at his post by pardoning the rebels and releasing the prisoners who had attacked the French. This moderate course brought him a reprimand from his own father, Charles Le Moyne, Baron de Longueuil, soon to be the governor of Montreal, who articulated the new policy of coercion. Governor de La Galissonière ordered the commanders to exact the surrender of all "Indian murderers and malefactors" and send them down to Quebec. In addition, each tribe was to produce two British prisoners for every Frenchman they had killed.[28]

Surrendering killers was by the 1740s customary in the *pays d'en haut*, but so was pardoning them. When the Ottawas and Saulteurs of Michilimackinac and Saginaw began to surrender the killers, they were astonished to find that the French not only put them in prison, with no promise of mercy, but refused the calumet until all murderers were surrendered. The French at Michilimackinac declared that there would be no more pardons since these only occasioned new crimes. When the Indians demanded mercy, the French replied that it was mercy to detain the prisoners and thus halt their crimes. Requests for mercy for the murderers, made in council to La Galissonière himself, only brought his renewed demand for the surrender of all the murderers and strengthened his determination to punish the guilty. The governor released a hostage who had previously been given for the murderers' surrender, but he warned the Indians: "The word pardon for any

---

[27] Gustave Lanctot, *A History of Canada*, 4 vols. (Cambridge, Mass.: Harvard University Press, 1965), 3:70–89.

[28] For arrival of convoy in 1747, see Journal, Nov. 23, 1747, *NYCD* 10:140. For actions of commanders, Saint Pierre at Michilimackinac, see Journal, Nov. 10, 1747, *NYCD* 10:137. For Longueuil and pardon to Saulteurs, and Ottawas and Chippewas of Saginaw, see Journal, Nov. 23, 1747, *NYCD* 10:141; his attempts to fortify loyalty of Mikinac and Kinousaki, Ottawa chiefs at Detroit, see Journal, Dec. 3, Dec. 23, 1747, *NYCD* 10:145, 149. For attack and pardon, see Journal, Nov. 29, 1747, Jan. 12, 1748, *NYCD* 10:150–52, 156–57; for Longueuil and La Galissonière, see Journal June 2, 1748, *NYCD* 10:161–62.

murderer must not be pronounced any more." La Galissonière, who by July had three murderers in custody, was pleased with the results of his policy and the renewed attacks by some Indians on the British. He informed Le Gardeur de St. Pierre, the commander at Michilimackinac, and Longueuil that the arrival of a convoy under the Sieur de Céloron in 1748 should give them the ability to act with even greater firmness in exacting the surrender of the murderers.[29]

The Algonquians, for their part, viewed this new French recalcitrance with growing confusion and alarm. That murderers should be surrendered was predictable. That the French should demand prisoners to raise up their dead was understandable. But in return, the murderers should be pardoned and restored to favor, and this was not being done. The Algonquian solution to the problem is apparent in the speech of Gros Serpent, an Ottawa married to an Iroquois woman of the village of Petit Rapide near Niagara. Gros Serpent was a mediator solicited by the wife of Agouachimagand, an Ottawa man who had led a party that had ambushed and killed some French voyageurs. She had asked his aid in obtaining pardon for her husband. Gros Serpent, accompanied by the Iroquois of Petit Rapide, spoke at Niagara in 1748. He gave the French a beaver robe that would symbolically hold the bones of the murdered men, and he raised up the dead with a slave. He asked that the past be forgotten and that mercy be granted. The French commander at Niagara accepted the gifts that Gros Serpent offered, but only Onontio, he said, could grant pardon. If Agouachimagand and his men went to Montreal and threw themselves on the mercy of their father, they would obtain mercy.[30]

But murderers were not receiving the usual reception at Montreal and Quebec. La Galissonière contended later that he intended to release one of the murderers he already had in custody to Achaoualina, a Saginaw chief who was the man's relative, but he gave no indication of this to the delegation of Michilimackinac chiefs who visited him at the time. He denied the request of the chiefs for the release of the murderers and ordered the killers conveyed from Montreal to Quebec. But as the French guard escorted their prisoners toward Quebec, an unknown party attacked them, slaughtered the French to a man, and freed the prisoners. The escapees joined the chiefs who were already on their way back to Michilimackinace and Saginaw and

---

[29] For surrender of killers at Michilimackinac, see Journal, June 25, 1748, *NYCD* 10:168–69. At Quebec, July 5, 1748, *NYCD* 10:170; surrender of murderer from Green Bay, Journal, July 14, 1748, *NYCD* 10:172. For greater firmness, see Journal, July 23, 1748, *NYCD* 10:173. For delivery of prisoners from Michilimackinac and Saginaw, Galissonière to Minister Oct. 23, 1748, *NYCD* 10:183.

[30] Parolles du Gros Serpend . . . dans le conseil tenus a Niagara, le 2 aout 1748, AN, C11A, v. 97, f. 402.

accompanied them home. It was an object lesson in the limits of French power and patriarchy, but it only renewed the French determination to reduce their allies. They would meet with little success. The Sinago Ottawas and many of the Saulteurs fled Michilimackinac and remained securely at Saginaw until they received French pardon in 1751.[31]

Although the reliance on force was failing to achieve its ends, the new minister of the marine, Rouillé, encouraged his governors to reject the older methods of the middle ground. He expressed understandable frustration at the escape of the Michilimackinac murderers, but the lesson he drew summarized the changing French view of the alliance. The officers at the posts, Rouillé wrote, were too "disposed to end disputes with the Indians by means of conciliation." Only "well placed examples of severity" would check the Indians, and governors should "neglect no occasions for procuring" such examples. The change was echoed by the governors. La Jonquière proclaimed that it was time "to lay down the law to the tribes which have rebelled against us and to force them even in spite of themselves back to their duty."[32]

Bringing the tribes back to their duty had in the past always involved working through the chiefs, but now French governors adopted policies that both alienated and enfeebled the alliance chiefs upon whom their own success depended. In a disastrous series of conferences at Quebec in 1749, Governor de La Galissonière insulted many of the visiting delegations by giving them either no presents or only token presents. Although he gave substantial presents to those tribes who surrendered men who had killed the French during the war, this had minimal effect since he simultaneously denied mercy to the murderers. Onontio had humiliated his chiefs, and he paid a price for it. The immediate result of the conference was increasing discontent among the Miami confederation. Les Ongles, the leading Wea chief at Ouiatenon, had to beg a little barrel of brandy from the Comte de Raymond at the Miami post so that "he might not arrive in shame at my village." But Les Ongles's small barrel of brandy did not save him from the scorn of other Weas. Le Comte, another Wea leader, mocked Les Ongles for having returned from Montreal with nothing.[33]

---

[31] For murderers, see Galissonière to Minister, Oct. 23, 1748, *NYCD* 10:184; Canada, Sauvages, 15 avril 1749, AN, C11A, v. 94, f. 73. For pardon, see Parolles, O8t8ois Sinagos du Saginaw, 13 juillet, 1751, AN, C11A, v.97, La Jonquière to Minister, Sept. 17, 1751, *WHC* 18:83. The figure "8" in "O8t8ois" is pronounced "dh."

[32] For first quotation, see Rouillé to La Jonquière, May 4, 1749, *IHC* 29:87–88; for second quotation, see La Jonquière to Rouillé, Nov. 12, 1749, *IHC* 24:124–25.

[33] For lack of presents, see Report of Sieur Roy, Apr. 1, 1750, *IHC* 29:170,173; Report of Porc Epic, Apr. 5, 1750, *ibid.*, 176; Report of Raymond, Feb. 15, 1750, *IHC* 29:177–78; Report of Le Pian, May 1750, *ibid.*, 198; Raymond to La Jonquière, May 22, 1750, *ibid.*,

Les Ongles was not alone in his humiliation, but he accepted it with more forbearance than other, lesser chiefs. La Graine, a subordinate Wea chief, and L'Enfant, a Piankashaw chief at Vermilion, also returned from Montreal empty-handed, and they fell into a rage when they discovered that in their absence their villages had been ravaged by disease. They blamed the epidemic on French witchcraft. La Graine, L'Enfant, Le Comte, and La Mouche Noire, another Piankashaw chief, all joined rebel Miamis who had already accepted belts from Orontony. At the Illinois settlements Mactigue de Macarty, a voluble self-important drunkard, became commander in 1751. Unlike earlier commanders, Macarty did not immediately understand the necessity of giving "the chiefs the wherewithal to maintain their prestige in the village."[34]

Undercutting the chiefs hurt the French for it rendered the warriors increasingly independent. During the best of times, as the French noted, "there is only voluntary subordination" among the western Indians. "Each person is free to do as he pleases. The village chiefs and war chiefs can have influence, but they do not have authority, still their influence over the young men depends upon how much they exert it, and upon their attention to keeping their kettles full, so to say." Les Ongles remained loyal, but the chief himself admitted that he could not hold his young men when the French refused to offer a *bon marché*. Quoting French prices that required a man to spend his entire year's hunt merely to clothe himself, he told the Comte de Raymond that this "rebuffs all our young men, and we are no longer able to hold them back." Without a *bon marché* – which it was the duty of their father to provide – the warriors could not be held to the alliance.[35]

The capstone on the edifice of failure erected by the French resort to dictation and subordination came with the Céloron expedition of 1749. Governor de La Galissonière decided to dispatch an expedition under Captain de Céloron to expel the British, to force Orontony either to return to Detroit or to drive him off, and to disperse other Indian rebels who had

205–6. For disease, see Report of the Nephew of M. the Commandant at Ouiatonon, Apr. 2, 1750, *ibid.*, 174. For Les Grands Ongles, see Raymond to La Jonquière, May 22, 1750, *ibid.*, 201, 207; for words of Les Grands Ongles, see May 17, 1750, *IHC* 29:214–25.

[34] For other chiefs, see Report of Sieur Roy, Apr. 1, 1750, *IHC* 29:170, 173; Report of Porc Epic, Apr. 5, 1750, *ibid.*, 176; Report of Raymond, Feb. 15, 1750, *IHC* 29:177–78. These were almost certainly the chiefs who entered the covenant chain of the Iroquois and English at la Demoiselle's town in Feb. 1750; see Treaty with Wawiagtas and Piankashas, Mulkearn (ed.), *George Mercer Papers*, 128–39. For Illinois visit and gifts, see De Guyenne to Vaudreuil, Sept. 10, 1752, *IHC* 29:719–20. For Macarty, see Duquesne to Rouille, Oct. 31, 1753, *IHC* 29:846–47.

[35] For chiefs, quotation, see Edward P. Hamilton (trans. and ed.), *Adventure in the Wilderness: The American Journals of Louis Antoine de Bougainville, 1756–60* (Norman: University of Oklahoma Press, 1964), 134. Raymond to La Jonquière, May 22, 1750, *IHC* 29:201, 207; Words of Les Grands Ongles, May 17, 1750, *IHC* 29:214–15.

congregated at Sonnontio on the Scioto River. Instead of restoring French hegemony at a stroke, Céloron's expedition demonstrated the weakness of the French.[36]

Céloron's progress from the Great Lakes to the Ohio with two hundred French, thirty mission Indians, and a load of lead plates, which he buried to mark the Ohio boundary of New France, provided the French captain with daily doses of humiliation. Any chance of success for the expedition vanished when the Detroit Indians, after great promises, refused to join Céloron. William Johnson, now emerging as the central figure in New York's Indian policy, sent messengers west to warn of Céloron's approach, and after some initial panic, the Ohio Indians grew increasingly defiant when they realized how few men accompanied Céloron. They could, after all, muster nearly eight hundred warriors on the upper Ohio alone.[37]

In the end, Céloron could only request the obedience that he was ordered to demand. In his various councils Céloron warned the Indians that the British now came for trade but eventually would seize the Indians' lands. Céloron did not himself dare execute his orders to pillage and evict the British traders who had flocked to the Ohio. Instead, he could do no more than tell the traders he encountered to leave and not return. He realized that their absence would not exceed his own stay in the villages. Indian promises to banish these Englishmen grew ever vaguer as he proceeded west. By the time he reached the towns of Chiningué (Logstown) and Sonnontio he, himself, feared attack.[38]

Similar defiance was apparent all across the *pays d'en haut*. In 1749 and 1750, large numbers of Ottawas and Chippewas from Lakes Superior and Huron continued to carry furs to Oswego. Here they received wampum belts, medals, and flags from the British to carry back to the *pays d'en haut*. Nouk8ata, a Michilimackinac Ottawa, became a British chief, and many warriors eagerly sought to follow him. Ottawas and Chippewas carried British brandy west to Green Bay, arousing fear of British influence there.

[36] For Céloron expedition, see Galissonière to Rouillé, June 26, 1749, *IHC* 29:97.

[37] *Ibid.* A complete text of Céloron's journal is in Margry, *Découvertes* 6:666–726. There is an abbreviated translation in *WHC* 18:36–59, which is valuable largely for the footnotes that give place locations. For expedition, see Journal de la Campagne, Margry, *Découvertes* 6:666. For initial terror, see *ibid.*, 671, 675, 680, 685. For refusal of Indians of Detroit, see *ibid.*, 714. For warrior strength, see Weiser, Journal, in Thwaites (ed.), *Early Western Travels* (Weiser counted members of all the Six Nations plus Shawnees, Wyandots, "Tisagechroanus," Mohicans, and Delawares). For Johnson's warning, see Hendricks Speech to Johnson, Feb. 2, 1749–50, *NYCD* 6:548.

[38] For fears of attack, see Journal, Margry, *Découvertes* 6:691–92, 703–5; for warnings about English, see *ibid.*, 6:681, 694–95; for signs of traders, see *ibid.*, 6:678, 683–84, 686, 688, 689. For promises, see *ibid.*, 6:678–80. By Sonnontio the Indians made no specific promises, they only said they would work for *bonnes affaires*, *ibid.* 6:713. For English in every village, see *JR* 69:185.

Farther east, near Lake Erie, nine villages of Mississaugas, having entirely forsaken the French alliance, moved closer to the Iroquois.[39]

Céloron's expedition was supposed to resolve French policy difficulties; instead, it underlined the continuing deterioration of the alliance and led to further drift. Céloron himself concluded that the Indians were "very badly disposed toward the French and entirely devoted to the English." Force would only drive them into the arms of the British and ally them to the Têtes Plattes. French traders, Céloron thought, could not meet British prices, and even if they could, this would only encourage the continuing migration south to lands "convenient to the English governments." La Jonquière, who succeeded La Galissonière, initially planned a much larger expedition to follow Céloron's, but when he found Céloron had not actually been attacked, he decided traders and a few officers would suffice. For the next several years he oscillated between threats of force and attempts at conciliation.[40]

Whatever its deficiencies, such drift had advantages over the steadfast pursuit of the disastrous policies of the preceding few years. The appeal of force and subordination remained strong for La Jonquière, but he channeled it into actions against the British. La Galissonière had already suggested to the court the necessity of new posts along the Ohio, but for the moment, La Jonquière contented himself with attacks on British traders. The French and their partisans seized British traders whenever they found them unprotected in the Ohio country. The actions threatened the rebels' interests without threatening their lives, but the British used the attacks to argue that the French sought both to deny the Algonquians liberty to trade and to enslave them.[41]

[39] The "8" in 'Nouk8ata" is pronounced "dh." La Jonquière to Minister, Sept. 20, 1750, WHC 18:67–68; La Jonquière to Minister, Sept. 17, 1751, WHC 18:80–81; Parolles de Pemant8euns [Pennahouel], 5 juillet 1751, AN, C11A, v. 97. For Green Bay, see La Jonquière to Minister, Sept. 16, 1751, WHC 18:78–79; Returns of Western Tribes Who Traded at Oswego, 1749, NYCD 6:538. Example of English message, Speech of English at Oswego to the Huron named Tahoké, n.d., IHC 29:127–28. Mississaugas were trading at Oswego, and the French in 1749 sought to provide both a regulated trade and to restrict their access to the English, Les journaux de M. de Léry . . . 1749, RAPQ, 1926–27, 339. For movement of Mississaugas, Clinton to Lords of Trade, July 17, 1751, NYCD 6:713–14; Lindesay to Johnson, July 10, 1751, NYCD 6:729–30. Colden credited this move to French inspired attacks by the Ottawas, but I have found no evidence of such attacks in the French records, Colden to Clinton, Aug. 8, 1751, NYCD 6:742.

[40] For quotation on attitude of tribes and French dilemma, see Margry, Découvertes 6:725–26. Céloron added that in any case French traders would only trade beaver to the English in exchange for menues pelleteries that brought a high price in France and a low price in England, La Jonquière au Ministre, 27 fév. 1750, AN, C11A, v. 95, f. 129.

[41] For La Galissonière's suggestion, see Memoir on the French Colonies, Dec. 1750, NYCD 10:230. For protests to English over traders' presence, see Jonquière to Phips, Mar. 7, 1750, NYCD 6:565–66. For attacks on traders, see Trent to Peters, July 22, 1750, PA, series 1, 2:50; Lindsay to Johnson, Sept. 7, 1750; JP 1:297; Johnson to Clinton, Sept. 25, 1750, NYCD 6:590–91; Deposition of John Patton, Mar. 8, 1752, IHC 29:490–99; Deposition of

Except for these attacks, French policy grew increasingly conciliatory. In 1750, La Jonquière began to act as a father and to restore the alliance. By declaring a general amnesty, he ended the fiascoes that had resulted from French attempts to punish the killers of Frenchmen during the war. He then moved to strengthen the alliance chiefs. In dealing with virtually every band that appeared in Montreal that year, he awarded medals to those men designated as alliance chiefs by either villagers or previous medal chiefs. He gave sizable presents to the chiefs to redistribute in their villages, and he mediated outstanding quarrels between the villages. Not satisfied with the rapprochement he had arranged at Montreal, La Jonquière, who had replaced the commanders at Detroit and at the Miami post, urged on the new officers a policy of conciliation in the Ohio Valley. Céloron arranged for a large delegation of chiefs from Detroit and Saint Joseph to visit the rebel Miamis in order to persuade them to return to Fort Miami. Simultaneously, he recruited Father de la Richardie to visit the Wyandots and convince them to return to Detroit. Governor de Vaudreuil of Louisiana advocated a similar policy of conciliation.[42]

La Jonquière's policy of reconciliation proved more successful than the earlier threats of punishment and demands of subordination. Some Wyandots deserted Orontony, who had moved south toward the British and the Ohio; the Ottawas at Saginaw accepted La Jonquière's amnesty and returned to Michilimackinac. Nouk8ata, the Ottawa chief at Michilimackinac who had traded and negotiated with the British at Oswego, begged forgiveness. By the time he held council with the tribes of the Great Lakes in 1751, La Jonquière had begun to understand the realities and rhetoric

Thomas Bourke, Mar. 8, 1752, *ibid.*, 503–05. For justification and rival imperial positions, see Jonquière to Clinton, Aug. 10, 1751, and Clinton's notes, *NYCD* 6:731–36. The Mohawks and English in 1750 interpreted French actions as preparation for an attack on both the Ohio Indians and the Iroquois, Johnson to Clinton, May 4, 1750, *JP* 1:276–77.

[42] For presents, see Jonquière au Ministre, 3 nov. 1751, AN, C11A, v. 97, f. 193. For medal chiefs, see Parolles des Sakis, Reponse, 29 juin, 1 juillet, 1750, AN, C11A, f. 251; Parolles des P8tet8atames, 29 juin 1750, AN, C11A, v. 95, f. 249; Parolles des Kiskakons ... de Michilimackinac et reponse, 4, 6 Juillet 1750, AN, C11A, v. 95, f. 241. For mediation, also see Parolles des Sakis, Reponse, 29 juin, 1 juillet, 1750, AN, C11A, f. 251; Parolles des Saulteurs de Chouagamegon, et reponse, 2–3 juillet 1750, AN, C11A, v. 95. For pardon, see Parolles des Kiskakons ... de Michilimackinac, et reponse, 4, 6 juillet 1750, AN, C11A, v. 95, f. 241; Parolles de 8ta8ois de la bande de la fourche, Reponse, 1 juillet, 6 juillet, 1750, AN, C11A, v. 95, f. 244; Puants de la Bay, (1750), AN, C11A, v. 95, f. 195. For actual mediation and another killing of a Frenchman, see Jonquière to Rouillé, Sept. 17, 1751, *IHC* 29:347–55. For instructions for De Villiers, see July 10, 1750, *IHC* 29:217–25. Raymond later claimed that he was on the verge of restoring many of the rebel Miamis when he was replaced, but this is doubtful. Raymond to Rouillé, Oct. 1, 1751, *IHC* 29:393–98.

The death of Frenchmen could still spawn initial demands for execution, La Jonquière to Ministre, Sept. 17, 1751, *WHC* 18:81–83. Vaudreuil was clearly contemplating more forceful actions against the rebels, Vaudreuil à Jonquière, 24 mars 1751, Cavagnal Letterbooks, LO9, v. 4, Huntington Library.

of alliance politics. His presents, unlike La Galissonière's, were large, and he honored and welcomed the chiefs. He was ready to forgive those who had had dealings with the British. He praised the chiefs and speakers in council. He acted quickly to mediate quarrels between his loyal children. He had learned to threaten only as a prelude to forgiveness. He received the Sinago Ottawas, who had fled to Saginaw after the murders of Frenchmen, and "forgot entirely all that you have done to the French. I no longer think of it." At the same time, he made it clear to the chiefs that he had eyes and ears of his own in the West. In council he repeated messages from the British that the chiefs assumed to be unknown to the French. He attempted to use the chiefs to force the Ottawas to raise warriors against the rebels of the Ohio and Wabash in order to demonstrate their own loyalty. Indeed he offered, and many of the Ottawas and Chippewas accepted, the British as a scapegoat on whose head all the previous problems of the alliance could be laid. La Jonquière had begun to reinvigorate the alliance.

Both La Galissonière and La Jonquière realized that any restoration of the alliance depended on a reform of the fur trade. They identified the policy of leasing the posts as a central problem, and they moved to end the policy at each post where disgruntled Indians had the option of seeking out the British. La Galissonière went farther and urged that the Compagnie des Indes maintain the higher price it had offered for beaver during the war in order to meet British competition. In this he partially succeeded. At the same time he urged the traders at Frontenac, Niagara, and Detroit to furnish goods at the same rate as the British for two or three years to come. La Jonquière also promised to intervene when traders cheated Indians. And for those Indians who insisted on journeying to Oswego, the French added posts at Toronto and Sault Sainte Marie and, eventually, a trading house at the Petit Rapide of the Niagara, to intercept them and offer them goods at competitive prices. Above all, the French were ready to offer the Indians brandy; for as Pennahouel, the speaker for the Michilimackinac Ottawa put it, the young men "love their drink."[43]

---

[43] There was substantial trade with the English at Oswego in 1750, La Jonquière to Minister, Sept. 20, 1750, WHC 18:67; Abstract of Despatches, 1749, NYCD 10:199–202. For end leases, see La Galissonière to Minister, Oct. 23, 1748, WHC 17:503; Jonquière au Ministre, 20 sept. 1749, AN, C11A, v. 93, f. 101; Jonquière and Bigot to Minister, Oct. 9, 1749, WHC 18:33; Jonquière to Minister, Aug. 18, 1750, WHC 18:63. Complaints that leases were alienating the western villagers had appeared as early as 1737, Bienville au Ministre, 21 juin 1737, AN, C13A, v. 22.

For brandy, see Parolles des P8tet8atames, 29 juin 1750, AN, C11A, v. 95, f. 249; 8ta8ois de Missilmakinack, 1 juillet 1750, AN, C11A, f. 248; Parolles de Pennant8euns, 7 juin 1751, AN, C11A, v. 97. Brandy was a central element in English trade gains, see Weiser, Journal, in Thwaites (ed.), Early Western Travels, 1:41. Trade, Parolles de 8ta8ois de la bande de la fourche, Reponse, 1 juillet, 6 juillet, 1750, AN, C11A, v. 95, f. 244. For Toronto, see La Jonquière and Bigot to Minister, Oct. 9, 1749, WHC 18:34. For Sault Sainte Marie, see La

Reform presented opportunities for La Jonquière that went beyond restoring the alliance. All French governors sought to enrich themselves, but La Jonquière was a ruler of exceptional greed even by Canadian standards. He saw in the *congés* the means of delivering the western fur trade to his favorites and, through them, of securing his own fortune. La Jonquière's desire for wealth seemed, however, but a passing and flickering fantasy alongside the passion of his intendant, François Bigot. Bigot arrived in 1748 to replace Hocquart and served until the end of the French period. For him the suffering of Canada was but a path of fortune. Despite the corruption, the end of leasing increased French supplies at the posts and the prices fell.[44]

Although La Jonquière's policy of reconciliation and the restoration of the fur trade gradually ended the revolt along the Great Lakes, rebellion continued along the Ohio and the Wabash. Here the breakdown of older hierarchies and the actual presence of the British had created too many new leaders and too many new opportunities for the alliance to be entirely restored. The Wyandots at their new village of Conchake on the Muskingum, along with the republicans of the Ohio and the rebel Miamis, continued to defy the French.

French reforms in the fur trade had little immediate effect among the rebels south of the Great Lakes, because the Ohio Valley trade differed in fundamental ways from the trade along the Great Lakes. On the Great Lakes the French had an effective and well-established supply network and had created a market not only for beaver and *menues pelleteries* but also for venison, canoes, fish, corn, and bear oil. Here concessions to the Algonquians yielded results. Only the Mississaugas persisted in rebellion. They increasingly withdrew toward the Iroquois. In the south, however, deerskins prized by the British, but less valued by the French, remained the heart of the trade. This gave the British a substantial advantage, and they gained a second one from the difficulties of canoe travel in the region. The frequent portages necessary along the upper reaches of the Maumee and Wabash rivers made French trading voyages far more arduous and expensive there than elsewhere in the *pays d'en haut*. Beyond the lakes, too, the northern birch from which canoes were made disappeared, and the heavier and more unwieldy pirogues dominated the waterways. French reforms had less of an

Jonquière au Ministre, 24 aoust 1750, AN, C11A, v. 95, f. 211. For strategic significance of Petit Rapide, see Mémoire sur les postes ... en 1754 ... Raymond, *RAPQ* 1927–28, 330–32. For location of posts, see R. Cole Harris (ed.), *Historical Atlas of Canada*, vol. 1, *From the Beginning to 1800* (Toronto: University of Toronto Press, 1987), plate 39, plate 40.
44 For La Jonquière and Bigot, see Lanctot, *A History of Canada* 3:80–81; Lawrence Henry Gipson, *The British Empire Before the American Revolution*, 15 vols. (New York: Alfred A. Knopf, 1958–70), 5:27–29.

impact on prices here, and in the Ohio Valley the rebels seemed more determined in their rejection of the French.[45]

The republican leaders on the Ohio and Wabash rivers also had more of a stake in the rebellion than the rebels of the Great Lakes for, like Orontony, many of them had used the rebellion to overthrow not just Onontio but an existing village hierarchy. To accept Onontio's pardon meant to accept renewed inferiority to the alliance chiefs who had remained loyal to their father. From Chiningué (Logstown), where the young men said they no longer possessed their old chiefs and spoke directly to the French in council, to the Wabash villages where alliance chiefs such as Piedfroid of the Miamis and Les Ongles of the Weas found their influence evaporating, the old political and social order was in the midst of change.[46]

The political revolution traveled backward along a network of intermarriage and kinship that had for generations tied the *pays d'en haut* into a single social unit. It reached into virtually all villages south of the Great Lakes. Particularly along the Wabash, the leaders of the rebellion were often men who had married women who were not members of their own tribes and villages, and in this they resembled many of the loyal chiefs: La Demoiselle of the Miamis may have been a Piankashaw by birth. One of his closest allies, La Mouche Noire, was a Kaskaskia who became a chief who numbered followers among both the Weas and the Piankashaws. Le Jarret, the stepfather of La Grue of the Miamis, was a Wea who had risen to the leadership of the Miamis of Tepicon. Le Loup was a Kickapoo who became a chief among the Piankashaws.[47]

---

[45] Trade goods in the Ohio Valley were not abundant. The Shawnees of Sonnontio said the English were their sole resource, Speech of Shawnees, n.d., *IHC* 29:128. In 1752 Macarty at the Illinois complained of the scarcity and high price of Canadian trade goods and of smuggling to the English, Macarty to Vaudreuil, Mar. 18, 1752, *IHC* 2:516–17; Macarty to Vaudreuil, Sept. 2, 1752, *IHC* 29:666–67. Macarty to Rouillé, June 1, 1752, *IHC* 29:641. There was always also a question of how many presents found their way into Indian hands; Raymond, who had been dismissed by La Jonquière and who was hardly disinterested, claimed embezzlement was widespread. Mémoire sur les postes du Canada ... 1754, *AQ*, 1927–28, 325, 349–50. He also criticized the domination of the posts by a small group of families; see *ibid.*, 334–37. Allowing favored officers to sell brandy was, apparently, a lucrative tactic, *ibid.*, 344.

For portages and trade with the English, see Projet pour s'opposer à l'agrandissement du Anglois en Canada..., 15 oct. 1729, AN, CIIA, v. 51, f. 467; Memorandum, Feb. 13, 1731, *WHC* 17:131–32. For deerskins, see Chapter 3. The Indians of the Ohio repeatedly complained to Céloron of the inability of the French to supply them, and Céloron thought that the French could never effectively compete in the region. Journal de la campagne ... Céloron, Margry, *Découvertes* 6:683, 698, 725. By 1749 supplies of trade goods at Michilimackinac were reportedly so abundant that merchants there were selling at a loss, La Jonquière au Ministre, 20 sept. 1749, AN, CIIA, v. 93, f. 101. For Mississaugas, see Colden to Clinton, Aug. 8, 1751, *NYCD* 6:742.

[46] Chiningué, Margry, *Découvertes* 6:690, 696–98.

[47] For La Mouche Noire, see Reports to Raymond, Mar.–Apr. 1750, *IHC* 29:176–77. As a Wea chief, Jonquière to Rouillé, Sept. 25, 1751, *IHC* 29:366–67; as a Piankashaw, Words of

Given strong ranked patrilineages, Indian men who intermarried from the outside should have had little influence. The only kinspeople they had within the village were affinal kin – their wives' kinspeople. Since such ties were not nearly as strong as those that bound members of the same patrilineage, these men should have been minor figures. Their simultaneous rise seems a clear sign of the fragmentation of the older hierarchies and ranked lineages of the Illinois and Miami confederations.

Why the influence of the older "kings" declined and this pattern of intermarried leadership emerged is not clear, but the answer may lie in disease. From French descriptions, for the early Miamis and, presumably, the Illinois, "kings" were ritual leaders or shaman-chiefs. Disease killed such leaders as readily as it killed their followers. It would have both shattered belief in the power of shaman-chiefs to protect their people and encouraged the incorporation of outside groups in order to maintain numbers. If this happened, then the old relationship of chief with people would have collapsed. This could explain the rise of outsiders to leadership. With the old ranking of patrilineages now in dispute, outsiders may have been able to reconcile quarreling patrilineages precisely because they had been born into none of them. Like Onontio, they could gain influence because they were mediating outsiders. Outsiders, too, may have been better able to appeal directly to all warriors in a village in a way that another man whose social identity was more firmly fixed in a specific lineage could not. Seniority in a strong lineage still brought political standing, but it was no longer the only route to influence.

At the same time as the emergence of intermarried outsiders as chiefs diminished the political influence of kinship within the village, it strengthened kinship ties between villages. Le Jarret and La Mouche Noire, for example, retained ties to their own patrilineages in their native villages. As the rebellion developed, such ties gave rebel chiefs the ability to influence people in distant towns. La Mouche Noire was the brother of Rouensa, a leading Kaskaskia alliance chief. La Mouche Noire persuaded one of his brothers, perhaps Papechingouya, to visit the British at Pickawillany, the seat of the Miami rebels, in 1751. Rouensa remained loyal to the French, but he also remained tied to his brothers. He was unwilling to countenance French attacks on his kinspeople. La Mouche Noire thus used his kin connections both to recruit allies and to secure protection for his efforts.[48]

Les Grands Ongles, May 17, 1750, *IHC* 29:209. La Mouche Noire later joined the Piankashaws, De Guyenne to Vaudreuil, Sept. 10, 1752, *IHC* 29:719. For Le Jarret, see Words of Les Grands Ongles, a Wea Chief, May 17, 1750, *IHC* 29:207. That he was a Wea is indicated by the Miamis carrying gifts to the Weas in order to cover his death, Report of Sieur Roy, Apr. 1, 1750, *IHC* 29:169.

[48] Rouensa bore the same name and was head of the same lineage as the father of Aramepinchieue, but the half century separating the two had eroded the power of the

Rouensa, in any case, could not have struck the rebels without alienating his own people. Just as La Mouche Noire had moved to the Wabash, so Illinois villages contained many Miami, Wea, and Piankashaw women and children. As Ousaouikintonga, a Kaskaskia headman, later asked the French after their initial attack on the Miamis: "Why, my father, why do you not strike me myself? Why do you strike a tribe allied to me where all my relatives are?" Governor de Vaudreuil of Louisiana realized that neighboring tribes were unlikely to attack the rebels because the rebels were in large part their relatives.[49]

The political boundaries of village politics had extended beyond the limits of any one village, but what complicated matters even further was that these boundaries also encompassed French villages in the Illinois country at Vincennes, Saint Joseph, and Detroit. Sexual relations between Frenchmen and Indian women continued to create unease among Jesuits and French officials. In the late 1730s the French court had even attempted to ban further intermarriage in Louisiana, but the Jesuits in Illinois country had protested. Such marriages were undesirable, they admitted, but the alternative was *métis bâtards* among all the tribes. They explained to the court that *métis legitimes* invariably became French in outlook, culture, and loyalty. In the last twenty-one years only one, they claimed, had left to live among the Indians. *Métis bâtards*, however, were invariably Indian, remaining among their mothers' people.[50]

Métis bâtards may have become Indian, and *métis legitimes* French, but both, nonetheless, represented significant ties between the two peoples. The Jesuits admitted as much. Indian women maintained worrisome connections

Rouensas. Population decline had brought the consolidation of previously separate groups. In 1733 the Tamaras and Rouensa's Kaskaskias inhabited a single village. This combination eventually resulted in the absorption of the Tamaroas by the Kaskaskias, but the immediate result was the rise of two village factions, one led by Louis Rouensa of the Kaskaskias, the other by Le Chat of the Tamaras. The French recognized no single chief for the village. Neither Rouensa nor Le Chat exerted effective control. They and other Illinois chiefs were, according to the Jesuits, "chiefs only in name, but without any power or authority." Where the earlier Rouensa had been a shaman-chief whose conversion had, in turn, made the Kaskaskias Christian, this later Rouensa had to divide power within a reduced village with rivals. Les P. P. Boullenger et Mercier au Ministre, 22 avril 1733, AN, C13A, v. 17, and *ibid.*, 25 aout 1733, AN, C13A, v. 17. For Papechingouya, etc., see Jonquière to Rouillé, Sept. 25, 1751, *IHC* 29:366–67. For earlier trade overtures and journey of son of Louis Rouensa, see Extrait de particuliers . . . pendant les mois d'avril et may 1742, AN, C13A, v. 27, f. 85.

49 Macarty to Vaudreuil, March 18, 1752, *IHC* 29:518. For intermarriage, see *ibid.* 714; Vaudreuil to Rouillé, Apr. 8, 1752, *IHC* 29:578–79; Macarty to Rouillé, June 1, 1752, *IHC* 29:642. For Illinois visit and gifts, see De Guyenne to Vaudreuil, Sept. 10, 1752, *IHC* 29:719–20. For Macarty, see Duquesne to Rouillé, Oct. 31, 1753, *IHC* 29:846–47.

50 Mémoire sur les mariages des sauvagesses avec les françois 1738, AN, C13A, v. 23, and Mémoire concernant les Ilinois, 1732, AN, F3, v. 24. For discussion of marriages, see Bienville et Salmon au Ministre, 16 may 1735, AN, F3, v. 20, f. 85.

with their kinspeople even though, the priests claimed, such ties diminished over time. At any time, a French village would hold intermarried Indian women, their children, and an array of visiting relatives. Priests and officials in France feared betrayal and corruption, but local commanders realized that such connections could be useful. Macarty was quick to remind the Illinois of their kinship ties and obligations to the French when La Mouche Noire urged them to join the rebels. To keep the villagers loyal, French commanders depended, too, on the *métis legitimes* and on the Frenchmen who had intermarried and traded among the Indians. The relatives of such men were often prominent. Le Porc Epic of the Miamis was related to the French, and the sister of Le Maringouin, the chief of a village on the Vermilion River, had married a Frenchman.[51]

The French deployed the *métis legitimes* in their attempts to restore order in the *pays d'en haut*, but in the end neither the efforts of the *métis* nor the economic reforms achieved the French goals. In 1750, La Jonquière dispatched the Sieur Chabert de Joncaire, a *métis* whose mother was Iroquois, to the Ohio. He brought French trade goods and sought to establish French trading houses. His ultimate object was to detach the republican villages of the Ohio from the British either by having these Indians evict the British traders or by persuading the Iroquois to withdraw the villages, whose inhabitants were largely Iroquois or Iroquois dependents, from the Ohio country. He failed on both counts. The Cayugas frankly told him that the republics were now a fact of life:

> Father, it appears that you wish all the Indians who are on Beautiful river to withdraw; you know that is a Republic composed of all sorts of Nations, and even many of those who lived near you have settled there. It is a country abounding in game, and this it is that attracts them thither.

The Ohio republicans were not universally hostile to the French. They would trade with Joncaire and he secured partisans among them, but they would not evict the British nor abandon the area.[52]

IV

Rebellion persisted on the Ohio and among the Wyandots, but it was farther to the west, on the Wabash and its tributaries, that the final stage of the

---

[51] Macarty to Vaudreuil, Mar. 18, 1752, *IHC* 29:511–15. For Le Maringouin, see Macarty to Vaudreuil, Mar. 18, 1752, *IHC* 29:507–8. For women among French, see *ibid.* 521. See also n. 50.

[52] For Cayuga speech and Joncaire, see Conference of...Jonquière with the Cayugas, May 15, 1750, *NYCD* 10:205–9. See also Conference between Colonel Johnson and a Cayuga

rebellion developed. By the time Orontony died in 1750, La Demoiselle – the leader of the rebel Miamis – had already eclipsed him, and La Demoiselle's town of Pickawillany on a branch of the Great Miami had become the center of the revolt. Like Orontony, La Demoiselle's original defection from the alliance had looked more toward village than imperial politics. But the widening rebellion and French attempts at reconciliation had eventually forced him to choose between broadening his own ambitions or succumbing to the alliance chiefs. La Demoiselle had chosen to move into deeper waters.[53]

Like Orontony, La Demoiselle had originally been a minor figure in his village. In 1747, when he led a party of warriors to sack the French post at the Miamis' village, La Demoiselle was not even a band or a clan leader. Apparently, he was not even a Miami but an intermarried Piankashaw. Le Porc Epic, who was tied by marriage to the French and remained loyal to them, was "the first chief of the band of La Demoiselle." La Demoiselle was most likely only a war leader in Le Porc Epic's band. Understanding his rise from a minor war leader to a threat to the French empire involves a detour into Miami politics and an examination of puzzling leadership patterns among the Miamis.[54]

In the late 1740s, there were two main Miami villages – Kekionga (or Kiskakon), on the upper reaches of the Maumee, and Tepicon, on the upper Tippecanoe. The village of Kekionga, where La Demoiselle lived, was led by Piedfroid (or Wisekaukautshe), whom the French regarded as the head chief of the Miamis. The village of Tepicon was led by Le Jarret until his murder in 1749. After the death of Le Jarret, his stepson La Grue (or Le Gris) nominally led the village, but the actual leader seems to have been La Grue's mother, who served as a sort of regent.[55]

There are signs that these two villages themselves reflected a previous and significant fracturing of the Miami. The name of Le Jarret's stepson, La

Sachem, Dec. 4, 1750, *NYCD* 6:608–10. For Joncaire and Ohio Iroquois, see Croghan's Journal May 18–27, 1751, in Thwaites (ed.), *Early Western Travels*, 1:58–69.

[53] For death of Orontony, see Jonquière to Minister, Oct. 10, 1750, *WHC* 18:74–75.

[54] The English called La Demoiselle, the old Piankashaw, "king," which was apparently a reference to his original tribal origins. William Trent, *Journal of Captain William Trent from Logstown to Pickawillany, A.D. 1752* (New York: Arno Press and the New York *Times*, 1971), 88. For attack and English connections, see Occurrences in Canada during the year 1747–48, *NYCD* 10:139–40, 143. For Le Porc Epic, see Raymond to La Jonquière, Jan. 5, 1750, *IHC* 29:154. Le Porc Epic's brother-in-law was the Sieur Roy, a prominent *métis* and interpreter at the post, *ibid.* For a summary of clan structure and social organization, see *HBNI* 15:684–85.

[55] For bands and Piedfroid as head chief, see Boishébert's Report, 24 July 1733, *MPHC* 34:109; Raymond on the Miami, Oct. 1749, *IHC* 29:122–23. For Le Jarret, see Raymond to La Jonquière, Oct. 11, 1749, *IHC* 29:121. For Le Gris or La Grue, see *ibid.* 123; for his mother, see Reports to Raymond, Mar.–Apr. 1750, *IHC* 29:173; Raymond to La Jonquière, May 14, 1751, *IHC* 29:290–91.

Grue, is a French rendering of Atchatchakangouen, or sandhill crane, the self-denomination of the Miamis. Among many Algonquians, names remained the possession of a lineage or clan and were recirculated from generation to generation. Given that the leading lineage would be the one most likely to possess the tribal name, La Grue is a logical representative of that lineage. Certainly the rank he inherited possessed marks of a ritual status greater than that of civil leaders among neighboring peoples. The regency exercised in his behalf by two older men and his mother is one sign of this. They maintained custody of the wampum belts and other marks of power. The lineage of La Grue thus may have been the chiefly lineage that had once produced the chiefs whom the French had mistaken for kings.[56]

But if La Grue was the hereditary chief of the Miamis, how did Piedfroid come to be recognized by the French as the "head chief"? The answer seems tied to disease and the rise of the midewiwin. Although the seventeenth-century Miami had been known for the unusual power of their hereditary chiefs, in the early eighteenth century, amid large losses to epidemics, the French had noted increasing rivalries and divisions between the leaders of the confederation. Since Miami chiefs originally had priestly functions, it is quite possible that their inability to halt losses to epidemics considerably weakened their position. It is notable that Miami tradition records Le Gris, the other name for La Grue, as one of the two survivors of an epidemic that destroyed Tepicon. In the oral tradition, Le Gris later became chief of the Turtle clan. What is significant here is not the literal historicity of the story but the identification of Le Gris, or La Grue, with epidemics that destroyed his village. He became the hereditary chief whose people were victims of epidemics.[57]

Similarly, Piedfroid became the chief who rescued his people from epidemics. In the documents, he emerges first as a chief who led his people when they fled their village in 1733 after an outbreak of smallpox. In Miami oral tradition, too, Piedfroid was connected with disease. Nearly a century after his death, the nineteenth-century Miami remembered him as the most powerful of the midewiwin priests. The midewiwin was, among other things, a curing society, and among the Miami its origins seem to date to the late seventeenth century, when the nation lived by the Saint Joseph River,

---

[56] For Le Gris, see Raymond to La Jonquière, Oct. 11, 1749, *IHC* 29:190–21, 123; for name as La Grue, see Parolles du Grue, Oct. 6, 1749, AN, C11A, v. 95, f. 376. Note his portrayal of himself as a timid young man and the protestations of loyalty both on his part and that of his father and stepfather before him. For crane, see *HBNI* 15:681. For similar circumstances in nineteenth century, see C. C. Trowbridge, *Meearmeear Traditions: Occasional Contributions from the Museum of Anthropology of the University of Michigan*, no. 7, ed. Vernon Kinietz (Ann Arbor: University of Michigan Press, 1938), 13.

[57] Trowbridge, *Meearmeear Traditions*, 12–13.

precisely the time when epidemics were ravaging the nation and deep divisions were appearing in the social fabric. An old man wandering in the woods while mourning for a son who had died discovered an immense lodge. Within it were animals who had taken human shape, and they revealed to him the source of their powers as a way of assuaging his grief. They gave him powers both to kill and to cure and promised that in exercising the powers he would achieve both a long life and the enjoyment of the good things of the world. They told him:

> We saw you very much afflicted, and were disposed to relieve your troubles. The power which has been given you, and the ceremonies which you have seen, are half bad and half good: that is to say, men will be disposed to divert them to purposes equally vicious & laudable. When you go home you will find this to be a valuable profession, and we enjoin it upon you to keep it secret from the world. You will have the authority to form a new branch of this society, but you must never initiate members, without a heavy fee; and have a care that you do not bring the society into disrepute, by extending it too much. Conduct every part of ceremony with gravity and secrecy and suffer no one to contemn it or to ridicule its proceedings.[58]

The animals of this revelation have all the marks of the other-than-human beings, or manitous, of earlier Algonquian accounts, but they are now united into a single powerful lodge or society. As before, they bestow power, but this power, being the sum of their individual powers, is far greater than that of the older visions. More significantly, it is a socially organized power. The animals instruct the old man to form a society of his own and to initiate others into its secrets. The appeal of such a society of hierarchical curers in a nation ravaged by disease and with an older hierarchical tradition seems apparent. By the 1730s, at least, Piedfroid had combined chieftainship and the midé priesthood.

The critical question here is one of whether Piedfroid represented members of the older hierarchy, who assumed leadership of the midewiwin to buttress their own positions, or whether he represented previously subordinate figures who used the midewiwin during a period of epidemics to rise to political leadership. Harold Hickerson has interpreted the midewiwin among the Chippewas as a centralizing and unifying force that created a single tribe from a group of totemic bands. Chippewa midé priests remained largely distinct from the civil chiefs of the villages, but among the Miami the midewiwin priesthood appears to have been part of the fracturing of an existing hierarchy. The midewiwin represented a new route to political

[58] Boishébert to Beauharnois, July 24, 1733, *MPHC* 34:109. Trowbridge, *Meearmeear Traditions*, 77–85; quotation, 83.

leadership. Piedfroid combined leadership in the midewiwin and political leadership, and he eclipsed the older lineage of La Grue.

If Piedfroid rose to prominence outside of the older channels, he opened a route, as Miami oral tradition attested, that others could follow. In Miami oral tradition, the members of the midewiwin society became so jealous of Piedfroid that they resolved to kill him. These conspirators, who were "the principals of their respective bands," succeeded in murdering him through trickery. But Piedfroid's son made a great medicine and killed them in turn, and the society was never so powerful again. This oral tradition of a struggle between midewiwin priests roughly parallels the actual revolt of La Demoiselle and others against Piedfroid in the late 1740s, a struggle that climaxed in the early 1750s. In 1752 Piedfroid died of smallpox – precisely the disease from which he had earlier saved his people. So, too, did one of his sons. La Grue also died of smallpox, and before the year was out La Demoiselle was dead at the hands of the French and the Indians loyal to them. The death of men of "power" in the legend paralleled the death of men of power in fact.[59]

In Miami memory, the fall of Piedfroid involved a contest over power, but the power both sides mustered was the only power Algonquians recognized – the power other-than-human people bestowed on those who properly appealed to them. In Miami history, the power that La Demoiselle mustered against Piedfroid also came from outside. The sacking of the Miami post marked La Demoiselle as an ally of Orontony, who had sent him a belt soliciting the attack, and, through Orontony, the attack made him an ally of the Iroquois and the British. Orontony was during these years strongly promoting the Wyandot-Iroquois connection, describing the two as "one people." The British connection was more recent and more formal. The Wyandots met with official representatives of Pennsylvania in 1748, the same year La Demoiselle's Miamis negotiated a treaty with the Pennsylvanians at Lancaster. For both the French and the British, La Demoiselle's attack had meaning largely within their own imperial struggle, but for La Demoiselle himself the blow was significant within a different power struggle. The support he gained among the Wyandots, the Iroquois, and the British enabled him to challenge effectively his rivals – and erstwhile superiors – in Miami village politics.[60]

[59] Harold Hickerson, "The Sociohistorical Significance of Two Chippewa Ceremonials," *American Anthropologist* 65 (1963): 67–85; Trowbridge, *Meearmeear Traditions*, 85–87. For deaths, see Longueuil to Minister, Apr. 21, 1752, *WHC* 18:108. This account has Le Gris's mother also dead of smallpox, but she appears at a conference the next year. See next chapter.
[60] For Wyandots and English, see Journal of Conrad Weiser, 1748, *PCR* 5:350–51. For Miamis, see Treaty at Lancaster, July 19, 1748, *ibid.*, 307–19. For Wyandots-Iroquois, see Weiser Journal, *ibid.* 350.

La Demoiselle's revolt thus reflected both the imperial struggle between France and Great Britain and a village struggle among the Miamis themselves. La Demoiselle, like Orontony, having rejected his existing village leadership with its connections to the French, necessarily began to rely on alliances with other peoples to fortify his position. British trade was essential to La Demoiselle's success against Piedfroid, but the way he used his trade to seek a new political order across the *pays d'en haut* gave him significance far beyond his village.

Pickawillany, the village Piedfroid established after this attack on the French, was initially only a new Miami town. It was not a republic. When Céloron visited Pickawillany he had already traveled through Rocher Ecrit, where Alquippa, a woman and a Mingo, held sway. At Chiningué (Logstown) he had found a "very bad village" of Mingos, Shawnees, and Delawares, with a scattering of mission Indians, Abenakis, Nippisings, Ottawas, and other nations. Sonnontio was a jumble of Mingos, Shawnees, mission Indians, Delawares, a few Miamis, "and some from nearly all the tribes of the *pays d'en haut*." Even at a small Miami village below Pickawillany there were some Senecas. Pickawillany itself, however, consisted only of Miamis.[61]

Events forced La Demoiselle to broaden his following. As late as the fall of 1749, he was still only an ambitious Miami factional leader engaged in a struggle with Piedfroid. Two years later, he had won over Le Cigne, Piedfroid's war leader, and left the old chief with a following consisting only of his own lineage. Still, this was only a local triumph, a victory in Miami politics. Such small successes bred their own dangers. Even as he attracted new followers, La Demoiselle also attracted new rivals for leadership. When Céloron visited Pickawillany, Le Baril, another Miami chief, maintained a separate village by the White River. More recruits brought more divisions, and by 1750 two *principeaux considéres*, Le Sac à Petun and Le Pean, had apparently grown jealous of La Demoiselle's pretensions and opened negotiations with the French to return to Kekionga.[62]

---

[61] For Chininguè, see Margry, *Découvertes* 6:690, 696–98. For quotation on Sonnontio, see *ibid.*, 707; for Senecas among Miamis, see *ibid.*, 715.

[62] La Demoiselle had unsucessfully tried to get Piedfroid's and La Grue's warriorts to help him against Céloron earlier in the summer, Raymond to La Jonquière, Sept. 4, 1749, *IHC* 29:108–10; Parolles du Grue, 6 oct. 1749, AN, C11A, v. 95, f. 376. For La Demoiselle's promise, see Margry, *Découvertes* 6:722; for Piedfroid's reaction, see *ibid.*, 723; for Piedfroid's loss of influence, see Raymond to La Jonquière, Oct. 11, 1749, *IHC* 29:120; Raymond to La Jonquière, May 22, 1750, *IHC* 29:202; Parolles du conseil tenu a Miamis, 8 oct. 1750, AN, C11A, v. 95, f. 378; Raymond to Minister, Oct. 1, 1751, *WHC* 94–96; Raymond to La Jonquière, Sept. 5, 1749, *IHC* 29: 108–10; Oct. 11, 1749, *IHC* 29:119, 122–23; Raymond to Jonquière, Jan. 5, 1750, *IHC* 29:149.

For Le Baril, see Margry, *Découvertes*, 6:720. For Le Pean, see Report of Le Pean or Le Pian, May 1750, *IHC* 29:197–200; for Le Sac à Petun, see Report of Sieur Roy, Apr. 1750,

La Demoiselle, however, proved more than capable of meeting the French challenge. He adroitly used both the alliance's successes and failures to subvert it. He used the appeal of British goods, French mistakes, and the by-now pervasive kin connections created by intermarriage in the *pays d'en haut* to attract new followers. At the time of Céloron's visit, Pickawillany contained only forty or fifty warriors. A year later there were four hundred families. La Demoiselle had attracted the minor chiefs of the Weas and Piankashaws who were angry about La Galissonière's parsimony and the warriors who were furious about French prices. If La Demoiselle was actually a Piankashaw, some of these people may have been his kin. In the spring of 1750 he obtained promises from the Ottawas and Chippewas of Saginaw, then unreconciled with La Jonquière, to join him the next year. He also began to send belts into the Illinois country and up the Mississippi inviting other more distant peoples to come to Pickawillany.[63]

By the fall of 1751, La Demoiselle's influence had begun to stretch far beyond the Miamis. The Sieur de Benoist feared a "revolution" of the tribes of the region for bad reports had been constant for over a year. The Sieur de Ligneris, in command at Vincennes, thought the Piankashaws at the Vermilion River were entirely in the British interest. Piankashaw warriors sacked his canoe and only through the intervention of Le Loup and other alliance chiefs did he regain his goods. In the Wabash region only the Kickapoos and Mascoutens had rejected the message of La Demoiselle and the rebels, and many Frenchmen suspected that they were more neutral than loyal. The size of British presents and the failure of the French to match them made the Comte de Raymond at the Miami post fear the loss of the entire country. The possibility of revolt continued to flicker as far north as

---

ibid., 173. Raymond claimed that these chiefs were on the verge of returning to Kekionga when he was relieved, Raymond to Minister, Oct. 1, 1751, *WHC* 18:96; Raymond à Vaudreuil, n.d., Cavagnal Letterbooks, LO 9, v. 4, Huntington Library. The Miamis never united behind any single leader. La Grue's band remained independent. They seemed ready to relocate at Fort Miami in 1749, but did not do so. Parolles du Grue, 6 oct. 1749, AN, C11A, v. 95, f. 376.

[63] For population 1749, see note 88, *WHC* 18:50. For population 1750, see Gist Journal, Mulkearn (ed.), *George Mercer Papers*, 109. For La Mouche Noire, the Piankashaw king, see Gist Journal, Mulkearn (ed.), *George Mercer Papers*, 111. For invitations and English support, see Raymond, to La Jonquière, Jan. 5, 1750, *IHC* 29:149, 154–56; Benoist to Raymond, Feb. 11, 1750, *IHC* 29:164–65; Jonquière to Rouillé, Oct. 1750, *IHC* 29:241; Report of Porc Epic, March 15, 1750, *ibid.* 166–67. For Weas and Piankashaws, see Report of Chaperon, May 1750, *ibid.*, 194. For Ottawas and Chippewas, see Report of Le Pean, May 1750, *ibid.*, 199. For Menominees, see Extrait du conseil, 27 juillet... 1 aoust 1750, AN, C11A, v. 95, f. 130. For Illinois, see Vaudreuil to Rouillé, Oct. 10, 1751, *IHC* 29:401–3. La Demoiselle grew more and more arrogant in his treatment of medal chiefs of other nations who came to lure him back to the alliance, Parolles de Pennant8euns, 7 juin 1751, AN, C11A, v. 97. For arrival of pro-French delegation to Pickawillany, see Gist Journal, Feb. 17, 1751, Mulkearn (ed.), *George Mercer Papers*, 19–21.

among the Potawatomis of Saint Joseph. A small group of Miamis living and intermarried among the Potawatomis, previously considered the most loyal of tribes by the French, had apparently begun to act as agents for La Demoiselle. The danger in the region from Saint Joseph south to the Illinois villages was not the complete defection of the allies of the French but, rather, the alliance chiefs' piecemeal loss of their followings. At the Miami and Wabash posts, the French might retain the alliance chiefs and their immediate kinspeople, but the others would slip into the rebel orbit.[64]

By the early 1750s, working from this tangled skein of intermarriage, factional rivalries, and declining hierarchies, men like Chartier, Orontony, and La Demoiselle had begun to construct a new political order in the *pays d'en haut*. The republics of Pickawillany, Sonnontio, and Logstown all marked the change. Village and imperial politics had become inseparable, and the small tragedies of Piedfroid, Nucheconer of the Shawnees, and Sasteretsy of the Huron-Petuns, as they suffered defeat or humiliation at the hands of their village rivals, created powerful reverberations that eventually involved empires.

---

[64] For revolution, see Vaudreuil to Rouillé, Oct. 10, 1751, *IHC* 29:401. For Kickapoos, see Report of son and son-in-law of Bourbonnais, May 1750, *IHC* 29:196. For Mascoutens, see Raymond to La Jonquière, May 22, 1750, *ibid.*, 206. For Potawatomis, see Report of Le Pian, May 1750, *ibid.*, 200. The Piankashaw king – apparently La Mouche Noire – was the leading chief at Pickawillany in La Demoiselle's absence, Gist Journal, Mulkearn (ed.), *George Mercer Papers*, 111. For Piankashaws of Vermilion, see De Ligneris to Vaudreuil, Oct. 25, 1751, *IHC* 29:414–15. For intervention of Le Loup, see Macarty to Vaudreuil, Jan. 20, 1752, *IHC* 29:454–55. For Potawatomis, see Question of M. Le General, Council, AN, C11A, v. 97. For intermarried Miamis, see Raymond on the Miami, Oct. 1749, *IHC* 29:123. The Sauks and Menominees had traded with the English, and La Jonquière warned them and the Winnebagos about foreign Indians in their villages. Both are indications of rebel activity among them. Parolles des Folles Avoines, 27 juillet 1750, AN, C11A, v. 95; Parolles des Sakis, 27 juillet 1750, AN, C11A, v. 95; Puants de la Bay, *ibid.*

6

The clash of empires

Inform'd by Thomas Kinton that before ye Ind^n War, he being out here at a
Town a little way up ye Alegheny, where the Indians found a Rat & Kill'd it
which yet antiants of them seem'd Concearned & told him that ye French or
British should get that Land from them, ye same prediction being made by their
Grandfathers on finding a Rat on Delaware before ye White People Came there.

"Journal of James Kenny," March 19, 1762

I

As long as Pickawillany and the Ohio republics survived, Onontio regarded
them as a knife poised to sever Canada from Louisiana. The British, or so
the French believed, wielded the knife. By the early 1750s, both the British
and the French had convinced themselves that the outcome of the political
struggle in the villages along the Ohio and the Wabash would decide the
imperial struggle on the American continent. To William Johnson, soon to
emerge as the most critical figure in formulating British Indian policy, the
Indians of the Ohio seemed

> the only Body of Indians now upon the Continent whose Friendship or
> alliance is most worthy of courting or continuing wherefore if we lose
> them (who have been for these three years past so firmly attached to the
> British Interests as by sundry instances can be made appear) it must be
> our own faults & the consequences may be very bad.

On the French side, Governor de La Galissonière made the Ohio Valley the
key to the continent. He concocted an eighteenth-century domino theory in
which the loss of the Ohio Valley would doom not only Canada and
Louisiana but eventually the French Caribbean and even Spanish Mexico.[1]

Although both England and France asserted claims of sovereignty over the
Ohio Valley, each initially sought to control the area indirectly through
Indian proxies. The revolt thus became a critical factor. If the rebels

[1] La Galissonière, Memoir on the French Colonies on North America, Dec. 1750, *NYCD*
10:220–32; Johnson to Clinton, Feb. 19, 1749/50, *NYCD* 6:547.

maintained themselves and the British traders remained in their villages, the British gained. If they failed, the French took the upper hand. This situation presented an obvious threat to the Algonquians, whose choices seemingly narrowed to a choice of masters; but as La Galissonière astutely recognized in 1750, there was a potential opportunity here for them, too. It was in the Indians' interest, he wrote, that "the strength of the British and the French remain nearly equal, so that through the jealousy of these two nations, those tribes may live independent of, and draw presents from, both." The failure of the republicans to exploit effectively this lucrative balance of power brought European armies into the region, turned the contest into one of imperial force, and threatened to destroy the political middle ground.[2]

The escalation toward imperial conflict was gradual, complicated, and often hard to follow. In terms of practical politics, both the French and English empires in the Ohio Valley translated into quarreling amalgams of separate colonies and allied groups. The French empire in the region consisted of the border regions of two colonies, Canada and Louisiana, and allied Indians, many of whom the French, with good reason, feared would join the rebels. The French saw the British as a united and diabolical force bent on seducing their old allies, but the rebels actually were dealing with representatives of three separate colonies (New York, Pennsylvania, and Virginia), a private company (the Ohio Company), many independent traders, and the Iroquois. The attempts of these various interests to win over the rebels yielded a tangled and mutually contradictory set of treaties and agreements that lacked a cornerstone. Lean on any single promise and the whole structure would tumble down.

The various agreements that joined the Ohio republicans and the Miami rebels to the British and Iroquois resulted from diplomatic and commercial opportunism rather than a coherent imperial strategy. The rebels sought access to the English goods necessary to sustain and broaden their own influence, and they sought British and Iroquois protection from the French. The Iroquois sought to legitimize their own claim to the Ohio region, restore the migrants from the east to the covenant chain, and establish new ties with Algonquian groups. British traders sought profitable commerce. William Johnson sought to use the Iroquois to extend British influence in the area, but the New York assembly failed to support either him or the Iroquois. Virginia and Pennsylvania sought to validate their conflicting claims of title to the upper Ohio. The Ohio Company sought land for speculation. To

---

[2] The French claimed sovereignty on the basis of La Salle's discoveries. The Iroquois claimed it on the basis of conquest. The English claimed it on the basis of their supposed sovereignty over the Iroquois. For Indian opportunity, see Memoir of the French Colonies in North America, M. de la Galissonière, *NYCD* 10:223.

call this hodgepodge of ambitions and aims an alliance is like calling the occupants of a brothel on any given night a family.[3]

In the Ohio Valley, the implications of any one agreement between the rebels and the British virtually always contradicted the implications of another. The Ohio republicans and the Miami rebels linked themselves to the Iroquois covenant chain, thus ostensibly relying on the Iroquois to handle their diplomatic relations with the Europeans, and, at the same time, they established independent ties with Pennsylvania through a treaty signed at Lancaster in 1748. Pennsylvania, for its part, established direct ties with republicans while acknowledging Iroquois claims of primacy over them. Conrad Weiser, Pennsylvania's representative to the Ohio villagers, tried to cut through the problem by asking the Iroquois to "take the petticoat from the Delawares and Call them for the futter their Brethren or Children and leave out the word Cousin (because in the Indian language at Signifies a Subject or one that is under command)." By removing the petticoat, the Delaware would lose their symbolic status as women, that is, people with no direct say in diplomacy or war and no right to establish independent relations with the British or with the Miami rebels. Complicating the issue still more was the status of the *viceroys* or *half kings*, who were supposedly delegated by the Iroquois council at Onondaga to handle the diplomatic relations of the Ohio villagers. It is not at all clear, however, that Tanacharison, the half king of the Mingos and Shawnees, and Scarooyady, the viceroy over the Ohio Delawares, obeyed any instructions from Onondaga that they did not want to obey. Indeed, it appears more likely that they acted as the republicans' negotiators with the Iroquois rather than as Iroquois regents over the Ohio villagers.[4]

---

[3] For example of mutual distrust among various English principals involved, see Paul A. W. Wallace, *Conrad Weiser, 1696–1760, Friend of Colonist and Mohawk* (Philadelphia: University of Pennsylvania Press, 1945), 335–36; Promise of aid, Report of Le Pean, *IHC* 29:198.

[4] A Treaty at the Courthouse in Lancaster . . . , *PCR* 5:316. The covenant chain as a single grand alliance was a myth; for an account of the various Iroquois alliances and their tangled history, see Daniel K. Richter and James H. Merrell (eds.), *Beyond the Covenant Chain: The Iroquois and Their Neighbors in Indian North America, 1600–1800* (Syracuse: Syracuse University Press, 1987); Wallace, *Weiser*, 271, 321. For Delaware as women and their relation to the Iroquois, see Francis Jennings, " 'Pennsylvania Indians' and the Iroquois," in Richter and Merrell (eds.), *Covenant Chain*, 75–92. The exact status of Scarooyady, an Oneida, is not clear. He clearly was an Iroquois and may initially have had responsibility for relations between both the Shawnees and the Delawares and the Iroquois, but whether he was directly appointed by Onondaga or selected by the people of the Ohio themselves is uncertain. Richard Aquila, *The Iroquois Restoration* (Detroit: Wayne State University Press, 1937), 196–97. Monighotootha eventually became the Iroquois representative to the Shawnees, Council, May 30, 1753, *PCR* 5:615. Tanacharison (or Tanaghrisson) is even more problematic. The son of a Catawba mother and a Seneca father, he seems to have promoted himself to a position of influence by mediating between Iroquoia and the Ohio villages, Michael N. McConnell, "Peoples 'in Between': The Iroquois and the Ohio Indians, 1720–1768," in Richter and Merrell (eds.), *Covenant Chain*, 101–102.

Indeed, by 1750 it increasingly appeared to the British that on the Ohio River the servants had become the masters. William Johnson worried that the Ohio Indians were the key to controlling the Iroquois, and not vice versa. If French efforts to win back the Ohio Indians succeeded, he wrote, the Iroquois themselves would drift toward the French "as them very Indians are their Cheif and trustiest Allies." And that same year Governor Hamilton of Pennsylvania reported that the large increase in the number of Iroquois settled on the Ohio River worried the council at Onondaga as much as it worried the French. The "Refugees of the Six Nations," the Shawnees, the Delawares, the Wyandots, and the Miamis alone could now muster between fifteen hundred and two thousand warriors. Hamilton also thought that the Iroquois on the Ohio and their allies represented "a new Interest that in a little time must give them [i.e., the Iroquois] Law instead of taking it from them." So numerous and significant were the Ohio Indians that Hamilton despaired of Pennsylvania alone absorbing the cost of keeping them loyal to the British.[5]

The republics were on the rise and the Iroquois were in decline, but in the early 1750s both stood in common fear of empires. They only disagreed on which empire they feared more. La Demoiselle worried that the French attacks on British traders promoted by La Jonquière would cut him off from the supplies and trade he needed. Many members of the Iroquois council feared that the British were guaranteeing the independence of the Six Nations' former clients and thus increasing the migration of Onondaga's own people. British policies enhanced Iroquois fears that the British, no longer needing them, now disdained them. The British crown cut its presents to the Iroquois following King George's War, and the New York assembly refused to appropriate money for gifts.

Just as La Demoiselle's fear of the French brought him closer to the British, so Iroquois fear of the British increased the influence of the French among them. Conrad Weiser reported in October 1750 that the death of pro-British chiefs and the failure of New York to fulfill its obligations to the Iroquois had put openly pro-French chiefs in power on the council. The Onondagas, while pressing their own claims to the Ohio and denying the right of any Europeans to establish posts there, informed La Jonquière that they were demanding that British traders withdraw from the region and were summoning their own warriors home. William Johnson tried, without much success, to win over the French chiefs and to persuade the Iroquois that

---

[5] For Johnson quotation, see Johnson to Clinton, Aug. 18, 1750, *JP* 9:63; Hamilton to Clinton, Sept. 20, 1750, *NYCD* 6:593–94. For Iroquois relation with Ohio Indians, see McConnell, "People 'in Between'," in Richter and Merrell (eds.), *Covenant Chain*, 93–114.

French efforts on the Ohio threatened both their access to goods and their best remaining hunting grounds.[6]

Precisely because so many interests were at stake in a region where no single group exercised significant control, the road to conflict became more and more slippery. The dangers of doing nothing seemed great; the dangers of taking action seemed even greater since there was no reasonable way to control or even predict the outcomes of those actions. As the crisis built, some groups – Pennsylvania, New York, and the Iroquois, for example – refused to commit themselves. Others, particularly Canada and Virginia, took more and more forceful action and came to dominate the conflict. But like cars racing down an icy hill, these tactics produced predictable failures. The more events threatened to slip out of control, the more force the remaining contestants applied. Collisions were only a matter of time.

II

The irony of the eventual French resort to force on the Ohio River was that it may very well have been unnecessary. The French underestimated the underlying strength of the alliance and its ability to reabsorb the Miami rebels; they overestimated the strength of the British on the Ohio. By abandoning the politics of the middle ground, the French raised the stakes and bet Canada itself on a direct imperial confrontation that they would ultimately lose.

The French policy of force proceeded in several stages. In the spring of 1751 the French emissary Sieur Chabert de Joncaire traveled to the Ohio Valley to demand the expulsion of British traders. His actions angered and alarmed many Iroquois. As Joncaire's escort of Iroquois warriors demonstrated, the French still had partisans among the Six Nations, but his reception on the Ohio itself was hostile. The speaker for the Six Nations on the Ohio, probably Tanacharison, demanded to know by what right the French used force on Iroquois lands. "We the Six Nations will not take such usage." That same spring a delegation of Onondaga chiefs went to Montreal to forbid Joncaire's fort at the carrying place, but the British feared that in the end they would consent, for some Senecas and Onondagas clearly

---

[6] For Johnson and presents, see Colden to Clinton, Aug. 8, 1751, *NYCD* 6:739, 741; Weiser to Lee, Oct. 4, 1750; Wallace, *Weiser*, 318–19. Clinton blamed New York's failure to act on the assembly, Clinton to Lords of Trade, Dec. 2, 1750, *NYCD* 6:598–99; Conference between Johnson and a Cayuga Sachem, Dec. 4, 1750, *NYCD* 6:608–10; Johnson to Clinton, Dec. 20, 1750, *JP* 1:314. For Cayuga anger at English demands for land, see Conference with . . . Jonquière, *NYCD* 10:206. For Onondagas, see Conference between . . . Jonquière and the Indians, July 11, 1751, *NYCD* 10:233.

remained sympathetic to the French. The divided Iroquois could not achieve a consistent policy.[7]

Farther west, La Jonquière initially chose to work through the alliance. Ottawa and Chippewa war parties, largely from Michilimackinac, attacked the British traders. Only in the summer of 1751 did La Jonquière turn to his allies to strike La Demoiselle directly. He instructed Cèloron, now in command at Detroit, to organize the necessary expedition. When Cèloron attempted to recruit Detroit Indians and mission Indians from Canada to join the French, however, he again found so little enthusiasm among them that he began to fear that the original rebel conspiracy had been rekindled among the villages of the lakes.[8]

Cèloron's failure buttressed the belief of both Governor de Vaudreuil of Louisiana and La Jonquière and his officers in the *pays d'en haut* that the alliance could not be depended on in any test with the rebels. The French, they believed, would have to act unilaterally and decisively. They must resort to force on a scale that would obliterate La Demoiselle and the Ohio republicans and overawe the allies. The time had come to step outside the alliance and dictate a new order. The French prepared to act alone and with overwhelming force.[9]

And yet, even as the French prepared to abandon the alliance as a vehicle that no longer fitted their needs, village politics set it in motion again. Tired of the delay and wrangling at Detroit, a small party of Nippisings, a people marginal to the *pays d'en haut*, detached themselves from Cèloron's abortive expedition and took two scalps near La Demoiselle's village. The French

---

[7] For alarm at French, see Lindesay's Report of Indian News, Feb. 5, 1751, *NYCD* 6:706. For presents, see Report of Privy Council . . . Apr. 2, 1751, *NYCD* 6:638. For Joncaire and Ohio Iroquois, see Croghan's Journal, May 18–27, 1751, in Reuben Gold Thwaites (ed.), *Early Western Travels, 1748–1846* . . . , 38 vols. (Cleveland: Arthur H. Clark, 1904–7), 1:58–69, quotation, 68–69. For Montreal delegation, see Report of John Lindesay, May 24 – June 25, 1751, *JP* 9:80–83; Lindesay to Johnson, 15 July 1751, *DHNY*, 2:623–24.

[8] Vaudreuil to Macarty, Sept. 9, 1751, *IHC* 29:311–41; Gist Journal, in Lois Mulkearn (ed.), *George Mercer Papers Relating to the Ohio Company of Virginia* (Pittsburgh: University of Pittsburgh Press, 1954), 108. For preparation for war, see Croghan to Gov. of Pennsylvania, Dec. (Nov.) 16, 1750, Thwaites (ed.), *Early Western Travels*, 1:53–54. Declare for English, see Croghan Journal, 1751, Thwaites (ed.), *Early Western Travels*, 1:59–60, 62–69; Gist Journal, in Mulkearn (ed.), *George Mercer Papers*, 111–12, 113. For strike La Demoiselle, see La Jonquière to Rouillé, Sept. 17, 1751, *IHC* 29:349; Parolles, M. Le Gènéral, 7 juin 1751, AN, C11A, v.97. For seizure of traders and Miami response, see Gist Journal, Mulkearn (ed.), *George Mercer Papers*, 13–14, 101, 103. General Council, *ibid.* 104, 107. For Ottawa, see Report of John Lindesay, May 24 – June 25, 1751, *JP* 9:80–82. For La Jonquière's decision, see La Jonquière to Cèloron, Oct. 1, 1751, *IHC* 29:381–92; Vaudreuil to Rouillé, Oct. 10, 1751, *IHC* 29:403–05. For events at Detroit, see Longueuil to Minister, Apr. 21, 1752, *WHC* 18:104–9.

[9] For Vaudreuil rejects Indian attacks, see Vaudreuil to Rouillé, Apr. 8, 1751, *IHC* 29:578–79; De Ligneris to Vaudreuil, Oct. 3, 1752, *IHC* 29:730–33.

dismissed the raid as an act of stupidity that would anger and alarm the rebels without harming them. In this they were right, but the unatoned bloodshed nevertheless shaped events.[10]

The immediate result of the killing of La Demoiselle's people was further defections from the alliance among the villagers of the Wabash and Illinois country. The rebels demanded the aid of their relatives among the Piankashaws on the Vermilion, the Piankashaws of Vincennes, the Weas, and the Illinois. Two rebels had died, and now Frenchmen began to fall in combinations of two. The Miamis promptly killed two soldiers at Fort Miami. At Vincennes, two Frenchman were killed while making pirogues, and two slaves were also murdered. The Indians living around Vincennes withdrew from that post and joined those on the Vermilion. A war party of Piankashaws and Indians from the Wabash and Vermilion rivers, ostensibly destined for the Chickasaws, instead made a series of attacks on Frenchmen in the Illinois country. French counterattacks at the Illinois River killed several members of the Indian party. The French also captured, among others, two Illinois warriors and Le Loup, the Kickapoo who had become a Piankashaw chief and a French partisan, and who was the nominal leader of the war party. The toll in dead now escalated. In revenge for the losses at the Illinois, the Vermilion Piankashaws led by Le Maringouin killed five Frenchmen trading in their villages. One of the dead was Le Maringouin's own brother-in-law.[11]

All of this seemed to demonstrate the unreliability of the allies, but then, as quickly as they had begun, the killings stopped. The immediate reason was probably the outbreak of smallpox that swept over much of the *pays d'en haut*. Although it carried away the Miami alliance chiefs Piedfroid and La Grue and the loyal Detroit Ottawa chief Kinousaki, the French hoped it would continue its ravages, being "fully as good as an army against the rebels." Smallpox wielded a hatchet far more bloody than any the combatants possessed, and by halting the rebel attacks, it gave the French time to assess their situation. Months of interrogation of Le Loup and negotiations with the Illinois revealed a more complex pattern of betrayal. Le Loup had set out to kill Chickasaws in order to distract Piankashaw warriors from the trouble by the Wabash River. Angered at Le Loup's continued loyalty to the French, Le Gros Bled, another Piankashaw chief, had dispatched his own warriors to kill Frenchmen in the Illinois country, anticipating, quite cor-

---

[10] For Nippising attack, see De Ligneris to Vaudreuil, Oct. 25, 1751, *IHC* 29:416–17; St. Ange to Vaudreuil, Feb. 28, 1752, *IHC* 29:484–87.

[11] St. Ange to Vaudreuil, Feb. 28, 1752, *IHC* 29:484–87; Macarty to Vaudreuil, Jan. 20, 1752, *IHC* 29:433, 444; Longueuil to Minister, Apr. 21, 1752, *WHC* 19:110–11; De Ligneris to Vaudreuil, Oct. 25, 1751, *IHC* 29:415–16; *ibid.*. Oct. 3, 1752, *IHC* 29:730. For Le Maringouin, see Macarty to Vaudreuil, Mar. 18, 1752, *IHC* 29:507–8.

rectly, that the blame would be placed on Le Loup. Le Loup was twice betrayed, for some of his own warriors also attacked the French without his knowledge. Nor were the Illinois as hostile as they seemed. Alternately threatened and solicited by both the rebels and the French, they vacillated and squabbled, not certain of where to turn.[12]

Under the pressure of smallpox and internal jealousies, La Demoiselle's republic began to crack. The arrival of Le Gros Bled among the Miami rebels may have sparked new rivalries among the rebel chiefs. By the late winter of 1752, soon after Le Gros Bled came to Pickawillany, La Mouche Noire, Le Maringouin, and L'Enfant were seeking rapprochement with the French. Rivalries among chiefs had helped create republics; they could also dismantle them. But these rebel chiefs' desire for rapprochement may also have come from a pragmatic assessment of La Demoiselle's possibilities. La Demoiselle was unprepared for a major conflict. In a sense, his very strength was his weakness. La Demoiselle's success in increasing the size of Pickawillany had made it ecologically precarious in the best of years. Not enough land had been cleared to feed a steadily increasing population, and Pickawillany's warriors had to hunt in more and more distant circuits for game. The town was strong only in theory; its warriors were usually elsewhere. The combination of smallpox and widespread crop failures the year before made an already precarious town uninhabitable. La Demoiselle himself, however, remained defiant.[13]

With La Demoiselle reeling, the alliance delivered the death blow. On a June day in 1752, Charles Langlade, a *métis* from Michilimackinac, emerged from the woods surrounding Pickawillany with 250 Ottawa and Chippewa warriors. La Demoiselle, who had vowed to die rather than return to the French alliance, was about to keep his vow and, symbolically, break it.

Langlade took the town by surprise. Most of the men were absent hunting; the women were in the fields. The British traders rushed to their stockade, but they and the few warriors who joined them numbered only twenty in all and had no water. The Ottawas and Chippewas seized the women and a few British traders who had barricaded themselves in a

---

[12] For smallpox, see Longueuil to Minister, Apr. 21, 1752, *WHC* 18:108, 115–16. For action of Le Gros Bled, see Macarty to Vaudreuil, Mar. 18, 1752, *IHC* 29:521, 527–28. For betrayal by own warriors, see Macarty to Vaudreuil, Jan. 20, 1752, *IHC* 29:438; De Guyenne to Vaudreuil, Sept. 10, 1752, *ibid.* 713–14. For account of rivalries between Illinois and negotiations with rebels, see Macarty to Vaudreuil, Jan. 20, 1752, *IHC* 29:436–48; *ibid.*, Mar. 18, 1752, *IHC* 29:528–35; Macarty to Vaudreuil, Mar. 27, 1752, *IHC* 29:537, 545–46, 553. Macarty to Vaudreuil, Sept. 2, 1752, *IHC* 29:660.

[13] For rapprochement, see Macarty to Vaudreuil, Mar. 27, 1752, *IHC* 29:537; Macarty to Rouillé, June 1, 1752, *IHC* 29:660. For difficulty of provisioning Pickawillany, see La Jonquière to Rouillé, Oct. 29, 1751, *IHC* 420–22. Conditions in 1751–52, Longueuil to Minister, Apr. 21, 1752, *WHC* 18:108, 115–16.

storehouse. After a brief fight, the attackers asked to talk with the British, Mingos, Miamis, and Shawnees in the stockade. They offered to exchange the women for the British traders, whom they promised not to harm. The British and their allies agreed. The Ottawas and Chippewas returned the women as promised, but they immediately killed a wounded trader, ripped out his heart, and ate it. The Ottawas and Chippewas captured La Demoiselle, killed him, and, while his followers watched, cooked and ate him. La Demoiselle had died without returning to the alliance, but the alliance had nevertheless incorporated him once more.[14]

When Charles Langlade delivered up La Demoiselle's body to the Ottawa and Chippewa warriors, some of them Langlade's own kinsmen, to eat, both the host and the main course at this cannibal feast were united in more than the obvious way. Their brief encounter and union seemed to signal the collapse of the rebellion and the restoration of the alliance beside the Wabash River, but it was an ambiguous success. The leading actors here were neither French chiefs nor, properly speaking, alliance chiefs. They were a *métis*, Charles Langlade, with much "power... on the minds of the Indians," and La Demoiselle, a rebel chief. French allies had struck the blow that the French, despairing of their aid, had planned to strike themselves.[15]

In the aftermath of Langlade's victory, Onontio reincorporated his errant children back into the alliance. In May, some Wyandots came to announce they no longer had a separate existence but were now a single people with the Huron-Petuns of Detroit and at peace with their brothers, the Ottawas, Potawatomis, and Chippewas. By the fall they had resumed the attacks on the Chickasaws and Catawbas whose cessation years before had helped spark the rebellion. Then, in July 1753, the rebel Miamis themselves arrived. They came with a revealing escort: Potawatomis of Saint Joseph led by Topenebe, their senior civil chief; a party of Sauks who also lived at Saint Joseph; loyal members of the band of Piedfroid; and, finally, La Grue's mother, who represented the Miamis of Tepicon. They gave Onontio the

---

[14] For various French accounts of events at Pickawillany, see Longueuil to Rouillé, Aug. 18, 1752, *IHC* 29:652–53; Macarty to Vaudreuil, Sept. 2, 1752, *IHC* 29:680–81, 684; De Ligneris to Vaudreuil, Oct. 3, 1752, *IHC* 29:733. Duquesne refers to Langlade leading only Ottawas and Chippewas, Duquesne to Machault, Oct. 10, 1754, *IHC* 29:940–5. The English account is in William Trent, *Journal of Captain William Trent From Logstown to Pickawillany, A.D. 1752* (New York: Arno Press and *New York Times*, 1971), 86–88, Cellender to Gov., Aug. 30, 1752; Twightwees' Speech to Burney, *PCR* 5:599–601.

[15] For quotation on Langlade, see Duquesne to Machault, Oct. 10, 1754, *IHC* 29:905. For preparation of army and death of Jonquière, see Bigot au Ministre, 6 mai 1752, AN, C11A, v. 98, f. 90. The minister, Rouillé, rejected the idea of an Indian war on the Ohio and wanted efforts confined to driving off the English, Rouillé to Duquesne, July 9, 1752, *IHC* 29:648–51; Rouillé to Duquesne, May 15, 1752, *WHC* 18:118–22.

symbolic gifts of the alliance – wampum and a small kettle, a symbol of their union with Potawatomis. Their speaker, according to custom, begged Onontio for mercy. The Potawatomis, Sauks, and loyal Miamis, acting as intermediaries in the tradition of the alliance, asked Onontio to accord the rebels forgiveness. Governor Duquesne, who had succeeded La Jonquière, forgave them in the manner of a stern but loving father, crediting his mercy to the intercession of his loyal children and the French chief, Louis Colon de Villiers, commander at the Miami post. He warned them of their certain destruction should they stray again.[16]

Duquesne participated in a ritual of submission and forgiveness that he did not fully understand. He drew all the wrong lessons. "I have," he wrote the minister, "had much satisfaction . . . in seeing tremble before me all the Indians who came down this year." Duquesne believed himself a sterner patriarch than the middle ground allowed. The rituals had been enacted, but the alliance had only seemingly been restored.[17]

The French now believed irrevocably in force. They desired a West held by French forts and French settlements and not by the Algonquian children of a French father. Governor Duquesne redirected the army, once destined to strike the rebels at Pickawillany, to establish instead a permanent fort on the upper Ohio and cow the Ohio republicans.[18]

Pierre-Paul de la Malgue, the elder Sieur de Marin, led Governor Duquesne's army. No Indians resisted its approach as it moved southward toward the Ohio River in 1753, only the country itself resisted. Drought made the rivers low and the portages long. Marin had his men cut wagon roads across the portages, but as they did so scurvy broke out among the troops. Marin died that fall in the forests while disease and exhaustion claimed the lives of four hundred of his men. Captain Le Gardeur, who took command at Marin's death, reserved garrisons for two new French posts: Presque Isle, at the beginning of the portage from Lake Erie, and Fort Le Boeuf, at its end. He dispatched a small detachment to Venango, at the mouth of the Rivière-au-Boeuf. He sent the remainder of the sick and worn-out men home. Not until the next year, 1754, would an expedition under Claude-Pierre Pécaudy de Contrecoeur establish a strong French

---

[16] Conseil solemme tenu avec les Miamis rebeles . . . 6 juillet 1753, AN, C11A, v. 99, f. For Wyandots, see Conseil des Hurons, 3 mai 1753, AN, C11A, v. 99, f. 75. For attacks, see Duquesne to Minister, Oct. 31, 1753, *IHC* 29:849–50.

[17] For quotation, see Duquesne to Rouillé, Oct. 27, 1753, *IHC* 29:840.

[18] For forts, see Duquesne à Contrecoeur, 18 oct. 1752, in Fernand Grenier (ed.), *Papiers Contrecoeur et autres documents concernant le conflit anglo-français sur l'Ohio de 1745 à 1756*, (Quebec: Les Presses Universitaire, Laval, 1952), 16–17. For news of army in West, see Macarty to Vaudreuil, Sept. 2, 1752, *IHC* 29:681. For more troops to Illinois, see Longueuil à Vaudreuil, 30 juin 1752, London Papers, Box 7, LO 373, Huntington Library.

presence on the Ohio with Fort Machault, at Venango, and Fort Duquesne, at the forks of the river.[19]

A brief attack and a few casualties at Pickawillany, the march of an army that the country itself remorselessly reduced to a specter – such were the measures that ended a revolt whose adherents had once stretched from Iroquoia to the Mississippi and which had claimed the support of British colonies far more populous and rich than Canada. The ravages of drought and disease had aided the French, hindering the attempts both of the Wabash rebels to reorganize in the wake of La Demoiselle's death and of the Ohio rebels to resist Marin. But drought and disease obviously hurt Marin too. More than smallpox and crop failures were at work.[20]

What had failed was the rebels' alliance with the British and the Iroquois. Following the attack on Pickawillany, the Miami rebels invoked the covenant chain and the chain of friendship and instigated the necessary ritual measures to procure aid. Those Shawnees who had been present at Pickawillany, along with the "captains and warriors of the Twightwees," sent out a string of black wampum and a scalp to the "captains and warriors of all nations in alliance with them" calling for assistance. The Miamis also returned to the Six Nations a large white wampum belt given them on their first becoming allies, "to let them know the situation they were in was bad." The Delawares and Shawnees of Sonnontio and Chiningué added belts of their own. The skirmish at Pickawillany had left several Miamis, a Shawnee, a Mingo, and an Englishman dead and five British traders prisoners. The dead and the prisoners, in a sense, controlled what followed. The dead demanded revenge, but the British prisoners posed a different problem. They, potentially at least, blocked united action. Since the Miamis had surrendered them, the British could legitimately hold the Pickawillany warriors responsible for the prisoners' fate. Realizing this, the Ottawas and Chippewas had taunted the defenders of Pickawillany, telling them that whether they killed the warriors at Pickawillany or not did not matter, since

---

[19] For plans for expedition, see Duquesne à Contrecoeur, 14 nov. 1752, *Papiers Contrecoeur*, 17–19. For departure of Marin, fear of Indian opposition, see Duquesne à Contrecoeur, 14 avril 1753, Grenier, *Papiers Contrecoeur*, 31–32. He had problems with discipline, supply, and disease, e.g., Duquesne à Marin, 3 sept. 1753, *ibid.*, 60–61; Duquesne au Ministre, 5 oct. 1753, AN, C11A, v. 99, f. 14; Duquesne au Ministre, 2 nov. 1753, AN C11A, v. 99, f. 59; Gustave Lanctot, *A History of Canada*, 4 vols. (Cambridge, Mass.: Harvard University Press, 1965), 3:86; Duquesne au Ministre, 22 nov. 1753, AN, C11A, v. 99, f. 70. For orders to Contrecoeur, see Duquesne à Contrecoeur, 27 jan. 1754, Grenier, *Papiers Contrecoeur*, 92–96. For complaints of difficulties from outset, see Journal de Joseph-Gaspard Chaussegros de Léry...*RAPQ*, 1927–28, 18 mai 1754, 360; 16 juin, 365; 27 juin, 369.

[20] For continued drought and food shortages on Wabash, see Macarty to Vaudreuil, Sept. 2, 1752, *IHC* 29:675, 677. For hunger on Ohio, see *Virginia Gazette*, Aug. 16, 1753, quoted in Mercer, Case of Ohio Company, Mulkearn (ed.), *George Mercer Papers*, 12.

the British and the Six Nations would now put La Demoiselle's followers to death.[21]

The attack on Pickawillany created the first significant demand for a united British-republican-Iroquois response to the French. Under pressure, the precarious British-rebel alliance shuddered and collapsed. At Sonnontio in August 1752, the Miamis, Mingos, Delawares, and Shawnees instigated the necessary rituals to put Iroquois warriors and British militia into the field. They wiped away the blood and tears caused by the death of the British at Pickawillany and brightened the chain of friendship that bound them to Pennsylvania. They then called on "the English and the six Nations to put their hands upon your heads and keep the French from hurting you." Miami delegates called upon the Ohio republicans to intercede for them with the British that they might not resent the loss of the traders; they also asked assistance against the French.[22]

Neither Pennsylvania nor the Iroquois provided aid. Although a Seneca faction under Le Collier Pendu encouraged resistance on the Ohio, the Mohawks were so furious at the refusal of Governor Clinton of New York to redress land frauds perpetrated against them that they announced that the covenant chain with the British was broken. No aid would come from Iroquoia. To most of the beleaguered Iroquois, the French and British had merged into a single threat. As they told the British in 1753: "We don't know what you Christians, English and French together, intend; we are so hemmed in by both, that we have hardly a hunting place left." When in the summer of 1753, the Pennsylvanians asked guidance from Onondaga on how to act toward the Iroquois dependents on the Ohio, the Iroquois declared their neutrality. They said the conflict was a quarrel between the French and the British. If Iroquois allies were struck, they told Pennsylvania that it "would be very kind" of the Pennsylvanians to help the victims. As Peter Wraxall put the matter three years later, the Six Nations regarded the conflict on the Ohio as one of two thieves fighting over Iroquois property.[23]

[21] Trent, *Journal*, 89–90, July 7, 12, 1752; Wallace, *Weiser*, 354.

[22] Trent, *Journal*, Aug. 4, 1752, 93–101.

[23] For French and Iroquois sovereignty over Ohio, see Canada, Sauvages, 1752, AN, C11A, v. 98; Dr. Shuckburgh to Pownall, Oct. 30, 1753, *NYCD* 6:806; Conference between Gov. Clinton and the Indians, June 12, 1753, *NYCD* 6:781–82; Conference Between Mohawks and Colonel Johnson, July 26, 1753 *NYCD* 6:808–9. For Iroquois divided, see Journal of Conrad Weiser's Visit to the Mohawks, Aug. 13, 1753, *NYCD* 6:796–97; Minutes of Council, May 21, 1753, *PCR* 5:608. There were two chiefs with the name Le Collier Pendu; this one was a Seneca, La Chauvignerie à Contrecoeur, 11 mars 1754, *Papiers Contrecoeur*, 106–07; Conseil tenu avec les Cinq Nations, 12 oct. 1754, AN, C11A, v. 99; A Message . . . to the Governor of Pennsylvania, July 31, 1753, *PCR* 5:637. For quotation, see Conference at Onondaga, Sept. 10, 1753, *NYCD* 6:813. For same sentiment in negotiations with French, see Conseil tenu avec les Cinq Nations à Montreal, 12 oct. 1754, AN, C11A, v. 99, f. 11. Also see Meetings of Commissioners for Treaty with Six Nations, July 3, 1754, *NYCD* 6:869–

The rebel call for aid and renewal received only a slightly better response in Pennsylvania. Thomas Burney, one of the traders who had escaped Pickawillany, brought the Miami message to Carlisle, Pennsylvania, at the end of August 1752. From there it was forwarded to Philadelphia. The governor gave the message to the assembly, but the assembly was unwilling to act without interviewing Burney. They adjourned having done nothing.[24]

Only in May 1753, as the French army under Marin advanced toward the Ohio River, did Governor Hamilton ask the assembly to provide aid, and only then did they appropriate a present to condole the Miamis and aid their other allies. Even as they granted the aid, however, the assembly made it clear that the Indians should look to New York and Virginia for military assistance. Hamilton himself continued to believe that the Ohio Indians were dependents of Onondaga's and would act under its direction. He accordingly devoted most of his attention to the Six Nations. Not until the fall of 1753 did Benjamin Franklin, Richard Peters, and Isaac Norris meet with the Ohio rebels and a delegation of Miamis and Wyandots to perform the necessary ceremonies of condolence. Only then did they, bewildered by the necessary protocol, cover the dead and brighten the chain of friendship. But it was too late; the bulk of the rebel Miamis and the Wyandots had already returned to Onontio.[25]

By default, the ultimate British decision on whether to support the Indians on the Ohio River came to rest with the Virginians. But the Virginians were more interested in obtaining title to the Ohio country than in helping the republics defend it against the French. At nearly the same time that Langlade fell upon Pickawillany, representatives of Virginia were at Logstown informing Tanacharison that Virginia claimed present-day Kentucky, West Virginia, and western Pennsylvania by virtue of the Treaty of Lancaster of 1744. Asserting that the Six Nations had ceded all claims to the land, they asked the villages of the Ohio to confirm the treaty and permit

---

72. For Wraxall, see Wraxall, Some Thoughts upon the British Indian Interest, 1756, *NYCD* 7:23.

[24] Cellender to Gov. with Message of Twightwees, Aug. 30, 1752, *PCR* 5:599–601; Wallace, *Weiser*, 334–36.

[25] Governor to Assembly, 22 May 1753, *PCR* 5:608–9; A Message to the Governor from the Assembly, 31 May 1753, *PCR* 5:616–17. Report of Richard Peters, et al., Sept. 22, 1753, *PCR* 5:665–86. For controlled by Onondaga, see Hamilton to Dinwiddie, 2 Aug. 1753, *ibid.*, 633.

For return of Weas, see De Ligneris to Vaudreuil, Oct. 3, 1752, *IHC* 29:730–31. For decline of rebels, see Macarty to Vaudreuil, Dec. 7, 1753, *IHC* 29:760–63, 769; Vaudreuil to Rouillé, Sept. 10, 1752, *IHC* 29:727; Conseil des Hurons, 3 mai 1753, AN, C11A, v. 99, f. 75. For attacks on traders, see letter of Captain Trent, May 3, 1753, in Mercer, Case of Ohio Company, in Mulkearn (ed.), *George Mercer Papers*, 9. Duquesne was willing to pardon the Wabash rebels. His orders to the Sr. de Pean, who was to march to the Illinois, were to demand the surrender of the murderers and then pardon them in the usual manner. Instructions de Duquesne à Pean, 9 mai, 1754, Grenier (ed.), *Papiers Contrecoeur*, 120–22.

British settlement. As if such a huge and sudden land claim was not enough of a thunderbolt, the Virginians launched a second one. They demanded the surrender of a man accused of murdering a British woman on the New River, asserting the right of the British to try Indian murderers in their courts. Here was what the French had long warned: British goods only paved the road to a loss of land and slavery.[26]

Where the republicans had expected allies in defending their lands, they found only British colonists seeking to claim them. Although the situation seemed hopeless, Tanacharison, the half king, tried to tread a fine line that would allow him both to deflect British land claims and to obtain British aid against the French. In a closed meeting with the Virginia delegation, he expressed surprise at the Iroquois cession of the Ohio region, saying he had never heard of it, but he promised to "confirm whatever they had done." In council, too, he referred the matter to Onondaga. He seemed to yield to the Virginians by granting them permission to build a stronghouse, but not a settlement, on the Monongahela River where Pittsburgh now stands. Only at the last minute, after the British interpreter Andrew Montour, at the request of the Virginia commissioners, held a private meeting with Tanacharison, had the half king and the other Six Nations chiefs present signed the treaty confirming the cession of 1744 and allowing a British outpost at Pittsburgh. It appears that Montour, a *métis* of Iroquois and French descent, who worked for Pennsylvania and Virginia as his interest dictated, and Tanacharison thought of this last-minute agreement as a trap of their own. They reasoned, and the Ohio Indians later pressed the point, that if the Virginians had to ask permission to build on the land, then they did not own it. And in agreeing to recognize the larger cession, they were merely deferring the matter to Onondaga. Montour denied the next year that the Indians had ever sold or released the Ohio country. As John Mercer of the Virginia Company himself noted, Tanacharison in his later negotiations with the French stressed that the land belonged to the Indians and not the British or the French. And on this Onondaga, for the moment, seconded him.[27]

---

[26] There are two accounts of this council; the complete minutes are in Treaty at Logstown, 1752, CO 5, 1327; also see Council held at Logstown, June 1, 1752, Mulkearn (ed.), *George Mercer Papers*, 274, 276; for murder, see *ibid.*, 277; Wallace, *Weiser*, 334–36. For Ohio Company's position and instructions to Gist, see Mercer, Case for Ohio Company, 1762, Mulkearn (ed.), *George Mercer Papers*, 6–7.

[27] Logstown Treaty, 1752, CO 5, 1327. Council, Logstown, June 9, 1752, Mulkearn (ed.), *George Mercer Papers*, 275, 281–83. For Onondaga council upset about Virginia's negotiations on Ohio, see Extract of letter of Col. Johnson, Mar. 26, 1753, *DHNY* 2:39–40; Croghan's Journal, 1754, in Thwaites (ed.), *Early Western Travels*, 1:78–79. English traders, meanwhile, aggravated matters still further by fraudulently attaching to a written message

The council at Logstown helped spur the Virginians to defend land they now believed to be theirs. William Trent arrived at Logstown in 1753 as Marin approached, and in the fall of 1753 George Washington and Christopher Gist arrived to demand the withdrawal of French troops from the region. Then, in March 1754, William Trent returned to establish a stronghouse with a small garrison at the forks of the Ohio. Although Contrecoeur quickly forced its surrender in April, Washington was by then already on the march with a much larger contingent of militia to secure the Ohio. Direct imperial conflict had begun.[28]

The approach of rival bodies of troops drastically cut the options of the republicans. The upper Ohio River had ceased to be a haven between empires; it had become a battleground. Most of the republicans, like the Iroquois, had come to regard the British and the French as a single Christian threat. The Delawares were quite direct. If the French claimed all the land north of the Ohio, they asked, and the British all the land to the south, what was left for the Indians? When William Trent arrived in the summer of 1753, he did not "like the behavior of the Delawares." The Ohio Indians in the fall of 1753 readily accepted rumors that if neither the French nor the British could establish clear dominance on the Ohio, they would unite to dispossess the Indians. Resisting the French would be aiding the British, and this no longer made sense. And so resistance melted away.[29]

By 1753 the Ohio republicans regarded themselves as the objects of a general Christian conspiracy. In May 1754, as Washington and Contrecoeur steered toward the collision of empires, George Croghan clearly and percep-

from the Ohio Indians a cession of all lands east of the Ohio in payment for traders' debts. When Ohio Indians in the fall of 1753 pressed the point that the English could not own land they needed Indian permission to build on, Conrad Weiser – the chief Indian negotiator for Pennsylvania who had now agreed to assist the Virginians – exploded, calling Andrew Montour an "Impudent felow" for denying the cession. Weiser to Taylor, Fall 1753, in Wallace, *Weiser*, 348–49. Gov. Dinwiddie of Virginia contended the Indians on the Ohio had surrendered their land to Virginia at Logstown, Dinwiddie to Hamilton, May 21, 1753, *PCR* 5:630. For Tanacharison and the French, John Mercer, Case of the Ohio Company, 1762, Mulkearn (ed.), *George Mercer papers*, 13, 76. The Iroquois contended the lands on the Ohio belonged to the Indians "independent of both" the English and the French, Council, Philadelphia, May 21, 1753, *PCR* 5:608.
    Francis Jennings gives a much simpler interpretation of the treaty. He has Montour bribing Tanacharison. Francis Jennings, *Empire of Fortune: Crowns, Colonies, and Tribes in the Seven Years', War in America* (New York: W. W. Norton, 1988), 42–43.
28 For Trent, see Trent, *Journal*, 1753, CO 5, 1328. For Washington's mission, see John C. Fitzpatrick, *The Diaries of George Washington*, 1748–99 (Boston: Houghton Mifflin, 1925), 1:48–60. For Trent's fort and surrender, see *ibid.*, 76–77. Also see Journal of Mr. Christopher Gist, *Collections of the Massachusetts Historical Society*, 3rd series, vol. 5 (Boston: John H. Easburn, 1836), 101–08.
29 For Delaware quotation, see Gist Journals, Mar. 12, 1752, Mulkearn (ed.), *George Mercer Paprs*, 39; Fitzpatrick, *Washington Diaries*, 52–53. For Trent quotation, see Trent, *Journal*, July 14, 1753, CO 5, 1328.

tively gave the governor of Pennsylvania an account of conditions on the Ohio:

> The whole of ye Ohio Indians Dose Nott No what to think, they Imagine by this Government [i.e., Pennsylvania] Doing Nothing towards ye Expedition that ye Virginians and ye French Intend to Divide ye Land of Ohio between them, and if they should putt that Construction on ye Delays of this Government, itt will Certainly be of ill Consequence to the British in gineral, and itt is my opinion without the harty Concurrence of this Government that the Indians will Suspectt ye Virginians as only atacking ye French, on Account of Setling ye Lands ye Government may have what opinion they will of ye Ohio Indians, and think they are obligd to Do what ye Onondago Counsel will bid them, Butt I ashure yr honour they will actt for themselves att this time without Consulting ye Onondago Councel.

News of supposed Iroquois cessions of land along the Ohio River at the Albany Conference of 1754 only widened the breach with Onondaga. The Ohio Indians defined themselves as a separate people in a world where the French, the British, and the Iroquois were all threats.[30]

It was, ironically, the so-called Iroquois viceroys themselves – Tanacharison and Scarooyady – who forwarded the break with Ononadaga. Tanacharison was convinced that the French represented the primary danger and must be met with force, but he could obtain no aid from Onondaga, Pennsylvania, or the villages he supervised. The rebels, finding themselves isolated, were demoralized and fearful, a condition not helped by incredible importations of rum from Pennsylvania. On receiving news of Marin's advance, Tanacharison could not even convene a council. The Indians "being all drunk none of them came." When he did convene a council, the Delawares and Shawnees, whom Trent feared were already partially in the French interest, informed Tanacharison by two strings of wampum that they "looked upon them [the Six Nations] as their rulers and that they were ready to strike the French whenever they bid them." There was mockery in the reply. The Iroquois, as the Delawares and Shawnees knew, would not risk such an attack on the French. Tanacharison and Scarooyady, in a last series of desperate maneuvers, attempted to act unilaterally. Tanacharison warned off the French while Scarooyady asked the British for aid.[31]

---

[30] For Croghan, see Croghan to Governor, May 14, 1754, *PA*, Series 1, 2:144–45. For a later statement of fear of English, see Butler to Johnson, May 14, 1755, *JP* 1:495. The news of supposed Iroquois cessions of the Ohio to Pennsylvania at Albany in 1754 also greatly alarmed the Indians on the Ohio, Croghan's Remarks, Sept. 17, 1757, *DHNY* 2:756–61; Johnson's Remarks, 10 Sept. 1757, *NYCD* 7:329.

[31] For quotation, see Council, 30 May 1753, *PCR* 5:615. For delegations, see John Fraser to Young, Aug. 27, 1753, *PCR* 5:660. For rum trade, see Report of Peters et al., 22

Both Scarooyady and Tanacharison forthrightly claimed the Ohio as belonging to the republicans. At Winchester Scarooyady told the Virginians, "Now, Brother, I let you know that our Kings having nothing to do with our Lands; for We, the Warriors, fought for the Lands & so the right belongs to us, & we will take Care of them." He then told the Virginians to abandon their plan for a stronghouse on the Ohio for they wanted neither French nor British on their lands. In a second conference with the Pennsylvanians, he asked that records of his negotiations be forwarded to Onondaga. Scarooyady's motives are unclear, but the Pennsylvanians well knew by then that Onondaga did not countenance these direct negotiations with the Mingos and their dependents. The Iroquois were furious with Pennsylvania and Virginia for treating with "these Indians, whom they [the Iroquois] called Hunters, and young and giddy Men and Children; that they were their Fathers, and if the British wanted anything from these childish People they must speak to their Fathers."[32]

Tanacharison delivered essentially the same message of independence to the French. When he met Marin in early September to give him the last of three ritual warnings not to advance, he spoke to him not as the half king but rather as a speaker for the Iroquois warriors living on the Ohio. We are, he told Marin, warriors and not chiefs. The river where we are belongs to us, the warriors. The chiefs who supervise public affairs (*travaillent aux affaires*) are not its masters. The warriors claimed the land. If Marin insisted on building new forts, the warriors would strike.[33]

But few warriors actually followed Tanacharison and Scarooyady. The Delawares and Shawnees had agreed to strike only if asked and backed by Onondaga. Marin grasped this. Ignoring normal council etiquette, he told the warriors who had accompanied Tanacharison that he scorned all the stupid things that Tanacharison had said. He promised to brush aside any resistance they might be so foolish as to make. The Shawnees of the upper village immediately disavowed Tanacharison's speech to Marin. Tanacharison himself returned to Logstown where he "shed Tears, and ... actually warned the British Traders not to pass the Ohio." He could not protect them from the French.[34]

Sept. 1753, *PCR* 5:676. For Delawares and Shawnees, see Trent *Journal*, Aug. 23, 1753, CO 5, 1328.

[32] For Scarooyady and Virginia, see Lawrence Henry Gipson, *The British Empire Before the American Revolution* (New York: Alfred A. Knopf, 1942), 4:284; Pennsylvania, sentiment of Iroquois, see Report of Peters et al., 22 Sept. 1753, *PCR* 5:677; Message of Montour, *PCR* 5:635.

[33] For Tanacharison, see Conseil tenu par des Tsonnontouans Venus de La Belle-Riviere, 2 sept. 1753, Grenier (ed.), *Papiers Contrecoeurs*, 53–58. For the second notice, see *PCR* 5:666.

[34] For Tanacharison and French, see Marin à Joncaire, (après le 3) sept. 1753, Grenier (ed.), *Papiers Contrecoeur*, 58–59; Baby à Marin, 5 sept. 1753, *ibid.*, 63; Duquesne au Ministre, 2

The eventual appearance of the Virginia militia boosted Tanacharison's ardor, but it did not halt the erosion of his influence among the rebels who feared British intrusions upon the Ohio as much as they feared French intrusions. When Washington came to the Ohio in the fall of 1753, Tanacharison and Scarooyady attempted to get the Shawnees and Delawares to return all their wampum belts to the French and thus break off negotiations with them. Both groups refused to do so. But only with the arrival of Contrecoeur did the tide turn decisively toward the French. In 1754 the Shawnees and other Indians of Sonnontio sought rapprochement with the French even as Virginia committed troops to the Ohio.[35]

III

In the fighting between France and England that began with Sieur de Villiers's defeat of Washington in 1754, the Ohio Indians played a complicated and ambiguous role. They – along with French allies from all over the *pays d'en haut* – fought the British, but the war they waged was often a parallel war. Their goal was not the triumph of Onontio but an Ohio free of British and French domination. A full-scale account of the Seven Years' War is out of place here, but an account of the continued decline of the politics of alliance and the continuation of the republican ideal is necessary.

When Washington returned to the Ohio with Virginia militia in the spring of 1754, only Tanacharison and a small band of Mingos followed him. The Ohio Indians disavowed Tanacharison and, by and large, remained neutral. The French commander, Captain Claude-Pierre Pécaudy de Contrecoeur, dispatched Joseph Coulon de Villiers de Jumonville to warn the British off the Ohio. Washington, claiming that the Frenchman came as a spy and not an emissary, attacked him. Tanacharison and his warriors joined the British in the attack. It was Tanacharison who found the wounded Jumonville on the

oct. 1753, AN, C11A, v.99, f.14; Joncaire à Marin, 7 oct. 1753, Grenier, (ed.), *Papiers Contrecoeur*, 69–71; Baby à Marin, 12 sept. 1753, *ibid.*, 65–67; Joncaire à Marin, c. aug. 30, 1753, Contrecoeur Papers, Archives of Seminary of Quebec, copies in Ohio Valley–Great Laker Ethnohistorical Archives, University of Indiana, hereafter cited as GLEHA. Shawnees, Paroles Des Chaouanons, 3 sept. 1753, Grenier (ed.), *Papiers Contrecoeur*, 61–62. For actions on Ohio, see Report of Peters et al., Sept. 22, 1753, *PCR* 5:670. In November, only Tanacharison proved fully cooperative in Washington's and Gist's attempts to warn the French off, see Gist Journal, *Collections of the Massachusetts Historical Society*, 4:103–4, 106–7.

[35] For Tanacharison, see Washington to Dinwiddie, May 9, 1754, and June 3, 1754, *The Official Records of Robert Dinwiddie*... (Richmond: Virginia Historical Society, 1893, AMS repr., 1971), 1:152, 191–93 (hereafter, *Dinwiddie Records*), Fitzpatrick, *Washington Diaries*, 52–54, 56. For French fear, see La Chauvignerie à Contrecoeur, 11 mars 1754, Grenier (ed.), *Papiers Contrecoeur*, 108–9. The Shawnees of Sonnontio sought rapprochement even before learning of Washington's defeat, Duquesne à Contrecoeur, 20 juin 1754, *ibid.*, 190.

battlefield after the skirmish. He spoke to him in the old ritual terms of the alliance. "You are not yet dead, my father," he said. And then, raising his tomahawk, he struck until his father died.[36]

When Tanacharison buried his tomahawk in Jumonville's head, his bitter killing symbolized a deeper reality. The alliance on the Ohio was dead. Governor Duquesne, who had ordered Contrecoeur to the Ohio, followed the old forms, but his real appeal was force. He assured Contrecoeur that the Ohio Indians were savages and, like all savages, would die of fear when they saw French troops march to the borders of their villages.[37]

Duquesne was half right about the Indians. Threatened on both sides, the rebels had no desire to confront the immediately stronger power. Most Indians regarded the French as militarily superior to the British, and when the Sieur de Villiers, accompanied by mission Indians, revenged his brother's death and forced Washington's surrender at Fort Necessity, their opinion was confirmed. Most of Tanacharison's small band of warriors deserted him. The half king himself was dead soon afterward, killed, the Indians believed, by French witchcraft. The Ohio Indians unenthusiastically came to terms with the French. The mission Indians warned the French that the people of the Ohio had not welcomed the French victory and should not be trusted. The Indians of the Ohio greeted with alarm the substitution of forts and troops for treaties of peace and alliance.[38]

[36] Shingas proclaimed Delaware neutrality because, he said, the Six Nations had ordered it. Since the Iroquois representatives on the Ohio were all pro-English, such a declaration only solidified Delaware independence under the pretense of obedience to Onondaga. Onondaga had apparently simultaneously ordered the Shawnees from the Ohio, an order that had absolutely no effect. Fitzpatrick, *Washington Diaries*, 75–76, 87, 93, 96–99. The Ohio Indians had asked the Six Nations to withdraw Tanacharison from the Ohio. Duquesne was pleased and satisfied with their neutrality during the first half of 1754. Duquesne à Contrecoeur, 1 juillet 1754, Grenier (ed.), *Papiers Contrecoeur*, 207. For Tanacharison and English, see *Virginia Gazette*, May 1754, in Mulkearn (ed.), *George Mercer Papers*, 86–88. For French report that Jumonville was attacked by Washington while under a flag of truce, see De l'Isle Dieu au Ministre, 12 oct. 1754, AN, C11A, v. 99, f. 470. As the orders to his brother, M. de Villiers, demonstrate, the French regarded his killing as murder. Ordres, M. de Villiers, 22 juin 1754, AN, C11A, v. 101, f. 16.; Tanacharison and death of Jumonville, Journal . . . De Lery, 20 juin 1754, *RAPQ*, 1927–28, 367.

[37] For fear, see Duquesne à Contrecoeur, 15 avril 1754, Grenier (ed.), *Papiers Contrecoeur*, 106–7. For settlements and garrisons, see Vaudreuil to Rouillé, Sept. 24, 1750, *IHC* 29:226; Mémoire sur les postes du Canada . . . en 1754 . . . Raymond, *RAPQ*, 1927–28, 329; Jonquière and Bigot to Minister, Oct. 5, 1759, *WHC* 18:30–31.

[38] For Washington's defeat, see Journal de la Campagne de M. De Villiers au Ft. Necessite, Grenier (ed.), *Papiers Contrecoeur*, 196–202; note that the chiefs of the mission Iroquois tried to avoid accompanying him, but were overruled by the warriors, p. 197. For death of Tanacharison, see Morris to Dinwiddie, Oct. 3, 1754, *PA*, Series 1, 2:177. For dispersal of followers, see Duquesne au Ministre, 3 nov. 1754, AN, C11A, v. 99, f. 399. The English recognized that Washington's defeat meant the Indians would return to the French, Croghan to Hamilton, Sept. 27, 1754, *PA*, Series 1, 2:178–79; Johnson to Shirley, Dec. 17, 1754, *JP*, 1:429–31. For Ohio discontent, see Duquesne à Contrecoeur, 14 aoust 1754,

But Duquesne was only half right because although force had secured renewed allegiance on the Ohio, that force could only be effectively deployed with Indian consent. In forest warfare Canadians and French regulars routinely defeated and humiliated greater numbers of British colonials and regulars, but these Frenchmen in their posts on the Ohio hung like cannonballs on a string; formidable as they were, they would eventually fall of their own weight. French soldiers could not fight without food, without supplies, or without the eyes the Indians provided in the forest. Nowhere were the logistical difficulties of forest warfare more apparent than in the Ohio country. From Marin's expedition to the eventual fall of Fort Duquesne, supplying the posts remained a constant preoccupation and hazard. Maintaining the long and tenuous supply lines to the Ohio occupied far more men than defended Fort Duquesne itself and limited the number of troops the French could deploy. Meanwhile, the cost of provisions strained the royal treasury as Intendant François Bigot and his cronies made fortunes from supply contracts. The French had to depend on the Indians to help supply and defend the very garrisons dispatched to intimidate them. The supposed prisoners had become their own jailers.[39]

Superficially in 1754, the French had never been stronger in the *pays d'en haut*. They had subdued the republicans, banished British traders, and repulsed British troops. Their new post secured the dangerous Ohio country. The rituals of the alliance were once more observed from Montreal to the Mississippi and from the Great Lakes to the Ohio. But, in reality, French power gleamed like a new uniform on a sick soldier. Reasonably healthy only along the Great Lakes and in the Illinois country, elsewhere the alliance had become the creation of French force and would not outlive the application of that force. The older ideal of the alliance would long hold the affection of many Algonquians, but its present reality bred resentment.

Grenier (ed.), *Papiers Contrecoeur*, 247; De l'Isle Dieu to Machault, Oct. 12, 1754, *IHC* 29:909. For fear of French allies, see Duquesne au Ministre, 25 juin 1753, AN, C11A, v. 110.

[39] For difficulties of supply, see Bigot au Ministre, 6 mai, 1752, AN, C11A, v. 98, f. 90; for Marin's problems, e.g., see Duquesne à Marin, 3 sept. 1753, C11A, v. 98; Duquesne au Ministre, 5 oct. 1753, AN, C11A, v. 99, f. 14; Duquesne au Ministre, 2 nov. 1753, AN, C11A, v. 99, f. 59; Lanctot, *History of Canada*, 3:86; Duquesne au Ministre, 22 nov. 1753, AN, C11A, v. 99, f. 70. For orders to Contrecoeur, see Duquesne à Contrecoeur, 27 janvier 1754, Grenier (ed.), *Papiers Contrecoeur*, 92–96. For complaints of difficulties, see Journal de Joseph-Gaspard Chaussegros de Léry... *RAPQ*, 1927–28, 18 mai 1754, 360; 16 juin, 365, 27 juin, 369; Vaudreuil to Moras, 12 July 1757, *NYCD* 10:583; for corruption, see Edward P. Hamilton (ed. and trans), *Adventure in the Wilderness; The American Journals of Louis Antoine de Bougainville, 1756–60* (Norman: University of Oklahoma Press, 1964), 195–97. Reliance on Indians, Parole des Chaouanons, 3 sept. 1753, Grenier (ed.), *Papiers Contrecoeur*, 61–62. For weakness of Fort Duquesne, see John M'Kinney's Description of Fort Duquesne, Grenier (ed.), *Papiers Contrecoeur*, planche vii. Also De l'Isle Dieu to Machault, Oct. 12, 1754, *IHC* 29:909.

Yet, despite this, for four years, the French and their Indian allies waged a brilliant and cruel war against the far richer, more populous, and more powerful British. In 1755 the French and their Great Lakes and mission Indian allies routed the British under Edward Braddock. They left the forest floor strewn with the dead, and outside the walls of Fort Duquesne the Indians avenged their own losses by burning alive a few of the prisoners they had taken. What appeared a united effort, however, was an often uneasy parallel effort. The French fought an imperial war, and their Great Lakes and Illinois allies assisted their father until he proved incapable of fulfilling his paternal obligations. The Ohio republicans, however, fought their own war, for their own reasons, and made their separate peace.

The roots of the war the Ohio republicans waged against the British reached back to 1753 when South Carolina imprisoned some Shawnees who had taken the war road south against the Catawbas. The leader of the party, The Pride, died in prison. Although Pennsylvania secured the release of the remainder of the Shawnees and returned them to the Ohio region, The Pride's relatives became a war faction. By January 1755 they were circulating war belts as far north as Sandusky.[40]

Most Shawnees and Delawares refused the war belts and also refused to join the mission Indians, the Great Lakes Indians, and the French in the defense of Fort Duquesne against Braddock, but the British continued to drive the republicans into the arms of the French. Pennsylvania sought, and received, a cession of lands along the Ohio from the Iroquois, and the British reportedly seized and hanged emissaries that the Shawnees and Delawares had sent them. The Shawnees and the Delawares retaliated by sending belts to all the surrounding nations inviting them to help avenge these deaths. They accepted, and slaughter reigned on the British frontiers.[41]

[40] For original imprisonment and release, see Croghan Journal, Jan. 12, 1754, Thwaites (ed.), *Early Western Travels*, 1:74–75. The Indians were striking the English frontier as early as the fall of 1753, but which Indians are not clear. Fitzpatrick, *Washington Diaries*, Dec. 14, 1753, 1:60–61. Trent suspected the Ottawas and Chippewas, Trent *Journal*, Aug. 4, 1753, CO 5, 1328. The Shawnees, far from joining them, feared attacks from the Ottawas and Chippewas, *ibid.*, Aug. 6, 9, 1753.

[41] For Shawnee and Delaware hesitation, Contrecoeur à Vaudreuil, 21 juin 1755, Grenier (ed.), *Papiers Contrecoeur*, 365. Shingas claimed that the Delawares would have joined the English except for Braddock's arrogance and refusal to guarantee them their lands, Beverly Bond, Jr. (ed.), "The Captivity of Charles Stuart, 1755–57," *Mississippi Valley Historical Review* 13:63. For specific incidents that angered Indians, see Abstract of Despatches from Canada, *NYCD* 10:423. These hangings were sometimes cited, as was the much earlier hanging of a Delaware chief in New Jersey, Meeting in the Court House at Lancaster ... May 19, 1757, *JP* 9:755. For mention of hangings, see Hamilton (ed.), *Adventure in the Wilderness*, May 5, 1757; Vaudreuil au Ministre, 17 avril 1757, AN, F3, v. 15, f. 5. Laputha, a "Sahunah King" took up the hatchet in October against the French. Dinwiddie to DeLancey, Dec. 17, 1754, *Dinwiddie Recorde*, 1:430; Dinwiddie to DeLancey, n.d., *Dinwiddie Records*, 1:311. Dinwiddie ordered his officers to take all Indians not clearly allied to the English

The relations of the French to this Shawnee-Delaware-Mingo war always remained equivocal. Although Frenchmen, Shawnees, and Delawares fought side by side, they remained, in a sense, only enemies of a common enemy. The French spoke of the Delaware and Shawnees' sending independent belts to solicit war parties instead of their taking up their father's hatchet. Similarly, Tamaqua (or Beaver), whom the Iroquois had appointed head chief of the Delawares, contended that the Delawares had taken up not the French hatchet but, rather, one offered by mission Iroquois and other members of the Six Nations who had joined the French. By 1756 the French recognized that the furious attacks on the British frontier had taken on a life of their own. Captain Dumas, now in command of Fort Duquesne, reported that the cruel war the Indians were waging had cost the lives of twenty-five hundred British men, women, and children by 1756 and would not necessarily cease once the French made peace.[42]

The Ohio Indians had opened a parallel war against the British, and there are indications that their war alongside the French only continued the strategy of the rebellion under a new cover. The Ohio Indians recognized both the extent to which the French depended on their aid along the Ohio and the opportunities that this presented. According to an escaped British prisoner, the Indians believed that the British and French had agreed to deprive them of their lands, but if the Ohio Indians could use the French to

---

prisoners, Dinwiddie to Lewis, Sept. 11, 1754. For Shawnee and Delaware belts soliciting war, Abstract of Despatches, *NYCD* 10:423.

[42] The French initially encouraged the Shawnees to avenge the death of The Pride, but by the time some Shawnees struck the North Carolina frontier in the fall of 1754, the French had reversed themselves and were urging restraint. Not until 1755 did the French again encourage the Shawnees, but then they worried about the desire of many Shawnees to remain neutral. Not until after the defeat of Braddock and the reported hanging of the Shawnee-Delaware embassy by the English were the Ohio Indians and the French clearly in agreement. Duquesne à Contrecoeur, 24 juillet 1754, Grenier (ed.), *Papiers Contrecoeur*, 222–23; *ibid*, 18 juillet 1754, 220. By the fall Contrecoeur ordered a halt in French-sponsored raiding and recommended only defensive action, Duquesne à Contrecoeur, 30 oct. 1754, *Papiers Contrecoeur*, 266, *ibid.*, 5 mars 1755, 289. By July and Aug. 1755, the French were actively encouraging raids, and many raiding parties went out, Sylvester Stevens, Donald Kent, and Emma Woods (eds.), *Travels in New France by JCB* (Harrisburg, Pa.: Pennsylvania Historical Survey, Pennsylvania Historical Commission, 1941), 67.

For Shawnee alliance against English, see Journal . . . de Lery, 1 jan. 1755, *RAPQ*, 1927–28, 409–10. Baby à Contrecoeur, 18 jan. 1755, *Papiers Contrecoeur*, 274. By April and May, the Shawnees were attacking with French approval, Duquesne à Contrecoeur, 27 avril 1755, *ibid.*, 322–24. Duquesne au Ministre, 31 mai 1755, AN, C11A, v. 100. Contrecoeur à Vaudreuil, 14 aoust 1755, Grenier (ed.), *Papiers Contrecoeur*, 419; Vaudreuil au Ministre, 19 sept. 1756, AN F3, Moreau St. Mery, v. 14, f. 341. Dumas a ?, 24 juillet 1756, AN, C11A, v. 101, f. 322. For anger at supposed cession, see Johnson's Remarks . . . 10 Sept. 1757, *NYCD* 7:331. For independent belts, see Abstract of Despatches, 1756, *NYCD* 10:423. A Delaware prisoner contended that the Delawares accepted a Shawnee war belt, Examination of a Delaware Prisoner, 1757, *PA*, Series 1, 3:147. For refusal to take French belts, see Council at Carlisle, Jan. 1756, Thwaites (ed.), *EWT* 1:85–86.

defeat the British, then "we may do afterwards what we please with the French, for we have [them] as it were in A Sheep Den and may cut them any time, for they had no liberty to plant any Corn yet tho they tryed but it was forbid them." The Ohio Delaware speaker, Ackowanothic, gave an identical account of the larger strategy when asked to explain the reasons the Indians attacked the British. He answered that to defeat the British who coveted their land they needed French aid, for the British were "such a numerous People," but "we can drive away the French when we please."[43]

This strategy for independence on the Ohio also involved an open renunciation of Iroquois overlordship. The British continued to urge the Iroquois to control and chastise their dependents on the Ohio, but the Delaware and Shawnee attacks were "as they say themselves . . . to shew the Six Nations that they are no longer Women, by which they mean no longer under their Subjection." And, indeed, the Iroquois were unable to exert any real influence over the Ohio Indians during the war.[44]

The tenuousness of the cooperation between the Ohio Indians and the French remained disguised beneath the tremendous military success achieved by the French and the Indians in 1755, 1756, and 1757. Brilliant victories against enormous odds allowed belief in a resuscitated and powerful French-Algonquian alliance whose skill, daring, and intelligence more than offset British numbers and wealth. But the heart of the alliance beat only along the Great Lakes and in the Illinois country, and even there it grew weak. On the Canada – New York border where much of the fighting occurred, the Great Lakes Indians and the French quarreled incessantly. Here the Indians fought alongside and under officers fresh from France who did not understand the compromises and rituals of the middle ground. General Montcalm sporadically attempted to treat Indians as soldiers, bound to military discipline, instead of as warriors who came and went as they chose and who consulted manitous and not French officers on the eve of battle. The cruel and bloody rituals of Algonquian warfare disgusted the French regulars and their officers. They were not accustomed to seeing prisoners tortured and cannibalized. Nor could the French make sense of the sudden and unexpected kindnesses the Indians bestowed on other prisoners they wished to adopt.[45]

---

[43] For first quotation, see Daniel Claus to Johnson, Apr. 5, 1756, *JP* 2:439. For Ackowanothio, see Wallace, *Weiser*, 530. For belief that both French and English wanted their land, see Remarks on An Indian Conference, Easton, Nov. 1756, *PA* 3:38–39.

[44] For quotation, see Robert Morris to Johnson, 15 Nov. 1755. *JP* 9:309–10. For similar assertion, see Proprietors of Pennsylvania's Observations, Dec. 11, 1756, *DHNY* 2:738–42; Atkin to Lords of Trade, Dec. 27, 1756, *NYCD* 7:209.

[45] For Indian-French disputes, see Vaudreuil au Ministre, 1 sept. 1756, AN, F3, Moreau St. Mery, v. 14, f. 297; Hamilton (ed.), *Adventure in the Wilderness*, 164–65. Vaudreuil to Massaic, Aug. 4, 1758, *NYCD* 10:780; Speeches, July 30, 1758, *ibid.* 805. For disgust at

The British denounced General Montcalm, the French commander in Canada, for permitting the Indians to slaughter prisoners at Fort William Henry, an event James Fenimore Cooper later immortalized in *The Last of the Mohicans*. But of more immediate concern to the French was the price of the efforts Montcalm did make to control his allies. Montcalm's relations with the Iroquois and Algonquians had become so bad that the last French governor, Pierre François de Rigaud, Marquis de Vaudreuil, who maintained a mutual and sustained enmity with Montcalm, accused the general of wrecking the alliance. At the peak of military success the alliance began to unravel. Once more, just as in King George's War, the British blockade took effect, and the presents and trade goods Onontio owed his children disappeared. Once more smallpox epidemics ravaged the Indians. Once more warriors became disgruntled and alienated, and once more the alliance began to fall apart in the *pays d'en haut*.[46]

As an English blockade brought the usual shortage of goods, French troubles expanded beyond the Ohio region. In the winter of 1757–1758, the Menominees of Green Bay attacked the French. Disease and scarcity of trade goods formed the familiar backdrop to the revolt, but exactly what precipitated an assault that killed twenty-two Frenchmen remains unclear. Whatever the immediate cause, the Menominees themselves were far from united, and alliance chiefs seem subsequently to have regained control. In the usual manner of the alliance, the chiefs sent seven of the killers to Montreal. The precedent was that Onontio would pardon the killers and the Indians would cover the French dead with British prisoners or scalps. In June of the previous year, two murderers of Frenchmen had come to

---

Indian treatment of prisoners, see Hamilton (ed.), *Adventure in the Wilderness*, 40–41; for cruelty and kindness, see *ibid.*, 144; for complaint of mode of war, see *ibid.*, 60, but need them, see *ibid.*, 144; Stevens (ed.), *Travels in New France*, 81.

[46] For Montcalm and Indians, see Vaudreuil au Ministre, 1 sept. 1756, AN, F3, Moreau St. Mery, v. 14, f. 297; Hamilton (ed.), *Adventure in the Wilderness*, 164–65; Vaudreuil to Massaic, Aug. 4, 1758, *NYCD* 10:780. Montcalm blamed the assault on the English prisoners on brandy and English insults to Abenakis, Montcalm to Webb, Aug. 14, 1757, *NYCD* 10:618–19. Serious shortages of trade goods became apparent in 1756 and 1757, Vaudreuil au Ministre, 15 juin 1756, AN, C11A, v. 101. f. 28. For desperate situation by 1758, see Vaudreuil, Mémoire, 3 nov. 1758, AN, C11A, v. 103. For smallpox, see Vaudreuil au Ministre, 15 juin 1756, AN, C11A, v. 101. f. 28. There were shortages at Niagara, Journal de Niagara, 29 juillet 1757, 31 juillet 1757, in Henri-Ramond Casgrain (ed.), *Collection des manuscrits de marèchal de Levis*, 12 vols. (Montreal and Quebec: L. J. Demers & Frere, 1889–1901), in vol. 11, *Relations & journaux des differentes expeditions . . .*, 113, hereafter Casgrain, *Relations*; Hamilton (ed.), *Adventure in the Wilderness*, 152, 180. For general shortages, see Vaudreuil to Minister, Oct. 30, 1757, *WHC* 18:200; Canada, 1757, AN, C11A, v. 101, f. 270. Louisiana was even worse off, Kerlerec au Ministre, 28 jan. 1757, AN, C13A, v. 40, f. 27. For Indians holding French responsible for smallpox, see Hamilton (ed.), *Adventure in the Wilderness*, 197. By the end of the summer of 1757, Indian enthusiasm was slackening, Stevens (ed.), *Travels in New France*, 88. Casgrain, *Relations*, 6 juin 1757, 88–89.

Montreal from the *pays d'en haut* "naked, smeared with black paint, slave sticks in their hands." Onontio had forgiven them, and they had joined warriors gathered to attack the British. Similarly, in 1758, Onontio pardoned four of the Menominees and sent them to war against the British. But Vaudreuil did not forgive the other prisoners. The accounts are confused, but he had them either shot or whipped in the town square at Montreal. It was a retribution that General Montcalm thought did "great honor to the French name."[47]

Such incidents were harbingers of the alliance's final demise. As the British advantages in wealth and population began to be felt and they closed in on Canada, *mémoires* addressed to the court from the colony pronounced the alliance a failure. The most interesting of these reports is a *mémoire* entitled simply "Des Sauvages." It is at once a backward glance at the policies the French should have pursued, a protracted denunciation of the policy of alliance they had followed, and an assault on the character of the Indians themselves. According to the writer, French expenditures on behalf of the alliance had been in vain. The king's agents had stolen vast amounts of the goods and provisions destined for the Indians; those that reached the Indians had only encouraged them in their indolence and drunkenness. Indians fought for the French, but ineffectually. They were only a band of robbers devoted to theft and cruelty. Indians were, the writer continued, a cowardly and traitorous people lacking both "any sort of feeling" and "ambition."[48]

To control these Indians and render them useful, goods should be given them only as a direct reward for services provided. But even this was only a poor substitute for the policy that ideally should have been followed. Canadian officials should have encouraged merchants to settle among the Indians as they had in Illinois. Living as traders and farmers and raising families in the *pays d'en haut*, these habitants would have served as examples of industry while providing a counterbalance against Indian conspiracies. The French, by constantly increasing Algonquian wants and selling them

[47] For attack and executions, see extracts, letter from Montcalm, May 15, 1758, and journal entry Aug. 13, 1758, in *WHC* 18:203–4. There are three different accounts of the fate of the Menominees. Montcalm says they were shot. Bougainville says they were flogged (Hamilton [ed.], *Adventure in the Wilderness*, 260); François Pouchot says two were turned over to the Indians in Montreal for them to "do justice" and they executed them: "the first event of this kind on the part of the Indians since Europeans had lived in the country," Pouchot Memoir, *WHC* 18:211. See also, Hamilton (ed.), *Adventure in the Wilderness*, 204, and Journal of Occurrences, 1757–1758, May 16, *NYCD* 10:840. For murderers of previous year, see Hamilton (ed.), *Adventure in the Wilderness*, 117–18.

[48] Mémoire, Des Sauvages, 1759, AN, C11A, v. 104, f. 481. The vast frauds perpetrated upon the crown during the war by Canadian officials in charge of expenditures for the Indians was a constant theme of these mémoires; see also, Mémoire, Canada, 1758, AN, C11A, v. 103, f. 511.

corn and trade goods, would have made the Indians dependent upon them. In the end, the French would have been masters of the Indians. Implicit in the denunciation was the reality of the alliance: The French were not masters of the Indians; they were only their allies.[49]

What makes this *mémoire* interesting is not its consequences: Since Canada would be ceded to England, the *mémoire* would have no consequences. Rather, it is important as an eerie prophecy of what British policy would be. The French writer, aware that France was on the brink of defeat, denounced Indians and the policy of alliance. His *mémoire* was a lament for the failure of the French to subordinate the Indians. Immediately after the war, the British under General Jeffrey Amherst in effect simply altered the tenses of this *mémoire*. What should have happened became, for Amherst, what was to happen.

IV

The British assertion of mastery over the Indians after the Seven Years' War flew in the face of a promise they had made to the Ohio villagers during the war. Initial British peace overtures to the Ohio Algonquians proceeded from a conviction that earlier British policies had failed and the British must now imitate the French. Sir William Johnson and the representatives of the government of Pennsylvania, with all the sincerity desperation could muster, had begun to make promises to reform. They vowed to act according to the procedures and customs of the middle ground; they claimed that they would alter those practices that had alienated the Ohio villagers. William Johnson and Edward Atkin, the king's new superintendants for the northern and southern Indians respectively, had agreed by the fall of 1756 that the "monstrous Frauds and Abuses" of the trade would have to be remedied. Exchange with the Indians would be uniformly regulated for the superintendents. The British would have to imitate the French by building a parallel infrastructure of forts, officers, gunsmiths, missionaries, medal chiefs, and annual presents. Johnson also pressed the board of trade to rescind the land grants along the Ohio that were "some of the most considerable causes of the weakness of our Indian interest and chief obstructions to the revival and encrease of it." In December 1756 the proprietors of Pennsylvania, all the while protesting their own virtue, unilaterally renounced the purchases of the western lands that they had made from the Iroquois at Albany in 1754. They retained, however, the exclusive right to purchase those lands lying within their colony's boundaries

---

[49] Mémoire, Des Sauvages, 1759, AN, C11A, v. 104, f. 481.

should the Indians decide to sell. By 1758 Johnson had taken the final logical step by advocating the creation of "clear and fixed Boundaries between our Settlements and their Hunting Grounds."[50]

The actual negotiation of peace took years and involved the Ohio villagers, the Six Nations, and the Susquehanna Delawares who followed Teedyuscung, their alternately shrewd, self-serving, bombastic, and pathetic leader. As the negotiations proceeded, three brothers of the Turkey phratry – Tamaqua (or Beaver), Pisquetomen, and Shingas – of the Delawares became increasingly influential. Tamaqua and Pisquetomen, a chief and a councillor, respectively, had a standing mandate to pursue peace.[51]

[50] For reforms, see Atkin to Loudoun, Nov. 26, 1756, Loudoun Papers, LO 2282, Huntington Library. For Johnson and land grants, see Johnson to Board of Trade, Nov. 10, 1756, *NYCD* 7:169–70. Pennsylvania, Proprietors Observations, Dec. 11, 1756, *DHNY* 2:738–41. For boundaries, see Johnson to Denny, July 21, 1758, *JP* 2:879.

[51] Both Teedyuscung and the Iroquois claimed to speak for the western villagers. For Teedyuscung's claims, see Conference, Mar. 15, 1758, *PCR* 8:35. For Iroquois pretensions, see Conference, Aug. 5, 1758, *ibid.*, 152. For example of Delaware refusal to acknowledge Iroquois hegemony, see Morris to Hardie, Feb. 15, 1756, *PA*, Series 1, 2:574–75. For Teedyuscung, see Anthony Wallace, *King of the Delawares: Teedyuscung, 1700–1763* (Philadelphia: University of Pennslyvania Press, 1949). The Delawares and Shawnees, however, did continue to accept advice from the Mission Iroquois and the Mingos on the Ohio, Council at Carlisle 13 Jan. 1756, Thwaites (ed.), *Early Western Travels*, 1:84–87.

The Iroquois in 1758 declared the Munseys or Minisinks (Unami Delwares) to still be women who could not negotiate independently. Conference, Aug. 7, 1758, *PCR* 8:157. For the Iroquois efforts at Easton, see Wallace, *Weiser*, 538–52. For lands and claim to make peace on Ohio, see Conference at Easton, Oct. 1758, *PCR* 8:182, 199. Independent of Six Nations, Croghan to Johnson, April 14, 1758, *JP* 2:620. For disavowal of Teedyuscung, see Post Journal in Charles Thomson, *An Enquiry into the Causes of the Alienation of the Delawares and Shawanese Indians from the British Interest, and into the Measures Taken for Recovering Their Friendship* (London: J. Wilkie, 1759), 138, 139.

The French responded to the presence of English belts carried by eastern Delawares by renewing their own efforts to win these Delawares over, see Vaudreuil au Ministre, 25 juillet 1758, AN, C11A, v. 103, f. 114.

Tamaqua and his brothers supplanted earlier efforts by Netawatwees and the Turtle phratry to dominate the negotiations. William Hunter, "Provincial Negotiations with the Western Indians, 1754–58," *Pennsylvania History* 18 (July 1951): 213–19; Michael Norman McConnell, "The Search for Security: Indian-English Relations in the Trans-Appalachian Region, 1758–63" (Ph.D. diss. William and Mary, 1983), 112–76. The 1758 delegation seems to have been the work of people of the Turtle phratry since Kelipma (or Gelapamund), the brother of Netawatwees, accompanied the delegation. For Tamaqua, see "Journal of James Kenny," *Pennsylvania Magazine of History and Biography*, 37 (1913): 18; Post Journal, Thomson, *Enquiry*, 135. For Kuskuski as settlement of four towns, see Post Journal, *ibid.* 138.

Tamaqua and others had long been eager to secure peace with the English, see Bond (ed.), "Captivity of Charles Stuart, 1755–57," 64–65. Tamaqua and his brothers claimed they had no satisfactory accounts of earlier negotiations undertaken in the name of the western Delawares, Post Journal, *PCR* 8:144. Message, Conference at Easton, Oct. 1758, *PCR* 8:187–89. For fuller version of message and explanation, see Post Journal, in Thomson, *Enquiry*, 160–61.

There are several mentions of Pisquetomen, Shingas, and Tamaqua as brothers, "Journal of James Kenny," 421, 425; Conference with Indians, July 8, 1758, Philadelphia,

Direct peace negotiations between the British and the Ohio Indians proceeded rapidly after the appearance of Pisquetomen and Keekyuscung (or Delaware George), a councillor of the Turkey phratry, in Teedyuscung's town of Wyoming in June 1758. That summer, Frederick Post, a German Moravian twice married among the Delawares and fluent in their language, returned to the Ohio region with the western-Delaware emissaries. Pisquetomen then came east with an offer by the Delawares on the Ohio River to restore their ancient peace and friendship with the British and to extend the peace westward "to the Nations of my colour." Post made a second trip to the Ohio in late fall of 1758. He brought an invitation to sign the Treaty of Easton, already negotiated with the Iroquois and the Susquehanna Delawares, and a British promise that they still held to the ancient chain of friendship. The king would receive the western Indians as a tender father receives his lost children, and Pennsylvania would relinquish its purchase of lands west of the Appalachians. General John Forbes's army, then advancing on Fort Duquesne, would not attack them. On this trip, Post was accompanied by Pisquetomen, Thomas Hickman, and two Cayuga chiefs, one of whom was the younger Scarooyady. Post also participated in the final stage of negotiations: direct talks between the Indians and Colonel Henry Bouquet, who sat in for the by-now gravely ill General Forbes. In these negotiations, Post was joined by Croghan and Andrew Montour. But the Pennsylvanians did not conclude a formal treaty with the Ohio Indians until 1762 at Lancaster, and by then the peace was rapidly unraveling.[52]

Abercromby Papers, 422, Huntington Library. That Shingas was a war leader is an inference. Kenny says he was a chief, the equivalent of King Beaver or Delaware George, but he did not sign early messages to the English as a captain or counsellor. "Journal of James Kenny," 428. Post Journal, Thomson, *Enquiry*, 159. For civil leaders as clan and phratry leaders, see William W. Newcomb, Jr., *The Culture and Acculturation of the Delaware Indians*, Anthropological Papers, Museum of Anthropology, University of Michigan, no. 10 (Ann Arbor: University of Michigan Press, 1956), 50. For civil and war chiefs, see *ibid.*, 53.

[52] Although Hunter, "Provincial Negotiations," 217, identifies Delaware George as Menatochyand, Keekyuscung appears to have been Delaware George since Hugh Mercer, who knew him well, later used the names interchangeably; see Mercer to Bouquet, Feb. 17, 1759, in Sylvester Stevens and Donald Kent (eds.), *The Papers of Colonel Henry Bouquet*, 19 vols. (Harrisburg Pennsylvania Historical Commission, 1940), 2:38–39, and Mercer to Bouquet, Dec. 23, 1758, *ibid.* 1:209–10. Message of Pisquetomen, Easton, Oct. 13, 1758, PCR 8:187–88. Governor Denny's Answer, Oct. 20, 1758, *ibid.* 8:206–7. For Hickman and Pisquetomen, see Instructions to John Null and William Hayes, 21 Oct. 1758, *PA*, Series 1, 3:556–57. The Delawares met in Philadelphia with Governor Denny where they agreed to take Post to the Ohio, Conference with Indians, July 8, 1758, Abercromby Papers, 411, Huntington Library; also July 7, 1758, *PA*, Series 1, 3:456–69. For these events in the colonial political and military contexts, see Gipson, *British Empire*, 9:50.
  For Post, see Journal of Frederick Post, . . . June 27 . . . 1758, Huntington Library. Frenchmen were present at most of the councils held by Post, Post Journal, Thomson, *Enquiry*, 137, 138, 139; goes to Fort Duquesne, 142. For French efforts with Delawares, see Vaudreuil to Minister, July 28, 1758, in Sylvester K. Stevens and Donald Kent, *Wilderness Chronicles of Northwestern Pennsylvania* (Harrisburg, Pa.: Pennsylvania Historical Commis-

The British-Delaware negotiations reintroduced the old ambiguity of the status of the Ohio villagers. Tamaqua had only the most tenuous control over the warriors of his own phratry and virtually no influence at all over other Delaware warriors. Tamaqua, Pisquetomen, and Delaware George repeatedly cautioned Post to pay no attention to the warriors, women, and young people while the chiefs tried to restore a consensus, but the resentment of many Delawares could hardly be ignored. At Saukunk that summer, Bemino or Killbuck, a renowned conjurer and war leader, and Kuckquetacton, another war leader, threatened and mistreated Post. The presence of the Iroquois further confused the situation. The Six Nations returned to the Ohio River in the person both of the Cayuga chiefs who accompanied Post and of the Six Nation warriors who marched with Forbes. Although Post negotiated directly with the Ohio Indians, thus buttressing their claim to independence, he maintained the old Pennsylvania line of Iroquois sovereignty and ultimate control of land on the Ohio.[53]

The Delaware chiefs of the Turkey phratry were willing to acknowledge a token Iroquois hegemony, which gave them precedence over other phratry chiefs, but they expected to be treated as British allies and not British or Iroquois subjects. Shingas and Tamaqua made their own expectations quite specific:

> Brethren, we let you know, that the French have used our people kindly, in every respect; they have used them like gentlemen.... So they have treated the chiefs. Now we desire you to be strong; we with you would take the same method, and use our people well: for the other Indians will look upon us; and we do not otherwise know how to convince them, and to bring them into the English interest, without your using such means as will convince them.

The civil leaders, at least, envisioned peace in the usual terms of an alliance maintained by British and Indian alliance chiefs.[54]

sion, 1941), 113. Eastern Delawares were simultaneously informing the French of English movements, Vaudreuil au Ministre, 28 juillet 1758, AN, C11A, v. 103, f. 114.

[53] For Saukunk, see Post Journal, Thwaites (ed.), *Early Western Travels*, 1:200, 210–11; Hunter, "Provincial Negotiations," 218. Killbuck's phratry is unclear. He was a member of either the Turtle phratry or the Turkey phratry; see his mark, Delaware Treaty, *NYCD* 7:741. Beaver and his brothers did win support from the Turkey phratry warriors of Kuskuski and rejected French demands for the surrender of Post, Vaudreuil au Ministre, 15 oct. 1753, AN, C11A, v. 103. For lack of control, see Post Journal, Thwaites (ed.), *Early Western Travels*, 1:246. For three tribes, see *ibid.*, 1:271.

The English were notably brothers rather than fathers, Post Journals, Thwaites (ed.), *Early Western Travels*, 1:240, 247. Post himself addressed the Indians as brother or brethren, as did the governor of Pennsylvania and Forbes, Post, *ibid.*, 1:259–60, Governor, 262, Forbes, 264. For Iroquois, "chief owners of the land," *ibid.*, 258.

[54] For quotation, see Post Journal, Thwaites (ed.), *Early Western Travels*, 1:277–78. See also Post Journal, Thomson, *Enquiry*, 157, for Pisquetomen's request to become an English alliance chief.

Over the course of the negotiations, a fairly consistent Delaware position emerged. The peace would rest on a mutual withdrawal of French and British from the Ohio Valley. Peace would not consist of the mere replacement of the French by the British, for the Delawares openly feared the intentions of both sets of Europeans.

> We have great reason to believe you intend to drive us away and settle the country, or else why do you come to fight in the Land that God has given us. . . . Why don't you and the French fight in the old Country, and on the Sea? Why do you come to fight on our Land? This makes every Body believe you want to take the Land from us, by force and settle it.

Europeans, they concluded, only fought for the right to plunder Indians. As evidence, the Delawares resurrected an old story that had circulated before the war that the French and British had actually allied to destroy the Indians and take their land.[55]

This goal of a dual British-French withdrawal from the Ohio region was not impossible. General Forbes, at the beginning of his march, lamented that he had no clear orders to leave a garrison at Fort Duquesne if he succeeded in driving the French from it. He also spoke in a letter to Shingas and Tamaqua of a peace "as sure as the Mountains, between the English Nation and the Indians."[56]

Even the British triumph at Fort Duquesne did not immediately erode the Indian bargaining position. The refusal of the Delawares and Shawnees to provide further aid to Fort Duquesne had made the rotten and crumbling post untenable. The French blew it up in November 1758 and withdrew to Fort Machault near the village of Custaloga's Wolf phratry at Venango on the Rivière-au-Boeuf. The British marched into a ruin at whose entrance the

---

[55] Post Journal, Thomson, *Enquiry*, 153–54, 155, 160–61; Post Journal, Thwaites (ed.), *Early Western Travels*, 1:240. For unwilling to join English army, see Easton Conference, Oct. 20, 1758, *PCR* 8:208. For earlier version of story, see Claus to Johnson, Apr. 5, 1756, *JP* 2:439. This story reappeared among the Iroquois again in 1757, Journal de la campagne de M. De Bellestre en oct. et nov. 1757, Casgrain (ed.), *Rélations*, 11:132. For French account of Indian attempt at joint withdrawal, see Vaudreuil au Ministre, 15 feb. 1759, AN, C11A, v. 104, f. 19.

[56] For garrison, see Forbes to Pitt, 6 Sept. 1758, in Alfred Proctor James (ed.), *Writings of General John Forbes Relating to His Service in North America* (Menasha, Wis.: Collegiate Press, 1938, Arno repr. 1971), 205. See also Forbes to Abercromby and Amherst, Nov. 26, 1758, *ibid.*, 263; Forbes to Pitt, Nov. 27, 1758, and Jan. 21, 1759, *ibid.*, 268. For quotation, see Forbes to Kings Beaver and Shingas, Nov. 9, 1758, *ibid.*, 252–53. For Indian solicitation to De Ligneris to abandon Fort Machault and wish of Indians to have both French and English off the Ohio, see Vaudreuil to Berryer, Mar. 30, 1759, *NYCD* 10:948. For suggestion by Montcalm that Ohio be abandoned, see Montcalm à Vaudreuil, 27 fev. 1759, AN, F3, v. 5, f. 255. Vaudreuil, however, continued to consider the Ohio to be of "the greatest consequence for this colony," Vaudreuil au Ministre, 5 mars 1759, AN, C11A, v. 104.

French had left a grisly guard: the severed heads of the Scots Highlanders who had died in an earlier attack by Major Grant on the fort. The fall of Fort Duquesne did not, however, immediately end the French presence on the Ohio. From Fort Machault they solicited aid among the Delawares and Shawnees and threatened for another eight months to return to evict the British.[57]

In negotiating with the British at Fort Duquesne, Tamaqua therefore still had opportunities for success and much to gain. He had several goals. He sought to use the Iroquois to buttress his own position among the Delawares – for they acknowledged him as head chief – and to use the threat of Iroquois retribution to keep Delaware warriors from rejoining the French. He wished to cement his ties with the British and secure trade goods, but at the same time he wanted to ensure the British withdrawal from the Ohio region. He stated the Delaware position clearly: the British were "to go back over the mountain." This was the means to peace with not only the Delawares but the "far Indians." All the chief men of the Allegheny and "all my young men, women and children that are able to understand" were well pleased with the governor's offers of peace, and Tamaqua himself was willing to extend it to the Shawnees and "all the nations settled to the westward." If the British promised to withdraw from the Ohio region, Shingas had earlier told Post, "I will use it for an argument to argue with other nations of Indians." A successful British peace could link the villages of the Ohio River, the Wabash, and beyond in a common league bound to neither the French nor the British. This common league, in turn, would guarantee a lasting peace. Tamaqua, Shingas, and Keekyuscung told Post, "Brother, we alone cannot make a Peace, it would be of no signification; for as all the Indians to the Sun Rise to Sun Set are united in one Body, 'tis necessary that the whole should join in the Peace or it can be no Peace."[58]

The league of Indian nations that Tamaqua claimed must ratify the peace

---

[57] Logistically, Fort Duquesne was in trouble by the end of 1755, Copie de la lettre ecritte à M. de Macarty, 10 nov. 1755, avec M. de Kerlerec, 1 juin 1756, AN, C13A, v. 39. The loss of Fort Frontenac in the summer of 1758 cost the French the supplies destined for the Ohio, Doreil to Belle Isle, Aug. 31, 1758, *NYCD* 10:821; Vaudreuil to Massiac, Sept. 2, 1758, *NYCD* 10:823; Bigot au Ministre, 22 nov. 1758, AN, F3, v.315, f. 221. For abandonment of Fort Duquesne, see Vaudreuil au Ministre, 20 jan. 1759, AN, C11A, v. 104, f. 13.

For heads, see Gipson, *British Empire*, 7:283.

Custaloga's town was a predominantly Delaware town on the west side of French Creek. It held about 40 warriors who remained loyal to the French, Patterson and Hutchins Journal, Oct. 1759, in *Bouquet Papers*, 4:167; Mercer to Bouquet, Apr. 24, 1759, 2:110.

[58] For Tamaqua and the Cayugas, see Post Journal, Thwaites (ed.), *Early Western Travels*, 1:273. Tamaqua opposed entry into war, A Council Held at Carlisle, 13 Jan., 1756, *ibid.*, 1:85–86. For negotiations, see Post Journal, *ibid.*, 1:258, 270–77. There is a brief and largely accurate French account of these negotiations in Casgrain (ed.), *Rélations*, Nouvelles sauvages, nov. et dec. 1758, 11:175–79. Tamaqua again acknowledged Iroquois hegemony over the Ohio in 1760, Council held by . . . Monckton, Aug. 12, 1760, *PA*, Series

became also a body potentially able to enforce the peace. As Keekyuscung told Post in secret:

> All the nations had jointly agreed to defend their hunting place at Alleghenny, and suffer nobody to settle there; and as these Indians are very much inclined to the English interest, so he begged us very much to tell the Governor, General and all other people not to settle there. And if the English would draw back over the mountain, they would get all the other nations in their interest; if they staid and settled there, all the nations would be against them; and he was afraid it would be a great war, and never come to a peace again.

Under the cover of subordination to the Iroquois and peace with the British, Tamaqua planned to reassert his own influence over the warriors and transform at least part of the French alliance into an independent body powerful enough to compel the British to withdraw. He and the Delawares would emerge as the center of an alliance on the Ohio so strong that Delaware subordination to the Iroquois could only be nominal.[59]

The Iroquois, at least, were not deceived about the rationale behind Tamaqua's pretended subordination to their wishes. They reported to the British that the Shawnees and Delawares were still all too ready to join the French "to shake off their dependence on the Six Nations." The British continued to take the position that they would withdraw as soon as the French left the region, but privately the Iroquois, who needed British assistance among their supposed dependents, were urging them to stay.[60]

In the end, the British did stay. They chose to rely on force and not an Indian alliance, and Tamaqua's elaborate plans collapsed. Without having received instructions, General Forbes decided to leave a garrison of two hundred men. Colonel Bouquet, who temporarily assumed command of this garrison at Fort Pitt (which replaced Fort Duquesne), told the Indians that the soldiers were not there to "take Posession of yr hunting Country" but only to protect British traders. When Tamaqua told Colonel Bouquet that the soldiers should go back over the mountains, Croghan and Andrew Montour, who were acting as interpreters, refused to translate the speech. Croghan instead told Bouquet the Indians had consented to a 200-man

---

1, 3:748. For his use of Iroquois, see Post Journal, Thwaites (ed.), *Early Western Travels*, 1:273, quotations, 271–73.

For quotations on peace in West, see Post Journal, Thomson, *Enquiry*, 141.

[59] Ketiushund, Post Journal, Thwaites (ed.), *Early Western Travels*, 1:278.

[60] Later the Delaware warriors would separately ratify the agreements made by Tamaqua and other chiefs, Council held by ... Monckton, Aug. 12, 1760, *PA*, Series 1, 3:748. For Iroquois fear, see Mercer to Bouquet, Jan. 8, 1759, *Bouquet Papers*, 15:33; Indian Conference at Pittsburgh, Jan. 8, 1759, *Bouquet Papers*, 15:28–29. For public declarations and Iroquois requests that they stay and reinforce Pittsburgh, see Indian Conference at Fort Pitt, Jan. 8, 1759, *Bouquet Papers*, 15:28–31.

garrison. Frederick Post, who had remained at the Ohio River, asserted that the Indians had consented to no such thing. An angry confrontation ensued with Croghan calling Post a damned liar. Tamaqua's brother, Shingas, however, upheld Post and accused Croghan of altering the message.[61]

This small British garrison at Fort Pitt was perched at the end of a tenuous supply line, and the French at Fort Machault, weak as they were, still had hopes of evicting the British. Although Tamaqua and Shingas worked to detach other Indians from the French, Colonel Hugh Mercer realized that "their old thinking People would gladly give over fighting, and have seen too much of both English & French to be very fond of a near connection with either." But hopes of a mutual withdrawal failed with the fall of New France. French plans to attack Fort Pitt collapsed when news arrived of the siege of Niagara and the French forces turned to a futile and disastrous attempt to raise the siege. When Niagara fell, Fort Machault and Presque Isle became untenable and their garrisons withdrew to Detroit.[62]

With the fall of Niagara, the French alliance unraveled with a speed and completeness that alarmed the Ohio Indians of every faction. Although the majority of Ohio Indians wanted the French off the Ohio, they did not want the French completely defeated by the British, for the collapse of the French

---

[61] Bouquet, Conference with the Indians, Dec. 4, 1758, Pittsburgh, *Bouquet Papers*, 15:18–19. For supposed Indian agreement, *ibid.* 20–21. For Post's account, Post Journal, Thwaites (ed.), *Early Western Travels*, 1:283–85. Denny promises no attempt on lands, see Denny to Indians at Wyoming, Apr. 24, 1759, *JP* 3:33–37. As late as July 1759, the English were indicating that they planned only to maintain a "strong house" to safeguard the trade on the Ohio, "Journal of James Kenny," 428.

[62] For Indians, French, and Fort Machault, see Abstract of Dispatches, *NYCD* 10:974. For plans of French, see Vaudreuil au Ministre, 20 jan. 1759, AN, C11A, v. 104, f. 13. For French negotiations with Indians, see Vaudreuil au Ministre, 15 fev. 1759, AN, C11A, v. 104, f. 19. For Indian solicitation of De Ligneris to abandon Fort Machault and wish of Indians to have both French and English off the Ohio, see Vaudreuil to Berryer, Mar. 30, 1759, *NYCD* 10:948. For French attempt to mount expedition, see Kerlerec au Ministre, 8 oct. 1759, AN, C13A, v. 41. For fear of cutting supply lines, see Bouquet to Amherst, Mar. 13, 1759, Amherst Papers (reel 32). For attacks, see Stephen to Stanwix, May 25, 1759, *Bouquet Papers*, 3:153–54; Curry to Bouquet, May 29, 1759, *ibid.*, 3:167. For resentment among Shawnee, Delaware, and Mingo warriors, see "Journal of James Kenny," 423–24, 426, 427. For quotation, see Mercer to Bouquet, Mar. 1, 1759, *Bouquet Papers*, 3:65. For Tamaqua's and English attempt to lure French allies over to the English, see Mercer to Bouquet, Mar. 1, 1759, *Bouquet Papers*, 3:65. Mercer, Indian Intelligence, 17 Mar. 1759, *Bouquet Papers*, 3:84–85. Mercer to Bouquet, Mar. 18, 1759, *Bouquet Papers*, 3:88–89. Journal of . . . Johnson's Proceedings, Conference held at Canajohey, Apr. 1759, *NYCD* 7:384; "Journal of James Kenny," 422, 425. Beaver later contended that he had thought what he carried to the western Indians was a copy of a peace treaty with the English, but it turned out to be merely a copy of Pennsylvania's renunciation of its land purchase from the Iroquois, Journal of Frederick Post, July 20, 1762, *PA*, Series 1, 4:96.

For diversion of French, see Croghan to Stanwix, July 15, 1759, *Bouquet Papers*, 3:191–93; Macarty à M. Kerelerec, 21 sept. 1759, AN, C13A, v. 41, f. 103. For Indians at siege of Niagara, defeat, and abandonment of other posts, see Journal of Siege of Fort Niagara, *NYCD* 10:986–87, 992.

would leave them no available counterweight to British power. When news of the fall of Niagara and the abandonment of Fort Machault and Presque Isle arrived, the Indians around Fort Pitt seemed sober and abandoned their singing and dancing.[63]

V

The British victory over France allowed the British to think that the *pays d'en haut* was ripe for the kind of imperialism that civilized men thought they should by right exert over "savages." There was no longer a need to indulge Tamaqua. General Amherst promised not to take Indian land, but he would not withdraw from it. He would treat the Indians according to the services they rendered, rewarding them when they were good, punishing them when they were bad. In the kinship terms of the alliance, the Indians had always been children, but now they were being infantilized.[64]

General Amherst's new vision of the *pays d'en haut* was a simple one: the British were conquerors; the Indians were subjects. It was a view that abolished the middle ground. The politics of villages no longer mattered. Only the politics of empire counted. And they counted quite literally. Imperial wars were expensive, and in the wake of victory, Amherst was under heavy pressure to reduce expenditures.[65]

With the imperial struggle resolved by the conquest of Canada, Indians no longer seemed of great significance to the British military. As General Thomas Gage recognized, "All North America in the hands of a single power robs them of their Consequence, presents, & pay." The mistake of the Indian agents and superintendents like Croghan and Johnson, Amherst confided to his officers, was that they thought the Indians of "more consequence than they really are." It was a view the officers at the western posts were prone, at least initially, to accept. With the fall of Niagara came an eagerness to adopt a tougher policy toward the Indians. "We must," Colonel

[63] For Indian reaction, see "Journal of James Kenny," 437. After the fall of Niagara, Johnson used a Chippewa prisoner to seek peace in the West and soon undertook negotiations with the Ottawas, Chippewas, and Mississaugas, Johnson to Amherst, July 31, 1759, *JP* 3:115–18, Journal of Indian Affairs, Aug. 22, Aug. 29, 1759, *JP* 13:118–20, 128–29. For French abandonment of forts at Venango and Presque Isle, see Croghan to Stanwix, Aug. 13, 1759, *Bouquet Papers*, 4:31. Some Ottawas who came to Fort Pitt to see the English killed two soldiers on their departure, Mercer to Stanwix, Aug. 6, 1759, *Bouquet Papers*, 15:67.

[64] Amherst Policy, Amherst to Johnson, Sept. 11, 1759, *JP* 3:136; Johnson to Amherst, Dec. 8, 1759, *JP* 3:183, Amherst to Johnson, Dec. 18, 1759, Amherst Papers, reel 30. Conference held by . . . Moncton, Aug. 12, 1760, *PA* 3:744–52.

[65] For a detailed discussion of the enormous debts the British had accrued during the war, see Gipson, *British Empire*, 10:1–222.

Bouquet wrote, "be brothers and friends, but not slaves." Similarly, Colonel Hugh Mercer, while promising to treat the Indians kindly, was relieved that we "can now speak to Indians in proper stile since services are not necessary." A worried George Croghan warned that although the military had conquered the French, they had "nothing to boast from the War with the natives" who must be conciliated.[66]

General Jeffrey Amherst was not interested in conciliation. He was a man who had little patience with Indians or with the limits negotiated on the middle ground. He thought categorically and universally. He had a soldier's veneration for obedience and a devotion to the standards of Englishmen that he regarded as decency and common sense writ large. Indians were savages who had to be brought to understand the necessity of obedience in their own particular relation to the British empire and who must conform to the universal laws of thrift, diligence, and trade. Before the fall of Niagara, Amherst was diffident. With Canada's soldiers still prepared to resist him, Sir Jeffrey tended to accept Sir William Johnson's advice in dealing with Indians. Experience, however, robbed Amherst of his diffidence in Indian affairs, and that diffidence unfortunately proved to have been his major asset. No longer deferring to William Johnson, Amherst had by 1761 blustered into Indian affairs with the moral vision of a shopkeeper and the arrogance of a victorious soldier. Years of experience in Indian affairs had taught Johnson and Croghan what weight the middle ground could bear; Amherst landed ponderously upon it and it cracked. The question would be, did it matter?[67]

At the center of Amherst's policy was a determination to eliminate the presents that served as a token of the entire middle ground. Amherst believed that presents were emblematic of the problems with existing relationships with the Indians. Presents cultivated the natural lassitude of savagery. If Indians got provisions by asking for them, they would "grow remiss in their hunting." Amherst had no objection to Indians receiving charity in cases of dire necessity, but regular presents would have to cease. Indians would have to support themselves by hunting. Amherst was prepared to pay for services rendered, but "purchasing the good behavior, either of

---

[66] For Gage quotation, see Gage to Gladwin, Feb. 19, 1762, Gage Letterbooks, Clements Library, University of Michigan. For Amherst quotation, see Amherst to Bouquet, June 7, 1762, Amherst Papers, Reel 33. For Bouquet quotation, see Bouquet to Croghan, Aug. 10, 1759, *Bouquet Papers*, 15:75–76. For Mercer quotation, see Mercer to Denny, Aug. 12, 1759, in Stevens and Kent, *Wilderness Chronicles*, 165. For not conquered, see Croghan to Johnson, Jan. 25, 1760, *JP* 10:134. For fear of Indians, see Croghan to Johnson, 22 Dec. 1759, *JP* 10:131. For tensions and theft and murder around Fort Pitt, see "Journal of James Kenny," 424–49.

[67] Amherst to Johnson, Dec. 18, 1762, Amherst Papers, reel 30; Amherst to Johnson, Mar. 16, 1760, *JP* 3:198–99.

Indians or any others is what I do not understand; when men of what race
soever behave ill, they must be punished but not bribed."[68]

Johnson and Croghan recognized the magnitude of the change Amherst's
new approach to Indian affairs involved. His rejection of the procedures of
the middle ground served to increase astronomically the difficulties involved
in settling all other outstanding differences. George Croghan wrote: "The
British and French Colonies since the first Settling [of] America . . . have
adopted the Indian Customs and manners by indulging them in Treaties and
renewing friendships making them large Presents which I fear won't be so
easey to break them of as the General may imagine." And Sir William
Johnson warned:

> The French . . . spared no labor, or Expence to gain their friendship and
> Esteem, *which alone enabled them to support the War in these parts so long*
> whilst we, as either not thinking of them of sufficient Consequence, or
> that we had not so much occasion for their assistance not only fell
> infinitely short of the Enemy in our presents &ca to the Indians, but
> have of late I am apprehensive been rather premature in our sudden
> retrenchment of some necessary Expences, to which they have been
> always accustomed.[69]

Amherst dismissed such warnings. He remained remarkably sanguine
about Algonquian and Iroquois resistance to unilateral changes in their
relationships with Europeans. He believed that he had the power to demand
"good behavior" of Indians because he was their conqueror. He dismissed
their power to resist, and those of his officers who did not command posts in
the Indian country shared his arrogance. When news of the first of several
attempts to muster resistance to the British emerged, the General wrote
Johnson that they "never gave me a moment's concern as I know their
incapacity of attempting anything serious." Amherst was confident that he
had the power to destroy the Indians totally "whenever any of them give me
cause."[70]

---

[68] Amherst to Johnson, Dec. 18, 1762, Amherst Papers, reel 30; Amherst to Johnson, Mar. 16,
1760 *JP* 3:198–99. Johnson alone spent £17,072 on Indian presents between Nov. 1758 and
Dec. 1759. For orders restricting presents, see Croghan to Hutchins, Oct. 25, 1761, *Bouquet
Papers*, 15:166. Gage to Le Hunte?, Oct. 7, 1762, Gage Letterbooks, Clements Library;
Croghan to Johnson, Oct. 8, 1762, *JP* 10:548–49. Amherst relented enough to allow
"trifles" to be given away at the posts (Campbell to Bouquet, Oct. 27, 1762, *MPHC* 19:173),
but he denied any system of regular presents, Amherst to Bouquet, Jan. 7, 1763, Amherst
Papers, reel 33.

[69] Croghan to Bouquet, Mar. 27, 1762, *Bouquet Papers*, 15:183; Johnson to Earl of Egremont,
May 1762, *JP* 10:461.

[70] Amherst to Johnson, Aug. 9, 1761, Amherst Papers, Reel 30; Amherst to Johnson, Dec. 20,
1761, *ibid*. For scorn among military, see Claus to Johnson, Dec. 3, 1761, *JP* 3:575–76.
This picture of Amherst is very different from the oddly narrow one that is presented by
Harry Kelsey in "The Amherst Plan: A Factor in the Pontiac Uprising," *Ontario History* 65

In the *pays d'en haut*, Amherst's increasingly direct role in Indian affairs gave British policy its particular form, but the specifics of British policy were not fully his doing. Decisions to occupy the posts formerly held by the French, demands for the return of all prisoners taken in the war, and the curtailment of expenditures in North America were part of larger government policies. And Amherst's decision to eliminate presents and to rely on trade as the sole mechanism for the exchange of goods between Indians and whites was only the means of implementing the new financial stringency.[71]

Despite their dismissal of the Indians and their insistence on dictating the future, the British did not seek conflict. Their policy, as Amherst repeatedly stated, was to guarantee the protection of Indian lands and to insure a regulated, fair, and abundant trade free of a reliance on rum. Their ways of dealing with the Indians might ignore French precedents, but, as they saw it, they asked little from the Indians that had not already been accorded the French. When, for example, the British demanded the return of all British prisoners, they saw themselves as led by both precedent and justice. And indeed, they did have a strong case. The Algonquians had at the conclusion of both the Iroquois wars and the first Fox war regarded the failure to return captives as a casus belli. Similarly, the British saw their occupation of the posts as merely a replacement of the French occupation. With the exception of Sandusky, the British asked for no new posts. The British instituted a policy of keeping the Indians deliberately short of powder, but although the Indians felt the result, they could only guess the intention. The British did not publicly proclaim this policy; they lied and denied it.[72]

Except for the elimination of presents and restrictions on the sale of gunpowder, Johnson and Croghan did not seriously question most British measures; they only criticized the speed with which they were taken and the failure to negotiate them according to the diplomatic procedures of the middle ground. Johnson thought denying the Indians powder caused unnecessary suffering and formed an obstacle to the very trade both he and

(Sept. 1973): 149–58. Kelsey basically blames the rebellion on Amherst's subordinates who were unable to provide the ships necessary to supply and reinforce the upper posts in accordance with Amherst's plans.

71 For a discussion of the cession of Canada, see Guy Frégault, *Canada: The War of the Conquest* (Toronto: Oxford University Press, 1969), 296–340. Gipson, *British Empire*, 8:208, 216, 300, 309.

72 For British assurances and policy, see Johnson to Amherst, Sept. 10, 1759, Amherst Papers, reel 31; Amherst to Johnson, Sept. 11, 1759, *JP* 3:136; Amherst to Hamilton, 30 Mar. 1760, *JP* 3:205; Amherst's Speech to the Western Indians, c. Apr. 24, 1760, *Bouquet Papers*, 15:90–93. At Detroit Campbell feared trouble if Indians knew of Amherst's intentions to keep them short of powder, Campbell to Bouquet, Oct. 12, 1761, *MPHC* 19:116; *ibid.*, 3 July 1762, *MPHC* 19:158. For scarcity and suffering, see Johnson, Private Journal, 19 Oct. 1761, *JP* 13:270. Croghan was denying to the Shawnees that such a policy existed as late as Dec. 1762, Report of Indian Conference at Fort Pitt, Dec. 8, 1762, *Bouquet Papers*, 15:194.

Amherst wanted to encourage. He and Croghan both regarded eventual subordination of the Indians as inevitable, but they thought it could be gradual and peaceful. In Johnson's words, there were "yet necessary Expences" that they "should be gradually weaned from, and that by a prudent Conduct, and due distribution of some little favours to them for a time, we may effect without much trouble, what we should find no small difficulty in compassing by force." For now, the precedents of the middle ground should be followed. Presents would serve to get prisoners returned and the posts occupied peacefully.[73]

Amherst's policies served both to validate the fears of the Ohio Indians that the British meant to subordinate – and, in their terms, enslave – them and to shatter the willingness of many other Algonquians to accept further extensions of the peace. The British had broken their original promise to evacuate the Ohio Valley after the defeat of the French, and they had also lied when they had claimed they would erect only a stronghouse at Pittsburgh to protect the trade. Instead they built and garrisoned a substantial fort at the forks of the Ohio. When they occupied the other posts of the *pays d'en haut* in 1760 and 1761, they surprised and alienated many of the Indians. The Detroit Indians told the French that they had been promised by the British at Niagara that a British garrison would not come to Detroit. When Robert Rogers's Rangers escorted such a garrison in the fall of 1760, the public welcome was cordial. The Detroit Indians confined themselves to reminding the British that "this country was given by God to the Indians." Privately, however, they told the deposed French commander, M. de Bellestre, that they had been betrayed.[74]

[73] For Johnson's position, see Johnson to Amherst, Mar. 21, 1761, *JP*, 10:244–47, *ibid.*, Apr. 23, 1761, *JP* 10:257–58. For quotations, see Johnson to Lords of Trade, Aug. 20, 1762, *JP* 3:866–67. For Johnson on present, see Johnson to Amherst, Dec. 6, 1761, *JP* 3:582; Johnson to Amherst, Jan. 1, 1762, Amherst Papers, reel 31; Johnson to Amherst, June 12, 1761, *JP* 10:286–87. Gives presents for prisoners, Croghan to Bouquet, Mar. 27, 1762, *Bouquet Papers*, 15:182–83. Croghan thought the posts would present no difficulty if presents were given, Croghan to Bouquet, Nov. 25, 1762, *Bouquet Papers*, 9:167.

Amherst's position on powder was contradictory. He wanted Indians to hunt commercially, but he restricted their access to the powder necessary to do this. He asserted, however, that if they were "industrious" they could barter for powder. Under pressure from Johnson, he was allowing small gifts of powder by the fall of 1762 when there was a shortage in the upper country, Amherst to Johnson, Sept. 12, 1762, Amherst Papers, reel 30; Johnson to Amherst, Sept. 24, 1762, Amherst Papers reel 31.

[74] For Indian version of original promise, see Rapport fait à M. de Ligneris . . . 4 jan 1759 par Casteogain, chef de Loups . . . joint a la lettre de M. de Vaudreuil, 15 feb. 1759, AN, C11A, v. 104, f. 23. As late as Jan. 1759, the British were still indicating that they would return home following the defeat of the French, Indian Conference at Pittsburgh, Jan. 8, 1759, *Bouquet Papers*, 15:31. For Fort as stronghouse, see "Journal of James Kenny," 428. For fear of Fort Pitt, see Johnson to Gage, Mar. 17, 1760, *JP* 3:200–1.

For Rogers at Detroit, see Howard Peckham (ed.), *Journals of Major Robert Rogers* (New York: Corinth Books, 1961), 157–67. For quotation, see Conference at Detroit, Dec. 3,

Strong British garrisons vindicated the Algonquians' greatest fear: that the British were determined to seize Algonquian lands. Not only the Ohio Indians but even the villagers at Detroit were apprehensive of British intentions. The British pledged themselves to protect Indian lands and observe the partition line agreed to at Easton by the Six Nation chiefs, but Indians hunting on the upper Ohio and its tributaries constantly found whites building cabins and cutting clearings in the woods. British troops evicted these "vagabonds," but more always appeared.[75]

The British demand for prisoners also came to be regarded as a breach of faith. The status of the hundreds of captured British prisoners living among the Algonquians varied widely. Some were little more than slaves, harshly treated and badly fed. Others had been adopted to replace dead villagers and were regarded by the Indians as their relatives. Still others, mostly women, had intermarried; some now had Indian children. Finally, many children had become almost completely Indian in appearance and culture.[76]

1760, *Bouquet Papers*, 15:99. For resentment, Conseil, 28 nov. 1760, AN, C11A, v. 105, f. 358. For Indians uneasy about blockhouse at Sandusky (1761), see "Journal of James Kenny," 39. For general unease, see Johnson to Amherst, July 29, 1761, Amherst Papers, reel 30. The Indians at Mackinac also made it clear that they regarded the land as theirs and the French could not dispose of it, Milo Milton Quaife (ed.), *Alexander Henry's Travels and Adventures in the Years 1760–1776* (Chicago: Lakeside Press, R. R. Donnelley & Sons, 1921), 42–46.

75 For fears of Detroit Indians, see Extract from Journal of Col. Hugh Mercer, Apr. 5, 1759, *Bouquet Papers*, 3:103 For fears of Mingos, see Croghan to Amherst, Dec. 2, 1762, Amherst Papers, reel 32. For general resentment, see Johnson to Lords of Trade, Aug. 20, 1762, *JP* 3:865–69. For British reassurances, see Johnson to Amherst, Sept. 10, 1759, Amherst Papers, reel 31; Amherst to Johnson, Sept. 11, 1759, *JP* 3:136; Amherst to Hamilton, 30 Mar. 1760, *JP* 3:205; Amherst's Speech to the Western Indians, c. Apr. 24, 1760, *Bouquet Papers*, 15:90–93. For Easton, see Conference Held at Fort Pitt, Apr. 6–12, 1760, *JP* 3:214. For Johnson's idea of appropriate policy, see Johnson to Lords of Trade, May 17, 1759, *NYCD* 7:377. For white hunters killing deer, see Angus McDonald to Bouquet, Oct. 25, 1761, *Bouquet Papers*, 7:173. For hunting as pretext for settlement, see Bouquet to Fauquier, Feb. 8, 1766, *Bouquet Papers*, 8:20–21. For prohibition of settlement west of Allegheny Mountains, see Proclamation, Oct. 30, 1761, *Bouquet Papers*, 15:178–79. For settlers, see Bouquet to Amherst, Apr. 1, 1762, Amherst Papers, reel 32.

76 Captain Charles Lee described the number of English prisoners among the Delawares near Venango as "prodigious," Capt. Charles Lee, Journal, Oct. 1, 1759, *Bouquet Papers*, 4:138. Charles Power, a prisoner among the Wyandots, said they were kind to prisoners, but other nations treated them cruelly, Croghan to Johnson, 26 Jan. 1760, *JP* 10:136. For a good account of an adoption by the Caughnawagas or French Mohawks then living on the Muskingum with the Delawares, see James Smith, *An Account of the Remarkable Occurrences in the Life and Travels of Col. James Smith, During His Captivity with the Indians in the Years 1755, '56, '57, '58 & '59* (Cincinnati: R. Clarke, 1870; Ohio Historical Society repr., Columbus, 1970), 28–31. Croghan reported that many prisoners were free to leave but refused to do so, Croghan to Monckton, July 25, 1761, *JP* 10:316–18; e.g., see Some Account of a Visit ... 1761, 8th month, 9th, Huntington Library HM 8249. For Indian captivity, see James Axtell, "The White Indians of Colonial America," in James Axtell, *The European and the Indian: Essays in the Ethnohistory of Colonial North America* (New York: Oxford University Press, 1981), 168–206. Axtell overemphasizes the success of Indians in assimilating adult white captives.

The British had initially led the Indians to believe that they could retain those adopted prisoners who wished to remain. By early 1759, however, the British had begun to demand the return of the captives. They made no immediate attempt to seize them. The British feared that a "squabble" about the captives would drive the Delawares, Shawnees, and Mingos back to the French. With the total defeat of the French in 1760, however, the British insisted on the immediate return of all prisoners. They initially refused to offer either gifts or ransom for their return. The Indians were simply to surrender them.[77]

The issue of prisoners became a constant irritant. Many of those prisoners who wanted to return to the British were surrendered willingly. James Kenny, a Quaker in charge of the Pennsylvania trading store at Pittsburgh, met an Indian named Jimmy Wilson, who, although he had never gone to war, had obtained a white woman and boy.

> He kept ye Woman as his wife, using her kindly; on finding she inclin'd to return to her own People he brought her & ye boy with ye Amount of his Estate to our Store & told ye Woman notwithstanding He Loved her, as she wanted to leave him, would let her go, so he divided his substance equally with her, giving half ye remained to ye Boy & set them both free & went with ye Woman home giving her a Horse to Ride; an Instance of more self-denial than many men of great Christian professions shews their poor Negros.

But other Indians grumbled about whites wanting back prisoners who "were satisified to live with ye Indians," and still others simply wanted them ransomed. Croghan recognized that giving presents was the easiest way to

---

[77] For decisions on prisoners, see Minutes of Meeting with a Delegation of Minisinks, July 11–16, 1760, HM 8249, Huntington Library; "Journal of James Kenny," 185; Croghan to Monckton, July 25, 1761, *JP* 10:316–18; An Indian Conference, Sept. 25, 1761, *JP* 10:327. For return of captives, Indian understanding of original British position, see Rapport fait á M. de Ligneris . . . 4 jan. 1759 par Casteogain, chef de Loups . . . joint a la lettre de M. de Vaudreuil, 15 feb. 1759, AN, C11A, v. 104, f. 23. The Pennsylvanians had, however, made their determination to get prisoners back from the beginning of peace negotiations, Conference, Philadelphia, July 7, 1758, *PA*, Series 1, 3:456–69. For English demands and actions, see Mercer to Bouquet, Feb. 7, 1759, *Bouquet Papers*, 3:34–35. Here Mercer fudged the issue of redeeming the captives, denying a present asked for the return of a small girl, but then giving a woman a present out of "charity." Pittsburgh, Mercer to Bouquet, Mar. 21, 1759, *Bouquet Papers*, 3:92. For squabble, see Mercer to Bouquet, Apr. 24, 1759, *Bouquet Papers*, 2:110. In Sept. 1759 Croghan was asking for the return of prisoners, "Journal of James Kenny," 428. For immediate return, see Conference Held at Fort Pitt, Apr. 6–12, 1760, *JP* 3:214: Indian Conference at Detroit, Dec. 3, 1760, *Bouquet Papers*, 15:95.
   The French had used the initial failure of the English to demand the return of their prisoners as a way to convince the Indians that if the English did not even care for those of their own blood, they would not care for the Indians, Vaudreuil au Ministre, 15 feb. 1759, AN, C11A, v. 104, f. 19.

redeem prisoners, and he ignored the strictures against giving them. By
October 1761, Croghan had received 338 prisoners from the western
nations, but many others refused to return. Amherst's complaints about
expenses cut the goods available for redeeming the prisoners, but the
independent efforts of Pennsylvania did secure the release of additional
captives. In the spring of 1762, Bouquet estimated that 200 to 300 prisoners
remained in Indian hands, apparently largely among the Shawnees and
Delawares, but by then a new element had entered into negotiations. The
Shawnees and Delawares believed that as soon as they released the last of
the prisoners, the British would attack them and seize their lands.[78]

As the Algonquians' greatest fears about British greed, ambition, and
faithlessness seemed vindicated, their greatest hopes were dashed. During
the war, the British blockade and the inability of the French to procure
goods had left many Indians nearly destitute of powder and European
clothing. They thought the British would restore an abundant trade, and,
indeed, the British intended to do exactly that. "Trade," William Johnson
wrote General Amherst in early 1759, "is one of the strongest cements to
bind our Indians connexions." But trade, as Johnson also realized, had
dangers for "Great Irregularities have formerly been committed in this
Article." Johnson wanted an abundant trade, but for it to succeed, it had to
take place under the direct supervision of his agents or the military, who
would issue passports and supervise the exchange.[79]

[78] "Journal of James Kenny," 7, 12, 161, 168, 169. Indian Conference at Detroit, Dec. 3,
1760, *Bouquet Papers*, 15:98; Croghan to Johnson, Oct. 12, 1761, *JP* 3:550; Bouquet to
Amherst, Mar. 7, 1762, Amherst Papers, reel 32. By the fall of 1762 Bouquet estimated that
400 prisoners had been surrendered at Detroit and Pittsburgh, Bouquet to Amherst, Oct. 9,
1762, Amherst Papers, reel 32. For presents, see Croghan to Bouquet, Mar. 27, 1762,
Bouquet Papers, 15:182–83, 200–330; for remain, see Bouquet to Amherst, Mar. 30, 1762,
Amherst Papers, reel 32. For Shawnees, see Alexander McKee, Report, Apr. 12, 1762,
Amherst Papers, reel 32; Council with Shawnees, Fort Pitt, Apr. 16, 1762, Amherst Papers,
reel 32; Instructions for Alexander McKee, Oct. 5, 1762, *JP* 10:545–47. The Shawnees of
the upper town blamed the delay on those of the lower town, Journal of Alexander McKee,
Oct. 21, 1762 *JP* 10:577; for promise of lower town, *ibid.*, 578. For Delawares, see Croghan
to Bouquet, Dec. 10, 1762, Amherst Papers, reel 30. For fear attack, see *ibid.* Amherst's
dissatisfaction, Amherst to Bouquet July 25, 1762, Amherst Papers, reel 33.
[79] Johnson to Amherst, Feb. 22, 1759, *JP* 10:103–4; *ibid.*, Apr. 21, 1759, *JP* 3:29; Amherst to
Johnson, Nov. 19, 1760, Amherst Papers, reel 30. For French difficulties, see Mémoire, 1
juin 1759, AN, C11A, v.105, f. 127; Vaudreuil au Ministre, 15 oct. 1759, AN, C11A, v. 104,
f. 106; Vaudreuil au Ministre, 24 juin 1760, AN C11A, v. 105, f.77. For Indian desire for,
see Journal of . . . Johnson's Proceedings, 16 Apr. 1759, *NYCD* 7:384; Conference Held at
Fort Pitt, Apr. 6–12, 1760, *JP* 3:213.
For need goods at Detroit, see Campbell to Bouquet n.d., c. Nov. 1760, *MPHC* 19:47.
For Indians destitute and "starving" at Michilimackinac, see Campbell to Bouquet, Detroit,
Dec. 23, 1760, *MPHC* 19:50. For promise of cheap trade at Detroit, see Conference at
Detroit, Dec. 3, 1760, *Bouquet Papers*, 15:99. To Chippewas, Johnson, Journal of Indian
Affairs, Aug. 1, 1759, *JP* 13:118. For supervision, see *ibid.* 96. Trading Permit, Dec. 22,
1760, *Bouquet Papers*, 15:102; Mercer to Croghan, Aug. 1, 1759, *Bouquet Papers*, 15:60. The

Trade never fulfilled Indian or British expectations. An abundance of whiskey, a scarcity of other goods, and high prices plagued the exchange. Trade goods began to arrive at Fort Pitt in January 1759, but so much of the cargo was whiskey that Colonel Mercer had to buy it up himself to keep it out of Indian hands. Goods remained scarce at Fort Pitt, and traders almost immediately began to ignore the published list of prices for a regulated trade of those goods they did possess. Johnson was forced to raise the regulated prices. The opening of a trading store operated by the province of Pennsylvania and the arrival of more Indian traders increased the supply of goods at Pittsburgh, but it also brought the usual problems of the trade, especially as the traders left Fort Pitt and began traveling to surrounding villages. Despite a ban on the rum trade, Indians pawned their clothes and wampum to get it. Tamaqua obtained six kegs of rum and his village went on a six-day binge. Custaloga's town was so drunk that Croghan could not hold a conference there.[80]

Instead of linking the British and the Algonquians, trade became merely another sign of the deterioration of the old arrangements of the middle ground. Papoonhoal, the Minisink religious leader from east of the Alleghenies, contrasted the present methods of exchange with their emphasis on gain against the older conception of a just price and exchange as a means of securing friendship:

> Brother, It comes into my mind to mention something to you that I think wrong in your Dealings with the Indians. You make it publick that you will give a certain price for our Skins, and that they are to be weighed and Paid for at that set price according to their weight. Brother there are two bad things in this way of Dealing. You alter the price that you say you will give for our Skins, which can never be right. God cannot be pleased to see the price of one & the same thing so often altered and changed. Our young men finding that they are to receive for their Skins according to their weight play tricks with them . . . to make them weigh more. . . .
>
> Brother you see that there is no love or honesty on either

British in Canada abolished the old French system of *congés* and monopolies of certain posts, Gage to Amherst, Mar. 20, 1762, *MPHC* 19:15–17.

[80] Indians themselves were actively soliciting traders, Journal of . . . Johnson's Proceedings, 16 Apr. 1759, *JP* 7:384; Niagara Campaign, Oct. 12, 1759, *JP* 13:156. For prices, see Mercer to Croghan, Aug. 1, 1759, *Bouquet Papers*, 15:60. For scarcity, see Croghan to Stanwix, Aug. 6, 1759, *Bouquet Papers*, 15:68; Mercer to Bouquet, Sept. 8, 1759. For traders contest regulations, see Petition of Reynell et al., July 9, 1759, *PA*, Series 1, 3:665–66. For raise price, see "Journal of James Kenny," 24. For provincial store, see *ibid.* passim. For traders to villages, see *ibid.*, 26. For liquor, see Mercer to Bouquet, Jan. 29, 1759, *Bouquet Papers*, 3:28–29. John Langdale to Bouquet, Mar. 5, 1761, *Bouquet Papers*, 6:53–56; "Journal of James Kenny," 14, 16, 17; Bouquet to Monckton, July 14, 1760; Stevens and Kent, *Wilderness Chronicles*, July 14, 1760, 182.

Side. . . . Therefore, Brother, we propose to fling this entirely away for it remains so we shall never agree and love one another as we ought to do. Now brothers, I desire you will not raise your Goods to too high a price, but to lower them so as you can afford it, that we may live and walk together in one Brotherly Love and Friendship as Brothers ought to live.

When gain rather than "love" ruled the trade, exchange remained chaotic. Theft, after all, procured gain as readily as trade. The British cheated and the Indians stole. Bouquet complained on the eve of Pontiac's Rebellion that since the suppression of presents, Indian war parties attacking the Cherokees had increased stock thefts to such an extent that country people were unwilling to provision Fort Pitt.[81]

The trade grew no better as it penetrated farther into the upper country, and Johnson's efforts to reform it proved unsuccessful. Johnson tried to confine trade to the posts so as to better regulate it, but traders from both Pennsylvania and Canada continued to go to Indian towns. The Indians complained of high prices and shortages of goods, while the commanders of the new British posts complained of the inordinate amount of rum carried into the country. There was a "general Clamour" among the Indians. Amherst, despite his own vocal devotion to trade, exacerbated the problem. He cut scalping and clasp knives, razors, tomahawks, gunpowder, flints, fowling pieces, and rum from Johnson's list of trade goods to be carried by traders to Detroit. When in 1762 reports of traders having been killed by the Chippewas of Sault Sainte Marie reached Thomas Gage, he was not surprised. "From the manner in which they traded & which Our traders now follow, I shall not wonder if I hear of many Accidents of this Nature in Other places," he wrote Amherst.[82]

The burden of blame for the trade's failure to pacify the Indians increasingly came to rest on rum. Amherst believed, with some reason, that if traders did not sell such vast quantities of rum, then the Indians would not

---

81 For quotation, see Minutes of Meetings with a Delegation of Minisink . . . Philadelphia, July 11–16, 1760, HM 8249, Huntington Library. For thefts, cheating, see "Journal of James Kenny," 439, 17, 30, 34, 40, 160; Amherst to Bouquet, Jan. 7, 1763, Amherst Papers, reel 33. For stock thefts, see Amherst to Bouquet, Jan. 7, 1763, Amherst Papers, reel 33. Among themselves, as prisoners testified, the Indians remained rigorously honest (*Colonel Smith's Journal*, 87), even when they stole from Europeans, *ibid.*, 94.

82 For rum and price, see Amherst to Johnson, July 11, 1761, Amherst Papers, reel 30; Niagara and Detroit Proceedings, July–Sept. 1761, *JP* 3:437–39; Johnson, Private Journal at Detroit, July 17, 1761, *JP* 13:219–20. For intervention, see Johnson to Bouquet, Sept. 18, 1761, *Bouquet Papers*, 15:163. For trade at villages, see Johnson to Amherst, Dec. 7, 1762, Amherst Papers, reel 31. For continuing complaints, see Ward to Bouquet, June 13, 1762, *Bouquet Papers*, 8:155. For cuts goods, see Amherst to Johnson, May 7, 1764, Amherst Papers, reel 30. For murder quotation, see Gage to Amherst, July 6, 1762, Gage Letterbooks, Clements Library.

be in such want. He also thought rum lay at the bottom of most violence between Indians and the British. The problem was that the British had pushed the rum trade for years, and its sudden curtailment simply became another example of British arbitrariness and stinginess. A few chiefs welcomed the prohibition, but among most Algonquians, curtailing the trade in rum compounded rather than removed discontent.[83]

Faced with this new British policy, Algonquian leaders attempted to protect the practices of the middle ground and buttress their own position as mediators. The chiefs, who sought to conciliate their people and the British, bore the brunt of the relentless British pressure on the middle ground. Algonquian speakers and chiefs persistently pushed the commanders to maintain the French practice of feeding Indians when they visited, repairing their guns and implements, and making them gifts. Instead, they found officers who acted like shopkeepers. Under Amherst's orders, officers bargained and quarreled over the price of the venison they themselves had asked the warriors to bring to the posts. When chiefs could not guarantee a bon marché, neither could they control their warriors' thefts and horse stealing.[84]

When murders and thefts occurred, the British turned to the chiefs to secure the guilty and then complained of their lack of influence when they predictably failed. Tamaqua was the first victim of the military policy. In the summer of 1759 some of Killbuck's people, probably Turtle phratry warriors, were suspected of killing a British wagoner. The British demanded that Beaver obtain satisfaction. When he failed to gain concessions from the warriors of another village and another phratry, the commander of Fort Pitt, Colonel Bouquet, derided Beaver for having "so little . . . influence among his own People." Unlike the French, the British officers did not yet understand that the influence of a chief was circumscribed, that the success

[83] For liquor ban, see Bouquet to Amherst, Mar. 7, 1762, Amherst Papers, reel 30. Gage at Montreal still allowed rum; Johnson asked for a total prohibition since Indians would travel any distance and pay any price for it, Johnson to Amherst Apr. 1, 1762, Amherst Papers, reel 31. For prohibition, see Amherst to Johnson, July 6, 1762, Amherst Papers, reel 30; Amherst to Gage, July 26, 1762, Amherst Papers. For smuggling, see Amherst to Johnson, Aug. 22, 1762, Amherst Papers, reel 30; Amherst to Johnson, Nov. 21, 1762, Amherst Papers, reel 30. Traders contended they never traded rum alone, but only in proportion to dry goods; without rum Indians will not trade, Andrews et al. to Johnson, Apr. 27, 1762, JP 3:720–21. For resentment of loss of rum, see Croghan to Amherst, Dec. 2, 1762, Amberst Papers, reel 32. For approval, see Journal of James Gorrell, Oct. 12, 1761–June 14, 1763, JP 3:708; Indian Proceedings, Apr. 21–28, 1762, JP 3:700.

[84] For requests of commanders, see Campbell to Bouquet, Mar. 10, 1761, Bouquet Papers, 6:61; Campbell to Bouquet, May 21, 1761, MPHC 19:67; Campbell to Bouquet, June 1, 1761, MPHC 19:70–71. (Sandusky) Meyer to Bouquet, Oct. 22, 1761, Bouquet Papers, 7:172. For venison, see Meyer to Bouquet, Nov. 29, 1761 and Dec. 9, 1761, Bouquet Papers, 7:213–14.

of a chief like Beaver depended less on his power than on the actions of the British themselves toward his people. He was influential insofar as he procured benefits from the British; his influence dissipated when they sought to use him simply as a conduit to convey their demands. The chiefs had to have presents to exert their influence, but Beaver's initial warning that the chiefs expected to be treated as the French had treated them was ignored. The chiefs along the Ohio River, Croghan explained, "seldom or ever hunt" and their "Necessities oblige them to be Mersinary." To deprive them of presents was to deprive them of influence.[85]

The British depended on the chiefs to exercise power that the chiefs had never possessed, even as they undercut the sources of their actual influence. The British, for example, pressed the chiefs to restore the prisoners, but decisions concerning prisoners were made by the families that had adopted or enslaved them, not by the village or tribe as a whole. The chiefs apparently did try to secure the return of all prisoners, but without the necessary presents, such attempts only made them enemies.[86]

All over the *pays d'en haut*, those chiefs who tried to mediate with the British lost influence. Many longed for a return of Onontio. Even among the Seneca, the western door of the Iroquois confederacy, the chiefs declined rapidly in influence. A speaker for the warriors of the important Seneca villages of Chenussio (or Geneseo) lying along the Genesee River told Johnson in council that "we ... are in fact the People of consequence for Managing Affairs, Our Sachems being generally a parcell of Old People who say Much but who Mean or Act very little, so that we have both the power and the Ability to Settle Matters."[87]

Among the Ohio villagers, too, warriors seemed ready to take control of events. Croghan reported in 1762 that the warriors of "Every Nation" were "very Sulkey & Ill Temper.d." As a Shawnee chief complained in early 1763, British actions seemed designed to cultivate Indian jealousy and create nostalgia for the French.

[85] For quotation, see Mercer to Bouquet, Aug. 20, 1759, *Bouquet Papers* 15:80–81. Killbuck himself had no desire for war with the English in 1759. When Delawares and Shawnees from Venango and Custaloga's Town struck the English, Delaware George and Killbuck successfully intervened to restore peace. Delaware George, Indian Intelligence, Apr.–May 1759, *Bouquet Papers*, 3:118. For Croghan quotation, see Croghan to Bouquet, Mar. 27, 1762, *Bouquet Papers*, 15:183. Croghan exaggerated. In the fall of 1762, Alexander McKee found Tamaqua at home when most of his people were hunting, but he said that he would go on a brief hunting trip soon. Journal of Alexander McKee, Oct. 16, 1762, *JP* 10:576. Colonel Smith, who lived among the Caughnawaga Mohawks, Delawares, Ottawas, and Wyandots, said the chiefs had to hunt like all others, *Colonel Smith's Journal*, 159.
[86] For decisions on prisoners, see Minutes of Meeting with a Delegation of Minisinks, July 11–16, 1760, HM 8249, Huntington Library; "Journal of James Kenny," 185; Croghan to Monckton, July 25, 1761, *JP* 10:316–18; An Indian Conference, Sept. 25, 1761, *JP* 10:327.
[87] For Seneca quotation, see Indian Proceedings Apr. 21–28, 1762, *JP* 3:697–98.

All the Indian nations are very Jealous of the English, they see you have a great many forts in this Country, and you are not so kind to them as they expected. The French were very Generous to the Indians and always gave them Cloathing, and Powder and Lead In Plenty, but you don't do that Brothers, and that is what makes the Indians so uneasey in their minds. This I assure you is the true Cause of all this Jealousy.[88]

In 1762, it seemed that the middle ground itself was about to crumble and cave in, leaving a cultural and political chasm yawning between Algonquian villagers and the agents of European empires. Algonquians and Europeans had risked the cultural formulations created on the middle ground against the events that followed the fall of New France, and the formulations had failed to hold: The British posts, the Algonquian horse thefts, the prisoners, and the paucity of presents were all more eloquent statements of reality than the increasingly hollow rhetoric of the council. Many of the fraternal kinship metaphors that had guided earlier British-Algonquian relations yielded to Amherst's counterformulation of conquerors and unruly subjects, which seemed, in fact, to offer a more coherent account of events. Yet the master metaphor of the middle ground – European fathers and Algonquian children – remained untested. In 1763, an Ottawa war leader, Pontiac, rose against the British to restore his French father and created a British father instead.

[88] For quotation, see Croghan to Bouquet, Nov. 25, 1762, *Bouquet Papers*, 9:167. For Shawnee, quotation, see Ecuyer: Indian Intelligence, Jan. 30, 1763, *Bouquet Papers*, 15:196.

7

Pontiac and the restoration of the middle ground

We know them now to be a very jealous people, and to have the highest notions of Liberty of any people on Earth, and a people, who will never Consider Consequences when they think their Liberty likely to be invaded, tho' it may End in their Ruin.

George Croghan to the Lords of Trade, 8 June 1764

The Six Nations, Western Indians &c. having never been conquered, Either by the English or French, nor subject to the Laws, consider themselves as a free people.

William Johnson to the Lords of Trade, 8 October 1764

The chief crazy enough to dream not so much of the abuse of a power he does not possess, as of the use of power, the chief who tries to act the chief, is abandoned.

Pierre Clastres, *Society Against the State*

I

The events of Pontiac's Rebellion are well known. In 1763, Indians from the Senecas west to the Illinois and from the Chippewas south to the Delawares attacked the recently occupied British posts in the *pays d'en haut* and, with the exceptions of Niagara, Detroit, and Fort Pitt, took them all. By the end of the year, British reinforcements raised the sieges of the surviving forts. They did not crush the rebellion but stymied it, and it slowed to an inconclusive halt. It was from these events that the nineteenth-century historian Francis Parkman created his *History of the Conspiracy of Pontiac.*[1]

[1] Francis Parkman, *History of the Conspiracy of Pontiac* (New York: Book League of America, 1929); Howard H. Peckham, *Pontiac and the Indian Uprising* (Princeton: Princeton University Press, 1947). Also see three articles by Wilbur R. Jacobs, "Gift-Giving and Pontiac's Uprising," "Pontiac's War – a Conspiracy?" and "1763 – Year of Decision on the Indian Frontier," all in Wilbur R. Jacobs, *Dispossessing the American Indian: Indians and Whites on the Colonial Frontier* (New York: Charles Scribner's Sons, 1972), 75–103. Michael McConnell, "The Search for Security: Indian-English Relations in the Trans-Appalachian Region, 1758–63" (Ph.D. diss., College of William and Mary, 1983) gives the most complete account of events along the Ohio in the years before the revolt.

Parkman created a Pontiac to fit his dramatic needs. He derived Pontiac from Robert Rogers's *Concise Account of North America* and his *Ponteach: A Tragedy*, but even though Rogers had actually met Pontiac, the Ottawa chief of his play was a literary invention. Both Parkman and Rogers needed a chief to symbolize a people. His fall would be his people's fall. Parkman's Pontiac was a chief who, from his entrance into the narrative, exerted a "singular control." He excited "the fierce passions of the Indians" for a fundamentally racial struggle. But the racial struggle reflected Parkman's own Victorian understanding of the world; the outlook of the Algonquians was far more complicated. Pontiac's Rebellion was not the beginning of a racially foreordained Indian demise; it was the beginning of the restoration of the middle ground.[2]

Pontiac's Rebellion was almost the reverse of the ultimate racial showdown Parkman imagined. Instead of revealing an unbridgeable chasm between Indians and whites, it succeeded in restoring, at least diplomatically, a common world and a common understanding. Out of the radically different British and Algonquian interpretations of the meaning of the British victory over the French, it forged a new, if tenuous, accommodation between the races. The British replaced the French as fathers. The true story of Pontiac's Rebellion is not just the dramatic assaults on the British forts that Parkman chronicled but also the accommodation of the Algonquians and the British.[3]

With the rebellion reconceived, Pontiac, too, must be reconceived. He is a figure who has, in some ways, been much diminished since Parkman had this "remarkable man" first meet Robert Rogers and "stand forth distinctly on the page of history." Parkman credited the planning and leadership of the revolt against the British to Pontiac and described it as a homogeneous conspiracy. Historians have since discredited his view. Parkman's Pontiac led a grand attempt that failed. The modern Pontiac is but a local leader who, in Howard Peckham's words, "had fought a losing war and made peace without attaining any of his objectives." Peckham's Pontiac and the other reduced modern Pontiacs conform better to the facts known about the man, but they distort his context, mistake the nature of his failure, and miss his success.[4]

Pontiac's world was a continuation of the old world of controversies

[2] Parkman, *Conspiracy of Pontiac*, 107; for Rogers and Pontiac, see Peckham, *Pontiac*, n. 59, 62.
[3] Parkman, *Conspiracy of Pontiac*, 111–21; quotation, 114.
[4] Quotation, Parkman, *Conspiracy of Pontiac*, 107. For reduced Pontiac, see Peckham, *Pontiac*, 111. For quotation, see Peckham, *Pontiac*, 319.
McConnell, "Search for Security," 415, also creates a reduced Pontiac, but he places him within a larger effort of an Indian attempt to retain their independence. For an attempt, I think misplaced, to reconceptualize the war as one of "self-determination," see Jacobs, "Pontiac's War," 83–93.

between the alliance and the republics. The British assertion of conquest and subjection forced both sides to create political alternatives to the alliance and alternative understandings of the relationship between whites and Indians. Neither side could, however, think in isolation; they could only, as it were, think together, and so the British and the Indians found themselves moving back onto the middle ground. Pontiac, in his attempt to kill the British, helped to turn them into fathers. Neolin, the Delaware prophet who inspired Pontiac, tried to create an Indian way and, in doing so, became part of a larger movement of religious syncretism.

II

Pontiac's revolt gestated in the long interlude between the fall of Canada in 1760 and the actual cession of Canada to Great Britain in 1763. It resulted, in a sense, from a series of failures – the failure of the Indians to create a confederacy that would prevent British occupation of the region, the failure of the British to act as either fathers or brothers, and the failure of Onontio to return. Each failure contributed to the dissolution of the *pays d'en haut* into the regional blocs that composed it and made the revolt a group of separate and loosely linked rebellions.

Algonquian attempts to forge unity collapsed one after another between 1760 and 1762. Tamaqua's plans to create a pan-Indian alliance centered on the Delawares had barely collapsed when, in the spring of 1760, the British received word of a new attempt: a meeting of the Indians of the *pays d'en haut*, the Iroquois, and Indians from the Susquehanna villages that was to take place "at Some Indian towns over the Ohio." One of the principal points of this council, Frederick Post learned, would be "how to secure the limits between them and they white people, so that they may live by themselfs a due distance from us, to secure theire hunting ground, for they are more affraid of loosing theire hunting grounds than theire lives and they are very much preposest and suspcious that that is our scheme to incroge upon them." The Pennsylvanians wanted to have representatives at this council, but the Iroquois turned back an attempt by Post and John Hays to attend. The meeting seems to have taken place without any Europeans present.[5]

In 1761, the British occupation of the forts at Niagara, Detroit, and Pittsburgh so alarmed the Chenussio Senecas that they attempted to create a

---

5 Meeting, Amherst to Hamilton, Mar. 30, 1760, *JP* 3:205. Missiweakiwa said the meeting was to consider how to regulate traders, Conference Held at Fort Pitt, Apr. 6–12, 1760, *JP* 3:216. For Post quotation, see Post to Governor Hamilton, Mar. 11, 1760, *PA*, Series, 1, 3:709. For representatives, see Logan to Peters, July 19, 1760, *PA*, Series 1, 4:62–63. For Post and Hays, see Journal of John Hays, 1760 *PA*, Series 1, 3:737–40.

western confederation to attack the new British posts. The Senecas feared that the occupation of Detroit by the British completed British encirclement of their territory. They feared, too, that the posts gave the British direct contact with the western nations and thus could only diminish the Iroquois' own standing as intermediaries in the West. Finally, the plan seems to have been the work of pro-French Iroquois. Teaatoriance (or Tahiadoris), the Seneca emissary who carried the plan, was the son of Phillipe-Thomas Chabert de Joncaire. To the British, the whole scheme seemed French-inspired. This plan supposedly won the consent of those Delawares and Shawnees alarmed at the British occupation of Fort Pitt, but it gained few other adherents.[6]

A meeting called at Detroit in 1761 to cement this anti-British confederation instead led to its dissolution. The council was, according to George Croghan, to be "a greatt Meeting of all ye. Western Nations [to take place] at Detroit Next Spring [1761] by there own apointment to wh. ye. Six Nations are Invited.... Many thing will be Disgusted [i.e., discussed] there Reletiff to what has past Sence ye. Warr and fixing on Some plan for thire futer Conductt." Iroquois, Delawares, Shawnees, Mohicans, Wyandots, Kickapoos, Miamis, Chippewas from Saginaw, Mingos, Detroit Chippewas, Ottawas, Potawatomis, and Huron-Petuns met together before Sir William Johnson arrived in Detroit that September to ratify the peace between the British and the western Indians.[7]

The Detroit Indians, jealous of Seneca pretensions in the West, betrayed the Chenussio plan to Johnson. After the usual ceremonies of condolence,

---

[6] For the Chenussios, a "brave and powerfull tribe of the Seneca Nation," who lived near Niagara and wanted the English to drive the French out, see Johnson to Lords of Trade, May 17, 1759, *NYCD* 7:376; Johnson, Private Journal, July 24, 1761, *JP* 13:227; Niagara and Detroit Proceedings, July–Sept. 1761, *JP* 3:453. For war messages and betrayal, see Copy of the Indian Council held near Detroit between the Deputies of the Six Nations, and the Western Indians, June 1761, Syluester Stevens and Donald Kent (eds.), *The Papers of Colonel Henry Bouquet*, 19 vols. (Harrisburg: Pennsylvania Historical Commission, 1940), 15:123–27; for the Ottawas and Chippewas, see Niagara and Detroit Proceedings, July–Sept. 1761, *JP* 3:456; letter, n.d., c. June 1761, *JP* 3:413–15. For Campbell's account of the conspiracy and involvement of Delawares and Shawnees, see *ibid.* 437–39. Croghan did not think the Ohio Indians were involved, Croghan to Monckton, July 25, 1761, *JP* 10:316. For son of Joncaire, see Niagara and Detroit Proceedings, July–Sept. 1761, *JP* 3:460. For Iroquois blame it on Seneca alone, see *ibid.* 440. For Seneca blame it on Ohio Mingos, see *ibid.* 463–64, and people of Chenussio, 491. The people of Chenussio said it was instigated by a message sent by the Wyandots and Potawatomis to a Cayuga chief named Awetharung'wahs, living at Presque Isle (Oughreni), probably before end of war. They claimed to have only been trying to learn the real sentiments of the western Indians and they blamed Tahiadoris (Teaatoriance) for misrepresenting the message.

For Gage's opinion, see Gage to Amherst, Aug. 21, 1761, Gage Letterbooks; for Croghan's opinion, see Croghan to Johnson, Mar. 31, 1762, *JP* 3:662.

[7] Croghan to Johnson, Jan. 13, 1751, *JP* 3:303; Niagara and Detroit Proceedings, 1761, *JP* 3:468–75.

Anáiása, the "Chief of the Hurons" who acted as speaker in the meetings with Johnson at Detroit, denounced the Seneca Kayashuta, who was sitting before him, as one of bearers of the Chenussio war belts. Kayashuta, who would for the next quarter century form the main link between the Senecas and the Mingos at the Ohio River, spent most of the remainder of the conference in long and tangled justifications of his actions. Having exposed the Iroquois as conspirators and, by contrast, affirmed the Huron-Petuns as agents of peace, Anáiása then accepted a Mohawk offer to renew the covenant chain between the Iroquois and the western nations. In establishing this link with the Iroquois, he emphasized that the Mohawks should be grateful for his acceptance. "We beg you will consider," he told the Mohawks, "that this Alliance which you have made is not an inconsiderable one, being made with all the Nations of the North and West." Sir William Johnson, grasping the opportunity to divide the Iroquois and the western villagers, recognized the Huron-Petuns as the titular heads of this supposed league of all the western and northern nations and lit the new council fire at their village near Detroit.[8]

Both the pretensions of the Detroit Indians to speak for the various nations of the *pays d'en haut* and their loyalty to the British were disingenuous. The so-called Ottawa confederacy that Johnson recognized at Detroit was nothing more than the regional bloc of villages at Detroit under another name. The Detroit Indians – Potawatomis, Ottawas, Huron-Petuns, and Chippewas – told the arriving British in 1760 that "all the Indians in this Country are Allies to each other and as one people," and they spoke truly if they meant the region around Detroit. A quarter of a century had largely healed the bitter quarrels at Detroit which now contained, by British count, 780 warriors. Within the bloc, tribal identity was flexible. Captain Donald Campbell marked one such transference of loyalty in a passing phrase: "Aron the Mohawk who is now a Wiandot." But Indians outside Detroit did not necessarily share identity or interests with this Ottawa confederacy. The Delawares, for example, had symbolically lit the council fire at Detroit, but considerable tension continued between the Ohio villagers and the people of Detroit. The allegiance of other villages from Saint Joseph through the

---

[8] Niagara and Detroit Proceedings, 1761, *JP* 3:469–71. For Iroquois recognition, see Report of Indian Council Near Detroit, July 5, 1761, *Bouquet Papers*, 15:125. The Delawares, by bringing a symbolic spark from the "first Council fire . . . which was a fire of peace" and kindling it in the Huron-Petun council house, acknowledged the shift and apparently abandoned their own pretensions to leadership.

The Iroquois, who accompanied Johnson, addressed the "other Indians" as "Brethern of the Huron and Ottawa Confederacy" (*ibid.*, 480–81), and in restoring the Covenant Chain, made a separate alliance with this alliance. For Hurons, see *ibid.*, 483–84, quotation, 488, Johnson, 494–95. Johnson later claimed to have encouraged discord, Johnson to Gage, Jan. 12, 1764, *JP* 4:295–96.

Wabash country to the Detroit council fire was tenuous, and the people between Lake Michigan and the Mississippi remained entirely marginal to the confederacy. Nor were the Detroit Indians devoted to the British. Like the Chenussio Senecas, they had dispatched belts to organize resistance against the British.[9]

The inability to unite against the British was only one sign of the underlying divisions of the *pays d'en haut*. Without the French, groups of associated villages, such as the ones at Detroit or along the Ohio, became planets without a sun. There was nothing to keep them in their orbits, and they collided and clashed. They betrayed one another to the British, and eventually they fought. In 1762, the Miamis, Ottawas, Chippewas, and Potawatomis were preparing to attack the Shawnees. The Michilimackinac Chippewas were on the verge of war with the Menominees and their allies, and the Sauks feared attacks from the Illinois in retaliation for earlier attacks of their own.[10]

The disarray of the Algonquians presented the British with an opportunity to ensure their own dominance in the *pays d'en haut*. Except in Illinois country, the British occupied the old French posts without Algonquian resistance. And despite the belts urging rebellion, most of Onontio's children apparently expected the British to act, if not as fathers, then as brothers. They did not anticipate conquerors. They did not know of Amherst's orders to curtail gifts and restrict the sale of powder. And the officers, marooned with small garrisons in an Algonquian sea, found themselves of necessity edging away from Amherst's orders and back toward the middle ground that Amherst had ordered abandoned.[11]

British policy in 1762, however, dashed Algonquian hopes for accom-

---

[9] Croghan, Indian Conference at Detroit, Dec. 3, 1760, *Bouquet Papers*, 15:98; Campbell to Bouquet, June 21, 1761, *MPHC* 19:78. For population, see Niagara and Detroit Proceedings, 1761, *JP* 3:501. Another 400 warriors lived around Detroit, putting the total Indian strength there at 1,180 warriors.

For Detroit message, see Conseil, 28 nov. 1769, AN, C11A, v. 105; Bellestre au Ministre, 16 juin 1762, AN, C11A, v. 105, f. 356. This message went out despite the friendly reception given Croghan and Rogers, Croghan's Journal, in Reuben Gold Thwaites (ed.), *Early Western Travels, 1748–1846 . . .* , 38 vols. (Cleveland: Arthur H. Clark, 1904–07), 104–13.

[10] For examples of failure and betrayals of rival plots and lack of unity, Bouquet to Amherst, Dec. 12, 1762, Amherst Papers, reel 32. The Senecas told the English that Aghstaghregck, a "chief man of Hurons," had not forgotten the death of his nephew in battle at Niagara. In the winter of 1761–62, the Senecas claimed Aghstaghregck had departed to seek his vengeance on the Virginia frontier, Indian Proceedings Apr. 21–28, 1762, *JP* 3:699. For Miami council with Shawnees, see Journal of A. McKee, Nov. 1, 1762, *JP* 10:577. For western quarrels, see Journal of James Gorrell, June 24, 1762, Aug. 13, 1762, *WHC* 1:33–35; Lieutenant Thomas Hutchins Journal, June 2, 1762, *JP* 10:521–29. Journal of A. Mckee, Nov. 1, 1762, *JP* 10:579.

[11] For example of pressure for presents, see Holmes to Bouquet, Mar. 17, 1762, *Bouquet Papers*, 8:52; Hutchins Journal, 1762, *JP* 10:528.

modation on the middle ground. Crop failures, epidemics, and famine, particularly severe along the Ohio River and in the Wabash country, swept the *pays d'en haut*, and the Algonquians begged for assistance from their British brothers. Events had now put both their lives and their conceptions of the British at risk, and the British by and large failed them. The local commanders either lacked the capacity to give aid or gave it grudgingly. In a disastrously timed and planned journey, Lieutenant Thomas Hutchins traveled from Michilimackinac, Green Bay, and Saint Joseph along western Lake Michigan and through the Wabash country without any presents. From Saint Joseph south, sick Indians unable to hunt for their families begged for aid that he could not supply. The British replicated such failures at virtually all the posts. A party of Mingos, citing the hunger and sickness of their women and children and their neglect by the British, assured Croghan "that your conduct makes all the Indian Nations around you very jealous, and that you have some bad designs against them."[12]

The bad designs the Mingos insinuated was an obvious conclusion in a world where those unattached by real or ritual kinship bonds were always potential enemies. If the British did not act as fathers or brothers, then they might very well plot the Algonquians' destruction. Men who refused to aid the victims of famine and pestilence could easily become identified as the source of famine and pestilence. Witchcraft and sickness remained closely linked, and no Algonquians would doubt that those with bad designs had the means to put them into effect. Famine and epidemic, coupled with British trade policies, created an Algonquian image of the British not as misguided brothers, but as enemies, a malevolent people bound by neither kinship nor ritual obligations.

This image of the British as merciless enemies gave renewed power to calls for revolt against them, and it also created nostalgia for Onontio – the good father who had united his children. Because the documents from this period are overwhelmingly British – by the very people the French, Iroquois, and Algonquians wished to keep in the dark – the politics behind the eventual revolt emerges as a puzzle with pieces missing and with the remaining pieces purposefully mismatched. The British interviewed Indians; the Indians gave contradictory accounts. These accounts implicated other

---

[12] McConnell, "Search for Security," 360, 377–80, emphasizes these famines and epidemics. For example of talk in fall of 1761 pleading hunger and poverty, see Talk of Kipimisaming "un Loup habitant parmi eux," 30 sept. 1761, enclosure with Amherst to Johnson, March 13, 1762, Amherst Papers, reel 30. This could be a ritual claim of poverty, however. For conditions among villages visited by Hutchins, see Hutchins Journal, 1762, *JP* 10:521–29. Sickness continued into the fall, Journal of Alexander Mckee, *JP* 10:578. For quotation, see Croghan to Amherst, Dec. 2, 1762, Amherst Papers, reel 32, letter may be misdated. See also Report of Indian Conference, Dec. 9, 1762, *Bouquet Papers*, 15:193.

Indians or Frenchmen, who either denied all or supplied wholly new versions of the story. The conspiracies were always on the verge of seeming to be chimeras called up by the anxieties of isolated post commanders, but their reality was proved by the telltale wampum belts that conveyed the messages from village to village. The belts existed, but what they meant confused the British. There was much reason to be confused. Between 1761 and 1763, war belts issued from at least four different sources: the Seneca town of Chenussio, Detroit, the missions around Montreal, and the Illinois country. Taken together, they created widespread belief that Onontio was on the seas to evict the British, reunite his children, and restore the alliance.

The belts from Detroit and Chenussio that circulated across the *pays d'en haut* were, whatever encouragement the French offered, primarily Indian in origin, but those from the Illinois country and Montreal definitely did originate with the French. The Montreal belts apparently represented a last-ditch attempt by the French to defend Canada. After its fall, the belts continued to circulate and took on a life of their own, as French Canadians spread rumors of Onontio's return. The Illinois belts similarly represented an attempt by that isolated outpost of Louisiana at the end of the Seven Years' War to muster Indians to its own defense and to halt British-encouraged Algonquian attacks on the Cherokees, who were waging their own war against the British colonies. French traders of the *pays d'en haut* also used the belts to persuade the Indians that Onontio was about to return.[13]

***

[13] The Montreal plot apparently grew out of the efforts of the French in Canada in 1760 to organize Indian resistance against the English. As early as 1758, Vaudreuil was planning to summon all the tribes of the *pays d'en haut* to Montreal for a last-ditch defense of Canada against the English, Reflexions Genérales, 1758, AN, C11A, v. 103. It was supposedly kept alive by M. Longueuil, traders, and the clergy; it was spread by the Caughnawaga Mohawks and the Ottawas and joined by the Mississaugas, Fox, Sioux, and others. The English detected traces of this conspiracy throughout 1761 and 1762. The Caughnawagas pled their own innocence and put the blame on the Chenussio Senecas. French traders denied participation, and Gage, although he believed it was evidence of the general bad disposition of the Indians, eventually dismissed the whole affair as the work of a few discontented Indians, Johnson, Private Journal, Oct. 7, 1761, *JP* 13:266; Gladwin to Amherst, Feb. 4, 1762; *JP* 10:380, Mar. 5, 1762; *JP* 10:392–93, Apr. 4, 1762, *JP* 10:422–23; Apr. 5, 1762, *JP* 10:424–25; Gage to Amherst, Feb. 17, 1762, Gage Letterbooks. For Caughnawaga version, see Conference with Canasadaga Indians, Mar. 15, 1732, *JP* 10:398–99. For Johnson takes seriously, see Johnson to Amherst, Mar. 20, 1762 and May 6, 1762, Amherst Papers, reel. 31. For Amherst doesn't, see Amherst to Johnson, Mar. 21, 1762, Amherst Papers, reel 30. For some increased concern, see Amherst to Johnson, Apr. 4, 1762, Amherst Papers, reel 30. For Gage blames it on Kanitchgouly, see Gage to Gladwin, Apr. 20, 1762, and Apr. 27, 1762. Gage Letterbooks. For Otquandageghte's confession and Caughnawaga of Swegacy (St. Regis), see Claus to Johnson, June 2, 1762, *JP* 3:751–54. For await French fleet, see Gage to Amherst, June 14, 1762, Gage Letterbooks. For denial, see Claus to Johnson, June 30, 1762, *JP* 3:819.

In the spring of 1762 the French at the "forks of the Ohio" (probably Fort Massac near the mouth of the Tennessee) gave a belt to the Weas. This was apparently the very belt the Senecas, Delawares, and Shawnees claimed to have given to the Miamis. Either the Senecas

In British accounts, the various belts – Iroquois, Algonquian, and French – tend to merge into a single conspiracy, but the movements actually remained largely distinct. The Chenussio belts linked the Senecas, Delawares, Shawnees, and Mingos. The second conspiracy revolved around Detroit. Canadian traders sponsored the third, although it intersected with the Indian attempts. Ironically, the French garrison at Illinois, after the first news of impending peace reached the *pays d'en haut* in 1762, seems to have remained largely aloof from plans to attack the British and restore Onontio.[14]

III

Not only did French aloofness from plans to evict the English fail to deter the various conspiracies, but accounts of the pending cession of Canada to

lied, for the French specifically ordered their belt be kept from the Delawares and the Six Nations, or two French belts were in circulation. The French told the Weas that the English, the Six Nations, and the Delawares had joined together to destroy the western Indians. To save themselves, they should be prepared to join the French the next spring and drive the English from the country. The immediate aim of the French, and the Cherokees who joined in the message, was to halt the attacks by the northern tribes on the Cherokees. In 1762, the French desperately needed Algonquian aid to maintain their last two weak bastions of resistance against the English: the Illinois country and the Cherokees. The surviving correspondence concerning the Illinois country during these years makes mention of no official attempt to encourage an Indian rebellion. For conditions there, see Kerlerec au Ministre, 21 mars 1762, AN, C13A, v. 43. Neyon de Villiers à Kerlerec, 1 juillet 1762, AN, C13A, v. 43, f. 165. For reports of French at Illinois stirring up western nations, see Croghan to Amherst, Oct. 5, 1762, *JP* 10:543. For French belt to Weas, see Indian Intelligence, Sept. 28, 1762, *JP* 10:534–35. For Shawnee chief says belt from Cherokees and French at Illinois, see Captain Simeon Ecuyer, Indian Intelligence, Jan. 30, 1763, *Bouquet Papers*, 15:196.

14 Which French dispatched these belts is not clear, but most likely they were traders and not officers. The report of a captive brought to Ouiatenon, the English post closest to the Illinois, said that the French soldiers at the Illinois wanted peace, but the Canadian traders were urging the Indians to murder the English. Amherst moved to shut off all communication with the Illinois country on the grounds that reports from the Illinois "tends to set them [the Indians] agog to think their old Friends are to come Again." But Indians continued to travel to the Illinois. Saint Joseph Potawatomis, Ottawas, and Michilimackinac Chippewas all supposedly received private presents from the French who urged them to attack the English. Jenkins to Gladwin, Ouiatenon, July 29, 1762, *JP* 10:476; Amherst to Gage, Aug. 11, 1762, Amherst Papers, reel 30; Johnson to Amherst, Dec. 7, 1762, Amherst Papers, reel 31; Illinois, Intelligence from a Waweotonan (Wea) Indian, July 11, 1763, *JP* 4:169. For sample of French attitudes, see Kerlerec to Berryer, June 8, 1761, *MPA* 5:272–73.

William Johnson in the summer of 1763 received reports from the Mohawks that the war hatchet had been passed from the French governor of Louisiana. If such a message had indeed existed, and there is no mention of it in the French records, it must have dated from 1762, because it refers to the Spanish alliance. There is no sign that this was the source of the actual rebellion, although the Indians obviously expected French aid, Journal of Indian Affairs, July 7, 1763, *JP* 10:767.

England, which reached the *pays d'en haut* in early 1763, actually fueled them. These reports came, as Captain Simeon Ecuyer at Fort Pitt put it, as a "thunderclap" to the Indians. According to Croghan, the cession "allmost Drove them to Despair." The Shawnees came to Alexander McKee, Croghan's assistant, and "desired to know if the French had given up their country and by what right they could pretend to do it. They said plainly that the English would soon be the Great People in the country." Netawatwees (or Newcomer), the chief of the Delaware Turtle phratry, declared the British had "grown too powerfull & seemed as if they would be too Strong for God himself." When news of the final peace settlement did arrive in 1763, the Indians found that the French had indeed ceded Canada and Louisiana east of the Mississippi to England. They had also, although the Indians did not yet know it, given Louisiana west of the Mississippi to Spain.[15]

The despair and surprise of the Algonquians at the cession was no greater than that of many French-Canadian traders and habitants of the *pays d'en haut*. Canadians could not fully believe that they had been abandoned. They submitted plans to the ministry both to excite rebellions to regain Canada and to sustain the Indians in their resistance to the British. These *mémoires*, as far as can be determined, obtained no official support; the ministry filed them and forgot them. Yet the men who supported petitions to ministers in France also continued to move, with more effect, among the Indians.[16]

In October 1762, George Croghan received reports that the preceding summer French emissaries in Indian dress had held a secret council at the Ottawa village at Detroit with the chiefs and principal warriors of the Wyandots, Chippewas, Ottawas, Potawatomis, and "some other Tribes who live amongst those Indians on Lake Superior, above Mechelemackinac and Fort Le Bay." The location of the conference at the Ottawa rather than the Huron-Petun village indicates a shift of influence. The Ottawas now apparently took precedence at Detroit, and they sought to expand their efforts beyond their own regional bloc. Messengers from this conference went to the Miamis, Weas, Kickapoos, Piankashaws, and Shawnees. In a

---

[15] For thunderclap, see Ecuyer to Bouquet, Mar. 11, 1763, *Bouquet Papers*, 10:69. For despair, see Croghan to Bouquet, Mar. 19, 1763, *Bouquet Papers*, 10:80. For don't want English to go further down the Ohio, see Council with Shawnees, Apr. 16, 1762, Amherst Papers, reel 32. For lands, see Croghan to Johnson, Apr. 24, 1763, *JP* 10:659–60. For fear of French in Louisiana, see Witham Marsh to Johnson, Jan. 30, 1763, *JP* 4:34. For rumors of French army, see Extract of letter from Lieutenant Jenkins to Gladwin, Mar. 28, 1763, Amherst Papers, reel 31. For newcomer, see "Journal of James Kenny," *Pennsylvania Magazine of History and Bioghaphy*, 37 (1913): 187.

[16] For two such plots, see Abstract of a Plan to excite a Rebellion in Canada, 1763, *NYCD* 10:1155–57; Projet d'opération pour la Nouvelle Orleans relativement au Canada, 1763, AN, C11A, v. 105, f. 421. For Canadians urging Indians to attack, see Extract, Lt. Jenkins to Gladwin, Mar. 28, 1763, Amherst Papers, reel 31.

demonstration of the continuing differences within the *pays d'en haut*, however, the Ottawas kept the Delawares and the Six Nations in the dark.[17]

In the cession of Canada, Algonquian warriors and Canadian habitants found, in their near despair, an engine to drive them toward at least partial unity. They conceived a desperate hope that revolt would both expel the British from the region and promote a French return. The habitants and traders told the Indians, and may have themselves believed, that French fleets were upon the seas. Onontio would return.

The dream of Onontio's return, however, existed alongside another, very different vision of the future of the *pays d'en haut*. Near the Ohio River, Neolin, the Delaware prophet, preached a message that seemingly left no room for European fathers. Neolin called upon Indians to reform themselves, to cast away European tools and clothes, and to prepare for a world where they would live independently of whites. Superficially, this vision seemed as dramatic a withdrawal from the middle ground as Amherst's determination to reduce the Indians to subjects, but Neolin and his vision were far more complicated.

In November 1762, James Kenny, a Quaker in charge of the trading store established at Pittsburgh by the commissioners of Indian affairs for the province of Pennsylvania, noted in his diary the teachings of an "Imposter which is raised amongst ye Delawares, in order to shew them ye right way to Heaven." The imposter was Neolin. He had received a vision from heaven, where, he said, there were no whites but only Indians. He preached that the Indians once had direct access to heaven, but since the coming of whites, they had been taught sins and vices that barred their way and diverted them to hell. To regain the "Good Road," they had to learn to live "without any Trade or Connections with ye White people, Clothing & Supporting themselves as their forefathers did." They must also pray to "ye Son or Little God," who carried their petitions and presents to the Great Being who was "too High and mighty to be spoken to by them."[18]

The Delaware prophet, with his references to the Christian God, to heaven and hell, to sin, and to a return to old ways, was part of a growing movememt of religious syncretism among the Delawares and Shawnees. In the 1750s, Papounhan, a Munsee Delaware, had begun to combine Quaker beliefs with advocacy of a return to "the ancient Customs and Manners of Their Forefathers." In 1760, John Hays had encountered at the village of Asinsinkm, then on the Chemung River east of the Appalachians, a

---

[17] Indian Intelligence, recd. Sept. 28, 1762, *JP* 10:534–35; Intelligence recd. Sept. 20, 1762, with Croghan to Amherst, Oct. 5, 1762, Amherst Papers, reel 31; also *JP* 10:534–35. For Catholic Huron-Petuns, see Rogers to Johnson, Oct. 7, 1763, *JP* 10:871–72, Peckham, *Pontiac*, 113.

[18] "Journal of James Kenny," 171–73.

Delaware "preast" and a "Book of Pickters" similar to the "bible" of the Delaware prophet. Most likely the old priest he encountered there was Wangomend, a Munsee who would later migrate west to the town of Goshgoshing. What all of these religious leaders had in common was the assimilation of segments of Christian doctrine that they used to effect an ostensible return to traditional customs.[19]

This ostensible return to old ways attracted the most attention from whites. Such a return threatened the fur trade and Christian missionary endeavors, and by the 1760s it was also often linked to rumors of a united Indian attempt to drive the British from the country west of the Appalachians. Neolin predicted that "there will be Two or Three Good Talks & then War," which at least some Delawares took to mean that "by following his instructions, they would, in a few years, be able to drive the white people out of their country."[20]

Whites feared the Indian prophets' nativism, but this nativism remained joined with the interest of the prophets in Christianity. Papounhan, with his affinity for the Quakers and his possible eventual conversion by the Moravians, shared much with Neolin. In 1766 the Presbyterian missionary Charles Beatty would find Neolin a particularly interested and courteous inquirer into Christian doctrine and eager to use it to supplement his original vision. Beatty even had hopes for his conversion. Although Neolin recognized whites as a source of Indian problems, he believed the core of the problems lay within the Indians themselves. His vision had come "while he was alone by himself musing & greatly concerned about the evil ways he saw prevailing among the Indians."[21]

Neolin's concern with the "evil ways" prevailing among the Indians was a recurring theme of Indian prophets and, although it was couched in terms of

---

[19] Charles Hunter, "The Delaware Nativist Revival of the Mid-Eighteenth Century," *Ethnohistory* 18 (Winter 1971): 42–43; Neolin himself was quite interested in Christian doctrine, see Guy Soulliard Klett (ed.), *Journals of Charles Beatty, 1762–69* (University Park: Pennsylvania State University Press, 1962), 67–68. The village of Assink reappears farther west later, see Helen Hornbeck Tanner (ed.), *Atlas of Great Lakes Indian History* (Norman: University of Oklahoma Press, 1987), 9; map 16, 80. For resurrection of old customs, see William A. Hunter (ed.), "John Hays' Diary and Journal of 1760," *Pennsylvania Archaeologist* 24 (Aug. 1954): 74–75.

For an interesting discussion of the prophets which differs in emphasis from the one I give here, see Gregory Dowd, "Paths of Resistance: American Indian Religion and the Quest for Unity, 1745–1815" (Ph.D. diss., Princeton University, 1986), especially, 282 ff.

[20] "Journal of James Kenny," 171; Hunter, "Delaware Revival," 43.

[21] For Papounhan's attachment to Quakers in 1760, see Minutes of Meetings with a Delegation of Minisinks, two Nanticokes, and three Delawares from an Indian Town Above Wyoming... Philadelphia, July 11–16, 1760, HM 8249, Huntington Library. Klett (ed.), *Journals of Charles Beatty*, 65, 67–69. See also Hunter, "Delaware Revival," 47, and Anthony Wallace, "Revitalization Movements," *American Anthropologist* 58 (1956): 264–81. For Moravians, see Dowd, "Paths of Resistance," 289–90.

a return to a purer past, it represented a break with older Algonquian views. Neolin and the other prophets took such interest in Christianity because, like the Christians, they were moralists. The various Delaware prophets, with their long exposure to Quaker and Moravian proselytizing, were actively integrating the concept of sin into the Algonquian world view. Algonquians in general already conceived of misfortune as a punishment that resulted from the anger of supernaturals. When angry manitous punished people, however, the manitous were reacting to failures in ritual observance. They punished particular omissions in the necessary rituals with particular brands of catastrophes. Neolin, however, lamented moral failings which offended not a particular manitou but a supreme being. When angered, this supreme being punished on a scale that threatened to destroy whole peoples.

The shift from ritual concern to moral concern came as a gradual change in emphasis and not as a sudden, sharp break with older views. Its first stages are apparent in an incident Conrad Weiser recorded in his diary in 1737. While among the Shawnees and Onondagas located on the Susquehanna, Weiser asked them how Indians could now suffer famine in a region that had once been among the most productive in the Indian country.

> They answered that now game was scarce, and that hunting had strangely failed since last winter; some of them had procured nothing at all; – that the Lord and creator of the world was resolved to destroy the Indians. One of their seers, whom they named, had seen a vision of God, who had said to him the following words: – You inquire after the cause why game has become scarce, I will tell you. You kill it for the sake of the skins, which you give for strong liquors, and drown your senses, and kill one another, and carry on a dreadful debauchery. Therefore have I driven the wild animals out of the country, for they are mine. If you will do good, and cease from your sins, I will bring them back; if not, I will destroy you from the end of the earth.
>
> I inquired if they believed what the seer had seen and heard? They answered, yes, some believed it would happen so; others also believed it, but gave themselves no concern about it. Time will show, said they, what is to happen to us; rum will kill us, and leave the land clear for the Europeans without strife or purchase.[22]

New and old religious ideas existed side by side in this response. Indians in an earlier period would have attributed the absence of game to failures to appease specific manitous or a keeper of the game. This seer made the offenses moral and caused by British rum, although a failure to honor the animals was implicit. The being offended by Indian immorality was not a

[22] Paul A. W. Wallace, *Conrad Weiser, 1696–1760, Friend of Colonist and Mohawk* (Philadelphia: University of Pennsylvania Press, 1945), 88. The town in the diary is given as Otsineky. It was largely inhabited by Shawnees and Onondagas.

keeper of the game but, rather, the "creator of the world." Angered, he threatened to exterminate the Indians. The only solution of the problem was moral reform.

Later Papounhan, whose views the Quakers widely reported because they seemed so close to their own, gave a similar account of God's anger at the Indians. When asked about "the alteration of times and why they are so changed from what they had been some years past," he answered:

> People are grown cross towards each other, if they lived in Love it would not be so but they grow proud the covetous which causes God to be angry & to send dry & hot summers & hard Winters and also Sickness amongst the People, which he would not do if they Loved one another & would do as he would have them.[23]

If a supreme being could single out Indians for punishment, however, by the same logic he could also single them out for favor. Implicit in Papounhan's remark was another idea that gained increasing currency among Algonquians in the late eighteenth century: separate Indian and white ways or paths toward a shared supreme being who had different purposes for each. Indians recognized God's punishing hand because they assumed his usual benevolence toward Indians in general. The Shawnee chief Kachhowatchiy told the proselytizing noblemen Count Zinzendorf in the fall of 1742 that:

> he himself was an Indian of God's creation and he was satisfied with his condition [and] had no wish to be European. . . . He liked the Indian Way of Life. God had been very kind to him even in his old Age and would continue to look well after him. God was better pleased with the Indians, than with the Europeans. It was wonderful how much he helped them.[24]

The emphasis on *Indians* in these different contexts was important if, as yet, tentative. Manitous helped individuals or discrete social units: clans, villages, and, perhaps, tribes. But God seemed to deal with Indians in larger units. Even when God helped Kachhowatchiy as an individual, it was because he was pleased with his life as an Indian. Despite the differences among them, Indians were thinking of themselves as a group that took on unity and coherence when opposed to whites.

The distinctions drawn between Indians and whites by the Shawnees and Delawares in their references to heaven, hell, sin, and other aspects of Christian dogma clearly betrayed British influence, but the Indians were

---

[23] Some Remarks made by a person who accompanied Papoonahoal and the other Indians from Philadelphia, n.d., Huntington Library.
[24] Wallace, *Weiser*, 144.

turning the supposed universality of Christianity on its head. They used it to emphasize Indian distinctiveness and a separate Indian path. This was not simply a phenomenon of British contact. As the alliance declined, and with it the idea of Indians and whites as the common children both of a heavenly father and of Onontio, their earthly father, similar ideas appeared among the French allies. In 1757, Louis Antoine de Bougainville, after reporting the continued dependence of the Ottawas on their manitous, said that they had more recently added two Masters of Life to their cosmology. One was brown and beardless and had created the Indians. The other, who had created the French, was white and bearded.[25]

Neolin's message, therefore, fell on well-tilled ground. Neolin might denounce white practices, but what he really preached was Indian guilt. Indians were guilty because they had accepted from the whites things that were unsuitable for an Indian way. The great advantage of accepting guilt in this way is that it restores power to the guilty party. To take the blame is, in a sense, to take control. In the 1760s, amid the widespread drunkenness and violence that accompanied the reopening of British trade at Pittsburgh, the fear of British attempts to settle the Ohio country, pressure from the British to return white prisoners, the occurrence of a devastating epidemic among the Shawnees, and the prophecies that the whites would once again drive the Delawares from their home, Neolin assigned guilt and promised power and well-being to those who reformed. Many Indians already accepted the reality of God's anger at them; Neolin assured them that they could allay this anger and regain control of events.[26]

In the beginning, Neolin's message, despite its emphasis on a broad Indian-white dichotomy, was apparently meant largely for the Delawares. Neolin instituted his religion among the Delawares with the introduction of a "bitter water . . . to purge out all that they got of ye White peoples ways & Nature." But such was the power of this bitter drink that, if any other nations drank of it, they would die. Bitter drink was an odd foundation for Delaware exclusiveness. It originated in the southeast and came to the Delawares through the Shawnees. Such exclusiveness would not last. Neolin's message, as a call to moral reform, spread beyond the Delawares.[27]

In 1763 Neolin's nativism, along with efforts to secure the return of Onontio, began to create the wider Algonquian unity that had so far

[25] Edward P. Hamilton (ed. and trans.), *Adventure in the Wilderness: The American Journals of Louis Antoine de Bougainville, 1756–60* (Norman: University of Oklahoma Press, 1964), 133. For a vision among the Onondagas, see Proceedings with the Sachems and Great Warriors of the United Six Nations, Sept. 10, 1762, *JP* 10:505–6.
[26] "Journal of James Kenny," 178, 193. Kenny identified the epidemic as ague or malaria, *ibid.*, 169, 172.
[27] *Ibid.*, 188. Dowd, "Paths of Resistance," 296.

eluded those discontented with British rule. One movement looked back nostalgically to the French alliance. The other grew from a sense of Algonquian separateness that opposed the patriarchal formulations of the alliance. The genius of Pontiac was his ability to fuse, at least temporarily, these contradictory tendencies into a common ideology of revolt. They had, after all, more in common than was immediately apparent: Both were cultural hybrids formed on the middle ground; both appealed to warriors and war leaders; and both were geared to ridding the *pays d'en haut* of the British.

Pontiac took Neolin's moral code and, while accepting the need for moral reform, made the message anti-British rather than generically antiwhite. Given the difficulties of translation of the various Delaware words for white, this may, indeed, have been Neolin's intention all along. Because Pontiac's career before the attack on Detroit is unknown, it is impossible to determine whether he heard the prophet directly or learned of his teaching through messengers. Pontiac had been, according to later accounts, one of the Ottawa delegates who visited Fort Pitt in the summer of 1760; he thus could have had his own connections with the Delawares. In the months before the uprising, converts flocked to Neolin. By adding the Detroit Indians to those who heeded Neolin's message, Pontiac forged a critical connection with the Delaware followers of the prophet.[28]

Pontiac greatly tempered Neolin's rejection of white ways. Neolin's morality became a social and political program of temperance, monogamy, self-sufficiency, and intertribal peace. Its purely religious aspects departed drastically from existing Algonquian practices: Neolin condemned medicine bags and bundles and substituted direct prayer to a spirit of life. The spirit of life demanded a stricter respect for "your brothers," that is, game animals, than had been practiced earlier and took over control of those animals usually credited to the various masters or keepers of the game.[29]

The Potawatomis of Saint Joseph gave Neolin's message an even more Christian gloss than Pontiac had. They interpreted Neolin's message to include both a rejection of older practices (in this case, personal medicine, polygamy, and guardian spirits) and an injunction to resist the British, who with their diseases and "their imprisoning you, will totally destroy you." The implications seemed so Christian to them that, as the French reported, "they all wish to be baptized."[30]

---

[28] For emissaries sent to Fort Pitt in summer of 1760, see Croghan Journal, Indian conference, Detroit, Dec. 3, 1760, *Bouquet Papers*, 15:95. For Pontiac as one of them, see Declaration of James Grant, 24 Dec. 1763, *JP* 13:320. For Neolin's converts, see "Journal of James Kenny," 188. For whites, see Dowd, "Paths of Resistance," 303.

[29] Milo M. Quaife (ed.), *Journal of Pontiac's Conspiracy* . . . (Chicago: R. R. Donneley & Sons, 1958), 8–17.

[30] This account is from Villiers to D'Abbadie, Dec. 1, 1763, *WHC* 18:259–61.

With the rise of Neolin's popularity and the adoption of his message by Pontiac, the simmering discontent of the previous four years boiled up into rebellion. The "Master of Life," as Pontiac said, "put Arms in our hands." It was a rebellion that both derived from the traditions of the middle ground and aimed at its restoration. After more than a century of sustained contact between Indians and whites, even a seemingly nativist rebellion could arise only from the middle ground. Ideas borrowed from European culture were used to justify an ostensible return to an Algonquian past that was, in fact, a new creation on the middle ground. There was no return to a pre-European past, and it is doubtful that many desired it.[31]

This was not the restoration of tradition but, rather, its invention. As Kenny recognized, these were "new devotions" being practiced by Neolin's followers. The anthropologist Anthony Wallace selected Neolin's new religion as one of his examples of a revitalization movement: a movement of conscious and sweeping cultural change initiated to construct a more satisfying culture. And Neolin largely did conform to Wallace's criteria, even if Wallace underestimated the differences between moral and ritual reform and stressed too much the revolutionary effects of such an attempt. For in Neolin's case, at least, both his moral emphasis and his general endeavor formed part of a continuous adjustment on the middle ground.[32]

IV

In the spring of 1763, Pontiac's efforts to combine the ideologies of revolt bore fruit at Detroit, but months earlier, many British traders and the chiefs who still harbored hopes for a British alliance had sensed the future. Tamaqua grew somber and withdrawn after his return from Lancaster, Pennsylvania, to ratify the final treaty of peace with the British. His brother Shingas appeared sullen, and rumors had it that he and Weindohelas had been at Guiyahoga raising warriors against the British. People attended Neolin's ceremonies in increasing numbers, and James Kenny heard that all the Ohio Delawares had accepted the prophet's teachings. Among the Miamis, the chiefs won a bitter struggle to get the long-circulating Seneca belt away from the warriors, but their eventual success hid a larger failure. The chiefs made no mention of the Detroit belt (or the Wea belt sent by the French) that still circulated. A Shawnee chief came to Fort Pitt to warn the British of the dangers they faced and of the growing alienation of the

---

[31] Council in Illinois, Apr. 15–17, 1764, in Farmar to Gage, Dec. 21, 1764, Gage Papers.
[32] For quotation, see "Journal of James Kenny," 172; Wallace, "Revitalization Movements," 264–81.

warriors. Giving such information was not an act of treason on his part but his fulfilling his duty as an alliance chief. The British, however, not only did nothing to help him restore calm; they purposely insulted a Shawnee delegation that the chiefs had persuaded to escort prisoners to Fort Pitt in the spring of 1763. What could chiefs do when the British acted this way?[33]

Amherst chose not to heed the warnings. By the fall of 1762, the most experienced Indian traders on the Ohio River expected war. Amherst thought the plots "Meer Bugbears," and he blustered that a revolt would be the "Greatest misfortune that befall them." Nevertheless, he dispatched reinforcements to Niagara and Detroit. Johnson, seeing the revolt as a defensive response to British policies, seized the opportunity to lecture Amherst once more on the realities of the middle ground and to urge the restoration of presents. But Amherst was not about to change his policy. Indeed, he informed Johnson that he wanted a total cessation of the supplying of provisions to the Indians. If necessary, he would combat a revolt; he would not prevent it.[34]

In the late winter of 1762–1763 the Indians of the *pays d'en haut* began seriously to prepare for war. The Algonquians were desperate, but they were also, as George Croghan recognized, confident because of past military successes against the British. If the Senecas, Shawnees, and Delawares rose, Croghan warned, the others, despite their differences, would follow. He was wrong only about which group would rise against the British first.[35]

In the weeks before the outbreak at Detroit, the divisions between the Miamis and the Detroit Indians, on the one hand, and the Delawares, Shawnees, Mingos, and Senecas, on the other, began to diminish. Johnson later received reports that a message from the Senecas and the Cayugas, calling on the Detroit Indians to revolt that spring, had reached the West in March, and almost simultaneously the Mingos and Delawares supposedly had fowarded belts to the Lakes. On April 20, Major Henry Gladwin, who had reinforced and now commanded the garrison at Detroit, reported that

---

[33] For Delawares, Shingas, see "Journal of James Kenny," 172; for Shingas and Weindohelas, see McKee Journal, Nov. 23, 1762, *JP* 10:580; for Tamaqua, see "Journal of James Kenny," 168, 175; for Neolin, see *ibid.*, 171–73. For Miamis surrender belt, see Indian Speech, Mar. 30, 1763, *MPHC* 19:181–82. For Shawnee chief, see Captain Simeon Ecuyer, Indian Intelligence, Jan. 30, 1763, *Bouquet Papers*, 15:196.

   For vow to receive 100 Shawnee "beggars" coming in with 5 prisoners, very coldly, see Ecuyer to Bouquet, Apr. 9, 1763, *Bouquet Papers*, 10:96. For leave very much dissatisfied, see Ecuyer to Bouquet May 29, 1763, *Bouquet Papers*, 10:107.

[34] For traders, see "Journal of James Kenny," 169. For bugbear, see Amherst to Johnson, Apr. 3, 1763, Amherst Papers, reel 30. For reinforcements, see Orders to Captain Dalyell, Jan. 16, 1763, Amherst Papers, reel 30. For Johnson's views, see Johnson to Amherst, Jan. 21, 1763, Amherst Papers, reel 31. For Amherst's response to news, see Amherst to Bouquet, Feb. 16, 1763, *MPHC* 19:178; Amherst to Johnson, Apr. 3, 1763, Amherst Papers, reel 30.

[35] For quotation, see Croghan to Johnson, Dec. 10, 1762, *JP* 3:964–65.

the Delawares, Shawnees, and Senecas had been "tampering" with the Indians there but, he thought, without effect. A week later Pontiac called the famous council to plan his assault on the fort. In early May, the British at Pittsburgh heard that the Miamis had accepted a war belt from the Senecas and Mingos only a month after surrendering an earlier belt to Ensign Robert Holmes, who commanded the British post among them. The Detroit Indians struck first, but they believed that surrounding peoples had already determined to go to war. Pontiac, in his speech to the Detroit Indians urging them to attack, asked them to do only what their neighbors had already decided to do. Clearly, he thought himself part of a revolt that extended far beyond Detroit.[36]

Like a burning brand dragged through tinder, the war belts that runners carried from Detroit sparked other attacks in their wake. The Delawares and Shawnees sent a belt east from Pittsburgh to the Senecas around Niagara. And the Senecas, after years of urging the western Indians to follow them into a war with the British, found themselves urged to join an actual Algonquian revolt. In June, Ottawas, Chippewas, Wyandots, and Senecas took Presque Isle and Fort Le Boeuf. Other belts moved north and west. The Weas, the Miamis, the Saint Joseph Potawatomis, the Mingos at Venango – all heeded the war belts and seized the small British posts among them. The Michilimackinac Chippewas took the fort at the straits, but there the revolt halted. The Ottawas of Arbre Croche and Saint Ignace denounced the attack, redeemed the British prisoners, and escorted them to Montreal. Ottawa messengers from Detroit appeared at Fort Edward Augustus at Green Bay, but planning for the revolt had never extended that far, and the Menominees, Winnebagos, Sauks, Fox, and Iowas sent messages assuring the British of their friendship. They helped the small British garrison flee to Montreal.[37]

---

[36] For Seneca and Cayuga belt, see Rogers to Johnson, Oct. 7, 1763, *JP* 10:871–72. For Detroit, see Extract, Gladwin to Amherst, 20 Apr. 1763, *JP* 4:95. For Miamis, see "Journal of James Kenny," 196. For Mingo and Delaware belt, see Extract of Letter of Mr. McGee [McKee], Nov. 22, 1763, Amherst Papers, reel 32. The Chenussio Senecas later blamed the war on Delaware belts sent to Detroit where Pontiac used them in his own efforts, Journal of Indian Congress, Dec. 15, 1763, *JP* 10:964–65. For Pontiac's speech, see Peckham, *Pontiac*, 120.

A later declaration by M. Jadeau said that Tiata, a Huron chief, told him Pontiac was not influenced by the Seneca belts, but rather by promises of certain habitants that a French army was approaching and by his own disillusionment with the English, Declaration by M. Jadeau, Apr. 5, 1764, enclosure with Gladwin to Gage, May 12, 1764, Gage Papers, AS 18.

[37] Couagne to Johnson, June 6, 1763, *JP* 4:137. Peckham, *Pontiac*, 112–242, provides a narrative of the revolt as does Parkman. For Ottawa and Chippewa actions at Michilimackinac, see Extract, Etherington to Gladwin, June 12, 1763, *JP* 10:695. For Presque Isle, Declaration of Benjamin Gray, June 22, 1763, *Bouquet Papers*, 10:176; Christie to Bouquet, July 10, 1763, *Bouquet Papers*, 10:211. For other attacks, see MacDonald to Bouquet, July 12, 1763, *MPHC* 19:216–17. For Venango, see Johnson to Amherst, July 7, 1763, Amherst Papers,

Compared to the prolonged struggles and rebellions of the French period, this rebellion flared more hotly and burned out more quickly. It was a war of great brutality and small kindnesses. At Detroit, Pontiac seized Captain Campbell under a flag of truce, and a month later, Wasson, a Chippewa war leader from Saginaw, had him gruesomely tortured and killed in revenge for the death of Wasson's nephew. The Indians ruthlessly killed many soldiers and traders; they spared and adopted others. Once more they fell on the frontiers, where by September the Pennsylvanians had lost six hundred persons. Amherst called on his troops to take no prisoners and recommended to Bouquet that smallpox blankets be placed where they might fall into Indian hands. Bouquet agreed and added the suggestion of imitating the Spanish and hunting the Indians with bloodhounds to "extirpate or remove that vermin." But it is notable, too, that the usual cruelties of Algonquian warfare no longer went unquestioned by the Algonquians themselves. The Chippewas of Michilimackinac denounced Pontiac for his cruelties saying that they violated the wishes of the master of life.[38]

The rebellion failed in its goal of evicting the British: Detroit, Fort Pitt, and Niagara held out. When both Pontiac and the Delawares, Shawnees, and Mingos who were besieging Fort Pitt separately asked the French commander at Fort Chartres in Illinois country for aid, they received only a demand that they stop fighting and an invitation to retire across the Mississippi and live under French protection. The siege of Detroit collapsed in the early fall, and Wabbicomigot, a Mississauga leader, began to negotiate for peace. Late in October, Pontiac himself dispatched a letter to Major Henry Gladwin, the commander at Detroit, saying that he accepted the talk his father in Illinois country had sent him. He was ready for peace.[39]

reel 31. Michilimackinac Ottawas and Green Bay Tribes Indian Conference, Aug. 9–11, 1763, *JP* 10:779–86.

[38] For Ottawa killing of prisoners, see Gladwin to Amherst, May 28, 1763, Amherst Papers, 2:5, Clements Library. For smallpox and dogs, see Bouquet to Amherst, July 15, 1763, Amherst Papers, reel 32. In December Gladwin received reports that the Delawares had lost 200 people to smallpox, Gladwin to Moncrieffe, Dec. 3, 1763, Amherst Papers, Clements Library. For take no prisoners, see Amherst to Bouquet, June 29, 1763, Amherst Papers, reel 33. For English lose 600 on frontier, see Bouquet to Hamilton, *Bouquet Papers*, Sept. 12, 1763, 11:48.

[39] Supposedly some of the French at Detroit told the Indians that a French army was advancing to their aid up the Mississippi, Johnson to Amherst, July 30, 1763; *NYCD* 7:533. Others, seconded by Montreal traders, placed the army and fleet in the River Saint Lawrence, Gladwin to Amherst, July 8, 1763, Amherst Papers, 2:6, Clements Library; Amherst to Gage, Aug. 1, 1763, Amherst Papers, 6:56, Clements Library. For Indian belief in promises of French aid, see Deposition of John Segar, Oct. 12, 1763, Court of Inquiry, Gage Papers, AS 15.

For Pontiac's request for aid and powder, see Deposition du nommé Charlot, Reponse, 27 oct. 1763, AN, C11A, v. 105. For Delaware request, see Parole des Iroquois, Loups et Chaouanons . . . 2 nov. 1763, AN, C11A, v. 105, f. 410; for refusal, see Noyan de Villiers à Gladwin, 27 sept. 1763, Amherst Papers, Clements Library; Noyan de Villiers, Proclama-

The result was a stalemate. Colonel Bouquet, marching to relieve Fort Pitt, defeated the Delawares, Shawnees, and Mingos at Bushy Run, but his initial dispatches hardly made the results seem like a victory. He was unable to follow up on his success and feared that an advance of any distance greater than a mile from Fort Pitt would lead to his total destruction. Bouquet's victory, in any case, was followed by a more costly British defeat when the Senecas ambushed the British at Niagara. Amherst continued to rave against the Indians, denouncing them for being "only fit to Live with the Inhabitants of the Woods, being more nearly allied to the brute than to the Human creation," but he could not "teach the whole race" the lesson he wished in 1763. Gladwin, for his part, said he needed at least fifteen hundred troops at Detroit to do anything effective, and even they could not act until the next spring.[40]

V

The military stalemate at the end of 1763 became an ideological stalemate. The British had not reduced the Algonquians to subjects. Amherst's return to England in November 1763, his policies condemned by the lords of trade, marked both his own failure and the larger failure of British policy. His successor, General Thomas Gage, and William Johnson were more interested in repairing the damage Amherst's policies had caused than in conquering the Indians. Gage admitted that the Indians, in opposing the British, "have acted upon principles of policy which would have excited more enlightened Nations," and he was willing to compromise with them in order to secure a peace. The opposing ideologies of the Algonquians had fared no better. Onontio had not returned; Neolin's dream of a return to an imagined older life had not brought that life into being. The British remained.[41]

tion, Sept. 27, 1763, Amherst Papers, Clements Library. See also De Villiers to D'Abbadie, Dec. 1, 1763, *IHC* 10:49–57. For powder, see Gladwin to Moncrieffe, Dec. 3, 1763, Amherst Papers, Clements Library.

For end of siege, see Peckham, *Pontiac*, 229–42. Pontiac's note and Gladwin's response of Oct. 30, in Gladwin to Amherst, Nov. 1, 1763, Amherst Papers, Clements Library. A copy of Pontiac's note is reproduced in Peckham, *Pontiac*, facing 236.

[40] For Bushy Run, see Bouquet to Amherst, Aug. 5, 1763, Amherst Papers, reel 32. For inability to attack, see Bouquet to Amherst, Oct. 24, 1763, *MPHC* 19:230–31. For ravings, see Amherst to Bouquet, Aug. 7, 1763, Amherst Papers, reel 33. For cannot teach lesson, see Amherst to Johnson, Sept. 30, 1763, Amherst Papers, reel 30. For Niagara, see Johnson to Amherst, Sept. 30, 1763, *JP* 4:209–11. For Gladwin, see Gladwin to Amherst, Aug. 10, 1763, and Oct. 7, 1763, Amherst Papers, 2:9 and 2:18, Clements Library.

[41] For return and repudiation of Amherst, see Peckham, *Pontiac*, 242; Croghan to Johnson, Feb. 24, 1763, *JP* 4:339. For quotation on policy, see Gage to Johnson, Jan. 12, 1764, *JP* 4:291. For compromise, see Gage to Johnson, Mar. 4, 1764, *JP* 4:355.

The acceptance of these ideological failures was admittedly not immediate. There were British officials who still demanded the conquest of Indians. There were French and Algonquians who still remained ready to welcome an Onontio who would surely come. But the initiative was gradually shifting to those who recognized failure and desired accommodation. Sir William Johnson, chief among the British accommodationists, half persuaded Thomas Gage that further fighting was unnecessary and useless. Despite Indian protestations of poverty, Johnson believe that the Algonquians were quite capable of continuing the war. They had lost few persons, and between the ammunition gained from plunder and that supplied by French traders, the western Indians had enough powder and balls to fight. Gage was more willing to believe that the Indians desperately needed a restoration of trade to survive, but he agreed with Johnson on a second reason for seeking peace: the difficulty of waging war in the West. As George Croghan pointed out to the lords of trade, victories by British troops consisted of burning some thatch huts and cornfields. Small triumphs came at the risk of ambush and catastrophic defeat. Even when British soldiers defeated Indians in battle, they won only a Pyrrhic victory for they destroyed the fur trade and drove the Indians farther west whence they could still fall on the undefended colonial frontiers. The third reason for seeking peace was the cost of waging the Indian wars. Amherst's cutting of Indian presents and the military aggressiveness in occupying the posts had turned out to be false economies, since maintaining the posts and fighting a war had cost the British treasury far more than conciliating the Indians would have. The final reason, at least initially, was fear that the Indians of the *pays d'en haut* would cross the Mississippi to settle with the French and provide a bulwark for Britain's enemies. When news of the cession of Louisiana to Spain reached Gage, he was elated. Both he and Johnson now anticipated an eventual French withdrawal, and they minimized the danger of an effective Indian alliance with the Spanish.[42]

---

[42] Gage was more inclined than Johnson to demand satisfaction and to doubt the ability of the Indians to continue their resistance, Gage to Johnson, Jan. 23, 1764, *JP* 4:302–4; Gage to Johnson, Feb. 6, 1764, *JP* 4:318–19; Gage to Johnson, Feb. 20, 1764, *JP* 4:334–35; Gage to Johnson, Apr. 30, 1764, *JP* 11:167–68. But he too was ready for peace, Gage to Halifax, July 13, 1764, *IHC* 10:282–85. For Johnson's assessment of Indian strength, see Johnson to Lords of Trade, Jan. 20, 1764, *NYCD* 7:599. The Indians had captured a three-year supply of powder at Michilimackinac (Gladwin to Amherst, Jan. 20, 1764, Amherst Papers 7:113, Clements Library), and they were apparently getting powder from the Illinois, Landoc's Declaration, June 4, 1764, in Gladwin to Gage, June 11, 1764, Gage Papers, AS 20; Croghan to Johnson, May 13, 1765, *JP* 11:737–38. For fear of Indian withdrawal, *ibid.*; Johnson to Gage, Jan. 12, 1764, *JP* 4:295–96. For destruction of trade, see Johnson to Lords of Trade Jan. 20, 1764, *NYCD* 7:600. For news of cession of Louisiana, see Gage to Johnson, Jan. 23, 1764, *JP* 4:303–4. For threat, see Johnson to Gage, Feb. 3, 1764, *JP* 11:36; Gage to Johnson, May 28, 1764, *JP* 4:434. The French, too, thought the Indians

Accommodation between the British and the Algonquians came, however, only after several years of additional diplomatic and military sparring. Johnson held peace conferences at Niagara, but agreements were secured only with the Chenussio Senecas and the Catholic Huron-Petuns of Detroit. Most of those attending his conferences were people who had refused to join in the war. The great bulk of the anti-British confederacy, despite earlier peace overtures, seemingly remained at war.[43]

In this atmosphere of uncertainty, the British dispatched two armies to the *pays d'en haut* on a rather quixotic mission of conquest. Gage allowed the commanders a great deal of discretion as to whether they should attack the Indians or conclude peace with them. The first army, under Colonel John Bradstreet, waited until Johnson's Niagara conference had concluded and then in early August moved west along Lake Erie. The second, under Colonel Henry Bouquet, was to proceed to the Ohio River as soon as Bouquet succeeded in raising troops in Pennsylvania and Virginia.

The result of these parallel efforts to seek peace without abandoning the war was nearly total confusion. Bradstreet, while vocal in his desire to attack Indians, lacked confidence in the twelve hundred men under his command and distrusted the Indians – Iroquois, Caughnawagas, and Chippewas – whom Johnson had secured to escort him. When, even before leaving Niagara, Bradstreet received word from Gladwin that parties of the Detroit Potawatomis, the Sandusky Wyandots, and even Pontiac's Ottawas, who had retreated to the Maumee River, had asked for peace, he decided that assaulting the Indians was not advisable. On August 12 he met a small delegation of Shawnees, Mingos, Delawares, and Wyandots east of Presque Isle. Despite the warnings of his Iroquois escort that these Indians were spies, Bradstreet negotiated a preliminary treaty with them.[44]

unlikely to ally themselves to the Spanish because of Spanish mistreatment of Indians elsewhere, Aubry to Minister Feb. 4, 1765, *IHC* 10:431. For George Croghan's arguments to the lords of trade, see Croghan to Lords of Trade, June 8, 1764, *IHC* 10:256–63. Johnson was willing to put the blame for the war on the French, Johnson to Lords of Trade, Jan. 20, 1764, *NYCD* 7:599.

[43] There were Chippewas from near Michilimackinac and Mississaugas from Toronto present at Niagara; whether they represented people who had been involved in the fighting is not clear, An Indian Congress, Niagara, July 17 – Aug. 4, 1764, *JP* 11:285. Gage himself was unsure as to whether the Chippewa and Mississauga delegates represented those who had been at war with the English, Gage to Johnson, Aug. 15, 1764, *JP* 4:509.

[44] Pontiac initially was absent in the Illinois country. For composition of his army, see Lawrence Henry Gipson, *The British Empire Before the American Revolution* (New York: Alfred A. Knopf, 1942), 9:117. For Bradstreet's evaluation, see Bradstreet to Gage, July 12, 1764, Gage Papers, AS 21. For these peace overtures, see Gladwin to Bradstreet, July 12, 1764, in Bradstreet to Gage, July 12, 1764; Bradstreet to Gage, Aug. 5, 1764; Gladwin to Bradstreet, July 28, 1764, in Bradstreet to Gage, Aug. 5, 1764, all in Gage Papers, AS 22. Johnson to Gage, Aug. 5, 1764, *JP* 11:324–25. For location of encounter, see Bradstreet to Gage, Nov. 4, 1764, Gage Papers, AS 26. For believed to be spies, see Coghnowagey & Ganughsadagey, Peter Spencer, Dec. 2–16, *JP* 11:507.

In early September, Bradstreet held a council at Detroit with various representatives of the Ottawas, Chippewas, Shawnees, and Wyandots from Sandusky, and a delegation of Miamis observed the proceedings. Potawatomis from Saint Joseph, some Mississaugas, and Chippewas from Saginaw arrived too late for the council but were clearly interested in peace. Pontiac, fearful of Bradstreet's intentions, did not attend. Bradstreet then proceeded to Sandusky to await the Ohio Shawnees, Delawares, and Mingos who were to bring in their prisoners and ratify a final peace. They never arrived.[45]

Gage disavowed Bradstreet's treaty with the Wyandots, Delawares, and Shawnees, who, it turned out, were as ambivalent about peace as the British. The Shawnees and Delawares later claimed that their chiefs did not go to meet Bradstreet because they were fearful of leaving home with Bouquet's army approaching, but this is questionable. In fact, many Shawnee chiefs could not meet Bradstreet, because they had already departed to see the French at the Illinois River in order to seek aid to continue the war. The French commander refused them aid, but the habitants and traders at the Illinois welcomed them, and French traders accompanied them home.[46]

[45] For Pontiac sends belt, see G. D. Scull (ed.), "The Montresor Journals," *Collections of the New York Historical Society for the Year 1881* (New York: New York Historical Society, 1882), 281. There is a copy of Bradstreet's negotiations of Aug. 12, 1764, in Frontier Wars, Draper Manuscripts, Wisconsin Historical Society. It is also printed in *JP* 11:328–33.

For councils, see Scull (ed.), "Montresor Journals," 287–90; Congress with Western Nations, Sept. 7–10, 1764, *JP* 11:348–55. Gage accused the Shawnee-Delaware-Wyandot delegation of being spies, Gage to Johnson, Sept. 4, 1764, *JP* 4:524–25. Gage was apparently right that the delegation had no more power than Bradstreet to secure a peace, but then all Bradstreet offered them was the opportunity to bring the chiefs in to make peace.

[46] For the lengthy Gage-Bradstreet controversy over his treaties, see Gage's denunciation, Gage to Bradstreet, Sept. 2, 1764, Gage Papers, AS 24; Gage to Bradstreet, Oct. 15, 1764, *IHC* 10:344–46. For quotation and definite orders to attack Shawnees and Delawares, see Gage to Bradstreet, Aug. 16, 1764, Gage Papers, AS 23. Johnson had news of peace overtures from Pontiac and wrote optimistically to Gage of establishing peace, Johnson to Gage, Aug. 5, 1764, *JP* 11:325–26. Gage thought that the peace overtures of the Wyandots, Chippewas, and Ottawas prevented Bradstreet from attacking them, Gage to Johnson, Aug. 15, 1764, *JP* 4:508–9. Why peace overtures from the Shawnees and Delawares should likewise prevent an attack was never made clear to Bradstreet.

Gage on August 18, before receiving news of Bradstreet's actions, wrote Bouquet: "It remains with him [Bradstreet] to make a formal peace with those Nations [Detroit], and he has orders unless he brings them to peace which to appearance shall be safe & lasting to fall on them," Gage to Bouquet, *MPHC* 19:270. Johnson in a letter to Gage of Sept. 1, 1764, expressed the ambivalent policy that trapped Bradstreet: "I apprehend tha Pondiac will follow the Example of the rest, as also all the Shaw^se & Del^s. Whom I w^d. rather wish severly punished (*which must prove a disappointment to the Army, if C. Bradstreet is obliged to accept their submission*)." Italicized portion crossed out in the original, Johnson to Gage, Sept. 1, 1764, *JP* 4:518–19.

Gage eventually insisted Bradstreet was authorized to offer peace but that this did not enable him to negotiate the terms of peace, Gage to Bradstreet, Sept. 2, 1764, Gage Papers, AS 24. Gage sent a copy of the negotiations to Johnson on the same day, Gage to Johnson, Sept. 2, 1764, *JP* 11:342–45.

Gage was particularly angry because of continuing attacks on the frontier, although he

Bouquet, after many difficulties in recruiting troops, did succeed where Bradstreet had failed: He secured a truce with the Ohio Indians. Bouquet did not even leave Fort Pitt with his small army of fifteen hundred men until October 1, but even that late in the year he managed to march them onto the Scioto Plains, an area at the center of the new Delaware, Mingo, and Shawnee villages. He negotiated a peace whose terms were not dissimilar to those demanded by Bradstreet and denounced by Gage. Gage desired the execution of the Shawnee and Delaware leaders responsible for the war, but Bouquet, like Bradstreet, chose to ignore this requirement. The major difference between Bradstreet's treaty and Bouquet's truce was that the Delawares and Mingos (but not the Shawnees) actually surrendered to Bouquet the prisoners whom they had only promised to Bradstreet, and they all agreed to meet with Johnson in the spring. All the Indians party to the treaty surrendered hostages to guarantee their participation in the final peace negotiations with Sir William Johnson.[47]

Bouquet's and Bradstreet's expeditions gave the Algonquians warning of

admitted that Bradstreet could have no knowledge of Delaware-Shawnee attacks, Gage to Earl of Halifax, Sept. 21, 1764, *NYCD* 7:655. Bradstreet wrote two long letters in his defense, Bradstreet to Gage, Sept. 29, 1764, Gage Papers, AS 25. Bradstreet to Gage, Nov. 4, 1764, Gage Papers, AS 26. Compare to Bouquet, Gage to Johnson, Dec. 6, 1764, *JP* 11:496–98.

For proposed visit of Shawnee and Delaware chiefs, see St. Ange to D'Abbadie, Aug. 12, 1764, *IHC* 10:295; St. Ange to D'Abbadie, Nov. 9, 1764, *IHC* 10:356–57. Charlot Kaské, "beloved man of the Shawnee Nation," left this delegation to go see D'Abbadie himself in New Orleans, *ibid.* For audience with D'Abbadie, see Journal of D'Abbadie, Dec. 20, 1764, *IHC* 10:203–4. D'Abbadie died soon after and Charlot Kaské finished his negotiations with Charles Philippe Aubry, his successor.

For secondhand account of their reception, see Croghan to Gage, Mar. 2, 1765, Gage Papers, AS 31; Journal of Indian Affairs, Mar. 2, 1765, *JP* 11:617. Shawnee cite Bouquet as reason for failing to appear and surrender prisoners, Indian Proceedings Oct. 20, 1764, *JP* 11:442.

[47] In recruiting, Bouquet found that although Pennsylvania offered a scalp bounty to spur enlistments, the settlers of western Pennsylvania were more eager to slaughter the peaceful Indians among them than to go to war. Bouquet sneered that they found "it easier to kill Indian in a goal [jail] than to fight them fairly in the woods." For Paxton Boys, see Peckham, *Pontiac*, 219. For scalp bounties, see Proclamation of John Penn, July 7, 1764, Ayer Collection, Newberry Library; Bouquet to Gage, June 7, 1764, *MPHC* 19:268. For troops, see Gipson, *British Empire*, 9:115–16.

For Bouquet's negotiations, see Conference of Henry Bouquet with the Indians of the Ohio, Oct. 16, 1764, HM 569, Huntington Library, and An Historical Account of Colonel Bouquet's Expedition Against the Ohio Indians in the Year 1764. Neville B. Craig, Esq. (ed.), *The Olden Time*, 2 vols. (Pittsburgh: Dumars, 1846, Millwood, N.Y.: Kraus Reprint 1976) 1:217–21, 241–61. A partial account is in Indian Proceedings, Oct. 13 – Nov. 16, 1764, *JP* 11:435–69. Gage twice had ordered Bouquet to "deliver the Promoters of the War into your hands to be put to death," but Bouquet never secured the war leaders. Bouquet did, however, draw up a list of those he wished to secure; among them was Neolin ("The Prist Delaware Negowland"), Memo, Sept. 22, 1764, *Bouquet Papers*, 13:142. Gage to Bouquet, Sept. 2, 1764, *MPHC* 19:272–73; Gage to Bouquet, Oct. 15, 1764, *MPHC* 19:277. For Bouquet's terms, see Bouquet to Gage, Nov. 15, 1764, *MPHC* 19:280.

the British ability to continue the war and carry it into their own country; they thus strengthened the position of those urging accommodation. But the expeditions had not established the terms of accommodation let alone reduced the Indians to subjection. When Bradstreet submitted the treaty he had negotiated at Detroit, Johnson was aghast. In the treaty Bradstreet asserted British sovereignty over the Indians. The expressions of subjection must, Johnson thought,

> have arisen from the ignorance of the Interpreter or from some other mistake; for I am well convinced that they never mean or intend, any thing like it, and that they cannot be brought under our Laws, for some Centuries, neither have they any word which can convey the most distant idea of subjection, and should it be fully explained to them, and the nature of subordination punishment etc., defined, it might produce infinite harm.

From Johnson's perspective the expeditions had, at the most, helped fragment the confederacy that had assaulted the British in 1763 and whose continuation would make the Algonquians, in Johnson's words, "very dangerous neighbors."[48]

The negotiations had unleashed an often bitter and divisive competition among village leaders who saw in negotiations with the British the possibility of restoring the old alliance chieftainships. Tamaqua and Custaloga, aided by Neolin, sought to make themselves intermediaries between the British and the Delawares as a whole and intermediaries between the British and the other villages of the *pays d'en haut*. They succeeded neither with their own people nor with the British.

Many warriors denounced Custologa, now the leading peace advocate, as an old woman. Most waited to see what terms Killbuck (or Bemino), the emissary sent to Sir William Johnson, was offered before firmly committing themselves to peace. The Delawares remained so bitterly divided that in negotiations with George Croghan at Fort Pitt in the spring of 1765, two war leaders quarreled violently in council "& stabb'd each other, in such a manner that their Lives are despaired of." Such violence was unheard of in council deliberations. Johnson and Croghan, meanwhile, refused to

---

[48] For sovereignty, see Congress with Western Nations, Sept. 7–10, 1764, *JP* 4:532–33; Johnson to Lords of Trade, Oct. 30, 1764, *NYCD* 7:674; Johnson to Gage, Oct. 31, 1764, *JP* 11:395; Johnson to Colden, Dec. 11, 1764, *JP* 4:616. For Croghan's assessment, see Croghan to Johnson, July 12, 1764, *JP* 4:462–64. For destroy confederacy, see Johnson to Gage, Jan. 12, 1764, *JP* 4:296; Johnson to Lords of Trade, Jan. 20, 1764, *NYCD* 7:599.

Johnson had put forward his position that the Indians were unconquered and sovereign quite forcefully in an earlier letter, Johnson to Lords of Trade, Nov. 13, 1763, *NYCD* 7:572–81. They were he thought "the most formidable of any uncivilized body of people in the World" (574).

countenance Neolin's ploy of allowing the Quakers to meddle in the peace
settlement. They also realized that the attempt of the Delaware chiefs to set
themselves up as mediators divided the Ohio peoples and actually delayed
negotiations.[49]

In practice, as the British gradually discovered, a secure peace among the
villages of the Great Lakes could not arrive from negotiations with any
set of "chiefs." Not even the rivals for influence within the villages claimed
so much. Although the Shawnee warriors negotiated an agreement with
Bouquet, they did not immediately act to fulfill it, being "unwilling to take so
much upon them in their [the chiefs'] absence." As Louis Chevallier, a
Frenchman residing at Saint Joseph explained to the British, "to make a
Solid Peace it was necessary that all the Chiefs of the Village and War
Chiefs" should be present.[50]

The great irony of Bradstreet's and Bouquet's negotiations of 1764 was
that since the negotiations were in and of themselves incapable of creating an
accommodation in the *pays d'en haut*, they increased the influence, in British
eyes, of those who refused to negotiate. If the agreements at Detroit and the
Scioto River had not calmed the Algonquians, then those who had not
negotiated must hold the real power. The British increasingly identified
Pontiac as the holder of this power. A local war leader, defeated at Detroit, a
man whose surrender and exile were initial conditions of peace, emerged by
the end of 1764 as the most significant figure in the entire *pays d'en haut*.
This was not simply due to his own considerable abilities. It was also a result
of British policy, which in a belated attempt to come to grips with the
political realities of the *pays d'en haut*, brought out these abilities.

Pontiac had lost influence among the Detroit villagers following the failure
of the siege at Detroit, but he gained it elsewhere. Precisely because neither
the world of the *pays d'en haut* nor the struggle against the British was

---

[49] For hopes to be mediators, see Croghan to Johnson, May 12, 1765, *JP* 11:736; Intelligence
Received from Kayashuta, May 9, 1765, in Croghan to Gage, May 12, 1765, Gage Papers,
AS 36; Murray to Gage, May 12, 1765, Gage Papers, AS 36. For Neolin, see Croghan's
Journal, Apr. 1, 1765, Apr. 29–30, 1765, *IHC* 10:4, 7–8. Neolin acted as an intermediary
with the English thereafter; see Intelligence Received from Neoland, July 15, 1765, Gage
Papers, AS 39. For Bouquet, see Conference of Henry Bouquet with the Indians of the
Ohio, Oct. 16, 1764, HM 569, Huntington Library. Croghan learned that two tribes (or
phratries) of the Delawares were averse to making peace, Croghan's Journal, Apr. 14, 1763,
IHC 10:5. Only Custaloga and his tribe were well disposed, Croghan to Gage, May 12,
1765, Gage Papers, AS 36. For fight in council, see May 1, 1765, *ibid.*, 8. For Killbuck, see
Proceedings of . . . Johnson with the . . . Six Nations & Delawares, May 7, 1765, *NYCD*
7:731. Killbuck was a member of the Turkey phratry. Treaty of Peace, May 1765, *NYCD*
7:741. The phratry chiefs were Custaloga, Tamaqua, and Teatapercaum (or Samuel).
[50] For Shawnees, see Journal of Indian Affairs, Mar. 2, 1765, *JP* 11:617; Chevalier to
Campbell, Nov. 23, 1763, Gage Papers, AS 30. The Wabash and Illinois Indians similarly
said no answer could be given on peace belts sent by Bradstreet until war chiefs as well as
civil leaders were present in council, Court of Enquiry, Feb. 21, 1765, Gage Papers, AS 31.

exclusively tribal or local, his defeat at Detroit was not final. By 1764, Pontiac had clearly become more than an Ottawa war chief. George Croghan would later claim that Pontiac "commands more respect among those Nations (i.e., the Wabash villages), than any Indian I ever saw could do amongst his own Tribe." Pontiac retained an Ottawa following in the villages along the Maumee River, but, in the tradition of the rebel chiefs, his power was not tribally based. Pontiac claimed to speak for a larger common cause. The belts he conveyed listed not tribes or nations but the villages that followed him. The British initially thought in terms of making peace with tribes, but Pontiac recognized that his world was a shifting set of factional alliances that transcended villages and tribes. In April 1764, Neyon de Villiers, commanding Fort Chartres in Illinois country, reported to Governor D'Abbadie in New Orleans that Pontiac, who had relatives among the Illinois, had undone in an hour his eight months of work in resigning the Illinois Indians to a British occupation. Pontiac made them part of the "common cause" of the Indians of the *pays d'en haut* against the British, and he fortified the resolve of the Wabash Indians, who said they "preferred dying to making peace with the British."[51]

Pontiac also continued to find critical allies among the French. By 1764 many French habitants of Detroit were more than ready for peace with the British, but others joined the habitants of the Illinois country, those of Vincennes, and numerous Canadian traders in continued resistance. They became an almost independent force that was beyond the control of the French commanders of Fort Chartres. The traders fed Algonquians' hopes of Onontio's return, and they supplied them with powder, ball, and trade

---

[51] Croghan to Johnson, Nov. 1765, *IHC* 11:53. Ponitac had a 40-year-old belt showing 210 villages, Journal of Captain Thomas Morris, 1764, in Thwaites (ed.), *Early Western Travels*, 1:309. Charlot Kaské's belt had 47 villages supposedly loyal to Pontiac, Journal of D'Abbadie, Dec. 20, 1764, *IHC* 10:203–4. For Pontiac in Illinois, see Villiers to D'Abbadie, Apr. 20, 1764, *IHC* 10:242; Villiers to Loftus, 20 Apr., 1764, *ibid.*, 244. In late 1763 Pontiac was still resolved on war and apparently had adherents among the Wisconsin tribes, Extrait de la lettre de M. de Neyon . . . à M. D'Abbadie, 27 dec. 1763, in Halifax to Gage, July 14, 1764, Gage Papers, ES 2; Extrait de la lettre de M. de Neyon . . . à M. D'Abbadie du 15 jan. 1764 in Halifax to Gage, July 14, 1764, ES 2, Clements Library. Pontiac by 1764 had convinced the Illinois to take part in the "common cause" of all the Indians of the *pays d'en haut*, Extrait de la lettre de M. de St. Ange . . . à M. D'Abbadie, enclosure in D'Abbadie à Gage, Aug. 16, 1764, Gage Papers, AS 23, Clements Library. For Wabash Indians, see Saint Ange to D'Abbadie, July 15, 1764, *IHC* 10:290. St. Ange said that the major Indian efforts in 1764 went toward strengthening and enlarging their alliance, St. Ange to Aubry, Nov. 9, 1764, *IHC* 10:359–60. For extension beyond Mississippi and resolution of Illinois, see Extrait de la lettre ecrit à M. le Duc de Choiseul le l avril 1764 par M. D'Abbadie in Halifax to Gage, July 14, 1764, Gage Papers, ES 2; St. Ange to D'Abbadie, April 7, 1765, *IHC* 10:469; Council at the house of M. de St. Ange, Apr. 4, 1765, *ibid.*, 477. For relatives, see Reponse de Pondiac . . . 10 mai 1768, in Turnbull to Gage June 14, 1768, Gage Papers 77.

goods. Their goal was to block the British occupation of the Illinois and Wabash country and to maintain it as a de facto French-Algonquian island in the midst of the British empire.[52]

Pontiac, as an agent of this "common cause," continued to define it as a joint French-Algonquian enterprise. In 1764 and 1765, he traveled widely across the *pays d'en haut*, cementing the commitment of the Wabash and Illinois villages to resist British occupation. As at Detroit, he claimed to be acting for the benefit of his French father, but the French commanders at Fort Chartres feared that any attempt to refuse the Indians small gifts or to resist Pontiac would lead to attacks on the French. Pontiac had, in effect, made loyalty to the Algonquian resistance the defining quality of "Frenchness," for any Frenchman who resisted him had almost by definition become an Englishman.[53]

Pontiac, in the manner of the old republicans, thus had created a real, if always tenuous, power base within the villages of the Wabash and the Illinois, but the British magnified this power. They made Pontiac the key to the peace that eluded them. A man whom they had initially scorned and sought to diminish they eventually elevated to nearly superhuman status. At Detroit in September 1764, Bradstreet had believed that Pontiac was a broken man. This proved to be a costly illusion. Bradstreet had abandoned his demand that Pontiac surrender and go into permanent exile (at British expense) as a condition of peace, but he had disdainfully chopped apart the peace belt that Pontiac had sent him. Such an act, roughly equivalent to a European ambassador's urinating on a proposed treaty, had shocked and

---

[52] Despite French denials, the English continued to suspect that the French officially encouraged the Indians. Gage singled out the activities of St. Vincent (who was among the Maumee Ottawas when Bradstreet's emissary, Capt. Morris, was captured) and Chabert Jonquière, whom he accused of participating in attacks on the English frontiers, Gage à D'Abbadie, 10 jan. 1765, Gage Papers, AS 30. The British emissary, Lieutenant John Ross, sent up from New Orleans initially blamed St. Ange for Indian resistance (Ross to Farmar, Feb. 21, 1765, in Farmar to Gage Mar. 24, 1765, Gage Papers, AS 32), but he later praised St. Ange and thought the traders acted on their own, copy of letter from Lieutenant Ross, May 25, 1765, *IHC* 10:481–83. For French denials, see Halifax to Gage with enclosures, July 14, 1764, Gage Papers, ES 2. Also see D'Abbadie à Gage, 26 sept. 1764, Gage Papers, AS 24, Clements Library.

Villiers felt threatened as early as the end of 1763, Journal of D'Abbadie, *IHC* 10:170–71. St. Ange complained that he could not control the traders, nor protect Fort Chartres against an Indian attack, Fraser to Gage, Apr. 27, 1765, Gage Papers, AS 137. The small tribes of the Mississippi attacked an English convoy attempting to go to the Illinois and blocked access from that region. For statement of anti-English position of these peoples, see Extract of letter of M. Desmazellieres to D'Abbadie, March 14, 1764, *IHC* 10:236.

[53] Villiers to D'Abbadie, Apr. 20, 1764, *IHC* 10:242. For French fear assaults in Illinois, see Aubry to Minister, Feb. 25, 1765, *IHC* 10:457; Extrait de la lettre de M. Neyon ... à M. D'Abbadie du 15 jan. 1764, in Halifax to Gage, July 14, 1764, ES 2, Clements Library. For Indian anger at St. Ange for speaking in behalf of English, see Letter of Lt. Ross, May 25, 1765, *IHC* 10:482.

angered the gathered Indians. It had also apparently convinced Pontiac that he had nothing to gain from negotiations with the British.[54]

One of Bradstreet's own subordinates soon disabused him of his illusions about the decline of Pontiac. In late August, Bradstreet had dispatched Captain Thomas Morris, under Indian and French escort, to go to the Illinois country and arrange its peaceful capitulation to the British. Morris never got beyond the Miami villages, but during his journey, he discovered firsthand how complicated the politics in the Maumee and Miami villages had become. With Bouquet not yet on the march, Shawnee and Delaware messengers circulated war belts across the *pays d'en haut*. French traders spread rumors of an approaching French army, and Algonquian warriors along the Maumee River and in the Wabash country remained hostile and angry. Although Attawang, the headman of Roche de Bout, one of the villages on the Maumee, had already entered into negotiations with the British and was part of Morris's Indian escort, he was unable to protect Morris in his own village. Drunken Ottawa warriors forced the captain to flee into a cornfield in order to save his life. Later, among the Miamis, two warriors actually tied Morris to the torture stake before Pacane, "king of the Miamis nation, and just out of his minority," shamed them into releasing him.[55]

Morris was a soldier of remarkable equanimity and detachment. Among the Miamis he sat in a canoe reading a volume of Shakespeare, the gift of Attawang, while angry warriors demanded that his escort surrender him. He was able to put aside his mistreatment and evaluate his experience with dispassion. Pontiac, Morris believed, was ready for peace. He wrote Bradstreet that Pontiac appeared "quite tractable" and urged the colonel – too late, as it turned out – to dismiss all thought of violent measures. He warned that "people driven to despair are capable of everything and that by leaving room for repentance we often make a zealous Friend of an inveterate enemy." He urged a general pardon and suggested that "Pondiac might

---

[54] For exile of Pontiac, see Bradstreet to Gage, Aug. 28, 1764, Gage Papers, AS 23. For destroys belt, see Remarks on Conduct of Bradstreet, Nov. 24, 1764, *JP* 4:601; Gage to Bouquet, Dec. 7, 1764, *MPHC* 19:287–88; Journal of Indian Affairs, Dec. 30, 1764, *JP* 11:515.

[55] For orders to Morris, see Bradstreet to Morris, Aug. 26, 1764, in Bradstreet to Gage, Gage Papers, AS 23. For Morris's account, see Morris Journal, Thwaites (ed.), *EWT* 1:301–19; Morris to Bradstreet, Aug. 31, 1764, in Bradstreet to Gage, Sept. 12, 1764, Gage Papers, AS 24. The Miamis acted before the observers at the congress at Detroit returned to the villages, Scull (ed.), "Montresor Journals," 298. They contended they would not have molested Morris if they had known of the negotiations at Detroit, Testimony of Thomas King, Oct. 3, 1764, *JP* 4:553.

The English treated Delaware emissaries little better. They seized two Delawares, one of them Captain Pipe, when he visited Fort Pitt, Reid to Bouquet, Sept. 18, 1764, *Bouquet Papers*, 12, 139.

be made a faithful Subject of the King of England and become of infinite Service." Morris may have overestimated Pontiac's current inclination toward peace, for the Ottawa had just sent a six-foot-long belt through the *pays d'en haut* to strengthen and expand the confederation against the British. But he had predicted the future drift of Pontiac's policy.[56]

Morris's letter fed Johnson's and Gage's growing conviction that Pontiac, rather than expensive military expeditions into the *pays d'en haut*, was the key to peace. Gage thought him "not only . . . a Savage, possessed of the most refined Cunning and treachery natural to the Indians, but . . . a Person of extraordinary Abilities." And Johnson agreed: "This fellow shou'd be gained to our Interest or knocked in the head. He has great Abilities, but his Savage Cruelty destroys the regard we Should otherwise have for him." Particularly after Bouquet's truce with the Shawnees and Delawares, Pontiac seemed the critical final element in making the peace secure and in making the British occupation of the Illinois country possible.[57]

VI

Even as Pontiac became the partial creation of British policy, he was also a man following a clearly Algonquian path. He had been, until the end of the siege of Detroit, a war leader, a man in some ways as rash and heedless in all but his plans for attack as the young warriors themselves. In the midst of the siege of Detroit, he had suffered a stinging rebuke from the son of the Le Grand Saulteur of the Michilimackinac Chippewas and from a Shawnee emissary for his lack of restraint in his treatment of prisoners and his abuse of the French habitants. And in his bitterness following the defeat at Detroit, he could be, particularly when in his drink, a violent and cruel man. In a horrible incident on the Maumee River in 1764, he ordered a Frenchman to drown Betty Fisher, a seven-year-old English prisoner who, sick, naked, and shivering from the cold, had sought to warm herself at Pontiac's fire. The Frenchman had done so. The man who ordered the murder of Betty Fisher was a war leader, a man without the patience, restraint, or self-control of the chiefs who mediated, made the paths smooth, and corrected the excesses of warriors.[58]

[56] Morris to Bradstreet, Aug. 31, 1764, in Bradstreet to Gage, Sept. 12, 1764, Gage Papers, AS 24. For belt, see St. Ange to D'Abbadie, 9 Nov. 1764, *IHC* 10:356–57.

[57] For quotation, see Gage to Halifax, Apr. 14, 1764, *IHC* 10:241. For Johnson quotation, see Johnson to Gage, July 2, 1764, *JP* 11:249–50.

[58] For the Betty Fisher murder, see Examination of John Maret, Aug. 4, 1767, in Turnbull to Gage, Apr. 25, 1768, Gage Papers, AS 76. For rebukes, see Milo M. Quaife (ed.), *The Siege of Detroit in 1763: The Journal of Pontiac's Conspiracy and John Rutherfurd's Narrative of a Captivity* (Chicago: Lakeside Press, 1958): 172–76, and Peckham, *Pontiac*, 186–88.

Yet already in 1764 and increasingly in 1765, Pontiac was metamorphosing in predictable Algonquian fashion from a war leader into a chief. This was the normal life cycle of a leader. Just as a generation earlier the Michilimackinac Ottawa Pennahouel had made the difficult passage from restless war leader to patient chief, so, too, Pontiac now followed the same well-worn if arduous path. Captain Morris glimpsed this Pontiac at the Maumee in the fall of 1764, and in 1765 other British emissaries sent to negotiate the peaceful surrender of the Illinois country found him nearly fully transformed. Pontiac, the chief and mediator, who protected Morris, also protected Lieutenant Alexander Fraser at the Illinois. Although Fraser, too, glimpsed a different Pontiac when the Ottawa was drunk, he still thought Pontiac the "most sensible man among all the Nations, and the most humane Indian I ever saw."[59]

Pontiac's predictable Algonquian evolution from war leader to chief connected with the British creation of what at times seemed an Indian emperor of the *pays d'en haut*, and in this intersection lay Pontiac's downfall. Pontiac was really the first Indian of the *pays d'en haut* since Kondiaronk to be celebrated among Europeans. Robert Rogers in his *Ponteach* created a literary Indian who was a great and commanding chief, but great and commanding chiefs did not exist in the *pays d'en haut*. And to treat Pontiac as if he were one was to detour his normal political evolution. A different man might have stayed on course, but the British would finally more than half convince Pontiac that he did, in fact, command the western villages.[60]

The British offered Pontiac both chieftainship and an escape from his ideological impasse. He could vault from being a nativist war leader in the service of a French father – a tenuous position increasingly hard to maintain – to being a new kind of alliance chief. Pontiac was already partially acting as an Algonquian chief and a mediator; the British promised him success on a scale no other Algonquian had ever achieved. Pontiac was not just tempted; he believed the influence that the British attributed to him was real. That belief would cost him everything, including his life.

This intersection of Pontiac's movement toward chieftainship with the British belief in his power took place in the Illinois country. A French garrison still maintained itself at Fort Chartres, but the real resistance to British occupation came from the habitants and the Illinois themselves. Both were linked to the anti-British rebels farther east by Pontiac and by another, less famous leader: Charlot Kaské.

---

[59] For Fraser quote, see Extract of letter of Lieutenant Fraser, May 18, 1765, *JP* 11:743. For Fraser's experience and Pontiac's drinking, see Fraser to Gage, Apr. 27, 1765, Gage Papers, AS 137; Fraser to Gage, May 15, 1765, Gage Papers, AS 36; Fraser to Campbell, May 20, 1765, *IHC* 10:496.

[60] Robert Rogers, *Ponteach, or the Savages of America: A Tragedy* (London: J. Millan, 1766).

Charlot Kaské took the road of resistance Pontiac declined to follow. Charlot Kaské was a Shawnee whose father was a German. His wife was a British captive raised among the Shawnees since early childhood. His children, therefore, were three-quarters European by descent. He was "of the prayer," raised as a Catholic, and unlike Pontiac, he never drank "anything stronger than water." But like Pontiac, he was a war leader, much respected "amongst all the nations for his Sense," and he was ardently devoted to resisting the British occupation of the *pays d'en haut.*[61]

Charlot Kaské functioned from 1763 to 1765 as an organizer of resistance, first in cooperation with Pontiac and then in opposition to him. In 1763 he appeared at Fort Chartres in the Illinois country, bringing a message and a request for French aid from Pontiac. In 1764 he was back at the Illinois River with a delegation of lower Shawnee chiefs. When they failed to obtain the French commitment of aid they hoped for, he traveled on to New Orleans to attempt to secure aid from the governor of Louisiana. In New Orleans he cast himself in the role of a representative of the Shawnee "great chief" seeking aid from his father. But Charlot Kaské no longer gave his loyalty primarily to the Shawnee chiefs or to his father. His loyalty went to the cause of anti-British resistance, and the British who attended his councils with the French regarded him as an agent of Pontiac. When Charlot Kaské heard from the governor, Charles Philippe Aubry, who had succeeded D'Abbadie, that the French had indeed ceded the *pays d'en haut,* he replied, "I am surprised that the emperor has ceded it; and since he rejects us, we are masters of our bodies and our lands." When Charlot Kaské returned to the Illinois, he dismissed news of the Shawnee truce with the British as quickly as he had dismissed the peace of the French and the British. Neither bound him, and he promised to disrupt them. He then falsely reported the talk he had had with Charles Philippe Aubry. Aubry had refused military aid and urged peace; Charlot Kaské claimed that the governor had promised assistance and demanded attacks on the British.[62]

By 1765 the political combat of the *pays d'en haut* took place in the villages where Pontiac's emissaries, supported by French traders, competed with the

---

[61] For his background and refusal to accept peace, see Fraser to Gage, May 15, 1765, Gage Papers, AS 36. Also Déposition du nomme Charlot sauvage français . . . 1763, AN, C11A, v. 105.

[62] As agent of Pontiac, see Déposition du nomme Charlot, sauvage français . . . 1763, AN, C11A, v. 105; De Villiers to D'Abbadie Dec. 1, 1763, *IHC* 10:49–56. Campbell to Gage, Feb. 20, 1765, Gage Papers, AS 31. New Orleans, Journal of D'Abbadie, Dec. 20, 1764, *IHC* 10:203–4. D'Abbadie died on Feb. 4, 1765, and Charlot Kaské finished his negotiations with Aubry, Aubry à Gage, 16, Feb. 1765, Gage Papers, AS 31. For full talk and Aubry's reply, see Speech made by . . . Charlot Kaské, Feb. 24, 1765, *IHC* 10:444–54, quotations, 450. For refusal to accept peace, see Fraser to Gage, May 15, 1765, Gage Papers, AS 36.

British for influence. It produced political instability. Groups such as the Chippewas of Saginaw and Michilimackinac, whom the British thought were ready for peace, began once more to conspire against the British in 1764 and 1765. The Miamis split into factions with the anti-British faction momentarily dominant. Publicly the Illinois deferred to the Ottawas' (in this case, Pontiac's) judgment on whether they should resist the British or negotiate, but in practice Pontiac's following depended on a day-to-day struggle to maintain his influence among these and neighboring peoples. News of Bouquet's truce with the Shawnees in the fall of 1764 hit Pontiac hard. It encouraged him to take British peace overtures far more seriously.[63]

Whereas Charlot Kaské allied himself with the French traders to urge continued resistance, Pontiac emerged as a mediator during the spring and summer of 1765. Lieutenant Alexander Fraser, who had ill-advisedly left Pittsburgh before George Croghan had finished his councils there, presented Pontiac with an opportunity to act as a chief. When Fraser arrived at Fort Chartres, in the Illinois country, he found the French commander, St. Ange (whom Fraser, unfairly, dismissed as "superannuated [and] timorous"), could not protect him from Charlot Kaské's followers. Pontiac even tentatively accepted a peace belt from Fraser. He did so, he said, both because his French father, St. Ange, recommended it, and because the Shawnees, Delawares, and Iroquois, who had started the war, had made peace. They would, he presumed, withdraw from his hand the hatchet that they had given him. He and the Illinois agreed to meet with Croghan, whom Fraser wrongly presumed was close behind him, at Ouiatenon.[64]

Pontiac's stance as a mediator, however, almost immediately collapsed. The Illinois told Fraser that they would follow Pontiac in accepting or rejecting the belt of peace, but, in fact, they maintained their own independent position. They intended to tell Croghan that they would not allow the British to occupy their country but only those lands north of the Wabash. When Croghan failed to appear at Ouiatenon at the appointed time in early May, Fraser and Pontiac's attempt at peace faltered. The Illinois chiefs, who

---

[63] Among Miamis, see Croghan to Gage, Mar. 2, 1765, Gage Papers, AS 31. For Miami factions, see Campbell to Gage, Apr. 28, 1765, Gage Papers, AS 35. Hostile, Courts of Inquiry, Detroit, March 11 and April 6, 1765, *JP* 11:670–79. For rumors of attacks from Chippewas and Ottawas, see Fraser to Gage, Apr. 27, 1765, Gage Papers, AS 137; Extracts of letter from William Howard, May 17, 1765, *JP* 11:739–40. At Illinois, see Fraser to Gage, Apr. 27, 1765, Gage Papers, AS 137.

[64] Lieutenant Ross had come up to the Illinois from Mobile before Fraser arrived. For his description of his negotiations, their failure, and his flight, see Ross to Farmar, May 25, 1765, *IHC* 10:481–83. See also Declaration of Hugh Crawford, July 22, 1765, in Gage to Halifax, Aug. 10, 1765, Gage Papers, ES 4. Description of St. Ange is from Fraser to Gage, Apr. 27, 1765, AS 137. Croghan's own departure was delayed by difficulty in holding conferences at Pittsburgh and initial unwillingness of Shawnees and Delawares to escort him, Gage to Halifax, Apr. 27, 1765, *JP* 4:731.

had gone to meet Croghan, abandoned the whole plan. Only Pontiac remained willing to wait for Johnson's assistant.[65]

By early May 1765, Charlot Kaské, not Pontiac, was in ascendancy among the Illinois. Pontiac himself stopped the Illinois from taking revenge on Fraser when false reports of a joint Cherokee-British attack on a party of Illinois arrived, but he could do nothing to curtail the rising tide of anti-British hostility after Charlot Kaské returned from New Orleans with his message of war. Although Pontiac remained friendly to Fraser, he advised the British officer either to accompany him back to the Maumee or to leave for New Orleans. Fraser fled down the river. The subsequent arrival of yet another British emissary, Pierce Sinnot, sent by the southern superintendent of Indian affairs, John Stuart, and escorted by a French officer, only slowed Charlot Kaské's momentum. Just when Sinnot thought that he had negotiated a peaceful British occupation, he, too, had to flee for his life.[66]

Pontiac's debut as a chief had thus far been largely a failure; all that saved the negotiations was a serious miscalculation on the part of Charlot Kaské and the French traders. They used the rumors of joint British-Cherokee attacks on the Illinois and Wabash villages to solicit war parties in the Wabash country. In late May 1765, one of these parties – made up largely of Kickapoos and Mascoutens – attacked George Croghan, who had finally begun his journey to the Illinois country, near the mouth of the Wabash. They killed most of Croghan's escort, including three Shawnee chiefs.[67]

As Croghan later realized, without this attack, his mission would have failed. The Illinois had driven out all the British emissaries sent to them;

[65] For attempt at peace, see Fraser to Gage, Apr. 27, 1765, Gage Papers, AS 137. For collapse, see Fraser to Gage, May 15, 1765, *IHC* 10:491–93; Extract of letter from Fraser, May 18, 1765, *JP* 11:743; Fraser to Gage, May 18, 1765, *IHC* 10:494–95.

[66] For Charlot Kaské, Fraser, Pontiac, and Illinois chiefs, see Fraser to Campbell, May 17, 1765, *IHC* 10:493–94; Extract of a letter from Lt. Fraser, May 18, 1765, *JP* 11:743–44; Fraser to Gage, May 18, 1765, *IHC* 10:494–95; Fraser to Campbell, 20 May, 1765, *IHC* 10:495–97; Fraser to Gage, May 26, 1765, *IHC* 10:515–16; McKee to Johnson, Aug. 12, 1765, *JP* 11:884. Governor Aubry believed that Fraser had bungled the negotiations by making promises about Croghan's arrival that only led to the disappointment and disillusionment of the Indians, Aubry à Gage, 24 juin 1765, Gage Papers, AS 38; Fraser to Gage, June 17, 1765, *IHC* 10:519.

Sinnot and the French captain, Harpain de la Gauterais, were in touch with Croghan by mid-June, Sinnot to Croghan, June 14, 1765, *JP* 11:788–89; Croghan to Johnson, July 12, 1765, *JP* 11:835–38; Croghan to McKee, Aug. 3, 1765, in Reid to Gage, Gage Papers, AS 41; Johnson to Lords of Trade, Sept. 28, 1765, *NYCD* 7:765.

[67] For attack and aftermath, see Croghan's Journal, *IHC* 11:30–52. The Weas blamed the attack on the French, *ibid.*, 34, as did the attackers themselves, Croghan's Journal, *IHC* 11:40. Charlot Kaské immediately sent a pipe and a speech by the hands of a Frenchman to have Croghan burned, *ibid.* 40–41. A letter from Vincennes written before actual news of Croghan's capture indicates French complicity in the attack, Capucin to Campau, June 7, 1765, *JP* 4:764–66.

they and the French habitants seemed determined to prevent a British occupation. He doubted if he could have overcome their resistance. But the attack changed everything; it threatened internecine war. By killing three Shawnee chiefs, the Wabash villagers now faced the near certainty of British-supported Shawnee, Delaware, and Iroquois attacks against them. They now desperately needed a mediator. The civil leaders and elders, with strong popular support, immediately disavowed the actions of their young warriors and solicited peace, asking both Croghan and the French to intercede for them with the Shawnees.[68]

Pontiac, who had increasingly been pushed into the background after Charlot Kaské's return to the Illinois, reemerged as a crucial figure. Having lingered ineffectually at the Illinois villages, he now found his services solicited not only by the Wabash villagers but also by Saint Ange, who apparently made it clear that Charlot Kaské and the traders did not enjoy his support. But above all, Pontiac could now successfully act as an alliance chief because the British – Croghan included – were eager to regard him as the leader of all the rebellious villages. Gage's disillusionment with Bradstreet made him regret more and more that officer's precipitous rejection of Pontiac's initial overtures at Detroit. In January 1765, Gage sent a message to Pontiac, informing him that the British desired him as a friend, but "as he has been a most Inveterate Enemy, it is necessary he should do us some Extraordinary Service to Convince us of his Sincerity." Colonel John Campbell forwarded the message from Detroit. Given this British predisposition to find a great chief, it is no wonder that when Croghan met Pontiac at Ouiatenon, he said he had never seen so influential a chief.[69]

The final negotiations took place at Ouiatenon, at Detroit, and at the Illinois villages. Croghan conducted the talks at Ouiatenon and Detroit, and Pontiac participated in both councils. Two years after initiating a revolt to restore his French father, he accepted the British king as his father. The next spring, fulfilling promises he had made at Detroit, he visited William Johnson and formally ratified the peace. Charlot Kaské attempted to continue the resistance, but events had turned against him. The arrival first of a small garrison sent from Pittsburgh under Captain Thomas Stirling and then, finally, of Major Robert Farmar, who came up the Mississippi with a

---

[68] For various Wabash villages disavowal of attack, see Croghan's Journal, *IHC* 11:32–33, 36, 43. For significance of attack and requests for English mediation, see Croghan to Johnson, July 12, 1765, *JP* 11:838; Croghan to Mckee, Aug. 3, 1765, in Reid to Gage, Gage Papers, AS 41.

[69] For Pontiac's influence and invitation to him to negotiate, see Campbell to Johnson, May 21, 1765, *JP* 11:746; Croghan to Johnson, Nov. 1765, *IHC* 11:53. For quotation, see Gage to Johnson, Jan. 18, 1765, *JP* 11:540. For regrets Bradstreet's actions, see Gage to Campbell, June 5, 1765, Gage Papers, AS 37. For influence on Wabash, see Croghan to Johnson, July 12, 1765, *JP* 11:839.

larger body of troops, ended the agitation for war. Charlot Kaské met Stirling forty miles below the Wabash. He futilely urged the French who accompanied him to attack the British. Unreconciled to the British, the Shawnee war leader withdrew among the French, many of whom, themselves, began to move across the Mississippi.[70]

VII

In 1765 and 1766, peace and alliance on the middle ground returned to the *pays d'en haut*. Given the early British demands for the execution of those who had fomented and led the revolt, the actual treaty stipulations were surprisingly mild. The basic British peace terms were predictable: the return of prisoners, the recognition of the rights of the British to the old French posts and the land surrounding them, and a guarantee of free passage through the *pays d'en haut*. These amounted to little more than a restoration of the status quo ante bellum. Other demands for the surrender of selected leaders and men accused of murder were far more extraordinary, but they were also quite selective. They fell largely on people marginal to the *pays d'en haut* proper, the Chenussio Senecas and the mixed peoples, largely Delawares, of the Susquehanna.[71]

The Chenussios, abandoned by the rest of the Iroquois, had to sign a humiliating peace. They ceded the Niagara portage, agreed to surrender murderers to the British, and promised to give up the leaders of the Susquehanna Delawares who had fled to them for protection. The British made them leave hostages until they fulfilled their promises. Johnson then compelled those Delawares who sought shelter among the Chenussios to

---

[70] Unlike Charlot Kaské, who wanted Croghan burned, Pontiac immediately departed to Ouiatenon to negotiate with him, Croghan's Journal, *IHC* 11:40–41. He was urged to do so by St. Ange, who immediately set to work to free Croghan, Aubry à Stuart, 1 sept. 1765, enclosure with Stuart to Gage, Jan. 21, 1766, Gage Papers, AS 47. For conducts negotiations, see Croghan's Journal, *IHC* 11:41–42. For Pontiac's influence among Miami, see Campbell to Johnson, May 21, 1765, *JP* 11:746. For conference at Detroit, see *ibid.* 43–47. Meeting with ... Ouiatonans, Kecopoes, etc., July 13, 1765, *JP* 11:847–50. For reconciliation with Pontiac, see Campbell to Johnson, Sept. 16, 1765, *JP* 11:938–39. For Stirling, see Stirling to Gage, Oct. 18, 1765, *IHC* 11:107. For withdraws, see Fraser to Gage, Dec. 16, 1765, Gage Papers, AS 46. For French movement, see Farmar to Gage, Dec. 19, 1765, Gage Papers, AS 46.
    As 1765 drew to a close, there was still unrest among the Saint Joseph Potawatomis and some Michilimackinac Chippewas who were threatening to attack Detroit, Johnson to Gage, Dec. 21, 1765, *JP* 11:981–83.
[71] For peace terms, see Johnson to Lords of Trade, Jan. 20, 1764, *NYCD* 7:600. For price on heads of Susquehanna Delaware leaders, see Johnson to Montour, Feb. 21, 1764, *JP* 4:336–37.

disavow all alliances except with the Iroquois and renounce all their claims to land along the Ohio.[72]

The British, for all their early threats of retribution, exacted no such price farther west. The Huron-Petuns, the first to make peace at Niagara in 1764, recognized the British inheritance of all the rights the French had enjoyed at Detroit, agreed to return British prisoners and slaves, and promised to submit disputes with the British to the commander at Detroit or to Johnson. The British, in return, agreed to recognize all original Huron-Petun rights and privileges and to restore a free trade, but only after all the Indians of the *pays d'en haut* were at peace. Later treaties, whether Bradstreet's at Detroit or Johnson's, exacted no harsher concessions.[73]

With Johnson having abandoned Bradstreet's claims of absolute sovereignty over the Indians, the political contours of the middle ground remained basically the same as in the French era. The Algonquians became allied with the British, and the British king became the father of the Algonquians. As negotiations came to a successful conclusion, the Algonquians abandoned the old ritual term *brother* when talking to the British and addressed them as *father*. But the precise meaning of patriarchy and the duties of fathers and children had once more to be worked out in practice.[74]

---

[72] Johnson put pressure on the Chenussios by recruiting war parties among the Iroquois to attack the villages on the Susquehanna. For eagerness of some Iroquois to "punish the Shawanese and Delawares," see Journal of Indian Affairs, Jan. 2, 1764, *JP* 11:24. For Opposition to such tactics, see Montour, Hare, and Johnson to Johnson, Feb. 21, 1764, *JP* 11:74–75. The Chenussios argued that the western Indians had forced them into rebellion, *ibid.* 26. The brunt of English and Iroquois attacks fell on the Susquehanna Indians. Johnson to Gage, Mar. 16, 1764, *JP* 4:372; Johnson to Colden, Feb. 28, 1764, *JP* 4:346; Johnson to Gage, Apr. 16, 1764, *JP* 11:132–33. For take no prisoners, see Johnson to Penn, Feb. 9, 1764, *JP* 4:323–24. For demands on Chenussios, see Indian Conference, Mar. 24 – Apr. 3, 1764, *JP* 11:154–55; Articles of Peace Concluded with Senecas, Apr. 23, 1764, *NYCD* 7:621–22. For flight of Susquehanna Indians, see Johnson to Stuart, Mar. 18, 1764, *JP* 11:104. For Chenussios seek to intercede for them, see Journal of Indian Affairs, Apr. 24. May 11, 1764, *JP* 11:181–84. Congress with Chenussios, Niagara, July 24, 1764, *JP* 11:291–324. For hostile Delaware leaders, see Indian Intelligence, c. July 1764, *JP* 4:494–95. By the fall the Chenussios had still failed to secure Squash Cutter (or Onusaraquedra) and Attiatawitseris, the Delawares the English demanded, Indian Congress, Oct. 10, 1764, *JP* 11:379. The English would eventually pardon all of those surrendered by the Senecas and Delawares, except for Squash Cutter who died while a hostage. See Johnson to Gage, June 19, 1765, *JP* 4:772.

[73] For invitation to Niagara, see Gage to Gladwin, Mar. 23, 1764, *JP* 11:115. For Johnson threatens Hurons, coupled with invitation for peace, see Indian Conference, Detroit, May 7–10, *JP* 11:176–80. For other Mississauga bands, see Indian Congress, Niagara, May 26, 1764, *JP* 11:202–3. For conference, see Conference with Indians, Niagara, July 11–15, 1764, *JP* 11:264–76; Indian Congress, July 17 – Aug. 4, Niagara, *JP* 11:278–94. For terms, see Articles of Peace, Niagara, July 18, 1764, *NYCD* 7:652–53.

[74] For example of father, see Proceedings of . . . Johnson with the Ohio Indians, July 4, 1765, *NYCD* 7:750; "Croghan's Journal," 13, 18; Relation of Proceedings of M. Marasac . . . July 29, 1765, Gage Papers, AS 40; "Croghan's Official Journal," *IHC* 11:43–44, 45–46, 52. The Mingos initially continued to address the English as Brethren, "Croghan's Journal," 15,

In restoring peace, Johnson carefully used the accustomed language of the covenant chain and the usual diplomatic procedures of the middle ground to assure the Indians of their continued independence. Although telling the Indians they were now subjects of the king of Great Britain, he modified the phrase with the clause "so far as the same can be consistant with the Indians native rights." Johnson's negotiating procedures, which coupled a demonstration of force with native diplomatic forms, were themselves staples of the middle ground. In London, George Croghan tried to convey to the lords of trade that such an approach was the only one that could succeed in North America. Indians were to be governed only by love and fear. They must not be allowed to entertain too great notions of their own importance, but neither could Europeans dictate to them. It required "a long Acquaintance with their Singularities, and study of their Dispositions, to know how to flatter their Vanity so as to gain their Confidence which can only fix their Love and Affection."[75]

Striking a balance between love and fear, between gratitude for a father's kindness, generosity, and mediation and fear of his wrath remained the great practical problem of British Indian policy. Johnson moved to remove one of the Algonquians' greatest anxieties: that the British would make a direct claim on their lands. One of Charlot Kaské's most effective arguments in the villages of the Wabash and Illinois country was that the British would deny the Algonquians any title to the land.

> The English come there and say that the land is theirs and that the French have sold it to them. You know well our fathers have always told us that the land was ours, that we were free there, that the French came to settle there only to protect us and defend us as a good father protects and defends his children.

The British, Johnson realized, had to persuade the Indians that the replacement of the French in no way changed their title to the lands nor the relationship between fathers and children. The British must remove Algonquian "jealousy" concerning their encroachments.[76]

but in the preliminary treaty negotiated by Croghan, they, along with the Shawnees and Delawares, accepted the English as their fathers, Copy of the Articles Subscribed by the Shawanese, Mingos, & c... May 1765, Gage Papers, AS 40.

[75] For native rights, see Proceedings... of Johnson with Ohio Indians, July 9, 1765, *NYCD* 7:754. For Croghan quotation, see Croghan to Lords of Trade, June 8, 1764, *IHC* 10:262–63. For example of care in ceremonies, see Murray to Gage, Feb. 17, 1766, Gage Papers, AS 48.

[76] For first quotation, see Speech by Charlot Kaské to D'Abbadie, Feb. 24, 1765 (delivered in Dec. 1764), *IHC* 10:445. For second quotation, Johnson to Colden, Feb. 27, 1765, *JP* 4:653. The primary reference here is to the Mohawks.

When Pontiac and the Illinois deputies met Croghan, they explicitly denied that they had ceded their country to the French, "Croghan's Official Journal," *IHC* 11:42. They repeated this at Detroit, *ibid.*, 47–48.

Johnson opposed encroachments, but the question of what defined an encroachment allowed a festering sore to develop on the British-Algonquian alliance. Even before Pontiac's Rebellion broke out, the British government had issued the Proclamation of 1763 forbidding British settlement on lands beyond the Appalachians. But Gage, while welcoming the plan, did not regard the prohibition as absolute. He allowed a path to settlement in his own plan to plant colonies based on "military tenures" around the posts. The British obviously did not regard all cessions and settlements as encroachments. Following Pontiac's Rebellion, the British widened Gage's path to create two huge avenues for obtaining cessions and settlements. First, in their treaty with the Delawares, Mingos, and Shawnees, the British partially resurrected the old doctrine of Iroquois ownership of the lands along the Ohio River by allowing the British and the Iroquois to decide where the borders between British and Indian lands were to be. This opened the possibility of the Iroquois, ceding away the land of their "dependents," as they had before. The second avenue resulted from General Gage's belief that the French had reached Illinois country before the Illinois themselves had fled there and thus had prior claim to the land that had, by right of conquest, descended to the British king. He thought the settlement of British citizens in the Illinois country absolutely necessary. These two exceptions gravely weakened what was on the surface a strong British commitment to reserve the *pays d'en haut* for Indians. How weak the commitment was, in fact, became all too apparent in Croghan's and Johnson's eventual involvement in attempts to acquire western lands.[77]

Having abandoned Amherst's attempt to treat the Algonquians as a conquered and subject people, Johnson moved to recreate an infrastructure

---

[77] For proclamation, see Proclamation of Oct. 7, 1763, *IHC* 10:39–45; for treaty of peace concluded with the Delawares, see 8 May 1765, *NYCD* 7:740. Gage welcomed the action as removing a major source of conflict, Gage to Johnson, Jan. 12, 1764, *JP* 4:290. Gage planned to plant colonies based on "Military Tenures" around the posts, and there were plans to plant an English colony on the Mississippi. For posts, see Gage to Johnson, Mar. 4, 1764, *JP* 4:355; Gage to Bouquet, May 14, 1764, *MPHC* 19:257–58. For Illinois, see Croghan to Lords of Trade, June 8, 1764, *IHC* 10:260; Croghan to Johnson, Dec. 27, 1765, *JP* 4:886–87. For Gage's position, see Gage to Croghan, Apr. 4, 1766, Gage Papers, AS 50, and Apr. 16, 1766, *IHC* 11:216–17. Stirling informed Gage that the French owned only the lands the posts stood on, Stirling to Gage, Dec. 15, 1765, *IHC* 11:126.

For Johnson and Iroquois claims, see Johnson to Lords of Trade, Oct. 30, 1764, *NYCD* 7:674. For "Suffering Traders" grant and cessions near Fort Pitt, see Johnson to Peters, Jan. 30, 1766, *JP* 5:22; Johnson to Lords of Trade, Jan. 31, 1766, *NYCD* 7:809; Croghan to B. Franklin, Feb. 25, 1766, *JP* 5:37–39. Pontiac and the Detroit Indians were willing to give the English the land necessary for carrying on the trade, "Croghan's Official Journal," *IHC* 11:48.

For recommendation of Johnson, Croghan, and Illinois land company that Gage be included, see Johnson to Benjamin Franklin, May 3, 1766, *JP* 5:196–97. Gage, whose rigorous honesty in such matters was exceptional, refused, Johnson to William Franklin, June 20, 1766, *IHC* 11:318.

for the western alliance. For, as he realized, peace and the "late great Acquisitions to the Westward, can have little permancy unless a proper fund & a regular System be established." Johnson believed the Indians must receive treatment equivalent to what the French had accorded them. He thought that "neither the Western Indians nor they [Senecas and Mohawks], who have tasted the French favours can ever be hearty friends until by like treatment we establish ourselves in their Esteem." Once peace had been restored, Johnson believed, the Indians would not violate it "if they meet with good treatment hereafter, but should they at any time be neglected, before we have established a fair and disinterested character among them, they will not fail to repeat their depredations neither will we be able to prevent them from doing considerable damage."[78]

Johnson and Gage were willing to go some distance on the middle ground to guarantee "good treatment." In late 1763, Johnson outlined his plans for rearranging the administration of Indian affairs, and Gage seconded his insistence on reform. The reforms came. In 1764, the board of trade offered a new plan for the centralization of Indian affairs under northern and southern Indian commissioners to end the "local interefering of particular Provinces." The new plan forbade private or colonial land purchases from the Indians, confined trade to the posts, banned the rum trade, gave commissaries serving at the posts the powers of justices of the peace, and, despite some reluctance, agreed to set a tariff of regulated prices on trade goods. Except in West Florida, however, the government never fully implemented the plan. Johnson did not obtain the full complement of commissaries and blacksmiths that the plan envisioned, nor did the commissaries receive judicial powers. And in 1765, under pressure from the traders and Johnson, who argued that without rum the trade would substantially diminish since the Indians could fill their needs for manufactured goods with relatively few furs, the lords of trade agreed to allow a supervised rum trade. This new policy responded to earlier Indian objections to colonial mismanagement and mistreatment, but it proved both expensive and ineffective in controlling either the Algonquians or British.[79]

---

[78] For quotation, fund and system, see Johnson to Peters, Jan. 30, 1766, *JP* 5:22; for quotation, imitate French, see Johnson to Gage, Apr. 27, 1764, *JP* 11:164; for quotation, treatment, see Johnson to Lords of Trade, Jan. 20, 1764, *NYCD* 7:600; see also Johnson to William Eyre, Jan. 29, 1764, *JP* 11:22.

[79] For background of plan, which was never fully implemented, see Gipson, *British Empire*, 11:429–30; for Johnson, quotation, pay for posts, see Johnson to Gage, June 9, 1764, Gage Papers, AS 19. For reform, see Johnson to Lords of Trade, Nov. 13, 1763, *NYCD* 7:573–80; Gage to Johnson, Oct. 14, 1764, *JP* 11:375–77; Gage to Johnson, June 24, 1764, *IHC* 10:268. For intent of plan, see Lords of Trade to Johnson, July 10, 1764, *NYCD* 7:634–36. For plan itself and presents, see Plan for Imperial Control of Indian Affairs, July 10, 1764, *IHC* 10:273–81; Johnson to Lords of Trade, Oct. 8, 1764, *IHC* 10:34–42. For Croghan's assessment, see Croghan to Johnson, July 12, 1764, *JP* 4:462–64. For rum trade,

The British tried to demonstrate their "love" for their children by allocating twenty thousand pounds annually for presents and contingent expenses in North America. Johnson assured the lords of trade that the best policy was to "conquer their prejudices by our generosity, they will lay aside their jealousies, and we may rest in security. This is much cheaper than any other plan, and more certain of success; our extensive frontiers renders it necessary." In a fit of judicious optimism, Johnson budgeted only £4,000 for annual presents and another £1,000 for presents for chiefs and other individuals. This sum, supposedly, would take care of all the Indians under his jurisdiction. Johnson made much larger presents at Niagara in 1764, and that fall British officers began once more to give presents to visiting Indians.[80]

By 1765, however, the real costs of patriarchy were once more becoming clear. Gage began to receive letters from the treasury ordering him to curtail expenses, and he, in turn, ordered the officers at western posts to be as sparing as possible in their presents, giving them only to "the chiefs and perhaps a few others." Following such directives, however, proved difficult, for good relations with the Algonquians depended on the favors and honors one could bestow. When John Campbell at Detroit refused the Huron-Petun chiefs a fat ox for a festival, "they went away abruptly saying that they were entirely neglected by the English." And Gage soon realized that his officers' presents had merely been rivulets flowing into a sea of red ink when George Croghan began to submit his accounts. Gage growled that the enormous expense of occupying the Illinois country made it hardly worth having. Johnson, however, forthrightly justified increasing Indian expenses to the lords of trade. The British must, he told them, meet expectations raised by French practices.[81]

---

see Johnson to Lords of Trade, Oct. 8, 1764, *IHC* 10:334–35. For trade regulations, see Orders of the Regulation of Trade, Jan. 16, 1765, *IHC* 10:400. Croghan, too, argued that rum and ammunition were critical to trade, Croghan to Gage, Mar. 12, 1765, Gage Papers, AS 32. For prices, see Equivalents for Barter, *JP* 11:990–93.

[80] For Johnson quotation, generosity, see Johnson to Lords of Trade, Aug. 30, 1764, *NYCD* 7:649; also see Johnson to Gage, Mar. 15, 1766, *JP* 5:80. For presents at Niagara, see Conference with Indians, Niagara, July 1764, *JP* 11:274–76; for presents at Michilimackinac, see Campbell to Gage, Nov. 10, 1764, Gage Papers, AS 26. Johnson estimated the expense for provisions alone at £25,000 New York currency. His estimate with the presents was £38,000 Sterling. Thus his estimate of £4,000 a year for presents seems odd indeed.

[81] For favors and honors, see Johnson to Lords of Trade, Oct. 8, 1764, *IHC* 10:331. For treasury, see Gage to Johnson, Dec. 16, 1764, *JP* 4:618; Johnson to Gage, Jan. 3, 1765, *JP* 11:520. For fat ox, see Campbell to Johnson, Aug. 17, 1765, *JP* 11:898–99. Gage ordered Captain Stirling at Fort Chartres to discover how the French had given presents and imitate them as sparingly as possible, Gage to Stirling, Dec. 30, 1765, Gage Papers, AS 46. By then Farmar was requesting a "proper assortment of goods" to distribute to the Illinois and their neighbors, Farmar to Gage, Dec. 16, 1765, AS 46. Croghan requested £3,445 of presents for his 1766 trip to the Illinois, Gage to Johnson, Apr. 7, 1766, *IHC* 11:212–13. For

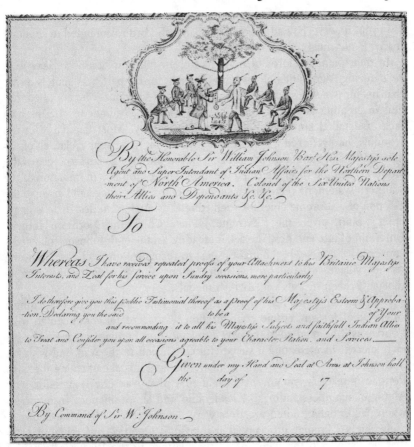

By the Honorable Sir William Johnson Bar.t Her Majesty's sole Agent and Super-Intendant of Indian Affairs for the Northern Department of North America. Colonel of the Six United Nations their Allies and Dependants &c. &c.

To

Whereas I have received repeated proofs of your Attachment to his Britanic Majesty's Interests, and Zeal for his Service upon Sundry occasions, more particularly

I do therefore give you this public Testimonial thereof as a Proof of his Majesty's Esteem & Approbation. Declaring you the said to be a of Your and recommending it to all his Majesty's Subjects and faithfull Indian Allies to Treat and Consider you upon all occasions agreable to your Character, Station, and Services.

Given under my Hand and Seal at Arms at Johnson hall the day of 17

By Command of Sir W. Johnson

This certificate from William Johnson was, like calumets, wampum belts, and medals, one of the visible signs of alliance on the middle ground. (Courtesy of the New-York Historical Society, N.Y.C.)

As essential as the resumption of present giving was in maintaining an Algonquian-British alliance, Johnson still had to reestablish the conduits along which the presents would flow. He needed alliance chiefs, both British and Algonquian. Like the French, Johnson planned to provide interpreters and smiths at each post. But instead of relying on officers and traders, whose ignorance and self-interest rendered them unreliable British chiefs, Johnson

Croghan overdrawn, see Johnson to Gage, Mar. 9, 1765, *JP* 11:624–25. For Gage's complaints of Illinois, see Gage to Croghan, Apr. 4, 1765, Gage Papers, AS 33. For must meet expectations raised by French, see Johnson to Lords of Trade, May 24, 1765, *NYCD* 7:714–15.

hoped to establish a network of commissaries and agents at the various posts. By 1766, however, it had become clear that the British intended to abandon many, if not most, of the smaller posts.[82]

In their plan, the lords of trade had given Johnson significant leeway in recognizing Algonquian chiefs, and Johnson, for his part, was acutely aware that his influence rested on the "Favours" and "honours" he could confer. But in creating alliance chiefs, Johnson was initially impeded by his own lack of detailed knowledge of Algonquian society. Most familiar with the Iroquois, he preferred a system that would simply recognize clan chiefs as alliance chiefs, but many Algonquians lacked the strong clan structure of the Iroquois. And he wisely rejected the lords' suggestion that in imitation of the southern system, he recognize a single chief for each village and arrange the election of a supreme chief for each tribe. Any attempt to designate a single chief would, given the "Extreme Jalousy which the Northern Indians Entertain of one another," be self-defeating. In the end, Johnson followed a conservative course. He thought it best to recognize those chiefs whom the various villages offered for his approbation. And at Niagara he began to replace French medals with British medals.[83]

But Johnson, for all his insight into the extreme jealousy that designating a single chief for any ethnic configuration would create, continued to treat Pontiac as if he reigned in the *pays d'en haut*. And Pontiac, impressed by his own success in mediating a successful conclusion to the war, and with his head turned by British attentions, made the fatal mistake of acting the part. Pontiac himself began to speak in a tone that was utterly at odds with Algonquian understandings of leadership and subordination. In a society where, as Croghan noted, warriors were "governed only by persuasions of their chiefs," Pontiac proclaimed at Johnson's Ontario conference in 1766 that he "spoke in the name of all the Nations to the Westward whom I command." This was not the language of a chief. It is not surprising that by

---

[82] For commissaries, see Johnson to Stuart, Sept. 17, 1765, *JP* 4:848; Johnson to Lords of Trade, July 1765, *NYCD* 7:747–48. For smiths and interpreters, see Johnson to Lords of Trade, Jan. 31, 1766, *NYCD* 7:808–9. For posts, see Johnson to Gage, Jan. 7, 1766, *JP* 5:1–2; Gage to Johnson, Feb. 3, 1766, *JP* 5:30. For Barrington's plan, see May 10, 1766, *IHC* 11:234–40; Gage's Remarks, *ibid.* 243–45.

[83] Plan for Imperial Control of Indian Affairs, July 10, 1764, *IHC* 10:276–77. For chiefs, Johnson to Lords of Trade, Oct. 8, 1764, *IHC* 10:331–32; for favors and honors, see Johnson to Lords of Trade, Oct. 8, 1764, *IHC* 10:331. Wabbicomigot, e.g., received a medal from Johnson, "which binds me to you," Journal, 1765, *JP* 11:820. As with the French, British officers in the West also bestowed medals, Howard to Johnson (Michilimackinac), June 24, 1765, *JP* 11:807. Johnson recognized their importance, Johnson to Gage, Jan. 30, 1766, *JP* 5:20.

The English, as the French had, exerted veto power over chiefs who refused to act as intermediaries and mediators. Bouquet, e.g., deposed a phratry chief of the Delawares who refused to negotiate, Indian Proceedings, Nov. 10, 1764, *JP* 11:457–58.

1766 reports reached Johnson that the "Indians are very Jalouse of pondiac & want to Chuse another Chief they think we make to much of him." More ominously, a Frenchman offered to bet Normand Macleod, Johnson's commissary at Ontario, that "Pondiac would be killed in less than a year, if the English took so much notice of him."[84]

Pontiac was drifting into dangerous waters. On his return to the Ottawas, he found that British esteem did not win him Ottawa loyalty. The young warriors openly threatened him, denied he was a chief, and, on several occasions, beat him. His declining influence at Detroit and along the Maumee River made his connections with the Illinois and Wabash peoples all the more important. Yet when the Illinois delegation to Johnson's peace conference reached Detroit, Pontiac stabbed an Illinois chief. The whole delegation returned home. His actions were hardly those of a chief.[85]

By 1768, Pontiac was both the most famous Indian in the *pays d'en haut* and a man without a home. His position among the Ottawas grew so intolerable that he decided to withdraw temporarily among his relatives in Illinois country. But the Illinois, who certainly had not forgotten his attack on their chief, feared Pontiac. He quarreled with them once more before retiring to hunt during the winter of 1768–69. By late March rumors were circulating among the Kaskaskias that he would return with 150 canoes full of warriors and cut off the Illinois. In the spring of 1769 Pontiac did return, but he came only with two of his sons and a few other warriors. On April 20, 1769, a nephew of Makatchinga (or Black Dog), a Peoria chief of the Illinois confederation, accompanied Pontiac on a visit to the trading store of Baynton, Wharton, and Morgan in the French village of Cahokia. As they left the store together, the Peoria clubbed Pontiac from behind, stabbed him, and fled. Pontiac died ignominiously in the dirty street of a French village, his death a monument to the limits of chieftainship.[86]

British alliance chiefs, as Pontiac learned, could no more pretend to power than could French alliance chiefs. In its structure of presents, diplomatic forms, and regulated trade with fixed prices, and with its emerging array of

[84] For Croghan, see Abstract from Croghan's Journal, May 24, 1766, Gage Papers, AS 51. For Pontiac, see Western Conference, July 25, 1766, *NYCD* 7:858. For jealousy, see Roberts to Johnson, Niagara, June 23, 1766, *JP* 5:279; MacLeod to Johnson, Aug. 4, 1766, *JP* 12:150. For other reports of opposition to him, see Hay to Croghan, Aug. 28, 1767, *JP* 5:644; Hay to Croghan, Aug. 22, 1767, *JP* 5:637–38.

[85] For Illinois chief, see Cole to Johnson, June 23, 1766, *JP* 5:278–79. For decline among Ottawas, see Réponse de Pondiac . . . 10 mai 1768, in Turnbull to Gage, June 14, 1768, Gage Papers, AS 77; Peckham, *Pontiac*, 305–6.

[86] Réponse de Pondiac . . . 10 mai 1768, in Turnbull to Gage, June 14, 1768, Gage Papers, AS 77. This essentially follows Peckham, *Pontiac*, 308–16, but also see Journal of Transactions and Presents given to the Indians from 28th of Dec. (Illinois), Mar. 29, 30, 1769, Apr. 20, 1769, Gage Papers. Pontiac intended to return to Detroit, Account of Baynton, Wharton, & Morgan . . . Sept. 13, 1768, *IHC* 16:407.

alliance chiefs, the British alliance was the French system reborn, but the British system was a Frankenstein monster. In its first years, it was only a soulless imitation of the old alliance; the missing soul was mediation. Onontio had ideally reconciled his warring children. He had covered and raised up the dead. But initially Johnson and the British did not conceive of themselves as mediators. Instead, Johnson envisioned separate alliances with the Iroquois and several western regional groupings whom the British would play off against one another and supply with arms for their internecine wars.[87]

Yet as the French had found, imperial ambitions often became deflected on the middle ground. The British found mediation hard to avoid. When the Piankashaws, Miamis, Weas, Kickapoos, and Mascoutens entered the British alliance after the attack on Croghan, their first request was that the British reconcile them with the Shawnees and Delawares. And it is revealing that despite dallying with the idea of fomenting intertribal war, the British did mediate this quarrel. Similarly at Michilimackinac, Captain Howard found himself mediating between the Menominees and the Chippewas.[88]

Sporadic mediation, however, did not make a stable alliance. Johnson realized as much. His treaties ritually concluded a war, but they only began the process of creating English fathers in the *pays d'en haut*. As Johnson put it after Croghan's journey restored tranquillity to the West, affairs must be properly attended to or "everything will fall to the ground." Johnson intended to resurrect the French alliance with the English at its head, but larger events both forced and tempted him to do otherwise. White and Algonquian villagers, not imperial officials, would determine events in the *pays d'en haut* for the next generation.[89]

---

[87] For prohibitions, see Imperial Control of Indian Affairs, July 10, 1764, *IHC* 10:279. For separate alliances, divisions, see Johnson to Gage, Feb. 19, 1764, *JP* 4:331. For fomenting jealousy between Iroquois and western Indians, Johnson to Gage, Mar. 16, 1764, *JP* 4:368. For new standards, see Indian Conference, Mar. 24 – April 23, 1764, *JP* 11:134–59. For must surrender murderers, etc., see Treaty ... with the Delawares, May 5, 1765, *NYCD* 7:740 (later subscribed to by Mingos and Shawnees).

[88] For mediation, see "Croghan's Official Journal," *IHC* 11:43; Howard to Johnson, June 24, 1765, *JP* 11:806–7. Captain Reid at Pittsburgh thought encouraging war between the Wabash villages and the Shawnees was a good idea, Reid to Gage, Aug. 2, 1765, Gage Papers, AS 40. Gage thought resentment should be kept up, but violence restrained, Gage to Reid, Aug. 19, 1765, Gage Papers, AS 41. But Johnson, knowing that if the English failed to mediate, fighting between the Kickapoos and Shawnees could close the Ohio, urged mediation, Johnson to Gage, Mar. 22, 1766, *JP* 5:91.

[89] Johnson to Gage, Oct. 26, 1765, *JP* 11:957–59.

8

The British alliance

They [the Indians] discovered that the back[country] inhabitants particularly those who daily go over the Mountains of Virginia employ much of their time in hunting, interfere with them therein, have a hatred for, ill treat, Rob and frequently murder the Indians, that they are in generall a lawless sett of People, as fond of independency as themselves, and more regardless of Govern^{mt} owing to ignorance, prejudice, democratical principles, & their remote situation.

Sir William Johnson to the Earl of Dartmouth, November 4, 1772

A nation scattered in the boundless regions of America resembles rays diverging from a focus. All the rays remain, but the heat is gone. Their power consisted in their concentration: when they are dispersed, they have no effect.

Samuel Johnson, *A Journey to the Western Islands of Scotland*, quoted in
Bernard Bailyn, *Voyagers to the West*

I

Although William Johnson aspired to model a British alliance on his image of the old French alliance, in the end he came to violate his most basic premises. Seeking to overcome the colonial mismanagement that had cost the British their Indian allies before the Seven Years' War, he had found himself "obliged to pursue those methods so successfully practised by the French." Johnson imitated the French system of gifts and medals, of officers and chiefs. He instituted a regulated trade. He replaced French fathers with British fathers, but he failed to persuade the British government to bear the costs such an alliance demanded, nor could he quickly call into being the cultural and social middle ground on which the alliance must finally rest. As a result, Johnson in the years just before his death had begun to pit his Indian children against one another rather than to reconcile them as a good father should.[1]

At the root of the alliance's weakness between 1765 and 1776 was the emergence west of the Appalachians of a third village world alongside those of the Algonquians and the French. This village world, too, was a

[1] Johnson to Lords of Trade, 20 Oct. 1767, *NYCD* 7:988. Lawrence Henry Gipson, *The British Empire Before the American Revolution* (New York: Alfred A. Knopf, 1942), 11:433.

heterogeneous mix of different peoples loosely linked by intermarriage and common loyalties. But this village world was white and British, and it was openly and aggressively expansionist. More tenuously attached to the empire than the villages of the Algonquians, these villages remained beyond the control either of the governors and the legislatures east of the mountains or of the British soldiers west of the mountains. Neither Johnson nor any other British official exerted effective control over backcountry settlers.

This third village world of British subjects resembled only superficially the second and earlier village world created by the French. The French habitants of Kaskaskia, Detroit, Vincennes, Michilimackinac, and smaller settlements had by the 1760s drifted into a practical independence of their own, but they had earlier sustained the French empire rather than defied it. And they had created a common world with the Algonquians of the *pays d'en haut*.

The British villages only partially re-created the familiar face-to-face relations with Indians that had allowed the French alliance to survive its many crises. George Croghan had grasped the essence of French-Algonquian relations and noted the absence of a British-Algonquian equivalent when he traveled through the French and Algonquian villages of the *pays d'en haut* after his capture by the Kickapoos and Mascoutens in 1765. The French and Indians, he said, had been "bred up together like Children in that Country, & the French have always adopted the Indians Customs & manners, Treated them Civily & supplyed their wants generously." It was an opinion British officers seconded. Viewing the "Five or Six Hundred" French traders and voyageurs who gathered in the early summer of every year at Michilimackinac, Captain Turnbull thought they had "adopted the very Principles and Ideas of the Indians and differ from them only a Little in color." Or as General Thomas Gage put it, the French had become "almost one People with them."[2]

There is no need to romanticize this relationship. Indians and French abused and killed each other; they cheated each other as well as supplying each other's wants. But their knowledge of each other's customs and their ability to live together – what Croghan described as their having been bred up together – had no equivalent among the British. Johnson, Croghan, and Gage recognized that the only secure basis for Algonquian-British relations lay on the middle ground, but at the outset their middle ground remained

---

[2] Croghan to Johnson, Nov. 1765, *IHC* 11:53–54. Croghan made similar comments in his journal, Aug. 17, 1765, *IHC* 11:37, and in an earlier letter about the inhabitants of Vincennes, Croghan to Johnson, July 12, 1765, *JP* 11:840. For Turnbull quotation, see Turnbull to Gage, July 5, 1771, Gage Papers, AS 112. For Gage quotation, see Gage to Hillsborough, Nov. 10, 1770, Clarence E. Carter (ed.), *The Correspondence of General Thomas Gage*, 2 vols. (New Haven: Yale University Press, 1931–33), 1:275.

almost exclusively diplomatic; it did not extend to day-to-day life. And as long as it was exclusively diplomatic – governed by paid officers with all the contingent expenses involved in maintaining an alliance amid the constant strife of British subjects and Algonquian villagers – it would remain expensive.[3]

There were in 1766 few likely candidates for extending the middle ground outside its formal, diplomatic sphere. First the Seven Years' War and then Pontiac's Rebellion had decimated the ranks of experienced British traders, those men most at ease on the middle ground. Nor had the British produced any religious figures who approximated the Jesuits. British missionaries seemed to Johnson "well meaning but Gloomy people," who wanted "to abolish at once their [the Indians'] most innocent Customs, Dances, Rojoycings." Such people were no match for the old French missionaries, "men of spirit, Abilities and a knowledge of the World." As for British settlers along the frontiers of the *pays d'en haut*, many of them hated, feared, and despised Indians.[4]

In the letters of Gage and Johnson, the British colonials who moved into the West emerge as uniformly "low," "the very dregs of the people," or "lawless banditti." They were men and women who were escaping the controls of their betters in a hierarchical society – "Idle Persons" who were not "under Landlord or Law," in Johnson's words, or as Gage put it, "a Sett of People . . . near as wild as the country they go in, or the People they deal with, & by far more vicious & wicked." Their characters appeared in particularly poor light, Johnson insisted, because French agents, "all Men of Ability and Influence," still moved about the *pays d'en haut*. Such characterizations, it is true, evoke images of the coureurs de bois of a century earlier, but with a critical difference. Unlike the earlier Frenchmen, these British settlers did not believe that their lives depended on good relations with Indians, nor did they seek a refuge among them. Although traders and settlers depended on the British military to support them in case of conflict, they resented the efforts of the same military to restrict their actions.[5]

---

[3] For the importance of forms and customs, see Gage to Wilkins (Fort Chartres), Apr. 8, 1772, Gage Papers, AS 110; Basset to Gage, Aug. 1, 1772 (Detroit), Gage Papers, AS 113. Basset replaced Captain Stevenson, noted for his mastery of the customs of the middle ground, Johnson to Gage, Aug. 13, 1772, *JP* 8:572–73. For connection with presents, see Johnson to Lords of Trade, Nov. 16, 1765, *NYCD* 7:776; Johnson to Lords of Trade, 28 June 1766, *NYCD* 7:838.

[4] For demise of old traders, see Johnson, Review of the Trade and Affairs in the Northern District of America, Sept. 22, 1767, *IHC* 16:35. For comparison of missionaries, see *ibid.*, 52.

[5] For Johnson quotation, landlords, etc., see Johnson to Gage, Nov. 24, 1767, *DHNY* 2:886. For "low", "dregs", see Review of the Trade and Affairs in the Northern District of America, Sept. 22, 1767, *IHC* 16:38, 44. For French, see *ibid.*, 45. For Gage quotation, see Gage to Shelburne, Feb. 22, 1767, *IHC* 11:510. For Indians form opinion of English from traders, see *ibid*, 49. For "banditti," see Wilkins to Gage, Jan. 8, 1767, Gage Papers, AS 61.

British Indian policy initially feared contact between Indians and whites and hoped to make it as restricted and supervised as possible. French officials had come gradually and reluctantly to view their traders in the West, their habitants in the small villages from Detroit to Kaskaskia and Cahokia, and the *métis* offspring of Algonquian-French intermarriage as essential to the alliance. Johnson and Gage feared, as the French had originally feared, the presence of uncontrolled Europeans in the West. When Johnson attempted to implement the board of trade's plan following Pontiac's Rebellion, he seemed at times to interpret it as a wholly secular reincarnation of the old Jesuit dream of the *pays d'en haut*. Like the Jesuits, he hoped to restrict access to the region to a few Europeans and then watch those few intensely. Johnson and Gage desperately wanted the clear dividing line between Indian and white lands that the British government had promised to create in 1765. They wanted to evict the white settlers who had ignored the Proclamation of 1763 and settled along the Cheat River and Redstone Creek in western Pennsylvania. The trade regulations Johnson issued for his northern superintendency early in 1767 restricted trade to the military posts of the *pays d'en haut* where commissaries, appointed by the crown, could supervise it. Unsupervised trade, Johnson contended, would only lead to widespread fraud. The Indians, who had "no other recourse" against fraud, would retaliate with robberies and murders. In the end, there would be war.[6]

The attempts of Johnson and Gage to restrict and supervise the activities of British subjects in the West involved them in endless difficulties that very quickly brought Johnson's entire system down. The traders, licensed by the governments of their particular provinces, chafed at restrictions confining their trade to the posts, particularly when French traders, who had moved across the Mississippi, continued to bring goods up from New Orleans and sell them in the villages of the upper Mississippi, Illinois, Wabash, and Ohio regions. Gage thought that the majority of furs trapped in the Illinois and Mississippi countries never reached British markets. They flowed down-river to New Orleans.[7]

---

[6] For boundary, see Johnson to Moore, Oct. 22, 1767, *JP* 5:741. Croghan to Johnson, Oct. 20, 1767, *IHC* 16:90. The Iroquois were willing to sell lands south of the Ohio to the mouth of the Cherokee river, lands the Cherokees claimed as a hunting ground. The Cherokees wanted the boundary fixed at the Cohohway. Lords of Trade to Earl of Shelburne, Dec. 23, 1767, *NYCD* 7:1004–5.

　　For settlers, see Gage to Edmonstone, Nov. 24, 1767, Gage Papers, AS 72; Murray to Gage, Dec. 10, 1766, Gage Papers, AS 58; Gage to Johnson, Dec. 20, 1767, *DHNY* 2:892.

　　For trade regulations, see Regulations for Indian Trade, May 1, 1767, *JP* 5:422–24. The regulations were apparently issued before this, since complaints about the regulations began in January. For discussion, see Johnson to Gage, Oct. 22, 1767, *IHC* 16:92; Gage to Johnson, Oct. 4, 1767, *JP* 12:367; Johnson to Earl of Shelburne, May 30, 1767, *NYCD* 7:928–30; Johnson to Gage, May 20, 1767, *DHNY* 2:853–54.

[7] Captain Gordon's Journal, Aug. 31, 1766, *IHC* 11:300–01; Gage to Johnson, Jan. 19, 1767, *IHC* 11:498.

British traders, even as they used the French presence as an argument to free themselves from confinement to the posts, cooperated in this illegal trade. According to George Croghan, prominent British merchants provided the trade goods that allowed these French traders to subvert the system. The British already in Illinois country sold their furs to the French. The sales yielded higher profits than they would if they bore the cost of transportation back to Philadelphia, for the French could ship their cargoes downriver to New Orleans. Johnson thought all the British traders would imitate those at the Illinois River if given the chance. Governor Carleton of Canada, in attempting to divert the trade into British Canada, defied Johnson's regulations. He asserted that Johnson's commissaries had no control over traders who carried his passes. Canadian traders obtained Carleton's passes to trade in villages north of Lake Superior, but once out of the range of officers and commissaries, they traded wherever they chose. Similarly, traders with passes to Fort Chartres in the Illinois country could, and did, stop to trade in villages along the way. During 1767 both British and French traders openly flaunted the restrictions, and the commissaries and officers complained that they lacked sufficient legal power to do anything about it.[8]

Attempts to evict illegal settlers proved no more successful. Colonial legislatures showed little interest in evicting settlers, and Gage believed that "men of Interest Abet these Encroachments." In the spring of 1767 Gage did order Captain Murray of Fort Pitt to evict settlers along Redstone Creek and the Cheat River and burn their cabins, but within months they had rebuilt and George Croghan reported that there were "double the Number of Inhabitants in those two settlements that ever was before." Gage himself grew so disgusted that he informed Johnson that he would not use the troops

---

[8] For approval of wintering among Indians north of lakes, see Earl of Shelburne to Johnson, June 20, 1767, *JP* 5:566. For sale to New Orleans, see Johnson to Gage, Dec. 12, 1766, *JP* 5:229; Gage to Johnson, Dec. 1, 1766, *JP* 12:225–26. For Carleton, see Carleton to Johnson, 27 March 1767, *JP* 5:520–23; Johnson to Gage, June 12, 1767, *DHNY* 2:855–57. For illegal trade by settlers near Fort Pitt, see Petition of Traders to George Croghan, Dec. 18, 1767, *JP* 6:19. For French traders on north shore of Lake Ontario, see Macleod to Johnson, Nov. 5, 1767, *JP* 5:777. For traders go up Ohio, see Croghan to Johnson, Oct. 20, 1767, *IHC* 16:90. For stop on way to Illinois, see McCleod to Johnson, Oct. 8, 1767, *IHC* 16:83; Turnbull to Gage, June 14, 1767, Gage Papers, AS 66. For defiance of regulations at Fort Pitt, see Johnson to Gage, Apr. 1, 1767, *DHNY* 2:843. Smallman to Murray, May 16, 1767, in Murray to Gage, May 16, 1767, Gage Papers, AS 65; Baynton, Wharton, & Morgan to Gage Oct. 24, 1764, Gage Papers, AS 58. For Detroit, see Turnbull to Gage, Sept. 9, 1766, Gage Papers, AS 56; *ibid.*, Sept. 13, 1767, Gage Papers, AS 69. For supply French, see Croghan to B. Franklin, Jan. 27, 1767, *IHC* 11:503.

For debate over regulation, see Van Schaak and Other Traders to Hay, Sept. 4, 1767, *IHC* 16:3–5. Memorial of Traders, Sept. 20, 1766, *IHC* 11:378–82. Cole to Croghan, Dec. 19, 1767, *JP* 6:21. Turnbull to Gage, Dec. 1, 1767, Gage Papers, AS 72. Review of the Trade and Affairs in the Northern District of America, Sept. 22, 1767, *IHC* 16:50; Johnson to Gage, June 14, 1766, *JP* 12:105–6. Johnson to Earl of Shelburne, Dec. 3, 1767, *NYCD* 7:999.

to halt Indian attacks on the new settlements without direct orders from the king.[9]

As this system limped along, it seemed to London but a conspiracy to increase expenses. Insofar as the attempt to restrict the trade to the posts succeeded, it increased the numbers of Indians who visited the forts. The greater the number of Indians present, the greater the number of provisions and gifts necessary to keep them content. Failure to evict illegal settlers around Fort Pitt and the many murders committed by settlers and traders forced the British to cover the dead and compensate the Indians even though they had announced that trials in colonial courts would replace the older practice of covering the dead. The failure to control traders demanded an expansion of the system of posts, the appointment of new commissaries, and a means to prevent the export of illegally obtained furs. And Johnson reiterated the need for annual congresses.[10]

Because of its expense and because of the legal problems resulting from the extraordinary powers Johnson's commissaries and Gage's officers required if they were to control British subjects in the *pays d'en haut*, Indian policy became a major concern of the British ministry in the 1760s and 1770s. Attempts to force the colonies to bear part of the costs of the North American military establishment not only failed but, in the Stamp Act crisis, precipitated a major challenge to imperial authority.[11]

---

[9] For Gage quotation, encroachments, see Gage to Johnson, Nov. 9, 1767, *JP* 12:379. For ordered off, see Notice of Alex MacKay to All People now Inhabiting to the Westward, *PA*, Series 1, 4:251–52. For evictions, see Gage to Murray, May 5, 1767, Gage Papers, AS 64; Murray to Gage, June 24, 1767, Gage Papers, AS 66; Gage to Murray, July 21, 1767, Gage Papers, AS 67. For resettlement, see Croghan to Johnson, Oct. 18, 1763, *JP* 12:374. Gage ordered Murray to avoid a general war and have the Indians confine their "Resentment to those who have injured them," Gage to Murray, June 28, 1767, Gage Papers, AS 66. These people settled largely within lands claimed by Virginia, Murray to Gage, Apr. 7, 1767, Gage Papers, AS 63.

[10] The original plan had been to cut down the number of posts, Gage to Johnson, Feb. 3, 1766, *JP* 5:30. For expenses and expansion, see Johnson to Gage, Jan, 7, 1766, *JP* 5:1–2; Gage to Reed, Apr. 14, 1767, Gage Papers, AS 63; Gage to Reed, July 22, 1767, Gage Papers, AS 67; Reed to Gage, Oct. 28, 1767, *IHC* 16:101; Reed to Gage, Oct. 5, 1767, *IHC* 16:81; Gage to Roberts, Sept. 14, 1767, Gage Papers, AS 69; Gage to Rogers, Sept. 21, 1767, Gage Papers, AS 70; Gage to Johnson, July 20, 1767, *JP* 5:601; Murray to Gage, June 1, 1767, Gage Papers, AS 65; Gage to Johnson, Apr. 13, 1767, *JP* 5:537. The cost of Croghan's trip to the Illinois, e.g., came to £8,408, Croghan's Account, Feb. 22, 1767, *IHC* 11:511. For congresses, see Johnson to Shelburne, Jan. 15, 1767, *JP* 7:892–93.

Johnson's lengthy Review of the Trade and Affairs in the Northern District of America, Sept. 22, 1767 (*IHC* 26:24–67), essentially appeals, as Gipson points out, for the implementation of the full 1764 plan of the Lords of Trade, Gipson, *British Empire*, 11:435. For posts, see *IHC* 26:59–60.

[11] For questions of power of superintendents, see Shelburne, Reason for Not Diminishing American Expenses This Year, Mar. 30, 1767, *IHC* 11:538–41; Wm. Grant to Gage, Oct. 3, 1766, Gage Papers, AS 57. For need for judicial power in West, see Gage to Johnson, Dec. 1, 1766, *JP* 12:226; Gage to Johnson, Jan. 25, 1767, *IHC* 11:499–500; Johnson,

In the wake of the Stamp Act, British Indian policy lost its center. The ministry surrendered control over trade to the colonies, and colonial officials failed to regulate the trade at all. The Crown cut back on gifts to the Indians, demonstrating to the Algonquians the king's lack of regard for his children. Patriarchal relations between British fathers and Algonquian children grew strained. The Crown now limited William Johnson to "a very Slender Allowance" for all the northern Indians, not just those of the *pays d'en haut*. Deprived of necessary funds, Johnson discharged his commissaries, that is, his British chiefs. And the British secretary of state, Lord Hillsborough, advised Johnson that rather than mediate disputes between the Indian nations he should let "natural enemies and jealousies" take their course.[12]

This abdication of so much of the diplomatic middle ground left the chiefs, both British and Algonquian, in the lurch. Both groups maneuvered desperately to maintain their positions. British officers and officials of the northern superintendency, particularly those in Illinois country, continued to act as fathers by securing advances from the traders. Gage recognized that such presents were necessary, but under pressure from the crown to reduce expenses, he was often outraged at the amounts spent. In a quarrel over

Review of the Trade and Affairs in the Northern District of America, Sept. 22, 1767, *IHC* 26:50, 56–57, 61–63. As Captain Turnbull reported, "there are Liberty Boys at Detroit as well as Elsewhere," Turnbull to Gage, Jan. 10, 1767, Gage Papers, AS 61. For accusations that Colonel Reed at Fort Chartres took bribes, see Morgan to Baynton and Wharton, Dec. 10, 1767, *IHC* 16:130–31. For accusations of the commissary, see Benjamin Roberts against Rogers, Roberts to Guy Johnson, Aug. 20, 1767, with Hay to Gage Oct. 1, 1767, Gage Papers, AS 70. Suspicions of Rogers's actions, Gage to Roberts, Sept. 21, 1767, Gage Papers, AS 70, and Gage to Speismacher, Sept. 21, 1767, Gage Papers, AS 70. For arrest of Rogers, Speismacher to Gage, Dec. 9, 1767, Gage Papers, AS 72; Rogers to Gage, Dec. 11, 1767, Gage Papers, AS 72. For Rogers's arrest of Commissary Roberts, Rogers to Gage, Sept. 22, 1767, Gage Papers, AS 70.

For British policy and the American colonies, see Jack M. Sosin, *Whitehall and the Wilderness: The Middle West in British Colonial Policy, 1760–77* (Lincoln: University of Nebraska Press, 1961), 79–171. Also see Gipson, *British Empire*, 11:437ff. For ideological and pragmatic aspects of policy dispute, see Shelburne, Reason for not Diminishing American Expenses This Year, Mar. 30, 1767, *IHC* 11:538–41; B. Franklin to W. Franklin, Aug. 28, 1767, *IHC* 16:1. In cabinet meetings Shelburne's objections were partly ideological (trade "can scarcely admit of any regulations which do not naturally flow from itself"), partly legal (the superintendents and commissaries had no authority rightly derived from either the civil or military power), and partly utilitarian (Britain could not bear the expense; the army should not be scattered in small posts; the colonies could take over supervision now that the French were gone; and the expansion of settlers into the interior would keep the colonies dependent on Britain by preventing them from concentrating their population and developing manufactures). For Shelburne's arguments, see Minutes Submitted to the Cabinet, Sept. 11, 1767, *IHC* 16:12–21. Considerations Submitted to the Board of Trade . . . , Oct. 5, 1767, *IHC* 16:77–81.

12 For do not mediate, see Hillsborough to Johnson, May 4, 1771, *NYCD* 8:270. For slender allowance, see Johnson to Blackburn, June 1, 1770, *JP* 7:707; Edmonstone to Gage, July 16, 1770, Gage Papers, AS 93. For Johnson's argument to encourage Indian wars, see Johnson to Gage, Jan. 4, 1771, *JP* 12:881–83; *ibid.*, Aug. 22, 1771, *JP* 8:232–34. For Johnson's evaluation of the failure of the trade policy, see Johnson to Gage, May 15, 1773, *JP* 8:799.

presents given to the Indians, George Croghan resigned his position in the fall of 1771. The declining authority of British chiefs was everywhere apparent. The Indians rightly judged that backcountry whites had escaped the authority of "their wise People."[13]

Algonquian chiefs fared even worse than British chiefs. Chiefs depended on British gifts and assistance to keep the paths clear and their young men smoking quietly on their mats. But without gifts and assistance, the chiefs found it impossible to control the discontented. The chiefs of the Potawatomis of Saint Joseph, perhaps the most troublesome village for the British in the entire *pays d'en haut* during the 1770s, complained that they could not stop the factionalization of their own people. Those who disputed the authority of the chiefs were "always doing Bad things as if on Purpose to Embarass the Old Chiefs." Not only did the British fail to support the chiefs as they should, they actively undermined the peace of the villages through the liquor trade which created havoc among the Algonquians. Young men traded for liquor instead of blankets and cloth. And liquor curtailed the hunt by debilitating the hunters at the same time as it reduced their number. "The chiefs," Major Henry Basset at Detroit reported, "complain much of the intention of the English to kill all their young men.... The Chiefs declare they loose more their young men by Rum than they used to do by war." Liquor, a Huron chief asserted, is the "Cause of a great deal of our Unhappyness, by it our Young Men not only [are] reduced to the Necessity of stealing to recover what they loose by Drunkeness, but deprived of their Reason and render'd incapable of listening to or taking the Advice of their Wise People." The British attempt to have the benefits of empire without sustaining the costs of the imperial alliance thus sent tremors through the *pays d'en haut.*[14]

---

[13] As they had earlier, British officers sought to evade the policy against presents, regarding them as essential to their own safety, Turnbull to Johnson, Sept. 9, 1769, *IHC* 16:594; Turnbull to Johnson Sept. 30, 1769, *JP* 7:196; Turnbull to Gage, Oct. 12, 1767, Gage Papers, AS 87; Gage to Edmonstone, Sept. 10, 1769, Gage Papers, AS 87; Edmonstone to Gage, Sept. 20, 1769, Gage Papers, AS 87; Gage to Turnbull, Apr. 9, 1770, Gage Papers, AS 91. For recognized as necessary, see Gage to Edmonstone, Nov. 5, 1770, Gage Papers, AS 97.

For Croghan's resignation, see Croghan to Gage, Aug. 29, 1771, Gage Papers, AS 105; Gage to Johnson, Oct. 1, 1771, *JP* 8:286; Croghan to Gage, Nov. 2, 1771, Gage Papers, AS 107.

The Journal of Transactions and Presents given to the Indians from Dec. 23, 1768, Gage Papers, gives a good account of how the officials at the Illinois, who were confronted with first a French and then a Spanish garrison just across the Mississippi, continued to act as fathers making presents, supplying the chiefs, and seeking to mediate quarrels. For escaped authority, see McKee's Journal, April 3–6, 1773, *JP* 8:756.

[14] For embarrass old chiefs, see Speech of Four Indian Chiefs, May 22, 1773, *JP* 8:803–5. For liquor, see Basset to Haldimand, 29 Apr. 1773, *MPHC* 19:296. For quotation, see Indian Conference, Pittsburgh, Oct. 9, 1773, *JP* 12:1035.

II

In the decade between Pontiac's Rebellion and the outbreak of Lord Dunmore's War in 1774, the diplomatic middle ground, like an island in a storm, eroded away on one side while slowly expanding on another. This rapid erosion of the diplomatic middle ground revealed the basic fragility of British-Algonquian relations. British Indian diplomacy did not rest on a bedrock of common life. British backcountry settlers usually hated and feared Indians, and many of the "meanest & most profligate traders," as Johnson scornfully remarked, relied on rum because they could sell it profitably without knowledge of either Indian ways or Indian language.[15]

Missing in the *pays d'en haut* was what the Algonquians often referred to as "antient custom," which was not so much inherited as created. It was a mutually comprehensible, jointly invented world rather than a traditional set of procedures. But in the 1770s, as the alliance and its forms rapidly wore away along with the deteriorating empire, traders and backcountry settlers were slowly building up a new customary world. Like a coral island growing beneath the sea, it remained invisible until it broke the surface. Unlike Johnson's restricted middle ground of diplomacy, which largely involved Algonquian men and British officers and officials, this new middle ground included a wider assortment of people: traders, Algonquian women, missionaries, ex-prisoners, some backcountry settlers, and eastern Indian refugees.[16]

The sources of this middle ground lay in both trade and the human legacy of the raids of the Seven Years' War and Pontiac's Rebellion: the white captives who had lived among the Indians. Such origins meant that the scale of this new accommodation initially remained limited and localized. The process advanced most quickly along the Ohio River and eastern Lake Erie; it was weaker at Detroit, Michilimackinac, and in the Illinois country. By 1770, it had barely penetrated the Wabash country or Saint Joseph, where French traders and habitants limited the access of the British; nor was it well advanced along the upper Mississippi, which also remained largely closed to the British.[17]

[15] Croghan to Johnson, Nov. 1765, *IHC* 11:53–54. Croghan made similar comments in his journal, Aug. 17, 1765, *IHC* 11:37, and in an earlier letter about the inhabitants of Vincennes, Croghan to Johnson, July 12, 1765, *JP* 11:840. For Johnson quotation, see Johnson to Hillsborough, Aug. 14, 1770, *DHNY* 2:976.

[16] "Antient Custom" in some ways corresponds to the "Invention of Tradition" in Eric Hobsbawm and Terence Ranger (eds.), *The Invention of Tradition* (Cambridge: Cambridge University Press, 1983), in the sense that "they are responses to novel situations which take the form of reference to old situations, or which establish their own past by quasi-obligatory repetition." But the examples I cited are unusual because, among other reasons, they involve the people of two societies.

[17] For French influence, see Thomas Hutchins, Remarks on the Country of the Illinois,

The presence of British traders and captives in Algonquian villages proved essential to the creation of a new middle ground. These people gained access to Algonquian culture largely through Algonquian women. As traders, mothers, and lovers, and as arbiters of prisoners' fates, women both mediated between two worlds and created people with a foot in each.

The most obvious form of mediation was sexual. Algonquian women readily formed liaisons with British traders. At Pittsburgh in 1772, the missionary David McClure found "the greater part of the Indian traders keep a squaw . . . they allege the good policy of it, as necessary to a successful trade." By giving their consorts access to Algonquian kinship networks, women eased the traders' entry into the villages, and the children that sprang from such unions offered the possibility of a more permanent connection between the cultures. This possibility, however, remained largely unrealized in the years before the Revolution. The offspring of British traders and Algonquian women remained the equivalent of the *métis bâtards*, that is, people deserted by their fathers who grew up culturally as Algonquians. Such paternal desertion was not always by choice. Many traders who died or fled during the turmoil of the 1750s and 1760s necessarily left their offspring behind.[18]

The earlier *métis* of the *pays d'en haut* grew up exposed to both their paternal and their maternal cultures; such people were few in the 1760s and 1770s. By far the most notable of them was Alexander McKee. The child of a union between Thomas McKee and a Shawnee woman, who was probably a white captive raised from childhood among the Shawnees, Alexander most fully assumed the kind of intermediary role common among the French *métis*. He served as a British Indian commissary – a British chief – but in George Croghan's words, the Shawnees considered him "as one of thire own pople his Mother being one of thiere Nation." McKee explained the Indians to the British and the British to the Indians.[19]

More significant than their literal creation of people of the middle ground

---

Sept. 15, 1771, Gage Papers, AS 138. Only in 1772 did Gage indicate that British traders were beginning to expand their range, Gage to Johnson, May 12, 1772, *JP* 8:480. In 1767 there were approximately 600 Frenchmen and 303 black slaves at Kaskaskia. In addition, there were 60 French families at Cahokia, 25 at Prairie de Rocher, 3 at St. Phillipe, and 3 at Fort Chartres. There were 232 permanent inhabitants and 27 Indian and black slaves at Vincennes in the Wabash country, along with 168 traders and voyageurs. There were, in addition, approximately 750 Frenchmen at Saint Louis and Sainte Genevieve or Misère in Spanish territory, Information on the State of Commerce in the Illinois Country . . . Capt. Forbes, enclosure with Gage to Hillsborough, Jan. 6, 1769, Gage Papers, ES 14.

18   For quotation, see *Diary of David McClure* (New York: Knickerbocker Press, 1899), Sept. 13, 1771, 53.

19   Croghan to Johnson, Sept. 18, 1769, *JP* 7:182. McKee spoke several Algonquian languages and knew "their customs and manners," Croghan to Gage, Jan. 1, 1770, Gage Papers, AS 89.

– the *métis* – was the role of women in ritually easing the passage of whites into the village world. Women in the Algonquian world reconstituted society; they created new social identities for people born in other foreign worlds. They did so through the adoption of prisoners. They restored social life to those of their own people who had died by replacing them with British and Indian captives. The degree to which women controlled the fate of captives varied from group to group, but among all the Algonquians and Iroquois of the *pays d'en haut*, women exerted significant control over prisoners. Whether a prisoner was condemned to death, spared but made a slave, or adopted to take on the social identity of a lost relative often depended at some critical point on the choice of a woman.[20]

Among the Shawnees there were two sets of female "chiefs" – war "chiefs" and civil "chiefs." Each was ritually connected with a major form of sustenance for the people. Just as women both produced crops in the fields and brought home the meat killed by the hunter, so the female peace chiefs supervised planting and prepared feasts of vegetable foods – "white corn & smaller vegetables" – while the female war chiefs prepared "meats and coarser vegetables." The female peace chiefs could stay war parties; the female war chiefs welcomed them on their return and thanked them for the "good meat," that is, the prisoners they brought home. In the late eighteenth century, these prisoners could still be literally "good meat" if they were burned at the torture stake and ritually cannibalized. During the 1750s and 1760s, the fate of the prisoners apparently depended on whether the peace women reached them and touched them before the Miseekwaa-weekwaakee, a hereditary society headed by four old women, did. If a Miseekwaaweekwaakee touched a prisoner first, she thanked the warriors for bringing her good broth, and the prisoner was burned and eaten.[21]

---

[20] See Sylvester Stevens, Dorald Kent, and Emma Woods (eds.), *Travels in New France by JCB* (Harrisburg: Pennsylvania Historical Survey, Pennsylvania Historical Commission, 1941), 100, but in some cases war parties burned prisoners at Fort Duquesne before traveling to their home villages, *ibid.*, 71–72. David Zeisberger, the Moravian missionary, said that Algonquian women frequently intervented to make sure that European women did not have to run the gauntlet on reaching an Algonquian village, Archer Butler Hulbert and William N. Schwarze (eds.), *David Zeisberger's History of the Northern American Indians* (Ohio State Archaeological and Historical Society, 1910), 105. Marie Le Roy and Barbara Leininger thought that the three soft blows given them on the back when they were received at Kittanning on the Allegheny was just to "keep up an ancient usage," "Narrative of Marie Le Roy and Barbara Leininger . . . ," *Pennsylvania Magazine of History and Biography* 29 (1905): 409. For an analysis of captivity that differs from mine, see James Axtell, "White Indians," in James Axtell, *The European and the Indian: Essays in the Ethnohistory of Colonial North America* (New York: Oxford University Press, 1981), 168–206.

[21] Vernon Kinietz and Erminie W. Voegelin (eds.), *Shawnese Traditions: C. C. Trowbridge's Account, Occasional Contributions from the Museum of Anthropology of the University of Michigan, no. 9* (Ann Arbor: University of Michigan Press, 1939), 13, 18–21, 53–54. The Miseekwa-aweekwaakee were drawn from the Linewaa m'soamee of the Piqua Shawnees. It appears

Among the Miamis also, there were female war and peace chiefs, but these women's ritual power over prisoners was not nearly so great. Among the Miamis, such a woman derived her office from her relation to a male chief. The eldest daughters of male war and village chiefs became female war and village chiefs. As among the Shawnees, the female village chiefs stayed the shedding of blood. They halted outbreaks of revenge killings and stopped war parties from going out. In most cases when prisoners arrived at the village, women could prevent their execution, unless the prisoners had been selected by the Amaumoaweeaukee, or man eaters, all of whom were members of the Sonkisia, or Sky moiety. If they were spared, however, prisoners passed into the hands of the male village chief. He distributed them, and the children of the deceased, both men and women, decided whether to accept the prisoner for adoption.[22]

Algonquians never intended this incorporation of prisoners into Algonquian society to be a means of extending the middle ground. They intended incorporation, whether as a relative, slave, or cannibal victim, to make the captive completely Algonquian, but the complete assimilation of adults rarely took place. Children often became completely Algonquian in appearance, culture, and manner, but slaves obviously remained marginal, and most adult adoptees failed to be fully woven into the social fabric of the villages. For example, although adopted among the Delawares, Marie Le Roy complained that "her Indian mother had been so cross and had scolded her so constantly" that she could not stay with her any longer. Hugh Gibson, captured by the Delawares, became the brother of Pisquetomen, Tamaqua, and Shingas, and "although in general, with a few painful exceptions, he was treated kindly by them," he "had no inclination to spend his days with the Indians."[23]

The Delawares realized full well how tenuous familial connections were in the first years of captivity. For years both Gibson and Le Roy were deterred

---

from Black Hoof's account that only those prisoners who no family wished to adopt were delivered to the Miseekwaaweekwaakee, Trowbridge, Black Hoof's Account, in *Shawneese Traditions*, 64.

Prisoners destined for death were painted black; see "An Account of the Remarkable Occurrences in the Life and Travels of Colonel James Smith during His Captivity with the Indians" (1799) in Wilcomb Washburn (ed.), *The Garland Library of Narratives of North American Indian Captivities* (New York: Garland, 1919), 9. "Even if adopted, apparently a prisoner who attempted to escape was liable to be tortured and killed," "Narrative of Marie Le Roy and Barbara Leininger," 410–11.

[22] C. C. Trowbridge, *Meearmeear Traditions: Occasional Contributions from the Museum of Anthropology of the University of Michigan*, no. 7, ed. Vernon Kinietz (Ann Arbor: University of Michigan Press, 1938), 14–15, 17, 21–22. Women were not allowed to be present when medicines were redistributed, 23. For prisoners, see *ibid.*, 24, 28–29. For adoption, see *ibid.*, 36–37. For Amaumoaweeaukee, see *ibid.*, 88.

[23] "Narrative of Marie Le Roy and Barbara Leininger," quotation, 416. "An Account of the Captivity of Hugh Gibson," in Washburn (ed.), *The Garland Library of Narratives*, 153.

from attempting to escape by the gruesome example the Delawares had made of the wife of Alexander M'Allister, who had tried to flee to the settlements. The Delawares forced the other prisoners to watch as she "was long made to writhe in the flames" in order to deter them from any thoughts of escape. Gibson may have been Pisquetomen's brother, but he was never fully a Delaware. Pisquetomen beat him on several occasions, something no sober Delaware would do to another, and he and other relatives threatened to burn Gibson. When Gibson refused to marry, Pisquetomen thrashed him with a hickory rod. Even captives such as James Smith, who reported that after his adoption by some Caughnawagas then living among the Mingos on the Ohio, "I never knew them to make any distinction between me and themselves," never became fully part of Indian society. Smith, too, contemplated running away, and for him the distinction between captives like himself and the Indians always remained clear. Prisoners like Marie Le Roy and Barbara Leininger, who were less well treated, never thought of themselves as anything but captives and longed for redemption.[24]

It was the resistance of adult British prisoners to complete assimilation, abandoning neither their culture nor their religion, that made them bridges to a new middle ground. They made an adjustment to village life that involved something less than taking it on its own terms. The critical part of this adjustment was not the simple exchange of skills by which prisoners, for example, learned to hunt or farm in the Indian manner but, rather, a search for mutually intelligible meanings by which a common life and sense of the world became possible. The winter that James Smith spent with Tecaughretanego, his Indian brother, in a hunting camp near the Scioto River was spent partly in a "chearful conversation" that much of the time consisted of a comparison of white and Iroquoian ways in which each gained instruction. Much of the talk centered on religion. Neither converted the other. Smith did not abandon his faith in Christian revelation, and Tecaughretanego thought he "was now too old to begin to learn a new religion," but both learned the terms of the other's discourse and understanding and, in the manner of the middle ground, sought to use them for their own purposes.[25]

The process need not be as elevated as Smith's and Tecaughretanego's

---

[24] "Captivity of Hugh Gibson," adoption, 143; beatings and threats, 145–46; escape, 149; torture of M'Allister, 143–44. Gibson escaped with a party that included Barbara Leininger and Marie Le Roy, but he does not name Le Roy, instead referring to a German from a family named Grove, "Narrative of Marie Le Roy and Barbara Leininger," for escape, 413–17, for quote, 416. For torture of M'Allister and others as warning, see 410. "Colonel Smith's Account," 11–13.

[25] "Colonel Smith's Account," 50–56, 78–81. On a more material level, white prisoners learned to hunt, and whites, in turn, taught on occasion more effective ways to fish, ibid., 56–57.

religious discussions on long winter nights; far simpler instances put shared meanings into action. When Pisquetomen kicked his brother Hugh Gibson down, denouncing him as a lazy "good-for-nothing-devil ... and trampled him under his feet," Gibson looked up "and in a soft and gentle manner, merely [said,] 'I hear you, brother.'" He thus instantly disarmed Pisqueto- men's rage, and the Delaware showed Gibson the greatest kindness. In the incident the men had reversed cultural roles. When Pisquetomen attacked Gibson, he not only used him as a slave rather than as a brother, but he also denounced him in European terms. The Algonquians regarded Satan as European; whites carried devils among them. Gibson, for his part, bore the attack like an Algonquian. He shamed Pisquetomen by addressing him in kinship terms and, in doing so, brought Pisquetomen to treat him as a brother.[26]

Prisoners learned through experience that actions took on quite different meanings in an Algonquian village than in the colonial backcountry. Alexander Henry's capture and adoption by the Ojibwas during Pontiac's Rebellion did not turn him into an Indian, but it did make him a person conscious of the multiple meanings of his actions and of the necessity of finding interpretations upon which both he and the Algonquians could agree. Common actions and events that had one meaning among the British had a different meaning among the Ojibwas. When Henry bled some Indians, he found himself transformed into a doctor. Among the Algonquians, medicine symbolically and actually often consisted of drawing out a poison or a foreign body presumed responsible for illness. Bleeding clearly fitted their concept of an appropriate remedy, and Henry became a healer. Henry inadvertently discovered that his actions could take on Algonquian meaning and so provide him, as a European, with a social role on the middle ground. Women especially sought to be bled, perhaps because of associations with menstruation. Henry found "this service was required of me; and no persuasion of mine could ever induce a woman to dispense with it."[27]

Henry did not have to believe himself a doctor, but he did have to understand what Indians believed. Henry, for example, had no faith in the ability of dreams to prophesy the future, but he found it necessary to act as if he did and to prophesy through his dreams, since "protestations of my ignorance were received with but little satisfaction, and incurred the suspicion of a design to conceal my knowledge." He accommodated his captors and relatives and gave the necessary prophecies. Similarly, Hugh Gibson told

---

[26] "Captivity of Hugh Gibson," 146. For devil, see below.
[27] Milo M. Quaife (ed.), *Alexander Henry's Travels and Adventures in the Years 1760–1776* (Chicago: R. R. Donnelley and Sons, 1921), 116–17.

Shingas that there would soon be peace with the whites. When asked how he knew, he replied "I dreamed so." When Pisquetomen arrived a few days later with Frederick Post, Gibson was called a prophet.[28]

With the end of Pontiac's Rebellion, these captives became logical agents for extending the middle ground. Most returned home, but many remained among the Indians or on the frontier near them. Henry returned to being a trader; Joseph Nickels, "who had been a captive among the Indians when young & well acquainted all their customs," became an interpreter at Fort Pitt. He interpreted not just language but social meaning. These captives had their Algonquian equivalents. The sizable postwar migration of Algonquians from east of the Alleghenies brought both Moravian converts and other Pennsylvania and New Jersey Delawares and Munsees well versed in British, Christian, and European meanings. Joseph Peepee, a Christian Delaware who migrated from the Susquehanna to the Muskingum in 1772, served as interpreter for David McClure, Charles Beatty, and David Jones in much the same manner that Nickels did at Fort Pitt. All these people formed bulwarks of the middle ground.[29]

The experiences of prisoners such as Smith, Gibson, and Nickels during the long years of war formed only a more extreme and concentrated version of an ongoing discourse in which more and more British subjects – traders, soldiers, missionaries, and some settlers as well as ex-captives – began to participate. In the winter of 1772–73 when David Jones visited the Shawnee town at Chillicothe, he found twenty whites living there. He also encountered David Owen, who resided in the white settlements but had a Delaware man living with him and who often traveled among the Indians. Jones found, too, that even fully assimilated captives served to extend the middle ground. Traders sought such women as wives, settled permanently with them, and the women in the usual manner bridged the two worlds.[30]

As such contacts increased in number and duration, the adjustment of meaning became more stable. Indians and whites had time to find parallel beliefs on which to build. An accommodation such as Henry's expedient

---

[28] For dreams, see *ibid.*, 148; "Captivity of Hugh Gibson," 148.

[29] For Delawares who spoke English, see "Journal of James Kenny," *Pennsylvania Magazine of History and Biography*, 37 (1913): 42, 423–25; For Joseph Peepee, see *Diary of David McClure* (New York: Knickerbocker Press, 1899), Aug. 23, 1772, 46. For Nickels, see *ibid.*, Sept. 13, 55; David Jones, *A Journal of Two Visits Made to Some Nations of Indians on the West Side of the River Ohio in the Years 1772 and 1773* (New York: Arno Press and *New York Times*, 1971, orig. ed., 1774), 100. For Moravians, see *Diary of David McClure*, Sept. 5, 1772, 50–51. McClure hardly considered either Peepee or Nickels fully assimilated into British culture, *ibid.*, Sept. 19, 1772, 59. For Peepee's own negotiation of social meaning, see *ibid.*, 82. McClure also met "a young man, of the name of Hamilton," who having grown up among the Indians, returned to the whites, but then decided to go back among the Indians as a trader, *ibid.*, 87–88.

[30] Jones, *Journal of Two Visits*, 18, 55, 58, 88.

resort to dreams was inherently tenuous; more lasting accommodations were possible when European and Algonquian beliefs actually overlappped. The Quaker belief in direct divine inspiration, for example, yielded not only an interest in Indian prophets but also a common interest with Indians in the meaning of dreams. In entertaining Indians at his Pittsburgh trading house, James Kenny took an interest in their dreams and often recorded his own. To talk of dreams and to talk of God created a discourse on the supernatural that drew from both cultures and moved both ways. Kenny, as a Quaker, pondering the meaning of Delaware dreams, had as a rough equivalent the Delaware George White Eyes, who had traders read him the Bible in his hunting camp.[31]

People far less sympathetic to the Indians than Kenny found the same route to the middle ground. In his memoirs of the white settlements of the West Virginia and Pennsylvania country, the Reverend Joseph Dodderidge connected backcountry superstitions with "ancient pagans," but their derivation more likely represented a fusion of old European and Algonquian beliefs:

> The croaking of a raven, the howling of a dog, and the screech of an owl, were as prophetic of future misfortunes among the first adventurers into this country, as they were amongst the ancient pagans; but above all, their dreams were regarded as ominous of good or ill success.[32]

This intellectual cross-fertilization found in the attention to dreams and omens remained inchoate and personal until tested in social action. Whites tried out interpretations of Algonquian beliefs, and Indians tried out interpretations of European beliefs. In the classic procedure of the middle ground, the testing often took place through an appeal to the values of others in order to try to manipulate them. In July 1759, for example, Pisquetomen, who often called himself a Quaker, demanded that James Kenny tell him what the British meant by bringing troops to the Ohio, "reminding me that

---

[31] "Journal of James Kenny," 12, 176; for White Eyes, see *ibid.*, 178. When McClure arrived among the Delawares at Kekalemahpehoong (or Newcomer's Town) on the Muskingum, he was told a story of a young Englishman who had been visited in a dream and spared from the destruction of an island upon which he lived because God had further work for him. He was asked if he was the young man and his work was to show Indians the way to heaven, *Diary of David McClure*, Sept. 24, 1772; p. 66.

The Baptist David Jones, by contrast, on his return from Newcomer's Town dreamed of his son's death. When he found that his son had indeed died, Jones was staggered, but instead of drawing the obvious parallels between this and Indian dreams, he dismissed it as an uncommon occurrence and said that usually "no notices should be taken of slumbering imaginations," Jones, *A Journal of Two Visits*, 113.

[32] Joseph Doddridge, *Notes on the Settlement and Indian Wars of the Western Parts of Virginia and Pennsylvania from 1763 to 1783* (Albany, N.Y.: Joel Munsell, 1876), 65.

ye Quakers always should speak truth & not lie." The same day Daniel, another Indian who sometimes called himself a Quaker, asked Kenny for a gun to fight the French Indians. When told that Quakers did not fight, he said "he could fight & be a Quaker too."[33]

Whites, too, tested in action their interpretations of Indian beliefs. Sometimes such interpretations involved denial of the truth of Indian beliefs, sometimes they involved acceptance. In either case, the resolution in action took place on the middle ground, and the final judgment involved people from both cultures. Perhaps no aspect of Algonquian culture aroused more differences among whites than witchcraft. Even among as tightly knit a group as the Moravian missionaries, some, such as David Zeisberger, accepted the actual ability of Algonquian shamans to attain their ends through magic and to harm their victims through supernatural means, while others, such as John Heckewelder, denied the power of witches. Both groups appealed to experience with Indians to make their case.[34]

In 1776, the Quaker trader John Anderson, "after vainly endeavouring to convince those people by argument that there was no such thing as witchcraft," dared Algonquian shamans to try to kill him with their magic. One shaman, an "arch sorcerer," obliged, and in front of many spectators he tried to dispatch the trader. His failure vindicated Anderson in his disbelief, but the test did not induce the Algonquians to abandon belief in witchcraft. Instead, this and other failures led the Algonquians and many Europeans to redefine witchcraft in racial and cultural terms. The shaman involved in Anderson's experiment explained his failure by declaring that whites ate too much salt and this inured them against the shaman's medicine. Indian witchcraft, in short, worked against Indians, not against whites. But this formulation, too, was subject to further testing.[35]

David Zeisberger, like Anderson, had originally been skeptical of the claims of shamans, "thinking it all to be a boasting and lying on their part." He had, however, become persuaded otherwise. Those who, like Anderson's shaman, made great claims, Zeisberger contended, knew the least of the dark arts. "The adepts do not boast of their knowledge for fear of their lives." There were, Zeisberger contended, "Indians who have the ability to bring about the death of any one by other than ordinary means, even in the short space of twenty four hours." Although the Indians claimed that their

---

[33] "Journal of James Kenny," 433–34.
[34] For Zeisberger, see Hulbert and Schwarze (eds.), *Zeisberger's History*, 84, 125. For Heckewelder, see John Heckewelder, *History, Manners, and Customs of Indian Nations who Once Inhabited Pennsylvania and the Neighboring States*, new and rev. ed. (Philadelphia, 1876; repr. ed., New York: Arno Press, 1971), 239. Doddridge, *Notes on the Settlement*, 179–84, noted the prevalence of belief in witchcraft among backcountry settlers.
[35] For Anderson, see Heckewelder, *History*, 243.

magic had no effect on whites "because they use so much salt in their victuals," this was "merely a pretense as there are instances of Europeans having fallen victims to their skill in poisoning." For Zeisberger the cause of failure in a case such as Anderson's was the insufficient skill of the practitioner. The power was real, and Indian denials of its efficacy against whites was only a subterfuge designed to conceal their murders.[36]

Debates over witchcraft summoned the Christian dévil and Algonquian manitous onto the middle ground where they themselves could be modified. In a syncretic fashion, some manitous could be associated with the devil, salt could protect Indian as well as European victims, and the less obvious witches were, the more dangerous they could become. British subjects and Algonquians had established a mutually comprehensible dialogue about witches.[37]

The same sort of common reasoning, however, could proceed from the opposite premise: Magical powers did not exist, and it was the weakness and suggestibility of the victim that created the effect. This, essentially, was John Heckewelder's position. Heckewelder thought that the Indians' belief in witchcraft allowed their fantasies to undo them. In defending this opinion, Heckewelder and other whites sought verification from the sorcerers themselves, and they claimed to have received it. One of the "most noted sorcerers" supposedly told a white man that his victims died only of "a disturbed imagination," victims not of witchcraft but of their own "credulity and folly." Like Zeisberger's interpretation, Heckewelder's involved an appeal not only to experience but to the stated beliefs of the other culture. It demanded confirmation from the Algonquians themselves.[38]

What Indians and Europeans did in arguing about the supernatural they also did in action. A serendipitous but notable example of achieving the aims of one culture through the mechanisms of another occurred in 1771. During the same attack that had led to the capture of Alexander Henry, "one Bruce, A Trader," had been plundered at Michilimackinac in 1763 by the Ojibwa war leader Grand Saulteur. The attack had ruined Bruce, and the trade had not treated him any more kindly after Pontiac's Rebellion ended. Bankrupt, he had sought refuge among the Fox. There he had become a "Chief," in this case almost certainly meaning a war leader. In 1770, the Chippewas accidentally killed some Fox, and Bruce led the Fox party that

---

[36] Hulbert and Schwarze (eds.), *Zeisberger's History*, 125–26. For early claims made by the Indians to Zeisberger on the power of witches, see "Diary of David Zeisberger's Journey to the Ohio . . . From Sept. 20 to Nov. 16, 1767," *Ohio Archaeological and Historical Quarterly* 21 (1912): 16–17.

[37] In 1772, David McClure entered into this dialogue about devils/evil manitous, sin/ witchcraft almost immediately, *Diary of David McClure*, Sept. 15, 1772, 56–57.

[38] Heckewelder, *History*, 239–41.

went to revenge the dead. The revenge Bruce achieved proved particularly sweet: Bruce's Fox warriors killed his old nemesis, Grand Saulteur. Grand Saulteur, plunderer of Bruce, enemy to the British, relative of Pontiac, and recognized avenger of Pontiac's death, proved a pleasing victim to the British military as well as to Bruce. The personal desires of a man of one culture and the collective hopes of others found fulfillment through the logic of a people of another culture. Bruce, as Algonquian war leader and bankrupt British trader, became at least momentarily whole in the death of Grand Saulteur.[39]

This melding of interests derived from two different cultures continued to be most common in the rituals of exchange. The British did not have to reinvent such rituals to initiate trade. Both ex-prisoners and French Canadians proved adept tutors in their meaning. Alexander Henry's experience as a captive and his close association with French Canadians, for example, quickly taught him the necessary trading rituals and changed him from the novice he had been at Michilimackinac into a seasoned operator on the middle ground. Exchange began with the giving of large gifts of food by the Indians. The trader returned gifts of powder, shot, and rum. The Indians might then give additional gifts, but at some point the gift exchange gave way to individual bartering, very often conducted by the women. In many such cases there was a connection between material exchange and sexual exchange. Trading sometimes ended, as it did in one of Henry's expeditions, with the women abandoning "themselves to my Canadians."[40]

Some British traders such as James Kenny probably had this sexual exchange in mind when they condemned the other traders for "joyning with ye Indian customs and abominations," but Kenny, too, had to re-create exchange on the middle ground. He hired an ex-prisoner to assist him and learned to speak Delaware. He gave small gifts and received the usual instruction from Indians who appealed to his own values to get him to act appropriately, as when they cautioned Kenny that he should not cheat for it would "offend ye Great Spirit above." When Algonquian women demanded to spend the night at his trading house, however, Kenny balked. They threw stones at his shutters after he had locked them out, but Kenny refused to budge.[41]

As Kenny's resistance demonstrates, reproduction of the rituals of ex-

---

[39] For Bruce, see Turnbull to Gage, May 29, 1771, *JP* 8:117. For Grand Saulteur, see Journal of Transactions and Presents . . . from 23 Dec. 1768 (Ill.), April 29, 1770, Gage Papers, AS 138.

[40] Henry, *Travels*, 235–36; "Journal of James Kenny," 169. The English traders regularly used Frenchmen to conduct the actual exchange, Gage to G. Johnson, May 29, 1768, *JP* 12:517; Gage to Turnbull, May 30, 1768, Gage Papers, AS 77.

[41] "Journal of James Kenny," for quotation, see 182; for cheating, 169; women, 17; ex-prisoners, 6.

change was often imperfect; they had to replicate themselves in the face of rival interpretations and struggles over meaning that could, in fact, alter them. One such change seems to have taken place in the years following Pontiac's Rebellion. Apparently, British traders reinterpreted the conjuncture of sexual exchange and gift giving as prostitution, and with the whole-sale introduction of rum as a trade good, the conjuncture did indeed become something very close to prostitution.

During the late eighteenth century, the old association of sexual exchange with commodity exchange seems to have reduced sexual acts themselves to commodities. Women had sexual intercourse with white men in exchange for a payment of rum. Sex became a business venture in a double sense, since the women did not consume this rum but instead carried it to Indian men to whom they sold it at high prices. The alteration of exchange between peoples thus carried over to alter the nature of exchange within a village. Algonquian men, who had earlier voiced few objections to sexual relations between Algonquian women and white men, denounced this new practice. By 1766, Delaware chiefs were condemning this kind of prostitution as "very bad" and trying unsuccessfully to halt it. As women increased their control over goods gained through this trade, the trade for rum became distinct from prostitution since women could exchange furs directly for liquor. The Shawnee chiefs asked whites in 1770 not to "sell [rum to] our women to sell to us again." And in a dispute over "slaves, cattle, Indian corn, wampum, silver works, and axes" claimed by the Frenchman Richardville when Marie Louisas, the Miami woman he lived with, left him, Marie's brother Pacane claimed that she had acquired this property partly by trading skins for rum at Detroit and then retailing the rum. Rum served as a lubricant that was gradually shifting the meaning of exchange on the middle ground toward a commodity transfer whose end was private profit. Such actions proved particularly alarming to Algonquians when engaged in by Indians themselves, and by 1770 the Susquehanna villagers, many of whom moved west, were denouncing Indian traders as far worse than white.[42]

Shifts in meaning could occur, but Algonquians continued to have the power to transmit intact most of the special rituals of the middle ground. Those novice white traders who failed to learn the necessary rituals of exchange from French Canadians, ex-prisoners, Algonquian women, or

---

[42] For Delaware complaint, Guy Soulliard Klett (ed.), *Journals of Charles Beatty, 1762–69* (University Park, Pa.: Pennsylvania State University Press, 1962), 67; Hulbert and Schwarze (eds.), *Zeisberger's History*, 117. For Shawnee complaint, see Croghan Journal, Aug. 1, 1770 in Croghan to Gage, Aug. 8, 1770, Gage Papers, AS 94.
For Pacane's sister, see Council held at Detroit 18 Sept. 1774 with Lernoult to Gage, Sept. 9, 1774, Gage Papers, AS 123. Women apparently also acted as agents of white traders, *Diary of David McClure*, Sept. 28, 1772, 73. For denunciation of Indian traders, see Sachems of Oquaga to Johnson, 22 Jan. 1770, *JP* 7:348.

other experienced traders necessarily learned the rituals from their customers themselves. In 1769, in a private venture, William Johnson equipped Ferrall Wade and C. Keiuser for a trading expedition to Toronto on Lake Ontario. Their letters over the next several years provide an account of the education of traders.[43]

Wade and Keiuser discovered that despite the inroads of rum, the trade along Lake Ontario remained a relationship very much anchored in the mix of reciprocity, profit, and politics established on the middle ground. Rum proved necessary to the trade, particularly in the spring when hunters returning from winter camps would not trade without rum and tobacco. But rum alone could not sustain the trade. Johnson, despite his condemnation of the rum trade, had apparently outfitted his own novice traders almost entirely with rum. They informed him that they needed a wider assortment of goods if they were to obtain a substantial number of furs. They also needed a larger relationship with the Mississaugas, and the Indians themselves took on the chore of establishing it. The Mississaugas used food to create reciprocity. Asking the traders to winter among them, they supplied Wade and Keiuser with venison and corn at a "mere triffle." In return, the traders had to "feed All the Indians that come hear whether they trade or not." The Mississaugas also initiated a political relationship. Perhaps because of the traders' relations with Johnson, the Indians granted them a status of "Verry Great Men," to whom they spoke with strings of wampum. Reciprocity seems, however, to have governed only the exchange of food and, to a lesser degree, rum, tobacco, powder, and ball, the last two because they obtained food. Other goods fell within the realm of profit, and the British sought to maximize their own gains while still underselling competing French traders. But even here, fair dealing seems to have carried as much weight in determining whom the Indians traded with as did price.[44]

Traders profited, but the trade embodied relationships beyond profit. A stable trade could evolve only as the basis of a stable social relationship, and competition between traders was often a competition for social place. Only those traders who established social place had opportunities for profit. In the fall of 1771, for example, Keiuser responded to an invitation from the Indians of Pemiskittyon to winter among them. When they received

---

[43] For first winter, see Wade & Keiuser to Johnson, June 14, 1770, *JP* 7:739–40.
[44] Rum, Wade & Keiuser to Johnson, June 14, 1770, *JP* 7:739–40; *ibid.*, Apr. 6, 1771, *JP* 8:62–63; *ibid.*, June 18, 1771, *JP* 8:149–51; Ferrall Wade to Johnson, May 29, 1771, *JP* 8:118; *ibid.*, June 7, 1771, *JP* 8:128. For evolution of exchange relationship, see Wade & Keiuser to Johnson, June 20, 1770, *JP* 7:756; Wade & Keiuser to Johnson, Mar. 1, 1771, *JP* 8:2–3; Ferrall Wade to Johnson, May 29, 1771, *JP* 8:118; Wade & Keiuser to Johnson, June 18, 1771, *JP* 8:149–51; C. Keiuser to Wade, Dec. 30, 1771, *JP* 8:854–56. Articles requested by Wade & Keiuser, c. Aug. 16, 1770, *JP* 7:824–25.

him, they made him a present of ten bearskins and immediately sent out messengers to bring surrounding people in to trade. But Keiuser's hopes for great profits collapsed when one French and two British traders arrived at Passkottejang, about a day's journey away. They spoke on a large belt and a large silken flag and claimed to be relations of Sir William Johnson who had "sent them hier to make them Charity, & to let them have their Necessary's Cheaper than any Trader yet sold them." The new traders had, with their claims of kinship to Johnson, preempted Keiuser's social place. He could only console himself with the hope that, because his competitors gave a blanket for each buckskin in order to validate their claims and status, they must soon go bankrupt.[45]

Wade, who remained at Toronto, also found social position the key to exchange. Wade was adopted by the "Great Chief," who "took me as his Child, and All the Indians should look on me as such." Wade's new father summoned Monoghquit, the headman of a village close to Toronto, upbraided him for pillaging traders, and denounced his young men for drinking at the expense of their hunt. Monoghquit and his people were fools, he said; "the English put Confidence in them, and they should not by there bad behaviour break the friendship that subsisted between them." As a good son, Wade, for his part, stressed his loyalty and commitment to the Indians. He urged them to trade only with him and not with visiting traders, for without him they would have to travel to Niagara in winter to obtain mere trifles. On his father's departure, Wade made the old man a present of one of his own coats, a keg of rum, a blanket, powder, and shot.[46]

Exchange had long been embedded in the middle ground, but a much larger and grander systematization of meaning also continued into the late eighteenth century. It involved an ongoing dialogue between Indians and whites about religion, with the most notable participants being Indian prophets – that is, proponents of religious syncretism – and Christian missionaries who were in this period largely Moravians. The issue at stake, in one sense, involved the middle ground itself. The prophets sought to understand the world as a shared setting with a common God for two different ways of life: an Indian way and a European way. The missionaries attempted to convince the Indians that they were "one people" who ideally should share a single Christian way.[47]

In making their case for an Indian way, the prophets were not traditional-

---

[45] Ferrall Wade to Johnson, Sept. 22, 1771, *JP* 8:270–77; C. Keiuser to Wade, Nov. 23, 1771, *JP* 8:324–25.

[46] Ferrall Wade to Johnson, Sept. 22, 1771, *JP* 8:270–77; *ibid.*, Oct. 28, 1771, *JP* 8:303–5.

[47] For one people, see Zeisberger, "Diary," 27; Klett, *Journals of Charles Beatty*, 62. The idea of separate ways was not confined to the prophets; see McClure's discussion with the speaker at Newcomer's Town, *Diary of David McClure*, Oct. 4, 1772, 80.

ists hostile to Christianity. They often sought out missionaries and appro-
priated parts of their doctrines. In 1767 when the Presbyterian Charles
Beatty reached Kekalemahpehoong (or Newcomer's Town) on the Mus-
kingum River, he found that his most attentive and interested listener was
Neolin. The same year David Zeisberger visited the Munsee town of
Goshgoshing on the upper Allegheny. He too met an "Indian preacher,"
Wangomend, who stayed near him during Zeisberger's visit and wanted to
preach with him and the Indian Moravians who accompanied him.[48]

Zeisberger often lumped the preachers together with "doctors and
sorcerers" as "apostles of Satan," but he also recognized the clear differences between them. Like the shamans, the preachers had access to
manitous, but unlike them, they also had direct revelations from God. They
demanded that the Indians follow a "very severe" moral code. They "made
themselves a bible, consisting of a sheet of paper, on which there is a
representation of God, of the Whites, the Indians, and the Blacks," and they
took to preaching like missionaries. They claimed "that there are two ways to
God, one for the whites and one for the Indians." Wangomend was quite
willing to admit that both Zeisberger and one of his Indian assistants, Anton,
knew God. When Zeisberger provoked a confrontation with Wangomend,
the Indian preacher defended his message of an Indian way, but then
admitted that he neither knew of Christ nor understood his message.
Zeisberger, in pressing his advantage, wandered unknowingly onto the
middle ground. To know Christ, Zeisberger told Wangomend, the preacher
would have to "give up your Indian abominations and come to the Saviour as
a poor, wretched lost man, who knows nothing." But such a stance was
exactly the posture of an Algonquian before the manitous. Wangomend
made the predictable response: he would be "glad to hear because he was
poor."[49]

Such confrontations between missionaries and Indians could yield
converts, but they were also grist for the syncretic mill. Wangomend
eventually became Zeisberger's enemy, but he also became the enemy of
witches and shamans, whom he and other Indians increasingly identified
with Satan. The Indians, Zeisberger later reported, accepted the existence of
Satan but made him an evil brought by the whites. "They declare that he is
not to be found among the Indians but only among the white people, for if he
were among the Indians they would long since have discovered him, and
their ancestors would have told them about him." By identifying older

---

[48] Klett (ed.), *Journals of Charles Beatty*, 65, 68–70; Zeisberger, "Diary," 23–25; Heckewelder, *History*, 293.

[49] Zeisberger, "Diary," quotations, 24, 25, 29, 31. Zeisberger realized that the preachers were a new group. He claimed they first emerged around 1750, 133. For moral code, see Hulbert and Schwarze (eds.), *Zeisberger's History*, 134.

A Moravian minister baptizes Delaware and Mohican Indians at the Moravian mission, Bethlehem, Pennsylvania, before the Moravians migrated farther west. (Rare Book Division, New York Public Library)

religious figures with Satan, a white introduction, the preachers made themselves defenders of an Indian way, which was now, in fact, their way, a syncretic blend of Christianity and older Algonquian beliefs. Many older shamans, such as the "grand Conjuror" of Kekalemahpehoong, found themselves banished for having too "much influence with the Devil."[50]

The Moravians came to regard these prophets, rather than the shamans, as their leading opponents and eventually claimed to have vanquished them. But they mistook the decline of individuals for the end of the syncretic process itself. The eclipse of individual prophets no more ended the process than Delaware rejections of missionaries who came among them ended Christian proselytizing. Missionaries continued to come and prophets returned.[51]

The Moravians opposed the prophets, but they also opposed more subtle Delaware attempts to lure them farther onto the middle ground than they wished to go. The Moravians, who joined the Indians "in the chace, & freely distribute to the helpless," became fathers to their followers and were addressed as such. But they wished their children to remain distinct from the Delawares as a whole. The chiefs, Zeisberger later wrote in his diary, "used all sorts of devices to involve us with themselves," seeking "to confound us little by little with themselves." Indeed, many of the headmen and chiefs had tried to join the church, seeking, Zeisberger thought, to "become masters of it." This the Moravians had resisted. Of necessity the Moravians dealt on the middle ground, but far more than the Jesuits, they sought to remain only on its margins.[52]

III

The erosion of the diplomatic middle ground and the accretion of a new cultural middle ground took place in tandem. In a complicated and paradoxical way each fed the other. Johnson could not keep the backcountry world of the white villagers separate from the village world of the *pays d'en haut*. The conflict between these worlds undermined the alliance, just as

---

[50] *Ibid.*, 133–36; Heckewelder, *History*, 291; becomes enemy, 294; opposes witches, 294–95. For "grand Conjuror," see *Diary of David McClure*, Sept. 25, 1772, 67.

[51] Heckewelder recognized the continuity between Neolin and Wangomend, and between Tecumseh and his brother, the Prophet, Heckewelder, *History*, 295; for rejection of McClure's mission, see *Diary of David McClure*, Oct. 6, 1772, 83–84. Wangomend himself apparently moved to the Munsee village at Wahlhanding, Heckewelder, The Names of all the different Indian Nations . . . (1777), Ms. Moravian Archives, copy in Ohio Valley–Great Lakes Ethnohistorical Archives, University of Indiana, hereafter cited as GLEHA.

[52] For Moravians as fathers, see *Diary of David McClure*, Sept. 5, 1772, 51; Zeisberger, "Diary," Oct. 18, 1781, 1:27–28.

their intermingling began to build a new popular middle ground. But because the new middle ground grew so slowly, and the whites who helped create it remained but a minority, the crumbling of the alliance remained far more visible than the simultaneous growth of a common world.

The white villagers, who, along with imperial parsimony, weakened Johnson's alliance, had emerged as an independent force in the back-country by the late 1760s. They were a people as heterogeneous as the Algonquians themselves. Presbyterian Scots and Scots-Irish, Pennsylvania Germans, and American-born Virginians all mingled in the early settlements along Redstone Creek and the Cheat River and at Pittsburgh. Between 1764 and 1773, they filled most of the valleys between these places and the foot of the Appalachians, crossed over the Monongahela, and pushed down the Ohio. By 1774, there may have been fifty thousand whites west of the Appalachians. The British military could not control them. They were, according to Gage, "too Numerous, too Lawless and Licentious ever to be restrained."[53]

Many of the emigrants from east of the Appalachians were ragtag refugees from a hierarchical society that would soon enough envelop them once again, but in the 1760s and 1770s they had for the moment escaped hierarchical controls. As among the Algonquians, there were only imperfect ways to restrain the young men of the white villages. "They are already," Gage wrote in 1770, "almost out of the Reach of Law and Government; Neither the Endeavors of Government, or Fear of Indians has kept them properly within Bounds." Most British settlers, particularly the Virginians, despised Indians and abused them "wherever they happened to meet them." And, as David McClure observed of the backcountry settlers at Pittsburgh, they seemed "to feel themselves beyond the arm of government & freed from the restraining influence of religion." On both sides of the Ohio unruly young men, white and Indian, stole horses, got drunk, and fought.[54]

This difficulty in controlling their young men was but one of a series of similarities between the two societies. The missionary David McClure

---

[53] For settlement, see Solon J. Buck and Elizabeth Hawthorn Buck, *The Planting of Civilization in Western Pennsylvania* (Pittsburgh: University of Pittsburgh Press, 1939), 135–55. Most of these settlers were squatters until Pennsylvania began land sales in 1769, *ibid.*, 143. For extent of settlement, see *Diary of David McClure*, Apr. 24, 1773, 119. For quotation, see Gage to Johnson, Apr. 3, 1769, *JP* 12:710. See also Gage to Johnson, Oct. 22, 1769, *JP* 7:225. Johnson to Gage, Apr. 14, 1769, *JP* 12:715. There were many Virginians in what is now Pennsylvania as well as in West Virginia. Both colonies claimed jurisdiction over western Pennsylvania.

[54] Croghan Journal, Aug. 1, 1770; for quotation, abuse, July 5, 1770, in Croghan to Gage, Aug. 8, 1770, Gage Papers, AS 94. For McClure quote, *Diary of David McClure*, Sept. 13, 1772, 53. For Gage quotation, see Gage to Hillsborough, Nov. 10, 1770, Carter (ed.), *Correspondence of Gage*, 1:277.

thought the Virginians seemed "generally white Savages, and subsist by hunting, and live like the Indians." Gage drew the same parallel in giving an account of a new settlement on the Ohio. "Many of these people," he noted, were "half naked . . . and they differ little from Indians in their Manner of Life. They have no means to purchase Clothing but by skins, and that induces them to hunt, and consequently to intrude on the Indian hunting grounds." Economically, both societies survived on the basis of a mixed agricultural, grazing, and hunting economy. Their economies grew steadily more similar as Virginia long hunters invaded Algonquian hunting territories, and as Algonquians added significant numbers of horses and pigs and lesser numbers of cattle to their villages. Conflict between the two groups was thus chronic, not just because each group understood the world and their place in it in very different terms but also because the economic basis and political organization of the two worlds were so close. Algonquians and Virginians, for instance, might attribute entirely different meanings to the human relationship with game animals, but they nonetheless competed for animals which the Indians saw as theirs by right. As the Delawares, resorting to the parallels of the middle ground to make their meanings clear, said: "The Elks are our horses, the buffaloes are our cows, the deer are our sheep, & the whites shan't have them."[55]

In regard to the Indians, the British villagers were proceeding in a direction opposite from that taken by the French villagers of the *pays d'en haut*. The French had established a world of common meaning while maintaining a partially separate world of practice. Algonquians conceived of a French economy discrete and complementary to their own. Frenchmen brought European goods into the West, but they rarely competed commercially with Indian warriors for game or fish. They acquired these from the Algonquians. When they did hunt or fish, the French exploited quite specific resources with Indian permission. The Algonquians permitted voyageurs and traders on the Mississippi and Ohio to hunt commercially for buffalo, but other large game belonged to the Indians. Similarly, the French failure to farm extensively outside of the Illinois country had been a cause of

---

[55] For quotation, see *Diary of David McClure*, 93. For Gage quotation, see Gage to Hillsborough, Oct. 7, 1772, Carter (ed.), *Correspondence of Gage*, 1:336. For claim to game animals, see Speech of Beaver, May 6, 768, Conference at Fort Pitt, *PCR* 9:537. For complaints and quotation, see *Diary of David McClure*, Oct. 6, 1772, 83, 85. For Indian attacks on white hunters, see Gage to Hillsborough, Oct. 9, 1768, *IHC* 16:415; Gage to Wilkins, Oct. 11, 1768, *IHC* 16:419; Croghan Journal, Aug. 1, 1770, in Croghan to Gage, Aug. 8, 1770, Gage Papers, AS 94; Johnson to Gage, Dec. 23, 1771, *JP* 8:348; Johnson to Dartmouth, Nov. 4, 1772, *NYCD* 8:316.

For horse stealing, see Croghan to Johnson, May 19, 1770, *JP* 7:689; Croghan Journal, July 26, 1770, in Croghan to Gage, Aug. 8, 1770, Gage Papers, AS 94.

chronic complaint for French colonial officials, but the limits on their fields meant they did not threaten neighboring Indians.[56]

Just as they did between the Algonquians and the French, exchanges established relationships between the Algonquians and the British. How exchanges proceeded identified givers and receivers as friends or enemies. But whereas exchanges between the French and the Algonquians had strengthened the connections between the two peoples, exchanges between the British and the Algonquians bred conflict. The French took wives from the Indians and produced children of mixed descent; the British took land and threatened the well-being of Algonquian children. The French were friends and relatives; the British often seemed enemies and thieves.

Rum, which became the major exotic good moving between Indian and white villages, only made things worse. Not only did traders carry rum into the Algonquian villages, but Algonquians traveling among the British obtained it at nearly any post or settlement. As contact grew more frequent, conflict grew more frequent, and it was often fueled by rum. Following the end of Pontiac's Rebellion, meetings between the backcountry settlers and the Indians became commonplace both east and west of Pittsburgh. Indians frequented the country between the Ohio River and the mountains, both to hunt and to travel south toward the southern tribes. Indian hunters camped near white farms and traded at white homesteads where each settler, Croghan said, soon became a sutler.[57]

The great advantage of rum for many British subjects was that it provided a way to gain their immediate ends without engaging in the slow and tedious process of creating a common world of meaning. To traders unwilling to master the rituals and logic of exchange, or to anyone seeking quick Indian consent, rum could short-circuit the creation of meaning on the middle ground. A drunken Indian would agree to what a sober Indian would never consider. All of this came at a cost; for a drunken Indian would also do what a sober Indian would never attempt. Rum, by dissolving social restraints, very often produced violence. But since the consequences of trading in rum did not always fall on the trader, and because the gains it could produce were so spectacular, the trade persisted.[58]

[56] French hunters from Louisiana heavily hunted buffalo along the Ohio, killing at least 2,000 in 1768, Forbes to Gage, Apr. 15, 1768, Gage Papers, AS 76. Buffalo still seemed abundant to travelers, however, Butricke to Barnsley, Sept. 15, 1768, *IHC* 16:409–10. Indians had long accepted French buffalo hunting, but they strongly objected to hunters taking bear, beaver, and deer, Gage to Hillsborough, Oct. 9, 1768, *IHC* 16:415; Gage to Wilkins, Oct. 11, 1768, *IHC* 16:419. By 1774 there was, however, real competition between the French and some Miamis over resources, Council held at Detroit, Sept. 18, 1774, in Lernoult to Gage, Sept. 24, 1774, Gage Papers, AS 123.

[57] For sutlers, see Croghan to Gage, Aug. 8, 1770, Gage Papers, AS 94.

[58] Croghan said Indians rarely instigated conflict unless they had been drinking, Croghan to Gage, July 13, 1770, Gage Papers, AS 93.

Murders, often related to rum, plagued the country; both sides feared the consequences. In the early 1770s the growing revolutionary crisis in the East brought colonial boycotts of British imports and forced traders to rely even more heavily on rum. So great were the ravages of this rising tide of rum that the Indians could only interpret the scale of its importation as a plot to destroy them. Liquor impoverished them, caused them to murder each other and whites, and shattered the social organization of their villages. At a time when the position of the chiefs once more was deteriorating, liquor greased the skids of their descent.[59]

Yet conflict, even the violent conflict sparked by rum, could also feed the middle ground. Murder had long acted as a catalyst for the formation of the middle ground. Sparking similar deep emotions but different social responses in Algonquians and Europeans, murders forced the two groups either to kill again or to reach a mutually agreeable accommodation. Controlling and settling murders had been a central facet of the French-Algonquian alliance, and settling murders became, along with trade and land, part of the triumvirate of challenges Johnson's policy faced in the *pays d'en haut*. Ironically, Johnson had originally sought to remove murder and its resolution from the middle ground and to place it firmly within the British domain of courts and law. By controlling whites and punishing them for murdering Indians, he believed that he could gain the right to punish Indians when they murdered whites. The treaties that Johnson had negotiated to end the war had sought to give the British a unilateral role in settling violence between Indians and British subjects. British courts assumed jurisdiction,

---

[59] In the Illinois country Wilkins stopped Morgan from setting up a still from fear of the consequences, Wilkins to Gage, Feb. 20, 1771, Gage Papers, AS 100. At Fort Pitt, Edmonstone complained liquor always led to violence, for the Indians "study mischief when sober and put it in execution when Drunk," Edmonstone to Gage, Mar. 9, 1771, Gage Papers, AS 100. At Michilimackinac the Indians were "debauched" by rum and neglected their hunting, Gage to Hillsborough, Carter (ed.), *Correspondence of Gage*, 1:308. For example of Indian complaints, see Edmonstone to Gage, Apr. 24, 1771, Gage Papers, AS 102; Speech of Shawnees, July 1771, *JP* 12:915; Johnson to Gage, Nov. 16, 177, *JP* 8:319. For rum as conspiracy, see Croghan Journal, July 5, 1770, in Croghan to Gage, Aug. 8, 1770, Gage Papers, AS 94. Croghan to Gage, July 13, 1770, Gage Papers, AS 93; Basset to Haldimand, 29 Apr. 1773, *MPHC* 19:296; Indian Conference, Pittsburgh, Oct. 9, 1773, *JP* 12:1035.

For rum and victims, see Proceedings of Sir William Johnson . . . July 1770, *NYCD* 8:243. On September 1, e.g., Charles Hanigam and two others murdered a Delaware named Jacob Daniel and his two male children. Taken into custody and delivered to Fort Pitt by whites, Hanigam escaped, Affidavit of David Owens before Charles Edmonstone, Sept. 10, 1769, in Edmonstone to Gage, Sept. 10, 1769, Gage Papers, AS 87; Gage to Edmonstone, Oct. 8, 1769, *ibid*.

Earlier in August, Croghan had reported the murder of three whites in the West, Croghan to Johnson, Aug. 8, 1769, *JP* 7:78–79. For attacks on boats on Ohio and sacking of Vincennes, see *ibid*.; Gage to Johnson, Aug. 27, 1769, *JP* 7:140–41; Turnbull to Gage, Sept. 9, 1769, Gage Papers, AS 87; Wilkins to Gage, Dec. 5, 1769, Gage Papers, AS 88.

and these courts gave Indians neither a say in the rules governing the outcome nor even a right to testify. The irony of British policy in the years between the French and Indian War and the American Revolution was that although it aspired to control Indians, it foundered on the British government's inability to control its own subjects. And the more British officials failed to control their own people through law, the more events forced them to appeal to the customs of the middle ground.[60]

The ubiquity of murder, armed robbery, and rape – particularly in the Ohio country – in the years following Pontiac's Rebellion forced the British into ideological retreat. In the emerging Algonquian formulation of a world that contained separate Indian and white ways, the Indians regarded law as a distinguishing European trait. Law was a European tool for the control and restraint of Europeans, and the Europeans were liable for blame when laws failed to restrain their people. The British, in contrast, asserted the universality of law. It covered all of the king's children. When, after Pontiac's Rebellion, law proved an ineffective mechanism for controlling British subjects, Algonquians were surprised and suspicious. Having been told that the law covered all of the king's children, both red and white, the Six Nations refused to believe that settlers could come onto Indian lands and murder and cheat Indians without the king's permission. If he had desired to stop them, "he would have done it before now as he made laws to rule his People by." Similarly, since Indians equated law with punishment, Johnson eventually told Gage that it was better not to arrest white murderers of Indians than to arrest and acquit them, for Indians were incapable of appreciating the "Nicetys of the Common Law." In the *pays d'en haut* proper, the inability of British commanders to halt the murders of Indians forced Captain Murray at Pittsburgh to take the ultimately self-defeating position that the settlers and murderers were "under no Laws." But if white settlers fell outside British laws, why should Indians fall within them?[61]

Those people who murdered Indians so readily after 1765 did not do so without cause. By 1766 over a decade of sustained terror and brutality had given the backcountry settlers of Pennsylvania, Virginia, and Maryland reason enough to hate. They had seen entire families killed, often with terrible cruelty; relatives and neighbors had been carried off into captivity.

[60] Johnson, to be sure, came to recognize the inability of English courts to act without Indian participation and sought to modify the rules, at least for Christian Indians, Johnson, Review of the Trade and Affairs . . . , *IHC* 26:63.

[61] For Seneca quotation, see Journal of Indian Transactions at Niagara, in the Year 1767 (Aug. 8), *DHNY* 2:873. For laws, see Croghan to Franklin, Oct. 2, 1767, Shelbourne Papers, v. 50, Clements Library. For better not to arrest, see Johnson to Gage, Dec. 24, 1767, *DHNY* 2:893–95. For a general review of problem with laws, see Johnson, Review of the Trade and Affairs in the Northern District of America, Sept. 22, 1767, *IHC* 16:57–58. For Murray quotation, see Murray to Gage, May 16, 1767, Gage Papers, AS 65.

Their homes and fields had been ravaged and laid to waste. And during all of this, most of their own attempts to retaliate had been feeble and ineffective. In the end, only the troops of the empire had eliminated such attacks.

A desire for revenge burned deeply in the backcountry after the fighting in the *pays d'en haut* ended, and for many backcountry people peace presented their first opportunity to kill Indians. The Algonquians, who knew well enough the desire for revenge, had buried their desires with their dead in the rituals of peace. The people of the backcountry acknowledged no such rituals. They murdered Indians in such large and increasing numbers that Croghan warned it was not safe for any Indian to come near the Pennsylvania frontier. As one murderer of two Indian women (one of the few who were punished) declared, "he thought it a meritorious act to kill Heathens whenever they were found." And this, commented William Johnson, seemed to be "The opinion of all the common people."[62]

By the late winter of 1765 and the spring of 1766, killings in the *pays d'en haut*, particularly around the Ohio, were reported with an alarming regularity. At Detroit, two soldiers were killed by the Saint Joseph Potawatomis in revenge, as it turned out, for the rape of two Indian women. An Iroquois was murdered in the Pennsylvania backcountry. Four more Iroquois were killed in Virginia, "more" on the headwaters of the Monongahela. A black slave at Detroit murdered two Indian women. In April, at the mouth of the Scioto, two employees of British traders murdered five Shawnee men and women while they slept. The victims died after having fed the starving Englishmen. Robbery was the apparent motive. The slain Shawnees were relatives of the chiefs who had died escorting Croghan to the Illinois the year before. The murderers stole the condolence presents that their victims had received at Fort Pitt. In the six months preceding August 1766, whites murdered nearly twenty Indians.[63]

[62] For unsafe, see Croghan to Johnson, Apr. 18, 1766, *JP* 5:181. For attitude of "country people," see Johnson to Gage, Apr. 17, 1766, *JP* 12:74–75. For quotation, see Johnson to Lords of Trade, Aug. 20, 1766, *NYCD* 7:852.

[63] For soldiers, see Campbell to Johnson, Feb. 24, 1766, *JP* 12:29–30. For British ambush party carrying slave to raise dead, capturing three, and apparently killing a child in the process, see Campbell to Gage, Apr. 10, 1766, Gage Papers, AS 50. Campbell did not mention that the murders were in revenge for rape nor the death of the child, but Croghan and Johnson did, Abstract from Croghan's Journal, May 24, 1766, Gage Papers, AS 51, and Johnson to Gage, May 27, 1766, *JP* 5:224–25. For backcountry and Monongahela, see Croghan to Gage, Mar. 16, 1766, Gage Papers, AS 49. For women at Detroit, see Croghan Journal, May 25, 1766, Gage Papers, AS 51. For total, see Johnson to Lords of Trade, Aug. 20, 1766, *NYCD* 7:852. For murder of Shawnees, see Murray to Gage, Apr. 24, 1766, Gage Papers, AS 50. Gage to Johnson, May 19, 1766, *JP* 12:91. For relatives, see Abstract of Croghan's Journal, May 23, 1766, Gage Papers, AS 51. For other murders, including a Wyandot at Sandusky, see Johnson to Gage, June 27, 1766, *JP* 12:115.

Besides actual murders, there were even more inflammatory rumors of murders; see Indian Proceedings, June 18, 1766, *JP* 12:123. This party returned safely; see Proceedings of . . . Johnson with Pondiac, July 23, 1766, *NYCD* 7:864.

It rapidly became apparent that the courts could not settle these murders and that some alternate way of proceeding was necessary. Gage fumed that the colonies failed to enforce the laws and, indeed, protected the murderers of Indians. Johnson admitted that "from the present disposition of our People we can expect little Justice for the Indians." The Ohio Indians both lamented the loss of the old practices of the French and condemned the new.

> Before when accidents [murders] happened of this kind we made up by Condoling with each other, which is the antient Custom of all Our Nations in this Country, but you have broke tho. our old Customs and made New Ones which we are not well acquainted with; And you Can't Expect, let us be ever so desirous of living in Peace, that we will Sit Still and See our People murdered by yours without having the Same Satisfaction from you that you Demand of Us.

The chiefs warned repeatedly that they would be unable to control their warriors who would seek revenge, and by June 1766 the Shawnees had committed at least one murder south of the Ohio. Gage, at least rhetorically, was willing to let them take revenge if it would fall on the guilty parties or, at least, on the guilty settlements, but virtually everyone feared renewed war.[64]

This wave of murders and the British inability to either prevent them or punish the killers forced officials to return to earlier methods of dealing with violence. In June 1766, Croghan was "agreeable to antient Custom of our forefathers," condoling the Ohio Indians for their losses and covering their graves with goods "that their Blood may no more Stain the Earth." This, the speaker for the Shawnees assured Croghan, "had made their young men's &

[64] For colonies don't enforce laws, see Gage to Johnson, May 5, 1766, *JP* 5:201. For can't expect justice, see Johnson to Gage, June 27, 1766, *JP* 12:115. For Ohio quotation, see Croghan Journal, May 27, 1766, in Croghan to Gage, June 15, 1766, Gage Papers, AS 52. For can't control warriors, Shawnees, see Shawnee Message, Apr. 20, 1766, enclosed with Murray to Gage, Apr. 24, 1766, Gage Papers, AS 50. Abstract from Croghan's Journal, May 23, 1766; *ibid.*, May 24, 1766; Campbell wished he could try the slave accused of murdering Indian women at Detroit instead of sending him to provinces for trial as the law required, Campbell to Gage, May 8, 1766, Gage Papers, AS 51. For murder by Shawnees, see Stuart to Johnson, June 1, 1766, *JP* 12:99. For fear of war, see Johnson to Gage, July 4, 1766, *JP* 12:129–32; Gage to Campbell, July 7, 1766, Gage Papers, AS 54.

Gage's position on the Indians taking revenge was contradictory. He wished that the Shawnees had caught and killed murderers, Gage to Johnson, May 19, 1766, *JP* 12:91; on other murders, he wanted to "point them to proper objects of their resentment, and . . . guide them to the Province where these Lawless and abandoned Crew reside," Gage to Croghan, Mar. 21, 1765, Gage Papers, AS 32. He also wished the Detroit Indians had killed the slave who raped and murdered two women. But when the Saint Joseph Potawatomis did kill the two soldiers who had, according to Croghan, raped a woman, Gage approved Campbell's seizure of hostages, Gage to Johnson, June 16, 1766, *JP* 12:272. Not all Indians had promised to surrender murderers, see Instructions for George Croghan, Apr. 20, 1766, *JP* 12:81–82.

women's hearts perfectly easy." Although publicly the British continued to tell the Indians that British courts would govern murders, Gage privately informed Captain Murray at Pittsburgh that if the Indians discovered murderers and took revenge upon them, the military was not to retaliate.[65]

The British inability to punish white murderers of Indians vitiated their demands that Indian murderers of whites be tried in British courts. In 1767 and 1768, two sets of murders – one of whites by Indians, the other of Indians by whites – put an end to the entire British pretense of a rule of law. The British might thereafter insist on the principle, but in practice the resolution of murders returned to the middle ground.

With many murders of Indians by whites having already taken place in the *pays d'en haut*, Indians began to attack whites. In 1767, a British vessel under the command of Captain Sinclair that was used to supply the Great Lakes posts had overwintered in a creek near the entrance to Lake Huron. On May 10, a party of drunken Saginaw Chippewas, whose reputation for unruliness had been strong among the French, visited the British. There was no hint of trouble except for a warning to a Scotsman named McDougall that he should spend the night aboard the ship. When the Saginaw Indians departed, two Indians – one named Pattoe and the other Coweskimagon – crossed the creek and approached a German, an indentured servant of Captain Sinclair, who was at work in a field. One of the Indians was by now quite sober; the other was still drunk. The sober Indian took up a garden hoe and killed the German, while urging his drunken companion to kill the German's wife, which he ineffectively tried to do. The other Indians, seeing the attack from a distance, quickly summoned Sinclair. He seized the two attackers, neither of whom resisted, and, indeed, the actual murderer had always professed himself a friend of the British. Sinclair placed the Indians on board his vessel, determined to send them back to the colonies to stand trial. Although the Chippewa chiefs immediately took steps to assure Sinclair that the murderers had not acted with the consent of the nation, they feared British retaliation. Many of the Saginaw villagers abandoned their fields and fled into the woods.[66]

---

[65] Croghan Journal, June 5, June 9, 1766, Gage Papers, AS 52. British officers were astounded at Croghan's ability to conciliate the Indians, Gordon to Gage, June 15, 1766, Gage Papers, AS 52. Croghan said that even with the aid of the chiefs it had cost him more trouble than he had ever had in his life to turn the warriors from revenge, Croghan to Gage, June 15, 1766, Gage Papers, AS 52. For should not take revenge, surrender murderers, see Proceedings of . . . Johnson with Pondiac, July 23, 1766, *NYCD* 7:856. Gage still expected satisfaction when Indians murdered whites, Gage to Johnson, Sept. 7, 1767, *JP* 5:659–60.

[66] For murder, see Sinclair to Turnbull, May 15, 1767, enclosure with Turnbull to Gage, May 29, 1767, Gage Papers, AS 65; Turnbull to Gage, May 20, 1767, Gage Papers, AS 65. For flee, see Gage to Johnson, 20 July 1767, *JP* 5:601. For Indians sorry, those who retired to woods return, see Turnbull to Gage, June 6, 1767, Gage Papers, AS 65. For worries of war, see Johnson to Gage, Dec. 24, 1767, *DHNY* 2:893–95.

The murderers quickly became an embarrassment to the British. The German servant was not, as it turned out, a random and innocent victim. He had repeatedly abused and attacked Indians. Nor was the chiefs' desire to disavow the attacks equivalent to their consenting to the murderers' arrest and trial. They reminded the British that they had not obtained satisfaction when a bateau man had murdered one of their people two years earlier, nor was there as yet any satisfaction for the two women raped and murdered by a black slave at Detroit. Even more ominously, the Chippewas apparently went beyond their own immediate grievances and cited the many murders committed by the Virginians. Murders of Indians by whites were becoming common in all of the villages of the *pays d'en haut*. As the Delawares later told Croghan, the Indians of the Great Lakes complained that whites killed Indians with impunity, while "every little Crime which any of their People committed in their drink – was taken great Notice of." But for all the general resentment, it was the relatives of the murderers who were, predictably, most incensed over the arrest of their kinsmen. One of these relatives was Pontiac's nephew. Gage, in what was becoming his standard response toward murderers of both races, wished that Sinclair had killed the Chippewas on the spot. Johnson merely wished that Turnbull at Detroit had not forwarded the murderers to him.[67]

Johnson decided that returning the murderers was the only way for the British to extricate themselves from the dilemma created by their own policy of arresting Indian murderers, but he was too late. The Chippewas retaliated for the arrest. News reached Detroit at the end of August that a war party from Saginaw had attacked British traders on the Ohio. As various accounts filtered in, it became clear that Pontiac's nephew had organized the war party from among the relatives (both Ottawa and Chippewa) of the two murderers. They had sacked two bateaus belonging to the trading company of Baynton, Wharton, and Morgan that were proceeding to the Illinois and killed the nine Englishmen and two Indians on board. The British made no attempt to retaliate or to seize the attackers. Instead, George Croghan arrived at Detroit to carry out Johnson's intentions and restore the two murderers to the Saginaw Chippewas.[68]

[67] For possible provocation, see Johnson to Gage, Aug. 21, 1767, *DHNY*, 2:862; Gage to Turnbull, Sept. 3, 1767, Gage Papers, AS 69; Gage to Johnson, Sept. 7, 1767, *JP* 5:659. For previous murders, see Johnson to Gage, Aug. 6, 1767, *DHNY* 2:860. News of the Virginia murders had reached Sandusky and almost certainly Detroit and Saginaw, Turnbull to Gage, June 21, 1767, Gage Papers, AS 66. For Delaware statement, see Croghan Journal, Oct. 28, 1767, in Howard H. Peckham (ed.), *George Croghan's Journal of His Trip to Detroit in 1767 with His Correspondence Relating Thereto* ... (Ann Arbor: University of Michigan Press, 1939), 33. Johnson complained sending murderers down made matters worse, Johnson to Gage, July 11, 1767, *IHC* 11:582. For Gage wishes St. Clair (*sic*) had made an immediate example of two murders, see Gage to Turnbull, July 13, 1767, Gage Papers, AS 67.
[68] Johnson to Gage, Aug. 21, 1767, *DHNY*, 2:862. For news of murder, see Turnbull to Gage,

The council held at Detroit by Croghan must have seemed to the Indians an echo of the councils of their French fathers. Croghan, "agreeable to an antient custom of theirs," opened the council by condoling them over the deaths of several chiefs who had died during the past year. He then spoke on belts citing "every part of their past ill Conduct toward His Majesty's Subjects Since the Peace," even back to their murder of Captain Campbell. They deserved, he told them, the "Severest punishments." But, to convince them of the "humanity and Clemency of the British Nations," Gage and Johnson had sent back the two Chippewas who had murdered Sinclair's servant. He then delivered them to the gathered council, along with a large belt that signified the British promise "for the future ... to punish with death, every Offender who dared be so hardy to break their Engagements with us."[69]

The Indian response conformed to the old pattern of submission and forgiveness. Speaking for his people, a Chippewa chief admitted "our Conduct has been very bad," but cited the people they had lost at British hands. He could not respond for all his people who had already dispersed for the winter hunt, but he hoped that "our future Conduct will merit the Approbation of Our Father." The Ottawas blamed their actions on one bad man (presumably Pontiac's nephew), "who they believe was tempted by the Evil Spirit." If Johnson and Gage would not forgive the attackers, then they promised to surrender them. This was the old ritual of submission and forgiveness, complete with threats of a father's wrath and demonstrations of his mercy. It was clearly not the rule of law that the British had intended to assert.[70]

But then the rule of law could not even be enforced among the British themselves. In many ways the crucial incident in the decline of British legal hegemony was a series of murders by two Germans, Frederick Stump and his servant John Ironcutter. Stump was a settler east of the Appalachians near Middleburg, Pennsylvania. Like many backcountry settlers, Stump doubled as a rum seller. In January 1768 a party of Indian customers became unruly. Stump and his servant quieted them by murdering the entire party, four men (a Seneca and three Mohicans) and two women. They then proceeded to the Indian camp and killed another woman, two girls, and a

Aug. 28, 1767, Gage Papers, AS 69. How many Englishmen died is unclear. The Saginaws claimed they killed 9 Englishmen and 2 Indians, mistaking them for Cherokees, Turnbull to Gage, Oct. 8, 1767, Gage Papers, AS 71. Turnbull reported 14 Englishmen killed, Turnbull to Gage, Sept. 25, 1767, Gage Papers, AS 70. For Pontiac's nephew and kinspeople of murderers, see McKee to Croghan, Sept. 20, 1767, *JP* 5:686; Croghan to Johnson, Oct. 18, 1767, *IHC* 16:88; Croghan to Gage, Oct. 1, 1767, in Peckham (ed.), *George Croghan's Journal*, 21–22. For Ottawas, see *ibid.*, 43.

[69] Croghan's Journal, Nov. 23, 1767, in Peckham (ed.), *George Croghan's Journal*, 42.
[70] *Ibid.*, 44.

smaller child. Stump scalped his victims, in one case taking all the hair and the ears, thus in Indian eyes turning drunken murders into a declaration of war. When Stump was arrested and ordered brought to Philadelphia for examination, he was freed by a mob who feared the precedent of back-country settlers being sent to Philadelphia for trial. The murders, Stump's subsequent rescue, and the incursions of settlers west of the Appalachians combined to outrage both the Iroquois and the Indians on the Ohio. The entire *pays d'en haut* was soon awash in rumors of war, and white settlers fled the frontiers.[71]

The British moved almost immediately to conciliate the Indians. The Pennsylvania legislature passed a law threatening the death penalty for settlers who failed to remove themselves after thirty days' notice, and it appropriated £2,500 to console the Indians. Johnson himself consoled the Iroquois, and he ordered Croghan to gather the Shawnees, Delawares, "and such other Tribes in that part of the Country as have any of their People killed by ours since the peace" at Fort Pitt as soon as possible. There he was to deliver £1,200 worth of presents from Pennsylvania "after having performed The Ceremonys usual on those Occasion and reconciled them to the late Act of Cruelty." Croghan believed that these ceremonies and the presents he bestowed in April and May were all that prevented war.[72]

Murders continued after 1768, but by then the British had abandoned any meaningful attempt to apply the jurisdiction of British laws. Instead they resorted to the middle ground. In 1769, a drunken Menominee killed a Scottish interpreter and a Winnebago crippled a trader. When the Winnebagos came to Michilimackinac, they brought the attacker and surrendered him and then, as was customary, begged for his release. Not thinking it prudent to force the issue, the commanding officer, Beamsley Glazier, decided to release him. Having Indians in custody was only an

---

[71] For murder and victims, see Indian Proceedings, Congress with the Six Nations, Cherokees, et al., Mar. 8, 1768, *NYCD* 8:48. James Galbreth and John Hoge to Governor, Feb. 29, 1768, and for description of Frederick Stump and John Ironcutter, see *PCR* 7:487–89. For account of Stump's rescue, see *Pennsylvania Gazette*, Mar. 3, 1768, copy in Gage Papers, AS 74. For reaction on Ohio, see McKee to Croghan, Feb. 13, 1768, Gage Papers, AS 74; Croghan to Gage, Feb. 17, 1768, Gage Papers, AS 74. For Iroquois, see Johnson to Gage, Feb. 18, 1768, *IHC* 16:171–72. For significance of scalping, see Croghan to Gage, Mar. 1, 1768, Gage Papers, AS 75.

[72] For conciliation, see Croghan to Gage, Feb. 17, 1768, Gage Papers, AS 74 (Croghan had the amount wrong; for correct figure, see Penn to Johnson, 18 Feb. 1768, *JP* 12:432.) For law, see "An Act to Remove the Persons Now Settled . . . on Lands . . . Not Purchased of the Indians . . . ," Feb. 3, 1768, *PA*, Series 1, 4:283. For conference, see Johnson to Croghan, Feb. 29, 1768, *JP* 6:122; for quotation see Instructions to George Croghan, Mar. 5, 1768, *JP* 12:463. For Iroquois, see Johnson to Wharton, Mar. 5, 1768, *JP* 6:141–42. For Croghan's assessment, see Croghan to Gage, May 9, 1768, Gage Papers, AS 76. For conference, see Minutes of Conferences held at Fort Pitt in April and May, 1768, *PA*, Series 1, 9:514–43.

embarrassment. As James Stevenson, who succeeded Turnbull at Detroit, asked on hearing that Captain Brown at Niagara had arrested four Senecas for murder, "What law will they try them by? & who are to sit as their judges? If they are hang'd the savages will look upon it as murder in cold blood, & revenge will ensue."[73]

IV

Despite their sympathy for the suffering of the Algonquians and their scorn for backcountry settlers, British officials themselves also undermined the alliance. They, too, desired Algonquian lands. And they could convince themselves that by acquiring it they were actually forwarding the cause of peace. The story of the land cessions and speculation is long and complex. It has been told often enough to require only a summary here.

The story revolves around the Treaty of Fort Stanwix. More than thirty-one hundred Indians – Iroquois and the members of their covenant chain – met with Johnson in 1768 to replace the temporary proclamation line of 1763 with a "permanent" boundary between white settlements and Indian hunting grounds. In the complexity of the motives of its negotiators and in the hidden agendas of its terms, the Treaty of Fort Stanwix stands as the most tangled agreement reached by Indians and whites in the eighteenth century. At root, it was a cynical compact born in the mutual weakness of its two major parties: the Iroquois and the British empire. Both spoke for peoples – the Algonquians and the backcountry settlers – whom, in fact, they could not control. Under the guise of reaching a permanent resolution of the problems of the *pays d'en haut*, the British effectively abdicated their role as fathers to their Algonquian children, and the Iroquois betrayed those people who were nominally under their protection.[74]

The scale of British migration had resigned the Ohio villagers to some sort of cession in 1768, and they feared that the exact terms of the cession would be largely out of their hands. The British had insisted on asserting

---

[73] For other killings, see Hay to Croghan, Feb. 19, 1768, enclosure with Croghan to Gage, May 9, 1768, Gage Papers, AS 76; Morgan to Baynton and Wharton, July 20, 1768; *IHC* 16:354–55, 363; Forbes to Gage, July 28, 1768, *IHC* 16:367. For Green Bay murders, see Glazier to Gage, June 10, 1769, Gage Papers, AS 86. For Stevenson quotation, see Stevenson to Johnson, Dec. 18, 1770, *JP* 7:1041.

[74] For treaty, see Treaty with 6 Nations Shawanese Delawares, Senecas of Ohio & Dependants &c opened at Fort Stanwix on Monday the 24 Oct. 1768, *NYCD* 8:112–34. For final numbers, see Johnson to Gage, Nov. 13, 1768, *JP* 12:635–36. Benevissica represented the Shawnees, Turtleheart and Killbuck, the Delawares, *ibid.*, 113. Johnson, admittedly for his own reasons, was later quite explicit about how the inability of the empire to control its people became a motive for the cession, Johnson to Dartmouth, Nov. 4, 1772, *NYCD* 8:316.

Iroquois suzerainty over the Ohio villagers when General Forbes captured Fort Duquesne in 1758. Johnson had claimed Iroquois sovereignty over the lands on the Ohio in even stronger terms at the end of Pontiac's Rebellion. Johnson had forced the Shawnees and Delawares to agree that the Iroquois, as their ancient conquerors, would negotiate the final boundary between the British and the Indians. Not all officials, however, confused expedient British claims and political reality. General Gage thought such a myth of Iroquois conquest had been useful enough in negotiations with the French, but he did not believe that the Iroquois could negotiate away Shawnee lands on the basis of such a conquest.

> If we are to search for truth and examine her to the Bottom, I dont imagine we shall find that any conquered Nation ever formaly ceded their Country to their Conquerors, or that the latter every required it. I never could learn more than that Nations have yielded and acknowledged themselves subjected to others, and some ever have wore Badges of Subjection.[75]

In this situation of paper sovereignty and no actual control there was a clear temptation for the Iroquois to maximize both their claims and their cession. By ceding lands they neither controlled nor occupied, they would lose nothing and gain whatever the British were willing to pay. The Iroquois had first explored the possibilities in 1765 when they had claimed that their territory ended not at the Great Kanawha River but at the Tennessee. By offering such lands for sale, they were alienating lands actually used by their old enemies, the Cherokees, and by their own unruly dependents, the Shawnees. If the covenant chain had existed as a meaningful political relationship on the Ohio, there would have been a cost: the alienation of their dependent people. But the Shawnees, Mingos, Delawares, and more recent immigrants to the Ohio had long been in the habit of going their own way. When Johnson forwarded this proposed boundary line, however, the ministry rejected it. Too large a cession only opened more land to unproductive and unruly backcountry settlers, who were already disputing imperial efforts to control them, and created the possibility of war with the Cherokees and the Algonquians. The whole point of the boundary was to concentrate troops and settlers, not spread them out; the British government sought to settle quarrels with the Indians, not to breed new ones. Johnson was under clear orders in 1768 to negotiate a boundary at the Great Kanawha.[76]

---

[75] Johnson contended that the Shawnees lacked any title to any lands, even those north of the Ohio where their villages stood, Johnson to Hillsborough, Apr. 4, 1772, *NYCD* 8:292. For Gage quotation, see Gage to Johnson, Oct. 7, 1772, *JP* 12:994–95.

[76] For the difficulties of the boundary line, see Sosin, *Whitehall and Wilderness*, 170–73; Gipson, *British Empire*, 11:440–46. Johnson insisted that the Shawnees, Delawares,

In the Fort Stanwix Treaty of 1768, the British government, nonetheless, accepted the larger cession and allowed its own agents to deviate from instructions. William Johnson, his policy in shambles, consulted his own private interests as much as he did imperial interests. Later, defending his actions, Johnson seized on widespread illegal settlement as a justification for his larger cession. He claimed that he had known all along that the frontier people would push beyond the Kanawha "without any title whatsoever" and that "the Colonies would not, or could not prevent them." Since such weakness would "disgrace" the government in front of the Indians, he thought it best to secure a larger cession and thus keep expansion on British and not Indian lands. There was, however, a simpler explanation: Johnson accepted Iroquois claims to much of what is today Kentucky because doing so served the interests of land speculators, among whom were both himself and George Croghan.[77]

The mania for Ohio lands spread to London and spawned intense political maneuvering among speculators and politicians even as the empire weakened in the West. Plans for new colonies appeared only to disappear under the shocks spawned by the growing revolutionary crisis. Revolutionary tremors and the unacceptable costs of maintaining garrisons in the West brought a partial military withdrawal from the region. With the Mississippi River undermining Fort Chartres, Gage abandoned it, leaving only a small garrison of fifty men at Kaskaskia. At the end of August 1772, he ordered Fort Pitt razed. Not only was the garrison expensive, but Pontiac's Rebellion, Gage argued, had demonstrated that it could not protect the frontier. By 1773, British troops remained at only Detroit, Michilimackinac, and Kaskaskia, and only the first two were garrisons of any strength. The white children of the imperial father continued to increase in number, but their father, despite plans for new colonies, seemed to be fading away.[78]

Munsees, and Mingos were all dependents of the Six Nations and thus different from other western Indians, Johnson to Penn, Jan. 29, 1772, *JP* 12:937.

[77] For later rationale, see Johnson to Dartmouth, Nov. 4, 1771, *NYCD* 8:316. There are numerous accounts of the intense speculative interest in the West and Johnson's involvement in it. See Sosin, *Whitehall and the Wilderness*, 161–64. For actions at Fort Stanwix and the "suffering traders," see *ibid.*, 172–73; Thomas P. Abernethy, *Western Lands and the American Revolution* (New York: Russell and Russell, 1959, repr. of 1937 ed.), 34; R. A. Billington, "The Fort Stanwix Treaty of 1768," *New York History*, 25 (1944): 182–94; Gipson, *British Empire* 11:447, 455–97.

Most shares of the Indiana Company, as the "Suffering Traders" came to be known, were held by the Quaker firm of Baynton, Wharton, and Morgan, and the Jewish firm of Simon, Trent, Levy, and Franks. See Gipson, *British Empire* 10:458–60. For Croghan and Johnson, see Albert T. Volwiler, *George Croghan and the Westward Movement: 1741–82* (Cleveland: Arthur H. Clark, 1926), 261–69.

[78] Gage increasingly saw the British garrisons in the West as extraneous, expensive, and useless, Gage to Hillsborough, Nov. 10, 1770, Carter (ed.), *Correspondence of Gage*, 1:274–81, also *ibid.*, 1:318–19, Mar. 4, 1772. For decision to reduce garrison at Illinois, see Gage

In the vacuum left by the empire's decline, the Shawnees tried and failed to create a league to oppose the Fort Stanwix treaty. They denied the right of the Iroquois to cede the land. For the first half of the 1770s, this incipient alliance haunted William Johnson and the British military. At first skeptical that so wide a league could even be contemplated, let alone long endure, they grew increasingly worried as the conferences and meetings along the Scioto continued. By February 1771, Johnson had become concerned that a league of northern and southern Indians, supported by the French and the Spanish, might be a reality. With rumors of a new war between England and Spain circulating, there seemed a real danger that once more an Indian alliance would be arrayed alongside Britain's imperial enemies.[79]

Johnson spent his last years subverting the Shawnee league. By 1774, Johnson was dying, but his dying efforts were perhaps the most brilliant of his career, for rarely had he had fewer resources at his command. It was a virtuoso effort in the service of a nearly phantom empire and in cooperation with a weak and rusted covenant chain. The chiefs of the *pays d'en haut* whom Johnson persuaded to abandon the Shawnees did not know they were

to Johnson, Mar. 9, 1772, *JP* 8:417; Gage to Hillsborough, Mar. 4, 1772, and Apr. 13, 1772, Carter (ed.), *Correspondence of Gage*, 1:318, 321–22. For fort razed, see Gage to Hillsborough, Sept., 2, 1772; *ibid.*, 1:331–33; Gage to Johnson, Sept. 7, 1772, *JP* 8:593. For Fort Pitt, see Gage to Edmonstone, Aug. 31, 1772, Gage Papers, AS 113; Gage to Penn, Nov. 2, 1772, *PA*, Series 1, 4:457–58. The British destroyed the walls of the fort but left several buildings standing. Part of the dismantled fort was taken by settlers and reerected nearby. The Indians called this stockade the new fort, Croghan to Gage, Nov. 24, 1772, Gage Papers, AS 115.

79 For speech of Red Hawk, see enclosure with McKee to Croghan, Feb. 20, 1770, *JP* 7:406–7. Croghan Journal, July 5, 1770, enclosure with Croghan to Gage, Aug. 8, 1770, Gage Papers, AS 94. Johnson rejected this "new Dialect" of the Shawnees, saying that they never before challenged Iroquois control, Johnson to Croghan May 11, 1770, *JP* 7:655–56. In 1769 Alexander McKee reported the new league had sent delegates "throughout the Western Nations as well as amongst the Chickasaws and the Cherokees to the Southward," McKee to Croghan, Feb. 20, 1770, *JP* 7:404. For Mingo, Shawnee, Delaware delegation to Detroit, see Croghan to Gage, Jan. 1, 1770, Gage Papers, AS 89. For Cherokees at Shawnee village, see Edmonstone to Gage, May 13, 1770, Gage Papers, AS 92. For Shawnees among Creeks, see Gage to Johnson, June 10, 1770, *JP* 7:722; *ibid.*, Oct. 8, 1770, *JP* 12:872. For success among Cherokees, see Stuart to Gage, 8 Feb. 1771, *JP* 7:1131. For Caughnawagas, Johnson to Gage, Nov. 8, 1770, *JP* 7:992–93. For French encouragement and involvement, see Croghan to Johnson, May 19, 1770, *JP* 7:689; Croghan to Gage, Sept 20, 1770, Gage Papers, AS 96. For rumors of imperial war, see Gage to Johnson, Mar. 18, 1771, *JP* 8:55; Gage to Johnson, Oct. 1, 1771, *JP* 8:285. For skepticism about success, see Gage to Johnson, May 20, 1770, *JP* 12:822; Croghan to Gage, July 13, 1770, Gage Papers, AS 93. For fear, see Johnson to Hillsborough, Feb. 18, 1771, *NYCD* 8:262–63.

The Shawnees later claimed that the league consisted of the Shawnees, the Illinois, and ten confederate nations between them. These would almost certainly include the Weas, Piankashaws, Miamis, Kickapoos, Potawatomis, Wyandots, Ottawas, Delawares, and Munsees. The tenth nation may have been the Mascoutens, then in the process of being absorbed by the Kickapoos, or perhaps the Chippewas. The Mingos would not have been considered a separate nation, Johnson to Hillsborough Apr. 4, 1772, *NYCD* 8:291.

negotiating with phantoms, but in some ways they were phantoms themselves. Their father was dying, and the empire was dying. Ghosts of past glory reappeared in the *pays d'en haut* in 1773 and 1774, trying to recall things that no longer existed. The Huron chiefs of Detroit, acting for Johnson, carried calumets to the Wabash villagers, to the Potawatomis, and to the villagers along the Ohio, just as their predecessors had done in the days of the French alliance. Apparently under strong pressure from the women of the villages who feared war with the Iroquois, the Miami chiefs accepted the Huron demand that they heed Johnson and abandon the Shawnees. Although they said that the British had treated them as bastards, that is, as illegitimate children, the Miamis proclaimed that they were ready once again to clear and open the road that their ancestors had followed to the British. In a separate response, Pitchibaon, speaking for the Potawatomis of Saint Joseph, thanked Johnson for the "good advice." He blamed the actions of the Potawatomis on the loss of their old chiefs. Since their deaths, "we who are appointed in their place are no more listened to, every one sets up for Chief and make Towns and Village apart and they are the Cause of all the Mischief." The subtext of both the Miami and the Potawatomi messages was that peace and alliance remained possible if the British supported the chiefs.[80]

Johnson's triumph was brilliant but negative. He destroyed the Shawnee league, but there was no longer any meaningful alliance for the chiefs to serve. The troops were withdrawing. The empire was disappearing. The Ohio villagers sensed this. The Shawnees and Delawares, in an attempt to subvert Johnson, tried to open direct negotiations with Pennsylvania. They tried to form a delegation to London. They tried to negotiate directly with the backcountry settlers. All of these efforts failed.[81]

Johnson's pruning away of Shawnee allies debilitated the Shawnee league, but the most obvious sign of its decline was the division of the Shawnees

---

[80] Speech of Miamis to Sir William Johnson, 18 Aug. 1773, *MPHC* 19:308–10. The Hurons did not apparently receive such a friendly reception among the other Wabash villages, Lernoult to Gage, Sept. 24, 1774, Gage Papers, AS 123. For Potawatomis, see Speech of Pitchibaon, Sept. 18, 1773, *JP* 8:887–88.

[81] For attempt to reestablish direct relations, Edmonstone to Gage, Apr. 24, 1772, Gage Papers, AS 102; Speech of Pipe, 1771, also Minutes of a Council, 28 Sept. 1771, *PA*, Series 1, 4:438–42. For Killbuck, see Council, 7 May 1771, *PCR*, Series 4, 9:735–42.
For intervention of Quakers, see T. Wharton to Johnson, Dec. 1, 1772, *JP* 8:648; Johnson to Wharton, Dec. 24, 1772, *JP* 8:674–75. For appeal to London, see Alexander McKee's Journal, Apr. 3–6, 1773, *JP* 8:756.
For wise people, see Speech of Red Hawk, Feb. 20, 1770, *JP* 7:406–8. Croghan reported that the Shawnee, Delaware, and Mingo chiefs feared war because their villages would be the most open to attack by the English, Croghan to Gage, Aug. 8, 1770, Gage Papers, AS 94. For negotiations with backcountry settlers, see Croghan to Gage, Aug. 8, 1770, Gage Papers, AS 94; Croghan Journal July 26, 1770, enclosure with *ibid.*, Invitation, Croghan Journal, Aug. 1, 1770, *ibid.*

themselves. The village chiefs were increasingly losing control. By the spring of 1774, they openly acknowledged that the lower towns contained no chiefs and they could not be responsible for their actions. And even in the upper towns, an informant told the British, it was the warriors who exerted real control. This growing division between chiefs and warriors fed, in turn, a second fragmentation based on the component Shawnee groups. Not all the Shawnees had reunited on the Ohio; most of the Hathawekela (Oawikila) Shawnees lived among the Creeks. But in the fall of 1773 a more serious split occurred: 170 warriors and their families, apparently almost all of the Kispoko and Pekowi, left the Shawnee towns along the Scioto and moved west after attempting to persuade the Shawnees of Wakatawicks on the Muskingum to accompany them. The Kispoko and Piqua anticipated that they would "soon be hemmed in on all Side by the White people, and then be at their mercy." They felt that only migration offered an escape. The migrants eventually settled among the Spanish. Far from being the center of a powerful confederacy, the Ohio Shawnees in 1774 were a weakened, isolated, and fragmented group who, it appears, sought to make up their losses by inducing the Mingos then living near Logstown and Big Beaver Creek to join them. Those Shawnees who remained in Ohio were, ironically, those who thought that it was possible to reach an accommodation with whites.[82]

But as the Shawnees and their confederation split, so too did the British on the other side of the Ohio. The withdrawal of the garrison from Pittsburgh was soon followed by a bitter jurisdictional quarrel over the Monongahela area between Virginia and Pennsylvania. Armed bands of Virginians and Pennsylvanians confronted each other around Pittsburgh. Many migrants west of the Monongahela claimed title to their land from Virginia and refused to pay taxes or recognize Pennsylvania officials. George Croghan initially favored Virginia in the dispute, but his main interest continued to be the attempt to bring the new colony of Vandalia into being. For quite different reasons, both he and the Shawnees grew alarmed when in 1773 Virginia surveyors moved beyond the Kanawha boundary to survey Virginia grants in Kentucky. On the basis of a grant from Virginia, Captain Thomas Bullit surveyed the area around Louisville. Farther west, William Murray, acting for the Wabash Land Company, claimed to have purchased

[82] For migration, see Conference with Kayaghshota, Jan. 5–15, 1774, *JP* 12:1052. For no chiefs, see McKee Journal, May 21, 1774, *NYCD* 8:466. For informant, see McKee Journal, Apr. 16, 1774, *JP* 12:1088. For recruitment of Mingos and others, see *ibid.*, 1090, 1095. For divisions, see Jerry Eugene Clark, "Shawnee Indian Migrations: A Systems Analysis" (Ph.D. diss., University of Kentucky, 1974), 63–66. Clark apparently did not consult the Johnson Papers. The withdrawal of the Kispoko – whose chiefs were in charge of war – was particularly significant, Thomas Wildcat Alford, *Civilization and the Story of the Absentee Shawnees* (Norman: University of Oklahoma Press, 1936), 62.

the lands between the Wabash and the Illinois rivers from the Piankashaw Indians. The British government later invalidated Murray's purchase, and Johnson protested Virginia's actions, but in the spring more Virginia surveyors moved into Kentucky, and the Shawnee chiefs warned the British that they could not control what would happen when the surveyors met their young men on Kentucky hunting grounds.[83]

Algonquian warriors and British surveyors clashed in Kentucky, but the war began independently of them. Michael Cresap would bear, somewhat unfairly, much of the blame for the war. He was more like an Algonquian war leader than he was like any sort of officer in colonial society. A failed farmer and merchant from a prominent Maryland backcountry family who was making a new start below Wheeling on the Ohio, the leader of the six or seven young men who accompanied him, Cresap was actually an advocate of restraint when word of skirmishes between Shawnees and surveyors in Kentucky came downriver in the spring of 1774. He turned to war only after receiving a letter from John Connolly, who claimed jurisdiction as justice of the peace for Virginia. Connolly, a local blowhard whose arbitrary actions made him much hated by the Pennsylvanians, told the settlers at Wheeling that they should be prepared for Indian attacks. Cresap interpreted the letter as war and joined the war party. The next day his men attacked a trader's canoe, killing a Shawnee and a Delaware engaged by the trader, and the day after, they struck a party of Shawnees who had stopped at Cresap's plantation for supplies, killing a chief. Cresap contemplated, but then decided against, attacking a small Mingo village on Yellow Creek.[84]

---

[83] Croghan interpreted the troop withdrawal from the Ohio as a move by opponents against the new colony but thought it would improve relations with the Indians, Letter of Croghan, Dec. 28, 1772, *PMHB* 15 (1891), 433. The Shawnees wanted direct negotiations with Virginia and Pennsylvania, McKee's Journal, Apr. 3–6, 1773, *JP* 8:755–57. For plan for treaty, see Croghan to B. Gratz, May 11, 1773, George Rogers Clark Papers, Draper Manuscripts, 7J136, Wisconsin State Historical Society. For claims, see Croghan to St. Clair, June 4, 1772, *PA*, Series 1, 4:452–53. For Virginia grants, see Letters of Croghan, May 11, 1773, Oct. 15, 1778, in "Letters of Colonel George Croghan," *Pennsylvania Magazine of History and Biography* 15 (1891): 434–36. For Murray purchase, see Lord to Haldimand, 3 July 1773, enclosure with Haldimand to Gage, Oct 6, 1773, Gage Papers, AS 119. For Wasbash Land Company, see Abernethy, *Western Lands*, 193. For British invalidated the sale, see Hamilton to Haldimand, Dec. 4, 1778, Haldimand Papers, 21781.

For conflict, see Johnson to Haldimand, Sept. 30, 1773, *JP* 8:898; Johnson to Dartmouth, Sept. 22, 1773, *JP* 8:889; McKee Journal, March 8–13, *JP* 12:1083–86; also see Buck and Buck, *The Planting of Civilization*, 158–65, and Randolph C. Downes, *Council Fires on the Upper Ohio* (Pittsburgh: University of Pittsburgh Press, 1969), 152–78. Downes, however, greatly oversimplifies and misinterprets the Indian politics of the war. For Ohio Company titles, see Croghan to St. Clair, June 4, 1772, *PA*, Series 1, 4:452–53.

[84] In February and March, rumors reached Pittsburgh of murders by the Shawnees in the southern backcountry and on the Ohio, McKee Journal, Feb. 27, 1774, Indian Records, RG 10, Series III, Western Post Records, v. 16, Public Archives of Canada (hereafter cited as PAC). McKee Journal, Mar. 8–13, 1774, *JP* 12:1083–86. In Apr. the Shawnees were seizing and robbing surveyors, John Floyd to Preston, Apr. 26, 1774, Reuben G. Thwaites

The leader of the village of Yellow Creek, Logan, was a man in many ways very similar to Cresap. He was not a chief. Kayashuta and White Mingo were the Mingo chiefs. Logan was merely a war leader, the Indian equivalent of Cresap. The villagers at Yellow Creek consorted regularly with a small settlement of Virginians living just across the Ohio. Logan's sister had a child by a white trader, John Gibson. On May 3, 1774, a party of Virginians decoyed two Indian men and women from Yellow Creek across the river to drink with them at the house of a man named Baker. They made them drunk and murdered them and, likewise, killed two more who followed. They ambushed six men who came to investigate, killing, they believed, four. Greathouse and Baker, the men who led the murderers, and their party murdered eight to ten people that day and wounded two more. They almost murdered another, but after killing Logan's sister, they decided to spare her infant son. In May, the murder of another Indian, Joseph Wipey, a Delaware, came to light.[85]

All these killings were brutal, all were unprovoked, but all, too, were actions on the middle ground. They took place at familiar intersections of Algonquian and European worlds. The Delaware and the Shawnee were employees of a trader; the Shawnee party was returning from Pittsburgh, where they had consulted with Croghan. The Mingos of Yellow Creek had lived amicably with the whites across the river for some time. On other days, the visit that left them dead would have resulted in nothing more notable

and Louise P. Kellogg (eds.), *Documentary History of Dunmore's War, 1774* (Madison: Wisconsin Historical Society, 1905), and the Cherokees attacked a trader's canoe near Little Beaver Creek, killing one man. The whites suspected they fled to the Shawnees and Mingos on the Muskingum and Scioto, McKee Journal, Apr. 17, 1774, *JP* 12:1090. For a list of murders blamed on the Shawnees, see Letter from Redstone, Oct. 1774, in Peter Force (ed.), *American Archives: Consisting of a Collection of Authentick Records ... in Six Series* (Washington, D.C.: M. St. Clair Clarke and Peter Force, 1837–53), Series 4, 1:1015 (hereafter cited as *AA*).

For white attacks and rationales, see McKee Journal, May 1, 1774, *NYCD* 8:463; St. Clair to Penn, May 29, 1774, *PA*, Series 1, 4:502. Remarks on the Proceedings of Dr. Connolly, June 25, 1774, *PA*, Series 1, 4:528–29. Richard Butler said that the murdered chief was returning from Pittsburgh, but the chronology of the murders is different. Two different attacks may have been involved. Richard Butler Account of the Rise of the Indian War, 23 Aug. 1774, *PA*, Series 1, 4:568–70. For death of chief, see Extract of Journal of the United Brethren's Mission on Muskingum, May 6, 1774, *PA*, Series 1, 4:495. For murder of Wipey, see *ibid.* 503. For a summary of attacks, and reference to Connolly's letter, see Devereux Smith to Dr. Smith, June 10, 1774, *AA*, Series 4, 1:467–70. For resentment of Connolly, see Mackay to Penn, June 14, 1774, *AA*, Series 4, 1:473; Memorial to Penn, June 25, 1774, *AA*, Series 4, 1:483–84. For George Rogers Clark's memory of Cresap, see Clark to Samuel Brown, June 17, 1798, *IHC* 8:3–9.

85 Richard Sparks, a prisoner among the Shawnees, said Logan did not blame Cresap and that one of the murderers had previously lost a brother to the Indians. Statement of Richard Sparks, Nov. 1812, George Rogers Clark Papers, Draper Mss., 14J34–37. For murder of Wipey, see Extract of Journal of United Brethren's Mission on Muskingum, May 6, 1774, *PA*, Series 1, 4:495.

than a few goods' changing hands. Even the bloodshed accented rather than washed away the common world. In killing, both sides used common symbols. Cresap declared war with scalps. Baker scalped the dead to make his slaughter an act of war and not a drunken murder. This was a world of common contact and common meaning.[86]

The scalps made the meaning clear enough, but the Shawnees remained a careful people, and it was the duty of chiefs to seek peace. The chiefs refused the condolence message sent them by Croghan, McKee, and Connolly, denouncing it as full of lies. And they warned the whites that when news of the murders reached the villages, there would be retribution. Within the message, however, was the possibility of reconciliation. Cornstalk and the other chiefs still hoped to control the warriors. When traders led by George Butler arrived at the Shawnee towns, the alliance chiefs protected them and returned them under escort. Cornstalk sent Butler, a man who had previously acted as a messenger and mediator, and who had employed the Shawnee and Delaware murdered by Cresap's men, home with a letter informing Alexander McKee, himself the son of an Indian woman, that they would sit quiet "till we knew what you meant." Would the dead be covered or was this war?[87]

Cornstalk held open the possibility of mediation, and mediators had already come forward from among the Delawares. The old generation of Delaware civil chiefs was passing away. Tamaqua was dead and his lineage no longer so prominent. Custaloga was old, and his village at Venango had broken up, its people moving up the Ohio away from the British. Newcomer still lived at Newcomer's Town – perhaps the most important town in the Ohio country – and presided over its council, but he too had grown old and feeble. Quequedegatha (or George White Eyes), a chief who had previously served as a speaker, emerged as the alliance chief of the Turtle phratry in the place of Newcomer. Captain Pipe, long a speaker and head warrior, would succeed his uncle Custaloga. The two older men continued as phratry

---

[86] For scalps, see McKee Journal, May 1, 1774, *NYCD* 8:463. As declaration of war, see Johnson to Haldimand, June 9, 1774, *JP* 8:1164–65. For Cresap, see Clark to Brown, June 17, 1798, *IHC* 8:5.

[87] Shawnee chiefs here were acting according to the ideal of alliance chiefs. When a Miami war party defeated by the Cherokees passed through Pittsburgh, the Shawnee chiefs there condoled with them but expressed shock that chiefs would go on such an expedition, McKee Diary, Feb. 26, 1774, Indian Records, RG 10, Series 11, Western Post Records, v. 16, PAC.
For Shawnee reaction, see McKee Journal, May 25, May 26, June 1, June 4, 1774, *AA*, Series 4, 1:479–81. For hopes for peace, see Extract of Journal of the United Brethren's Mission on Muskingum, May 20, 1774, *PA*, Series 1, 4:496–97; Speech of Shawanese, May 20, 1774, *PA*, Series 1, 4:497–98; Richard Butler Account of the Rise of the Indian War, 23 Aug. 1774, *PA*, Series 1, 4:568–70. Butler had carried a letter from the Shawnees to Kayashuta, Croghan, and McKee in the fall of 1773, Conference with Kayaghshota, Jan. 5–15, 1774, *JP* 12:1046.

leaders, but neither could travel to keep the paths clear and carry the calumet to keep the warriors smoking peacefully on their mats. The generation of leaders on the middle ground whose struggles had resulted in the passing of the French father and the coming of the British were now passing away together.[88]

George White Eyes became a leading alliance chief in the service of an impotent alliance, and he performed his tasks well, so well that later, when people had forgotten what the alliance aspired to be and what the role of men like White Eyes was, he seemed a quisling. White Eyes was already fully a figure of the middle ground. As the English rendering of his name indicates, he was familiar with whites and their world. In 1766, he had kept a tavern on Big Beaver Creek. He had closely linked himself with the traders and had become, it seems, a trader himself, for he operated neither on the scale of nor in the manner of an Indian hunter. In 1773, the proceeds of his hunt – fifteen hundred deerskins and three hundred beaver – were so large that he must have traded for part of them, particularly since he had been fitted out by a British trader in return for half the profits. White Eyes carried the skins directly to Philadephia and demanded part of the proceeds in money. White Eyes, as did other traders, maintained a cabin in Pittsburgh and apparently stored goods there; for, when Virginians robbed the cabin, "£30 worth of his property [was] taken." White Eyes was interested in Christianity, believed the Delawares would have to increase the scale of their farming, and advocated peace with the British; he was an ideal intermediary between the two societies. He traveled the dangerous trails between the white and Shawnee villages, coming close to being murdered by either Connolly's men or the Shawnees, to assist McKee in trying to smooth the paths.[89]

[88] Conference with Kayaghshota, Jan. 5–15, *JP* 12:1047–48. For George White Eyes, see Minutes, Apr. 26, 1768, *PA*, Series 1, 9:515. Pipe was related to the Shawnees and had apparently served as a chief warrior among them. The Pride, whose death in South Carolina had helped spark Shawnee entry into the Seven Years' War, had been his relative, Armstrong to Denny, Dec. 22, 1756, *PA*, Series 1, 3:83; Croghan Journal, May 9, 1765, *IHC* 11:10. For acts as speaker, see Message to Pennsylvania, Sept. 1771, *PA*, Series 1, 4:441.

For Delaware pretensions to authority from Johnson to gather themselves together and sit in the center among the whites, the Six Nations, and the western nations, see McKee Journal, June 6, 1774, RG 10, series 11, Misc. Records of Western District, 16:9, PAC.

[89] For tavern, see Klett (ed.), *Journals of Charles Beatty*, Aug. 21, 1766, 46. For trading venture with Smallman, see Croghan to Gratz, May 11, 1773, 7J13C, George Rogers Clark Papers, Draper Mss. Although he succeeded Newcomer, White Eyes was associated with Tamaqua and Delaware George's faction, "Journal of James Kenny," July 5, 1762, 8. For Christianity and agriculture, see Jones, *Journal of Two Visits*, Feb. 13, 1773, 89.

White Eyes met with Croghan after the initial murders and carried condolence speeches to Newcomer's Town and to the Shawnee towns, returning with a message for the whites, McKee Journal, May 5, 1774, *JP* 12:1100; McKee Journal, May 25, 1774, *AA*, Series 4, 1:479; McKee Journal, May 9, 1775, *PA*, Series 1, 4:496; Meeting, June 29, 1774, *PA*, Series 1, 4:532.

White Eyes and Pipe, along with Kayashuta and White Mingo, were in Pittsburgh on May 5, 1774, when, under the instruction of McKee, Captain Connolly and the Virginians conducted a condolence ceremony "conformably to you [sic] custom." They wiped the tears from the Indians' eyes, symbolically collected the bones of the deceased, wrapped them in presents collected for the purpose, and interred the dead so "that every rememberance of uneasiness upon this head may be extinguished, and also buried in oblivion." It was White Eyes who agreed to pursue "the great and good work of peace," carrying the messages himself for the business was "too serious to be trifled with, or boys to be employed on; it is the happiness of ourselves, our women and children, and everything dear to us, that we are endeavouring to preserve." So important was the work that Newcomer himself also took it in hand.[90]

But White Eyes, Newcomer, and the Shawnee chiefs could not control Logan, already a deeply disturbed man who believed himself pursued by evil manitous. Many of the people who fell at the hands of Greathouse and Baker were his relatives, and their blood cried out for vengeance. There was no civil chief at Yellow Creek, and when Logan went to the mixed Mingo-Shawnee village of Wakatomica on the Muskingum to recruit a war party, he went among people whom both the Shawnee chiefs and Kayashuta had already said were beyond restraint.[91]

The Shawnee and Mingo chiefs could not stop Logan's retaliation, but they managed to confine the retaliatory parties largely to the warriors of Wakatomica, whose people were related to those on Yellow Creek. Only two small parties, thirteen men in all, followed Logan. And the Shawnee chiefs managed to exact some concessions even from them. Logan's hatchet would fall only on the Virginians west of the Monongahela. He would not attack Pennsylvanians, and when he returned, his warriors would "sit down and listen to their Chiefs."[92]

Logan and his followers took their revenge in killings as gruesome as those that had prompted them. They cut down a man, his wife, and their three children on Muddy Creek, and took three other children prisoner.

[90] For Delaware and Six Nation efforts, see Speech of Baby, July 19, 1774, with Lernoult to Gage, Aug. 1, 1774, Gage Papers, AS 122; Extract from Indian Transactions, May 5, 1774, AA, Series 4, 1:476–77; Letter of The Cosh (John Bull), May 24, 1774, PA, Series 1, 4:499–500.

[91] For Logan, see Devereux Smith to Dr. Smith, June 10, 1774, AA, Series 4, 1:467–70. Logan later told George Morgan that his mother and sister were killed at Yellow Creek, Morgan Diary, June 17, 1776.

[92] For the issues and divisions, see McKee Journal, May 26, June 1, June 5, AA, Series 4, 1:481–82. The Moravians said 20 men went against the English, Letter of Zeisberger, May 28, 1774, PA, Series 1, 4:498, but they agreed that all came from Wakatomica. See also Indian Intelligence, June 5, 1774, PA, Series 1, 4:508–9; Richard Butler Account of the Rise of the Indian War, Aug. 23, 1774, PA, Series 1, 4:568–70.

Neighbors found William Speir, his wife, and four children dead and scalped. Logan's men had left a broadax sticking in Speir's chest. Elsewhere solitary travelers and members of parties sent in pursuit of Logan fell. Although in all these attacks the Indians tried to kill Virginians and spare Pennsylvanians, terror enveloped the entire region. A little more than a dozen Indians threatened to depopulate the backcountry. Hundreds fled; thousands forted up.[93]

Still, this was not yet war. Into July Croghan, McKee, and the Shawnee chiefs all believed peace was possible. Logan returned with thirteen scalps. Although he would raid again in the summer and the fall, he announced that he was satisfied. His vendetta was against Cresap and the Virginians. They had murdered his people; he had murdered them in return. Kayashuta went to the Shawnees and, in the name of the league of the Iroquois, whom the Shawnees had long ago disavowed, ordered them to await the decision of Onondaga on war. More important, White Eyes returned and announced that the Shawnees were ready to send their chiefs to negotiate. It was a time, he said, for prudent men to take control of matters. Connolly, however, was intent on war. He announced that Logan's raids represented a declaration of war by the Shawnees. He partially succeeded in an attempt to waylay the Shawnee escort that had brought the traders safely home. He proceeded to prepare for a general war and an invasion of the Indian country. Lord Dunmore, the governor of Virginia, backed him. There would be no peace until the Shawnees were "severly chastised." Virginia had committed itself to war. Although Guy Johnson, who had succeeded his dead father-in-law as superintendent of Indian affairs, continued to work actively to isolate the Shawnees, neither the British military nor Pennsylvania had any intention of joining the conflict. Indeed, General Haldimand told Gage that all the settlers on the frontier were not worth what a campaign against the Indians would cost.[94]

[93] For threatened depopulation, see St. Clair to Penn, May 29, 1774, *AA*, Series 4, 1:463; June 12, 1774, *ibid.*, 466–67; Montgomery to Allen, June 3, 1774, *AA*, Series 4, 1:463–64. For killings, see Devereux Smith to Dr. Smith, June 10, 1774, *AA*, Series 4, 1:467–70; Letter to Williamsburg, June 16, 1774, *AA*, Series 4, 1:405; St. Clair to Penn, June 15, 1774, *AA*, Series 4, 1:471–73. For sparing of Pennsylvanians, see St. Clair to Penn, June 16, 1774, *PA*, Series 1, 4:519; Thompson to Penn, June 19, 1774, *PA*, Series 1, 4:521–22.

[94] For return of Logan and attempt on escort, see Extract of Letter from Fort Pitt, June 19, 1774, *AA*, Series 4, 1:429. For wounds one, see St. Clair to Penn, June 26, 1774, *PA*, Series 1, 4:530. For Logan satisfied, see Montgomery to Penn, June 30, 1774, *PA*, Series 1, 4:534–35. For later raids, Christian to Preston, Thwaites and Kellogg (eds.), *Dunmore's War*, 304–5. Dunmore had at the end of May sent a speech denouncing the Indians as aggressors, but promising peace with the Delawares and Six Nation Indians around Pittsburgh, Message, May 29, 1774, *AA*, Series 4, 1:482. By the end of June, he was committed to war on the Shawnees, Letter of Dunmore, June 20, 1774, *PA*, Series 1, 4:522–23. Virtually every knowledgeable observer thought peace was possible into July, Extract of Letter, May 30, 1774, in *Maryland Journal*, June 18, 1774, Thwaites and Kellogg

Virginia's belligerence and the failure of the Shawnee chiefs' peace overtures ensured war. By July, British offensive operations and the attack on Shawnee escorts broadened the war faction among the Shawnees, who had already sent out war belts to their neighbors. By then Connolly was building forts and raising ranger companies, and Pennsylvania, while condemning the Virginians and blaming them for the war, necessarily began to take defensive measures. In August, the backcountry militia crossed the Ohio and destroyed Wakatomica on the Muskingum, which had already been abandoned, and five surrounding villages. Pennsylvania continued to try to confine the war, sending the Delaware chief Pipe to the Shawnees as a mediator. When Dunmore himself arrived on the frontier to lead an expedition against the Shawnees, Pipe and White Eyes, despite Shawnee threats against him, met Dunmore in council with messages from the Shawnee chiefs assuring him that the Shawnees would welcome negotiations. The attempts by the alliance chiefs to secure peace, however, only served to limit the war to a battle between the Shawnees and the Virginians. The Hurons at Detroit, under British pressure, refused the Shawnees permission to remove to Sandusky and turned down their war belts. In the unequal test of strength between the Virginians and the Shawnees, the Virginians prevailed. To forestall a Virginian invasion of the Scioto country, the Shawnees attacked the Virginia army gathering at the Kanawha. The result was the battle of Point Pleasant and Shawnee defeat.[95]

(eds.), *Dunmore's War*, 28–29; Croghan to St. Clair, June 4, 1774, *AA*, Series 4, 1:465–66; Letter of Mckee, June 10, 1774, *PA*, Series 1, 4:511; Richard Butler Account of the Rise of the Indian War, Aug. 23, 1774, *PA* Series 1, 4:568–70. St. Clair condemned the Virginians for seeking war, St. Clair to Penn, June 22, 1774, *AA*, Series 4, 1:472–74. Pennsylvania wanted peace, Penn to Johnson, June 28, 1774, *JP* 8:1182–83. The Shawnees were ready to talk, Meeting with the Indians at Pittsburgh, June 29, 1774, *PA*, Series 1, 4:531–33, but had to arm, Message from the Governor, July 18, 1774, *PCR* 10:196–97. Johnson denied the Shawnees aid, Johnson to Gage, Aug. 26, 1774, *JP* 13:673–75.

For Connolly's message, see Letter, June 9, 1774, *AA*, Series 4, 1:394. For Virginians want war, see Devereux Smith to Dr. Smith, June 10, 1774, *AA*, Series 4, 1:467–70. For build forts, etc., see St. Clair to Penn, July 4, 1774, *PA*, Series 1, 4:539; Mackay to Shippen, July 8, 1774, *PA*, Series 1, 4:540–42. For Dunmore's account of the war, which is riddled with lies, see Dunmore to Dartmouth, 24 Dec. 1774, Thwaites and Kellogg (eds.), *Dunmore's War*, 368–95.

For Haldimand, see Haldimand à Gage, 12 juin 1774, Gage Papers AS 120, and juin le 23, 1774, *ibid.*

The Shawnees could not expect help from the Cherokees, Campbell to Preston, June 23, 1774, Thwaites and Kellogg (eds.), *Dunmore's War*, 48–49.

95   For Shawnee war belts, see Speech of Baby, July 19, 1774, with Lernoult to Gage, Aug. 1, 1774, Gage Papers AS 122. For refuse permission, see Speech of Sasteretsy, Aug. 19, 1774, Speech of 22 of the Principal Chiefs, Aug. 23, 1774, both with Lernoult to Gage, Aug. 31, 1774, Gage Papers, AS 122. The Weas, Kickapoos, and Mascoutens remained hostile to the English-Iroquois-Huron attempts to ensure peace, but they appear to have been responding to Ottawa and Fox overtures to block English passage to the Illinois, Council at Detroit, Sept. 11, 1774, with Guy Johnson to Gage, Nov. 10, 1774, Gage Papers, AS 124.

For White Eyes and Shawnee threats, see Indian Speeches, July 23, 1774, *PA*, Series 1,

The battle meant that Kentucky could be settled and that Lord Dunmore and the Virginia elite could now become rich. Dunmore demonstrated how murders occasioned by rum and backcountry settlers could serve the desires of more discreet men to become wealthy. To the Shawnees, reluctant participants in the battle, defeat meant a loss of their Kentucky hunting grounds. But that the battle took place at all signified that in the villages on the Scioto the desire for revenge and the anger of young men were stronger than the efforts of the chiefs for peace. That the Shawnees stood largely alone that day also meant, however, that anger and revenge were not everywhere ascendant; for elsewhere in the *pays d'en haut* and on the Ohio itself, warriors, despite extreme provocation, sat on their mats. The civil chiefs had prevailed. If there had been more Delawares at Point Pleasant, if there had been Kickapoos, Mascoutens, Miamis, Piankashaws, Potawatomis, or Weas, if there had been more Ottawas, Chippewas, or Wyandots, if there had been Cherokees – if there had been only a part of the league the Shawnees had envisioned – the outcome certainly would have been far different. But if the league had been there, so too, most likely, would have been Pennsylvania militia and British regulars. Who was not at Point Pleasant mattered as much as who was.[96]

Under Dunmore's peace terms, the Shawnees agreed not to hunt south of the Ohio in Kentucky, in effect recognizing the Fort Stanwix cessions and more. But with colonials gathering to face British troops at Boston and the vast majority of the warriors of the *pays d'en haut* uninvolved in Lord Dunmore's War, what a colonial governor at the head of white villagers

---

4:552–54. For attack on Wakatomica, St. Clair to Penn, Aug. 8, 1774, *PA*, Series 1, 4:558–60; Letter from Redstone, Aug. 8, 1774, *AA*, Series 4, 1:722–23; Extract McDonald to Connolly, in Thwaites and Kellogg (eds.), *Dunmore's War*, 151–56. For Pipe, see St. Clair to Penn, Aug. 25, 1774, *PA*, Series 1, 4:573–75. For final effort of Pipe and White Eyes, see Council between Lord Dunmore and the Indians, Oct. 14, 1774, *AA*, Series 4, 1:872–76.

[96] There were 1,100 men in the Virginia militia at Point Pleasant, Fleming's Journal, Oct. 17, 1774, in Thwaites and Kellogg (eds.), *Dunmore's War*, 288. The Virginians claimed that there were 800 to 1,000 Shawnees, Mingos, Delawares, and Ottawas at Point Pleasant, but since the vast majority of the Delawares, most of the Mingos, and all but a few stray Ottawas remained neutral, there was nowhere near this number present, Letter from Point Pleasant, Oct. 17, 1774, *AA*, Series 4, 1:1016–17. Guy Johnson, presumably from information from the Six Nations, thought the Virginians outnumbered the Shawnees two to one, which would have put about 550 warriors in the field, Johnson to Gage, Nov. 24, 1774, *JP* 13:695. Even this is probably high, since the Ohio Shawnees numbered, according to Johnson, only 300 warriors and had just suffered a substantial loss with the emigration of about half of them toward the Mississippi. In addition to the Shawnees, there were only some Mingos and a few Delawares and Wyandots in the battle, Johnson to Dartmouth Dec. 14, 1774, *NYCD* 8:517. The Shawnees put their losses at 30 men, including 3 Mingos, Proceedings of Col. Guy Johnson, 20 Jan. 1775, *NYCD* 8:535. Some Wyandots and Caughnawagas also died at Point Pleasant, Treaty, Oct. 7, 1775, Reuben G. Thwaites and Louise P. Kellogg, *Revolution on the Upper Ohio, 1775–1777* (Port Washington, N.Y.: Kennikat Press, 1970), 81.

could extort from a single group of Indians meant little. Point Pleasant signified that a war between Indian and white villagers for Kentucky had begun, not ended. Gage informed Captain Lernoult at Detroit that he should inform the Indians that the king disapproved of the action of the Virginians whom he had ordered out of the Shawnee country.[97]

For the moment, the *pays d'en haut* was once more a world of villages. North of the Ohio the Shawnee confederacy had failed miserably; the league of the Six Nations was a shadow; the empire was no more than a few small garrisons huddled in the woods. South of the Ohio, the backcountry villagers had only been under the most tenuous imperial control, and now the colonies they belonged to would soon be in revolt. In December the Iroquois and Guy Johnson met. The Iroquois had sent the Shawnees a message demanding they lay down the hatchet. They desired that the empire tell the same to the Virginians, "who are white Men, and supposed to be under command." These were specters speaking. Neither the Iroquois nor the empire could command on the Ohio.[98]

[97] Gage to Lernoult, Dec. 28, 1774, Gage Papers AS 125.
[98] Proceedings of a Congress with the Chiefs and Warriors of the Six Nations, Dec. 1, 1774, *NYCD* 8:521.

9

The contest of villagers

Every child thus reared, learns to hate an Indian, because he always hears him spoken of as an enemy. From the cradle, he listens continually to horrid tales of savage violence, and becomes familiar with narratives of aboriginal cunning and ferocity. Every family can number some of its members or relatives among the victims of a midnight massacre. . . . With persons thus reared, hatred towards an Indian becomes a part of their nature, and revenge an instinctive principle.

James Hall, *Sketches of History, Life, and Manners in the West*

Our white Brethren who have grown out this same Ground with ourselves – for this Big Island being our common Mother, we & they are like one Flesh and Blood.

Cornstalk, June 1, 1776, Morgan Diary

We are sprung from one common Mother, we were all born in this big Island; we earnestly wish to repose under the same Tree of Peace with you; we request to live in Friendship with all the Indians in the Woods. . . . We call God to Witness, that we desire nothing more ardently than that the white & red Inhabitants of this big Island should cultivate the most Brotherly affection, & be united in the firmest bands of Love & friendship.

American Commissioners for Indian Affairs to Delawares, Senecas, Munsees, and Mingos, Pittsburgh, 1776, Morgan Letterbook

I

In one sense, the impact of the American Revolution on the *pays d'en haut* was simple. By creating another expansionist state, the Revolution re-created familiar dangers and equally familiar opportunities for the Algonquian villagers of the region. European-Indian alliances in the *pays d'en haut* had originated and thrived amid a contest of imperial powers; the independence of the United States once more restored serious imperial competition to North America. Algonquians could again test a father's love and once more judge between possible fathers. In this sense, the Revolution came to the *pays d'en haut* like a violent storm after a drought. For all its clamor and destruction, it watered the political middle ground parched by the conflicts of the 1760s and early 1770s.

Although useful up to a point, this kind of simple structural reading of the political dynamics of empire and village deceives by aggregating a collection of local groups into three coherent units: the British, the Americans, and the Indians. What the *pays d'en haut*, in fact, consisted of until at least the mid 1780s was distinct villages and settlements (some Anglo-American, some French, and some Indian). The Revolution and the Indian wars that followed were imperial contests for dominance in the region, but they were also village struggles for power. The particular interests of villages and factions within villages had as much to do with ultimate loyalties as did the imperial rivalry between the United States and Britain.

In 1781, General Frederick Haldimand complained of the independence of the Anglo-American villagers and the Algonquians, both of whom pursued local interests within the context of larger struggles. He reported that many backcountry settlers who had retired to the frontier "upon the Pretense of separating themselves from Rebellion are encroaching upon the most valuable Hunting grounds of the Indians and securing themselves rich settlements." These people often attacked British parties, but "when made Prisoners profess their loyalty." As for the Indians, "There is no dependence upon even those Indians who are declared in our favor, and there are a number in that country our avowed enemies . . . there has not been a single Instance where the Indians have fulfilled their engagements but influenced by Caprice, a dream or a desire of protracting the war, to obtain presents, have dispersed and deserted the Troops."[1]

The early years of the Revolution were, as Haldimand indicated, a trial for the British. Although they secured raiding parties from the Shawnees and the Mingos, from the Detroit villagers, from the Potawatomis of Saint Joseph, and, to a lesser extent, from Saginaw and Michilimackinac, most other Indians remained either neutral or proved to be unreliable allies. Those Indians who fought the most effectively did so to deny Kentucky to the Americans rather than from loyalty to their British father. And many French, never fully reconciled to British rule, welcomed the Revolution, particularly after the American alliance with France.[2]

This comparative British weakness in the West, however, was not immediately apparent to the backcountry Americans whom the Indians now

[1] Haldimand to Clinton, Sept. 29, 1781, Clinton Papers, v. 176, Clements Library.
[2] For British allies in the *pays d'en haut*, see letter to Hamilton, 19 July 1776, *MPHC* 10:262; letter to De Peyster, 19 July 1776, *ibid.*; Gautier's Journal of a Visit to the Mississippi, 1777–78, *WHC* 11:101–11; Hamilton to Dartmouth, Sept. 2, 1776, *MPHC* 10:264–70; Council, 17 June 1777, in Louise P. Kellogg (ed.), *Frontier Advance on the Upper Ohio, 1779–1781* (Madison: State Historical Society of Wisconsn, 1917), 7–13; Bowman to Clark, Oct. 14, 1778 *ibid.*, 69–71; Clark's Memoir, *ibid.*, 260. Hamilton to Carleton, Apr. 25, 1778, *MPHC* 9:434; Gage to Haldimand, June 9, 1773, Haldimand Papers, Add. Mss., 21665. Abbott to Carleton, May 25, 1777, *IHC* 1:313, Abbott to Carleton, April 25, 1778, *IHC* 1:317; Abbott to Carleton, June 8, 1778, *IHC* 8:46–47; Bentley to Carleton, 10 April 1777, *IHC* 1:295.

lumped together under the old name for Virginians – the Big Knives. The Americans overestimated the number of Indians against them. They counted eighty-five hundred warriors arrayed against them, and this did not include the Sauks, the Fox, the Winnebagos, the Menominees, or any of the Illinois tribes. They assumed so many warriors were acting against them because Indian raiders, equipped by the British, took a heavy toll on the backcountry, particularly on the new settlements of Kentucky. The Americans looked for revenge and relief from the raids, but they had only a hazy idea of the origins of the raiders.[3]

It was to gain relief from these raids that the Americans launched a series of expeditions into the *pays d'en haut* and in the process made the initial fighting between villagers a contest of empires. An examination of George Rogers Clark's invasion of the *pays d'en haut* in 1778, the first and most famous of these expeditions, reveals the complexities of the ensuing struggle with particular clarity. It shows how the concerns of villages could, as in earlier wars, complicate imperial concerns. And it demonstrates, too, how the war itself forced a continuing accommodation with Algonquian custom among both British fathers and revolutionary Indian haters.[4]

II

George Rogers Clark hated Indians; he expected, he later told the captured Henry Hamilton, the British governor of Detroit, to see the whole Indian race extirpated, and "for his part he would never spare Man woman or child of them on whom he could lay his hands." Clark hated Indians because he loved Kentucky, and Indians, resisting its occupation by backcountry whites, had turned its land into a dark and bloody ground. Clark, a speculator in Kentucky land, had lost friends and neighbors in Algonquian attacks. He intended in 1778 to undertake a campaign to halt the Indian raids that threatened to depopulate the new settlements which were the seat of both his fortune and his emotional loyalties.[5]

Like many Indian haters, Clark believed, not always unreasonably, that he understood Indians and how to deal with them. He was also a man who acted

[3] Clark's belief in attacks from the Wabash apparently came from information provided by a group of Delawares who moved west to settle in that region, Petition of Committee, Harrodsburg, June 20, 1776, *IHC* 8:15. For his rationale, see Clark to Patrick Henry, 1777, *IHC* 8:30–32. For the American estimate of warrior strength, see Morgan to Zeisberger, Mar. 27, 1778, Morgan's Letter Book, Book 3.

[4] For Clark's views on significance of Kentucky, see Clark's Memoir, 1791, *IHC* 8:215–18.

[5] John D. Barnhart (ed.), *Henry Hamilton and George Rogers Clark in the American Revolution with the Unpublished Journal of Lieutenant Governor Henry Hamilton* (Crawfordsville, Ind.: R. E. Banta, 1951), 25 Feb. 1779, 189.

at times as if he were an Indian. "I suffered them," Clark wrote of his small
army's advance on Vincennes, "to shoot game on all occasions and feast on
them Like Indians war Dances each company by Turns Inviteing the other
to their feasts which was the case every Night." When his men hesitated,
confused in the midst of the watery waste through which Clark had led them,
Clark blackened his face, "gave the war hoop and marched into the water
without saying a word." A motive any Indian could understand kept the
Virginians in Clark's little army going through the dismal waterlogged land.
"Never [were] Men so animated," Major Bownman reported, "with the
thoughts of revenging the wrongs done to their back Settlements as this
small Army was."[6]

Indian hating provided its own odd routes to the middle ground, but Clark
also found other, older routes as he stumbled into the tangled village politics
of the *pays d'en haut*. Clark's expedition went in the wrong direction to
relieve pressure on Kentucky. Few raiders came from the Illinois country or
the Wabash. But Clark was shrewd enough to realize that in Illinois country
he had discovered an opportunity to detach a huge chunk of territory and
people from the British empire and open up the way to Detroit.

Once established at Kaskaskia, however, Clark recognized that he could
ill afford to act like a conqueror: "My situation and weekness convinced me
that more depended on my own Behaviour and Conduct, than all the Troops
that I had far removed from the body of my country: Situated among
French, Spanyards and numerous Bands of Savages on every Quarter."
Proper behavior promised great rewards among both the French and the
Algonquians, since the French had "great Influance among the Indeans
in Genl. and [were] more beloved by them (the Inds) than any other
Europeans." Clark could use the French trading connections with the
Indians of the upper Mississippi River, Illinois country, southern Lake
Michigan, and the Wabash River to spread American influence throughout
the region. To do so, Clark consciously emulated French methods. He dealt
with the Indians in the "French and Spanish mode which must be preferable
[to] ours, otherwise they could not possibley have such great influence
among them."[7]

---

[6] Clark's Memoir, *IHC* 8:269, 274. For quotation, see Bownman's Journal, Feb. 23, 1779, *IHC*
8:159. For Clark's army, see Clark to Mason, Nov. 19, 1779, *IHC* 8:139, 142.

[7] For quotation, see Clark's Memoir, *IHC* 8:23. At Vincennes, Clark to Mason, Nov. 19, 1779,
IHC 8:122–23. See also Instructions to Clark from Virginia Council, Dec. 12, 1778, *IHC*
8:78–82; Instructions from Gov. Patrick Henry to John Todd, Dec. 12, 1778, *IHC* 8:83–87.
For French influence, see Clark's Memoir, *IHC* 8:224. For emulation, see Clark to Chief of
the Winnebago, Aug. 22, 1778, *IHC* 8:65; Clark's Proclamation to the Fox Indians, Aug. 28,
1778, *IHC* 8:66; Clark to Mason, Nov. 19, 1779, *IHC* 8:124; Clark's Memoir, *IHC* 8:239.
Crooked Legs, a Wea chief, said the French were key in his decision to join the Americans,
Barnhart (ed.), *Hamilton Journal*, Dec. 10, 1778, 142.

Clark's dependence on the "French mode" complicated his Indian hating. He tried to construe the French mode as making Indians fear him, but French methods inevitably made him act at times as if he were an Indian lover. As a result, Clark came to misunderstand both the nature and the conditions of his triumphs. He only vaguely knew the Indians with whom he was dealing and why they cooperated with him. He imitated French methods without fully sympathizing with them, and he played the village politics of the *pays d'en haut* without comprehending local rivalries and ambitions. Yet for a brief golden period everything seemed to go his way.

Clark shrewdly and, to an extent, accurately presented the Big Knives to the various Algonquians of the western lakes, the Mississippi River, and the Wabash who visited him at Kaskaskia in 1778 as people much like themselves: "The Big Knife are very much like the Red people they dont know well how to make Blanket powder and cloath &c they buy from the English (whom they formerly desended from) and live chiefly by making corn Hunting and Trade as you and the French your Neigh(h)bours do." He argued that the Revolution was a result of the Big Knives' attempts to make guns and weave cloth, and British efforts to suppress their attempts. In his telling, the Revolution became a parable of escape from dependency and an assertion of the real commonalities of backcountry life among the Indians, the French, and the Virginians. The response of the Wabash Indians to this message, according to Clark, was that the "Indians had as great a right to fight the English as they [the Virginians] did."[8]

In establishing a common life, Clark was acting on the diplomatic middle ground, but here Clark the Indian hater-lover inevitably confused matters. Clark thought it a mistake to speak "soft" to Indians. In council with the Indians at Kaskaskia, Clark presented them with both a "Blody Belt (war) and a white one (peace)," telling them to choose. Clark did not give a full account of the Indian response to this mixed message in Illinois country, but the same message delivered to the Piankashaws brought only scorn. Old Tobacco, who eventually did join Clark, "told the Americans they did not speak to be understood, that he never saw an instance or heard tell of such a thing, as at a conference to present good and evil at one and the same time, therefore he kicked their belts from him." The response of Clark and the Americans to such Algonquian scorn at their ignorance of the diplomacy of the middle ground was to proclaim themselves warriors and not counselors as, indeed, they were.[9]

---

[8] Clark's Memoir, *IHC* 8:242–44. For response, see Clark to Mason, Nov. 19, 1779, *IHC* 8:124.

[9] Clark's Memoir, *IHC* 8:243–44; Clark to Mason, Nov. 19, 1779, *IHC* 8:124. For Old Tobacco, see Barnhart (ed.), *Hamilton Journal*, Oct. 14, 1778, 111. Old Tobacco (or Grand Coete) was at this time anti-Virginian, Beaubin's Account . . . Sept. 27, 1778, Haldimand Papers, 21782.

Clark the warrior could be understood. Because the role of war leader in a backcountry settlement was structurally so similar to that in an Algonquian village, and because Clark himself was an experienced Indian fighter, he seemed a familiar figure to the Algonquians. The Indians had a high opinion of the Big Knives as warriors. Blunt, remorseless, often cruel, and seemingly fearless, Clark swaggered and disdained his enemies. He was most successful in dealing with war leaders like himself. But since Clark's triumphs were those of a war leader, that is, the products of fear, pain, and opportunity, they were not stable. Clark's mistake was to think them the larger triumphs of alliance.[10]

The Western Algonquian accommodation with Clark was complicated. The villages of the Illinois and Wabash country initially feared him. It was this fear, together with French influence and the mistaken beliefs that Detroit had fallen and from now on the Americans would be the only source of supply, that brought many villagers to accept peace with the Big Knives once it was proposed in a comprehensible form. It made little sense to these villagers to lose trade and put their wives, children, and homes at risk out of loyalty to the British, when the French who were their relatives and friends had joined the Americans.[11]

But more was at work than expediency. Largely unwittingly, Clark served the village politics of the *pays d'en haut*. He buttressed the de facto republican independence of the French villages against the British Empire, and he also, in the old manner of Algonquian factional politics, was useful to ambitious Algonquians – particularly to the Piankashaw chief known as Grand Coete (or Old Tobacco) and his son, variously called Tobacco's Son or Young Tobacco. Clark grandiosely compared Young Tabacco to Pontiac and claimed that "nothing was be undertaken by the League on the Wabash without his assent." Tobacco's Son was, however, only a minor chief, at odds with other Piankashaw leaders.[12]

---

[10] For high opinion, see Hamilton to Carleton, Nov. 30, 1775, in Reuben G. Thwaites and Louise P. Kellogg, *Revolution on the Upper Ohio, 1775–1777* (Port Washington, N.Y.: Kennikat Press, 1970), 129. For Clark's rationale of his tactics, see Clark's Memoir, *IHC* 8:255, 257. Clark claimed to have treated with Chippewas, Ottawas, Potawatomis, Mississaugas, Winnebagos, Sauks, Fox, Osages, Iowas, and Miamis in addition to Piankashaws and Kickapoos, *IHC* 8:125. One group of "Meadow Indians" tried to seize Clark. To settle the incident, Clark, without fully realizing it, enacted the usual ceremonies of surrender and forgiveness with the gathered Indians, *IHC* 8:124–29. Clark's Memoir, *IHC* 8:249–52. For failure to secure real alliance, see Barnhart (ed.), *Hamilton Journal*, 110–49.

[11] For rationales for American alliance, see Barnhart (ed.), *Hamilton Journal*, 131, 136–37, 142.

[12] Clark's Memoir, *IHC* 8:241. Despite Clark's belief that Tobacco's Son remained loyal until his death, he actually sought rapprochement with Hamilton and accepted the British war ax, Barnhart (ed.), *Hamilton Journal*, Jan. 6, 1779, 162. For differences with and subordination to other chiefs, see *ibid.*, Dec. 8, 1778, 143; Dec. 20, 1778, 153; Feb. 21, 1779, 176.

Despite Old Tobacco's original disdain for Clark's message as conveyed by Captain Helm, he and his son had gone over to the Americans. Their dalliance with Clark arose at least partially from their need of support for a land sale they had earlier made to the Wabash Company without the consent of the other Piankashaws or of the Weas. By hitching their own ambitions to the Americans, Tobacco and his son might recoup their own precarious position in the village politics of the Wabash. Clark, who won so much by bluff and bluster, could himself be taken in by the bluff and bluster of others.[13]

Against the war leader Clark came the British father Hamilton, the man whom Clark held responsible for the attacks on Kentucky. By the fall of 1778, Hamilton had served at Detroit for nearly two years, but his march against Clark was his first venture deeper into the *pays d'en haut*. Just as Clark depended on the Illinois French to sustain him, so Hamilton depended on the Detroit French. And Hamilton depended, too, on the Indians. Familiar Algonquian rituals paced, punctuated, and eventually controlled Hamilton's march south from Detroit in the fall of 1778. These rituals – the calumet ceremony, war feasts, "eat all" feasts, the giving of war belts, the accepting of the hatchet, war dances, war songs, the whetting of the grindstone with rum to sharpen the hatchet of war, ceremonies to secure the approval of manitous – were by 1778 either customs of the middle ground (that is, rituals shared and performed jointly by Algonquians and Europeans in the *pays d'en haut*) or else Algonquian customs that Europeans had long recognized and discussed. Hamilton was not ignorant of them. His administration at Detroit had allowed him to master council decorum, and he had significant experience in soliciting Algonquian children to fight for their British father. He also had excellent advisers. Jehu Hay, an experienced Indian agent, accompanied him, and so, too, did the elite of the Detroit villages. Agushiway (or Egushewai), the leading Ottawa war leader from Detroit, counseled him on the march and acted as his intermediary to the chief's councils, and Dawatons – the reigning Sastaretsy of the Huron-Petuns – marched with him to Vincennes.[14]

Yet, out of Detroit, Hamilton's whole performance was off-key. He was at once condescending ("affected by the humble and reverential worship of these poor ignorant but well meaning creatures"), astonished, and inef-

---

[13] For sale, see Barnhart (ed.), *Hamilton Journal*, Nov. 28, 1778, 132, Nov. 30, 1778, 134, Dec. 20, 1774, 152.

[14] Hamilton to Haldimand, c. Sept. 1778, Haldimand Papers, 21781; Haldimand to Hamilton, Aug. 26, 1778, Haldimand Papers, 21781. Hamilton left Detroit with seventy Indians, all chiefs or picked men, Hamilton to Haldimand, Oct. 1779, *MPHC* 9:486–87. He picked up more as he proceeded. Hamilton to Haldimand, Nov. 1, 1778, *WHC* 11:180. Agushiway (or Egushewai), *Hamilton Journal*, Oct. 27, 1778, 116, Dec. 2, 1778, 135, Dec. 8, 1778, 140. For Dawatons, see Barnhart (ed.), *Hamilton Journal*, Aug. 23, 1778, 104, Jan. 1, 1779, 159.

fectively insistent on maintaining British military discipline on an expedition that included virtually no British soldiers. He recognized the necessity of allowing the ceremonies and rituals of the Algonquian warriors but tried to censor those parts of them that conflicted with military order. The whole march sporadically degenerated into wranglings over ritual. Hamilton willingly and successfully imitated the war dance, presented war belts, and sang his war song, but, fearing disorder, he resisted the symbolic pouring of rum on the grindstone to sharpen the war ax. Hamilton's omission of this distribution of rum when fourteen warriors joined him from the Ottawa village at Grand Glaize delayed the expedition until he apologized and provided two bottles of rum to the warriors. But at the Miami village at the portage, which he entered after a ritual mock battle between the Detroit Indians and the Miamis, Hamilton again purposefully failed to wet the grindstone. Although he produced the war belts and sang the war song, "in which I was followed by the Deputy agent, the chiefs, and principal warriors of the different nations," the Indians complained about the lack of rum. During the march, Hamilton wanted to control where the Algonquians camped, but this placed the Miamis in the rear and violated their custom of having the war bundles "advanced toward the Enemy's country" so that no one could pass in front of them. The Miamis complained bitterly about this slight to their manitous. Hamilton capitulated.[15]

For the Miamis, who had maintained only sporadic contact with the British after Pontiac's Rebellion, this whole experience proved disconcerting. To allay discontent among his young warriors, the Miami clan chief Waspikingua, or Necaquangai (Le Petit Gris), delivered a speech whose subtext was the need of the middle ground for undertakings such as Hamilton's.

> We are here mixed with the English, the French and several different tribes of brownskins, let us not take offense at any thing which may be said, since we are unacquainted as well with their language as their customs – however, let no man even in joke use a threatening gesture with his knife, or his War axe – These people [the Christians] have not the same religion with us. We believe in the Dieties of the woods and rivers, as well as in the supreme lord; they believe only in one sovereign being presiding over all – Our method of making war is by surprise, Our father the Englishman has another method, however, let us act our part as men.... The various nations have different customs, I will not

---

[15] Hamilton watched amazed as first the Chippewas and then the Ottawas hosted an "eat all" feast in which they consumed an entire bear, including the skin, Barnhart (ed.), *Hamilton Journal*, Sept. 14, 1778, 111–112. For Grand Glaize, see *ibid.*, Oct. 19, 1770, 113; for Miami, *ibid.*, Oct. 24, 1778, 114, Oct. 26, 115. For war bundle, *ibid.*, Nov. 15, 1778, 122. See also Dec. 13, 1778, 145.

implore all their Deities, but pray for the protection of those of our own
Nation and ask of them victory for my followers.[16]

Hamilton surrendered on the honor due to the medicine bundles and,
thereafter, conducted the expedition in a way that paid more attention to the
demands of the middle ground. The Indian shamans sang at night to the
bundles, hoping, Hamilton said, for a sign from their manitous. By the time
he reached Ouiatenon, Hamilton had resigned himself to observing the
Indian customs and, indeed, was being overruled in tactical decisions by the
chiefs who accompanied him. Outside Vincennes, he visited the Indian fires,
not, he assured them, from "idle curiousity to pry into their ceremonies."
Instead, he commended "their praying to the great Spirit, that he probably
was pleased with their adoration." One of the chiefs thanked him, saying,
"Who is there on earth that does not adore the Master of life, the giver of all
things, all who consider the various productions of nature, must worship
the supreme Lord." The next day, the son of Masgaish, a Chippewa war
leader, had an inauspicious dream that could have wrecked the expedition.
Hamilton quieted him, explaining in his journal: "It is necessary to endeavor
to find some method to quiet their superstition, rather than mock or insult
them." Just as Clark consolidated his role as war leader, Hamilton, after a
rocky start, was acting as father.[17]

Like Clark at Kaskaskia, Hamilton at Vincennes found that imperial
politics inevitably put him at the mercy of village politics. His army was
overwhelmingly French and Indian, and his negotiations in the various
villages along his route deeply involved him in Algonquian politics. He
proved more successful among the Algonquians than among the French
whom, on the whole, he disdained. Although the militia at Vincennes offered
no resistance to Hamilton and dutifully trooped to the chapel to renounce
their recent oaths to the United States and swear new ones to Great Britain,
Hamilton's arrival dismayed the French. He represented the first effective
British presence on the Wabash. Hamilton's little army, however, began to
disintegrate soon after reaching the town. The Detroit militia had come
under duress, and they had no intention of serving lengthy garrison duty.
They demanded to go home, and Hamilton, after disarming half of them,
dismissed them. Soon afterward, many Algonquian warriors, tired of the
inaction at Vincennes, began to depart. This left Hamilton increasingly
dependent on his French volunteers from Detroit and on the newly loyal

---

[16] For sporadic contact, see Lernoult to Gage, May 14, 1775, Gage Papers, AS 128. For
quotation, see Barnhart (ed.), *Hamilton Journal*, Nov. 15, 1778, 121–22.
[17] For bundles, see Barnhart (ed.), *Hamilton Journal*, Nov. 24, 1778, 128 . For customs, see
ibid., Dec. 8, 1778, 139. For overruled, see *ibid.*, 140. For Master of Life, *ibid.*, Dec. 13,
1778, 145. For dream, see *ibid.*, Dec. 14, 1778, 146.

Vincennes militia, whom Hamilton despised and who, in turn, despised and resented him.[18]

The final confrontation between Clark's 200-man army of Americans together with the "principal Young men of the Illinois" and Hamilton's little army of British, Frenchmen, and Indians came in February 1779. Young Tobacco with about a hundred Kickapoos and Piankashaws offered to diversify Clark's army even further, but Clark refused. He wanted to demonstrate that the Big Knives and their French companions did not need Indian aid. What decided the outcome of Vincennes was not the fighting, of which there was relatively little, but the decisions of the French and the Indians. The Vincennes militia, resentful of Hamilton, immediately deserted to Clark. The French volunteers "said it was hard they should fight against their own Friends and relations who they could see had joined the Americans." The bulk of the British Indians who had not already withdrawn now did so.[19]

In Hamilton's journal and Clark's various narratives, the American triumph at Vincennes is reconstructed as if it were a staged drama. The same accounts of events can be read on two levels: as texts structured to give meaning in terms of the larger conventions and symbols of Anglo-American society and as a less conscious delineation of the actual social bonds that held the people of the *pays d'en haut* together.

Hamilton attempted to organize his account of the siege and the surrender in conventional dualistic terms quite familiar in the later empire. The brave, disciplined, but outnumbered representatives of empire – the thin red line – confronted the rebels – "an unprincipled motley Banditti." But, to explain their downfall, reference to a third group – the French, whose "poltronnerie and treachery" betrayed the brave British – was necessary. Such an organization initially omitted the Indians who had dominated Hamilton's journal up to the siege. Indians became symbolically redundant once whites had taken their predictable roles as banditti or traitors.[20]

---

[18] On leaving Detroit, Hamilton had 3 officers and 30 British regulars; 14 officers and 71 rank-and-file militia from Detroit; 35 men in Captain La Mothe's volunteer company, 3 artillery men, and 70 Indians. For taking of Vincennes, militia, etc., see Barnhart (ed.), *Hamilton Journal*, Dec. 17, 1778, 147–49, Dec. 30, 1778, 159, and Hamilton to Haldimand, Dec. 18, 1778, Haldimand Papers, 21781. Also see Helm to Clark, c. Dec. 1778, Haldimand Papers, 21782. For Algonquians depart, see *Hamilton Journal*, Jan. 19–25, 1779, 165–67; Hamilton to Haldimand, Jan. 24, 1779, *IHC* 1:392. Hamilton also distrusted the devotion of the Wabash villagers, Hamilton to Haldimand, Dec. 18, 1778, Haldimand Papers, 21781.

[19] Clark's Memoir, *IHC* 8:269, 274. For quotation, see Bowman's Journal, Feb. 23, 1779, *IHC* 8:159. For Clark's army, see Clark to Mason, Nov. 19, 1779, *IHC* 8:139, 142. One hundred and seventy men marched with Clark; 46 men went by water, Bowman Journal, *IHC* 8:156. For quotation, see Barnhart (ed.), *Hamilton Journal*, Feb. 23, 1779, 178–83. Agushiway, Chamintawa (Ottawas), Sastaretsy (Hurons), Petit Gris (Miamis), and others were outside the fort and escaped capture, Hamilton, Apr. 1779, *IHC* 1:424.

[20] Barnhart (ed.), *Hamilton Journal*, Feb. 23, 1779, 185. His disdain for the French was long-

Clark organized the story of the siege in similar structural terms but with a predictable reversal of meanings. He emphasized the small size of his army, and although his army was partially French, he wrote as if their united resolve was to stop the attacks on Kentucky organized by the "hairbuyer" Hamilton. The men inside the fort – the British and their French partisans – were murderers and barbarians. He refused Hamilton's initial offer of terms because he wanted "an excuse to put them to Death or other ways treat them as I thought proper that the Cries of the Widows and Fatherless on the Frontiers that they had occationed now Required their Blood from my Hands. " The refusal of the people of Vincennes to aid Hamilton was a sign that they were in part "true Citizens & willing to Injoy the Liberty" Clark brought.[21]

When the Indians reemerged in the descriptions of the siege, Hamilton gave them center stage as victims of Clark's barbarity. For Clark the fact that Indians were victims was something of an embarrassment, underlining the reversal of symbolic roles. The techniques of both authors emerge in their treatment of the capture and murder of an Indian scouting party by the Americans. In Clark's memoir, this incident is relegated to a brief mention. The Americans tricked a returning Indian party, "killed three on the spot and brought 4 in." The Indian prisoners then "were Tomahawked by the Soldiers and flung into the River." Clark's diminishment of the incident is purposeful. In a much earlier letter, Clark had made the execution central as a matter of policy and an exercise in revenge.[22]

In contrast, Hamilton made the execution the critical event of the last stages of the siege:

> On their arrival, they were placed in the street opposite the Fort Gage, where these poor wreches [sic] were to be sacrified – one of them a young Indian about 18 years of age the son of Pontach, was saved at the intercession of one Macarty a Captain of Colol. Clarkes Banditti, who said he was formerly owed his life to the Indian's father – One of the others was tomahawked either by Clarke or one of his Officers, the other three foreseeing their fate, began to sing their Death song, and were butchered in succession, tho at the very time a flag of Truce was

standing, Hamilton to Dartmouth, Sept. 2, 1776, *MPHC* 10:264–70. The British high command was worried about Hamilton's tactics and actions from the beginning, see Remarks on Lt. Governor Hamilton's Letter, c. Dec. 1778, Haldimand Papers, 21782.

[21] Clark's Memoir, *IHC* 8:277, 284, 287. I have used Clark's Memoir as the most finished version of his account of the siege. There are other versions in his letter to Mason, Nov. 19, 1779, *IHC* 8:144, and his journal, Feb. 24, 1779, *IHC* 8:167. These are historically more accurate, but they are not the finished symbolic message that the Memoir presents.

[22] Clark Memoir, *IHC* 8:288. The numbers taken differ. See Clark Journal, *IHC* 8:167, Bowman Journal, *IHC* 8:161. See also copy of Clark Journal in Haldimand Papers, 21782; Clark to Mason, Nov. 19, 1779, *IHC* 8:144–45.

hanging out at the fort and the firing had ceased on both sides – A young chief of the Ottawa nation called Macutté Mong one of these last, having received the fatal stroke of a Tomahawk in the head, took it out and gave it again into the hands of his executioner who repeated the stroke a second and third time, after which the miserable being, not entirely deprived of life was dragged to the river and thrown in with the rope about his neck where he ended his life and tortures – This horrid scence was transacted in the open Street, and before the door of a house where I afterward was quartered, the master of which related to me the above particulars – The blood of the victims was still visible for days afterwards, a testimony of the courage and Humanity of Colonel Clarke –

Clark met with Hamilton after the execution: "His hands and face still reeking from the human sacrifice in which he had acted as chief priest, he told me with great exultation how he had been employed."[23]

The various accounts of the incident, for all their differences, manipulate the same symbols. In his letter and his journal, Chark depicted himself as acting sternly as an avenger of the widows and orphans created by the savage hair buyer Hamilton. Hamilton made Clark the savage "chief priest" in a "human sacrifice." In all of Hamilton's surviving accounts of the murder of the Indians, he attempted to paint his white opponent as an Indian, that is, a bloodthirsty savage. Clark's attempt, in his later account, to downplay the incident shows the advantage Hamilton gained in such a war of symbols. Hamilton the supposed "savage" hair buyer paled before Clark the sacrificial priest, reeking of the blood of Indian victims.

But even in this war of symbols arrayed for an audience outside the *pays d'en haut*, the more complicated social world continuously intruded. The dualities broke down. Ducoigne, an Illinois chief who was a *métis bâtard*, the son of a man who was a British interpreter at Niagara, served as an American messenger to the Wabash. The Michilimackinac trader Macarty, who had joined Clark, saved Pontiac's son because Pontiac had once saved him. As a Detroit partisan who had accompanied the ill-fated Indian war party was about to be dispatched, he was recognized and saved by his own father, a habitant from Illinois country who had accompanied Clark. After the surrender, another suspectd partisan of Hamilton's was saved by the inter-cession of his sister, who was from Vincennes. Raimbault, a trader from Quiatenon and a suspected partisan of the Indians', was being hanged when French from Illinois country intervened and saved him. Hamilton's Detroit volunteers marched home "huzzaing for the Congress." Kinship, friendship,

[23] Barnhart (ed.), *Hamilton Journal*, 183.

old obligations, and new obligations everywhere intruded and subverted Clark's and Hamilton's simpler stories and conficts.[24]

III

The messy and complicated village world that Clark and Hamilton encountered in the Illinois and Wabash country had more to do with the shaping of events in the West during the Revolution than did republican ideologies or imperial commands. Algonquians who depended on the Kentucky hunting grounds, or who had lost relatives to the Big Knives, fought bitterly and well; most of those who lacked such immediate concerns, faded in and out of the war. French habitants and traders considered their immediate interests, their local prerogatives, and acted accordingly. Backcountry Anglo-American, Scots-Irish, and German-American patriots lost relatives and property to Indians, and most of them became Indian haters. They killed Indians – friend and foe alike, where and when they found them – without much thought of the consequences to the revolutionary cause. As for backcountry Tories, loyalty to the king often mattered less than revenge for private grievances against revolutionary neighbors.[25]

In a war that eventually spanned much of the globe, and in the midst of a revolution that would alter world history, the *pays d'en haut* remained a small world where many of the principals – Algonquians, French, Iroquois, British (that is, Scots, Germans, English, Irish, and Anglo Americans) – knew one another personally. In this world only a handful of British regulars were really soldiers, men who could be compelled to fight. The others – white as well as Algonquian – were warriors, men who fought when they chose. Brave in defense of their homes and families, cruel in search of revenge, they lacked discipline; attempting to control them drove British and revolutionary officers alike to distraction.

The people who mattered in the West were often men and women of considerable shrewdness but of limited aims. They loaded village interests onto imperial or revolutionary wagons and rode them as far they could go.

[24] For Decoigne, see Hamilton to Haldimand, Aug. 7, 1778, *IHC* 1:351. For son of Pontiac, see Barnhart (ed.), *Hamilton Journal*, Feb. 24, 1779, 182–83. For French father and son, see *ibid.* For volunteers, Clark to Mason, Nov. 19, 1779, *IHC* 8:146. For Raimbault, see Barnhart (ed.), *Hamilton's Journal*, 188.
[25] For accounts of fighting during the war and immediately after, see Randolph C. Downes, *Council Fires on the Upper Ohio* (Pittsburgh: University of Pittsburgh Press, 1969), 179–310, and Solon J. and Elizabeth H. Buck, *The Planting of Civilization in Western Pennsylvania* (Pittsburgh: University of Pennsylvania Press, 1939), 175–203. For example of difficulties of protecting even allied Indians, see Brodhead to Reed, Nov. 2, 1780, Neville B, Craig, Esq. (ed.), *The Olden Time* (Pittsburgh: Dumars, 1846; Millwood, N.Y.: Kraus Reprint Co., 1976), 2:375.

The Algonquian leaders whom the Revolution thrust into prominence were typical. Except along the Ohio River and at Detroit, the older alliance chiefs had largely disappeared. The village leaders were either elderly men, long ignored by the Europeans, or a new generation far more parochial and less sophisticated than the alliance chiefs of a generation before. The village world had closed in around these *okemas*: the war leaders, clan leaders, shamans, councillors, speakers, and village headmen. Once familiar with Quebec, Montreal, Philadelphia, and New Orleans, once practiced in negotiations with all the peoples between the Mississippi and the Atlantic, they now dealt only with their immediate neighbors, with French nearly as isolated as themselves, and, to a much lesser degree, with British traders. What these leaders had borrowed from the Europeans only diminished them in European eyes. The two most influential Ottawa chiefs at Little Traverse, complained Patrick Sinclair, the lieutenant governor at Michilimackinac, were "the one a drunkard and the other an avaricious trader."[26]

Algonquian horizons had narrowed. In 1778, Henry Hamilton found the Wabash Indians "almost altogether in the dark with respect to the power of the British Nation, few but contemptible Renegadoes from the English having been seen among them, & the French traders from interest as well as mortified pride, decrying as much as possible every thing that was not French." And at Saint Joseph, Louis Chevallier spoke with condescension, but also from long experience, when he lamented the loss of old alliance chiefs in the largely Potawatomi villages around Saint Joseph:

> It does not seem to me . . . impossible to keep this nation in dependance, if they were united under the same chief, but divided as it is into six villages distant fifteen or twenty miles from each other, it is very difficult to impose this yoke. Each village has its own chief who disposes his young men according to his private ideas, too attentive to the poisoned speeches of certain traitors who sacrifice honor & duty to a sordid interests, they become deaf to the sweet words of their father & to any effort we can make to hold them after they are resolved.[27]

The British and, to a lesser extent, the Americans aspired to use these men to create a new alliance. Hamilton made an auspicious start for the British, but his defeat fragmented the *pays d'en haut* once more. Initially, the Americans did not seek to use the Indians against the British so much as to hold them neutral. There were chiefs willing to cooperate, but most Americans misunderstood the power of chiefs and what was necessary to give them influence. They tended to overestimate what the men they

---

[26] Sinclair to Haldimand, May 29, 1780, *WHC* 11:152.
[27] Barnhart (ed.), *Hamilton's Journal*, Nov. 27, 1778, 132; Chevallier to Haldimand, 28 Feb. 1779, *MPHC* 19:375.

encountered could do. As White Mingo complained, the Americans wrongly thought that chiefs had the power "to restrain or hold fast our young men against their will."[28]

The Americans, like earlier European powers, had to receive instruction in the meaning of the middle ground. The Americans failed to understand that presents were the visible evidence of love, devotion, and good faith. White Mingo reminded American Indian commissioners of "the ancient custom of our Forefathers, whenever they met together our Ancestors were always treated well," but most Indian commissioners interpreted such reminders as solicitations for bribery. Negotiations, by extension, became exercises in extortion. The "bad people" among the Delawares appealed to this logic when they claimed that the high prices asked for American goods showed that American friendship was not strong. In 1777, the neutral Delawares also used this logic when they complained that failing American supplies caused them to be "ridiculed by your Enemies for being attach'd to you who cannot even furnish us with a pair of stockings or a Blanket."[29]

One American who did understand was George Morgan, the ex-trader, the partner in Baynton, Wharton, and Morgan, who, fortunately for the United States, represented the Congress at Pittsburgh between 1776 and 1779. But Morgan himself was suspect along the frontier. Settlers lumped him with Alexander McKee and Simon Girty: Tories who knew Indians well and who went over to the British in 1778. General Edward Hand even arrested Morgan as a Tory in 1777. Eventually Morgan's quarrels with the military drove him from office in disgust. A skilled operator on the middle ground, Morgan struggled to maintain loyal chiefs who could hold the Delawares, Shawnees, Munsees, Mingos, and Wyandots neutral. Morgan, called Brother Taimenend (or Tammany, as the Americans later rendered it, after the prototype for Delaware chiefs), sincerely wanted peace. He told the Moravian minister David Zeisberger in 1778 that only the thought of securing it kept him at Pittsburgh. He knew how to support chiefs, and he knew they worked slowly and incrementally. The chiefs valued him in turn. John Killbuck of the Delawares called him "the wisest, faithfullest and best Man I ever had any thing to do with." The honor he paid to Kishanathathe

---

[28] For White Mingo, quotation, see Intelligence received from the White Mingo, Oct. 18, 1776, Morgan Letter Book, Book 2.

[29] For proper behavior, see White Mingo, Speech, Aug. 21, 1776, Morgan Letter Book, Book 2. For presents as bribes, see To the Honble Committee of Congress for Indian Affairs, July 39, 1776, Col. George Morgan Letter Book, Book 2. For agents in village, Commissioners of Indian Affairs to Newcomer, Aug. 17, 1776, Morgan Letter Book, Book 2. For impoverished, see Captain Pipe to Morgan, Apr. 5, 1777, Morgan Letter Book, Book 1. For lacks blankets, see Morgan to Delaware Council, Mar. 27, 1778. Morgan Letter Book, Book 3. For friendship, Morgan Diary, July 28, 1776. Not only did American presents fail, so too did American trade, Speech to Congress and Washington, May 10, 1779, WHC 23:318.

(or Hardman) who had previously been abused at Pittsburgh, moved the Shawnees to tell Morgan, "You have raised up our old Chief who lay dead & neglected – you have made him white to all Nations – this we shall forever thank you for."[30]

Morgan's goal of peace and Indian neutrality demanded concessions as well as presents on the part of the Americans. In the manner of an alliance chief, Morgan thought of his main task as restraining "our own people." He was more concerned with preserving an imperfect peace than "awing the different Nations by expeditions into their Country which may involve us in a general & unequal Quarrel with all Nations who are at present quiet but extremely jealous of the least encroachment on their lands." Morgan was willing to trade peace on the frontier for a withdrawal from Kentucky that would allow a concentration of revolutionary manpower and resources in the East, but virtually no one else was. George Rogers Clark and the string of frustrated American generals who operated out of Pittsburgh pushed a military solution which put increasing pressure on the Wabash villages, the neutral Delawares, the Shawnees, and the Allegheny Senecas to choose sides. They won the support of both the Continental Congress and Virginia's governor, Patrick Henry, who believed "Savages must be managed by working on their Fears."[31]

[30] McKee, Matthew Elliot, and Simon Girty all escaped from Pittsburgh and fled to the British in Mar. 1778, Hand to Yeates, Mar. 30, 1778, Kellogg (ed.), *Frontier Advance*, 249–50. Morgan worked largely with Captain Pipe, George White Eyes, and John Killbuck among the Delawares. The old Delaware chiefs Custologa and Newcomer died in the fall of 1776, Council Pittsburgh, Oct. 15 – Nov. 6, 1776. For Killbuck quotation, see Killbuck to Morgan, Jan. 20, 1779, *WHC* 23:204. For Shawnee quotation, see Morgan Diary, Oct. 29, 1776. For desire for peace, see Morgan to Zeisberger, Mar. 27, 1778, Morgan Letter Book, Book 3. For arrest of Morgan, see Hand to Congress, Dec. 21, 1777, Kellogg (ed.), *Frontier Advance*, 184–87.

Morgan quarreled with General McIntosh over his attempts to force the Delawares to abandon their neutrality and aid the Americans. The dispute led McIntosh to orchestrate accusations against Morgan for neglect of duty, Charges Against George Morgan . . . c. May 1779, *WHC* 23:328. Heckewelder and Zeisberger, given Moravian pacifism and Delaware neutrality, had become rather odd military advisors to American military officers such as McIntosh and Gibson, Brodhead, etc., Hackenwalder to Broadford (*sic*), May 28, 1779, *PA* Series 1, 7:516–18. Morgan, believing that American Indian polices would result in a general Indian war, resigned in May 1779, Morgan to Congress, May 28, 1779, *WHC* 23:345.

[31] For Morgan quotation, see Morgan to Hancock, Mar. 15, 1777, Morgan Letter Books, Book 1. For Morgan's position, see Morgan to Commissioner . . . in the Northern Department, Mar. 9, 1777, Morgan Letter Book, Book 1; Morgan and Nevill to Henry, Apr. 1, 1777, Morgan letter Book, Book 1. For danger of expanded war, see Morgan Diary, Nov. 7, 1776; for Henry, see Henry to Hand, July 27, 1777, Kellogg (ed.), *Frontier Advance*, 30. Meeting, July 24, 1776, Morgan Diary. For warning to Americans to vacate positions north of the Ohio, see A Message from the Chiefs of the Mohawks etc., Feb. 2, 1777, in letter from Moorhead to Morgan, Mar. 24, 1777, Morgan Letter Book, Book 1.

For plans for invasion, see Hand to Wharton, July 24, 1777 *PA*, Series 1, 5:443–44; Wharton to Hand, Aug. 22, 1777, *ibid.*, 540–41. For abandoned, see Hand to Washington,

Morgan's careful, nuanced diplomacy of the middle ground had to contend with the rough and ready variations on Indian ritual conjured up by military men who, like Clark, tried to improvise on diplomatic tunes they did not know. In 1778, three leading Delawares appeared at Fort Pitt for a treaty. John Killbuck was chief of the Turtle phratry; Quequedegatha (or George White Eyes) had abdicated his chieftainship to become first captain of the Turtle phratry; Captain Pipe, chief of the Wolf phratry, had similarly given up his office to act as war captain. General Lachlan MacIntosh was present; George Morgan was not. All of these Delaware chiefs were struggling to hold their people neutral and expected to reaffirm their neutrality, instead, however, the chiefs heard an American demand for their participation in General MacIntosh's projected expedition against Detroit.[32]

The Delawares desired, above all, to avoid fighting "against those Nations which with they were connected," and the Delaware chiefs continued to conceive of themselves as mediators who would try to prevent war between the Americans and the other villagers of the *pays d'en haut*. John Killbuck went to Fort Pitt as a phratry leader and a civil chief and, as such, had no power to declare war, for that power belonged to his captains. But as he explained later, after McIntosh presented the war belt at Fort Pitt in 1778, "I was looked upon as a Warrior, & which was the cause of so much confusion among my People." Because McIntosh did not understand the rituals and symbols of the middle ground, Killbuck did not realize the nature of McIntosh's request. He thought the Americans wanted their service as guides and mediators, not warriors:

> The Tomahawk was handed to me at Fort Pitt but not in a Warlike manner, we all standing & at no Council Fire, neither did I understand the meaning of it. I neither desired any Implements of War, all what I agreed to was to pilot the Army, 'till beyond our bound, & my great

Nov. 9, 1777, Kellogg (ed.), *Frontier Advance*, 154. As the Americans alienated village after village and Clark's expedition revealed British weakness, even Morgan eventually came to believe that an attack on Detroit was necessary, Morgan to Board of War, July 17, 1778, *WHC* 23:112–13.

[32] John Heckewelder, The Names of all the different Indian Nations in North America (1777), Mss. Moravian Archives, Box: Moravian Indian Missions, Heckewelder, copy, Ohio Valley–Great Lakes Ethnohistorical Archives, University of Indiana, hereafter cited as GLEHA. Treaty at Pittsburgh, Sept. 16, 1778, *Virginia Historical Magazine* 24 (Jan. 1916): 175–76.

John Heckewelder contended that Pipe never desired neutrality, but Heckewelder and the Moravians evaluated Indians largely on the basis of their attitude toward the mission and favored those, such as White Eyes, who were sympathetic to Christianity. Pipe and White Eyes were rivals, and so Moravian accounts of the period favor White Eyes. In fact, Pipe remained neutral even after Americans killed his relatives. John Heckewelder, *A Narrative of the Mission of the United Brethren Among the Delaware and Mohegan Indians, from Its Commencement in the Year 1740 to the Close of the year 1808* (Philadelphia: McCarty and Davis, 1820; Arno repr., 1971), 171–72.

Capt. White Eyes with several others to go before the Army & convey them to the Enemy in order to be of use to both Parties, in case they should desire to speak or treat with one another.[33]

Blunders on the middle ground had consequences. This one drove two hundred Delawares from the town of Coshocton and its vicinity into the arms of the British, but misunderstandings were also the stuff on whch the middle ground fed. Mistakes created innovations. In 1779 Killbuck, leading a Delaware delegation to meet with Washington and the Congress, announced a shift in the mechanisms of diplomacy. The Delawares had "thrown aside the use of wampum, they will wish to be indulged with your Excellency's [Washington's] written answer." They had abandoned the communication of messages through belts for communication through writing. Despite past experiences with Americans who had purposefully misinterpreted written documents to them, the Delawares apparently preferred to take their chances with intentional deceptions rather than with unintentional blunders by Americans who did not know how to use wampum belts, calumets, and war axes. With Moravian schools already among them, and relatives of the phratry chiefs' sent east for education at Princeton, illiteracy would not long be a problem. In the meantime, they petitioned Congress to assign them a secretary.[34]

When McIntosh blundered, he at least blundered upon the middle ground; backcountry settlers wished to obliterate the middle ground itself. White Mingo complained that the Americans spoke with two voices – one good and one bad. Morgan was the good voice. The bad voice came from the backcountry Indian haters, that is, from the Anglo-American residents inside stockades and in villages. Morgan warned John Hancock in March

---

[33] For Delawares desire to avoid war with people of own color, see Brodhead to Washington, Apr. 3, 1779, *WHC* 23:272. Only captains could declare war, George Henry Loskiel, *History of the Mission of the United Brethren among the Indians in North America...* (London: The Brethren's Society for the Furtherance of the Gospel, 1794), 1:144. For first quotation, Zeisberger to Morgan, Jan. 20, 1779, *WHC* 23:201. For second quotation, Killbuck to Morgan, Jan. 20, 1779, *WHC* 23:204. The news that the Delawares had accepted an American war belt put them at grave risk, Gibson to Morgan, Jan. 22, 1779, *IHC* 1:386; Morgan believed McIntosh's actions would increase the number of enemies, Morgan to Jay, Mar. 8, 1779, Morgan Letter Books, Book 3, Speech to Congress and Washington, May 10, 1793, *WHC* 23:320. Congress, however, insisted that the Delawares aid them, Speech of Congress to Delaware Chiefs, 26 May 1779, *WHC* 23:340–41.

[34] Morgan to Washington, May 9, 1779, *WHC* 23:313. Speech to Washington and Congress, May 10, 1779, *WHC* 23:319–20. Secretary, Delawares to Congress, May 29, 1779, *WHC* 23:353. For Moravian schools, see Heckewelder, *Narrative of the Mission*, 194.

The trip to Washington was an attempt by Morgan not only to cement peace and trade with the Delawares but also to wean the Wyandots, Ottawas, Chippewas, and others from the British, Taimenend to the Wise Men of the Delawares and Shawanese of Coohshoking: Jan. 5, 1779, Haldimand Papers, 21782. See also Galalemend to Montour, Jan. 4, 1779, Haldimand Papers, 21782.

1777 that he feared backcountry whites sought a war with neutral Indians "on account of the fine Lands these poor people possess." Morgan, like an Algonquian chief, could not restrain his young men who wished for a general Indian war and who organized "to massacre some who have come to visit us in a Friendly manner and other who have been hunting on their own Lands, the known Friends to the Commonwealth."[35]

The backcountry declared its own Indian policy in blood in much the same way that dissident Delaware and Shawnee warriors wrote their dissent from the policies of White Eyes, John Killbuck, and Cornstalk in the blood of white victims. Where the Delawares exiled their dissidents from the main villages in and around Coshocton, however, the backcountry tended to treasure, or at least defend, those of its people who killed Indians. The Delaware chiefs admitted that some of their people had killed whites, but in the manner of the middle ground, they appealed to parallels in white society. They argued that just as states contained Tories but the Continental Congress did not declare war on states, so Delawares should not be attacked for the actions of renegades. The backcountry settlers, however, lumped all Indians together and the results proved disastrous for American Indian policy. Indian haters killed or alienated the very men who were willing to act as alliance chiefs or mediators for the Americans. Along the Ohio in 1775, there were experienced chiefs cast in the old mold: Kayashuta, Cornstalk, Kishanathathe, George White Eyes, and Captain Pipe. Backcountry settlers proceeded to murder either these chiefs themselves or those closely connected to them.[36]

Given the size and success of the raids that ravaged the backcountry, the desire for revenge against an often brutal enemy was understandable enough, but Indian hating did not concentrate on enemies. Indian haters killed Indians who warned them of raids. They killed Indians who scouted for their military expeditions. They killed Indian women and children. They even killed Christian, pacifist Indians as they prayed. Murder gradually and inexorably became the dominant American Indian policy, supplanting the policies of Morgan, of the Congress, and of the military.

In 1777 and 1778, it became apparent that American officials could not control backcountry settlers either within or outside the militia. The most famous backcountry murder, that of Cornstalk, took place in spite of the opposition of militia officers, but General Edward Hand's so-called squaw campaign in the fall of 1777 was the work of a militia expedition. Attacking

---

[35] For two voices, White Mingo, see Intelligence received from the White Mingo, Oct. 18, 1776, Morgan Letter Book, Book 2. For murders by whites, see Morgan and Nevill to Henry, Apr. 1, 1777, Morgan Letter Book, Book 1.

[36] For Delaware analogy, see Delaware Chiefs to Congress, May 29, 1779, WHC 23:351–52. For exile, see Message of Delawares, May 1779, Morgan Letter Book, Book 3.

camps of women and children belonging to the neutral Delawares, the militia killed Captain Pipe's brother, two women, and a child. They took two other women prisoners. On learning of Hand's attack, Captain Pipe, a man regarded by the British as pro-American, took his losses with forbearance. He recalled a war party that had already departed to avenge the dead, saying "that though he had lost more of his friends than any of the rest, yet he had no thoughts of revenging himself, but keep fast hold to the Chain of Friendship." The Delawares continued to turn back those war parties that they could and to warn the Americans of others.[37]

Such warnings did not deter the Indian haters. In 1777, Colonel John Gibson warned that frontier whites were ready to murder George White Eyes, even though White Eyes had given warning of attacks on the frontier. In 1778, White Eyes, condemned by the Detroit and Sandusky Indians for betraying their raids and in desperate need of American assistance, guided the McIntosh expedition, which built Fort Laurens beside the Tuscarawas River. He hoped the Americans would protect the Delawares from the Detroit tribes he believed were about to attack him. According to accounts the Americans released at the time, White Eyes contracted smallpox on the expedition and died later at Fort Pitt. In fact, according to George Morgan, American militiamen murdered him.[38]

[37] For attacks, see Heckewelder, *Narrative of the Mission*, 159; Page to Hand, Kellogg (ed.), *Frontier Advance*, 85–86; Gibson to Washington, Dec. 5, 1777, *ibid.*, 172–74; Gibson to Hand, Dec. 10, 1777, *ibid.*, 178–81.

For Shawnees and Cornstalk, see Arbuckle to Hand, Oct. 6, 1777, Kellogg (ed.), *Frontier Advance*, 125–27; Arbuckle to Hand, 7 Nov. 1777, *ibid.*, 149–50; Narrative of John Stuart, *ibid.* 157–62; Hand to Henry, 9 Dec. 1777, *ibid.* 175–77. Morgan attempted to conciliate the Shawnees and cover the dead, Morgan to Shawnees, Mar. 25, 1778, *ibid.*, 234–37. Even this murder did not drive all of the Mequachake Shawnees to war. The Hardman, Nemwha, and Woweconeen moved with seventeen families to affiliate briefly with the Delawares of Coshocton, White Eyes and Killbuck to Morgan, March 14, 1778, Morgan Letter Book, Book 3. Meeting with Delaware Indians, Apr. 26, 1778, Morgan Letter Book, Book 3. For that they were Mequachake, see Treaty of Fort Pitt, Sept. 13, 1778, *Virginia Historical Magazine*, 24 (Jan. 1916): 174, and Kellelman to Maghingive Keeshuch, Sept. 21, 1779, Craig (ed.), *The Olden Time*, 2:316–17. For bulk of Shawnees took up hatchet, see Council at Detroit, Feb. 7, 1779, *WHC* 23:220.

The murder of Cornstalk brought denunciations of the backcountry people from Patrick Henry that rivaled the earlier opinions of Gage and Johnson, Henry to Fleming, Feb. 19, 1778, *ibid.*, 206–9. For squaw campaign, see Hand to Ewing, Mar. 7, 1778, *ibid.*, 215–16. For Pipe's relatives, see Recollections of Samuel Murphy, *ibid.*, 216–20. Morgan to Board of War, July 17, 1778, *WHC* 23:112–13. For Pipe as a Virginian, see Morgan Diary, July 24, 1776. White Eyes doubted his loyalty to the Virginians, *ibid.*, Oct. 24, 1776. He had, however, not only remained neutral until Hand's attack, but still sought peace afterward, Morgan to Zeisberger, Mar. 27, 1778, *ibid.*, 244. White Eyes and Killbuck to Morgan, Apr. 6, 1778, Morgan Letter Book, Book 3. The Americans condoled the Delawares for the attack, U.S. to Delaware Council, Apr. 13, 1778, *ibid.*, 269–70.

[38] For White Eye in danger, see Gibson to Hand, July 31, 1777, Kellogg (ed.), *Frontier Advance*, 35. For White Eye's warning, see *ibid.*, 54–68. White Eyes, Recollections of Stephen Burkam, *WHC* 23:157. For denounced at Detroit, see White Eyes to Morgan, July

Every major chief on the Ohio had thus felt the wrath of the Indian haters by 1779, and the blows continued as long as any remained either neutral or allied to the Big Knives. As Captain Leonard Helm wrote Clark, "If their is not a stop put to Kiling Indian friends we must Expect to have all foes." In 1779, when the Americans persuaded a delegation of Delaware chiefs to visit Philadelphia, backcountry settlers assembled to murder them on the road, and a soldier murdered a young Delaware man – "one of the best young men of the Delaware nation" – who had remained at Fort Pitt with the blind and aged Captain Killbuck. When it appeared that some of the Shawnees might be won over, Pennsylvania officials reported that so "violent are the Prejudices against the Indians" that the backcountry settlers would not let Indian goods designed to procure peace proceed over the mountains. The next year, Colonel Brodhead discovered a plan by men who had been militia officers to murder forty Delawares who had come to accompany his projected expedition.[39]

Unable to control the Indian haters, unfamiliar with the intricacies of the diplomatic middle ground, and short of trade goods and presents, American military officers, including Clark himself, squandered the advantages gained at Vincennes. Clark, without sufficient supplies and men, was unable to move on Detroit, and other American forays into the Indian country did only enough damage to make hostile Shawnees, Mingos, and Wyandots more dependent on the British. Clark's Indian policy soon became little more than what he called "mear political lies" and a series of blustering threats that only seemed to link him more tightly with the Indian haters. By the fall of 1781, Clark's gains had vanished, part of a general decline of American influence among both the Indians and the French, whom the Americans' levies of supplies had impoverished.[40]

19, 1778, Morgan Letter Book, Book 3; Zeisberger to Morgan, Aug. 25, 1778, WHC 23:132–33.

For guides, see Brodhead to Washington, Apr. 17, 1779, WHC 23:289. For Killbuck considers himself at war, see Kellelman to Brodhead, Sept. 21, 1774, WHC 24:73. For death of White Eyes, see Downes, Council Fires, 217.

[39] For Helm quotation, see Helm to Clark, May 9, 1779, IHC 8:317; Brodhead to Washington, May 3, 1779, WHC 23:306–7. Captain Killbuck the elder and Brodhead to Maginguapoos, Apr. 28, 1779, WHC 23:296–97. For goods and attack, see Reed to Brodhead, n.d., c. July 1779, PA, Series 1, 7:569. For plan to murder Delawares, see Brodhead to Reed, Nov. 2, 1780, PA, Series 1, 8:596.

[40] Clark's Memoir, IHC 8:293, 299; Helm to Clark, May 31, 1779, IHC 8:324–26; Clark to Mason, Nov. 19, 1779, IHC 8:146–49, 152–53; Clark to Nanaloibi, April 20, 1779, IHC 8:313–14; Clark to Fleming, Oct. 22, 1779, George Rogers Clark Papers, Draper Mss., 23J93.

British threats could alienate Indians as quickly as American, as Hamilton had found out in threatening White Eyes, William Wilson, Report, Sept. 26, 1776, Morgan Letter Book, Book 2; Hamilton to Dartmouth, Sept. 2, 1776, MPHC 10:270.

Petition of Inhabitants of Vincennes, June 30, 1781, IHC 8:430–33; Memorial of the Inhabitants of Vincennes to the French Minister, Aug. 22, 1780, IHC 8:438–49; Robert

IV

Indian hating destroyed Morgan's attempts to conciliate Algonquians on the middle ground, but Indian hating, despite itself, came to occupy a narrow and cramped corner of the middle ground. The Revolution began in the *pays d'en haut* with Americans and Algonquians talking of their common birth from a common mother, of their being like "one Flesh and Blood." These were the metaphors of peace and friendship. With war and Indian hating, the metaphors of a common birth gave way to the actualities of violent death. Yet in fighting and death, as well as in peace and negotiations, there were contacts, meanings to be deciphered, and understandings reached.[41]

When Macutté Mong at Vincennes took the hatchet from his own head and handed it mockingly back to his executioners, he acted the part of a warrior at the torture stake. He died confident that he would be avenged. The backcountry men who killed Macutté Mong understood his actions clearly enough; they could emulate them. In 1779 John Heckewelder wrote to Colonel Brodhead of the death of an American prisoner held by the Wyandots. Captain Henry Bird of the British Army had done all he could to save the man, even urging him to take up a gun and sell his life dearly; in rage and frustration Bird had denounced the Wyandots, saying he wished he was a rebel so that he could kill them all. But the prisoner himself, a man from the Indian-hating settlements, reacted like an Algonquian, "Seeming Pretty easy [he] only told them that the time would come that they would pay dear for all their commited Murders, and then was taken away by the Women and Murdered at a most horrid rate." In their last moments, an Algonquian warrior and a backcountry fighter might prove to be virtually indistinguishable.[42]

The meanings communicated by such deaths – the disdain for enemies, the certainty of revenge – were meanings of the middle ground, but such meanings were about as much of the middle ground as pure Indian hating

George to Clark, Oct. 28, 1780, *IHC* 8:461. For problems with supplies, etc., see Shelby to Clark, Oct. 10, 1779, *IHC* 8:370; Dodge to Jefferson, Aug. 1, 1780, *IHC* 8:437; Statement of Montgomery, Oct. 10, 1780, George Rogers Clark Papers, Draper Mss., 60J335–37. Brodhead to Washington, Oct. 17, 1780, *WHC* 24:283–84. The Spanish at Illinois, themselves short of goods, could do little to aid the Americans, Lebya to Gálvez, July 13, 1779, Lawrence Kinnaird, *Spain in the Mississippi Valley, 1765–94 . . . Part I: The Revolutionary Period, 1765–81*, Annual Report of the American Historical Association for the Year 1945, vol. 2, (Washington, D.C.: Government Printing Office, 1949), 346–47. *Ibid.*, Oct. 28, 1779, 361.

41 For quotations, see headnotes, The Cornstalk, June 1, 1776, Morgan Diary; American Commissioners for Indian Affairs to Delawares, Senecas, Munseys, and Mingos, Pittsburgh, 1776, Morgan Letter Book, Book 2. For death of Macutté Mong, see above.

42 For Wyandots, see Hackenwelder (*sic*) to Brodhead, June 30, 1779, *PA*, Series 1, 7:524–25.

could grasp. Indian hating reached only the barren edges of the middle ground; all planted there died. Later, ironically, when the middle ground itself had nearly vanished from sight, only literary and mythic versions of Indian hating preserved its traces. Herman Melville, D. H. Lawrence, and modern scholars like R. W. B. Lewis and Richard Slotkin discerned accurately enough that these stories of death implied a common world; that to hate and kill Indians – and to be captured and killed by them – involved, at some level, understanding them and imitating them.[43]

Pure Indian hating penetrated the middle ground the way backcountry fighters penetrated an Algonquian village – just far enough to destroy it. The middle ground blurred boundaries, and what pure Indian haters sought above all was to keep boundaries intact. Captives and converts, white or Indian, proved the greatest danger to Indian hating because they passed across borders. Whites, like Algonquians, killed captives, but unlike Algonquians, whites killed virtually all male captives and rarely adopted or attempted to assimilate any Algonquians. Clark's first retaliatory attack on the Shawnee towns of Chillicothe and Piqua took five or six male prisoners, whose fate was unknown, and one woman, who was killed by "ripping up her Belly & otherwise mangling her." In both Algonquian and backcountry attacks, women's bodies became bloody metaphors. Warriors, Indian and white, killed women more rarely than they killed men, but when they killed them, they often butchered them. Fighters who had rejected peace with its images of a common mother and common births now assailed actual mothers, ripping out their wombs. Men denied their common humanity by mutilating women.[44]

More often men struck each other directly, and this too was, like the symbolic slaying of women, a rejection of a common world. When Brodhead took Coshocton in 1781, he and his militia spared women and children but executed all male prisoners who did not have papers from the Continental Congress. Although Brodhead told the Indians the militia "would not be under his Command" and had forced him to execute prisoners, this was still official killing of a sort; the Indian haters went farther. Lewis Wetzel, a man who devoted much of his life to Indian hunting and was in many ways the prototypical Indian hater, tomahawked a Delaware chief from behind while the Indian negotiated with Brodhead.[45]

---

[43] Richard Warrington Baldwin Lewis, *The American Adam: Innocence, Tragedy, and Tradition in the Nineteenth Century* (Chicago: University of Chicago Press, 1955); Richard Slotkin, *Regeneration through Violence: The Mythology of the American Frontier, 1600–1860* (Middletown, Conn.: Wesleyan University Press, 1973.)

[44] In principle, whites distinguished themselves from Indians because they did not kill women and children nor torture prisoners, see, e.g., Thomas Hartley to the Chiefs and principal Indians of Chimung . . . Oct. 1, 1778, Haldimand Papers, 21782.

[45] Homan to Bird, Aug. 15, 1780, *MPHC* 10:418–9. For Brodhead expedition, see Butter-

The Delawares, who had previously made Brohead a member of the Turtle phratry, expected the American to act like a Turtle; they sought an accommodation on the old middle ground. But Wetzel with his tomahawk and his insatiable thirst for revenge was the dominant figure. He entered the middle ground only to destroy it. He and those like him never accepted its underlying beliefs. Herman Melville later captured the essence of their Indian hating: "The backwoodsman still regards the red man in much the same spirit that a jury does a murderer, or a trapper a wild cat – a creature, in whose behalf mercy were not wisdom; truce is vain; he must be executed."[46] Like Wetzel, Indian haters sought to terminate with a tomahawk blow to the skull more complicated searches for common meaning.

Many Algonquians, however, retained the older sense of the middle ground, beliefs not only that the boundaries between societies and cultures were permeable but also that identities were interchangeable. People could move between cultures; a person could become someone else. Metaphorically, Algonquians made kinship universal. Indian haters believed that birth and race ought to make whites and Indians permanent strangers.

Indian haters distrusted all who crossed the boundaries. They did not believe Indians could become "civilized." To them, becoming civilized invariably meant becoming white, which Indians could never do. They did not trust Christian Indians like the Moravians; as even Daniel Brodhead told Heckewelder, "I conceive that much confidence ought never to be placed in any of the colour, for I believe it is much easier for the most civilized Indian to turn Savage than for any Indian to be civilized."[47]

The most infamous American massacre, that of the Moravian Indians at Gnaddenhutten in 1782, illustrated where the American obsession with cultural boundaries could lead. The travail of the Moravians began when the majority of the Delawares joined the British in 1781. Captain Pipe of the Delawares and Half King of the Wyandots then forced the Moravian Delawares to abandon their mission towns and withdraw farther into the interior, to around Sandusky. The ministers, especially John Heckewelder, had become increasingly strong American partisans over the years, and the British and their allies wanted them out of the way so that they could no longer betray war parties against the American frontier. The Indian haters,

---

field's narrative of Brodhead's Coshocton Expedition, *WHC* 24:376–81. Brodhead released the women and children and 4 men with papers from Congress; he executed the remaining prisoners, Girty to De Peyster, May 4, 1781, *MPHC* 10:478–79.

[46] For Brodhead as Turtle, see Brodhead to Killbuck, Feb. 4, 1781, *WHC* 24:329–31. Herman Melville, *The Confidence Man, His Masquerade* (Evanston and Chicago: Northwestern University Press and the Newberry Library, 1984), 144. Clark took some women prisoners also, for he was advised to use one as a peace emissary, Tardiveau to Clark, Mar. 12, 1783, GRC Papers, Draper Mss., 52J79.

[47] For Brodhead quotation, Brodhead to Heckewelder, Jan. 21, 1781, *WHC* 24:321.

however, regarded all Indians as being of a kind. They had long believed that the Moravian Indians abetted attacks on the frontier and perhaps even participated in them. There had been earlier attempts to attack and kill the pacifist villagers.[48]

In the winter of 1782 a group of about 150 Moravian Indians returned to their abandoned villages to gather supplies of corn. The Americans had released some of the Moravian Delawares, whom they had seized earlier, with the message that they would not be molested if they returned to save their crops. While at their old villages, the Moravians met a returning war party that had murdered a woman and child on the Ohio, and who warned the Christian Indians that they expected pursuit. The Moravians, feeling they had nothing to fear from the Americans, delayed their own return to Sandusky. The pursuing Americans murdered and mutilated two Indians on their approach to Gnadenhutten, but the Moravian Indians of Gnadenhutten and Salem did not learn of this until later. They recognized some of the Americans as men who had earlier peacefully removed some Christian Indians to Pittsburgh; by and large, they believed the American claim that they had come to rescue the Moravians from the privations at Sandusky. Once the Americans had gathered the Moravians at Gnadenhutten, however, they accused them of being warriors and raiders. Their evidence was the particular white artifacts that the Moravians had adopted – axes, pewter basins, spoons, tea kettles, pots, cups, and saucers – and the fact that their horses had been branded. For Indian haters boundaries remained clear. All these things were marks of whites; that they were found in the hands of Indians could only mean theft. Indians, as they said, used wooden bowls and spoons.[49]

The Americans, not without division, condemned the captured Moravians – men, women, and children – to death. The Indians spent the night praying, singing hymns, and reconciling themselves to God's will. The militia dragged the Indians two or three at a time into two slaughter-houses and killed them with a cooper's mallet. They then set the houses on fire. More than ninety Indians died, the majority women and children.[50]

[48] For Heckewelder's pro-Americanism and aid, see Hackenwelder (*sic*) to Brodhead, May 28, 1779, Hackenwelder (*sic*) to Brodhead, June 30, 1779, Heckewelder to Brodhead, July 8, 1779, *PA*, Series 1, 7:516–19, 524–26; 541–42. For removal of Moravians, see Heckewelder, *Narrative of the Mission*, 223–306. Heckewelder said the British and Iroquois had considered killing the Moravians, but there seems to be no evidence for this beyond his accusations, *ibid.*, 231.

[49] For message, see McKee to De Peyster, 10 Apr. 1782, Haldimand Papers, 21782. For utensils, see Heckewelder, *Narrative of the Mission*, 317.

[50] For massacre, see Heckewelder, *Narrative of the Mission*, 310–25. The Indians of Shonbrun found the body of the first murdered Indian and, forewarned, escaped, *ibid.*, 324–25, 327. Relation of Frederick Lineback, 1782, *PA*, Series 1, 9:524–25. For an American account, see Letter from Fort Pitt, Mar. 30, 1782, Craig (ed.), *The Olden Time*, 2:478–79. For

The Indian haters adopted what they regarded as Indian means – massacre and torture – to keep the boundaries between Algonquian and white societies intact. To the east, the Iroquois complained that the many false reports of Indian cruelty that appeared in American newspapers merely served as a pretext for American cruelties practiced on Iroquois women and children. When the Americans took British prisoners, the Iroquois noted, "the Rebels don't put them to death; But we have no mercy to expect, if taken, as they will put us to death immediately, and will not even spare our Women and Children." By such killings, Indian haters kept their boundaries firm.[51]

It was the Algonquians who undermined the boundaries by adopting whites. Those whites whose own Indian hating remained pure and undiluted distrusted anyone who failed to resist Algonquian attempts to prove the boundaries permeable and who, as a result, entered deeper into the middle ground. When George Rogers Clark attacked the Shawnees of Chillicothe and Piqua, they held among their other captives some adult male prisoners. Distrusting the loyalty of these men, people for whom the boundaries remained intact, the Shawnees killed them when Clark approached. But the Shawnees spared Joseph Rogers, the cousin of George Rogers Clark. Rogers had been their prisoner for two years, and they harbored "too good an opinion of him to think" he would desert. Rogers did not desert; he fought the Kentuckians when they attacked Piqua, and Clark's men captured him after he was mortally wounded. As his cousin lay dying, Clark struggled between affection for kin and the reproaches of an Indian hater to a man who had become tainted. Indian hating won. Clark "soon rode up & expressed an opinion that as he knew that army was coming in time to have escaped & joined his countrymen, he shd have done it. He said he had no opportunity, & couldnt." Taken to the rear, Rogers died in a matter of hours. A captured Indian hater should have died or escaped. To remain raised the uncomfortable possibility that the Algonquians were right, that accommodations and transformations were possible.[52]

Indian captivity, even torture, blurred boundaries in the way quick and summary executions and murders did not. The possibilities of communica-

division in settlements, see Croghan to Dorsey, Apr. 28, 1782, GRC Papers, Draper Mss., 30J41; Cook to Moore, Sept. 2, 1782, *PA*, Series 1, 9:629.

51 For Iroquois complaints, see Council held at Niagara, 1 Apr. 1783, Haldimand Papers, 21779. For quotation, see Meeting of the principal Chiefs and Warriors ... Dec. 11, 1782, Haldimand Papers, 21779, f110.

52 Homan to Bird, Aug. 15, 1780, *MPHC* 10:418–19. For quotation, see Henry Wilson, Account of the Campaign against the Shawnee Indians, in *IHC* 8:452. Charles Talbert, *Benjamin Logan: Kentucky Frontiersman* (Lexington: University of Kentucky Press, 1962), 114, says that Rogers tried to escape but was killed by mistake. Wilson's account directly contradicts this.

tion and shared meaning increased; multiple identities became possible. Many captives resisted adoption successfully, but others, including some of the most famous Indian fighters, did not, and it compromised their Indian hating. R. G. Thwaites, the nineteenth-century historian and biographer of Daniel Boone, wrote that during Boone's captivity "his fellow prisoners . . . marveled at the ease with which their old leader adapted himself to the new life, and his apparent enjoyment of it." Thwaites, the fastidious Victorian, was unwilling to believe that Boone could have live pleasantly and profitably in an Indian village, but Boone certainly did. As a captive, Boone became temporarily and partially Algonquian, the adopted son of the Shawnee chief Black Fish of Chillicothe. Adoption tainted him; the great Boone eventually found himself on trial as a traitor when he returned from his captivity.[53]

The manner in which Algonquians sought to assimilate or kill captives showed that they had no exact equivalent for Indian hating. Algonquians distrusted the Big Knives, killed them, and tortured them, but Algonquians, for all their murders, took far more prisoners, particularly far more adult male prisoners, and tried to integrate many of them into their own society. Black Fish, a bitter enemy of the Kentucky settlements, told Hamilton that he loved Boone "too strongly" to let him go. When, after Boone's escape, Black Fish encountered him at the siege of Boonesborough, he wept over his son's ingratitude. No pure Indian hater could have acted like Black Fish, but not all Indian hating remained pure.[54]

The remarkable saga of Simon Kenton's captivity illustrates how the persistent Algonquian pursuit of a wider middle ground caused the separate logics and identities of Kenton and his Algonquian captors to merge, even as the Indians prepared to torture and kill him. Kenton, first as he prepared to die, and then as he lived, advanced beyond the Indian haters' vocabulary of stoicism and revenge.

The Shawnees took Kenton while he was on a horse-stealing expedition in the midst of war, and they took pains to explain to Kenton the logic of his death. Kenton took equal pains to rebut them. They appealed to their rendering of white morality; he appealed to the contradictions of their own actions:

> "Young man, didn't you know it was wrong to steal Indians' horses?"
> No, I did not, for you come and steal our horses. Don't you know the

---

[53] Reuben Gold Thwaites, *Daniel Boone* (New York: D. Appleton, 1991), 152–58. One of Boone's party, Joseph Jackson, elected to remain with the Shawnees, John Bakeless, *Daniel Boone* (New York: William Morrow, 1939), 176.

[54] Thwaites, *Boone*, 161. At the end of the Revolution, the Hurons objected strongly to returning their prisoners saying the British had promised them they would be able to keep prisoners "to strengthen their Nation," McKee to Haldimand, Sept. 8, 1783, Haldimand Papers, 21783.

Great Spirit don't love people that steal? No – did you ever know it? Yes, 20 years ago. Indians have got no cattle about their doors like white people – the buffalo are our cattle, but you come here and kill them; you have no business to kill Indians' cattle: Did you know that? No, I did not. He then whipped me pretty smartly, and told me it was for stealing Indians' horses.

In this dialogue of moral condemnation and defense, Kenton's captor, Bonah, and Kenton prey each on other's beliefs and logic in much the same way they preyed on each other's horses.[55]

Part of Kenton's ordeal simply involved the toughness and courage of Indian hating: the common ordeals of warriors. In the terrible agonies inflicted on him before his final torture, Kenton acted the warrior. As a captive, Kenton, in a more picaresque and less bloody way, communicated his meanings through women's bodies. When a woman, to deride the staked-out and helpless Kenton, sat on his face, "he gave his teeth a death-like set somewhere in the region of her inexpressibles and held a deathlike grip with his teeth and his mouth was well filled with her sporting flesh. Alas, she began to screach screach and yell like a loon. Now the Indians were convulsed with frantic and savage laughter, loud and sportive yells and howlings." Kenton the warrior also remained very much the backcountry settler. While awaiting his death as a captive at Wakatomica, on the Mad River, he still thought that "one day he would own some of that fine country."

But at Wakatomica the boundaries began to dissolve. There Kenton, the backcountry fighter, met his old friend, Simon Girty – the most notorious of the "white savages" and a man to whom the boundaries meant nothing. Captured by Indians as a child, Girty had returned to the white settlements only to desert to the Indians and the British in 1778. Girty pleaded for Kenton's life. And the Shawnees initially granted it. They immediately called Kenton brother, expressed admiration for his bravery and skill, and named him Cutta-ho-tha, the Blackened or Condemned man. An old woman took him to replace her slain son, and the Shawnees told him, "You [are] no more a white man but an Indian and a brother." Kenton later told an interviewer, "They say when a man comes among a parcel of people that are harsh to him, and they moderate towards him, he will be more attached to them, and I believe it." Kenton had abandoned orthodox Indian hating.[56]

Among adults, however, adoption remained a function of the middle ground; despite what the Algonquians said, adoption did not make Kenton

---

[55] Edna Kenton, *Simon Kenton: His Life and Period, 1755–1836* (Garden City, N.Y.: Doubleday, Doran, 1930), 108.
[56] For quotations from Kenton, see *Kenton*, 123, 124.

an Indian, and both sides knew it. Kenton plotted his escape, and a party of defeated warriors, on their return home, regarded him as a Big Knife; they demanded his execution in revenge for lost comrades. The council rescinded his adoption; they ceased to address him as brother. They sentenced him to die at Sandusky. On the way there, the Indians broke his arm and collarbone. Only a fortuitous rainstorm saved Kenton from his second appointment with death by burning. And then, just before the third attempt at his execution, Pierre Drouillard appeared and ransomed him. Drouillard came at the summons of Logan, a man who might have seemed the most likely candidate for white hating. Logan, however, remained more complex. The friend of whites who became their worst enemy, he had taken his revenge. Having known Kenton earlier, he now sought to save him. Drouillard ransomed Kenton on the ruse that the British would return him after information on Kentucky had been extracted at Detroit, but the British never returned him. Eventually, Kenton escaped from Detroit, made his return to Kentucky, and resumed fighting Indians with George Rogers Clark.[57]

Yet, despite his sufferings, adoption worked on Kenton; it tempered his Indian hating. Twenty years later, two Indian families lived on Kenton's land in Ohio, and his old captor Bonah used to visit him and eat at his table. When asked why he didn't kill Bonah, he replied that now it was peace, and what Bonah had done was an act of war. This was conventional white logic of honor, but it also rejected the grimmer logic of Indian hating in which Bonah was by virtue of his birth a killer awaiting execution. Later still, Kenton supposedly faced down more consistent Indian haters who sought to murder the Indians who lived with him.[58]

Indian hating could itself partially dissolve as boundaries blurred, but it could also create among Algonquians the boundaries that the Indian haters so ardently sought. In 1781, Pachantschihilas (or Buckongahelas) admitted that there were good white men, but "they bear no proportion to the bad." Indians could place no faith in their words for they were "not like the Indians who are only enemies, while at war, and are friends in peace." Buckongahelas had come to know the Long Knives; in the same way Indian haters had come to know Indians. He knew they were not to be trusted.[59]

The Algonquians had previously contrasted their own relatively lenient treatment of prisoners with the butchery of the Americans, but the killing of the Moravian Indians made the Delawares vow to spare no white man. They

[57] *Ibid.*, 102–44.
[58] *Ibid.*, 251–55.
[59] For Pachantschihilas, see John Heckewelder, *History, Manners, and Customs of Indian Nations Who Once Inhabited Pennsylvania and the Neighboring States*, new and rev. ed. (Philadelphia, 1876; repr. ed., New York: Arno Press, 1971), 80–81.

were for a period afterwards "exceeding cruel to all the prisoners they have taken," although they spared the prisoners already among them. Their most famous victim was Colonel William Crawford, head of the Pennsylvania militia expedition whose members bragged they were coming to exterminate the Wyandots.[60]

But Crawford, ironically, was no Indian hater, and he sought to avoid his fate. Sentenced to die, he sent for Wangomend, the Indian prophet who had long worked for peace with the Americans. Crawford had known and entertained him at Pittsburgh, and Wangomend, in turn, had treated visiting Americans kindly. But now the Delaware told Crawford that by associating himself with the men who had murdered the Moravians, he had placed himself beyond the power of friendly intercession for the Indians demanded revenge. At the end of the conversation, as the torturers, under the direction of Captain Pipe, came for him, both Crawford and Wangomend burst into tears, and "took an affectionate leave of each other." Crawford died pitifully at the stake; when nearly dead, he was scalped by Joseph, a baptized Moravian. Indian hating determined Crawford's fate; it drew lines across which friendship could not pass. It turned pacifist Christians into vengeful torturers.[61]

The alternative to the torture fire, the image of common children of a common mother, this path always remained dimly visible, but it remained the road untaken; Indian hating controlled backcountry attitudes and eventually American policy during and immediately after the Revolution. As Kenton's experience showed, Indian haters could not always keep the rigid boundaries between Algonquian and white villagers intact. There were times when the harsh demands of the warrior's code broke down. The Algonquians expected this and ritualized such breakdowns; their enemies could become their brothers. But such lapses took the whites by surprise and momentarily, at least, they had no defense when the human tragedy that

[60] For contrast in treatment, see De Peyster to Haldimand, May 13, 1782, *MPHC* 10:573–74. For Delawares, see Croghan to Davies, July 6, 1782, *IHC* 19:71. The Shawnees and other tribes continued to spare prisoners, *ibid.*, 72–73; McKee to De Peyster, Apr. 10, 1782, Haldimand Papers, 21781. For battle, see Caldwell to De Peyster, June 11, 1782, *MPHC* 20:25. For resumption of torture, see De Peyster to Haldimand, June 23, 1782, Haldimand Papers, 21781. De Peyster set to work to stop the Shawnees and Delawares from renewing the routine torture of prisoners, De Peyster to McKee, Aug. 6, 1782, *MPHC* 10:623–24. For extermination threat, see De Peyster to Haldimand, 18 Aug. 1782, *MPHC* 10:628–29.

[61] Wyngenund as prophet, Heckewelder *Narrative of the Mission*, 103–4. For Crawford and Wyngenund, see Heckewelder, *History*, 284–88; for examples of Wyngenund's treatment of Americans, see Butler, Journal, Aug. 29, 1775; Cuchaghunk, etc., to Morgan, June 7, 1777, *PA*, Series 1, 5:444–45; Big Cat to Brodhead, June 24, 1779, *WHC* 23:381. For Crawford's death, see W. Croghan to Davies, July 6, 1782, *IHC* 19:71–73; Letter to Washington, July 11, 1782, Craig (ed.), *The Olden Time*, 2:538. For Joseph, see *Diary of David Zeisberger, A Moravian Missionary among the Indians of Ohio*, tr. and ed. by Eugene F. Bliss, 2 vols. (Cincinnati: R. Clarke, 1885), Aug. 2, 1788, 1:431.

underlay the backcountry settlers' attempts to wrest away Algonquian land by force suddenly appeared before them. At Harrodsburg, Ann Harrod dreamed that her husband, James, had run out to aid men attacked by Indians outside the fort. The Indians had shot him and, when he fell, stooped over and stabbed him. It was a dream no Indian warrior would have disregarded, but the next day when Indians did attack three woodcutters outside the fort, Harrod forcibly tore himself from his wife's arms and ran to their aid. Harrod shot the nearest Indian who ran a short distance along a creek and then collapsed. Harrod stooped over him and stabbed him. The husband in the dream changed places with the Indian in actuality, and when James Harrod returned, Ann Harrod remembered, "he did not exult but seemed distressed, and said he wished never to kill another of the poor natives, who were defending their fatherland; and that this feeling was forced upon by the rebound of his knife, when he plunged it into the heart of the fallen Indian, who looked up so piteously into his face. He shed a tear when telling me." Husband as Indian, children of a common mother – the older options and metaphors of the middle ground still hovered as villagers, white and Algonquian, killed each other with enthusiasm and regret.[62]

V

The decline of American influence in the *pays d'en haut* under the assault of Indian hating allowed British imperial influence to expand, but the empire, too, had trouble imposing its will on both Indian and French villages. A nostalgia for Onontio still pervaded these villages. The American alliance with France gave the discontented habitants a formidable weapon in the *pays d'en haut*, and they used it to full advantage. They encouraged Algonquian villages from the Mississippi to Sandusky to believe, as they themselves hoped, that the Revolution was a harbinger of the imminent return of their French father. As Clark went into decline, these French villagers of the Wabash and Illinois country, with their kinship and trading ties to the Indians, became once more a virtually independent force. The French in the Illinois and Wabash country often operated under Spanish auspices, for Spain too had entered the war against England. The habitants and traders, however, used Spain to secure their own interests. In 1780, a French expedition from Illinois country, with the help of the French and the Indians at Vincennes, seized and burned the Miami post established by the British, in an abortive attempt on Detroit, where, apparently, the habitants were

---

[62] Kathryn Harrod Mason, *James Harrod of Kentucky* (Baton Rouge: Louisiana State University Press, 1971), 147–48.

waiting to join them. All of this was done, as Jonathan Dodge, the outraged agent for the state of Virginia, noted, in the name of the king of France "in order to evade the government of America."[63]

In 1780 and 1781, two other "Spanish" expeditions attacked Saint Joseph. The first was undertaken by French traders from Illinois country. Lieutenant Governor Patrick Sinclair of Michilimackinac, neither a subtle nor a particularly astute man, had suspected the loyalty of Louis Chevallier and the French traders Saint Joseph and had had them removed and replaced by Michilimackinac traders, the majority of them English. A result was the "Spanish" attacks on Saint Joseph. The first failed, but a second attack followed. Francisco Cruzat, the Spanish commander at Saint Louis, admitted that he had to agree to this expedition on the insistence of the Milwaukee Indians, a mixed group, who desired to plunder the post. Siggenuak, the Potawatomi chief who suggested the attack, apparently acted with the cooperation of Louis Chevallier's son who sought both to revenge his father's removal by the British and to eliminate the traders who had replaced the older Chevallier. Aided by the Potawatomis, the expedition stole all the English goods "and all the fruits of their industry for the season."[64]

The French intended these attacks to help neither the Spanish, whom they hated, nor the Americans, toward whom they had grown increasingly resentful; instead they appear to have been attempts to recapture the fur trade of the *pays d'en haut* that was being threatened by English traders. During the Revolution, English traders, with privileged access to the sloops the British government maintained on the Great Lakes, increasingly penetrated what had remained a French trade north of the Ohio Valley. Most

[63] For Promises and disloyalty of French, see Brehm to Haldimand, May 28, 1779, *MPHC* 9:410. For French kinship, see De Peyster to Haldimand, 1 June 1779, *MPHC* 9:382. For return of French father, Haldimand to Clinton, Sept. 4, 1779, *MPHC* 19:463. For attack on Miami, see De Peyster to Haldimand, Nov. 16, 1780, *MPHC* 10:448–49; De Peyster to Powell, 13 Nov. 1780, *MPHC* 19:580–81. Only British presents induced Miamis to attack, De Peyster to Haldimand, May 27, 1781, Haldimand Papers, 21781. For Dodge quotation, see Dodge to Cruzat, Nov. 11, 1780, Kinnaird, *Spain*, 2:393. For De la Balme, the leader of the expedition, and his lack of authority, see Cruzat to Gálvez, Nov. 12, 1780, *ibid.*, 395.

[64] For attempts to mobilize Potawatomis, Chevalier's loyalty, and messages from the Illinois, see De Quindre à De Peyster, 14 juin 1780, Haldimand Papers, 21782. For withdrawal of traders from Saint Joseph, see De Peyster to Bolton, July 6, 1780, *MPHC* 19:540; Sinclair to Haldimand, July 8, 1780, *MPHC* 9:560. For De Peyster opposes, see De Peyster to Sinclair, Sept. 17, 1780, *MPHC* 9:617. For English traders and losses, see Memorial and Petition, n.d., *MPHC* 10:367. For Cruzat and Indians, see Cruzat to Gálvez, Jan. 10, 1781, Kinnaird, *Spain*, 2:415. For attack on Saint Joseph by party from Cahokia and seizure of goods, see De Peyster to Haldimand, Jan. 8, 1781, *MPHC* 10:450–51; Cruzat to Gálvez, Aug. 6, 1781, Kinnaird, *Spain*, 2:431–34; R. David Edmunds, *The Potawatomis: Keepers of the Fire* (Norman: University of Oklahoma Press, 1978), 109–12. For English traders and losses, see Memorial and Petition, n.d., *MPHC* 10:367.

small French traders of the *pays d'en haut* lacked the capital to exploit the lucrative new northwest trade, and so maintaining their hold on the *pays d'en haut* was particularly critical. Wabash and Illinois traders who had access to goods from New Orleans were openly hostile to the English; Michilimackinac and Detroit traders, who depended on goods from Canada, had to be more circumspect lest their supplies be cut off. These northern traders had to maneuver delicately when the British attempted to limit their trade for strategic reasons or when the trading area of a French partnership overlapped areas of British and American influence.[65]

In principle imperial power might be great in the *pays d'en haut*, but in practice the Indians and the French repeatedly detoured the engine of empire. In 1780, a large British-Indian expedition against Illinois country and the Spanish outposts around Saint Louis failed, the English asserted, because of the treachery of Joseph Calvé, whose wife was a Sauk, Jean Marie Ducharme, "& others who traded in the country of the Sacks." These Frenchmen allegedly conspired with the Sauks and Fox to subvert the expedition in order to protect their own "Profits arising from the Lead Mines & from a commerce with the Illinois."[66]

Most Indians remained just as resolutely localistic and independent in their concerns as the French; few acted as tribal units. Most were consistently

---

[65] Hamilton reported in 1776 that "the Industry and enterprising Spirit of the traders at this Post [Detroit], so far outgo the Canadians, that I am persuaded the latter will in a very few years be dependants on or bought out of their possessions by the former – The navigating the Lakes in large Vessels, is entirely in the hands of the new Settlers ...," Hamilton to Dartmouth, Sept. 2, 1776, *MPHC* 10:270.

For changing fur trade, see Memorandum Relative to Trade in the Upper Country, n.d., c. 1777 (or 1778), *MPHC* 10:272–74; Memorandum for ... Carleton, Jan. 1778, *MPHC* 19:337–39; De Peyster to Haldimand, 14 June 1779, *WHC* 11:133–35; Haldimand to Campbell, June 28, 1779, *MPHC* 19:441; Grant to Haldimand, Apr. 24, 1780, *MPHC* 19:508–11; Jeanne Kay, "The Land of La Baye: The Ecological Impact of the Green Bay Fur Trade, 1634–1836" (Ph.D. diss., University of Wisconsin, 1977), Table 5.1. For conflict between English and French traders, see Petitition of Daniel Murray, Apr. 10, 1777, *MPHC* 19:321–22; Sinclair to Haldimand, July 8, 1780, *MPHC* 9:561–62; Sinclair to Haldimand, n.d., c. July 1780, *MPHC* 9:562–63. De Peyster to Haldimand, Sept. 21, 1778, *MPHC* 9:371–73; Haldimand to Indians, July 2, 1779, *WHC* 11:181–83; Sinclair to Brehm, Oct. 29, 1779, *MPHC* 9:530–31; Sinclair to Haldimand, 2 Aug. 1780, *WHC* 11:157–58.

In 1778, a list of licenses granted between April and June for traders going out of Michilimackinac included 19 French names and only 5 English or Scots; the French averaged 2.2 canoes each; the English 4. Many English merchants such as John Askin acted as wholesalers to the French, Askin to Barthe, June 26, 1778, in Milo Milton Quaife (ed.), *The John Askin Papers, 1747–1820*, 2 vols. (Detroit: Detroit Library Commission, 1928–31), 1:149.

[66] For difficulty of controlling traders, see Sinclair to Haldimand, n.d., c. July 1780, *MPHC* 9:562–63. Calvé et al., Sinclair to Haldimand, July 8, 1780, *WHC* 11:155–57; Calvé to Haldimand, Aug. 23, 1780, *MPHC* 10:422. For lead mines, see Sinclair to Haldimand, Aug. 3, 1780, *MPHC* 9:572–73.

loyal to neither the empire nor the Americans. The Delawares split and the Shawnees remained divided even after Cornstalk's death. The Wabash Indians joined the British when Hamilton came among them and then abandoned the British when Clark took Hamilton and Vincennes. They rejoined the British late in the Revolutionary War. The Potawatomis of Saint Joseph participated hardly at all before 1780. They followed Chevallier until his removal and remained of dubious loyalty thereafter. The Indians west of the lakes remained largely out of the war until 1780, and even then the Sauks and Fox were not dependable allies. The heart of the war against Kentucky and Pennsylvania came from what amounted to a group of warriors' towns stretching from Pluggy's Town on the Oletangy north to Half King's village on the Upper Sandusky, and also from the Shawnee villages whose occupants withdrew from the Scioto to the Mad River and its vicinity. Warriors recruited from Detroit and Michilimackinac also took part, but enthusiasm for the British waxed and waned in the Indian villages surrounding the British forts between 1776 and 1781. As late as 1780, a year in which the British and their allies made considerable gains, General Haldimand thought that little could be expected of the Indians in the *pays d'en haut*. Only gradually did the British use their great advantages in trade and presents to repair the damage and to resurrect their alliance.[67]

The Delawares of Coshocton provided the key to British success in finally uniting the Indians of the *pays d'en haut* against the Americans. The growing disillusionment of Captain Pipe with the Americans and his rivalry with John Killbuck, who as leader of the Turtle phratry was titular head of the town, brought Pipe's withdrawal from Coshocton. With British backing, Pipe then lured warriors and their families away from Coshocton and its satellite villages. Colonel Brodhead reported from Fort Pitt that Pipe and other "Indian Captains appointed by the British commandant at Detroit are

---

[67] Seventeen Shawnee families moved to Coshocton after Cornstalk's death, Account of Meeting, Apr. 26, 1778, Morgan Letter Book, Book 3. Hamilton had originally promised to act as father, Hamilton to Haldimand, Sept. 22, 1778, *IHC* 1:342, but this and other British promises went unfulfilled after his defeat, Brehm to Haldimand, May 28, 1779, *MPHC* 9:410. For British troubles, see De Peyster to Campbell, May 13, 1779, *MPHC* 19:411; McKee to Lernoult, May 26, 1779, *MPHC* 19:423; Haldimand to Clinton, May 26, 1779, *MPHC* 19:419; Chevallier to Lernoult, May 29, 1779, *IHC* 1:443; Bennett to De Peyster, Aug. 9, 1779, *MPHC* 9:392–93, Aug. 15, 1779, *MPHC* 19:456. For Shawnees, see Lernoult to Shawnees, July 19, 1779, Haldimand Papers, 21782. For Mequachake Shawnees, see Kellelman to Brodhead, Sept. 21, 1774, *WHC* 24:73. For Americans solicit Wyandots and Ottawas, see Brodhead to Wyandot, Apr. 8, 1779, *WHC* 23:278. For Wyandot response, see Heckenwalder to Broadford (*sic*), May 28, 1779, *PA*, Series 1, 7:516–18. Nonycondat to Maghenguia Kashuck, Sept. 17, 1779, and reply, Sept. 18, 1779, Haldimand Papers, 21781. Discours d'un députe huron de Sandoské, 19 juillet 1779, Haldimand Papers, 21782. American invasions of the Indian country forced the issue, Brehm to Haldimand, July 5, 1779, *MPHC* 9:417–18. For very little to be expected from them, see Haldimand to Clinton, Jan. 31, 1780, *MPHC* 19:497.

clothed in the most elegant manner, and have many valuable presents made them." John Killbuck and other "captains I have appointed by authority of Congress, are naked, and recieve nothing but a little whiskey, for which they are reviled by the Indians in general." By 1781, the Coshocton council had reversed itself and abandoned neutrality; John Killbuck had lost power and Pipe negotiated the entry of Coshocton into the British alliance. In 1782 the Wabash villages and the Peorias followed the Miamis, who had joined the British earlier, into the British alliance. Only the Kaskaskias, the mixed villages around Milwaukee, and John Killbuck (who had resigned as chief of the Turtles), and a few Turtle phratry warriors remained pro-American at the end of the Revolution.[68]

The British effort to create, at last, a real alliance in the *pays d'en haut* was also, however, never fully successful. In 1782, Arent De Peyster thought the "immense" treasure he had bestowed on the Indians had served to create a

---

[68] For Brodhead quotation, see Brodhead to Reed, Jan. 22, 1781, Craig (ed.), *The Olden Time*, 2:383. For people leaving him, see Killbuck to McIntosh, Mar. 15, 1779. For Pipe, see Killbuck to Brodhead, July 17, 1780, *WHC* 24:217. Speech to Delawares, June 7, 1781, J. Watts De Peyster, *Miscellanies by an Officer (Colonel Arent Schuyler de Peyster), 1774–1813*, 2 vols. (New York, A.E. Chasmar, 1888 (vol. 1) and C. H. Ludwig, 1888 (vol. 2)), 2:8–9. The Iroquois sought to resettle Ohio Delawares on the Genesee River, Proceedings of a General Meeting... 20 Mar. 1780, Haldimand Papers, 21779, f. 86.

For Coshocton and Americans, see William Penn and the councillors of Cooshockung to Brodhead, Jan. 13, 1781, *WHC* 24:314–15; Heckewelder to Brodhead, Feb. 26, 1781, *WHC* 24:337–38; Brodhead to Beeler, Mar. 4, 1781, Craig (ed.), *The Olden Time*, 2:389; Brodhead to Clark, Apr. 4, 1780, *IHC* 8:408; Killbuck to Brodhead, Jan. 15, 1781, *WHC* 24:316–317; Brodhead to Shepherd, Mar. 8, 1781, *WHC* 24:342; Brodhead to Washington, Mar. 27, 1781, *PA*, Series 1, 9:39. Brodhead to Reed, May 22, 1781, *PA*, Series 1, 9:161–62; Speech to Delawares of Cooshawking, June 7, 1781, in De Peyster, *Miscellanies*, 2:8–9.

For British gain Indians, Clark to Todd, Mar. 1780, *IHC* 8:404; Dodge to Jefferson, Aug. 1, 1780, *IHC* 8:437–38; De Peyster to Bolton, June 27, 1780, *MPHC* 19:536–37; Le Gras to Clark, Dec. 1, 1780, *IHC* 8:469; Speeches to Crozat, 1780, Kinnaird, *Spain*, 2:401–2; Lincot to Slaughter, Jan. 11, 1781, *ibid.*, 490–91; Lincot to Jefferson, Apr. 2, 1781, *ibid.*, 518; Floyd to Clark, Apr. 26, 1781, *ibid.*, 543; Lincot to Clark, July 18, 1781, *ibid.*, 574–76; Dalton to Clark, Nov. 3, 1781, Clark Papers, Missouri Historical Society, copy in GLEHA; Williams to Clark, Jan. 12, 1782, *ibid.*; Legrave (*sic*) to Clark, n.d. (c. Aug. 1782), G. R. Clark Papers, Draper Mss, 5J31; Clark to Harrison, Nov. 30, 1782, *IHC* 19:164–65; *ibid.*, 8 Mar. 1783, 213; Indian Council, Detroit, Feb. 25, 1782, *MPHC* 10:550; Council, 14 June 1782, *MPHC* 10:587–91. Clark to Kentucky County Commissioners, Sept. 5, 1781, *IHC* 8:596–98; Cruzat to Gálvez, Nov. 14, 1780, Kinnaird, *Spain*, 2:398–99; Sinclair to Haldimand, June 15, 1781, *MPHC* 19:639–40.

For shortages of goods, see Delawares to Brodhead, Feb. 17, 1780, *WHC* 24:139; Brodhead to Washington, Oct. 17, 1780, *WHC* 24:283–84; Brodhead to Washington, Jan. 23, 1781, *WHC* 24:326. Dodge to Jefferson, Aug. 1, 1780, *IHC* 8:437. The loyal Piankashaws in 1780 had been reduced to hunting with bows and arrows, Dalton to Clark, May 16, 1780, Clark Papers, Missouri Historical Society, copy in GLEHA, and by 1782, three-quarters of the Wabash tribes were hunting with bows and arrows and dressing in buffalo skins, Williams to Clark, Jan. 12, 1782, *ibid.*, Haldimand threatened to cut off all trade unless the Americans were expelled, Haldimand's Speech... to Michilimakinac... 2 July 1779, Haldimand Papers, 21779.

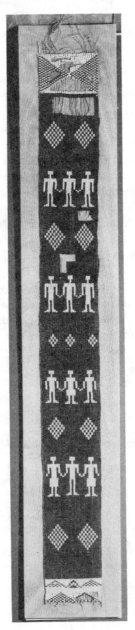

A wampum belt, made from white and purple shell beads, given to the commander at Detroit, Arent De Peyster, during the Revolution. (The Board of Trustees of the National Museums and Galleries on Merseyside-Liverpool Museum, England)

body of irregulars who had prevented inroads into the *pays d'en haut*, but who were in no sense under British command. "If too severe with them," he told Haldimand, "they tell us we are well off that there are no Virginians in this Quarter, but such as they bring here against their inclinations." The British paid a price for the long years of neglect in the *pays d'en haut*.[69]

For all its failings, however, the alliance the British had forged by the end of the Revolution was as close to the Algonquian conception of an alliance as they had thus far come. The British Indian department created a network of alliance chiefs in the *pays d'en haut*. Many of the early British chiefs were, in fact, Frenchmen recruited from among the more influential and trustworthy traders at Michilimackinac and Detroit. By the fall of 1778, the Detroit district alone had twenty-four men on the payroll of its Indian department, and these did not include Hamilton or military officers who also worked with the Indians. The British Indian establishment remained large as the war dragged on, but it grew less French. In 1778, the flight of Alexander McKee, Matthew Elliott, and Simon Girty to Detroit, followed later by two of Girty's borthers, created a core of skilled Tory chiefs. They proved invaluable in the Ohio Valley. McKee, in particular, could manage "the Indians to a charm." At Michilimackinac, Lieutenant Governor Patrick Sinclair tried to anglicize the Indian service with less success. Quarrelsome and opinionated, Sinclair regarded Charles Langlade and his nephew Claude Charles Gautier, perhaps the most adroit men on the British payroll, as "men of no understanding, application or steadiness." Instead of them, he chose to rely on an English trader and ex-soldier named Hesse.[70]

---

[69] De Peyster to Haldimand, Jan. 26, 1782, *MPHC* 10:547–48.

[70] For cultivation of chiefs, see Johnson to Gage, Mar. 31, 1775, Gage Papers, AS 127; Gage to Carleton, Aug. 18, 1775, Gage Papers, AS 134. For Montreal, see Foy to De Peyster, Aug. 28, 1778, *MPHC* 19:350. For methods, see Remarks on the Management of Indians in North America . . . end of Feb. 1777, Haldimand Papers, 21775; Claus's Remarks on the Management of Northern Indian Nations, Mar. 1, 1777, *NYCD* 8:702. Following the war Haldimand used these remarks to formulate his instructions to Sir John Johnson, William Johnson's son, for governing Indian affairs, Haldimand to John Johnson, Feb. 6, 1783, Haldimand Papers, 21775.

For recruitment, see Letter of De Peyster, June 13, 1777, *MPHC* 10:276–77; letter to Caldwell, 6 Oct. 1776, *MPHC* 10:270; De Peyster to Carleton, 17 June 1777, *MPHC* 10:278. Sinclair to Brehm, Oct. 29, 1779, *MPHC* 9:530. For Langlade and Gautier, see De Peyster letter, June 4, 1777, *MPHC* 10:275; De Peyster to Haldimand, Sept. 21, 1778, *MPHC* 9:372; Gautier's Journal, 1777–78, *WHC* 1:100–11; De Peyster to Haldimand, June 27, 1779, *WHC* 11:136.

For British chiefs, see Haldimand to Lernoult, Aug. 29, 1779, *MPHC* 10:357; Haldimand to De Peyster, Aug. 29, 1779, *MPHC* 10:358; List of officers, Interpreters & C., Sept. 5, 1778, *MPHC* 9:470; Brehm to Haldimand, May 28, 1779, *MPHC* 9:410; Haldimand to De Peyster, July 6, 1780, *MPHC* 10:409.

For Sinclair, see Sinclair to Haldimand, c. Feb. 1780, *WHC* 11:149. For Hesse, see Sinclair to Haldimand, Feb. 17, 1780, *WHC* 11:147–48; Sinclair to Haldimand, May 29, 1780, *WHC* 11:153. For McKee, Elliott, and Simon Girty, see Hamilton to Carleton, Apr. 25, 1775, *MPHC* 9:435; De Peyster to McKee, Nov. 2, 1777, Claus Papers, v. 2:139–40,

In seeking quickly to re-create a network of reliable Algonquian alliance chiefs, the English retained the correct theory of chieftainship but often blundered badly in putting theory into practice. Commissions fell "to such of their Great Chiefs as were recommended by their Leaders." Chiefs, as in the French alliance, moved between two worlds. They were those "who have listen'd to him [the king] and gained the esteem of their nation." In practice, however, early in the war inexperienced English officials often mistook Algonquian warriors arriving in Canada as chiefs and gave them gifts too lavish for their status.[71]

By 1783, however, British officials had mastered the protocol of appropriate gifts and ranks enough to codify it. General Haldimand spelled it out in his instructions to the new superintendent general of Indian affairs:

> Presents exceeding the Value of theirs are to be given them, in which Cases the Chiefs are always to be distinguished, for by pleasing them their Parties are pleased, and this is usually done in Silver Trinkets, for Instance, if an old Chief of their Council has no Medal, a large one with a red, or blue Ribbon should be given to him – A Young Counsellor, a smaller Medal – and to a War Chief, a gorget with the King's Arms engraved upon it. These Marks of Distinction are to be put on by the Officer of their affairs, when they are to be told that their Installation into those offices is then performed in Behalf of the King, their Father who expects they will fulfil the Duties of their Station and will at all Times recommend to their Warriors and young Men Fidelity and a firm attachment to their Father.

And, Haldimand suggested, not only should the British recognize such village notables, but each officer should have "one or two sober intelligent Chiefs" living near the posts as "their Friends and Confidents." These chiefs would act as speakers for the officers – "speeches so delivered will always have more influence than coming from an Interpreter."[72]

Recognizing and recruiting alliance chiefs was but a necessary first step;

PAC. McKee to De Peyster, Aug. 22, 1780, Haldimand Papers, 21782. For praise of McKee, see Bird to De Peyster, June 11, 1780, *MPHC* 19:533–34.
    West of Lake Michigan, the French traders had assumed the role formerly exercised by French officers, Memorandum for Carleton, 1778, *MPHC* 19:337–39; Sinclair to Haldimand, Feb. 5, 1782, *MPHC* 10:549; Sinclair to Haldimand, Mar., 9, 1782, *MPHC* 10:553–54.
[71] For esteem of king and nation, see Council held at Detroit, June 14, 1778, *MPHC* 9:446–47, 451. For buttress influence of chiefs, see *ibid.*, 444, 447. Chippewa, Ottawa, Fox, Sauk, Sioux, Menominee, and Winnebago warriors e.g., all arrived in Montreal in 1778, Raport général des sauvages arrive d'enhaut ... printems 1778, Haldimand Papers, 21779. For mistakes, see Sinclair to Brehm, Oct. 7, 1779, *MPHC* 9:526–27; Brehm to Sinclair, Apr. 17, 1780, *MPHC* 9:536.
[72] For instructions for Brigadier General Sir John Johnson, see Feb. 6, 1783, Haldimand Papers 21776.

they were but the means through whom the English father demonstrated his benevolence. As Ay-ou-wi-ainsh, a Mingo chief, told De Peyster, he must "use our Warriors well, in supplying them with such things as they require, if not, what effect will my advice have upon them to enforce what you may direct." And making the alliance work, with the Algonquians half believing that Onontio was about to return, demanded a substantial benevolence indeed. The Weas claimed to remember when Onontio's presents filled a cabin to the roof. As Captain De Peyster argued, "the Indians must have presents, whenever we fall off from that article they are not more to be depended upon." De Peyster was only translating into terms that Haldimand could understand the reasoning of the middle ground expressed by Ay-ou-wi-ainsh: "Father! I, and my people expect that you will give us necessaries in abundance, as also, such ornaments which is acceptable and pleasing to young men, if otherwise we shall imagine, you do not speak from the Heart."[73]

To speak from the heart and have their counsels followed, the British had to do what the French had done. They had to restore a system of annual presents, as well as give the special presents necessary to cover the dead, to hold councils, and to reconcile warring nations. They had to equip Indian warriors who fought for them, and since at Detroit, at least, the women customarily stripped off the clothing of returning warriors before they entered the Fort, "they must be Equipd anew and also rewarded for their Exploits however trifling." Warriors attacking the frontier lost their income from hunting and so the British had also to provision and support their families. When American counterstrokes against the Iroquois and Shawnees produced refugees, the British had to feed them too. The crown also resumed the French custom of gifts of gunpowder to hunters and warriors, and they fed all those who visited the forts. To provide the foodstuffs, the British at times had to buy from the Indians corn and fish, which they then restored to them in the form of rations and presents. And presents formed only part of the costs. They had to provide blacksmiths, interpreters, and commissaries. And, finally, all of this did not remove the need for British troops. This being an English war, the Indians often refused to fight unless accompanied by English or French partisans and regulars.[74]

[73] For Onontio's presents, see Abbott to Carleton, May 25, 1777, *IHC* 1:313; for Ay-ou-wi-ainsh, see Council, Detroit, Dec. 1, 1784, *MPHC* 11:326–27. For necessity of, see De Peyster to Haldimand, Oct. 24, 1778, *MPHC* 9:375; Brehm to Haldimand, May 8, 1779, *MPHC* 9:405.

[74] See Remarks on the Management of Indians . . . Feb. 1777, Haldimand Papers, 21775. For example of use of goods, see Gautier's Journal, 1777–78, *WHC* 11:100–11. For gunpowder, see Hamilton to Carleton, Apr. 25, 1778, *MPHC* 9:438. For provisions, see Askin to Day, June 9, 1778, Quaife (ed.), *Askin Papers* 1:121. For goods, see A List of Goods for Indian Department, Detroit, Sept. 5, 1778, *MPHC* 9:471. For Indian demands, see De Peyster to

These presents always remained reciprocal – the Indians presented gifts of fur and food – but they were unbalanced, and the cost of maintaining an Indian alliance had always dismayed the British. As the price of resurrecting it became clear, some British officials again quailed at the consequences. On taking command in Canada in 1778, General Haldimand was surprised to find £30,000 (NY) in bills from Detroit alone awaiting him, and what he called "these Amazing demands" continued to come out of Detroit. The Indians, Haldimand complained, had become "accustomed to receive so very liberally, that now their Demands are quite unlimited." He urged discrimination in the bestowal of presents, rewarding only those who provided services. Lieutenant Colonel Bolton at Niagara was dismayed at the slaughter of civilians frontier warfare involved. He thought that the costs of keeping the Indians "in good temper" were more than the entire trade and all the upper country were worth. Haldimand, himself, shared this kind of accounting. The cost of the Indian department had come to be "a considerable part of the National Expence," but the "Services performed by it" were "very inadequate." The Indians, he believed, wished to protract the war "that they may live in Indolence, receiving Presents which were at first indispensably necessary, & cannot now, with safety, be withheld from them."[75]

The English clearly did not think like fathers, but the Algonquians had never demanded that of them; all they asked was that the British understand how fathers should behave and then, as Hamilton said, "act the part of Father to them." But maintaining proper British actions demanded constant attention. In 1782, for example, Haldimand considered reducing expenses by having his officers refuse reciprocal gifts from the Indians. He reasoned

Haldimand, Oct. 7, 1778, MPHC 9:373. For demand British accompany them, see Hamilton to Cramhé, Aug. 12, 1778, MPHC 9:462. For need for support, see Brehm to Haldimand, May 9, 1779, MPHC 9:405. For refugees, Haldimand to Clinton, Aug. 29, 1779, George Rogers Clark Papers, Draper Mss., 58J38–39. For explanation, see De Peyster to Haldimand, June 8, 1780, MPHC 10:399–400. For cut back, see Haldimand to De Peyster, July 6, 1780, MPHC 10:408. For stripped by women, see De Peyster to Haldimand, May 27, 1781, MPHC 10:482.

The consumption of rum alone at Detroit was an "astonishing" 17,520 gallons a year, Haldimand to Lernoult, 23 July 1779, MPHC 10:345.

[75] For reciprocity, see Outlines for a Reformation of Expenses, c. Feb.–Mar. 1782, MPHC 10:555–57. For bills, see Haldimand to Robinson, 28 July, 1778, MPHC 10:290. For Bolton's complaint, see Bolton to Haldimand, Feb. 8, 1779, MPHC 19:371–72. For expense, see Hamilton to Carleton, Dec. 4, 1775, GRC Papers, Draper Mss., 45J101–104; Gage to McKee, Sept. 12, 1775, Gage Papers, AS 135; Letter to De Peyster, Aug. 21, 1776, MPHC 10:263. For unlimited demand, see Haldimand to De Peyster, 10 Aug. 1780, MPHC 10:416. For quotation, see Haldimand to Germain, Sept. 17, 1780, MPHC 10:431. In 1780 he simply described the expenses of the Indian department as "enormous," Haldimand to De Peyster, Feb. 12, 1780, MPHC 10:377. For "amazing," see Haldimand to De Peyster, Apr. 10, 1781, MPHC 10:465–66. For cost/services, see Haldimand to Powell, June 24, 1781, MPHC 10:492–93.

that this would give the Indians less inducement to come to the posts to receive their presents, would cut down on the expense of feeding them, and would make the Indians more economical with the king's goods. He was, in effect, undercutting the whole logic of reciprocity and patriarchy on which the Indians and the British had constructed a familial alliance. In the end, however, Haldimand backed off. Not only did his officers have an obvious interest in the Indians' presents, but the Indians were "inflexibly wedded to their antient Customs"; reforms could come only gradually. What Haldimand meant was that change remained a matter of the middle ground and not a matter of imperial dictation.[76]

This patriarchal union of empire and village had by the end of Revolution begun to restore the *pays d'en haut* as a coherent unit. Mediation remained at the heart of any alliance, for unsettled wars were "of great detriment to the Service & disadvantage to trade." British agents reconciled Winnebagos and Chippewas, Potawatomis and Miamis, Menominees and Chippewas, and Sauk and Fox and Chippewas. By 1780, just when Haldimand was despairing of Algonquian aid, sizable expeditions struck the Americans and Spanish from the Allegheny to the Mississippi. And yet the unity and the alliance remained tenuous, held together in large part only because of the pressure Indian haters exerted from outside. Lieutenant Colonel Bolton at Niagara thought that if the American General Sullivan had acted with "more prudence & less severity" in his invasion of Iroquoia, "we would not have had one third of the Six Nations in our interests at this time." The same could probably have been said of much of the Ohio and Wabash country.[77]

Within the alliance the old struggles over meaning and proper action that created the middle ground continued. Haldimand denounced the actions of the Shawnees and the villagers of the Great Lakes as "highly

---

[76] The Outlines for A Reformation of Expenses, c. Feb.–Mar. 1782, *MPHC* 10:55–57. Instructions for Officers, Feb. 6, 1783, Haldimand Papers, 21775.

[77] For suggestions on steps necessary to restore an effective alliance, see Claus's Remarks on the Management of Northern Indian Nations, Mar. 1, 1777, *NYCD* 8:702. For act as father, see Hamilton to Haldimand, Sept. 22, 1778, *IHC* 1:342. For mediation, see Letter to De Peyster, Aug. 21, 1776, *MPHC* 10:263. For Gautier's efforts among Winnebagos and Chippewas, see Gautier's Journal, Jan. 25, 1778, *WHC* 11:103. There was also danger of war between the Sauk and Fox and Chippewas, *ibid.*, May 26, 1778, 109, and the Menominees and Chippewas, De Peyster to Carleton, May 30, 1778, *MPHC* 9:365. For quotation, see De Peyster to Carleton, June 29, 1778, *WHC* 11:111–12. See also De Peyster to Haldimand, June 8, 1780, *MPHC* 10:400. The Miamis attacked a Potawatomi war party, Chevallier à De Peyster, 29 juin 1780, Haldimand Papers, 21782

For British gains, Pierre Prevost to Clark, Feb. 20, 1780, *IHC* 8:394–96. For attacks depopulating frontier, see McClay to Council, Apr. 9, 1780, *PA*, Series 1, 8:172–73. The British policy of mediation should be contrasted with the American policy of setting the tribes against each other, Washington to Brodhead, Jan. 10, 1781, *WHC* 24:314. For Bolton quotation, see Bolton to Haldimand, May 16, 1780, *MPHC* 19:521. For tenuous, see De Peyster to Haldimand, May 27, 1781, *MPHC* 10:484–83.

reprehensible" when in 1780 they refused to obey Captain Bird who "led" a British-Indian expedition against Kentucky. Instead they followed their own "wild schemes." Although the expedition destroyed two Kentucky settlements, captured all their inhabitants, and caused the Americans to abandon two other forts, Bird returned furious at Indian tactics. The Indians had refused to attack the American post at the falls of the Ohio and, by slaughtering captured cattle, had eliminated the provisions necessary for a march through Kentucky to empty it of settlements.[78]

As Captain Bird and other British officers discovered, the Indians retained their own methods of warfare and their own aims; these yielded victories but did not dislodge the Americans from the Kentucky stations. As the Americans drove more and more Indians into the arms of the British, Algonquian victories became more numerous and substantial. The Algonquians defeated Crawford and the Pennsylvania militia at Sandusky in June 1782 and turned their retreat to the Ohio into a rout. Joseph Brant, a Mohawk war leader who fought in the West in 1781–82, ambushed and defeated a large detachment Clark's troops near the Ohio in 1781. At Blue Licks in 1782, the Algonquians slaughtered the cream of the fighters of the Kentucky stations. Kayashuta burned Hannastown, the seat of Westmoreland County, Pennsylvania, to the ground in 1782 and ravaged the countryside around it. But the lasting results were few. The Algonquians were warriors, not soldiers; their victories proved their courage, their fighting ability, and the strength of manitous, but they did not drive out the Americans, for Algonquian warriors would neither submit to discipline nor remain long in the field. They fought to kill their enemies and to defend their homes, not to take and hold territory. The result was a war of small parties in which each side's settlements were vulnerable to attack but in which neither side gained lasting advantage.[79]

And then in 1782, with more warriors engaged in the British cause than ever before and with those warriors inflicting costly defeats on the Americans, the British made peace. They sent word to the Algonquians to

[78] Haldimand to De Peyster, Aug. 10, 1780, *MPHC* 10:416; Bird to De Peyster, July 1, 1780, *MPHC* 19:538. For a more restrained account, see McKee to De Peyster July 8, 1780, *MPHC* 19:541–43.

[79] For an example of the disintegration of an expedition, see Thompson to De Peyster, 26 Sept. 1781, *MPHC* 10:515–16; McKee to De Peyster, Sept. 26, 1781, *MPHC* 10:517–18. For British frustration, see Letter of Haldimand, Nov. 1, 1781, *MPHC* 10:534–35; Haldimand to Maclean, 10 Feb. 1783, *MPHC* 20:92. For example of how weakened Americans had become, see Floyd to Nelson, Oct. 6, 1781, *IHC* 19:1–3.

For victories, Brant, see Macomb to Claus, Sept. 14, 1781, Haldimand Papers, 21774; Downes, *Council Fires*, 268–76. For Sandusky, see Turney to De Peyster, June 14, 1782, Haldimand Papers, 21781. For Blue Licks, see Extract of letter of Captain Caldwell, Aug. 26, 1782, Haldimand Papers, 21783. For Hannastown, see "The Destruction of Hanna's Town," in Craig (ed.), *The Olden Time*, 2:354–59.

halt all but defensive measures, and the Algonquians, for the most part, complied. They specifically asked, however, that they be remembered in the peace.[80]

The terms of the peace, which ceded virtually the entire *pays d'en haut* to the Americans, coupled with delays in the arrival of British presents and reductions in the British Indian establishment, threatened to destroy the still tenuous alliance. The Six Nations, forgetting for the moment their own actions at Fort Stanwix, complained that the British cession of country – the *pays d'en haut* and Iroquoia – that did not belong to them was an act of treachery and cruelty that only Christians could be capable of. Or, as a Wea speaker poignantly complained on hearing of the cession: "In endeavouring to assist you it seems we have wrought our own ruin." British officers and officials had their own mortification over defeat at the hands of the Americans, compounded by the recognition that they had, by the "Infamous treaty," betrayed their own allies, a people whom the Americans had not defeated. Even in the midst of being "harassed out of all patience by the Indians," Arent De Peyster hoped that "we shall have it in our power to acquit ourselves honourably of our promises to the Indians."[81]

In their defeat and humiliation, the British officers began to think like fathers. That the Americans dared to send emissaries to the Indians outraged General Allan Maclean at Niagara, who complained to De Peyster not as the officer of a defeated army but as an old Highland patriarch, or the father of an Indian alliance.

[80] For stop war parties, see De Peyster to McKee, Jan. 24, 1783, *MPHC* 11:340–41; Robertson to McBeath, Apr. 25, 1783, *MPHC* 11:360–61; De Peyster to Haldimand, *MPHC* 11:362–63; Maclean to Washington, May 4, 1783, *MPHC* 20:112. For will aid in defense, see Haldimand to Johnson, Feb. 6, 1783, May 3, 1783, Haldimand Papers, 21775. For Indians asked to be remembered in peace, see Council, Lower Sandusky, Apr. 19, 1783, *MPHC* 11:354–55.

[81] For the treaty and the Indians, see Barbara Graymont, *The Iroquois in the American Revolution* (Syracuse: Syracuse University Press, 1972), 259–71. For apprehension of trouble, see Haldimand to J. Johnson, May 26, 1783, *MPHC* 20:124. For Six Nations' response, see Maclean to Haldimand, May 18, 1783, *MPHC* 20:118. For first news of peace, see De Peyster to McKee, May 6, 1783, Claus Papers 3:217, PAC. For Wea complaint, see Council, June 28, 1783, *MPHC* 11:370–71. The Iroquois made an identical complaint, Extract of a Council held with the Chiefs & Warriors of the Six Nations, July 2, 1783, Haldimand Papers, 21779, f. 116. De Peyster complained of Wabash impertinence, De Peyster to Haldimand, June 28, 1783, *MPHC* 11:372. Michilimackinac Ottawa chiefs, too, feared abandonment, De Peyster to Haldimand, 7 Jan. 1783, Haldimand Papers, 21781. For loss of presents, see Haldimand to Johnson Nov. 13, 1783, Haldimand Papers, 21775. For De Peyster quotation, see De Peyster to Maclean, June 18, 1783, *MPHC* 20:128. For "infamous," see J. Johnson to Haldimand, June 2, 1783, Haldimand Papers, 21775. At Niagara, Colonel Butler wished to leave and avoid the diagreeable business of informing the Indians of the terms of peace, *ibid.* Reductions took place at the end of the year, Johnson to Haldimand, Dec. 11, 1783, Haldimand Papers, 21775. There was the usual pressure to reduce expenses following the war, Haldimand to J. Johnson, Dec. 18, 1783, Haldimand Papers, 21775.

A portrait of Arent De Peyster, one of the most successful British chiefs at Detroit. (Burton Historical Collection, Detroit Public Library)

He wrote:

> The Indians get this day from the King's Stores the bread they are to eat to morrow, and from his magazines the clothing that covers their nakedness; in short, they are not only our allies, but they are a part of our Family; and the Americans might as well (while we are in possession

of these Posts) attempt to seduce our children & servants from their
duty and allegiance, as to convene and assemble all the Indian Nations
without first communicating their intentions to His Majesty's
Representatives in Canada.[82]

Such thinking greatly complicated the politics of the empire over the next
quarter century. General Haldimand himself thought that "Interest,
Humanity & Gratitude" demanded that the English support the Indians; the
safety of Canada and the fur trade depended on the British-Indian alliance.
The treaty itself left the terms and timing of the evacuation of the posts
"vague and indefinite." Haldimand urged the retention of the posts until the
United States agreed to allow the territory reserved for the Indians by the
Treaty of Fort Stanwix to be permanently set aside for the Indians, with both
British and Canadian settlers excluded. Other British officers and Indian
officials, while espousing the same goal, began to "adapt" imperial policy to
Indian interests – or rather to the interests of the alliance. They began by
actively working to undermine the cession that the treaty explicitly promised.
The British assured the Indians that they still considered them the rightful
owners of the *pays d'en haut* and allies of the king. The Fort Stanwix Treaty
line was the limit of the king's claims, and he could not cede what he did not
own. They told the Indians that they could not believe that the Americans
would "act so unjustly or impolitically as to endeavour to deprive you of any
part of your country under the pretext of having conquered it." The Indians
pressed for assurances of aid and believed that if the Americans threatened
their lands, the king would assist them.[83]

While empires and states went about making peace, the villages continued
to act on their own. De Peyster recognized that even with peace between
England and the rebels, the backcountry villagers would continue to attack
the Algonquians and encroach on their lands, and the Indians would

---

[82] MacLean to De Peyster, July 8, 1783, *MPHC* 20:139.

[83] Means suggested as the most probable to retain the Six Nations and Western Indians in the
Kings Interest, c. 1784, Haldimand Papers, 21779; Haldimand to Townshend, Oct. 23,
1782, *MPHC* 10:662–64; A. L. Burt, "A New Approach to the Problem of the Western
Posts," Canadian Historical Association, Report of Annual Meeting (Ottawa: Department
of Public Archives, Canada 1931), 61–75. For adapting, see Colin G. Calloway, *Crown and
Calumet: British-Indian Relations, 1783–1815* (Norman: University of Oklahoma Press,
1987), 71–72. For British reassurance, see Council at Sandusky, Aug. 26, 1783, *MPHC*
20:177; Meeting held at Niagara the 2 Oct. 1783, Haldimand Papers, 21779. The British
council speeches appear to have varied little from tribe to tribe. The same words appear in
Sir John Johnson's speech to the Iroquois, Proceedings . . . July 1783, Haldimand Papers,
21779, f. 124.
  For terms vague, Haldimand's position, see Wayne E. Stevens, *The Northwest Fur Trade,
1763–1800*, Illinois Studies in the Social Sciences, vol. 14, no. 3 (repr., Urbana: University
of Illinois Press, 1928), 87, 92. For Henry Hamilton's suggestion that British retain posts,
see State of Trade with the Indian Countries, Shelburne Papers 88:67, Clements Library.

retaliate. Although the Algonquians chafed under British restraints, the British were astonished at their forbearance. The Shawnees and the Iroquois, for example, longed to avenge the burning of Standing Stone village, attacked by Clark in the late fall of 1782 when the hunters were absent, but they remained quietly on their mats. The Indian haters were less willing to end the fighting. They voiced threats to exterminate the "whole savage tribe," and settlers, some sponsored by George Rogers Clark, pushed across the Ohio, seeking to establish claims. The Kentuckians obtained a prisoner exchange, but at it they informed the Shawnees that peace with the British did not include them, for they were bastards and their father had abandoned them. The Shawnees would have to make a separate peace with the Americans. The chronic murders, horse thefts, and raids typical of relations between Anglo-American and Indian villagers before the Revolution resumed once more. The fighting that had diminished in 1783 began in 1784 to mount again.[84]

In May 1783, George Rogers Clark had distilled his judgments about how the Americans should treat the Indians. He recognized Indians'

---

[84] For Clark, see Downes, *Council Fires*, 278–79, and Clark to Harrison, Nov. 27, 1782, *IHC* 19:157. For attack, see McKee to De Peyster, Nov. 15, 1782, Haldimand Papers, 21783. The Iroquois had apparently received exaggerated accounts of the attack, Meeting of the Principal Chiefs and Warriors, Dec. 11, 1782, Haldimand Papers, 21779. Extract from letter from Capt. Joseph Brant to J. Johnson, Dec. 25, 1782, Haldimand Papers, 21775. For De Peyster quotation, see De Peyster to Haldimand, Sept. 29, 1782, De Peyster, *Miscellanies*, 2:11. De Peyster refers to an attack on Standing Rock or Standing Stone, which had been the name of Assink, a Delaware village, but he is referring to the Shawnees, De Peyster to McKee, Apr. 20, 1783, Claus Papers, 3:213, Public Archives of Canada. For the Delaware village, see Helen Hornbeck Tanner (ed.), *Atlas of Great Lakes Indian History* (Norman: University of Oklahoma Press, 1987), 9.

For prisoner exchange, see De Peyster to McKee, June 5, 1783, Claus Papers 3:221–22, PAC. For peace does not include them, see Major Wall's Speech to the Shawaneese . . . July 7, 1783, Haldimand Papers, 21779. For lands were forfeited by British defeat, see Extract of a Council held with the Chiefs & Warriors of the Six Nations . . . 2 July 1783, Haldimand Papers, 21779.

The Shawnee and Delaware young men reportedly conducted a raid in May, Proceedings with the Indians of the Six Nations . . . July 1783, Haldimand Papers, 21779, f. 124. For forbearance, see Haldimand to Johnson, Oct. 2, 1783, Haldimand Papers, 21775. For settlement and fighting, see Pentecost to Dickinson, May 4, 1783, *PA*, Series 1, 10:167–68; Lee to Clark, July 27, 1784, GRC Papers, Draper Mss., 53J12. Journal of General Butler, Oct. 1, Oct. 2, Oct. 9, Oct. 18, Oct. 31, 1785, Nov. 14, 1785, in Craig (ed.), *The Olden Time*, 2:437–38, 442–43, 451–52, 459, 481. Samuel Hindman, one of the men who took part in the massacre of the Moravians, declared "he thinks robbing the Indians of their horses justifiable." It was an opinion shared by many Kentuckians, but not, significantly, by Daniel Boone, *ibid.*, Jan. 1–2, 1786, 506–7.

For Clark's role, see Harrison to Clark, Aug. 17, 1784, Draper Mss. 53J14. Buckongahelas's town on the upper Miami drainage and the Weas apparently took the lead in Indian resistance to white incursions and raids on the frontier, G. Girty to McKee, Sept. 5, 1784, Haldimand Papers, 21779; W. Croghan to G. R. Clark, Nov. 3, 1785, Draper Mss., 53J21; Journal of General Butler in Craig (ed.), *The Olden Time*, 2:436, 440, 444.

independence ("They have no notion of being dependant on Either the brittish or americans, But would make war on both if Equally Insulted"), but he thought their notion of their superiority to the Americans must be immediately crushed:

> We shall be Eternally Involved in a war with some nation or other of them, until we shall at last in order to save blood and treasure be Reduced to the necessity of convincing them that we are always able to crush them at pleasure, and determined to do it when Even they misbehave.... A greater Opportunity can never offer to Reduce them to Obedience than the present moment.

The United States would not adopt Clark's plan for an immediate invasion, but his attitude pervaded American thinking following the Revolution. Out of the struggle against it would emerge the confederations of the *pays d'en haut*.[85]

---

[85] Clark to Harrison, May 22, 1783, *IHC* 19:237. As usual, George Morgan enunciated a milder, less influential American position. The Americans, he informed the Senecas, would treat the Indians as brothers, Morgan to She-qui-an-sah-que (All-Face) and Kiandenané (Big Tree), Aug. 14, 1783, Haldimand Papers, 21983.

For American policy, see Reginald Horsman, *Expansion and American Indian Policy, 1783–1812* (East Lansing, Mich.: Michigan State University Press, 1967), 1–15.

10

Confederacies

> There is no need to discard theoretically all conceptions of "cultural" difference, especially once this is seen as not simply received from tradition, language, or environment but also as made in new political-cultural conditions of global relationality.
>
> James Clifford, *The Predicament of Culture*

I

Knowing by hindsight that the United States became a powerful state and that the Algonquians suffered defeat, death, and eventual removal, it is easy to misunderstand the complexity of their confrontation along the Ohio between 1785 and 1795. It is even easier to miscategorize the political units that confronted each other there. The conflict along the Ohio always remained, in part, a village conflict; but it was only partially a conflict of villages, because larger political units were forming on both sides. Until 1788 the American state consisted only of the Congress convened under the Articles of Confederation. The Indian confederation first took hazy shape at Sandusky in 1783. The Americans understood the confederation to be an alliance of tribes, but tribes in the *pays d'en haut* were less meaningful as political than as ethnic units. The identity of Algonquians as Shawnees, Delawares, or Weas influenced their actions and political loyalties just as the identity of backcountry settlers as Scots-Irish, Germans, or Anglo Americans influenced their actions. But this did not mean that the Weas, Shawnees, and Delawares acted as unified political entities any more than the Scots-Irish, Germans, and Anglo Americans formed unified and independent political groups. The basic political unit remained the village, which sometimes corresponded to the smaller tribal divisions of phratry and clan but most often did not. These various ethnic and village groups took on a common identity only when they opposed other groups. Thus the Scots-Irish, Germans, and Anglo Americans all became Americans when opposed to the Algonquians; the Shawnees, Delawares, Piankashaws, and others became Indians when opposed to the backcountry settlers.

In some respects the confederacies were strikingly similar. The con-

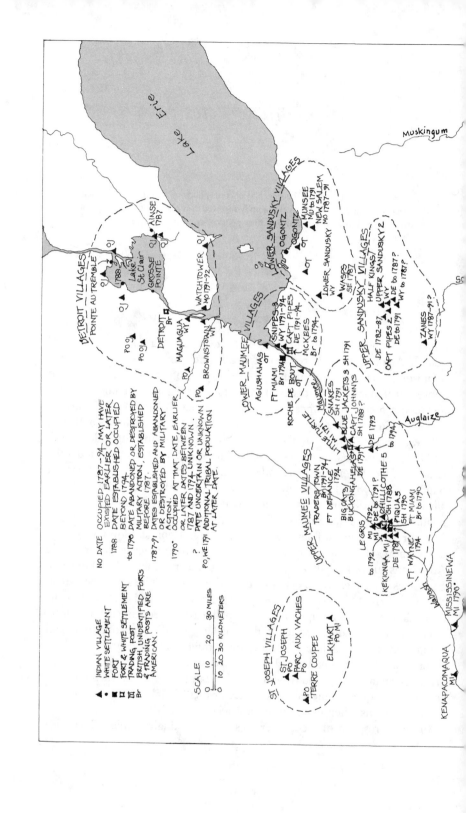

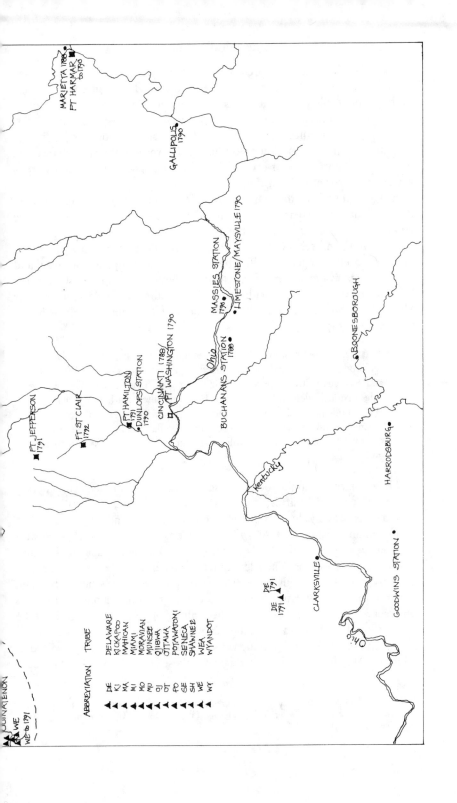

ORIENTATION
WE
WE to 1791

MARIETTA 1788
FT HARMAR
to 1790

GALLIPOLIS
1790

MASSIES STATION
1790
LIMESTONE/MAYSVILLE 1790

BOONESBOROUGH

FT JEFFERSON
1791

FT ST CLAIR
1792

FT HAMILTON
1791
DUNLOPS STATION
1790

CINCINNATI 1788/
FT WASHINGTON 1790

Ohio

BUCHANANS STATION
1788

Kentucky

HARRODSBURG

DE
1791

DE
1791

CLARKSVILLE

GOODWINS STATION

Ohio

ABBREVIATION   TRIBE

DE   DELAWARE
KI   KICKAPOO
MA   MAHICAN
MI   MIAMI
MO   MORAVIAN
MU   MUNSEE
OJ   OJIBWA
OT   OTTAWA
PO   POTAWATOMI
SE   SENECA
SH   SHAWNEE
WE   WEA
WY   WYANDOT

gresses of both contained representatives of independent political units each of which claimed to occupy a single territory. Both confederacies had problems controlling their members; both tended to make grand pronouncements they could not enforce. The leaders of both confederacies saw themselves as the cutting edge of history; their actions would mold forever the fate of their peoples. Before examining the world of the confederacies in detail, I shall give a brief overview of their conflict and provide, as it were, a roster of the social units of the *pays d'en haut*.

At the point where the two confederations met, they were most likely to dissolve back into villages. On both sides of the Ohio lay villages whose young men remained beyond the effective control of higher authorities. Indian hating and years of bloody war had bred deep animosity and endless cycles of revenge. The similarities between white and Algonquian social and political organizations served only to make both sides capable of pursuing local and private vengeance with little fear of hindrance. As Secretary of War Henry Knox summarized the situation for the Continental Congress in the summer of 1787:

> The deep rooted prejudices, and malignity of heart, and conduct, reciprocally entertained and practised on all occasions by the Whites and Savages will ever prevent their being good neighbours. The one side anxiously defend their lands which the other avariciously claim. With minds previously inflamed the slightest offence occasions death – revenge follows which knows no bounds. The flames of a merciless war are thus lighted up which involve the innocent and helpless with the guilty.[1]

The similarities should not be pressed too far. The American confederacy had a treasury and an army; it was, no matter how weak, a centralized state with agents present along the Ohio. General Harmar and his officers led a confederation army. In July 1787, the Congress passed the Northwest Ordinance to govern the lands north of the Ohio and dispatched Arthur Saint Clair as governor. The Algonquian confederacy had neither an army, a treasury, nor any form of coercive central authority. It was not a state and never aspired to be one. Such differences, however, loomed larger as abstract political categories than in the realities of power on the Ohio in the mid 1780s. The American confederacy was feeble. Its armed strength along the Ohio averaged about 350 men. Its treasury, as Henry Knox reported in March 1788, "has been declining daily for these last two years – if it is not in

[1] Report of the Secretary at War to Congress, July 10, 1787, Clarence Carter (ed.), *The Territorial Papers of the United States*, 28 vols. (Washington, D.C.: Government Printing Office, 1934–75), 2:31.

the last gasp I am mistaken." The Congress enlisted troops and then had to disband them for lack of funds.[2]

Knox and other officials of the central government yearned for the power to coerce both their own citizens and their Indian adversaries. The government, Knox thought, either must "keep them both in awe by a strong hand, and compel them to be moderate and just" or must compel either the whites or the Indians to withdraw. Such compulsion was, however, impossible. The Congress did not command sufficient troops to practice such a policy, and the state governments would not tolerate it. An Indian war, Knox had already decided, while "disagreeable at all times would be peculiarly distressing in the present embarassed state of the public finances." In attempting to inspire awe, the centual government more often reaped contempt. Unable to fight Indians, neither could the Congress intimidate the backcountry settlers, who laughed at congressional proclamations banning them from lands north of the Ohio.[3]

The American republic that claimed to have conquered most of the *pays d'en haut* was in fact but one of a group of powers competing for the region. The Congress negotiated three treaties – one with the Iroquois at Fort Stanwix in 1784, one at Fort McIntosh in 1785, and one at the mouth of the Great Miami in 1786 – that procured large cessions based on the supposed American conquest of the Algonquians. These treaties, the products of American illusions, launched the republic into a confrontation with the western Indian confederation and the British.

The theory of conquest foundered on the weakness of the new republic. Unable to afford a war against the Indians, yet needing revenue from the sale of lands north of the Ohio to fund the national debt, Congress sold land to former congressman John Cleve Symmes and his New Jersey syndicate and to the Ohio Company. By 1788 the United States was ready to renegotiate the earlier treaties, but it could not actually surrender the treaty cessions themselves. Negotiations between the American confederation and the Indian confederation were actually approaching when the Continental Congress dissolved in the fall of 1788. There would not be a new government of the United States until the nine states that ratified the Constitution established the federal government in 1789.[4]

[2] See Horsman, *Expansion and American Indian Policy 1783–1812* (East Lansing: Michigan State University Press, 1967), 32–52, quotation, 35–36. Report of the Secretary at War, Indian Affairs, Mar. 31, 1788, Carter (ed.), *Territorial Papers*, 2:101.

[3] Report of the Secretary at War to Congress, July 10, 1787, Carter (ed.), *Territorial Papers*, 2:31. For quotation, see Knox to Harmar, May 12, 1786, 3:39, Harmar Papers, and Knox to Harmar, Jan. 22, 1787, 5:9, Harmar Papers. For settlers, see Armstrong to Harmar, Apr. 13, 1785, v. 2, Harmar Papers.

[4] *Ibid.*, and A. L. Burt, *The United States, Great Britain, and British North America from the Revolution to the Establishment of Peace after the War of 1812* (New Haven: Yale University

Even as the Congress had rethought its relation to the Indian villagers north of the Ohio, Arthur St. Clair, the new governor of the Northwest Territory, admitted that peace depended as much or more on the back-country settlers who lived along the Ohio as it did on the Congress. Immigration from the older states was flooding the backcountry with settlers. General Harmar had his officers keep count of the boats passing on the Ohio, and he reported an "almost incredible" migration. From October 10, 1786, until May 12, 1787, a total of 177 boats containing 2,689 persons passed Fort Harmar on their way down the Ohio. From June 1, 1787 until December 9 of the same year, Harmar's officers counted 146 boats and 3,196 persons. And then from December 9 to June 15, 1788, a total of 308 boats and 6,320 persons passed the fort. These settlers were nominally under the jurisdiction of Pennsylvania and Virginia, but the Kentucky settlements were well on their way to becoming a separate state.[5]

Together these new migrants and the older settlers formed a volatile mix. They spilled north of the Ohio and squatted on lands claimed by both the U.S. government and the Indians. They raided Indian territory both independently and as Kentucky militia. As St. Clair reported: "Though we hear much of the Injuries and depredations that are committed by the Indians upon the Whites, there is too much reason to believe that at least equal if not greater Injuries are done to the Indians by the frontier settlers of which we hear very little."[6]

Restless, aggressive, and eager for land, these settlers were at once the strength of the new republic and the greatest threat to it. Thousands had moved to Kentucky only to discover that the price of land there was "beyond their reach." American officials feared that these people who had "no country" and no "attachment to the natale Solum" would settle across the Mississippi in Spanish territory and lay "the foundation for the Greatness of a rival country." Some, indeed, did migrate across the Mississippi into Spanish territory where Spain initially promised to offer land on better terms than were available in Kentucky.[7]

Backcountry settlers disputed both federal and Algonquian claims to the land. There were supposedly more than twenty-two hundred families north

Press, 1940), 102–5. For change policy, see Report of the Secretary at War: Indian Affairs, May 2, 1788, Carter (ed.), *Territorial Papers*, 2:103–5.

[5] St. Clair to the Secretary at War, Jan. 27, 1788, Carter (ed.), *Territorial Papers* 2:91. For Harmar's censuses, see Harmar to Knox, May 14, 1787, and Dec. 9, 1987, both in Harmar Letter Book B, Harmar Papers. See also Harmar to Knox, June 15, 1788, Letter Book C, Harmar Papers.

[6] For St. Clair quotation, see St. Clair to the Secretary at War, Jan. 27, 1788, Carter (ed.), *Territorial Papers*, 2:89. For similar sentiments, see Knox to Harmar, Dec. 19, 1789, in Gayle Thornbrough (ed.), *Outpost on the Wabash, 1787–1791*, Indiana Historical Society Publications, vol. 19 (Indianapolis: Indiana Historical Society, 1957), 211.

[7] Burt, *The United States, Great Britain, and British North America*, 101, 104–6.

of the Ohio by the spring of 1785 on lands closed to settlement. They ignored posted instructions to stay out. Settling "by the forties and fifties," they were, John Armstrong reported to Harmar, "banditti whose actions are a disgrace to human nature." Harmar thought that:

> These men upon the frontiers have hitherto been accustomed to seat themselves on the best of the lands, making a tomahawk light or Improvement as they term it, supposing that to be sufficient title. I believe them in general to be averse to federal measures, and that they would wish to throw every obstacle in the way to impede the surveying of the Western territory.... I shall take care to counteract the views of these vagabonds and support the authority of Congress.

To "support the authority of Congress" involved burning out these "fellows who wish to live under no government." And yet burning them out stirred their resentment without keeping them away. To pacify them and hold them for the republic, St. Clair wanted to purchase the Illinois country from the Algonquians and dispose of it in small tracts.[8]

Ignoring the government's land laws, the backcountry people ignored, too, its Indian policy and threatened to ignore its foreign policy. Angered by Spain's refusal to open the Mississippi to American commerce, some of them plotted to seize Natchez and New Orleans from Spain and thus open the river. Others conspired for an independent trans-Appalachian republic in alliance with France or England, nations, they thought, better able to maintain their rights. These were the "white savages" whom John Jay feared would "become more formidable to us, than the tawny ones who now inhabit" the region.[9]

The new federal government became as interested in imposing its authority over these "white savages" as it was in subduing the Algonquians. The subjugation of white and Indian villagers indeed became linked. The federal government felt threatened by both Indian attacks and backcountry retaliation on the Indians. An expedition by George Rogers Clark on the Wabash, and another by Benjamin Logan against the Shawnees, posed as much of a threat to federal authority as they did to the Indian villages. The *Maryland Journal* reported that Clark not only intended to "kill and scalp as many as he may conquer" along the Wabash, but he would also end the federal treaties

[8] For price and fear of migration across Mississippi, see St. Clair to Secretary for Foreign Affairs, Dec. 13, 1788, Carter (ed.), *Territorial Papers* 2:166–70. For squatters, see Harmar to Settlers West of Ohio, Apr. 21, 1785, v. 2, Harmar Papers; Harmar to Knox, Aug. 4, 1786, Letter Book A, Harmar Papers. For Armstrong quotation, see Armstrong to Harmar, Apr. 13, 1785, v. 2, Harmar Papers. For Harmar quotation, see Harmar to Knox, May 14, 1787, Letter Book B, Harmar Papers.

[9] Burt, *The United States, Great Britain, and British North America*, 101, 104–6.

that benefited only a few designing men. Harmar complained of Clark's "very irregular proceedings."[10]

Harmar and his officers saw the Kentucky and backcountry fighters not as allies but as enemies of the state and of good order. Harmar wished to hang one of them, Patrick Brown, after his raid on friendly villagers along the Wabash. He was enraged that Brown had set "the sovereign authority of the United States at defiance." Major John F. Hamtramck, who commanded the federal garrison at Vincennes, found it "very mortifying . . . to see the authority of the United States so much sneered at." Daniel Sullivan and Michael Duff, backcountry settlers who walked around Vincennes with Wea scalps on a stick and conspired with the Illinois Piankashaws to steal French horses to sell to the Spanish, threatened American authority as much as they threatened Indian well-being. Hamtramck felt they must be subdued.[11]

The failure of the Algonquians to accept the American claims to their territory by right of conquest precipitated a federal war that proceeded alongside the village wars of the border, but in waging it the federal government established its authority over white as well as red "savages." The government sought to subdue its own citizens, who thought they could "insult her authority with impunity," as well as reduce Indians to subjects and drive the British troops at Detroit and Michilimackinac from American soil.[12]

To portray the confrontation along the Ohio simply as a conflict between the new American state and Indian tribes misses the complexity of the relationships between the various groups involved; it neglects the extent to which confrontation itself was rearranging the organization and relationships of the region. Rather than providing yet another detailed account of the military confrontations that racked the *pays d'en haut* after 1785, it is more profitable to look at these relationships. Doing so discloses a more complicated world than the one visible only at Harmar's and St. Clair's defeat and Anthony Wayne's triumph at Fallen Timbers. War unarguably was a critical factor in the *pays d'en haut* during these years, but war also obscured the tangled politics and social relations that put, or failed to put, soldiers and warriors in the field.

The emergence and decline of the western confederation formed the

---

[10] Harmar to Knox, May 14, 1787, Letter Book B, Harmar Papers. Harmar thought the victims of Indian attacks had settled contrary to orders and were "not much to be pitied," Harmar to Knox, July 1, 1785, Letter Book A, Harmar Papers. For treaties, see *Maryland Journal*, Oct. 20, 1786, GRC Papers, Draper Mss., 11J118–20; Clark to Harmar, 25 June 1786, 3:64, Harmar Papers; Harmar to Knox, May 14, 1787, Letter Book B, Harmar Papers.

[11] For quotation, see Harmar to Hamtramck, Feb. 15, 1789, Thornbrough (ed.), *Outpost*, 150. For Sullivan and Duff, see Hamtramck to Wyllys, May 27, 1789, *ibid.*, 171; Asheton to Hamtramck, May 31, 1789, *ibid.*, 17; Hamtramck to Harmar, Aug. 14, 1789, *ibid.*, 183; Edgar to Hamtramck, Oct. 28, 1789, *ibid.*, 198–99.

[12] For quotation, see Putnam to Knox, Aug. 21, 1792, Rowena Buell (ed.), *The Memoirs of*

central feature of this complicated world, but the confederation cannot be understood in isolation. Indeed, the confederation did not exist except in its relation to outsiders. The confederation ruled no villages; its leaders could not compel allegiance. The only way to understand the evolution of the confederation is to place it within the context of the multiethnic world of the late eighteenth-century *pays d'en haut.*

II

In 1785, John Filson sailed up the Wabash River on his way to the French village of Vincennes. He enjoyed an idyllic passage. Heretofore "unaccustomed to indians," Filson met "numbers every day floating in Cannoes or encamped on the river's bank." Filson had to shake hands with every member of each party and exchange gifts. The Americans gave "flower, Salt or tobacco &c they in return frequently gave us flesh, fish, & fowl, these friendly exchanges never failed to ensure friendship and a hearty farewel."[13]

Not a year later, in the spring of 1786, warriors from the Wabash villages struck the Americans who had settled along the river. In late May, seven miles from Vincennes, they killed one man and took another prisoner. They burned him and then left his remains hanging in a tree. No chief stepped forward to cover these dead or raise them up. Instead, the warriors killed again and again. That things fell apart so quickly on the Wabash marked the seeming inability of the middle ground to incorporate any sizable numbers of Americans in the years following the Revolution. The gentler communications of Filson's trip up the river had vanished. Filson himself would die at Indian hands in the fall of 1788 while exploring the lands between the two Miami rivers with Judge Symmes.[14]

Filson had come "to this remote and dangerous part" to speculate in land, trade for furs, and gather material for stories of "danger and frequent death." This mix of motives and its result made Filson into something of a republican Baron Lahontan. And like Lahontan's, Filson's stories lasted a long time. Lahontan's own search for wealth in the *pays d'en haut* had yielded only Adario, the prototype for later noble savages. Filson's search had already

Rufus Putnam and Certain Official Papers and Correspondence (Boston: Houghton, Mifflin, 1903), 325.

[13] Beverley Bond, Jr. (ed.), "Two Journeys of John Filson," *Mississippi Valley Historical Review* 9 (1923): 320–30.

[14] Henry to Clark, June 12, 1786, GRC Papers, 53J32, Draper Mss. For death of Filson, see St. Clair to Knox, Oct. 26, 1788, William Henry Smith (ed.), *The St. Clair Papers: The Life and Public Services of Arthur St. Clair*, 2 vols. (Freeport, N.Y.: Books for Libraries Press, 1970, repr. of 1881 ed.), 2:94. For a description, see Narrative of John S. Gano, Frontier Wars, 2U144, Draper Mss.

yielded "Col. Daniel Boon" of Filson's *Discovery, Settlement, and Present State of Kentucky*. Filson had created his literary Boone the year before, and in the Kentuckian he had produced the longest-lasting embodiment of America's mythic frontier. Filson, a Pennsylvania schoolmaster, had described a Boone who adopted Indian virtues in order to kill actual Indians. He had transmuted Indian hating into something more appealing and fine. Lacking Indian vices, embodying only their virtues, Boone rose above the Indians whom he conquered. The best part of them lived on in him. Filson's Boone embodied a middle ground of a sort, but it was a mythic middle ground in which Indians died and ceased to be. They yielded to whites who incorporated them, not physically and in everyday life as the French at Vincennes did, but spiritually and only in myth. Actual Indians were but a hindrance.

It is fitting that Filson, one of the formative figures in creating the enduring American middle ground of myth, should enter into the middle ground of history at a place like Vincennes. Vincennes, perhaps more than any other site in the Ohio Valley, captured the social, ethnic, and political diversity of the *pays d'en haut* in the 1780s. If the Algonquians and the Americans could have created a post-Revolutionary middle ground on the Ohio border, this would have been the place.

Vincennes, when Filson reached it, had "upwards of 300 houses, most of which make a poor appearance but in general are convenient and clean." The houses made a poor appearance because they were, as a later visitor explained, "chiefly frame work . . . many of them covered with bark." They were, in short, mixtures of Algonquian and French styles. The people of Vincennes, whom the British governor Hamilton had so despised, Filson found friendly. "Numbers" of the French lived "as savages in some Respects" and were intermarried with the many villagers whom the Europeans lumped together as the Wabash Indians. The Kickapoos, Mascoutens, Piankashaws, Weas, Delawares, Shawnees, and Miamis who lived near the Wabash and its tributaries had "contracted a friendship and acquaintance" with the French that "time will never be able to irradicate." The French lived largely by trade, but by 1786 the French and the Indians had been joined by about seventy American families that had claimed lands around the posts. Some of these claims derived from the Virginia occupation of the region during the war; some of the claims were mere squatters' rights.[15]

---

[15] Bond (ed.), "Two Journeys of John Filson, " 326–28; L. C. Helderman, "The Northwest Expedition of George Rogers Clark, 1786–87," *Mississippi Valley Historical Review* 25 (1938): 318. Claims, Petition to Clark, Mar. 16, 1786, Petition to Clark, June 1, 1786, *Indiana Magazine of History* 34 (1938): 456–57. For Indian villages, see Helen Hornbeck Tanner (ed.), *Atlas of Great Lakes Indian History* (Norman: University of Oklahoma Press,

At Vincennes the Americans had entered a political netherworld that lay just beyond empire, alliance, and state. When in 1778 George Rogers Clark had conquered the town and overawed the Indians of the Wabash, he had made the French of the town into Americans and attached them to the Republic. Over the next decade his political and military accomplishments had melted away. The Indians had joined the British; the French had drifted into neutrality; Virginia had withdrawn her garrison and ceded her claim to Congress in 1784. After the war, American traders and farmers moved into the region; they claimed it was "entirely anarchial," and the French complained of being abandoned to a "state of nature." These were exaggerations. Before departing, Virginia's representative John Todd had "Comissioned a number of Magistrates to form a Court and appointed Col.° Legras Commandant and Judge of the Court." Le Gras served as a kind of chief, or as Major Ebenezer Denny called him, a "little governor" in the town. He organized the community and arbitrated disputes. The magistrates were, in effect, his council.[16]

This mix of peoples, the absence of state authority, and the inability of any one group to raise overwhelming force against the others had, in the past, contributed to the rise of the middle ground. Why did it not do so, even temporarily, along the Wabash? Or, rather, since a long-standing middle ground existed for the French and the Indians at Vincennes, why could it not incorporate in Americans? Why did Filson's idyll so quickly yield to bloodshed?

Part of the answer of liquor; the rest lies in sentiments and ambitions of the Americans. The first Americans who entered the region, like their predecessors on the Ohio twenty years earlier, turned their corn into liquor and sold the liquor to the Indians. The French magistrates banned the trade but could not suppress it, and they themselves came under suspicion of dealing in liquor clandestinely. The liquor trade provoked violence among everyone involved but largely between the Americans and the Indians. Drunken murders had long been the bane of the American frontier. It was the duty of the chiefs to step forward and cover the dead and control the drinking. But along the Wabash in 1786 no chiefs were able or willing to

1987), maps 17 and 18. Harmar later mentioned a "half French" man married to a "Wea squaw" who had great influence among them, Harmar to Knox, Nov. 24, 1787, Letter Book B, Harmar Papers. A year later Harmar put the population of Vincennes at 900 French and 400 Americans living in 400 houses, Harmar to Knox, Aug. 7, 1787, Letter Book B, Harmar Papers. For houses, see "A Military Journal Kept by Major E. Denny, 1781–95," *Memoirs of the Historical Society of Pennsylvania* (Philadelphia: J. B. Lippincott, 1860), Sept. 15, 1787, 311.

16 Helderman, "The Northwest Expedition," 320–21; Bond, "Two Journeys of John Filson," 327; Petition to Clark, Mar. 16, 1786, *Indiana Magazine of History* 34 (1938): 456–57. "Denny Journal," July 28, 1787.

act. In 1787 Harmar still found the Wabash Indians "amazing fond" of drinking.[17]

Among the French and the Indians there were men acknowledged as chiefs, but their power was in decline. Quarrels over the liquor trade had sapped the authority of Le Gras and the magistrates, who "began to experience... disobediance too frequently." And since Le Gras lacked any military authority to sustain him, he like a chief, could do nothing once people refused to acknowledge his authority.[18]

The chiefs among the Wabash villagers also proved incapable of ending the bloodshed and mediating the quarrels; they lacked fathers to provide them with the necessary gifts, and equivalent American chiefs with whom they might negotiate. Patriarchy was in sad disrepair along the Wabash. Some of these chiefs, like the old Wea Quiquapoughquáa (or Crooked Legs), had known several fathers over the preceding decade. He had accepted Clark's flags eight years earlier only to repent of his American alliance on the arrival of Hamilton. He had disavowed Hamilton after his defeat by Clark and later sought an alliance with Spain in preference to the Americans, French, or English. The Weas had joined the English in the last years of the war, only to be abandoned by them. By 1787 this chief, who had had so many fathers, was now without a father to serve and thus without gifts to conciliate his warriors. Power had passed to "fools," and Quiquapoughquáa kept himself concealed.[19]

Like the Weas, the Americans were led by "fools," men who were not old and wise but young and rash. When the French attempted to mediate, the Americans insisted that they were protecting the Indians from retaliation. In the neighboring Illinois country the Americans at Bellefontaine near Kaskaskia forted up, and on the Wabash the Americans at Vincennes constructed a blockhouse for refuge. Their leader was Daniel Sullivan, a borderer of the kind Harmar feared endangered the Republic and whom Le Gras described as "very dangerous... and pernicious to the public peace."[20]

---

[17] See Gibault to the Bishop, June 6, 1786, *American Historical Review* 14 (1908): 552–56; Harmar to Knox, Nov. 24, 1787, Letter Book B, Harmar Papers.

[18] Bond, "Two Journeys of John Filson," 327; Gibault to the Bishop, June 6, 1786, *American Historical Review* 14 (1908): 552.

[19] They were the chiefs who spoke to Clark in Oct. 1786, Clark to Wabash Indians and Replies, Oct. 1786, GRC Papers, 11J 108–117, Draper Mss. For Crooked Legs, see John D. Barnhart (ed.), *Henry Hamilton and George Rogers Clark in the American Revolution with the Unpublished Journal of Lieutenant Governor Henry Hamilton* (Crawfordeville, Ind.: R. E. Banta, 1951), Dec. 1, 1778, Dec. 4, 1778, 134–38; Talk to Cruzat, 1780, Lawrence Kinnaird, *Spain in the Mississippi Valley, 1765–94... Part I: The Revolutionary Period, 1765–81*, Annual Report of the American Historical Association for the Year 1945, vol. 2 (Washington, D.C.: Government Printing Office, 1949)

[20] Le Gras to Clark, July 22, 1786, *Indiana Magazine of History* 34 (1938): 465. There is a different version of this letter in Kinnaird, *Spain*, 2:175–81.

Until June 1786 the French managed to remain uninvolved in what was a
blood feud between the villagers and the Americans. On June 20, however,
Indians ambushed Sullivan and a party of Americans who were working in
their cornfields. They wounded two men, one of whom the Americans
thought certain to die. Sullivan and his men stalked into Vincennes, seized
the first Indian they found – a sick man under the care of the French – and
killed him. They scalped their victim and dragged his dead body "like a pig
at the tail of a horse." Unlike Indian killings which took place in the woods
and fields, this killing took place in a French settlement and thus implicated
the French.[21]

The murder threatened to turn the blood feud to war. Le Gras, who
regarded many of the Americans as outlaws who had brought all this trouble
on themselves, ordered all Americans without passports to leave Vincennes.
When Sullivan produced a passport, Le Gras ordered him to go anyway.
The Americans apparently made no move to leave, and in July from 450 to
700 warriors appeared before Vincennes to exterminate the Big Knives.
Such numbers represented more than the retaliation expected from the
kinspeople of the victims. A "chief of the river Languille" presented the
Piankashaws with a string of black wampum, urging them to join with "other
Redskins" in order to "destroy all the men wearing hats who are occupying
this island and who seem to be leagued against us to drive us away from the
lands which the Master of Life has given to us." The Indians demanded that
the French join them. In this crisis, chiefs at last managed to act effectively.
With calumets, flags, gifts, speeches, and threats, Le Gras and Major
François Bosseron negotiated a truce with the Wabash chiefs who persuaded
their warriors to depart. Promising to return "in roasting ear time," the
warriors left after shooting up Sullivan's house and destroying his crops.[22]

This abortive attack proved the prelude to Clark's last expedition against
the Wabash villagers. With the outlook already "very dark and altogether
barbarous," both French and Americans appealed to Clark. In 1786, Clark
was a war hero, an Indian commissioner for the confederation of states, and
the "first Citizen of the West." He was also a man operating in a political
vacuum. The Continental Congress and the new confederation of states
were not at war with the Indians, and General Harmar doubted that he had

---

[21] Small to Clark, June 23, 1786, GRC Papers, 53J36, Draper Mss.; Helderman, "The
Northwest Expedition," 324–25; Small to Clark, GRC Papers, 53J36, Draper Mss., copy in
Indiana Magazine of History 34 (1938): 459–60; Account in Le Gras to Clark, July 22, 1786,
Kinnaird, *Spain* 2:177.

[22] Helderman, "The Northwest Expedition," 324–25; Small to Clark, June 23, 1786, GRC
Papers, 53J36, Draper Mss.; Spring to Clark, July 22, 1786, Clark Papers, Missouri
Historical Society, copy in Ohio Valley–Great Lakes Ethnohistorical Archives, University of
Indiana (hereafter sited as GLEHA); Le Gras to Clark, July 22, 1786, in Kinnaird, *Spain*
2:175–81.

the authority to commit federal troops to any expedition against the Indians. Initiative thus passed to the Kentucky militia, to whose officers the Virginia government gave the authority to undertake their own defense. The officers appointed Clark commander-in-chief. The confrontation would be, as before the Revolution, villagers against villagers.[23]

In the fall of 1786 Clark moved against Vincennes for the second and last time. Clark had changed little in ten years. He was by temperament a war leader who thought that force was power and conciliation was a tactic to be adopted only from weakness. Clark was not ready to make the transition to chief let alone to father, although that is what the situation demanded. The man who had originally made his reputation at Vincennes would lose it there.

Clark marched to Vincennes, adding French and American volunteers to his force of Kentucky militia, and then proceeded toward the Indian villages of the upper Wabash. At the mouth of the Big Vermilion, a cry rose among his troops: "Who's for home?" Like an Indian war expedition confronted with bad dreams, Clark's expedition disintegrated. The rebellion had been the work of subordinate officers jealous of Clark. Left with only about half his men, Clark retreated to Vincennes. What made this doubly humiliating for Clark was that he had announced his presence and purpose to the Indians with his usual bluster and threats, and the Indians had mocked him. An unnamed war chief of the Weas replied to Clark's threats of bloody retribution: "Thou American, I am charmed to hear thee speak; probably thou are not a chief since thou speakst so ill. . . . Hope to hear from thee soon." On retreating to Vincennes, Clark was himself forced to resort to negotiations, but he had no authority to make a treaty, and the chiefs to whom he appealed had lost control over their own warriors. Despite Le Gras's attempts to act as a mediator, and conciliatory promises from the chiefs to meet in the spring, there would be no treaty. Clark garrisoned Vincennes and turned his attention to other enemies of Kentucky.[24]

Clark was a war leader who antagonized not just Indian war leaders and chiefs but the agents of the empire and the officials of the new American state as well. Convinced, as were most backcountry settlers, that the British

---

[23] See, Helderman, "The Northwest Expedition," 324–25. Harmar vacillated on allowing troops to join Clark, Petition to Clark, Mar. 16, 1786, Petition to Clark, June 1, 1786, Petition to Clark, June 12, 1788, *Indiana Magazine of History* 34 (1938): 456–59.

[24] Clark to Wabash Indians and Replies, Oct. 1786, GRC Papers, 11J108–117 Draper Mss.; Helderman, "The Northwest Expedition," 328–29. For jealousy, see "Denny Journal," July 38, 1787, 307. For attack and Clark's failure, see Girty to McKee, Oct. 11, 1786, *MPHC* 24:34; Letter of Ancrum, Oct. 13, 1786, *MPHC* 24:35–39; Harmar to Secretary of War, Nov. 15, 1786, Smith (ed.), *St. Clair Papers* 2:18–19; Information from Lewis, Nov. 14, 1786, 4:88, Harmar Papers, and Harmar to Knox, Dec. 7, 1786, Letter Book B, Harmar Papers. Also see Isabel Thompson Kelsay, *Joseph Brant, 1743–1806: Man of Two Worlds* (Syracuse: Syracuse University Press, 1984), 401–2; Harmar to Irvin, Dec. 10, 1786, Letter Book B, Harmar Papers.

were behind Indian resistance, Clark dispatched troops to Kaskaskia to dislodge the trader Jonathan Dodge, who, he thought, ruled Kaskaskia as a British agent. He then seized the property of three French traders at Vincennes whom he accused of being Spanish subjects trading illegally in American territory. This seizure was in retaliation for Spain's refusal to open the Mississippi to Kentucky exports. The seizure alarmed both Virginia officials and Congress who feared Spanish retaliation. Virginia revoked Clark's authority; Harmar disputed his right either to call treaties or to garrison Vincennes, and Secretary of War Knox ordered Harmar to disperse Clark's men. By the winter of 1787, however, the ill-supplied garrison had disbanded at its own volition. Clark, in disgrace, faced the threat of criminal charges and the reality of civil suits that would plague him for years. He had been crushed in the dangerous crevices between empires, states, and villages.[25]

Clark's failure did not deter others from seeking opportunity in those cracks that remained open between villages, empires, and the new American state. Pacane had moved in such cracks throughout his career. By one account, he was a Potawatomi by birth; more likely, he was the child of an intermarried Potawatomi. His name was the French rendering of the title or ritual name of the second ranking chief of the leading Miami clan. In 1785, however, he had left the Miamis with a band of followers because he was disturbed by the disorderly conduct of the warriors and their hostility to the Americans. He had settled near Vincennes, and he had remained neutral during the troubles along the Wabash even after Kentuckians had killed his father-in-law and some of his hunters and then "cut and hacked them to pieces." When Clark appeared, Pacane became his intermediary with the Wabash tribes. He and a chief named La Demoiselle, like the earlier subordinate Miami chief of the same name who had forged an alliance with English-speaking backcountry men, remained the American conduits to the Wabash despite the slaughter of their people by the Big Knives.[26]

Clark's fall did not hurt Pacane; he found other Americans in need of

---

[25] Helderman, "The Northwest Expedition," 329–31. For dispersal of garrison, see Harmar to Knox, May 14, 1787, Letter Book B, Harmar Papers.

[26] A young Pacane first appears in the record following Pontiac's Rebellion. Butler said he was a Potawatomi name Petequcica. The Americans were suspicious of him, see Butler Journal, in Neville B. Craig, Esq. (ed.), *The Olden Time* (Pittsburgh: Dumars, 1846; Millwood, N. Y.: Kraus Reprint Co., 1976), 2:514; for ranks second to Petit Gris, moves to Vincennes, see Samuel Montgomery, "A Journey Through the Indian Country Beyond the Ohio, 1785," *Mississippi Valley Historical Review* 2 (1915): 267. For hunters killed, see Spring to Clark, July 22, 1786, Clark Papers, Mo. Historical Society, copy in GLEHA; Le Gras to Clark, July 22, 1786, Kinnaird, *Spain*, 2:180–81. For carries Clark's message, see Clark to Wabash Chiefs, GRC Papers, 11J108–117, Draper Mss. A "Demoiselle" briefly appears as a messenger at this same time, *ibid.*; Le Gras to Clark, July 22, 1786, *Indiana Magazine of History* 34 (1938): 466.

Elizabeth Posthuma Simcoe, the wife of John G. Simcoe, the British lieutenant governor of Canada, probably drew this sketch of Pacane, a leading alliance chief of the Miamis during the 1780s and 1790s, when he attended a conference with the British in 1793. (Archives of Ontario [175(e)])

mediators to the Wabash villagers. Wabash raids on Kentucky, the desire of Harmar to establish a legitimate American presence at Vincennes, and the necessity of evicting squatters from lands that the Indians had never ceded and the Americans had not surveyed, all combined to bring federal troops north in 1787. Both the French and the Indians distinguished the troops from Sullivan's backcountry people. They called the federal troops the "real Americans." In collaboration with Le Gras, Pacane became Harmar's intermediary with the Wabash villages and later accompanied him to Illinois.[27]

Harmar's visit resulted in a conference at which the gathered Indians breathed "nothing but peace and friendship for the United States," but Harmar did not succeed in making the Wabash Indians children of an American father. He failed, in part because, like Clark, he scorned the middle ground even as he entered it. When the "old chiefs attended, expecting, as was customary, some presents," Harmar informed them that the Americans were warriors who "did not come to purchase their friendship with trinkets, but barely to take them by the hand if they chose to give it; if they did not, it was a matter of indifference." He relented only insofar as to give the old chiefs small personal presents. How could the chiefs intervene effectively with such people? How could orderly relations be established?[28]

Harmar's ambition to intimidate rather than conciliate meant that the Wabash would remain a site of conflict beyond the effective intervention of the American state even after Major John F. Hamtramck established a military post at Vincennes late in 1787. Despite the efforts of friendly chiefs, the French, and Hamtramck, the Wabash country became the domain of rash young men and a scene of raids and retaliation. This violent world remained, however, very much a face-to-face world of independent villagers and tangled personal relations. On July 8, 1788, Jean Baptiste Taitre, who had taken his family to Petit Rocher, on the Wabash River, three miles from Vincennes, met eight Indians. They entered his camp half an hour after sundown. Taitre knew only one of them, La Grosse Tête, but he knew him well. The Indians asked him to cross them over the Wabash, and after he had done so, they robbed him of his tools and provisions. They told him they had murdered two men that day beside the Little River, near the hated Daniel Sullivan's plantation. They warned him to take his family home for

---

[27] Harmar to Knox, May 14, 1787, Letter Book B, Harmar Papers. For evict squatters, see Knox to Harmar, Apr. 26, 1787, 5:67, Harmar Papers; Harmar to Knox, June 7, 1787, *ibid.*; Harmar to Knox, Nov. 24, 1787, *ibid.* For Le Gras, see Speech addressed to all the Indian Nations on the Wabash, Harmar Papers 6:54. For real Americans, see "Denny Journal," July 25, July 28, 1787, 306–7.

[28] For conference, see Harmar to Knox, Nov. 24, 1787, Letter Book B, Harmar Papers; Harmar to Knox, Dec. 22, 1787, Letter Book B, Harmar Papers; for talk with chiefs, see "Denny Journal," Sept. 8–10, 1787, 310–11.

other war parties were out that might not treat him so kindly. Taitre returned to Vincennes and reported the encounter to Antoine Gamelin, one of the magistrates at Vincennes.[29]

The little incident at Petit Rocher and its consequences reveal much about the texture of life on the Wabash even as violence ripped it apart. Taitre knew La Grosse Tête and was able, either in French or Piankashaw, to converse with him. The Indians robbed Taitre – for the French had cooperated with the Big Knives – but they also warned him to save his life and his family's. In 1788, Indians distinguished the French from the Big Knives they sought to kill and distinguished the Big Knives from the "real Americans" – those Americans who manned the post. But La Grosse Tête could not promise that such distinctions would bind all war parties. Taitre, perhaps more resentful at his own loss than solicitous of Americans, reported the encounter and implicated La Grosse Tête in the murders, but only after a week had elapsed. When Taitre swore before the magistrates of the district of Vincennes, Antoine Gamelin took his statement with both French and American witnesses. The next winter the American commander, Hamtramck, imprisoned La Grosse Tête when he appeared as usual in Vincennes. In the spring an Illinois-Wabash delegation came to ask for his release, which Hamtramck, unknowingly conforming to the older patriarchal pattern of repentance and mercy, was willing to grant. He failed to do so only because La Grosse Tête had already escaped. Americans, French, and Indians still inhabited a common world whose events echoed those of a century earlier.[30]

The common world was, however, becoming ragged, as murders cut into it and the patches applied by Hamtramck and the chiefs failed to hold. No one remained exempt from the spreading violence. In the summer of 1789, Patrick Brown of Kentucky, out to revenge Indian raids, attacked, as other Kentuckians had earlier, the friendly bands of Pacane and La Demoiselle. His men killed nine Indians and stole horses, including those of Pacane who was on a mission for Hamtramck to the Maumee River. The Vincennes magistrates refused to allow the Kentuckians to enter the town, and an outraged Hamtramck wanted to arrest Brown. He could do nothing, however, for he had only nine men fit for duty, and the American militia at Vincennes refused to act against Kentuckians. The Kentuckians, in turn, threatened to march on Vincennes. Hamtramck disavowed Brown's actions

[29] For post, see Hamtramck to Harmar, Jan. 1, 1788, 7:4, Harmar Papers. Deposition of Jean Bapt. Taitre, July 14, 1788, 8:23, Harmar Papers. Despite the troops at Vincennes, Hamtramck could not stop Wabash raids on Kentucky, Hamtramck to Harmar, May 21, 1788, 7:100, June 18, 1788, 7:119, Harmar Papers.
[30] For arrest, see Hamtramck to Harmar, Mar. 28, 1789, Thornbrough (ed.), *Outpost*, 161–62. For escape, see Hamtramck to Harmar, June 15, 1789, *ibid.*, 176.

to any Indian who would listen, but he could not halt a new cycle of revenge. By then, in any case, many Wabash Indians had already ceased to distinguish between the "real Americans" and the Big Knives. Three hundred Kickapoos attacked an American army convoy at the mouth of the Wabash inflicting heavy casualties. The bulk of the Piankashaws and many of the Indians on the Vermilion withdrew to the Kaskaskias, with whom they had long intermarried. There they raided American settlers and sold the plunder to Spanish subjects across the Mississippi.[31]

The withdrawal of the Piankashaws was but one sign of the decline of the face-to-face world at Vincennes. The French, fearful of the Kentuckians' threat to their land, sought to put themselves under the protection of the American state while trying to maintain trade connections with the British on the Miami. In July 1787, the French of Vincennes sent a petition to the Congress asking that the Congress survey and distribute their lands – received supposedly from a grant given by the Piankashaws and never legally divided. The French could no longer rely on their status as "fathers and friends" of the Wabash villagers' to ensure their security. Forced to choose between the Indians and the Americans, Le Gras and the other leading men chose the United States and asked for American title. Acting to protect their property, the French at Vincennes and the Illinois instead found it threatened. The Northwest Ordinance of 1787 prohibited slavery north of the Ohio, and Congress refused to say whether the act freed the slaves the French already held. Fearing that it did, many French slaveholders withdrew to Spanish territory following those Delawares and Shawnees who were withdrawing for other reasons.[32]

A common fear of the Americans and even a partial flight from them could no longer hold the French and the Indians together at Vincennes and the Illinois. As Indian attacks mounted in 1789, Hamtramck reported that the "discrimination of French & English is done with." At Kaskaskia, the French complained of Indian thefts and threats and the withdrawal of most

[31] For attacks, see Hamtramck to Harmar, Aug. 31, 1788, *ibid.*, 114–19; Hamtramck to Harmar, Oct. 13, 1788, *ibid.*, 124. In the wake of Brown's expedition, relatives of the dead killed two men and a child at Vigo's farm, Hamtramck to Harmar, Nov. 28, 1788, *ibid.*, 139. For Piankashaws, see *ibid.*

[32] Petition of the Inhabitants of Post Vincennes, July 26, 1787, Carter (ed.), *Territorial Papers* 2:58–60; Tardiveau to St. Clair, Mar. 20, 1788, *ibid.*, 2:99–100. For removal, see Harmar to St. Clair, May 8, 1789, Letter Book E, Harmar Papers; Hamtramck to Harmar, Mar. 28, 1789, and n. 6, Thornbrough (ed.), *Outpost*, 160–61; Tardiveau to St. Clair, June 30, 1790, Smith (ed.), *St. Clair Papers*, 2:117–18; St. Clair to President, Report of Official Proceedings . . . Mar. 5 to June 11, 1790, *ibid.*, 2:175–76; Hamtramck to Harmar, Apr. 14, 1791, Thornbrough (ed.), *Outpost*, 281. For continuing trade relations between the British and Vincennes, see George Sharp to Paul Gamelin, 7 July 1789, and Adhemar St. Martin to Paul Gamelin, Aug. 18, 1789, both in Christopher Coleman (ed.), "Letters from Eighteenth-Century Indiana Merchants," *Indiana Magazine of History* 5 (1909): 155–56, 158.

of their people to Spanish territory. The chiefs and those directly related to the French resented this decline most deeply, but they could not control the young warriors. Quiquapoughquáa (Crooked Legs), the old Wea chief, first threatened to abandon the warriors and then did so, bringing in his own followers, a band with about eighty warriors, to settle under the protection of the garrison at Vincennes. At Kaskaskia, the Piankashaws threatened to kill the Kaskaskia chief Ducoigne because he was a friend of the Americans, but he, too, remained allied to the United States. The efforts of Pierre Gamelin of Vincennes to act for Saint Clair in securing peace with the majority of the Wabash villages failed, deterred, ironically, by his very familiarity with the Indians. A personal enemy threatened him at the Vermilion and forced him to return. Antoine Gamelin finished the mission, but it achieved nothing. When some bands of Potawatomis and Weas did come in to negotiate peace, Hamtramck, who lacked goods, told them that he was unauthorized to do so, but he demanded the return of white prisoners as a sign of good faith. They went away "much disatisfyd."[33]

The old ties never completely vanished at Vincennes, but the common world narrowed. Although the French avoided a wholesale assault from the Wabash villagers, trade declined and murders occurred. When Hamtramck marched against the Wabash villages in November 1790, the Indians did not attack him on his retreat. They "suspected the French I had with me had been forced to march, and that they would not kill them." But this was, in the end, a small grace. Looking back, the French at Vincennes saw that their inability to avoid alliance with the Americans had destroyed them. For, as they told the French traveler Constantin-François Volney, the Indians, "embittered by the remembrance of their ancient friendship and alliance," killed their cattle and kept them from the plow and hoe. The Americans, meanwhile, cheated them of their lands. The Wabash villagers shared the

---

[33] For discrimination, see Hamtramck to Wyllys, May 27, 1789, Thornbrough (ed.), *Outpost*, 169–70. In the fall of 1790 Indians twice attacked a boat owned by Francis Vigo on the Wabash. The first time they mistook the boat for one carrying Governor St. Clair, the second time the boat was in company with an American boat. The Indians allowed the surviving crew to depart but warned them if they found them in the company of Americans, they would put them to death, St. Clair to Secretary of War, Sept. 19, 1790, Smith (ed.), *St. Clair Papers*, 2:184; Secretary Sargent to Gov. St. Clair, Carter (ed.), *Territorial Papers*, 2:300–01. For Kaskaskia, see Le Dru et al. to Hamtramck, Sept. 25, 1789, Thornbrough (ed.), *Outpost*, 190–91; Edgar to Hamtramck, Oct. 28, 1789, *ibid.*, 198–99; Hamtramck to Harmar, Nov. 2, 1789, *ibid.*, 205.

For Weas, see Hamtramck to Harmar, July 29, 1789, Thornbrough (ed.), *Outpost*, 178–79; Hamtramck to Harmar, Nov. 2, 1789, *ibid.*, 205; Hamtramck to Harmar, Nov. 2, 1790, *ibid.*, 264. For Gamelin, see Hamtramck to Harmar, Mar. 17, 1790; *ibid.*, 222–27; Gamelin's Journal, *American State Papers, Indian Affairs*, 2 vols. (Washington, D.C.: Gales and Seaton, 1832–34), 1:92–93 (hereafter cited as *ASPIA*); St. Clair to Secretary of War, May 1, 1790, Smith (ed.), *St. Clair Papers*, 2:135–36. Hamtramck to Harmar, Aug. 20, 1790. Thornbrough (ed.), *Outpost*, 247.

French sense of loss. As a Wea chief informed Volney: "Before the war . . . we were united and peaceable; we began to raise corn like the whites. But now we are poor hunted deer, scattered abroad without house or home, and unless somebody comes to our assistance, no trace of us will be left."[34]

III

The fighting that came to dominate life around Vincennes provided the heat that forged the western confederation. Initiated as a purely Indian political organization, the confederation, like the earlier republics, gradually became reabsorbed into a European alliance despite the efforts of its early leaders to keep it functionally separate. Joseph Brant, an English-educated Mohawk who had fought in the West during the Revolution, was the confederation's guiding light in its early years, and his complicated loyalties did much to mold the confederacy. Brant was devoted, in roughly descending order, to the league of the Iroquois, to the Indians as a race, and to the British Empire.

Brant would have preferred a western confederation that was an extension of the Iroquois covenant chain, but deep divisions among the Iroquois themselves, and the obvious western suspicion of the Six Nations, made this impossible. Attempts to convene the confederacy in Iroquoia had failed. Brant had then agreed to light the council fire at the Shawnee village of Wakatomica. But the destruction of that town by Benjamin Logan in 1786 had forced the confederation's removal to the Huron village of Brownstown (or Sindathon's village), at the mouth of the Detroit River. And this move forced the issue of the confederation's relationship with the British.[35]

Before Joseph Brant and the Iroquois agreed to light a council fire at Brownstown, they demanded that the Hurons clearly separate themselves from the British. Although the Hurons were the eldest nation in the West and "the ablest bretheren we have in this quarter,"

---

[34] Hamtramck to Harmar, Nov. 28, 1790, Thornbrough (ed.), *Outpost*, 267. For French, see Constantin-François Volney, *A View of the Soil and Climate of the United States of America . . .* (Philadelphia: T & G Palmer, 1804, repr.), 33–34; for Wea quote, see 382. See also "Narrative of John Heckewelder's Journey to the Wabash in 1792," *Pennsylvania Magazine of History and Biography*, 12 (1888): 169–70.

[35] The Iroquois had tried to convene a general meeting of the confederacy at Buffalo Creek in the spring of 1786, but the western nations had not attended. Western delegates had, however, attended a conference with the Six Nations in July 1786 seeking their aid if resistance to the Americans became necessary, and Six Nation delegations, in turn, came west, Speech of the Five Nations to the Western Indians, Nov. 1786, Frontier Wars, 23U39, Draper Mss; Heart to Harmar, 12 June 1787, 5:120, Harmar Papers; Heart to Harmar, 2 Feb. 1788, 7:20, Harmar Papers; Kelsay, *Joseph Brant*, 399–400; Saunders to Harmar, 30 July 1786, Harmer Papers.

> We have never yet been able rightly to Distinguish your fire place. When
> ever we the five Nations come to you on private Business, you intro-
> duced us to the English fire when you Should have had one under your
> own roofs, we therefore now brighten your fire that we may see it at a
> distance, if you look upon yourselves as a free people you Should keep
> up a fire of your own.[36]

In kindling the new council fire at Brownstown, the Hurons and the chiefs
in general remained outside the framework of the old alliance. Alexander
McKee did dispatch "trusty persons" to the council, but official British
representatives were not present at Brownstown. Instead, at the end of the
meetings, a delegation from the council met with the British at Detroit. They
demanded that the British give them a "determined answer" regarding
British relations with the confederacy and their willingness to aid it in a
conflict with the Americans. The confederacy thus represented not just an
attempt to forge a new set of relations with the Americans; it was equally an
attempt to forge a new set of relations with the British. In the old alliance,
the British had paternal relations with each of their individual children. Any
relations the British now had with the Algonquians were supposed to be with
a united confederacy.[37]

The Revolution had left the British relationship to the Algonquians
ambiguous. The British had announced peace, but they had not followed
either Algonquian or Iroquoian ritual and buried the hatchet. Later British
actions had not clarified the situation. They had retained their posts in the
pays d'en haut until the Americans honored loyalist claims guaranteed in the
Treaty of Paris. And although Britain was never willing to guarantee military
aid against American aggression, the British left open the possibility they
would aid their Indian allies against the Americans. London instructed
Canadian officials to supply in emergencies secret aid that Britain might
deny giving, and then, in 1787, went farther and allowed Indians to receive
the ammunition necessary to protect themselves. The British made large
presents to the Indians and sent provisions to the Shawnees after American
raids destroyed their winter food supplies. By 1788 the British had begun to
take steps to repair and strengthen their posts as British policy became a
sort of deathwatch, waiting for the United States to disintegrate so that
boundaries might be readjusted and separate agreements reached with the
settlers in the interior. The vagueness of British intentions, the lack of
specific instructions, and the hope of favorable future developments allowed
relatively minor British officials in the interior a great deal of leeway. In some
respects, they were as independent as Kentucky backcountry leaders.[38]

---

[36] Indian Council, Dec. 24, 1786, *MPHC* 11:470–72.

[37] *Ibid.*; Claus to Nepean, 5 May 1787, CO. 42/19:128–29.

[38] At Detroit, the British urged the Indians to make peace, Zeisberger to Helpers Conference,

The confederacy's odd fate was that its military success against the Americans, achieved without significant British participation, only increased Algonquian dependence on the British for the supplies necessary to wage war. The more the Algonquians fought, the less independent they grew. Yet to fail to fight was to lose the confederation's greatest political accomplishment: the acceptance among confederation members that the land belonged equally to all Indians of the *pays d'en haut*, could not be ceded without the consent of the entire confederation, and would be defended by all.

The principle of common ownership was central to the confederacy. The treaties of Fort Harmar and the Great Miami had revealed that the alternative was cessions of land by village chiefs and headmen weakened by the Revolution and eager for American aid in reestablishing their influence. All across the *pays d'en haut*, the Revolution had diminished the power of chiefs and increased that of the warriors and war leaders. And in the hazy half war–half peace that followed the Revolution, neither chiefs nor war leaders could restore political order to the villages nor assert uncontested leadership. David Zeisberger spoke of the Delaware leadership as "those who have made themselves chiefs." The chiefs could not control most Shawnee, Wyandot, Mingo, and refugee Cherokee warriors. At the Miami villages, the American emissary for the Great Miami Treaty, Samuel Montgomery, found that Petit Gris, the leading Miami chief, was in Detroit, and that Pacane, the second chief, had withdrawn "offended ... by their unpacific and disorderly conduct." A man called Orson, who was not a chief, presided over the council and he proved incapable of preventing the warriors from robbing and threatening Montgomery's delegation. Conditions were little different in the Wabash villages.[39]

Feb. 25, 1787, B 229, F 6, no. 2, Box 153, folder 10, Moravian Archives, copy in GLEHA. John Heckewelder pointed out the failure to bury the hatchet, Heckewelder to Schweiniz, Sept. 21, 1786, B 215, F 4, no. 5, Moravian Archives, Box 153, folder 10, copy in GLEHA. McKee's speech to the Miamis, etc., Sept. 1787, Frontier Wars, 23U60, Draper Mss.; Transactions with Indians at Sandusky, Aug. 1783, *MPHC* 20:174–183. The Hurons, too, pointed out the failure later on, Speech of the Five Nations to the Western Indians, Nov. 1786, Frontier Wars, 23U48, Draper Mss. The Michilimackinac Ottawas similarly seem to have left a war pipe (pipe hatchet) in Sir John Johnson's hands at the end of the Revolution, Extract, James Goddard to Davison, 15 Dec. 1785, CO. 42/17; Burt, *The United States, Great Britain, and British North America*, 98–105. For an example of how ambiguous promises by English agents could be, see McKee's speech to the Miamis etc., Sept. 1787, Frontier Wars, 23U60, Draper Mss. Harmar by the summer of 1787 had come to blame British traders rather than British officers for the trouble, Harmar to Knox, July 7, 1787, Letter Book B, Harmar Papers. British officials in Canada presumed as late as 1788 that the Indians would reach a satisfactory boundary settlement with the Americans, Precis of Dispatches for Lord Dorchester, July 20, 1788, CO. 42/20:97–98. For posts, see Instructions to Capt. Mann, May 29, 1788, CO. 42/20:44–46.

[39] For quotation, see *Diary of David Zeisberger, Moravian Missionary Among the Indians of Ohio*, tr. and ed. by Eugene, F. Bliss, 2 vols. (Cincinnati: R. Clarke, 1885), Oct. 9, 1782, 1:115. For war leaders as chiefs, see *ibid.*, Dec. 28, 1782, 1:126. For Butler quotation, see Butler's

The leading chiefs who signed the treaties at Fort McIntosh (1785) and the mouth of the Great Miami River (1786) – Captain Pipe of the Wolf phratry of the Delawares, Half King of the Wyandots, and Molunthy of the Mequachake Shawnees – were neither minor leaders nor fearful men. Captain Pipe and Half King had inflicted terrible defeats on the Americans and had turned back American invasions of their country; they, nonetheless, in the words of a Shawnee, "sold their lands and themselves with them" to the Americans. In the view of the general council of the fledgling confederacy, which rejected the treaties as invalid, these men had betrayed the confederacy to which they belonged.[40]

They had betrayed the confederacy partly from personal ambition and partly from devotion to the interests of their own villages. The Delawares and the Wyandots, after all, shared a long history of attempted accommodation with English colonists and traders, and it was a heritage Pipe and Half King had not easily discarded. Repeated American provocations had forced Captain Pipe into the arms of the British, but even during the war, Half King had proven receptive to American peace overtures. The military victories these two men had won against the Americans came at the cost of severe personal losses. Two of Half King's sons died in the fighting, and by October 1781 Wyandot casualties and smallpox epidemics had reportedly reduced their strength to only a hundred warriors. These heavy, and apparently disproportionate, Wyandot losses alienated Half King from the Hurons. In 1781, David Zeisberger reported that Half King cared nothing for the Hurons; his only concern was the Wyandots of Sandusky.[41]

Journal, Jan. 17, 1786, Craig (ed.), *The Olden Time*, 2:515. Montgomery, "A Journey Through the Indian Country," Sept. 17, 1785, 268–69. Butler wrongly thought Pacane to be anti-American, Butler's Journal, Jan. 16, 1786, Craig (ed.), *The Olden Time*, 2:514. For messages and replies, see Clark to Wabash Indians, Oct. 1786, GRC Papers, 11J108–117, Draper Mss.

For American policies, see Horsman, *Expansion and American Indian Policy*, 16–24; Substance of what the Americans said to the Delawares, n.d., c.1785, Frontier Wars, 23U20–21, Draper Mss. For Half King and Captain Pipe's efforts, see Montgomery, "A Journey Through the Indian Country," 260–273; Butler Journal, Nov.–Jan. 1785, Craig (ed.), *The Olden Time*, 2:487–501.

40 For Shawnees, see Message to McKee, Apr. 14, 1785, Frontier Wars, 23U, Draper Mss. For widespread sense of betrayal, see McKee to Johnson, Apr. 24, 1785, Frontier Wars, 23U23, Draper Mss. For rebuke of council, see Meeting held by the Several Nations of Lake Indians, ... 1785, Frontier Wars, 23U, Draper Mss. For denunciations of Pipe, see Butler Journal, Jan. 24, 1786, Craig (ed.), *The Olden Time*, 2:512.

41 For Half King and peace overtures, see Speech, Apr. 1, 1779, *WHC* 23:265; Speech of Doonyontat, Sept. 17, 1779, *WHC* 24:67. For loss of sons, see *Zeisberger Diary*, Oct. 10, 1781, 1:22. For only 100 men, cares nothing for Hurons, see *ibid.*, Oct. 18, 1781, 1:25. For wants to absorb Moravians, see *ibid.*, Oct. 3, 1781, 1:20; Zeisberger to Helper's Conference, June 15, 1787, B 229, F. 7, no. 1, Moravian Archives, Box. 153, folder 10, copy in GLEHA. The Detroit Hurons numbered about 250 warriors in 1785, Census, Claus Papers, 4:65, Public Archives of Canada (hereafter cited as PAC).

Pipe had suffered in other ways. Having outlasted his rivals in the struggles at Coshocton, he had begun to forget his place. In 1782, he had aroused the anger of the other Delaware war captains for "doing everything himself without their consent" during the long negotiations over the fate of the Moravian Delawares after their removal from the mission villages. The other captains informed him that "he had therefore nothing more to say and should be of no further account" in the negotiations. This was a sharp rebuke, and Captain Pipe had not taken it well. His own slipping position among the Delawares contributed to his subsequent willingness to act as a chief rather than as a war leader and to negotiate a peace rather than oppose the advancing Americans. By resuming his position as a phratry chief – a position he had resigned during the war – Pipe could outflank the war leaders for "a captain has no more right to conclude peace than a chief to begin war." In making peace with the Americans, Pipe gained preeminence over his rivals.[42]

Peace came at the price of a cession of a huge tract of land that the Americans had been unable to conquer. Neither Pipe nor Half King had the authority to make such a cession. Even as a chief, Pipe could act legitimately only for the Wolf phratry, not for the Delawares as a whole. The Turtle and Turkey phratries – badly split by the Revolution and migration – were not properly represented at Fort McIntosh and neither were the now quite powerful warrior villages that followed Buckongahelas. Half King was in an even more precarious position. Having previously acknowledged his rightful subordination to the Huron council at Detroit, he had proceeded to usurp their right to negotiate a peace. The general council of the confederacy sharply reminded him of this when they told him his role was "to receive Speeches or Messages, and not to determine upon them." And even if all the Delawares and Wyandots had been present, the cessions still would have been invalid for, as the American trader David Duncan later wrote, "the Wyandots, Delaws. & Shawnees do not own one foot of land." They lived on land granted by the Hurons and Miamis.[43]

---

[42] For denunciation of Pipe, see *Zeisberger Diary*, Mar. 3, 1782; Oct. 9, 1782, 1:115. For war leaders as chiefs, see *Zeisberger Diary*, Dec. 28, 1782, 1:126. For quote on peace, see Archer Butler Hulbert and William N. Schwarze (eds.), *David Zeisberger's History of the Northern American Indians* (Ohio State Archaeological and Historical Society, 1910), 100. Buckongahelas seemed to acknowledge the preeminence of chiefs at the treaty, Minutes . . . of Commissioners, Jan. 20, 1786, Frontier Wars, 3U 181–203, Draper Mss.

[43] Gelemund's (or John Killbuck's) retreat to the Americans with a fraction of the Turtle phratry and his war against his own people left him a nonentity. He resigned his chieftainship of the Turtle phratry, took the name Bill Henry, and joined the Moravians, *Zeisberger Diary*, Jan. 26, 1790, 2:81–82, Oct. 9, 1794, 2:377–78. Welapachtschien (Captain Johnny, Israel, or Gerard) of the Turkey phratry had also joined the Moravians. He largely disappeared from the record. By 1788 he was dead and his nephew had assumed his name and the chieftainship. *Zeisberger Diary*, July 28, 1788, 1:429. Pipe tried to get all the tribes (phratries)

Pipe and Half King justified the cession to the other villages of the *pays d'en haut* by reversing the actual American logic of Fort McIntosh. In the account of the treaty Pipe and Half King circulated among the Shawnees, an account that helped lure them to the second treaty at the mouth of the Great Miamis, the Americans had asked the Indians to "take pity" on them and give them a piece of ground, much indeed as the Delawares, Munsees, and Shawnees had earlier applied to the Wyandots and Hurons for land. The Americans had not claimed the land was already theirs by right of conquest; they had paid "a great many Thousands of Dollars." And finally, the advantages of the land were not lost to the Indians for the Americans shall "give your Children what they want, and will always continue giving them." This remarkable account of the treaty may have been a conscious attempt to deceive on the part of the Delawares and the Wyandots, but it may also have reflected their initial understanding of the cession. If it was the latter, it represented an Algonquian version of what an acceptable cession consisted of. It was an act of pity by the Indians such as they often practiced among themselves. They settled needy people among themselves and put them under obligation. And because white use of the land was to be perpetual, so the obligation of the Americans to aid Indians should be perpetual. Any such initial Algonquian interpretation of the treaties, however, soon collapsed when Weylendeweyhing and Buckongahelas relayed very different interpretations of American claims to the British. The Americans claimed, they said, to have conquered the Indians, and the English had ceded all the lands as far as the Mississippi.[44]

For the Treaty of the Great Miami, the Americans pressured Molunthy and the Mequachake Shawnees into recognizing the cessions already made at Fort McIntosh. This, however, proved to be the high mark of accommodation. Angry at the cessions, the warriors vowed resistance independent of the treaty chiefs if necessary. Sheminetoo (or Blacksnake) and other Shawnee chiefs and war leaders asked the British and Iroquois for aid and

---

of the Delawares to negotiate, "Denny Journal," Dec. 28, 1785, 269. For reprimand to Half King, see Message to the Half King, Sept. 20, 1785, *MPHC* 11:466. For Duncan quotation, see Duncan to Harmar, Mar. 28, 1786, 3:22, Harmar Papers.

The cession seemed to assure Half King that Delaware villages would remain clustered around the Wyandot villages on the Sandusky. He and Pipe who now heard "with the same ear, and spoke with the same tongue" had, in effect, confederated their villages on the Sandusky. A new multiethnic coalition in the tradition of the republics of the 1740s was emerging. For location of villages at end of war, see Tanner, *Atlas of Great Lakes Indian History*, map 18. For quotation, see map 18. Quote, Montgomery, "Journey Through the Indian Country," Sept. 1785, 264.

44 Message from the Shawnees, Apr. 11, 1785, Frontier Wars, 23U, Draper Mss.; Substance of what the Americans said to the Delawares, Frontier Wars, 23U20–21, Draper Mss. Harmar, on the contrary, described the treaty as being "entirely on the Commissioner's own terms," Harmar to Carleton, Jan. 24, 1785, Letter Book A, Harmar Papers.

war belts. The war leaders said, "Old Counsillors & Kings have given up the lands to the Big Knife. But ... the Chiefs of the Warriors have not given our consent & ... if the surveyors come to survey the land or if any of the white people come to set down on it ... we will putt our old men and chiefs behind us." Events had drifted so far out of the Shawnee chiefs' control that the warriors prevented them from calling councils even to consider messages from the Americans. Under such pressure, accommodation with the Americans collapsed. Half King reneged; Molunthy immediately sought British aid to resist the Americans, and Pipe saw his following dissipate. Wyandot, Delaware, and Shawnee warriors pursued their own course, and the villagers who had not signed threatened the conciliatory chiefs. As Half King later explained to the Americans, he was "between two fires for I am afraid of you and likewise the back nations." Before his death in July 1788, Half King had joined in western confederation councils designed to overturn the treaties he had helped make. By then Arthur St. Clair, the governor of the Northwest Territory, thought him the "greatest enemy we had amongst the Wyandots."[45]

The reabsorption of Pipe, Half King, and Molunthy into the confederation and the repudiation of their treaties came amid escalating raids along

[45] The best accounts of the Great Miami treaty council are the Journal of General Butler, in Craig (ed.), *The Olden Time*, 2:442–525, 529–31, and "Denny Journal," 263–80. For events leading up to the treaty, see Minutes of the Proceedings of the Commissioners, Frontier Wars, 3U181–203, Draper Mss.

Substance of What the Americans said, n.d., c. 1785, Frontier Wars, 23U 20–21, Draper Mss. For invalidity of treaties, see Meeting held by the Several Nations of Lake Indians, c. Sept. 1785, Frontier Wars, 23U, Draper Mss.

For Half King, see "Denny Journal," Jan. 1, 1786, 278–80; Indian Council Detroit, Sept. 20, 1785, *MPHC* 11:466. For Delaware divisions, see *Zeisberger Diary*, Apr. 25, 1789, 2:29; *ibid.*, Jan. 26, 1790, 2:81–82.

For fear of hostility of Delaware and Wyandot warriors, see Doughty to Knox, Oct. 21, 1785, Smith (ed.), *St. Clair Papers*, 2:10. For Wyandot horse thefts, quotation, see *Zeisberger Diary*, July 4, 1787, 1:354. For murders, see Roberts to Harmar, 28 Aug. 1785, v. 2, Harmar Papers.

For Molunthy, see Montgomery, "Journey Through the Indian Country," Sept. 25, 1785, 272; letter of Obidiah Roberts, Sept. 25, 1786, 4:43, Harmar Papers; Message of Malontha, Shade, and Painted Pole, Apr. 11, 1785 Frontier Wars, 23U, Draper Mss. There were also Piqua (Pekowi) Shawnees represented at the treaty, e.g., White Horse, Butler Journal, Jan. 12, 1786, Craig (ed.), *The Olden Times*, 2:511. For Blacksnake, see Message to McKee, Apr. 11, 1785, Frontier Wars, 23U, Draper Mss.. The war leaders' declaration is a sign that they did not ratify the treaty either; for quotation, see Duncan to Harmar, Mar. 28, 1786, 3:22, Harmar Papers. For prohibit councils, see Report of Unnamed Informant, Sept. 14, 1786, 4:28, Harmar Papers.

For Shawnee and Cherokee attacks and hostility, see Roberts to Harmar, 21 Aug. 1785, v. 2, Harmar Papers; Finney to Clark, Mar. 24, 1786, GRC Papers, 53J25, Draper Mss. Piqua (Pickaway), Saunders to Harmar, c. July 1786, 3:96, Harmar Papers; "Denny Journal," Oct. 3, 1786, 297. These warriors appear to have been from Wakatomica; they thus appeared to act in defiance of their chiefs who had signed the Treaty of the Great Miami.

the border. Mingos, Cherokees, Shawnees, Weas, Miamis, Potawatomis, Piankashaws, Kickapoos, Mascoutens, Munsees, Sauks, Ottawas, and Chippewas struck the frontiers. These raids cut off all other intercourse between backcountry whites and Indians, and killing became, as it were, normal communication between them. Each side refined its killing, sending gruesome messages through the bodies of the slain. After the Revolution, torture less often took place in its original ritualized form than as a random and unpredictable exercise in individual cruelty. Sacrifice – that is, ritualized public murder – had become simply murder. In September 1786, a party of Cherokees returned with four captive women to the village of Wakatomica. Algonquians rarely tortured women, but the Cherokees took two of these prisoners, a mother and a daughter, scalped them alive, cut their ears and arms off, hamstrung them, and threw them into a fire. Traders witnessed these brutal killings, and news of them soon reached the Americans. The Kentuckians took revenge in Benjamin Logan's attack on the Shawnees. His men burned the village of Mequachake despite the American flag flying above it. When the village chief Molunthy met them, holding up the Treaty of the Great Miami, the Americans killed him. By one account, he "was burnt and blown up [by] gunpowder set around him in small bags." The Americans answered gruesome death with gruesome death.[46]

By 1786, raiding warriors had replaced independent village chiefs as the main internal danger to the confederation. The Americans had no incentive to negotiate with a confederation that could not prevent border raids. And border raids brought backcountry retaliation that killed Indian women, children, and old men while disrupting the confederation councils themselves.[47]

---

[46] For burning, see Deposition of George Brickell, c. Sept. 1786, 4:28, Harmar Papers; letter of Obidiah Roberts, Sept. 29, 1786, 4:43, Harmar Papers. For some of numerous murders, see letter of Park, May 17, 1786, *MPHC* 24:29–31; Duncan to Harmar, Mar. 28, 1786, 3:22, Harmar Papers; Duncan to Harmar, May 16, 1786, 3:48, Harmar Papers. Chiefs of the Delawares and Chief of Wiandott at Sandusky to Americans, June 1, 1786, 3:54, Harmar Papers; Moses Henry to Clark, June 12, 1786, GRC Papers, 53J32, Draper Mss.; Sullivan to Clark, June 23, 1786, GRC Papers, 53J36, Draper Mss.; Small to Clark, June 23, 1786, GRC Papers, 53J36, Draper Mss.; Information of Capt Teacnise, a Delaware Indian . . . July 6, 1786, 3:75, Harmar Papers; "Extract of Major North," Aug. 23, 1786, *Maryland Journal*, Oct. 31, 1786, GRC Papers, 11J121–22, Draper Mss.; letter of D. M. Christian, Mar. 22, 1786, Frontier Wars, 2U140, Draper Mss. For Illinois, see Cruzat to Miró, July 19, 1786, Kinnaird, *Spain* 2:173–74. Whites also murdered Indians but in lesser numbers, see, e.g., Butler to Harmar, Mar. 11, 1787, 5:48, Harmar Papers. For Molunthy's death, Account, n.d., Frontier Wars, 23U39, Draper Mss. For a discussion of sacrifice societies, see Tzvetain Todorov, *The Conquest of America: The Question of the Other* (New York: Harper & Row, 1987, orig. ed., 1982), 143–44.

[47] Speech of the Five Nations to the Western Indians, Nov. 1786, Frontier Wars, 23U48, Draper Mss. Of the 10 Shawnees killed in Logan's attack, 5 were chiefs and thus those most likely to mediate the conflict, Coon and Hair to Butler, Oct. 21, 1786, 4:66, Harmar Papers.

Delegates from the Six Nations, the Hurons, Miamis, Delawares, Shawnees, Ottawas, Chippewas, Potawatomis, refugee Cherokees, and the Wabash villages met at Brownstown in November and December 1786. They represented villages and factions of villages rather than tribes. For all their stress on unity, the members of the confederation never considered themselves a single people, nor were individual villages bound by decisions of council. The confederation council became in effect a village council writ large, but the confederation lacked the intimate ties that bound a village, and it lacked fathers to mediate disputes.

The sachems of the Six Nations, given their own experience with the covenant chain, emerged as the basic political theorists of the confederation. Why, they asked, was "that large tract of Country between our present habitations and the Salt water, inhabited by the Christians, and ... not still Inhabited by our Colour?" The answer was that their forefathers had "wanted [lacked] that Unanimity which we now so Strongly and Repeatedly recommend to you." The sachems did not blame their forefathers who, they said, had viewed the first Europeans with "awe and veneration." But the Indians had learned that the whites "were beings like our Selves," who had conquered only "through the unanimity they were prudent enough to preserve ... and consequently none of the divided efforts of our ancestors to oppose them had any effect. ... Let us," the sachems urged, "profit by these things and be unanimous, let us have a Just sense of our own value and if after that the Great Spirit, wills, that other Colours Should Subdue us, let it be, we then cannot reproach ourselves for Misconduct. If we make a War with any Nation, let it result from the Great Council fire, if we make peace, let it also proceed from our unanimous Councils. But whilst we remain disunited, every inconvenience attends us. The Interest of any one Nation should be Interests of us all, the welfare of the one should be the welfare of all the others." The Mohawk Joseph Brant later explained the conception of the *pays d'en haut* that underlay the confederacy's doctrine of common ownership. A hundred years ago a "Moon of Wampum was placed in this country with four roads leading to the center for the convenience of the Indians from different quarters to come and settle or hunt here. A dish with one spoon was likewise put here with the Moon of Wampum." To eat from a common dish was a standard Algonquian metaphor of peace, alliance, and friendship.[48]

Taken together, these Iroquois speeches indicate how deeply the middle ground had influenced "native" political thinking. Indians, as well as whites,

---

[48] Speech of the Five Nations to the Western Indians, Nov. 1786, Frontier Wars, 23U45–47, Draper Mss.; Kelsay, *Joseph Brant*, 410. To eat out of the same dish was a common metaphor of peace, alliance, and friendship, see e.g., Le Gras, Speech addressed to all the Indian Nations of the Wabash, Aug. 7, 1787, Harmar Papers.

had come to define themselves in terms of the Other. Just as Benjamin Franklin before the Revolution had urged unity on the colonies by citing the example of the Six Nations, so the Six Nations urged the Indians to unite by citing the example of the ex-colonials. These were both appeals on the middle ground; their meaning came from the perceived experience of others. The dichotomies employed by the Iroquois speakers ranged beyond unity and disunity to those of "colour," or race, another concept developed by Indians on the middle ground. The sachems urged the disavowal of tribalism, which accepts many divisions; they appealed for unity on the basis of race, which accepts fewer divisions. Race and "colour," which loomed so large in Indian speeches of the period, could not be original native concepts for the continent had once been inhabited by a single race.[49]

But there are even more interesting aspects of this speech and of Brant's account of the origins of the *pays d'en haut*. The world the sachems and Brant appealed to was very much a historical world; they thought of themselves as living and acting in historical time. This they admitted had not always been the case. Their forefathers had treated whites "with awe and veneration," that is, like manitous. But now Indians knew the whites were "beings like our Selves." In historical time meaning is contingent, not constant or mythic. It is the result of testing belief against action. This was the meaning the Iroquois appealed to.[50]

Both Iroquois speeches were attempts to appeal to the past to create a future in the *pays d'en haut*; that future necessarily confronted a very similar American vision. Brant's symbol of the common dish paralleled an American republican vision of a common land of plenty, open to all migrants who would live together in harmony and peace. But for the American vision to reach fruition, the Americans would have to destroy the Indians' competing vision.

On one level, the Iroquois speech at Brownstown succeeded in obtaining agreement on the basic ideal of confederation unity. The belt of the confederation bound the villagers tightly together, leaving "only a Small opening to Westward for those Nations of our own colour, who will in time become a further acquisition to our Confederacy." The villagers pledged themselves to demand the Ohio as the boundary between Indians and Americans. They agreed that all Indian nations held the land in common and

---

[49] For Franklin's quotation and an excellent evaluation of the evidence on the associated issue of actual Iroquois influence on the constitution, see Elisabeth Tooker, "The United States Constitution and the Iroquois League," *Ethnohistory* 35 (1988): 305–36.

[50] On the question of time, see Calvin Martin, "Time and the American Indian," in Calvin Martin (ed.), *The American Indian and the Problem of History* (New York: Oxford University Press, 1987), 192–220. For a critique of Martin, see Michael Harkin, "History, Narrative, and Temporality: Examples from the Northwest Coast," *Ethnohistory* 35 (1988): 120–22.

unanimous consent was necessary to cede it. All the delegates pledged cooperation in maintaining the boundary. For any action with the Americans to be legitimate, the confederacy must be "all of one mind and one voice." Because of previous cessions were "illegal and of no effect," a new treaty was necessary, and the delegates suggested that a council be held in the spring of 1787.[51]

Agreements on principle did not, however, eliminate factional divisions and rivalries; nor did they give chiefs the ability to control warriors. With the council fire established at the Huron-Petun village of Brownstown and with the Mohawk Brant the most articulate advocate of the confederation, Huron and Iroquois competition became almost inevitable. And although the council's repudiation of the cessions won warrior approval and a promise of temporary peace until further negotiations could take place, the promise was limited in scope. If negotiations did not take place by spring, the warriors would resume their raids.[52]

Brownstown was the political peak of the confederation. The events leading up to the Treaty of Fort Harmar in 1788 revealed the political weaknesses that the confederacy would never be able to overcome. For unknown reasons, the message to Congress asking for renewed negotiations did not reach that body until July 18, 1787, already well past the date of a projected spring conference. By December 1787, when Richard Butler and Arthur St. Clair called the Indians to a new conference at the falls of the Muskingum, renewed border raiding had sparked rumors of inevitable war by the spring of 1788. The chiefs struggled to gain control. Hoping both to negotiate with the Americans and to convince the warriors of their intentions to protect their lands, the confederation chiefs altered their original demand for an Ohio boundary. They now resolved to "give the American a district of land [that is, the Muskingum boundary], and if they will be satisfied therewith, there is to be everlasting peace," and if not, they would unite and fight.[53]

---

[51] For Pipe and Half King, see Half King and Capt. Pipes Answer (c. 1787), Frontier Wars, 23U58, Draper Mss.; Speech of the United Indian Nations, 28 Nov.–18 Dec. 1786, MPHC 11:467–69; Speech of the Five Nations to the Western Indians, Nov. 1786, Frontier Wars, 23U44–55, Draper Mss. This did not mean that the Indians no longer recognized any difference in village or ethnic rights to the land. Many of the chiefs who agreed to the message at Detroit had only recently ceded land to British officers and French métis traders. And at the Brownstown conference, the Hurons, at the request of the Iroquois, granted the Shawnees the right to settle at the Glaize, Speech of the Five Nations to the Western Indians, Nov. 1786, Frontier Wars, 23U48, Draper Mss.. Treaty, Five Nations, etc. to the Congress of the United States of America, Dec. 18, 1786, ASPIA 1:3–5.
[52] Speech of the Five Nations to the Western Indians, Nov. 1786, Frontier Wars, 23U49–51, Draper Mss.; Indian Council, Dec. 24, 1786, MPHC 11:470–72.
[53] For delay, see Kelsay, Joseph Brant, 406. Resolution of Congress, Carter (ed.), Territorial Papers, 1:51; Butler to the Wyandots and other Indian chiefs, n.d., Frontier Wars, 23U57–

The chiefs succeeded in neither mollifying the Americans nor restraining the warriors; instead, their own internal divisions intensified. During a long wait for Brant's arrival from Iroquoia, the council extinguished the Brownstown fire and reconvened at the Miami towns. The rumors that came out of the chaotic conference attended by 1,000–3,000 Indians indicated both bitter divisions and increasing reliance on the British, who now took a far more active role in confederation deliberations. Alexander McKee attended and supposedly made large presents, but even with the support of a British father, the chiefs proved unable to forge a consensus.[54]

In July 1788, while the chiefs wrangled, a band of Ottawas and Chippewas attacked the American soldiers erecting buildings at the council grounds at the Muskingum, killing two of them with a loss of two warriors. Wabash warriors mounted a second more successful attack on American troops that killed or wounded half of a 36-man American detachment bringing supplies to Hamtramck at Vincennes. St. Clair sent an angry message to the confederation declaring that if the council was to convene, it would be beneath the guns at Fort Harmar. On receiving it, Brant, who had at last arrived, supposedly threw the message into the fire. It was not until late fall that the Americans heard from the confederation and learned that, despite continuing raids, the Indians still intended to negotiate and peace might be possible.[55]

58, Draper Mss.; Butler to Chiefs and Warriors . . . of the Shawano, Dec. 23, 1787, Cass Papers, Clements Library. For disposition of Indians, see David Duncan to Harmar, June 17, 1787, 6:2, Harmar Papers. For confederation position, see Zeisberger to General Helper's Conference, June 15, 1787, B 229, F. 7, no. 1, Box 153, folder 10, Moravian Archives, copy in GLEHA. For chiefs and captains cannot control young men, see Zeisberger to Ettwein, Oct. 1, 1787, Box 153, Folder 10, Moravian Archives, copy in GLEHA. For council, see St. Clair to Knox, Jan. 27, 1788, Smith (ed.), *St. Clair Papers*, 2:40–41. For rumors of war, see Heart to Harmar, 5 Dec. 1787, 6:119, Harmar Papers.

54 For delays, see St. Clair to Secretary at War, July 5, 1788, Carter (ed.), *Territorial Papers*, 1:119–20; Butler to St. Clair, July 18, 1788, Smith (ed.), *St. Clair Papers*, 2:60–61; Brant to Butler, July 8, 1788, *ibid.*; Heart to Harmar, July 20, 1788, 8:26, Harmar Papers.

For confederation, see Butler to St. Clair, July 14, 1788, *St. Clair Papers*, 2:51–52; St. Clair to Knox, Oct. 26, 1788, *ibid.*, 2:92–93; Zeisberger to Ettwein, Nov. 5, 1787, Box 153, Folder 10, Moravian Archives, copy in GLEHA. For 1,000, see Spear to Harmar, Dec. 4, 1788, 9:40, Harmar Papers.

I have found no accurate account of what happened at Detroit or on the Miami, but rumors circulated widely, Hamtramck to Harmar, Apr. 15, 1788, 6:2, Harmar Papers; St. Clair to Secretary of War, Aug. 17, 1788, Smith (ed.), *St. Clair Papers*, 1:81–82; St. Clair to Knox, Oct. 26, 1788, *ibid.*, 1:92–95.

55 For attack, see McDowell to Harmar, c. July 1788, 8:25, Harmar Papers; St. Clair to Secretary of War, July 13, 1788, Smith (ed.), *St. Clair Papers*, 2:50–51. For attack on troops, see Harmar to Knox, Sept. 14, 1788, Letter Book D, Harmar Papers. For withdrawal, see Harmar to Secretary of War, July 23, 1788. Smith (ed.), *St. Clair Papers*, 1:64. For St. Clair's message, see St. Clair to Indians in Council, July 13, 1788, Carter (ed.), *Territorial Papers*, 1:127–28.

For Brant and message, see Proceedings between a part of the Six Nations Indians and a part of the Western Confederate Indians and Governor St. Clair at Fort Harmar on the

But before negotiations could begin, the confederation's fragile unity began to collapse. At Sandusky, Brant paused and exchanged messages with St. Clair. He demanded that the council be held at "the falls of Muskingum . . . the place appointed by Congress." He also demanded that the United States disavow the earlier treaties since they were "only with a few Nations and those not authorized to transact any Business which Concerned the whole." The Indians looked on themselves as the "Masters and only true proprietors" of the lands of the *pay d'en haut*. The English had no right to cede such lands. They would, however, "to avoid further trouble . . . give to the United States all the Lands lying on the East side [of the] Muskingum."[56]

In response, St. Clair sent a final message "wherein I entered fully into the pretences they have made to be discharged from the obligation of former treaties – showed them the futility of them and gave them a view of the consequences of peace and War to themselves." It was a stupid and unnecessary mistake. Brant "on receipt of the Message immediately determined to go back with his people by way of Detroit." He persuaded the Wabash villagers, the Shawnees, most of the Delawares, and some of the Hurons to follow him. The majority of the Huron-Wyandots, however, saw in Brant's refusal to proceed an opportunity. If they could wring a compromise out of the Americans, they would become the unrivaled leaders of the confederation and restore the council fire to Brownstown. Although only the Delaware Wolf phratry, delegations from the Detroit Ottawas, Potawatomis, and Chippewas, and a stray group of Sauks went on to Fort Harmar with the Hurons, the negotiations proceeded.[57]

The result of the Huron-Wyandot bid for leadership within the confederation was a disastrous but revealing treaty. In the negotiations, the Huron-Wyandots both provided a variant on the Iroquois logic of Brownstown and tried, in the usual way of the *pays d'en haut*, to use negotiations

Muskingum River to the treaty made at that place on the 9th of Jan. 1789, Frontier Wars, 23U75–175, Draper Mss., 94 (hereafter cited as Fort Harmar Proceedings).
   Willys to Harmar, 8 Aug. 1788, 8:54, Harmar Papers' Harmar to Knox, Oct. 26, 1788, Letter Book D, Harmar Papers; St. Clair to Knox, Sept. 14, 1788, Smith (ed.), *St. Clair Papers*, 2:88.
[56] Address of the Six Nations and Western Confederacy to Governor St. Clair, 19 Nov. 1788, Frontier Wars, 23U66–74, Draper Mss..
[57] Address of the Six Nations and Western Confederacy to Governor St. Clair, Nov. 19, 1788, and Answer of Brant, Nov. 30, 1788, Frontier Wars, 23U66–74, Draper Mss.; St. Clair to the Secretary at War, Carter (ed.), *Territorial Papers* 1:164–65. The Indians at the Miami had supposedly agreed to go no farther than the falls of the Muskingum, Speer to Harmar, Dec. 4, 1788, 9:40, Harmar Papers. For division of Delawares, see Fort Harmar Proceedings 82, 111. For turning back of delegations, see *ibid.*, 93. For those in attendance – Wyandots, Delawares, Ottawas, Chippewas, Munsees, Potawatomis, and Sauks – see St. Clair to Knox, Dec. 13, 1788, Smith (ed.), *St. Clair Papers*, 2:106–7. Harmar to Knox, Jan. 13, 1789, Letter Book E, Harmar Papers.

with outsiders to settle village rivalries. The Huron-Wyandot speakers, Dyentente and T'Sindatton, devoted much of their time at the conference to discrediting Iroquois claims of ascendancy and promoting Huron claims. In a long speech that embodied the double nature of these negotiations, T'Sindatton, the leading chief at Brownstown, employed the full range of the logics of the middle ground to assert Huron ascendancy in the confederation and to deflect American demands for land. He spoke of dreams; he appealed to a common God; he cited earlier treaties. He appealed to Indian rights; he asked for American pity on "a poor and helpless people." In the end, he proposed that the Americans accept the confederation suggestion proposal of the Muskingum boundary. St. Clair pointed out that this offer was the same as Brant's, which he had already declined.[58]

With St. Clair's refusal to accept their proposal, the Huron-Petuns' strategy collapsed. They had come in the hope of gaining the confederation's ends and thus its leadership, but the treaty the Americans and the delegates of the western confederates signed at Fort Harmar validated the earlier cessions. The Americans understandably believed that they had broken the confederation and upheld the old treaties. But there were two inauspicious elements. Because of an American mistake, St. Clair had no white wampum – the color of peace – to make treaty belts. He had only black wampum. Thus he could not give belts to confirm or validate the treaty – an omission in the protocol of the middle ground equivalent to the failure of one party to sign the treaty. On the Algonquian side, T'Sindatton, the most creative of the Indian negotiators trying to reach a new accommodation on the middle ground, did not sign the treaty. The failure of the Brownstown chief to put his mark on the treaty was an ominous indication of how little it had achieved. Except for the Delaware chiefs of the Wolf phratry, Dyentente, and some other Huron-Wyandot chiefs, most of those who signed the treaty were making their first appearance in negotiations with Europeans. They were neither established chiefs nor war leaders. Their signatures meant little. The Hurons and Wyandots who signed had, perhaps, done so for a reason that the Americans considered relatively insignificant. In a memorandum to the treaty, the United States acknowledged the superior right of the Hurons and the Wyandots to the lands granted the Shawnees. Major Ebenezer Denny, observing the proceedings, regarded the whole episode as a farce.[59]

---

[58] Fort Harmar Proceedings, 119–21; Great Spirit, *ibid.*, 83, 89, 92, 105, 108, 125–26, cession 126.

[59] Fort Harmar Proceedings, 143, 152. See also Treaty of Fort Harmar, Carter (ed.), *Territorial Papers* 1:174–79 – the signatures have been compared to a list compiled of all those participating in negotiations since the outbreak of the Revolution. The Wyandots had the largest number of signatories, but by May, Abraham Coon was writing on behalf of the

The real consequence of the treaty was to discredit both the Hurons and the Iroquois. Their shared failure delivered the initiative to the warriors of the western villages unrepresented at Fort Harmar. The confederation's council fire now burned amid the villages grouped around Kekionga (or Miami Town), where the great council had met the previous summer and fall. The Miamis and Shawnees who lived in the region emerged as the guiding force of the confederation. In 1790, when Antoine Gamelin set out as an American emissary to try to bring the Wabash and Miami Indians to a treaty conference at Vincennes, the Piankashaws, Weas, and Kickapoos along the Wabash told him they could not act without "the consent of our elder brethern the Miamis." And when Gamelin reached Kekionga, the council there refused to act until it had notified all neighbors and the "Lake nations," as well as the British at Detroit.[60]

Iroquois influence declined as precipitously as that of the Huron-Petuns. Brant, before his departure east, had delegated the Shawnees near Kekionga to act for him. The Shawnees had sent out war belts, one of which the Wyandot chief Teynadat'on'tic, who had signed the treaty at Fort Harmar, managed to stop, but the others proceeded. By late summer of 1789, the Shawnees felt they had a consensus for united resistance. In September, a delegation of war leaders proceeded to Buffalo Creek to explain their actions to the Iroquois and to request aid. The failure of either Brant or his Seneca

nonsignatory Wyandots warning the Americans not to try to possess the land, Spear to Harmar, May 5, 1789, Harmar Papers 10:32. See also St. Clair to President, May 2, 1789, Smith (ed.), *St. Clair Papers* 2:112; Fort Harmar Proceedings, 129–33; Indian Speech to Sir John Johnson, Aug. 16, 1790, *MPHC* 20:308. The Miami chief Petit Gris (or Le Gris) also claimed that few legitimate chiefs had signed the treaty, Gamelin Journal, Apr. 29, 1790, Smith (ed.), *St. Clair Papers*, 2:159. For farce, see "Denny Journal," Jan. 11, 1789, 334. For other documents relevant to the treaty see compilation Document number 1, The Six Nations, The Wyandots, and Others communicated to the Senate, May 25, 1789, *ASPIA* 1:5–12.

The Americans were not without potential allies, Hamtramck to Harmar, Oct. 13, 1788, Thornbrough (ed.), *Outpost*, 122; Hamtramck to St. Clair, Apr. 19, 1790, and St. Clair to the Secretary of War, May 1, 1790, both in Smith (ed.), *St. Clair Papers* 2:135–37.

For raids, see Wyllys to Harmar, Apr. 15, 1789, 10:15, Harmar Papers. It appears that besides all the Wabash villages, the Shawnees, the Miamis, the Cherokees north of the Ohio, some of the Wyandots, and many Chippewas were ready for war in May 1789. But by fall, reports reached the Americans that the Chippewas were for peace, McDowell to Harmar, Nov. 1, 1789, 11:79, Harmar Papers; Spear to Harmar, May 31, 1789, 10:55; Harmar Papers. The Senecas and Munsees, while seeking peace, could not stop horse raids by their young men, Heart to Harmar, June 1, 1789, 1:57, Harmar Papers.

For U.S. policy, see Harmar to Asheton, Nov. 13, 1789, Letter Book F, Harmar Papers; Secretary of War to St. Clair, Dec. 19, 1789, Carter (ed.), *Territorial Papers*, 1:224–26. For summary, see Horsman, *Expansion and American Indian Policy*, 84–98.

60 For Miamis, see Gamelin Journal, Apr. 1790, Smith (ed.), *St. Clair Papers* 2:157–59; St. Clair considered the Wabash deferral to the Miamis "tantamount to a declaration that they will continue their hostilities," St. Clair to President, May 1, 1790, Carter (ed.), *Territorial Papers*, 2:245. Proceedings of a Council Held at Buffalo Creek, Frontier Wars, 23U172, Draper Mss. Tayendeght = Tyeandat'on'tic.

rivals to promise such aid underlined the demise of the Iroquois as a force in the West.[61]

The Treaty of Fort Harmar did not end the confederation. It merely increased the scale of raiding by angry warriors and launched the confederacy into a second phase, in which leadership passed to the Shawnee, Miami, and Delaware villages along the Maumee. The British would take a much larger role in this second phase until, by the time of Anthony Wayne's confrontation, the confederation had in some ways become indistinguishable from a British alliance.[62]

IV

If Vincennes was a symbol of the failure of the Americans to enter the middle ground, then Kekionga, which became the seat of the confederacy, was a monument to the middle ground's persistence among the British and the French. Despite the tendency of speakers within the confederation councils to stress color and the need to resist the whites, the confederation did not become racially separatist. The exclusion of whites was not necessarily a corollary of unity among Indians, who continued to adopt whites and to marry them. Indians drank with whites, fought with and alongside them, ate with them, had sexual relations with them, and exchanged goods with them. Whites lived intimately among Algonquians as they had lived intimately among Indians in the *pays d'en haut* for more than a century.

The movement of the confederation's council fire to Kekionga was not a removal to a remote "Indian" location. Kekionga sat at a juncture where the Saint Marys and Saint Joseph rivers commanded the Maumee-Wabash portage. Functioning as a commercial outpost of Detroit's, it was the center of the fur trade in the Ohio Valley and only slightly less a strategic commercial and military site than Detroit or Michilimackinac. There were fewer whites at Kekionga than at Detroit, where for some miles before reaching the town from the south, houses formed an almost continuous village along the Detroit River. But the upper Miami, as much as Detroit or Vincennes, was part of a long-standing multiracial, multiethnic world. French and English traders lived in Kekionga, and by 1790 there were approximately six Shawnee, Delaware, and Miami villages nearby. And just to the northwest lay the four largely Potawatomi villages around Saint Joseph. Politically, the confederation remained distinct from the old British alliance,

[61] Proceedings of a Council Held at Buffalo Creek, Frontier Wars, 23U172, Draper Mss.
[62] For a compilation of Indian raiding, see Document no. 14, Northwestern Indians, communicated to Congress . . . 9th of Dec., 1790, *ASPIA* 1:84–104. See also The Causes of the existing Hostilities, Jan. 26, 1792, Carter (ed.), *Territorial Papers*, 2:359–66.

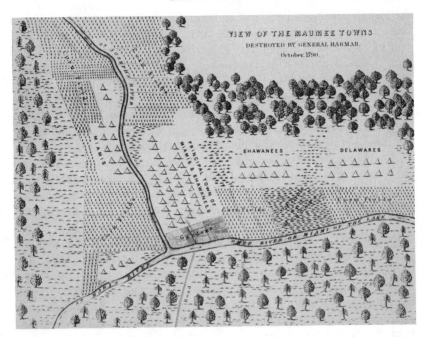

VIEW OF THE MAUMEE TOWNS DESTROYED BY GENERAL HARMAR. October 1790.

This map of the towns on the Maumee shows the extensive cornfields surrounding the villages. (Journal of Major E. Denny)

but the daily life of Kekionga revealed the extent to which the confederation itself drew sustenance from the middle ground and active intercourse with whites.[63]

In 1789, after the confederation's first attempt to negotiate with the Americans collapsed, Henry Hay set out to winter at Kekionga. He came with ready access to the diverse community of the place. He was the son of Jehu Hay, the deputy Indian agent at Detroit during the Revolution who, after being captured at Vincennes by George Rogers Clark, had languished for years in a Virginia prison. After his release, the elder Hay had become lieutenant governor of Detroit in 1784, but he had died the next year. His son's given name was Pierre, but self-consciously English, Henry had dropped the French name for his English middle name. He was, nonetheless, French on his mother's side, and his uncles were the Reaume brothers of Detroit. As a child, Hay had been intimate with the family of Petit Gris,

[63] Thomas Hughes, *A Journal by Thos. Hughes for his Amusement & Designed only for his Perusal by the time he attains the Age of 50 if he lives so long (1778–89)* (Port Washington, N.Y.: Kennikat Press, 1970), 155. For center of fur trade, see Merchants Trading at Detroit to Johnson, Aug. 10, 1791, *MPHC* 24:305–6.

the highest-ranking Miami chief and the village chief at Kekionga. Hay had been a "very great friend" of Le Gris's daughter, now dead. Le Gris reintroduced Hay to his son, Hay's "brother and old play fellow as he called him." Unlike Detroit or Vincennes where distinct Indian and French villages existed side by side, the French, English, and Miami lived together in Kekionga. Nor were the lines of authority easily disentangled in this society. When Little Turtle, Le Gris's brother-in-law and a war leader, brought a returning war party to Kekionga, Le Gris, as the civil chief of the village, "ordered a Pirogue (which happened to be just arrived from the forks of the river with wood) to be unloaded by some of the french lads who stood on the bank, and sent one of them over with it." He then billeted the warriors among the French, taking care "to trouble the families as little as possible." "This he ordered in a very polite manner, but quite like a general or a commandent."[64]

In Kekionga, Europeans obeyed a Miami chief, but across the river was Pacane's village where Miamis acknowledged a French *métis* chief. Jean Baptiste Richardville (a trader whose father was French and whose mother was Pacane's sister) acted as chief in the place of his uncle, Pacane, who had moved to the Wabash. Of all the inhabitants of the area, Richardville most clearly bridged the two worlds. His father was in Montreal, but Richardville's mother, Marie Louisas, was a "very clever" woman who had become a trader herself. She acted as speaker for her son, who was too shy to speak in council. With *métis* chiefs, Miami women acting like European traders, and warriors billeted like soldiers upon French villagers, this was a place where clearly separate groups created a common social and political world.[65]

The contours of this social world appear in Hay's visits, his meals, and the casual remarks about people that he recorded in his journal. This was a world where perhaps because so much did overlap, people preserved a strict accounting of origins, of who was who and who they had been before. Hay himself was quite alert to distinctions of race and even class. Hay's wandering eye for French women skipped over the daughter of the Paillets who was "very brown," and he dismissed the daughter of Rivard as "Un peu à la Paysan." But Paillet's daugher was brown, after all, precisely because intermarriage occurred. In other contexts, Hay readily socialized regardless of race. When he took a cariole ride to visit James Girty at his house two miles from Kekionga, he went with Jean Baptiste Richardville, the *métis* chief. And while at James Girty's, George Girty arrived with his "wife & two sisters in law (Indians)."[66]

[64] M. M. Quaife, "Henry Hay's Journal from Detroit to the Mississippi River," State Historical Society of Wisconsin, *Proceedings*, 62:214, 221–222.

[65] *Ibid.*, 220–21, 230. Either the supposedly patrilineal Miamis were matrilineal or Pacane was childless, Richardville would not otherwise have succeeded him, *HBNI* 15:685.

[66] Quaife (ed.), "Hay's Journal," 219, 221–22, 244.

This common world had boundaries. Not all was permissible. For a white "to go native" completely, for example, was a disgrace. Hay dismissed a man named Montroille as "a fellow who has abandoned himself totally & lives amongst the Indians, those kind of people are of the worst, they are very pernicious to the Trade who fill the Indians Heads with very bad notions & think nothing of Robbin the Traders Property ... such Rascalls ought to be ... totally excommunicated from the Indian country." Montroille had crossed over an unseen line.[67]

Where such boundaries started – where social worlds separated and merged – was a matter decided in the daily course of social action. What people did and did not do, whom they saw and whom they ignored, whom they praised and whom they censured revealed the boundaries. Hay found little profit at Kekionga where "almost every individual (except the engagés) is an Indian trader, everyone tries to get what he can by fowle play or otherwise" in a "Rascally Scrambling Trade," but he still enjoyed his stay immensely. Partially this was from his participation in a largely French and English round of drinking, dinners, dances, and parties. The Europeans drank more steadily and just as prodigiously as the Indians, and Hay ate well – "roasted Loine of Veal – a kind of wilde salled which they have here all winter ... some very [good] cocombers pickels cheese, &c. ... all served up in the french Stile."[68]

But only part of this social life was European; Indians, too, entered this world. Hay's journal survives only for the winter when the bulk of the Indians were absent in hunting camps, thus limiting their participation in the daily round of Kekionga. But when present in the village, they entered common society, although only at certain points and in a certain manner. Little Turtle and Le Gris, for example, commonly ate with Hay and George Ironside, but they did not take dinner. They came in the evening when "they drank tea, also maderia," or, more commonly, they breakfasted with the whites. Le Gris and his son, Hay's "brother," made gifts of venison and turkey to Hay. Le Gris expected occasional bottles of rum in return. On New Year's, according to "a common custom," the young warriors and their families flocked back to Kekionga "to Salute, and of course expect some little matter." The startled Hay found on New Year's Day that women had come into his house in such numbers that by three o'clock in the morning the house was full and he could not sleep. The tumult having awakened Hay, one woman came up to his bed to shake hands with him. As the winter wore on, more Indians entered the daily round of Hay's social activities. The Snake, a leading Shawnee chief, stayed three days with Hay, and on the

---

[67] Ibid., 257.

[68] Ibid., 224, 226–227. This duplicated Detroit on a smaller scale, where, Thomas Hughes said, there was "a ball once a week, which with carrioling and parties of all kinds made time go away faster than we had imagined," Hughes, Journal, 159.

return of Marie Louisas, Hay visited her, noting "she has been a handsome woman." Meanwhile, Marie Louisas's son, Richardville, joined Hay's Most Light Honorable Society of Monks. The Monks celebrated Mardi Gras at Richardville's house.[69]

The politics of the place were as mixed as the social life. In December what later turned out to be a false alarm was raised – news that the Weas had seized Antoine Lasselle, a Kekionga trader then visiting the village at Petit Piconne (or Tippecanoe). The Weas, supposedly, had accused Lasselle of betraying a Wea war party to the Americans. The mixed community at Kekionga acted to free him. A messenger from Marie Louisas brought the alarm, and Petit Gris dispatched three warriors to obtain his release. Petit Gris lamented that Lasselle had not asked his aid earlier "for . . . I should have sent one of [our] Chiefs with him, or given him a belt, as a Guard and which would have prevented any thing of this kind happening." M. Dufresne provided Le Gris with the gifts necessary to obtain Lasselle's release. Hay, while sorry for Lasselle, thought he had brought the trouble upon himself.[70]

As it turned out the quite confused Lasselle, who returned to Kekionga in early January 1790, had brought nothing on himself. It appeared that a trader name Fouché had betrayed a Wea party. Indians who had a grievance against Lasselle had blamed him instead. They had used Le Gris's name in sending out messages by one La Lache, a Wea *métis*, demanding vengeance against Lasselle.[71]

The confrontations with the Americans that nearly claimed Lasselle were almost constant during the winter of 1789–90, and they threw into stark relief the junctures of the various political and social relations in the area. Indians, including those from Kekionga, raided along the Ohio, killing some of their prisoners, adopting others, and ransoming still others to British traders. Within a week of Hay's arrival, he had met one prisoner, an Irishman, whom the Indians had freed and promised to take back to the Ohio in the spring. He had also seen the dried heart of another American, murdered after his capture by a warrior who had recently lost some of his own relatives. The warrior had incorporated the victim's heart and scalp into his war bundle.[72]

---

[69] "Hay's Journal," 228–229, 232, 235, 239–40, 242. For The Snake (or Blacksnake) and Marie Louisas, see *ibid.*, 246. For Richardville, see *ibid.*, 246, 250.

[70] Quaife (ed.), "Hay's Journal," 230–32; for false alarm, see *ibid.*, 233. For conspiracy, see *ibid.*, 23–39.

[71] *Ibid.*, 236–39.

[72] For accounts of attacks along the Ohio and the fates of some victims, see Wiley Sword, *President Washington's Indian War: The Struggle for the Old Northwest, 1790–95* (Norman: University of Oklahoma Press, 1985), 69–78. For Hay, see "Hay's Journal," 219–20, 222.

In 1789, the fighting remained on both sides very much a village war of revenge and plunder. Murder and torture were, as Hay wrote, the Indians' "way of retaliating" for their own losses, and the losses for which Indians retaliated sometimes included the loss of whites. In the fall of 1789, a Miami war party had struck the Americans, and in their pursuit the Americans had stumbled across a hunting camp of Shawnees from Mississinewa. They attacked and killed several women and children and "one Joseph Sovereigns who had been a prisoner since his infancy." In revenge for the death of an adopted white, Shawnee warriors attacked an American hunting party along the Ohio in "much about the same place w[h]ere their own people were killed." They took a young man named McMullen prisoner who was lately from Virginia and thus previously uninvolved in the border fighting. The Mississinewas gave McMullen to the Chillicothe Shawnees, and they brought him in painted black, usually a sign that a prisoner was condemned to death by torture. He held in his hands "a Shishequia which he kept ringing in his hand (its made of deer's hoofs) singing out lowde the words Oh Kentuck." McMullen was, however, a lucky man, for Blackbird (or Nonasekow) the civil chief of the Chillicothes, decided to adopt him into his own family. The French and British traders explained to the thoroughly confused and frightened McMullen that he was safe "and very lucky in being in the hand that he was." The British and French traders acted as cultural interpreters for an American about to become a Shawnee to replace another American Shawnee killed by Americans. This was not a simple world, nor were racial boundaries firm.[73]

It is necessary to keep both the complexity of this world and its strong village orientation in mind when considering the years of direct conflict with the Americans. Little Turtle became the most skillful confederation war leader. He helped defeat General Harmar in 1790 and Governor St. Clair in 1791. The Little Turtle who breakfasted with Hay did not become a ferocious nativist when he led the warriors against the Americans. The traders and their families with whom Hay had danced, sung, eaten, and drunk did not suddenly become uncomplicated agents of the British Empire because the Americans imagined them to be so.

When, in 1790, General Harmar finally mobilized the resources of the American state and marched against Kekionga, he was marching against the middle ground in both a figurative and literal sense: literally because Kekionga was the site of a mixed community, figuratively because by 1790 the confederation itself had ceased to be a purely Indian political formation. It had developed a tangled set of relations with British subjects and representatives of the British empire.

---

[73] *Ibid.*, 248–49.

V

When the United States decided to settle by force what it could not achieve by negotiation, it helped bestow on the British an influence within the Indian confederation that had previously been only imagined. Algonquian military success against the Americans exceeded everyone's expectation. The defeat of General Harmar in 1790 and the slaughter of St. Clair's army in 1791 shocked and dismayed both the backcountry settlements and the Congress. Given the numbers engaged, the defeat of St. Clair was one of the most severe American forces would ever experience. The Americans abandoned their equipment and their wounded and fled the field. The warriors slaughtered many of their prisoners, torturing some. They stuffed the mouths of the dead with soil – satisfying in death their lust for Indian land. Roughly two-thirds of St. Clair's more than fourteen hundred men were casualties – six hundred of them killed. Twenty-one Indians were killed. Major Ebenezer Denny, having faced the Indians twice, thought they were "perhaps superior to an equal number of the best men that could be taken against them."[74]

These victories, however, came at the price of dependence on the British. When the confederation council mustered its warriors at Auglaize to meet St. Clair, it could not feed them. In June 1791 approximately two thousand warriors reached the upper Maumee. They found little food but abundant liquor, for the British had chosen this inopportune time to deregulate the trade. The lack of food forced five hundred Sauk and Fox warriors to depart for home after only four days. Warriors from other villages arrived to replace them, but they, too, lacked supplies. By the time St. Clair marched, the confederation could muster only a little over a thousand warriors. The Wabash warriors, chastened by Kentucky attacks on their villages, remained at home.[75]

[74] For accounts of fighting, see Richard Kohn, *Eagle and Sword: the Federalists and the Creation of the Military Establishment in America, 1783–1802* (New York: Free Press, 1975), 91–128; Sword, *President Washington's Indian War*, 107–16; Paul A. Hutton, "William Wells: Frontier Scout and Indian Agent," *Indiana Magazine of History*, 74 (Sept. 1978): 187–89.

For numbers versus St. Clair, see Girty to Mckee, Oct. 28, 1791, *MPHC* 24:329–30. For no Wabash, see McKee to Johnson, Nov. 1, 1791, *MPHC* 24:330–31. There were also only about a dozen Six Nations warriors among them, McKee to Johnson, Dec. 5, 1791, *MPHC* 24:336–37.

For St. Clair's supply problems, lack of discipline, see St. Clair to Hodgdon, Oct. 21, 1791, St. Clair to Knox, Nov. 1, 1791, Diary of Denny, Sept.–Nov., all in Smith (ed.), *St. Clair Papers*, 2:248–62; for Denny quotations, see 262.

[75] For restrict war parties, see Answer of Missass, July 3, 1791, Claus Papers C1478, M. 6. 19, F1, v. 4, PAC. For estimate, see Smith to Clarke, June 5, 1791, *MPHC* 24:248. For food, see Journal, Detroit, June 8, 1791, *MPHC* 24:251; Brant to Johnson, June 23, 1791, *MPHC* 24:270. For Auglaize, see Reginald Horsman, *Matthew Elliott, British Indian Agent* (Detroit:

The defeats of St. Clair and Harmar demonstrated how formidable Algonquian warriors were in battle, but they also demonstrated the warriors' weakness in a long campaign. The Indians lacked the logistical capability to keep large numbers of men in the field, and they lacked the artillery necessary to storm fortifications. And even if they had possessed such capabilities, warriors, like militia, sought to fight and then return home. After a battle, decisive or not, Indian forces melted away. Time was on the Americans' side. They did not have to win battles; they only had to avoid disastrous defeats.

The only possible way for the Algonquians to compensate for these weaknesses was with British aid. Necessity and the bonds of common life made the gradual increase of British influence within the confederation a natural development. British agents at Detroit – Alexander McKee, Matthew Elliott, and the Girtys – marginal to the early councils of the confederation, became stronger advocates of Algonquian unity than many Algonquians. There was nothing odd about this. McKee's mother was probably an adopted white Shawnee captive, and his wife was Shawnee. Elliott and Girty, too, were married or had once been married to Shawnee wives. All of them had Shawnee children, and McKee's son appears to have fought for the confederation. All of them had lived among the Indians for years.

The reabsorption of the confederation into the British alliance was not, however, complete until 1794. When Elliott overstepped his bounds and asked the Delaware chiefs the business of the Stockbridge Indian delegation to the western council led by Hendrick Aupaumut in 1793, the Delaware Big Cat replied:

> Did you ever see me at Detroit or Niagara, in your councils, and there to ask you where such and such white man come from or what is their Business: Can you watch, and look all around the earth to see who come to us? or is what their Business? Do you not know that we are upon our own Business?[76]

Wayne State University Press, 1964), 69; Mckee to Johnson, Jan. 28, 1792, *MPHC* 24:366. For an excellent account of the Auglaize community, see Helen Hornbeck Tanner, "The Glaize in 1792: A Composite Indian Community," *Ethnohistory* 25 (Winter 1978): 15–40.

[76] Reginald Horsman's unusually nuanced work provides the standard account; see "The British Indian Department and the Abortive Treaty of Lower Sandusky, 1793," *Ohio Historical Quarterly* 70 (July 1961): 189–213; Reginald Horsman, "The British Indian Department and the Resistance to General Anthony Wayne, 1793–95," *Mississippi Valley Historical Review* 49 (Sept. 1962): 269–90; Horsman, *Matthew Elliott*, passim. At the important council in the fall of 1792 at the Glaize apparently only Simon Girty attended, Kelsay, *Joseph Brant*, 481. For McKee's ancestry, see *ibid.*, 484, and chap. 8. Aupaumut said Mckee was half Shawnee, *A Narrative of an Embassy to the Western Indians from Original Manuscript of Hendrick Aupaumut*, Memoirs of Historical Society of Pennsylvania 2 (1827), 105; for Big Cat, see *ibid.*, 103. For McKee's son, see *ibid.*, 125.

In Big Cat's rebuke of Elliott, however, Big Cat hardly spoke as an Indian nationalist, and Elliott was an ambiguous agent of empire. Life in the backcountry as traders and kinship ties with the Indians gave British agents only a loose loyalty to the distant empire. As had happened so often in the French empire, the politics of villages – Indian and white – became the tail wagging the imperial dog. As Reginald Horsman has observed: "Generalizations concerning 'the policy of the British government' or the 'policy of the British authorities in Canada' mean little unless it is realized that at the last instance this policy depended upon men who had lived among the Indians for many years, had taken their wives from among them, and had developed great sympathy of the Indian point of view." In the negotiations among the Americans, the English, and the Indians, McKee and the others acted as British chiefs. They were at once mediators and men advancing their own positions and their own interests.[77]

The meaning of the tangled negotiations between the Americans and the confederation that followed the defeat of St. Clair and the simultaneous rise of British influence becomes clear only by stripping away the seemingly substantive matters under discussion and looking at how each side constructed images of the other. Ostensibly the issues dividing the Americans and the Algonquians were the terms of peace: boundaries, payments for lands, and the legal status of the confederation and the individual villages. But negotiations over these issues never took place in any conventional diplomatic forum. Instead of being specific negotiations of agreed-upon differences, the diplomatic conversation was a struggle over images and it took place within rather than between groups. This was a diplomacy of mirrors, and image making became the real basis of negotiations. Once established, the image of the enemy as the Other demanded certain responses regardless of what the Other said or what concessions the Other offered. What the confederation was to do about the Americans, for example, ultimately depended on who the Americans were – what their true nature was – just as what the Americans would do about the Indians and the British depended on who they were. Interpreting the actions of the Other, deciding what those actions meant was the critical activity on both sides. Images of the Other were not set in stone; they had to be constantly tested against the world of action and alternate images. This process was not new, but what complicated it immensely was that between the Americans and the Indians it had ceased to be face-to-face. The common world yielded to a frontier over which people crossed only to shed blood. When warriors murdered two of the American envoys, Major Alexander Trueman and Colonel John Hardin,

---

[77] For quotation, see Horsman, "The British Indian Department and the Resistance to General Anthony Wayne," 270.

and most of their parties before they reached Auglaize, the meaning of the killings rather than the peace proposals the emissaries brought became the diplomatic issue.[78]

This struggle over image occurred on both sides of the battle lines. In the early 1790s, Congress and the nation were badly divided over a thus far expensive and futile war. "Indian war," as Henry Knox wrote, "was destructive to the interests of humanity and an event from which neither dignity or profit can be reaped." According to Secretary of State Thomas Jefferson, the war's unpopularity forced the government to attempt negotiations if only "to prove to all our citizens that peace was unattainable on terms which any one of them would admit."[79]

Attempts to negotiate peace involved little change in the substantive boundary issues. They did involve, however, a change in America's image. Both among many of its own citizens and among Europeans, the new republic seemed a greedy aggressor. To counter this image, the United States sacrificed what had been the cornerstone of its Indian policy. Officials conceded that the United States had not conquered the Indians during the Revolution and did not have title to their lands by right of conquest, and that England had no right to, and had not ceded, the Indians' land. The land was the Algonquians to sell to the United States or to keep as they chose.

Assumption by the Americans of this new stance as seekers of peace and reconciliation rather than as conquerors was an adroit tactical move. The lands ceded in the existing treaties threatened only the Shawnees, refugee Cherokees, Delawares, Wyandots, Mingos, and various fragments of more recent immigrants from the East such as the Munsees. As the American negotiator Rufus Putnam explained, the Indian confederation gained much greater strength by using American claims of conquest and demands for new cessions to persuade other Indians that the Americans "are after your lands they mean to take them from you and to drive you out of the country . . . they will never rest until they got the whole." By renouncing their claims to conquest and abstaining from immediate requests for more land, American negotiators hoped to split the confederacy. Obtaining the lands north of the Ohio still remained the ultimate goal of American policy. If the Indians made peace, federal officials believed, cessions would come as a matter of course, as American settlers killed game and encroached on Indian lands. If the Indians refused peace, then the negotiations would at

---

[78] For murder of American emissaries by Indians, see An Account of the Fate of Col. Hardin, Major Trueman, and several other persons . . . Frontier Wars, 5U28, Draper Mss.

[79] Horsman, *Expansion and American Indian Policy*, 90–96. For Jefferson quotation, see Horsman, "The British Indian Department and the Abortive Treaty of Lower Sandusky," 195. For treaty instructions, see Instructions to Rufus Putnam, May 22, 1792, in Buell (ed.), *Memoirs of Rufus Putnam*, 258–67. For Knox quotation, see *ibid.*, 267.

least gain time for Anthony Wayne, who was raising and training a new army, and would perhaps split the confederacy, making military victory easier.

While remaking their own image, the Americans remained divided over their image of the Indians. To make peace, Americans had to believe that the conduct of the Indians resulted from, in the words of Henry Knox, "more the misrepresentation of bad people, than any hardened malignity of the human heart." To press the war, on the other hand, savagery had to be deep-seated. The Indians had to be the ultimate Other – the bloodthirsty *sauvage*. They could not be the alternate image some Americans and Europeans offered – a people driven to war to defend a homeland threatened by invaders. If they were savages, their bloodthirstiness was explained, but not necessarily their targeting of the Americans. For this the British as Other – as scalp buyers profiting from the blood of innocents – became necessary. As Wayne, eager to fight the Indians, put it, they were a "victorious, haughty and insidious enemy, – stimulated by British emissaries to a continuance of war," whose terms for peace were "disgraceful to the American Character."[80]

For the Indians themselves, the struggle over image becomes most apparent in the journal kept by Hendrick Aupaumut at the Glaize, the villages on the Auglaize, in 1792. The sometimes shrewd, sometimes bewildered Aupaumut was a Stockbridge Indian, one of a group of Connecticut Mohicans, Hudson River Indians, and Long Island Indians who had sought refuge from white encroachments among the Oneidas. He was Christian and literate, and he acted as an American emissary in the western councils, for, like other Stockbridges, he believed that farming, Christianity, and the adoption of American gender roles would allow the Indians to incorporate themselves peacefully into American society. Aupaumut would for the next twenty years urge such accommodation, but he never secured it for the Stockbridges, who had to move repeatedly to avoid conflict with whites and other Indians.[81]

Aupaumut recorded and participated in the Algonquian debate over image while he delivered an American message urging a negotiated peace. The message itself contained the contending images of Americans, for it distinguished between the United States, which in metonymic imagery became the fifteen fires or George Washington, and the Big Knives, which now included most, but not all, frontier whites. Aupaumut persuaded Pipe, (who had resettled along the Maumee) Big Cat, and even for a while Buckongahelas (now the most influential Delaware leader) to become

---

[80] Instructions to Rufus Putnam from Henry Knox, May 22, 1792, Buell (ed.), *Memoirs of Rufus Putnam*, 261, 267. For Wayne quotation, see Wayne to Wilkinson, Aug. 5, 1792, *ibid.*, 331.
[81] For Stockbridges, see *HBNI*, 15:181, 209–11.

proponents of the image of the Americans as George Washington. The Shawnees, the Miamis, and some of the Hurons and Wyandots held out the counterimage of the Americans as Big Knives. The course of future actions and negotiations depended on whether the Indians were dealing with Big Knives whose forts were "blood" or George Washington and his "good message." Neither Aupaumut nor his rivals sought to persuade each other of the real American identity as much as they wanted to convince the "back nations" – the Ottawas, Chippewas, Potawatomis, Sauks, Fox, and Wabash villagers who provided the bulk of the confederation's potential strength.[82]

Aupaumut, who at the end of the narrative summarized his own and his opponents' arguments, clearly recognized that the central issue was who the Americans were. The Americans were, the Shawnees argued, inevitably "deceitful in their dealings with us, the Indians." Their promises of benevolence were their most potent weapons. They missionized Indians "to gain their attention, and then they would [have] killed them, and have killed of such 96 in one day at Cosuhkeck, few years ago." They had promised the Shawnee chief Molunthy that their flag would always protect him, but when he hoisted his flag the "Big knifes did not regard it, but killed the Chief and numbers of his friends." The Big Knives "know how to speak good, but would not do good towards the Indians." What Big Knives said could not and did not matter.[83]

Aupaumut countered by distinguishing the Big Knives from the United Sachems or George Washington. If all Americans were Big Knives, he and his people "would have been along ago anihilated," but the Americans sought to lift them up that "we may stand up and walk ourselves, because we the Indians, hitherto have lay flat as it were on the ground, by which we could not see great way." The United Sachems, chosen from all Americans, "must be very honest and wise, and they will do Justice to all people." The Big Knives were "thieves and robbers and murderers" who had run away to escape the laws. They were no different from the Cherokee renegades among the Shawnees. The expansion of the United States was subduing the Big Knives. The "law now binds them." Although Joseph Brant, like Aupaumut, sought peace, he attempted to buttress his own fading credibility at Aupaumut's expense. Brant feared that his own earlier visit to Philadelphia at the invitation of the Americans might be taken as a betrayal of the confederation, and he sought to establish his own credibility by sending word to the council that neither Washington nor Aupaumut were to be trusted. There were rivalries even among the accommodationists. Aupaumut had to

---

[82] Aupaumut, *Narrative*, 92–110, 121, 124. For Buckongahelas, see Account of the fate of Col. Harden, Major Trueman, etc., Frontier Wars, 5U28, Draper Mss.
[83] Aupaumut, *Narrative*, 122–31, quotations, 126–27.

remind the Algonquians that Brant was a Mohawk, and the "Mauquas have deceived you repeatly."[84]

The Shawnees and Miamis won the argument. The warriors justified the murders of Trueman and Hardin by using the Big Knife argument: They had already been deceived by the Americans and had no intention of being deceived again. Having killed the peace emissaries and continuing to raid themselves, the warriors then denounced the actions of American soldiers during the summer and fall of 1792 as the actions of Big Knives. The Americans talked peace, but their preparations were for war. The Big Knives killed some Delawares even as Aupaumut praised the Americans' peaceful intent. The Delaware chiefs Big Cat and Captain Pipe could not carry the council and make peace, but they sent a message to Washington telling him that if he demonstrated that he could "govern the hostile Big knifes" by withdrawing them from "the forts which stands on our land," then they could secure peace for the "war party will be speechless."[85]

The efforts at peace in 1792 yielded only Rufus Putnam's treaty at Vincennes with the remaining Wabash villagers (for by now many of the Piankashaws and all of the Kickapoos had withdrawn to Illinois country) and the Peorias, Kaskaskias, and Illinois Potawatomis. These villages signed largely to get back their women and children who had been seized by Kentucky raiders, but there were also signs of possibilities for real accommodation. The Potawatomis present made the Americans their father; a Wea clan matron spoke in council, desiring an end to the war and denouncing her sons for preferring confederaton councils to the treaty council at Vincennes; and the Wabash villagers made Jean Baptiste Ducoigne, the pro-American chief of the Kaskaskias, the council speaker. These actions all signified a movement toward a peace based on no further land cessions or settlements beyond the Ohio. When Putnam made no demands for land and acknowledged Indian title, a delegation of chiefs, at a clear risk of their lives, even agreed to go to Philadelphia. The delegates survived attempts by Kentuckians to murder them, but more than half of them succumbed to smallpox. The remnant, however, addressed Washington as father and, in the manner of the old alliances, asked his pity and protection. Ducoigne quite specifically envisioned an American alliance that would emulate the old French alliance: "The times are gloomy in my town. We have no commander, no soldier, no

---

[84] *Ibid.*, 113. For Brant's visit to Philadelphia and his position, see Kelsay, *Joseph Brant*, 458–82.

[85] For justification, see Wayne to Putnam, Aug. 6, 1792, Buell (ed.), *Memoirs of Rufus Putnam* 312. For peace messages, see Speech of Knox to Indians, Apr. 4, 1792, *MPHC* 24:394–96. The Delawares agreed with the Shawnees and Miamis in the spring but then wavered, Extract from the Speech of the Shawanoes, Delawares and Miamis, Apr. 15, 1792, Wayne Papers, Clements Library. For triumph of warriors, see Proceedings of a General Council of Indian Nations, 30 Sept. 1792 ... until the 9th day of Oct., *MPHC* 24:483–981.

priest. Have you no concern for us, father? If you have, put a magistrate with us to keep the peace. I cannot live so. I am of French blood." Such hopes were futile. The Senate rejected the treaty because it failed to grant the United States exclusive right to purchase Indian lands in the future. The delegation returned home with nothing. The Americans, however, would have one more chance at peace. The United States accepted an invitation sent by the confederation council to meet at Lower Sandusky the next year.[86]

The Sandusky council never took place. The American delegation of Benjamin Lincoln, Timothy Pickering, and Beverley Randolph got as far as Matthew Elliott's farm across from Detroit. There they stalled while the confederation council at the Maumee argued over whether to receive them. The sticking point was the Ohio boundary which first Iroquois messengers and then a delegation of confederation chiefs led by Brant had neglected to inform the Amercians had once more become the sine qua non for peace. Brant, who desired a Muskingum boundary, seemed "inclined to give up some cultivated settlements on the north of the Ohio," and supposedly said he was pledged to Congress to do so. Lieutenant Governor John Simcoe

---

[86] For attacks and prisoners, see Wabash Indians . . . Oct. 27, 1791, no. 20, *ASPIA* 1:129–35. For withdrawal of Kickapoos, see Articles of Agreement with the Wabash Indians, Mar. 14, 1792, Carter (ed.), *Territorial Papers*, 1:375. For Weas and Eel River, see Putnam to Knox, July 5, 1792, Buell (ed.), *Memoirs of Rufus Putnam*, 276. For council, see Journal of the Proceedings at a Council Held with the Indians of the Wabash and Illinois at Post Vincents (Sept. 24, 1792), *ibid.*, 335–67, particularly 339–40, 342–43; Speech of Rufus Putnam, Oct. 5, 1792, *ASPIA* 1:319; A Treaty of peace and friendship . . . Sept. 27, 1792, *ASPIA* 1:338–40. For Wells, see Instructions to Wells, Oct. 7, 1792, *ibid.*, 370. For chiefs to Philadelphia, see Putnam to Knox, Dec. 20, 1792, *ibid.*, 372. The prisoners were released to the Indians at the treaty, Putnam to Knox, Feb. 14, 1793, *ibid.*, 379; "Narrative of John Heckewelder's Journey," 40, 167–82; Knox to President, Jan. 2, 1794, *ASPIA* 1:470. See also R. David Edmunds, " 'Nothing Has Been Effected': The Vincennes Treaty of 1792," *Indiana Magazine of History* 74 (1978): 25–35. Edmunds asserts the Wabash and Illinois chiefs were already pro-American. This is true of La Gesse and Ducoigne, but the great majority of the Weas, Piankashaws, Kickapoos, and others were anti-American. They had been raiding Kentucky and attacking American troops for years. For groups and chiefs signing the treaty, see List of Signers of 1792 Treaty, Putnam Papers, v. 2, no. 142, copy in GLEHA.

Ducoigne, who the secretary of the Northwest Territory thought commanded only a dozen Kaskaskias, was a surprising choice as speaker. The Indians probably selected him for his pro-American sympathies, not knowing that Sargent thought him "of no consequence or Influence and . . . a monstrous beggarly rascal even for an Indian and an Arrent Paltroon," Sargent to Secretary of War, Oct. 29, 1792, Carter (ed.), *Territorial Papers*, 1:413. For his speech to Washington in Philadelphia, see Speeches of John Baptist de Coigne in H. A. Washington (ed.), *The Writings of Thomas Jefferson* (New York: Derby & Jackson, 1859), 8:178. Two of the delegates accompanied the Senecas to the projected conference at Lower Sandusky, Isaac Craig to Henry Knox, June 7, 1793, Isaac Craig Collection, v. 11A, Carnegie Library, Pittsburgh, GLEHA. For Lower Sandusky conference, see Proceedings of a General Council of Indian Nations, 30 Sept. 1792 . . . until the 9th day of Oct. *MPHC* 24:495.

reported Brant's statements to McKee urging him to "fix upon Brandt's mind the necessity of union."[87]

As an issue dividing the Americans and the confederation, the boundary was largely meaningless. The Americans would have rejected a Muskingum boundary just as quickly as an Ohio boundary. As a mark of continued factionalism within the confederation, however, the boundary was critical. An already reduced confederation tore itself apart. Putnam's treaty had effectively detached the Wabash villages, and with the Wabash neutral, the Sauks and Fox disappeared from the confederation. In effect, the confederation had lost its western flank, and promises of aid from the distant Creeks, Cherokees, and Seven Nations of Canada hardly repaired such a loss. Among the remaining confederation members, the Maumee villagers, bitter at the Iroquois who had failed to help in the defeats of Harmar and St. Clair, opposed Brant. Buckongahelas, the Delaware war leader, interrupted "in a very abrupt manner" a speech that Brant made in council. He, in effect, called Brant a liar, but his flagrant break with council ritual in interrupting a speaker sounded louder than anything he said. The old forms, the old symbols, could not hold the tensions within the confederation. Later, the Iroquois produced the symbol of the confederation itself, "a Moon of Wampum and dish with one Spoon ... which Signified that the Country was in Common." It sat forlorn, barely acknowledged, amid the wrangling.[88]

[87] Horsman, "The British Indian Department and the Abortive Treaty of the Lower Sandusky," 189–213; Horsman, *Expansion and American Indian Policy,* 96–98; Horsman, *Matthew Elliott,* 69–91. For American commission, see Benjamin Lincoln, Journal of a Treaty Held in 1793 with the Indian Tribes North-West of the Ohio, by Commissioners of the United States, *Collections of Massachusetts Historical Society,* 3rd Series, 5:131–70; Instructions ... 26 Apr. 1793, *ASPIA* 1:340–42; Journal, *ibid.,* 342–61; Message to Commissioners, July 31, 1793, *ibid.,* 579–85. Brant was originally somewhat vague about the boundary, see Brant to Clinton, Jan. 1793, Brant Papers 11F133, Draper Mss.; Captain Brant's Journal, July 1–23, 1793, in E. A. Cruikshank (ed.), *The Correspondence of Lieutenant Governor John Graves Simcoe,* 5 vols. (Toronto: The Society, 1923–31), 2:6. For quotation and Simcoe, see Simcoe to Clarke, July 10, 1793, *MPHC* 24:568–69. For minutes of a subsequent meeting with the British and Americans, see Minutes of a Council ... at Free Masons Hall, Niagara, Sunday the 7th of July, *MPHC* 24:560. For council and boundary, see Speech of Confederate Nations at the Glaize, Feb. 17, 1793, *Simcoe Papers,* 5:34–35. For Simcoe's desires, Simcoe to Hammond Aug. 24, 1793, *MPHC* 24:599–605. For Shawnee and boundary, see Speeches, Buffalo Creek, Nov. 16, 1792, *ASPIA* 1:323–24; Speech of Cornplanter and New Arrow to Major Wayne, 8 Dec. 1792, *ASPIA* 1:337.

[88] For Brant's concern over Wabash Indians, see Brant to McKee, May 17, 1793, *Simcoe Papers,* 5:41. For absence of Sauk, Fox, and Wabash, see confederation signatories, Lincoln, Journal of a Treaty ... 1793, 154–67. The Creek and Cherokee delegations and arrived with news that they had already commenced war to the south on the Shawnee promise of British aid, Letter to McKee, Feb. 6, 1793, McKee Collection, PAC; McKee to Simcoe, July 15, 1793, *Simcoe Papers,* 5:58–59. Simcoe feared the inclusion of the Creeks and Cherokees in the confederation would make peace impossible, Simcoe to Hammond, July 24, 1793, *Simcoe Papers,* 2:64–65; Simcoe to Clarke, July 29, 1793, *MPHC* 24:573–75;

The increasing assertiveness of the Maumee villagers, in turn, alienated the Lake Indians, that is, the Detroit villagers (with the exception of the Hurons), the Saginaw Indians, the villages from Arbre Croche to Michilimackinac, and the Potawatomis around Saint Joseph. They sided with Brant largely from their own sense that the Maumee villagers unduly dominated the confederation. Indeed, many Lake Indians paid more attention to their British fathers than to their brothers within the confederation. The Saginaw Indians initially refused to attend the council at all and had come only on an invitation from the British. Brant, for his part, blamed these widening divisions on McKee. He cited Buckongahelas, who had supposedly claimed that McKee had aborted a compromise between the factions and had persuaded Maumee villagers to refuse to compromise and, instead, to hold onto the Ohio boundary.[89]

In creating the Americans as Other, the Algonquians simultaneously resurrected the British as fathers. They did so with wariness and hesitation, but they had little choice. Their only hope was British aid. Believing war inevitable, Governor Carleton, Lieutenant Governor Simcoe, and McKee struggled, as fathers should, to unite and support their children. McKee actively intervened in confederation councils and countered the efforts of French traders who, spurred by news of England's war with France, intervened to urge peace with the United States. Antoine Lasselle, a trader from Kekionga, was the son-in-law of the erratic and often drunken Shawnee war leader Blue Jacket. His success in urging Blue Jacket to open private negotiations with the Americans forced McKee to have Blue Jacket watched.[90]

Simcoe to McKee, July 23, 1793, *Simcoe Papers*, 5:62–63; Brant to Simcoe, July 28, 1793, *Simcoe Papers*, 1:401.

For anti-Brant and anti-Iroquois feeling, see Brant Journal, June 9, 1793, *Simcoe Papers*, 2:6. The Delaware antagonism toward the Iroquois, which already ran deep, had received new fuel during the winter with reports that the Senecas had murdered two Delaware hunters, McKee to Simcoe, Jan. 30, 1793, *MPHC* 24:528; Brant to McKee, Mar. 27, 1792, Claus Papers 5:3, PAC. For Buckongahelas, see Brant Journal, July 23, 1793, *Simcoe Papers*, 2:23. For dish, see Brant Journal, July 25, 1793, *Simcoe Papers*, 2:12.

89 For divisions, see Brant Journal, July 23–25, 1793, *Simcoe Papers*, 2:8–11; Porter to Littlehales, July 5, 1793, *Simcoe Papers*, 1:376. For Saginaw Indians, see *Simcoe Papers*, 1:376. For Saginaw Indians, See Schefflin to McKee, Mat 7, 1793, Claus Papers 5:111–12, PAC. For Brant's analysis, see Brant to McKee, Aug. 4, 1793, *Simcoe Papers*, 5:66–67; Brant Journal, Aug. 5, 1793, *Simcoe Papers*, 2:15–16.

90 For Blue Jacket, see England to McKee, July 6, 1793, Claus Papers, 5:215–16, PAC; England to McKee, July 15, 1793, *Simcoe Papers*, 5:59; Duggan to McKee, July 17, 1793, Claus Papers 5:259–60, PAC. For Lasselle, see McDonell to McKee, May 3, 1794, *Simcoe Papers*, 2:227; Journal, Aug. 5, 1793, *Simcoe Papers*, 2:17.

For British policy, see Clarke to Simcoe, May 19, 1793, *Simcoe Papers*, 1:331; Simcoe to Clarke, May 31, 1793, *Simcoe Papers*, 1:339; Simcoe to Clarke, June 14, 1793, *Simcoe Papers*, 1:354–55; Simcoe to McKee, June 23, 1793, Simcoe Papers 5:50–51; McKee to Simcoe, July 5, 1793, Simcoe Papers, 5:56; McKee to Simcoe, July 28, 1793, *MPHC* 24:572–73;

The insistence of the Algonquians on the Ohio boundary as a precondition for negotiations killed the Sandusky conference, but the deeply divided confederation was unprepared to wage war. The Shawnees sang the war song and cited promises of British aid, but the Lake chiefs went privately to Brant and asked him to promote a peace with the Americans on the basis of the Muskingum boundary. The Maumee villages did get the Ottawas to join them in petitioning the British for aid, which the British, for all their earlier assurances, were unwilling to promise. As Simcoe wavered over what policy to pursue, Algonquian indecision, divisions, and impotence increased. The advance of Wayne's army and renewed fighting returned some Lake Indian warriors to the fold, but to the dismay of the British, only seven hundred Indians gathered to oppose Wayne in the fall of 1794. Despite the pleas of the Shawnees, most of these warriors dispersed when they received news that Wayne had retreated because of the onset of winter. Lieutenant Colonel Richard England reported from Detroit that never were the Indians known "to be so little united, (and) the army (Wayne's) has literally nothing to oppose their Progress." By January 1794, the unity of the Maumee villagers cracked as a Delaware faction sent a delegation to Wayne to ask peace terms.[91]

With the confederation unable to muster effective resistance, the burden fell on the British, and the confederation began to look more and more like a patriarchal alliance. In the fall of 1793, Governor Carleton made what would become a notorious speech to the Seven Nations of Canada. He told them he thought war between the United States and Great Britain was inevitable

McKee to Simcoe, Aug. 22, 1793, *Simcoe Papers*, 2:34–35; Simcoe to Hammond, Sept. 8, 1793, *MPHC* 24:507–9. Brant blamed McKee for insistence on the Ohio boundary, Brant to Chew, Sept. 26, 1793, *MPHC* 24:614. Simcoe believed McKee, Simcoe to Dorchester, Nov. 10, 1793, *Simcoe Papers*, 2:101–5.

[91] Chiefs of Western Nations to Simcoe, n.d., c. Aug. 1793, *MPHC* 24:597–99; Simcoe to Hammond, Aug. 24, 1793, *MPHC* 24:599–605. For clear British reluctance for conflict, see Dundas to Simcoe, Oct. 2, 1793, *Simcoe Papers*, 2:81–82. Brant, on his return, sought to obtain peace terms from the Americans, Simcoe to Dundas, Sept. 20, 1793, *Simcoe Papers*, 2:59; Proceedings of a Council, Oct. 10, 1793, *MPHC* 24:615. For Chippewas etc., see Simcoe to Dundas, Nov. 10, 1793, *MPHC* 24:623; Meeting . . . Indians of the Six Nations and their Confederates . . . Oct. 8 1793, *ASPIA* 1:473. For Lake Indians aid to Indians at Auglaize, see Journal of McKee, Sept. to Dec. 1793, *Simcoe Papers*, 2:126–29. Smith to McKee, Oct. 22, 1793, Claus Papers 6:49, PAC. For 700, see Dorchester to Dundas, Nov. 22, 1793, *MPHC* 24:625–26. For England quotation, see England to Simcoe, Dec. 14, 1793, *MPHC* 24:628. For Delawares, see McKee to England, Jan. 28, 1794, *MPHC* 24:631; McKee to Chew, *Simcoe Papers*, 2:138–39; England to Simcoe, Feb. 2, 1794, *MPHC* 24:632. The Shawnees and Miamis refused to listen to the Delaware delegation, Report of Captain Elliot, Feb. 11, 1794, *Simcoe Papers*, 2:152. It was led by George White Eyes, Wayne to Indians, Jan. 14, 1794, *Simcoe Papers* 2:131; Wayne to Delany, Jan. 21, 1794, Wayne Papers, Clements Library. By Mar., Wayne considered the peace attempt the work of spies, Wayne to Knox, Mar. 20, 1794, Richard C. Knopf (ed.), *A Name in Arms: The Wayne-Knox-Pickering-McHenry Correspondence* (Pittsburgh: University of Pittsburgh Press, 1960), 311.

and that a new western boundary would be set by the warriors. In mid February, Carleton ordered the reconstruction and reoccupation of a fort at the rapids of the Maumee and instructed Simcoe to prepare to meet Wayne "should he attempt by force to take possession of the country." Simcoe, who believed that resistance to the Americans was impractical as long as the Indians remained divided, now thought "circumstances may arise to reunite them."[92]

The circumstances arose from both the Algonquian and European borders of the middle ground. An Indian, most likely a shaman, dreamed "they should obtain Victories similar to those which heretofore has attended them, and they were in the highest spirits." The Chippewas "in consequence of some superstitious circumstances ... unanimously determined upon war." Agushiway (or Egushewai), the leading Detroit Ottawa chief, abandoned his partnership with Brant and pledged resistance to the Americans, and by May, Brant himself had abandoned negotiations and was urging the Lake Indians to united resistance. Simcoe, meanwhile, offered the first clear evidence of direct British military assistance. In April, troops prepared for the construction of a new fort at the Miami rapids between the village at Roche de Bout and Captain Pipe's village. This too put the Indians "in great spirits." And then in mid April at the Glaize, Elliot repeated Carleton's speech to the Seven Nations of Canada, with its prediction of a British-American war and a new boundary. "You have," they told Elliot, "set our hearts right, and we are now happy to see you standing on your feet in our Country." Word came from the Delawares across the Mississippi of a new alliance among them, the Spanish, and the southern Indians, all of whom were ready to cooperate with the confederation against the Big Knives. Renewed enthusiasm held despite efforts of French traders at the Glaize to persuade the Indians that their old father, Onontio, was at war with England and would soon return. Even many of the Wabash Indians reconsidered their peace with the Americans and sought readmittance to the confederacy.[93]

[92] Dorchester to the Seven Nations of Canada, Feb. 10, 1794, *Simcoe Papers*, 2:148–49; Dorchester to Simcoe, Feb. 17, 1794, *MPHC* 24:642–43. Dorchester thought the confederation "broken" at the end of Feb., Dorchester to Dundas, Feb. 24, 1794, *Simcoe Papers*, 2:163, also *ibid.*. Feb. 28, 1794, *MPHC* 24:646, but Simcoe had hopes of reuniting them, Simcoe to Dorchester, Mar. 14, 1794, *Simcoe Papers*, 2:181–84. For troops at Fort Miami, see Simcoe to Dorchester, Apr. 29, 1794, *Simcoe Papers*, 2:220–22. For Chippewas, see Simcoe to Dorchester, Apr. 29, 1794, *MPHC* 24:659–60.

[93] For dream, Agushiway, see Simcoe to Dorchester, Mar. 16, 1794, *Simcoe Papers*, 2:189. Brant did not regard Agushiway's answer as a break with him, Simcoe to Dorchester, Mar. 26, 1794, *Simcoe Papers*, 2:194–95. The Americans had, in any case, provided only an "evasive" answer to Brant's proposal for a Muskingum boundary, Brant to Chew, Mar. 25, 1794, *Simcoe Papers*, 2:193–94. By May Brant was for war, Brant to McKee, May 8, 1794, *Simcoe Papers*, 5:86–87. For great spirits, see Duggan to Chew, Apr. 6, 1794, *Simcoe Papers*, 2:209; Speech of the Shawanese, etc. Apr. 14, 1794, *MPHC* 24:656. For Spanish, see

By early May, as McKee reported to Joseph Chew, the secretary for Indian affairs, things were "considerably altered for the better," with "a very extensive union of the Indians Nations . . . the immediate consequence." This union, however, was really a pair of reconstituted European alliances. As Wayne approached, it became clear that the Indians expected the British to join them. Indeed, as Delawares from the Auglaize informed the commander at Fort Miami, they depended on the British to summon their children to the Glaize for the confederation had thus far been unable to do so. At Michilimackinac, the commander summoned and supplied Ottawas from Arbre Croche and Ojibwas from near the straits of Mackinac to resist the Americans. He even recruited a small group of Menominees, never members of the confederation, who were visiting the post.[94]

But the alliance was a mirage, for Carleton and Simcoe were acting without authority, and were unprepared to meet Algonquian expectations. Simcoe informed Carleton that the "Indians still intimate their hopes that their English father will assist them." Within a few days, the Algonquians ceased intimating such hopes and compelled both the traders and British officers at the Auglaize to march with them against the Americans. Their effort ended in a botched and unsuccessful attack on Wayne's advance post of Fort Recovery. Although there were roughly two thousand warriors gathered in the region between Detroit and the Auglaize, the delay of the Delawares and others meant only about eleven hundred men were available for the battle. The Indians defeated an American detachment outside the fort but failed to take the stockade itself. McKee tried to disguise the defeat at Fort Recovery as "unconsequential," but the setback was potentially disastrous. The Indian losses, despite Wayne's claims, were minor; indeed, it was the much heavier American losses that weakened the Indians, for the scalps and prisoners the Lake Indians had taken "accomplished the call of their Belts," and they departed for home. The battle thus ensured a significant diminution of Indian strength just as Wayne was ready to renew his advance.[95]

Speeches of the Western Indians, May 7, 1794, *Simcoe Papers*, 2:231–33. Less auspiciously, this message singled out the Piankashaws and Illinois as friends to the Big Knives. For French, see Ironside and Ranald McDonell to McKee, May 3, 1794, *Simcoe Papers*, 2:227–28. For Wabash and Kickapoos ask readmittance, see McKee to Simcoe, 26 July 1794, *Simcoe Papers*, 2:344–45. For fort, see map, *MPHC* 24:689.

[94] McKee to Chew, May 8, 1794, *Simcoe Papers*, 2:234–35. For troops, see Duggan to?, May 24, 1794, *Simcoe Papers*, 2:247–348. For British role, see Message Delivered by two Delaware Chiefs, May 25, 1794, McKee Papers, PAC. For Michilimackinac, see Entrés aux conseil les Court Oreilles de l'Arbre Croches et les Sauteux de la bande de Matchekioieh . . . 28 mai 1794, Claus papers, C–1470, MG 19, F1, v.6, PAC. Entrés . . . Conseil les Folles Avoines . . . 11 juin 1794, *ibid*. See also Doyle to Chew, June 9, 1794, *Simcoe Papers*, 2:262–63. For other recruitment efforts out of Detroit, see England to Simcoe, May 29, 1794, *Simcoe Papers*, 2:252; McKee to Chew, June 10, 1794, *Simcoe Papers*, 2:263.

[95] Diary of an Officer, *Simcoe Papers*, 5:90–94. For other assessments, see England to Simcoe,

Although no one knew it, the war essentially ended at Fort Recovery. British policy, as enunciated in London, and Canadian policy, as enunciated by Governor Carleton, Simcoe, McKee, and Elliot, now completely diverged. In England, John Jay was about to negotiate a British withdrawal from the posts. He assured the British that Wayne would not attack them and that instructions were on the way to Canada to avoid hostility. But in Canada, Algonquian demands become specific, and Simcoe's conviction that war was inevitable grew more certain. On his return from Fort Recovery, Little Turtle went to see Lieutenant Colonel England at Detroit. Little Turtle, whom England thought the "most decent, modest, sensible Indian I ever conversed with," asked two cannons and twenty men to renew the attack on Fort Recovery. Without it, he said, the Indians would "be obliged to desist in their plan of attempting to stop the progress of the American Army." Simcoe informed Henry Dundas, the secretary of state for war in the British Cabinet, that "assistance must absolutely be extended to the demolition of Fort Recovery & if possible, that of Fort Jefferson."[96]

As Wayne marched toward the Maumee, it became apparent that what he did mattered less than what the British did, for only the British could unite and supply the Indians. The Wyandots followed Little Turtle to Detroit, demanding that the British fulfill their promises and "rise upon your feet with your warriors and help us. If you do not, we cannot go to war any more." A few days later, the Indians abandoned the villages at the Auglaize and resettled near the new British fort at the Miami rapids. An American attack on the villages would now have to take place virtually under the eyes of a British garrison. There the Indians expected, with the aid of the Detroit militia, to fight the Americans.[97]

The end of the confederation and, so it seemed at the time, the British alliance was an anticlimax. On the morning of August 20, 1794, several hundred Indians and some English militia engaged the American army near

June 19, 1794, *Simcoe Papers*, 2:278–79; Simcoe to Dorchester, June 15, 1794, *Simcoe Papers*, 2:228; McKee to Simcoe, July 5, 1794, *Simcoe Papers*, 8:95–96; McKee to Chew, July 7, 1794, *Simcoe Papers*, 2:310. For losses, see Duggan to Chew, July 10, 1794, *Simcoe Papers*, 2:317. La Mothe to Chew, July 19, 1794, *WHC* 18:442. For Wayne's claims, see Wayne to Knox, July 7, 1794, Knopf (ed.), *A Name In Arms*, 345–49.

[96] Dundas to Simcoe, July 4, 1794, *MPHC* 24:679; Dundas to Dorchester, July 5, 1794, *MPHC* 24:679–82. For assurance of safety, see Grenville to Hammond, July 15, 1794, *MPHC* 24:691. For Little Turtle, see England to Simcoe, July 22, 1794, *Simcoe Papers*, 2:334. For forts, see Simcoe to Dundas, Aug. 5, 1794, *Simcoe Papers*, 2:353–54. For war certain, see Simcoe to McKee, Aug. 6, 1794, *Simcoe Papers*, 5:99; Simcoe to England, Aug. 19, 1794, *Simcoe Papers*, 2:392–93.

[97] A speech delivered to Colonel England, Aug. 6, 1794, *Simcoe Papers*, 2:357. For rapids, see McKee to England, Aug. 10, 1794, *Simcoe Papers*, 2:365; Examination of a Shawnee Prisoner, Aug. 11, 1794, *Simcoe Papers*, 2:366–67. England did muster the militia, England to Simcoe, Aug. 14, 1794, *Simcoe Papers*, 2:374–76; England to Baby, Aug. 20, 1794, *Simcoe Papers*, 2:395.

Alexander McKee's house on the Maumee. The main Indian force was several miles off receiving provisions. The Indians drove the American advance back, inflicting heavy casualties, but when they reached the main American army, they had to retreat for lack of reinforcements. When the main Indian force arrived, the warriors were winded and soon found themselves outflanked. Demoralized by the wounding of Little Otter and Agushiway, two leading Ottawa leaders, and by the deaths of several Huron chiefs, they retreated. The real defeat came during the retreat; for when the Indians fell back to Fort Miami, the garrison shut the gates on them and refused them aid.

In council that October, the chiefs asked British aid in an attack on the American posts; instead of granting such aid, Simcoe only promised that the next time American troops approached a British post, British troops would fire. A few war parties went out, but the conviction grew that, despite Simcoe's promises, the English would not assist the Indians, and they grew steadily more demoralized. A Shawnee reported that the French were likely to beat the English in Europe. Blue Jacket now thought of the English as nothing. And other Indians suspected the British of colluding with the Americans to drive the Indians from the country. The Indians prepared to come to terms with the Americans.[98]

[98] Fallen Timbers, Campbell to England, Aug. 20, 1794, *Simcoe Papers*, 2:395–96; McKee to Chew, Aug. 27, 1794, *Simcoe Papers*, 3:7–8. The French militia proved mutinous and worthless, England to Simcoe, Aug. 23, 1794, *Simcoe Papers*, 2:414; Wayne to Knox, Aug. 28, 1794, Knopf (ed.), *A Name In Arms*, 351–55. England denounced the Indians for leaving Fort Miami unprotected, England to Simcoe, Aug. 24, 1794, *Simcoe Papers*, 2:419. Some whites did fight with the Indians, Simcoe to Hammond, Nov. 10, 1794, *Simcoe Papers*, 3:179–80. For request aid, see Simcoe to Duke of Portland, Oct. 24, 1794, *Simcoe Papers*, 3:147. For Simcoe's promise, see Simcoe's Reply to the Indian Nations, Oct. 13, 1794, *Simcoe Papers*, 3:121–25. For Shawnee, see Smith to McKee, Oct. 11, 1794. *Simcoe Papers*, 5:112–13. For demoralization, see England to Simcoe, Aug. 30, 1794, *Simcoe Papers*, 3:20–22; Simcoe's Diary of a Journey to the Miami's River, Sept. 28, 1794, *Simcoe Papers*, 3:99–100. Brant to Chew, Oct. 22, 1794, *Simcoe Papers*, 3:140–41; W. Chew to J. Chew, Oct. 24, 1794, *Simcoe Papers*, 3:150; Smith to McKee, Oct. 28, 1794, *Simcoe Papers*, 5:118. For war parties, see Smith to McKee, Oct. 14, 1794, *Simcoe Papers*, 3:106–7. For collusion, see Simcoe to Duke of Portland, Oct. 24, 1794, *Simcoe Papers*, 3:145–46. The French were actively working to turn the Indians against the English, McKee to England, Nov. 18, 1794, *Simcoe Papers*, 3:183–84. For Wayne solicits negotiations, see Wayne to Western Indians, Sept. 12, 1794, *Simcoe Papers*, 3:79–80.

11

The politics of benevolence

Until the end of the eighteenth century . . . native American groups were sought as allies by the rival European powers. . . . The Indians were still independent military and political agents – "nations," in the parlance of the time whose support had to be gained with supplies of goods. . . . As a result the exchange of goods and services between Indians and Europeans resembled the giving of gifts more than an exchange of commodities.

Eric Wolf, *Europe and the People Without History*

As we are more powerful, and more enlightened than they are, there is a responsibility of national character, that we should treat them with kindness, and even liberality. It is a melancholy reflection, that our modes of population have been more destructive to the Indian natives than the conduct of the conquerors of Mexico and Peru. The evidence is the utter extirpation of nearly all the Indians in most populous parts of the Union. A future historian may mark the causes of this destruction of the human race in sable colors.

Henry Knox to the president, December 29, 1794

Ultimately, the white man's sympathy was more deadly than his animosity. Philanthropy had in mind the disappearance of an entire race.

Bernard Sheehan, *Seeds of Extinction*

I

Benjamin Lincoln kept a journal in 1793, during his fruitless attempt to negotiate a treaty with the Indian confederation, and he recorded how the Bible justified the future of the *pays d'en haut*. A New Englander who had served with distinction during the Revolution and crushed Shays' Rebellion afterward, Lincoln had little experience with Indians. He knew virtually nothing about how they lived. The vast cornfields and the herds of cattle, horses, and pigs surrounding many villages were unknown to him. Indians were hunters. He also did not know that the Indians of the *pays d'en haut* were probably increasing in numbers in the late eighteenth century, for from his Bible Lincoln had deduced that the Indians as Indians must disappear. Lincoln did not hate Indians; he presumed hatred was unnecessary. His logic foreshadowed the conventional nineteenth-century logic of the vanishing Indian. God had foreordained the earth to be fully populated, and "no men will be suffered to live by hunting on lands capable of improvement." Thus, "if the savages cannot be civilized and quit their present pursuits, they will in consequence of their stubbornness, dwindle and moulder away." The Indians were the children of Ishmael; the Americans, the children of Abraham. They had no common father.[1]

Lincoln's reasoning lay behind a kind of imperial benevolence that made it possible to reconcile saving the Indians with stripping them of their lands. Lincoln assumed, unlike the Indian haters, that Indians could change, but change could move only one way. Indians, having no right to oppose progress, could become "more laborious," or they could die. Their death would then be part of the divinely ordained order of things and Lincoln, at least, faced their extinction with equanimity.[2]

For more than a decade after Fallen Timbers, the American imperial benevolence personified by Lincoln held full sway in the *pays d'en haut*. For,

[1] Lincoln, Journal of a Treaty ... 1793, *Collections of the Massachusetts Historical Society*, 3rd Series, 5:139.

Those groups around the Great Lakes and in the upper Mississippi Valley were actually increasing in population during this period following the epidemics of the seventeenth century. The various members of the Miami confederation seem to have at least stabilized their numbers by the 1770s and 1780s, when the British counted 774 Wea and Miami warriors, as well as an additional 200 Piankashaws. What was surprising – and an ill omen for further population growth – was that among them, and also among virtually all other groups in the *pays d'en haut* south of Detroit, men outnumbered women. With the stabilization of the Miamis and the migration of new groups – the Delawares, Shawnees, Mingos, Mascoutens, Kickapoos, and smaller numbers of Ottawas, Wyandots, and Potawatomis – over the previous half century, the population was also growing in this region. For Ohio Valley and Miami figures, see De nombrement des Indiens résidents des le district du Détroit pour l'année 1782, Haldimand Papers 21783. The census counted 11,403 Indians: Hurons, Ottawas, Chippewas, Potawatomis, Miamis, Weas, Piankashaws, Mingos, Delawares, Kickapoos, and Mascoutens. It included the area from Detroit and Saint Joseph south to the Ohio and from Detroit west to the Wabash country.

The number of women is surprising, given the presumably higher mortality of males through warfare. It may be an artifact of the census takers' concentration on warriors, or it may represent other factors from higher mortality among women and killing of female infants to extensive outmarriage among Europeans. Only the Ojibwas had significantly more women than men, and they were, of all these groups, the ones who would best maintain their population over the next two centuries.

For mentions of corn surplus, Wyandots, see Gladwin to Amherst, Dec. 3, 1763, Amherst Papers, Clements Library, 7:96. For Saint Joseph, see Burnett to Meldrum, May 14, 1786, Burnett to Hands, May 25, 1786, Wilbur M. Cunningham (ed.), *Letter Book of William Burnett* (Fort Miami Heritage Society of Michigan, n.d.). For Ottawas of Arbre Croche, see Burnett to Hand, Feb. 6, 1791, *ibid.*

For vanishing Indian, see Brian W. Dippie, *The Vanishing American: White Attitudes and U.S. Indian Policy* (Middletown, Conn.: Wesleyan University Press, 1982).

[2] Lincoln, Journal of a Treaty ... 1793, 141. The best examination of the complexities of this benevolence is Bernard Sheehan, *Seeds of Extinction: Jeffersonian Philanthropy and the American Indian* (Chapel Hill: University of North Carolina Press, 1973).

When the Americans arrived, both the Huron mission and Detroit itself (pictured here in 1804) were products of more than a century of European–Indian accommodation on the middle ground. (William Clements Library)

despite substantial British aid to the Indians immediately after Fallen
Timbers, British influence declined precipitously over much of the *pays d'en
haut*. British provisions could not erase the memory of the king's soldiers
shutting Fort Miami against the retreating Indians. British aid could not
compensate for the wholesale defection of the French to the Americans,
and it could not compensate for the news of Jay's Treaty, which guaranteed
the evacuation of the British posts at the Miami River, Detroit, and
Michilimackinac. Wayne made good use of Jay's Treaty in securing Indian
agreement to the Treaty of Greenville, which ceded all but the northwestern
corner of Ohio to the Americans and guaranteed the United States military
reservations within the remaining Indian Territory.[3]

On the surface, Wayne negotiated with the Indian confederation, its
council fire now restored to Brownstown, but in reality he negotiated with
quarreling and embittered groups of villagers. Various villages sent separate
delegations to seek negotiations with Wayne. At the council itself, the divisions repeatedly opened. Although both Tarhe of the Sandusky Wyandots
and the Shawnee Red Pole asserted that the "Great Spirit gave us this land
in common," the gathered Indians openly quarreled over their respective
rights and claims. The gathered Indians asked Wayne to choose which
nation should speak for the whole and argued over the ownership of the
lands to be ceded, and the Wyandots, Delawares, and Shawnees even asked
Wayne to supervise the division of the lands among them. At the end of
the treaty council, Red Pole, Buckongahelas, and Mashipinnashiwish, a
Chippewa chief, all acknowledged the Americans as their father. Although,
at best, American imperial benevolence contemplated a cannibal father
absorbing his Indian children, to many Algonquians making the Americans
behave as an Algonquian father seemed the only means to reunite the *pays
d'en haut*.[4]

---

[3] Accounts of the negotiations are available in Harvey Carter, *The Life and Times of Little Turtle:
First Sagamore of the Wabash* (Urbana: University of Illinois Press, 1987), 145–55. For the
treaty and council, see *American State Papers, Indian Affairs*, 2 vols. (Washington, D.C.:
Gales and Seaton, 1832–34), 1:562–83 (hereafter cited as *ASPIA*). For Jay's Treaty, see
ibid., 573.
    For separate peace overtures and divisions, Wyandots under Tarhe (The Crane), see
Wayne to Knox, Dec. 23, 1794, Richard C. Knopf (ed.), *A Name in Arms: The Wayne-Knox-
Pickering-McHenry Correspondence* (Pittsburgh: University of Pittsburgh Press, 1960), 370. For
preliminary articles with Chippewas, Ottawas, Potawatomis, Sauks, and Miamis, see Wayne
to Knox, Feb. 12, 1795, Knopf (ed.), *A Name in Arms*, 384. See also Wayne to Pickering, Mar.
8, 1794, *ibid.*, 386–87. The chiefs, as Wayne mentions without fully understanding,
immediately sought American recognition of their status, *ibid.*, 390. For French, see
Information of Paul St. Bernard, Jan. 24, 1795, E. A. Cruikshank (ed.), *The Correspondence of
Lieutenant Governor John Graves Simcoe*, 5 vols. (Toronto: The Society, 1923–31), 3:272;
Burke to Little Hales, May 27, 1795, *Simcoe Papers*, 4:19–23; Brant to Butler, June 28, 1795,
Simcoe Papers, 4:33. Colonel R. G. England tried to maintain that the Indians remained
devoted to the British, England to Simcoe, Sept. 8, 1795, *Simcoe Papers*, 4:91–92.
[4] For father, see Minutes of Treaty, 10 June . . . 10 Aug. 1795, *ASPIA* 1:581–82; Letter of

But the Algonquians had lost the ability to force whites to act as fathers. George Washington accepted the title of father; the Americans established a system of annuities; Americans came to see the benefits in mediating disputes among Indians. But the Americans no longer feared Indians. The federal government put the functions of patriarchy to other uses; officials desired to establish control over villagers, both Indian and white, and to make the world of the villages but a transient stage in the larger march of progress. Those villagers, whether the mythical frontier people who could not stand to live in sight of smoke from their neighbors' chimneys, or Indians who refused to become farmers, would, as Lincoln predicted, have no choice but to disappear or withdraw. Congress passed the Trade and Intercourse Laws as mechanisms of control over backcountry whites, while relying on treaties and government trading houses to transform Indians. Although none of these measures worked as planned, and although backcountry Indian haters took their steady toll and angry warriors resisted cessions and avenged murders, this federal Indian policy withstood challenge until the 1820s.[5]

Jeffersonian Indian policy originally sought the coexistence of Indians and whites in the *pays d'en haut*, but it was not to be coexistence on the middle ground. Jefferson sought to make the Indians one with the Americans and culturally indistinguishable from them. The key was labor and property. As he told the Delawares:

Simcoe, Mar. 2, 1794, CO 42/22. The United States was willing to concede that the interests of the various villages were "blended together" thus necessitating treating with them as a group, Pickering to Wayne, Apr. 8, 1795, Knopf (ed.), *A Name in Arms*, 396–97. For select speaker, see Minutes of Treaty, 10 June … 10 Aug. 1795, *ASPIA* 1:568; for land, see 569–71, 581. For divisions, see A Sketch of a Speech from the Wyandot Chiefs … 10 Oct. 1794, *ASPIA* 1:548. Messages, Speeches and letters from Sandusky and replies, Sept. 17–27, 1794, *ASPIA* 1:525–27.

5 For Washington as father, see Washington to Chiefs and Warriors … of the Wiandots, etc., Nov. 9, 1796, Wayne Papers, Clements Library. For mediation, McHenry to Confederated Indian Nations, Dec. 2, 1796, Cass Papers, Clements Library; St. Clair to Secretary of War, Apr. 8, 1801, Clarence Carter (ed.), *The Territorial Papers of the United States*, 28 vols. (Washington, D.C.: Government Printing Office, 1934–75), 3:129; Dearborn to Harrison, July 3, 1802, National Archives, War Department, Records of the Office of the Secretary of War, Letters Sent, Indian Affairs, Volume A, M 15, roll 1 (hereafter cited as National Archives, WD, SO, LS, IA). By 1800, the commanders at the garrisons were under orders to deny provisions to Indians except in cases of "indispensable charity to travellers." Secretary of War to St. Clair, Apr. 25, 1800, Carter (ed.), *Territorial Papers*, 3:83.

For intent of U.S. policy, see Francis Paul Prucha, *The Great Father: The United States Government and the American Indians* (Lincoln: University of Nebraska Press, 1984), 89–114.

For a notorious example of Indian hating and murder, see Harrison to Secretary of War, July 15, 1801, in Logan Esarey (ed.), *Messages and Letters of William Henry Harrison*, in vol. 7 of *Indiana Historical Collections* (Indianapolis: Indiana Historical Commission, 1922), 25. For Indian anger at murders, see Harrison to Pierce, July 1806, *ibid.*, 191–92; Harrison to Jefferson, July 5, 1806, *ibid.*, 195–96. See also Moses Dawson, *A Historical Narrative of the Civil and Military Services of Major General William H. Harrison* (Cincinnati, Orio: Moses Dawson, 1824), 45. For federal frustration, see Secretary of War to Harrison, July 17, 1806, National Archives, WD, SO, LS, IA, B:240.

When once you have property, you will want laws and magistrates to protect your property and persons, and to punish those among you who commit crimes. You will find that our laws are good for this purpose. You will wish to live under them; you will unite yourselves with us, join in our great councils, and form one people with us, and we shall all be Americans. You will mix with us by marriage. Your blood will run in our veins and will spread with us over this great island.

This was a policy of amalgamation and imperial benevolence that in some ways hearkened back to the dreams of some early French imperialists. It enabled Jefferson to "believe, we are acting for their greatest good," even as he demanded more and more land. Under Jefferson, the permanent line guaranteed earlier at Greenville proved short-lived. After 1800 the president encouraged his governor of the new Indiana Territory, William Henry Harrison, to seek further cessions, and Harrison gladly did so. Harrison played the divided villagers against each other, getting substantial cessions. Because villages often contained members of several tribes and because different tribal groups shared common areas, one group rarely had exclusive claim to the land. If Harrison induced representatives of one group to make a cession, then others had to follow or else risk getting no payments at all for the land.[6]

After initial attempts to resettle their allies on the Canadian side of the boundary failed, the British watched American expansion at the expense of the Indians with relative equanimity. The British wanted good relations with their American neighbors on the Great Lakes. Alexander McKee, seeing the drift of British policy in early 1795, feared that "the distressed situation of the poor Indians who have long fought for us and bled fairly for us, will be no bar to a Peaceable accommodation with America and that they will be left to shift for themselves – but those who live a few years longer will Probably have cause to deplore the short sighted Policy of such a measure." The older agents – Elliott, the Girtys, and McKee – lost influence. Lieutenant

[6] See Sheehan, *Seeds of Extinction*, 119–28; for land, see 171. For a succinct statement of Jefferson's views, see Jefferson, Message to Congress, Jan. 18, 1803, *ASPIA* 1:685. See also Jefferson to Miamis, Powtewatamies, and Weeauks, Jan. 7, 1802, H. A. Washington (ed.), *The Writings of Thomas Jefferson* (New York: Derly & Jackson, 1859), 8:34–35. For long quotation, see Jefferson to Delawares, Dec. 1808, Esarey (ed.), *Harrison Messages*, 333. For Harrison's treaties, See *ASPIA* 1:687–97. The most notorious of these treaties was with the remnants of the Kaskaskias under Ducoigne, a band that numbered, according to the United States, only 30 men, women, and children in 1796 but that ceded southern Illinois to the United States in 1803, Articles of a Treaty between . . . the United States . . . and the head chiefs and warriors of the Kaskaskia tribe of Indians, Aug. 13, 1803, *ASPIA* 1:687; Sargent to Secretary of State, Sept. 30, 1796, Carter (ed.), *Territorial Papers*, 1:576; Harrison to Secretary of War, Feb. 26, 1802, Esarey (ed.), *Harrison Messages*, 45. Jefferson phrased such cessions as a favor the United States did for the Indians so that they could use the revenue to better develop their remaining lands. Jefferson to Little Turtle, Dec. 1808, National Archives, WD, SO, LS, IA, B:201.

Governor Simcoe criticized the agents for "their want of Education, Ignorance of all but the separate Nations, upon an interest with whom, their own consequence is grafted, their immoral Habits, and the Indolence and depravity which in them, seems to be derived from the persons with whom they are so conversant." As had happened with the French, defeat spawned disillusionment with the middle ground among higher British officials. They cut back on presents and provisions, sought to keep the Indians as disunited as possible, and tried to reduce contacts with their old allies to a minimum in order to lessen expenses. Their old allies, in turn, considered themselves orphans, although they still sought British mediation and gifts.[7]

The only ripple of crisis on this calm political surface came in the closing years of the century. Spurred by the sale of Louisiana to France, rumors spread in 1798 and 1799 that Onontio had returned and, with the southern Indians, was coming up the Mississippi to the *pays d'en haut*. The British believed they were the targets of this phantom conspiracy; the Americans thought it was a British plot to launch an Indian war against them. The Shawnees called a conference of the villagers to renew the confederacy and demand changes in the Treaty of Greenville. The Americans accused McKee of instigating a crisis, but McKee had died in January 1799. The French army never materialized; Napoleon ceded Lousiana to the United States, and tensions dissipated.[8]

[7] For British policy during this period, see Reginald Horsman, *Matthew Elliott, British Indian Agent* (Detroit: Wayne State University Press, 1964), 104–56, particularly 155. See also Prescott to Russell, Sept. 28, 1797, Lt. Governor's Office, Upper Canada, 1796–1816, 1:92, Public Archives of Canada (hereafter cited as PAC). There were only 167 Indians resettled in Oct. 1797, Return of Indians . . . at the Chenail Ecarte, Oct. 26, 1797, *MPHC* 20:564. For McKee quotation, see McKee to Chew, Mar. 27, 1795, *Simcoe Papers*, 3:335. For Simcoe quotation, see Simcoe to Duke of Portland, Feb. 17, 1795, *Simcoe Papers*, 3:302. Brant found he could agree with his old adversary McKee that the Indians had again been "left in the lurch," Brant to Chew, Jan. 19, 1796, *Simcoe Papers*, 4:178. Sir John Johnson, the head of the British Indian department, thought the Indians were to blame for their problems. They "have sold their country and have not a just claim on us." Chew to McKee Oct. 17, 1796, Supt. General's Office, v. 10, Sir John Johnson Correspondence, PAC, IA, RG 10. For beginning of cutbacks, see Johnson to Selby, Dec. 30, 1796, Claus Papers 7:296–97, PAC; McLean to Johnson, May 24, 1799, *MPHC* 20:633; Claus to Green, Sept. 14, 1801, Lt. Governor's Office of Upper Canada, 1796–1816, v. 1, Indian Affairs, RG 10, PAC. For seek disunity, see Duke of Portland to Hunter, Oct. 4, 1798, *MPHC* 20:665. The Americans initially suspected British intentions, Sargent to Secretary of State, Sept. 30, 1796, Carter (ed.), *Territorial Papers*, 1:579–80. For orphans, see Message of Ottawas to John Johnson, June 17, 1797, with Prescott to Russell, June 22, 1797, Lt. Gov. of Upper Canada Correspondence, 1796–1806, 1:48, PAC.

[8] Plot against Canada, Prescott to Russell, Oct. 5, 1798, Lt. Governor's Office, Upper Canada 1796–1816, v. 1, PAC. McKee did seek to resurrect an alliance among American Indians, but it was against this French and Spanish threat, McKee to Selby, Jan. 10, 1799, Dept. Superintendent General's Office, v. 26, IA, RG 10, PAC.; Instructions to Joseph Jackson, Jan. 15, 1799, Claus Papers 8:71–72, PAC. For Shawnees and confederacy, see Brant to Russell, Jan. 27, 1799, Lt. Governor's Office, Upper Canada, 1796–1816, v. 1, PAC. For death of McKee, see J. Selby to Russell, Jan. 18, 1799, *ibid.* For crisis of 1799, see Secretary

Politically uneventful, the years following the Treaty of Greenville nevertheless brought widespread economic and environmental change. In the Ohio country, American settlers were the main agents of change. Deeper in the *pays d'en haut*, it was British trading companies that altered the land and its people. Socially, economically, and environmentally, the decade following the Treaty of Greenville witnessed greater transformations in the *pays d'en haut* than any period since the Iroquois wars had created the region.

II

The ancient linkage between alliance and commerce had long served as one of the anchors of the middle ground in the *pays d'en haut*. Originally, Europeans had consented to the marriage of alliance and trade because the Indians would only have commerce with allies, but by the early eighteenth century the rationale of this marriage had shifted. The European empires maintained the marriage because without trade, the alliance would die. British imperialists, like the French before them, had found maintaining the marriage expensive. Therefore, when after the Revolution the British negotiators abandoned their allies and their posts, the British accepted the projected loss of a direct trade with the Algonquians, for "the annual profits of the fur trade were as dust in the balance when weighed against the annual cost of the military posts and garrisons." The Americans would now gather the furs, but the British believed furs and skins would still ultimately find their way to the London emporium. And since the Americans lacked industries of their own, British trade goods would still find a market in Indian villages. In exchange for renouncing the profits of but a single component of the trade, the British believed they were freeing themselves from its most expensive burden.[9]

Although the empire as a whole would little notice the loss of the direct fur trade, the cession of much of the *pays d'en haut* to the United States did threaten the men who gathered the furs. The most important of these men were the Montreal traders, the largely Scottish merchants – the McGills, Frobishers, McCraes, McTavishes, and others – who had settled in Canada

of State to British Minister, Apr. 30, 1799, Carter (ed.), *Territorial Papers*, 3:22; St. Clair to Pickering, *ibid.*, 3:28–29. See also *ibid.*, n. 97. For cession and rumors, see Powell to Askin, May 11, 1798, in Milo Milton Quaife (ed.), *The John Askin Papers, 1747–1820*, 2 vols. (Detroit: Detroit Library Commission, 1928–31), 2:139.
[9] For discussion, see A. L. Burt, *The United States, Great Britain, and British North America from the Revolution to the Establishment of Peace after the War of 1812* (New Haven: Yale University Press, 1940), 21–35, 83–85, dust quote 34. The connection between trade and alliance continued for many Americans, Extract of James Madison's Speech ... Opposing the Ratification of the Treaty with Great Britain, Apr. 6, 1796, *Simcoe Papers*, 4:236.

after its conquest. Their superior connections with the trading houses in England, from whom they obtained goods on commission, had given them an incalculable advantage over their French rivals in Montreal, whom they quickly supplanted as the suppliers of the Great Lakes trade. The middle link of the trading chain – the smaller merchants with their headquarters at Michilimackinac and Detroit – also became less markedly French. Here not only Scotsmen but also Scots-Irish, English, and a few Jewish traders joined the French. Only at the last link of the chain – the traders who carried goods into Indian villages – did French traders remain dominant.[10]

After the Revolution, the Montreal traders had vainly urged the British government to modify the treaty and retain the posts, and, when this proved impossible, they had delayed the evacuation of the posts and supported the Indians in their resistance to the Americans. The long delay in the British withdrawal from Detroit and Michilimackinac did not protect the fur trade over the southern *pays d'en haut*. Warfare disrupted hunting and the fur trade dwindled. The merchants involved took considerable losses.[11]

The center of the fur trade shifted toward the north and west, and new trading companies dominated the lands of the upper Mississippi. Long the most isolated area of the *pays d'en haut*, it was also the richest in furbearers and the most expensive and arduous to tap. These lands were thus the hardest for small traders to exploit. By cooperating among themselves and with the most prominent Michilimackinac merchants, the Montreal traders sought to forge a monopoly in these lands and the even richer Canadian lands beyond them. The Montreal traders were at once the spigot through which trade goods and credit flowed west and the drain through which furs moved to England. All actual traders in the *pays d'en haut*, from Englishmen like Alexander Henry to the French traders, depended on them and were at least seasonally in debt to them. In the winter of 1783–84 the leading Montreal merchants had combined their resources with those of the leading Michilimackinac traders to create the North West Company, which was really less a company than an extended partnership.

---

[10] For British and Scottish merchants, see E. E. Rich, *The Fur Trade and the Northwest to 1857* (Toronto: McClelland & Stewart, 1967), 133. Wayne E. Stevens, *The Northwest Fur Trade, 1763–1800*, Illinois Studies in the Social Sciences, vol. 14, no. 3 (repr., Urbana: University of Illinois Press, 1928), 122–25.

[11] Burt, *The United States, Great Britain and British North America*, 84–105. Stevens, *The Northwest Fur Trade*, 68–98, 168. For operation of trade in late 1770s, see Memorandum relative to the Fur Trade in the Upper Country, c. Mar. 1777, *MPHC* 10:272–74. For increasing volume during last years of the Revolution, see Stevens, *The Northwest Fur Trade*, 65. For figures from 1778 to 1782, see Annual Imports of Skins from Canada, CO. 42/17:91. In all Michilimackinac and its dependencies yielded approximately 4,000 packs of furs annually by 1784, Robertson to Haldimand, Aug. 5, 1784, *MPHC* 11:442. For losses from war, see Merchants Trading at Detroit to Johnson, Aug. 10, 1791, *MPHC* 24:305–6; Simcoe to Dundas, Aug. 12, 1791, *Simcoe Papers*, 1:50.

The growth of the North West Company and associated and competing companies eventually transformed the structure of social relations among the English, French, and Algonquians in the villages of the northwest *pays d'en haut*. In time, the North West Company would act as if it were a government as well as a trading company, but initially it needed the services of the empire. In July 1787, at the request of the traders, British officers and agents gathered the Sioux, Fox, Sauks, Menominees, Chippewas, and Ottawas together to end the wars impeding the fur trade of the upper Mississippi. Although the council ended up causing an imbroglio between traders and British officials, each of whom accused the other of fraud and of attempting to manipulate village politics for their own gain, the effort remained that of a father reconciling his divided children. But the need for the services of empire did not mean that the traders welcomed imperial regulation no matter how ineffective. In 1790 the Montreal merchants secured the repeal of the trade ordinance of 1777, thus ending the licensing system and opening a virtually unrestricted trade in liquor.[12]

Only the fringe of the *pays d'en haut* – the Lake Superior country and the lands draining the upper Mississippi – fell within the North West Company's area of concern, but within these northern lands it aspired to reign supreme. In 1793 the company had three ships operating on Lake Superior and sloops on Lakes Huron, Erie, and Michigan. These ships transported goods to the Grand Portage, and from there canoe brigades moved them north and west. By 1795 the North West controlled 11/14 of the fur trade of Canada, leaving only 1/14 to the older Hudson's Bay Company, much farther north, and the rest to independent traders. When reorganized in 1798, the company employed 50 clerks, 71 interpreters, 1,120 voyageurs, and 35 guides, most of them French and French *métis*.[13]

The rise of the North West Company prompted other combinations. The most important arose in 1798 when independent Montreal traders and dissident North West wintering partners formed the X Y Company. Together, these various companies represented a concerted effort to consolidate the trade. They never fully succeeded in banishing competitors, but they did elevate competition to battles between larger and larger units.

[12] For mediation, see Indian Council Michilimackinac, July 11, 1787, *MPHC* 11:490–96; Representation of Merchants, Aug. 10, 1787, *MPHC* 11:497–99; Extracts from Mr. Dease's Journal, *MPHC* 11:499–501; Report of Joseph Ainse, Aug. 16, 1787, *MPHC* 11:501–6; Proceedings of Court of Inquiry, June–July 1788, *MPHC* 11:541–77. For Northwest Company, see Stevens, *The Northwest Fur Trade*, 140–41. For repeal of ordinance, see Stevens, *The Northwest Fur Trade*, 118–19; An Act . . . to Promote the Trade in the Western Country, *MPHC* 24:204–5. See also Memorial of Montreal Merchants, Oct. 26, 1790, *MPHC* 24:111–13.

[13] For details of the trade, see Stevens, *The Northwest Fur Trade*, 120–43. For employees, see *ibid.*, 141.

Between 1777 and 1790 the number of individual traders and companies
licensed to carry goods from Montreal to the upper country fell by about
half. For well over a century small traders with a single canoe load of goods
had formed a substantial part of the trade. By 1790 only a single such trader
remained.[14]

As the companies stepped into the vacuum left by the decline of alliance,
consolidation and rationalization of the exchange became increasingly
important. Rationalization meant, above all, extricating the fur trade from its
intricate and expensive nexus of social relations. The bourgeois of the North
West Company who employed the French voyageurs and interpreters often
complained that their employees were too soft with the Indians. They
thought the voyageurs and interpreters too inclined to be generous with their
relatives and friends and to yield to their demands too easily. Kin connections facilitated trade, but they also necessitated the outward flow of goods as
gifts to kinspeople. Company officials put pressure on the traders in the field
to cut back on presents. They wanted trading partners more clearly treated
as customers rather than relatives. The companies tried to make gifts into
loans, and they tried to use credit to reduce hunters to a form of debt
peonage, but they did not succeed before 1812.[15]

The companies achieved only limited success because of competition
among themselves and also because, until after 1812, the British empire
proved unwilling to ignore fully the obligations of alliance even in the far
corner of the *pays d'en haut*. The trade war between the North West and X Y
companies in the early nineteenth century resulted in gluts of goods and
falling prices for trade goods. The number of gifts rose as trading companies
sought to steal each other's customers. In this war the companies resorted to
rum – whose import into the region doubled between 1800 and 1803 – and
violence. The war ended only when the two companies merged in 1804.[16]

Even when competition slackened, the companies found it difficult to
push the fur trade toward a simpler and more direct market exchange.
Except for liquor, the wants of most Indian groups remained relatively
inelastic. Comparison of fur returns at Michilimackinac before the de-

---

[14] For licenses and companies, see Stevens, *The Northwest Fur Trade*, 141–43; Rich, *The Fur
Trade*, 190–91.
[15] For such relationships and complaints, see Malhoit's Journal, *WHC* 19:182–84, 194,
200–1. The *WHC* journal is in translation. For the original French, see L. R. Masson, *Les
bourgeois de la Compagnie du Nord-Ouest* (New York: Antiquarian Press, 1960), 227–63. For
the intermarriage of employees and Indians, see Malhoit's Journal, July 24, 1804, *WHC*
19:178; Aug. 3, 1804, 184; Nov. 30, 1804, 204; May 24, 1805, 211. For example of
complaint of excessive generosity of intermarried voyageur, see Jean Baptiste Bazinet, *ibid.*,
Sept. 28, 1804, 200; for his Indian relations, Oct. 18, 1804, 204.
[16] Rich, *The Fur Trade*, 190–91. Stevens, *The Northwest Fur Trade*, 141–42. For an example of
an agreement between the Miamis Company and a trader, see Instructions for Gabriel
Hunct, Sept. 13, 1787. Quaife (ed.), *Askin Papers*, 1:298–99.

regulation of liquor, for example, shows Indians trading a nearly identical total of packs of fur there in 1767 and 1788. The trade of the post expanded only by drawing on new areas to the northwest of Lake Superior. Indians desired a certain number of goods of certain kinds, available at predictable prices. As late as the 1830s, traders operating in Wisconsin complained that once the Indians had "obtained their necessities for a few peltries" they "would not hunt afterwards." Indians hunted to feed their families and to acquire a limited number of furs for exchange. When these requirements were satisfied, they then ceased to hunt intensively.[17]

Traders used credit as well as rum to increase Indian demand, but Indians usually treated credit as a gift. The British government, passively but effectively, protected Indians from the potential consequences of their debts by providing no certain means to collect them. Until the merchants could guarantee the transformation of gifts into loans and guarantee the collection of debts, they could not turn the system into a straightforward market exchange. Merchants gradually managed to use British courts to insure the collection of debts from the French. They did not, however, secure means – short of violence – to convince Indians that credits were debts that had to be repaid on demand. To achieve this goal, they needed imperial aid, which after 1796 could not be obtained in Wisconsin and Michigan even if the empire had been willing. Outside of cutting off further credits, company control over Indian debtors remained virtually nil until the early nineteenth century. Thus despite the rise of powerful new companies, what was called the fur *trade* remained in reality a precarious amalgam of exchanges that ranged from gifts to credit transactions, to direct commodity exchanges, to extortion, to theft. Violence remained a constant possibility. The pressure the companies put on this older system was intense, but because the British remained interested in sustaining Indians as a counterweight to the Americans, those Algonquians of the *pays d'en haut* most involved with the larger fur trading companies sustained a tenuous economic independence.[18]

---

[17] E.g., Jeanne Kay, "Wisconsin Indian Hunting Patterns, 1634–1836," *Annals of the Association of American Geographers* 69 (Sept. 1979): 403. Demand could be quite specific. See Barthelemi Tardiveau, Mémoire concernant le commerce avec differentes nations sauvages ...mars 1784, Chicago Historical Society. For returns, see Jeanne Kay, "The Land of La Baye: The Ecological Impact of the Green Bay Fur Trade, 1634–1836" (Ph.D. diss., University of Wisconsin, 1977), 155–56. At Detroit British woolens still formed the core of the trade, Letter to Lean Neapeau, Detroit, Sept. 1, 1784, *MPHC.*, 24:19. For spending on liquor, see Edwin James (ed.), *A Narrative of the Captivity of and Adventures of John Tanner* (New York: Garland, 1975), 84, 93.

[18] For difficulty in collecting debts, see Archer Butler Hulbert and William N. Schwarze (eds.), *David Zeisberger's History of the Northern American Indians* (Ohio State Archaeological and Historical Society, 1910), 117; Todd and McGill to Askin, Dec. 29, 1786, *Askin Papers*, 1:278–79. Presents established a relationship of mutual aid, not one of debt, *ibid.*, 124. See, e.g., François Malhoit's unhappy winter at Lac du Flambeau in 1804, Malhoit's Journal,

Traders operating south of Michilimackinac also attempted to consolidate the fur trade, but here the reorganization of the trade and the campaign to divorce trade from the alliance made even less headway than they did in Wisconsin and Minnesota. In 1785, Michilimackinac merchants trading to the south and west organized the General Society of the General Store, which duplicated an earlier attempt in 1780. Before the company failed in 1787, their brief monopoly and attempts to make the trade a more purely commercial transaction had greatly antagonized the neighboring Ottawas of Arbre Croche. Farther south, in Detroit, the General Society spawned an imitator and a potential competitor when in about 1786 the merchants of Detroit formed the Miami Company. This company, too, collapsed. Without the leadership and control exerted by powerful Montreal traders, the companies of the *pays d'en haut* turned out to be feeble and fragile. In 1792, however, leading merchants in Detroit – Todd, McGill, and Company; Forsyth, Richardson, and Company; Alexander Henry and Company; and Grant, Campion, and Company – did link up with the powerful Montreal houses. They agreed to use the services of McTavish, Frobisher, and Company and McTavish, Fraser, and Company to import their trade goods and sell their furs in London. Since these two companies were the real powers within the North West Company, the Detroit trade, in a sense, became allied to that huge concern. This partial consolidation, however, struggled to control a Detroit fur trade in decline. American competition and declining numbers of furbearers were part of the problem, but particularly between 1789 and 1794 the fur trade suffered from war, which restricted the hunt, and from American expeditions and raids that hurt traders as well as Indians.[19]

WHC 19:163–233. See also Stevens, *The Northwest Fur Trade*, 155–56. The problem with credit existed over much of the continent, Colin G. Calloway, *Crown and Calumet: British-Indian Relations, 1783–1815* (Norman: University of Oklahoma Press, 1971), 152–53. For early problems at Detroit and results, see Hamilton to Dartmouth, Sept. 2, 1776, *MPHC* 10:264–69; for Michilimackinac, see Sinclair to Haldimand, Aug. 3, 1780, *WHC* 11:158–59. For examples of forcible exchange, see Langlade to Robertson, Mar. 5, 1783, *WHC* 11:164; Burnett to Hands, Feb. 2, 1790, Cunningham (ed.), *Letter Book of William Burnett*, 34; Baubin to Smith, Feb. 18, 1792, *MPHC* 24:378.

19 For 1780, see Sinclair to Haldimand, c. July 1780, *MPHC* 9:562–63; Sinclair to Haldimand, July 8, 1780, *MPHC* 9:561–62; Rich, *The Fur Trade*, 189; Stevens, *The Northwest Fur Trade*, 101. British traders anticipated capturing the Spanish trade in 1784, Letter to Lean Nepeau, Sept. 1, 1784, *MPHC* 24:19. Ottawas, Council, Aug. 3, 1787, *MPHC* 11:493–95. For a sense of the declining fur trade, see Christopher Coleman (ed.), "Letters from Eighteenth-Century Indiana Merchants," *Indiana Magazine of History* 5 (1909): 137–59. For impact of war, see Burnett to Hand, Feb. 6, 1791, Burnett to Todd, Feb. 10, 1792, both in Cunningham (ed.), *Letter Book of William Burnett*, 47–48, 52. François Malhoit wrote of the Chippewas in his diary in 1804: "If they went (to war), I should get no furs." Malhoit's Journal, Aug. 31, 1804, *WHC* 19:195. The Indians, Captain Dederic Brehm reported to General Haldimand during the Revolution, expected "providions [sic] for themselves and families, ammunition & cloathing" since they could neither hunt nor be sure of a harvest

By the mid 1790s, the defeat of the confederation and the consolidation of the fur trade threatened the Algonquians with economic dependency. Their use of European goods was, of course, long-standing. The personal attire of Algonquians – the vermilion with which they painted their faces, the jewelry they wore, and the clothing that covered them – consisted of products of European commerce. In their daily dress most Indians made only the moccasins on their feet, and in manufacturing these, they used European awls. The weapons the warriors carried were also of European manufacture. Finally, their household utensils – the knives with which they cut food, the kettles in which they cooked and the tools with which women sewed or fashioned wooden bowls and spoons – came from European traders.[20]

Mere reliance on European manufactures, however, is not the equivalent of dependency. In an obvious sense, people become clearly dependent when they cannot live without the material goods provided by another people. That the Algonquians deeply desired European manufactures and would hunt to obtain them goes without saying, but that they would starve or die without them does not follow. A Sauk chief threatened with the loss of trade in 1779, answered that "he & all others had arrows for their living & . . . they were not alarmed by that." There is no need for hypothetical arguments over the practicality of the Sauk chief's retort. In 1783 the Wabash villagers deserted the Americans and went over to the British in part because of the Americans' failure to supply them. These Algonquians clearly desired trade goods, but for the previous two years they had lived largely cut off from European trade. They had not starved. Instead, they reverted to older methods of feeding and clothing themselves. As early as 1780, the Piankashaws had returned to hunting with bows and arrows. By 1782, three-quarters of the Wabash villagers were using bows and arrows and wearing buffalo skins in place of blankets. Algonquians did not like living without European goods, but they could do so at least temporarily. Indians refused to buy when goods were expensive.[21]

when at war, Brehm to Haldimand, May 28, 1779, MPHC 9:405. At Michilimackinac Captain De Peyster reported that "the Indians since the beginning of the War are becoming very idle, even in the hunting Season," De Peyster to Haldimand, June 1, 1779, MPHC 9:383. During the Revolution the English asked the Shawnees to give up hunting and keep their warriors in the field, Speech of the Chavenous to Capt. Lernoult, Sept. 26, 1779, MPHC 19:468. For war disrupting hunt on Mississippi, see Memorandum for Sir John Johnson, Apr. 4, 1786, MPHC 11:486–87. On the White River, see Lorimer to Askin, Nov. 24, 1786, Askin Papers, 1:271. For excessive competition in region, see Burnett to Young, Oct. 7, 1792, ibid.

[20] For a good description of goods in the Indian trade and the uses Algonquians had for them, see Barthelemi Tardiveau, Mémoire concernant le commerce avec differentes nations sauvages . . . mars 1784, Chicago Historical Society.

[21] For Sauk chief, see Gautier to De Peyster, 19 Apr. 1779, MPHC 19:397–98. Piankashaws, Dalton to Clark, May 16, 1780, Clark Papers, Missouri Historical Society, copy in Ohio

Dependency, however, also has more complex meanings. Despite significant differences between them, historical dependency theory and Marxist studies of capitalist expansion both assert that peripheral regions – such as the *pays d'en haut* – are rendered dependent when representatives of the European core penetrate the peripheries, extract their surpluses, and thwart the inhabitants' efforts to regain control of surplus production. In the periphery, first merchants and then capitalists appropriate the fruits of the labor of primary producers in an unequal exchange; the resulting profit fuels the further development of the core. In one Marxist version of this process, merchants capture a kinship mode of production and transform it into an essentially tributary mode, which reduces the producers to a kind of debt peonage in which they depend on outsiders for essential elements of survival. Both Marxists and dependency theorists use the fur trade as an example of such an unequal exchange that results in the transformation of existing patterns of labor and social relations and the reduction of a region and its peoples to dependency. In a multiple sense, therefore, for these theorists the history of the periphery comes to depend on decisions made in the core.[22]

That this eventually happened over much of the *pays d'en haut* is clear, but the question is one of when this took place. Before the War of 1812, this transformation of existing patterns and social relations had, by and large, not occurred. The Indians remained, in Eric Wolf's words, independent

Valley-Great Lahes Ethnohistorical Archives, University of Indiana (hereafter cited as GLEHA). For Wabash villages, see Williams to Clark, Jan. 12, 1782, *ibid.* Haldimand had cut off trade to those villages that did not expel the Americans, Haldimand's Speech . . . to Michilimakinac . . . 2 July 1779, Haldimand Papers, 21779. Heckewelder emphasized that the Indians still maintained the ability to manufacture their own clothing, John Heckewelder, *History, Manners, and Customs of Indian Nations Who Once Inhabited Pennsylvania and the Neighboring States*, new and rev. ed. (Philadelphia, 1876; Repr. ed., New York: Arno Press, 1971), 202. As late as 1807, the Moravians described "old widows" making coats from hemp and turkey feathers. "They made their coats in that fashion in former times." Gottfried Oppelt and Christian F. Denke, Diary, Mar. 31, 1807, 1:55, Box 157, Folder 4, Moravian Archives, copy and trans. in GLEHA. For would not buy expensive goods, see Burnett to Patterson, Apr. 3, 1788, Cunningham (ed.), *Letter Book of William Burnett*, 26.

22 Here I have in mind Eric Wolf, *Europe and the People Without History* (Berkeley: University of California Press, 1982), particularly 21–23, 86–88. I agree with much of what Wolf says. In principle he makes the Indians independent actors. But his particular account of the fur trade is badly flawed and ignores the very common history he claims to want to emphasize. His account of the fur trade, 161–75, finds little support in the history detailed above. For a dispute over similar issues of the influence of the periphery, see Steven J. Stern, "Feudalism, Capitalism, and the World System in the Perspective of Latin America and the Caribbean," *American Historical Review* 93 (Oct. 1988), and the exchange between Stern and Immanuel Wallerstein that follows.

Francis Jennings asserts dependency by the mid eighteenth century. But he has not looked at the primary French sources, and his evidence is largely the assertion that the use of goods they were unable to manufacture themselves must have made Indians dependent, Francis Jennings, *Empire of Fortune: Crown, Colonies, and Tribes in the Seven Years' War in America* (New York: W. W. Norton, 1988), 50.

political agents. Independent political agents could still be economically exploited. The British might have raked off large surpluses from the fur trade and transferred the profits to Montreal and London. But determining whether this, in fact, happened may be impossible. Calculating profit involves reducing all the complicated exchanges of the *pays d'en haut* to a single unit of value. The middle ground, it is true, had by the late eighteenth century operated to create a common system of exchange and even unit systems of values. Traders in the southern *pays d'en haut* had, for instance, instituted the *buck* – the hide of a large male white-tailed deer – as the standard unit in whose terms they calculated both the value of other furs and of European manufactures. The buck, in turn, became equated with an American silver dollar. Similarly, in the northern region the *plus* – one beaver skin – became the standard unit of value. But the realm of the buck and the plus remained relatively narrow: It covered direct trade between a trader and his Indian customer, and this comprised only a portion of the total exchange system.[23]

Commercial exchanges continued to occur amid a complicated array of gift exchanges, extortions, and thefts. The Indians might lose on direct trade but balance their losses by gaining on the gifts they received, on the debts they refused to pay, and on thefts that went unpunished. When Lieutenant Governor Simcoe visited the Shawnees in 1794, he was astonished at "the richness of their Dresses and Ornaments (which upon an Average were worth forty or fifty pounds per man)." The trade had certainly not yet impoverished them. In this sense the real key to dependency was political. And, indeed, the great crisis of the trade in the years just before the War of 1812 was political. As William Henry Harrison noted in 1810, "These remote savages have felt their full share of the misfortunes which the trouble in Europe have brought upon the greater part of the world." Cut off from their Continental markets, the British could not sell furs and "the price of those articles" dropped "almost to nothing." But it was at this juncture that British gifts increased dramatically as the British sought allies in case of war. Only when they ceased giving adequate gifts, when the American and British governments were willing to deploy enough force to secure the collection of debts and to suppress theft, would the Indians slide into dependency.[24]

As long as the empire, for political reasons, remained willing to under-write the trade through gifts and other services, however, it remained possible for both traders and Indians to profit from the exchange. During

[23] For plus, see Stevens, *The Northwest Fur Trade*, 145. For buck equals dollar, see Jeffry to Harmar, Dec. 1789, Harmar Papers l11:99.

[24] Simcoe to Privy Council on Trades & Plantation, Dec. 20, 1794, *Simcoe Papers*, 3:228. For Harrison quotation, see Harrison to Secretary of War, June 14, 1810, Esarey, *Harrison Messages*, 426.

prolonged periods in the late eighteenth and early nineteenth centuries, the total costs of the trade – when the expenses both of the empire and of Montreal merchants and local traders are calculated – exceeded the profits merchants derived from the trade and the duties the crown collected from it. The net exchange between center and periphery was thus not necessarily unequal. An assertion of dependency on the basis of the consequences of unequal exchange makes little sense unless unequal exchange itself can be demonstrated.[25]

[25] Gifts, though important, seldom if ever met the Indians' total demand for goods. In the fall of 1778, e.g., the British gave presents to the Ottawas of Arbre Croche and Kishkacon (apparently a nearby village). The two villages contained 250 warriors or 875 persons (by British reckoning of 2.5 persons for each warrior). This semiannual present represented roughly half of the gifts given to the village as a whole during the year, although individuals might receive other gifts. To take two common trade goods: The Indians received 178 blankets (assuming a pair of blankets in the invoice means 2) and 120 shirts at this distribution. This was not even a shirt and a blanket for each warrior, although each warrior might have received one or the other. Since the gift was semiannual, over the course of the year a warrior might expect a blanket or a shirt, but this would still leave his family unclothed and would necessitate hunting, List of Goods . . . fall of 1778, *MPHC* 9:655.
    This basic ratio apparently applied to Michilimackinac as a whole. In August 1781 the British at Michilimackinac received 1,832 blankets (again assuming that a pair of blankets signifies 2) for presents to be distributed over the next year. In 1782, there were 4,020 Indians dependent on Michilimackinac, but this underestimates the total population since, except for the Ottawas and Chippewas of Grand River, Arbre Croche, Michilimackinac, and points in between, the British counted only the chiefs and heads of families who visited the posts. Goods received by the 150 Winnebagos, e.g., would have to be redistributed to a far larger number of people.
    If the list is revised to count only adult men, then 2,660 persons received the blankets. This means that there was not even one blanket for each person who received a gift directly; therefore, hunters still had to provide for their families. In addition to this, there would be blankets given by traders and charged to the Crown, but such gifts were most common when supplies did not arrive. Gifts on this scale represented a significant contribution to the limited demand for European goods, but Indians would still have to hunt. See Invoice of Goods, Aug. 31, 1781, *MPHC* 19:658–61. Number of Indians Resorting to Michilimackinac, Sept. 10, 1782, *MPHC* 10:635.
    The number of presents at Detroit was considerably larger – 9,400 blankets (or 4,700 pairs) in 1782 – but so was the number of Indians dependent on the post. A census in 1782 counted 11,403 Indians. The Detroit distributions came closer to meeting annual demand, but then, these Indians were more actively involved in the war, Estimate of Merchandise Wanted for Indian Presents . . . to 20 Aug. 1782, *MPHC* 10:632–33; De nombrement des Indiens résidents dans le district du Détroit pour l'année 1782, Haldimand Papers, 21783.
    This argument pertains only to areas like the *pays d'en haut* where two particular conditions applied: (1) Indians remained independent political agents able to force competing powers to give them the gifts necessary to maintain peace and alliance, and (2) they faced not a single large monopoly, or even several large firms, but many small competing traders whom they partially integrated into their own kinship systems. In areas such as the Hudson's Bay region where such conditions did not apply, trade could take different forms, and profit and loss were more easily determined. See Arthur J. Ray and Donald Freeman, *Give Us Good Measure: An Economic Analysis of Relations Between the Indians and the Hudson's Bay Company Before 1763* (Toronto: University of Toronto Press, 1978), passim.
    For Haldimand's complaints about frequency of bills drawn on traders, and the "Exorbitant Charges of the Merchants at the Posts," see Haldimand to De Peyster, May 8,

III

Dependency is an economic, political, and social relationship, but it can also be an environmental relationship. Economic change can produce environmental changes that undermine people's ability to feed and clothe themselves. Although the Algonquians retained a precarious hold on economic independence into the nineteenth century, they did have to face increasingly serious changes in the material world around them. In 1807, Trout, an Ottawa visionary, conveyed a message from the Great Spirit to the Indians living around Michilimackinac that was similar to several other prophetic messages of the period: "You complain," he told the Ottawas and Chippewas, "that the animals of the Forest are few and scattered. How should it be otherwise? You destroy them yourselves for their Skins only and leave their bodies to rot or give the best pieces to the Whites. I am displeased when I see this, and take them back to the Earth that they may not come to you again. You must kill no more animals than are necessary to feed and cloathe you."[26]

The diminished natural world Trout and other visionaries complained of was less a product of the inexorable depletion brought on by the fur trade than it was a result of changes in the nature of that trade. Accounts of poor hunts and famines in the 1780s, for example, are not easily attributable to depletion due to the fur trade. All changes in the environment are not the direct result of human actions, and all cases of starvation among humans are not indicators of environmental decline. Climatic variations – drought or heavy winter snows – have direct and immediate, although often short-lived, effects on game populations. Fur trade returns vary not only with the abundance of game, but with the weather and the market. Mild winters in

---

1781, Haldimand Papers, 21781. Haldimand to De Peyster, Apr. 20, 1781, *MPHC* 10:471; see also, Henry Hamilton, State of the Trade with the Indian Countries, Shelburne Papers, 88:67, Clements Library; Hamilton to Haldimand, c. Sept. 1778, Haldimand Papers, 21781; De Peyster to Haldimand, May 27, 1781, Haldimand Papers, 21781.

In justifying the cession of most of the *pays d'en haut* to the Americans, Lord Shelburne repeated earlier French arguments: It cost the government more to hold the territory than the fur trade yielded, Stevens, *The Northwest Fur Trade*, 76–78. It was an argument with much merit, see A. L. Burt, "A New Approach to the Problem of the Western Posts," Canadian Historical Association, *Report of the Annual Meeting* (Ottawa: 1931), 71.

The British government derived duties from the fur trade that averaged £22,021.15.4 between 1793 and 1801, Harold A. Innis, *The Fur Trade in Canada: An Introduction to Canadian Economic History* (Toronto: University of Toronto Press, 1956), 178.

[26] Substance of a Talk delivered at Le Macouitonong . . . by the Indian Chief Le Maigaouis or the Trout coming from the first man created . . . May 4, 1807, PAC, M.G. 19, F 16. See also the vision of "an old Indian woman," Oct. 24, 1803, Lawrence H. Gipson, *The Moravian Indian Mission on White River*, in vol. 23 of *Indiana Historical Collections* (Indianapolis: Indiana Historical Bureau, 1938), 262, and the vision of Tenskwatawa, Dec. 3, 1805, *ibid.*, 392.

which deer do not yard up in sheltered areas and in which inadequate snow cover hinders the ability of hunters to track or see deer and other game reduced fur trade yields. In more southerly areas, where Indians did not usually use snowshoes, heavy snows could disrupt the hunt. When natural factors affected the hunt, a report of a poor hunt might quickly be followed by reports of abundant game. Similarly, the chronic warfare of the 1770s and 1780s in the Ohio Valley kept hunters out of many areas, often restricted the duration of the hunt, and hurt food production, but it might have increased overall game populations. Lieutenant Governor Simcoe thought the increase in deer because of the war was "prodigious," and the Moravians reported that the area between the Muskingum and the Ohio rivers had become a war ground making game "very plentiful." Many travelers during the 1780s and early 1790s remarked on the abundance of game. When humans killed each other, animals received a respite.[27]

[27] Famine and want were prevalent in the Ohio country in the 1780s, but this was the result of war, crop failures, and terrible weather rather than game depletion. In 1782 there was famine in the Ohio Valley. And in 1784 famine returned again when the harvest failed and then a bad winter depleted deer populations. In 1787 once more there was a general famine in the Indian country from Detroit to the Miami, and in 1788 widespread hunger followed a winter in which the snow was six feet deep between the Ohio and Lake Erie. The Indians said it was the worst winter in living memory. This culminated in a severe famine in 1789 when Indians delayed planting because of fears of American invasion. Then worms attacked the corn – both at the Indian towns from Niagara to the Miami and at the white settlements in Detroit – and, finally, frost killed much of the remaining corn. The Indians were reduced to eating their horses; there were reports of starvation, and widespread sickness took many lives at Detroit. The next year brought little relief, for everywhere, David Zeisberger noted, there was "famine and want."

All of this does not mean permanent game depletion, see, e.g., Beverley Bond, Jr. (ed.), "Two Western Journeys of John Filson, 1785," *Mississippi Valley Historical Review* 9 (1923): 324, 328; Butler's Journal, Oct. 12–13, Oct. 17, 1785, in Neville B. Craig, Esq. (ed.), *The Olden Time* (Pittsburgh: Dumars, 1846; Millwood, N.Y.: Kraus Reprint Co., 1976), 445–47, 450; "Narrative of John Heckewelder's Journey to the Wabash in 1792," *Pennsylvania Magazine of History and Biography*, 12 (1888): 37, 51, 165, 173–74, 176; Sargent to Symmes and Putnam, Aug. 5, 1792, in Rowena Buell (ed.), *The Memoirs of Rufus Putnam and Certain Official Papers and Correspondence* (Boston: Houghton, Mifflin, 1903), 310; Speeches . . . Feb. 1, 1793, in H. A. Washington (ed.), *The Writings of Thomas Jefferson* (New York: Derby & Jackson, 1859), 8:181. For "prodigious" increase, see Simcoe to Committee of the Privy Council, Sept. 1, 1794, in *Simcoe Papers*, 3:55. For abundance, see Gipson, *Moravian Mission*, Sept. 30, 1802, and Autobiography of Abraham Luckenbach, in Gipson, *Moravian Mission*, 484, 599; Constantin-François Volney, *A View of the Soil and Climate of the United States of America* . . . (Philadelphia: T & G Palmer, 1804, repr.), 341.

William Burnett reported a poor hunt at Kankakee in 1789–90, Burnett to Hands, Feb. 2, 1790. It was followed by relatively good hunts in the early 1790s, and then a very poor hunt in 1795–96, Burnett to Chaboiller & Young, May 17, 1796. Two years later (1797–98) he reported a good year, Burnett to Parker Gerrard & O'Gilivy (*sic*), Burnett to John O'Gilvie & Co., May 26, 1798. But it was followed in 1798–99 by a mild winter and a poor hunt, Burnett to Robt. Innes & Co., Dec. 20, 1798, all in Cunningham (ed.), *Letter Book of William Burnett*, 32, 70, 89, 94–95, 113.

Around Detroit, the winter of 1784–85 was mild, which meant a poor hunt, but, supposedly, there was good hunting to the south of there, John MacPherson to Gray, Mar.

In areas less affected by war, however, depletion did occur. Such depletion tended to be local or species specific, and it often affected areas that had always been marginal game habitats. In the late eighteenth century, the pinelands of northern Michigan and Wisconsin could no longer support hunting. The Ottawas of Arbre Croche lamented in 1787 that "no more animals remain to call us out to the Woods." They lived on fishing and farming. The local depletion of beaver and deer in the area immediately around Green Bay forced the Menominees, Winnebagos, and Chippewas there to choose between continuing to maintain winter fishing villages and continuing to engage in the fur trade. The distance it was necessary to travel for the fall and winter hunt made it impossible to do both. A result was a sharp decline in fishing the fall and winter spawning runs, and the emergence of an annual migration to the hunting lands of the upper Mississippi. Although beaver remained only locally abundant even in the upper Mississippi, white-tailed deer and raccoon did abound, and they became the staples of the local fur trade.[28]

The decline of beaver was the most notable result of the fur trade, but even here depletion is more accurate than extinction. Given a respite, beaver populations could recover. Barthelemi Tardiveau asserted that beaver remained locally abundant in the Ohio and Wabash country following the Revolution, and although populations had dwindled in Michigan and Wisconsin by the nineteenth century, local populations, apparently not numerous enough for hunters' attention, remained. When a species declined, hunters and traders shifted their attention elsewhere. The trade shifted over time from a reliance on beaver to a reliance on the white-tailed deer and the raccoon. By the 1780s, the white-tailed deer was already the most significant animal in the fur trade from the Ohio as far north as Mackinac. Indeed, even raccoon pelts exceeded beaver pelts in terms of the

23, 1785. Another mild winter ruined the hunt on the Miamis in 1786–87, Ironside to Gray, Feb. 10, 1787, both in Coleman (ed.), "Indiana Merchants," 142–43, 149. For heavy snows, see Message from Chiefs at the Glaize, c. Apr. 1792, *MPHC* 24:401.

28 Ottawas of Arbre Croche, Council at Arbre Croche, Aug. 3, 1787, *MPHC* 11:494. Tribal names serve as easy referents at Green Bay and Milwaukee, but most of these people intermarried extensively, and their villages usually contained members of other groups. Kay, "Hunting Patterns," 412. Kay, "The Land of La Baye," 156 (data from Lart 1922, O'Callaghan 1851), 158, 160. For the fishery, see Charles Cleland, "The Inland Shore Fishery of the Northern Great Lakes: Its Development and Importance in Prehistory," *American Antiquity* 47 (1982): 761–84. De Peyster described winter fishing at Michilimackinac as precarious, De Peyster to Haldimand, June 1, 1779, *MPHC* 9:383. For description of hunting grounds and trade, see R. Dickson to Hamilton, July 14, 1793, *Simcoe Papers*, 1:387–91; Simcoe to Dundas, Sept. 20, 1793, *Simcoe Papers*, 2:59; Gottfried S. Oppelt, Diary, Sept. 30, 1805, Box 157, Folder 2, Moravian Archives, copy and translation in GLEHA. To the north, the Chippewas of Sault Sainte Marie and Michilimackinac who had not migrated toward the west relied far more on the fisheries than on the hunt for subsistence. Robertson to Matthews, Sept. 7, 1783, *MPHC* 11:394.

volume of trade. The beaver trade had shifted largely to the area northwest of the Great Lakes. Much later in the nineteenth century, as deer and raccoon declined, muskrat served as the staple fur of the trade.[29]

The decline of small furbearers had less of an impact on Indian subsistence than did the decline of large game animals – deer, bear, elk, and buffalo. This was at the heart of the crisis visionaries described in the early nineteenth century. The decline of these animals was most pronounced in the Ohio Valley, but it extended into the western Great Lakes region. It was the work of changes in habitat, of white hunters, and of changes in Indian hunting.

Wholesale depletion of large game animals became obvious only in the very late eighteenth and early nineteenth centuries. In southern Indiana, Ohio, and Illinois, whites, not Indians, were the main agents of the slaughter. William Henry Harrison, no friend of the Indians, termed the slaughter of buffalo, deer, bear, and elk on Indian lands by whites a "monstrous abuse." One white hunter, Harrison complained, killed more game "than five of the common Indians – the latter generally contenting himself with a sufficiency for present subsistence" while the whites were uniformly hide hunters.[30]

Complicating this slaughter of game was the habitat transformation that accompanied it. In settling farms, backcountry Americans destroyed game habitat. They also limited Indian villages to more and more narrowly circumscribed areas. Indians usually hunted out animals within easy range of their villages, but abandoning a village and moving to a new area allowed game to recover. The lands the Moravians reported full of game in the late 1790s had been depleted in the 1770s. With American settlement, habitat was permanently lost and the older cycle of depletion and recovery now had to take place on a circumscribed land base. Depletion was more likely to be permanent, and hunting pressure on remaining lands greater.[31]

Whites helped transform the habitat and diminish game even in unsettled areas. By 1805, white settlers were putting great pressure on Indians to stop

---

[29] For beaver, see Kay, "Hunting Patterns," 402–17. Beaver had begun to decline as early as the 1740s in eastern Wisconsin, but it was not eliminated, Kay, "Land of La Baye," 156, 158, 160. Barthelemi Tardiveau, Mémoire concernant le commerce avec differentes nations sauvages . . . mars 1784, Chicago Historical Society.

[30] For Harrison description, see Harrison to Secretary of War, July 15, 1801, Esarey (ed.), Harrison, 25–30. Indian complaints, Conference with the Delaware and Shawanoe Deputation, Secretary of War, Letters Sent, Indian Affairs, v. A, National Archives, M 15, roll 1. The Delawares and Cherokees living among the Delawares were hide hunters, Gipson, Moravian Mission, Dec. 1, 1801, Oct. 26, 1804, 132, 315.

[31] The Muskingum took its name "Elk's Eye" from the abundance of elk, but that animal had declined by 1780 although some remained, Hulbert and Schwarge (eds.), Zeisberger's History, 44. Bison were retreating from Indian settlements on the Muskingum by 1780, ibid., 59. As early as 1793, the British commented that Detroit hunters had to travel farther for game than they used to, Smith to McKee, Oct. 22, 1793, Claus Papers 6:49, PAC.

the annual burning of the forests that provided browse for deer. Algonquian hunters complained that "if we are not permitted to set fire we cannot live . . . if we set fire to the weeds or grass, it is to live on the game, we have no other means to subsist. All that the maker of Life placed on the Earth is to live upon and we endeavour to live as in the times of our first fathers. Why do you reproach us of setting fires?" As the settlements encroached, Indians could not manage neighboring lands in the usual manner.[32]

The final ingredient in this pattern of depletion was changes in the habits of Indian hunters. Harrison denounced white hunters, but in 1804 there were already many Indian hunters who resembled them. Foremost among the new market hunters were the Delawares. David Zeisberger described extraordinarily wasteful hunts by Ohio Delawares in the 1780s:

> Because there is considerable trade in skins, deer are killed mainly for their hides and only so much flesh is used as the Indians can consume while on the chase, wherefore, most of the meat is left in the woods for the wild animals. . . . As an Indian shoots from fifty to a hundred and fifty deer each fall, it can easily be appreciated that game must decrease.

But in the 1780s the Delawares were unusual. Other Indians thought them exceptionally profligate and dangerous and resented the appearance of their hunters. In 1787, the Miamis denied the Delawares access to their land "for the Delawares shoot the deer for the sake of the skins and leave the flesh lying in the bush." The Ojibwas similarly resented the Moravian Delawares for destroying their game. When in the 1790s Delaware hunters persisted in their practices, they were attacked by other hunters. But as Trout's rebuke to the Ottawas and Chippewas showed, Delaware methods had become widespread after the turn of the century.[33]

The acquisition of horses by the Algonquians also contributed to increased game kills. Acquired during the wars of the late eighteenth century, horses greatly aided the hunting of buffalo on the prairie lands of Illinois, Wisconsin, and Iowa. Unlike other groups, the Sauks and Fox maintained large winter villages, and they began to rely on bison to sustain these villages. Although Indian hunters undoubtedly contributed to the reduction of bison, here, too, it was white market hunters – in this case, French hunters who shipped meat south to New Orleans – who were probably the

---

[32] The Answer of Pawatamo, Chasso, and Oulaqua . . . Dec. 16, 1805, Esarey (ed.), *Harrison Messages*, 179.

[33] For Zeisberger quotation, see Hulbert and Schwarze (eds.), *Zeisberger's History*, 14. For Miami quotation, see *Diary of David Zeisberger, A Moravian Missionary Among the Indians of Ohio*, tr. and ed. by Eugene F. Bliss, 2 vols. (Cincinnati: R. Clarke, 1885), May 26, 1787, 1:346. For attack, see *ibid.*, Sept. 24–25, 1795, 2:421. For Moravians, Zeisberger, Heckewelder, see Edwards to Ancrum, Feb. 26, 1786, *Askin Papers*, 1:218–21. For waste, see Gipson, *Moravian Mission*, Oct. 26, 1804, 315.

leading factor in the animal's decline. Elk, another herd animal, also went into decline as far west as Wisconsin in the late eighteenth and early nineteenth centuries.[34]

The spread of skin hunting – the killing, only for their skins, of large animals critical to subsistence – sprang from several causes, but the liquor trade played a critical role. The end of the wars of the confederation and the abandonment of the British posts brought a decline in presents, increasing the burden on the trade. The deregulation of the liquor trade by the British also brought an increase in Indian demand, particularly in areas around the Great Lakes where ships could transport bulky kegs of liquor. And the settlement of the Ohio country made liquor easily obtainable in white settlements.[35]

In lamenting the changes brought by the fur trade, Trout was describing a physical world with less deer, less elk, less beaver, less large game of all kinds; but he was also describing a social world where, to paraphrase Maurice Godelier, a deer was more than meat and skins and a beaver was more than a source of fur. Animals remained persons with whom human beings maintained social relations, and Indian prophets such as Trout and Tenskwatawa, like Neolin before them, condemned the fur trade for altering the relations between humans and animals. Struggling to restore proper ritual relations between animals and humans, they spoke in terms of a Great Spirit who regulated the game in the same manner as keepers of the game had done earlier. If the Indians heeded the message of the Great Spirit, as given to the first man created and now again brought to life, then the first man would "cause the animals such as they were formerly when I created them, to come forth out of the Earth."[36]

[34] For Sauks and Fox, see Kay, "The Land of La Baye," 169–70; James Clifton, "From Bark Canoe to Pony Herds: The Lake Michigan Transportation Revolution, 1750–55" (paper presented at the Chicago Maritime Conference, 1984). All the herd animals – elk as well as bison – were declining in the late eighteenth-century *pays d'en haut*. For elk, see Kay, "Wisconsin Indian Hunting Patterns," 403.

[35] As a present, rum reached "astonishing" quantities at Detroit during the Revolution. In 1779, Indians were consuming rum at 17,520 gallons a year, Haldimand to Lernoult, July 23, 1779, Haldimand Papers, 21781. In 1793, R. G. England complained of the arrival at Detroit of two merchant vessels laden with rum, England to Simcoe, July 18, 1793, *Simcoe Papers*, 1:392. For other references, see Simcoe to McKee, July 23, 1793, *Simcoe Papers* 5:63. Perrault, 1795, Cass Lake Chippewa, *MPHC* 37:574; McKee to Johnson, June 20, 1791, *MPHC* 24:263–64. Because liquor was bulky, problems of transportation provided some limits on its use at least in those areas accessible only by canoe or horse, Memorial of Montreal Merchants, Apr. 23, 1792, *MPHC* 24:406.

Europeans sold rum directly to Indians, but Algonquians, often women, became the main purveyors of alcohol because of the danger drunken Indians presented to traders, Hulbert and Schwarge (eds.), *Zeisberger's History*, 90, 117; *Zeisberger Diary*, Sept. 28, Oct. 29, 1790, 2:126–27, 133; Gipson, *Moravian Mission*, Aug. 17, 1801, Apr. 13, 1802, July 27, 1803, Aug. 1, 1804, Feb. 26, 1806, 121, 158, 247, 305, 409.

[36] For quotation, see Substance of a Talk, May 4, 1807, PAC, M.G. 19, F 16. See also Gipson,

Tenskwatawa and Trout tried to create ideological obstacles to over-hunting and the fur trade. That they had to condemn overhunting, however, shows that existing Algonquian religious beliefs were proving insufficient to the task. Tenskwatawa explicitly related the decline of game to the fur trade and to Indian actions within the fur trade, but his position remained only one of competing explanations among reasons for the decline of game. Precisely because hunting was a holy occupation, a demonstration of spiritual power in which animals delivered themselves to the hunter with the consent of the spiritual masters of the game, refusing to kill an animal made no sense to many Algonquians. It was true that hunters should not kill gratuitously, but an Algonquian hunter who killed a deer for its skin and left the meat could very easily see his act as one necessary to obtain his *besoins*. And such killing, hunters believed, was not necessarily detrimental to deer. Long after Tenskwatawa had preached his doctrine, Shawnee hunters, for example, continued to believe that each deer, when killed in proper ritual manner, had four lives. It would immediately reincarnate itself and return. The whites, they said, were responsible for the disappearance of deer. They killed deer improperly and so the deer no longer returned. When the Delawares, the earliest and most ruthless market hunters, were unable to kill deer despite their use of powerful *besoins* or medicines, they blamed their failure on the presence of white missionaries who defeated the hunting medicine.[37]

For virtually all Algonquians the decline of game remained something to be explained by the neglect of ritual. Conserving game thus made sense only in terms of keeping out those hunters who were enemies or those who killed game in an improper manner. Thus the Sioux fought to preserve the hunting grounds of the upper Mississippi from encroaching Chippewa hunters, and the Chippewas attacked Sioux hunters they found on disputed grounds. The aim of this fighting was not, however, to protect game per se. Both groups allowed Menominee and Winnebago hunters to take game in the disputed area, for the Menominees and Winnebagos were enemies of neither and killed game properly. Similarly, some of the Chippewas north of Detroit blamed incoming Moravian Delawares for doing "great harm and damage in their hunting," perhaps because the Moravians had given up their hunting rituals.[38]

Moravian Mission, Dec. 3, 1805, 392. Maurice Godelier, *The Mental and the Material: Thought, Economy and Society* (Norfolk, England: Verso, 1986): 35.

[37] This was the belief of early twentieth-century Shawnees, C. F. Voegelin, *The Shawnee Female Deity*, Yale University Publications in Anthropology, no. 10 (repr., New Haven: Human Relations Area Files Press, 1970), 20, but it corresponds to earlier Shawnee cosmology. See also Jeanne Kay, "Native Americans in the Fur Trade and Wildlife Depletion," *Environmental Review* 9 (1985): 118–30. For Delaware and *besons*, and also for other rituals of the hunt, see Hulbert and Schwarze (eds.), *Zeisberger's History*, 84.

[38] For Menominees and Winnebagos, see Kay, "The Land of La Baye," 158–60; Kay, "Hunting Patterns," 412. For renunciation of hunting rituals, see John Heckewelder, *A*

To offset the spreading decline in game animals critical to subsistence, Indians in the southern part of the *pays d'en haut* adopted domestic animals: horses, cattle, pigs, and chickens. The Moravian Delawares and the Detroit Hurons led this movement. Indians could easily fit pigs – which foraged in the forests for food – into their subsistence cycle, but cattle presented more of a difficulty. Indians had to leave their cattle behind during winter hunts. Delawares living near the Moravians paid the Christian Indians to care for their cattle over the winter; others left them to forage in the forest. Such foraging, however, threatened fields in the summer, and the Hurons of Detroit, who had a "great many cattle," took to fencing their fields to protect them from roving animals. Indians adopted horses far more widely than they did cattle. Horses not only aided in certain kinds of hunting, they also allowed hunters to pack skins out and to pack food and supplies in.[39]

The increase in domestic livestock and the decline of game became a major indicator of the changes overtaking Indians in the early nineteenth century. The change was gradual. A Moravian family had "a number of horses, and perhaps an equal number of cows, a number of pigs, and a number of dogs, which serve them while hunting." And the Hurons of Brownstown in 1804 were set apart from their neighbors by their "few Cattle and . . . a large number of hogs" and their desire to increase their cattle herds. Deer and cattle, bears and hogs became markers of different modes of subsistence and also symbols of the new social constructions of Indians and whites.[40]

IV

The chiefs who tried to manage this rapidly changing world of first neglectful and then demanding fathers failed in their attempts. They failed most obviously in the Ohio Valley and the southern Great Lakes country, less obviously in the villages of the northwest *pays d'en haut* among the Winnebagos, Chippewas, Sauks and Fox, and Menominees. They failed as mediators; they failed to hold support among their own people; they failed to

Narrative of the Mission of the United Brethren Among the Delaware and Mohegan Indians, from Its Commencement in the Year 1740 to the Close of the Year 1808 (Philadelphia: McCarty and Davis, 1820; Arno repr., 1971), 123. For Chippewa anger at Moravians, see *Zeisberger Diary*, Nov. 9, 1784, 1:215–16.

[39] For early adoption of livestock, see Hulbert and Schwarze (eds.), *Zeisberger's History*, 45–46. For cattle, see *Zeisberger Diary*, Nov. 12, 1789, 2:65. For Hurons, see *ibid.*, May 9, 1791, 2:181.

[40] Autobiography of Luckenbach in Gipson, *Moravian Mission*, 598. Joseph E. Walker (ed.), "Plowshares and Pruning Hooks for the Miami and Potawatomi: The Journal of Gerard T. Hopkins, 1804," *Ohio History* 88 (Fall 1979): 402–3.

preserve the peace of their own towns. Many of them fell as victims of their own relatives and warriors. The final crisis of the political middle ground was marked by the blood of chiefs.

The Treaty of Greenville served as an augury of the chiefs' future. Sixty Potawatomis, among them many of the chiefs who had signed the treaty, died soon after the council with Wayne. The Potawatomis accused the Americans of poisoning their leaders. So many other chiefs died soon after the treaty signing that the British too suspected poisoning, but they thought the opponents of the treaty had poisoned those who had signed. Among the Shawnees, the death of Red Pole – the leading Shawnee negotiator – and another Shawnee brought accusations of witchcraft and then murders and retaliations.[41]

The deaths of so many chiefs only exacerbated the already touchy problem of who was a chief. Struggles between war leaders and peace or village chiefs spawned bitter rivalries and divisions. In the wake of a generation of nearly constant war, war leaders in many villages acted as if they should be the intermediaries with outsiders. In 1795 Anthony Wayne reported in some confusion that Blue Jacket, the Shawnee war leader, had visited him and "appeared to set an inestimable value upon a piece of printed Paper – enlisting[?] him as a War Chief & directing the Indians to consider him as such." The paper was dated 1784 and signed by Sir John Johnson. When Wayne showed him a decorated American commission, Blue Jacket expressed a desire for one "when he made peace," since the American commission was on parchment with decorations while his was "only paper." For Wayne, not understanding the nature of chieftainship, Blue Jacket's desire for such "trifles" was a sign of Indian childishness that he was glad to gratify. Certificates would, he believed, allow him to manipulate the Indians at no cost.[42]

But it was Blue Jacket who had just manipulated Wayne, for Wayne had in effect promised to recognize him as a chief. News spread that Wayne had recognized Blue Jacket as the "principal of the Shawnanoes Chiefs & could do with them what he pleased." The Mequachake (Mekoce) village chiefs blamed all this on the British certificate and denounced the British. "For having made any chiefs among them especially the younger brothers, if any were, made they say it ought to have been some of them." In terms of the traditional duties of the Shawnee divisions, the Mequachake complaint

[41] Wainway, the nephew of Old Shade, a Shawnee chief, foretold the death of Red Pole and Pemenewa. Quilawa then killed Wainway as a witch. Old Shade shot Quilawa, and Wessillawy killed Old Shade, Elliott to McKee, Sept. 30, 1797, Deputy Supt.'s Office, IA, RG 10, PAC. For poisoning of chiefs, see McKee to Chew, Jan. 29, 1796, *Simcoe Papers*, 4:186. For Potawatomis, see Selby to Chew, Oct. 13, 1795, *Simcoe Papers*, 4:104.
[42] Wayne to Pickering, March 8, 1795, Knopf (ed.), *A Name in Arms*, 390.

itself represented a bid for status and not a maintenance of older ways. By Shawnee reckoning, the Calaka and Oawikila divisions, not the Mequachake, had charge of political affairs. The Mequachakes had preeminence in matters of medicine and health. But Shawnee migrations west of the Mississippi, and the long history of mixed villages in Ohio country and along the Maumee, had altered the old pattern in which each division maintained its own villages. Now villages were often mixed, and the majority of Shawnees left in the *pays d'en haut* were Mekoce and Calaka (or Chillicothe); the older apportioning of duties failed to hold. The Mekoce were trying to increase their influence. In the wake of the incident, Black Hoof, a village chief among the Mequachakes, became the leading Shawnee advocate of accommodation with the Americans and Blue Jacket's leading rival. Black Hoof proclaimed the desire of the Shawnees at Wapakoneta to live like the Americans, and he complained that Blue Jacket and his followers received a disproportionate share of the Shawnee annuities.[43]

Similar contests emerged elsewhere. Buckongahelas, the most prominent war leader among the Delawares of the White River, remained a more influential figure than the phratry chiefs, and he acted as a chief to the Americans. "Mild and affable in his manners; friendly and humane, and sincerely desirous to promote the welfare of his people," he fulfilled the chiefly model. The Delawares, in the language of the middle ground, said he was "such a man among them as General Washington was among the white people." Already of "venerable appearance," his appearance nonetheless shocked whites unused to Algonquian customs. Buckongahelas had long drooping ear lobes created from the Algonquian custom of piercing the ear and decorating the lobe with rings. The weight gradually caused the lobe to stretch until eventually it reached the shoulders. When listening attentively, Buckongahelas had the habit of sucking on his ear lobe.[44]

Finally, among the Miamis, Little Turtle, perhaps the greatest Algonquian war leader, emerged from the shadow of Le Gris and became the leading chief to the Americans. The hereditary Miami chiefs, especially Pacane and Richardville, resented his dominance. They probably held the loyalty of as many or more Miamis than did Little Turtle, but he proved the more adept politician with the Americans. American negotiations with the Miamis were often just as much contests for influence between Little Turtle and Owl,

---

[43] *HBNI*, 15:624; Ironside to McKee, Feb. 6, 1795, *Simcoe Papers*, 3:288–89. See also R. David Edmunds, *Tecumseh and the Quest for Indian Leadership* (Boston: Little Brown, 1984), 47. For Black Hoof's position, see Talk to the Shawnee Nation, Feb. 19, 1807, National Archives, WD, SO, LS, IA, B:279.

[44] For quotation, see Gipson, *Moravian Mission*, Dec. 9, 1799, 32, Description, June 27, 1801, 108–9.

who acted as speaker for Pacane and Richardville, as they were negotiations between the Americans and the Miamis.[45]

The ideal of chieftainship had not changed significantly in the early nineteenth century; war leaders who aspired to be chiefs still had to act like chiefs. Chiefs took care of the people. At times, Tetapuska, one of the phratry chiefs of the Delawares, did not even own a horse: "Thus it is with the chiefs, they are almost poorer than many an Indian who calls them his king." Little Turtle had to be careful of the jealousy of every member of his clan. He had white clothes, tea, and coffee; he kept a cow; and his wife made butter. But he could not "indulge himself in these things, but [had to] reserve them for the whites." A warrior killed his first cow, and "he was obliged to feign ignorance of the man who did it, and to report that she died of herself." Chiefs could not "strike or punish the meanest warrior, even in the field, and at home nobody obeyed him, but his own wife and children."[46]

Chiefs could not rule, but they could persuade and influence. Chiefs, or their speakers, spoke well, using, as among the Delawares, chiefly language – a special ritual address. They advised and counseled, and they backed their words with gifts; they had knowledge others lacked; they could mediate disputes; they had standing among the whites. But chieftainship, as it had evolved in the alliance, had come to depend on European gifts, and with the British becoming increasingly distant and parsimonious fathers, the chiefs depended on the Americans. The Americans, however, offered the chiefs only limited goods for redistribution, and they demanded land in exchange. The chiefs acted in behalf of people resentful of further land cessions, and at times the chiefs protested cessions as fraudulent. But the chiefs could ill oppose such cessions in principle since their own generosity – their ability to act as chiefs – depended on the annuities the treaties yielded. And as Harrison pushed his treaties, chiefs signed from fear that if they refused, chiefs of other villages would gladly make the cessions in their stead. Landless groups, particularly the Delawares and Shawnees, saw such negotiations as a way to get Americans to grant them land. Black Hoof pressed the Americans to give him a deed for land, and soon other chiefs urged the Americans to draw lines between them and their neighbors.[47]

[45] For political maneuvering, see Harrison to Secretary of War, March 3, 1803, Esarey (ed.), *Harrison Messages*, 76–84. See also Journal of the Proceedings at the Indian Treaty at Fort Wayne and Vincennes, Sept. 1 to Oct. 27, 1809, *ibid.*, 370–75.

[46] For Tetapuska and quotation, see Gipson, *Moravian Missions*, July 31, 1801, 116–17. For quotation on power, see Volney, *A View of the Soil and Climate*, 355. For property, see *ibid.*, 378.

[47] "Language of the Chiefs," Jan. 8, 1802, in Gipson, *Moravian Mission*, 54. For an account of one such chief, see Carter, *Little Turtle*, 156–208. For complaints of chiefs, see Dearborn to Harrison, Feb. 21, 1803, Secretary of War, Letters Sent, Indian Affairs, v. A, M 15, roll 1, National Archives. For example of chiefs, cessions, and annuities, see Journal of the

Compounding this pressure from the Americans was the dissolution of village comity under a flood of liquor that washed across the villages closest to the American frontier. Many villages dissolved into nests of social pathologies. Some chiefs were opposed to this trade; some were complicit in it. Some were both. All were its victims. Drinking had long been a problem in the villages, and there had been periods, such as in the late 1760s and early 1770s, when liquor and violence had reached dangerous proportions, but few villages had seen conditions such as those that arose along the Wabash and White rivers in the late 1790s and early 1800s. Weas, Piankashaws, and Eel River Miamis flocked daily to Vincennes, and the village often had thirty to forty drunken Indians in its streets. Having traded their guns as well as most of their other possessions for liquor, they reeled through the village armed only with their knives, which they used to stab and slash hogs, cattle, Americans, French, and (mostly) one another. Many mornings, dozens of Indians lay "wallowing in the filth with the pigs." Most finally roused themselves, but often one or two, dead from wounds or exposure, never moved again. On the worst day, the citizens of Vincennes woke to four dead bodies in the streets of the village. Harrison estimated that the traders brought in annually six thousand gallons of liquor to sell in villages that numbered no more than six hundred warriors.[48]

Liquor threatened to destroy the villages themselves. Kinspeople murdered kinspeople. Chiefs, responsible for the peace of the village, died first. The son of Little Beaver, a Wea chief, killed his father. Little Fox died at the hands of one of his own people. There was, Harrison believed, scarcely a chief left alive among the villages neighboring Vincennes. The deaths from drinking, disease, and violence brought such an "astonishing annual decrease" as to form a "reproach . . . to the American Character." Federal and territorial attempts to restrict and ban the liquor trade failed

Proceedings at the Indian Treaty at Fort Wayne and Vincennes, Sept. 1 – Oct. 27, 1809, Esarey (ed.), *Harrison Messages*, 362–78; list of articles to be purchased for the annuities due the following nations of Indians for the year 1802, National Archives, WD, SO, LS, IA, v. A, M 15, roll 1. Similar annuity lists exist for other years. To get an idea of how the annuities had expanded, see A Statement of Indian Annuities showing in what they are to be paid in 1809, Jan. 1809, National Archives, WD, SO, LS, IA, B:419. Secretary of War to Wells, Apr. 24, 1807, National Archives, WD, SO, LS, IA, B:310.

For chiefs and tribal territories, see Conference Held with the Delaware and Shawanoe Deputation, Feb. 5, 1802, National Archives, WD, SO, LS IA, v. A; Dearborn to Harrison, Feb. 23, 1802, *ibid.*; Talk to Chiefs of Shawanee, Feb. 19, 1807, National Archives, WD, SO, LS, IA, B:279.

[48] Harrison to Secretary of War, July 15, 1801, Esarey (ed.), *Harrison Messages*, 28–30; Volney, *View*, 354. The Miamis, Potawatomis and Kickapoos, people living just beyond the Wabash, did not suffer so greatly from the trade, Harrison to Secretary of War, July 15, 1801, *ibid.* The Kickapoos had the reputation of not drinking at all, Oppelt Diary, Aug. 14, 1804, Moravian Archives, box 157, Folder 1, copy in GLEHA.

miserably; traders, backcountry settlers, and Indian middlemen easily evaded the laws.[49]

Liquor did the most damage along the Wabash where the proximity of the Indian villages to Vincennes made distribution easiest, but it also plagued the White River villages (accessible by the Greenville road) where many Delawares and some Shawnees had resettled, the Miami villages, the villages of the Shawnees, and the Munsee, Mohawk, and Chippewa villages in Canada east of Detroit. Joseph Brant killed his own son Isaac in self-defense when the young man attacked him in a drunken rage. The Moravians near the White River provided a detailed and grim chronicle of drunken murders and maimings in surrounding Indian villages that paralleled those on the Wabash. Indian middlemen – or, just as often, middlewomen – introduced whiskey in up to hundred-gallon lots, and the villagers drank until none of it remained. Brothers attacked brothers; others died from alcohol poisoning. Elders complained that they lost their young people, one after another. After four years of witnessing these debauches, the Moravians could generalize: "This drinking never passes without the shedding of blood. Most of them usually look as if they had passed through some great sickness. In this way they destroy themselves."[50]

Chiefs almost uniformly urged their people to stop drinking and urged the government to halt the trade. Little Turtle even succeeded in getting the Miamis to ban liquor in their hunting camps, although not in their villages. Many of these same chiefs, however, drank themselves, and some became liquor dealers. Among the Delawares, liquor had become embedded in ceremonies – particularly the annual Big House ceremony – in condolence rituals, and in the fabric of hospitality and sharing. The Moravians reported their converts could not refuse liquor without giving offense for to do so violated norms of mutuality and sharing. Delaware chiefs spoke against liquor at the ceremonies only then to join in the bacchanal. And in need of goods to sustain their influence, some chiefs such as Tetapuska became traders in liquor, using it and the goods they acquired through it to meet their obligations.[51]

---

[49] Proclamation: Forbidding Traders from Selling Liquor to Indians In and Around Vincennes, 1801, Esarey (ed.), *Harrison Messages*, 31. For attempts to control liquor traffic, see Francis Paul Prucha, *American Indian Policy in the Formative Years: The Indian Trade and Intercourse Acts, 1790–1834* (Cambridge, Mass.: Harvard University Press, 1962), 102–38.

[50] Gipson, *Moravian Mission*, Aug. 17, 1801, 121; May 18, 1802, 165; June 23, 1801, 107; May 31, 1802, 167; June 4, 1803, 235; Oct. 5–6, 1804, 314; July 10, 1805, 367. For quotation, see *ibid.*, Sept. 9, 1807, 378. For Munsees in Canada, see Christian Father Denke Diary, Feb. 8, 1808, box 157, Folder 5, Moravian Archives, GLEHA Transcription. For Brant, see Isabel Thompson Kelsay, *Joseph Brant, 1743–1806: Man of Two Worlds* (Syracuse: Syracuse University Press, 1984), 564–65.

[51] For restrict liquor, see Dearborn, Circular, 14 Sept. 1802, Secretary of War, Letters Sent, Indian Affairs, v. A, M15, roll 1, National Archives; Conference held with Little Turtle

No matter how the chiefs dealt with the depletion of land and the dissolution of comity, their influence seemed to decline. The fall of Tetapuska of the Delawares was particularly tragic. He had served as a village chief and counselor since before the Revolution and had invited the Moravians to open their mission near the White River. He had achieved some successes, winning for the Delawares the acknowledgment by some of the Miamis of Delaware rights along the White River and thus ending their status as a landless people. But he felt the larger failure of chieftainship. In 1801 he gathered his young people together for a feast and addressed them while they ate.

> My children you see how old I am, how gray my hair is; I am still not on the right road as God desires it of us. We have also often admonished you not to drink, nor to commit any evil, but nothing came of it. We remained as we were. We chiefs have now discovered why you have not changed either, because we ourselves do not do what we tell you to do.

Such speeches did not change his actions. He told the Moravians the chiefs had agreed to break the barrels of anyone who brought whiskey into the villages; at the same time, two barrels of whiskey were being lashed to his horse.[52]

In 1804, he attempted to deny the cession to Harrison at Vincennes, and in the spring of 1805, his role in land cessions to the Americans rendered his situation precarious. Fearful of repudiation by the young men, he lost his major ally Buckongahelas, and his influence slipped further as he found himself accused of bewitching Buckongahelas and causing his death. Removed from the chieftainship, he continued to sell whiskey, although he briefly flirted with living with the Moravians. In March 1806, Delaware warriors seized him, and, under torture, he admitted witchcraft and implicated Joshua, the only male Delaware Moravian convert in the White River region. Although Tetapuska later disavowed the confession, Tenskwatawa, the Shawnee prophet, identified Tetapuska and Joshua as witches. Warriors, including his own son, who hated him for having left his mother for a younger woman, took him to the Moravian town, tomahawked him, and threw him still alive into the execution fire.[53]

and other Chiefs, Jan. 7, 1802, *ibid.* For sharing and liquor, see Christian Father Denke Diary, Feb. 8, 1808, box 157, Folder 5, Moravian Archives, GLEHA Transcription. For Tetapuska, see below; for the Owl bringing liquor among the Miamis, see Gibson and Vigo to Harrison, July 6, 1805, Esarey (ed.), *Harrison Messages*, 145.

52 For Tetapuska invites Moravians, see Gipson, *Moravian Mission*, Apr. 14, 1800, 33. For quotation, see *ibid.*, July 9, 1801, 111. For transporting whiskey, see *ibid.*, March 22, 1803, 218. For gains Miami acknowledgment, see Harrison to Secretary of War, March 3, 1803, Esarey (ed.), *Harrison Messages*, 82–83.

53 For repudiates cession, see Delaware Indians to Wells, March 30, 1805, Esarey (ed.), *Harrison Messages* 117–18; Patterson to Wells, Apr. 5, 1805, *ibid.*, 121–23. For motives and

Other chiefs took a more decisive role in trying to halt the turmoil of the villages, but they too ran risks. Little Turtle of the Miamis was the most prominent of the chiefs opposing the liquor traffic and seeking to create a modus vivendi with the Americans. A man of commanding abilities, widely praised by American leaders and memorialized by Constantin-François Volney in his account of his travels in the United States, Little Turtle had sense enough to avoid the fate of Pontiac. He understood the limits of his influence and power within his own society. Little Turtle to a remarkable degree accepted many of the basic Jeffersonian premises for the Northwest. He imagined a gradual evolution among the Miamis away from hunting and horticulture, first toward stock raising and eventually toward male plow agriculture instead of female hoe agriculture. With whites spreading like "oil on a blanket," and Indians melting away "like snow before the sun," something had to be done before his people disappeared entirely. He successfully sought aid from the Quakers to advance such a program while working strenuously to restrict the liquor trade among his people.[54]

In attempting to implement this program Little Turtle worked closely with William Wells, a figure as thoroughly a product of the middle ground as any person in the *pays d'en haut*. Captured and adopted by Miamis as a child, Wells in his eventful life fought first against Harmar and then, joining the Americans, for Wayne, leading white scouts who dressed and fought as Indians. Wells had married Little Turtle's daughter Sweet Breeze, and after the wars he returned to live among the Miamis. Slipping in and out of personal controversies that at times cost him his office, he served as Indian agent for the Miami confederation, the Potawatomis, and the Delawares during much of the period between the Treaty of Greenville and the War of 1812. He was the closest equivalent to the British agents McKee, Girty, and Elliott that the Americans possessed. He was a servant of empire but had deep loyalties to the people whose interests the country he served sought to subvert. He died in 1812, when the Indians attacked Chicago. The warriors

fears, see Gibson and Vigo to Harrison, July 6, 1805, *ibid.*, 142–46. For accused of witchcraft, see Gipson, *Moravian Mission*, May 24, 1805, 357–58. For sells whiskey, see *ibid.*, Dec. 22, 1805, 394–95. For asks to settle, see *ibid.*, Jan. 8, 1806, 399–401. For witchcraft accusations and execution, see *ibid.*, March 14–17, 1806, 411–15; Kluge to Loiskel, Apr. 1, 1806, *ibid.*, 556–64. A second old phratry chief, Hinguapoos, or Big Cat, was also accused as a witch, but armed warriors from his clan saved his life, *ibid.*, March 15, 1806, 414; Apr. 9–10, 1806, 420.

R. David Edmunds says that Tetapuska was a former Moravian convert, R. David Edmunds, *The Shawnee Prophet* (Lincoln: University of Nebraska Press, 1983), 44, but while the Moravians thought of him as a friend, he was opposed to Christian doctrines, Gipson, *Moravian Mission*, Apr. 14, 1800, Apr. 3, 1805, 32, 344.

54 Volney, *A View of the Soil and Climate*, 334–35. Conference held with Little Turtle and other Indian Chiefs, Jan. 7, 1802, Secretary of War, Letters Sent, Indian Affairs, v. A, National Archives, M 15, roll 1.

who killed him ripped out his heart, divided it, and ate it. Even dead, he was in part among them.[55]

All the efforts of Little Turtle and Wells neither stopped Harrison's wheedling of cessions nor persuaded the Miamis to farm. Little Turtle and Wells's efforts to negate Harrison's Delaware-Piankashaw Treaty of 1804, which ceded land claimed by the Miamis, foundered on Jefferson's desire for expansion. Quaker efforts came to naught among the Miamis, for whom old gender roles largely held firm – Indian men refused to farm. Little Turtle, whom Secretary of War Henry Dearborn thought a man of extraordinary talent, inspired great jealousy among the other chiefs, probably because the Americans thought so highly of him. By 1808 Little Turtle, too, found himself subject to death threats, but the old and sick war chief faced down his opponents, vowing that although they might kill him, his would not be the only blood shed.[56]

Little Turtle and his counterparts – Black Hoof of the Shawnees, Five Medals of the Potawatomis, Adam Brown and Walking in the Waters of the Wyandots, and even Little Turtle's rival Owl – were all willing to accommodate the Americans. Such accommodation was the mark of the chief on the middle ground. They would urge the adoption of new technologies and gender roles; they had no fear of intermarriage, for intermarriage had long been a part of the *pays d'en haut*. They recognized a crisis among their people, and they sought aid from their fathers to resolve it. They had, however, a father who ignored their limits; who knew nothing of chieftainship. He expected what they could not achieve. In 1812, with the *pays d'en haut* on the brink of war, Gomo, a western Potawatomi chief then living on Lake Peoria, sought to find some accommodation with the Americans. He stood in council and addressed Ninian Edwards, the governor of the Illinois Territory. The speech he gave had been given in one form or another for a century and a half:

> Can a Chief sell land? I am a chief, but I am poor and worthy of pity, and I want to live in peace on our land. My father, If there could be found one Chief among us who had influence enough to deliver a murderer, I would be happy to see such a Chief. My father, you probably think I am

---

[55] There are two accounts of Wells and Little Turtle, Paul A. Hutton, "William Wells: Frontier Scout and Indian Agent," *Indiana Magazine of History* 74 (Sept. 1978): 183–222, and Carter, *Little Turtle*, for death, see 231–33. For loyalties, see Gibson and Vigo to Harrison, July 6, 1805, Esarey (ed.), *Harrison Messages*, 145. But also see Harrison to Secretary of War, Dec. 3, 1809, *ibid.*, 395.

[56] For jealousy, see Dearborn to Harrison, Feb. 23, 1802, Secretary of War, Letters Sent, Indian Affairs, v. A, National Archives, M 15, roll 1. See Hutton, "William Wells," 203–15; Carter, *Little Turtle*, 156–209. For Quakers, see Walker (ed.), "Hophins Journal," 361–407. Little Turtle rashly threatened war over the cession; for response, see Secretary of War to Wells, Dec. 24, 1804, National Archives, WD, SO, LS, IA, B:35.

a great Chief. I am not. I cannot control my young men as I please. My father. I am a red Skin, I am not a Great Chief, I am a Chief whilst my young men are growing, but when they become, I am no more master of them. My father, The Great Spirit created us all, we have not the same power as you have, you have troops & laws, when a man does ill, you have him taken & punished, but this I cannot do. My father, I could very easily seize or kill the murderers you mention, but unless the whole of my Chiefs & young men are consenting – otherwise I would be killed.[57]

For a century and a half, such chiefly powerlessness had paradoxically been transmuted into power of a sort, as Europeans, to gain their ends, had aided chiefs and had come to rely on the tools of chiefs: gifts, persuasion, kindness, and obligation. The Europeans had adopted Indian means because Indians, as a whole, commanded sufficient force to compel them to compromise. But when Gomo spoke, those days were ending. The chiefs were left to lament the passing of an age, an age that in retrospect seemed golden. Governor Harrison, the father who failed to be a father, noted:

The happiness they enjoyed from their intercourse with the french is their perpetual theme – it is their golden age. Those who are old enough to remember it, speak of it with rapture, and the young ones are taught to venerate it as the Ancients did the reign of Saturn "you call us" said an old Indian chief to me "your Children why do you not make us happy as our Fathers the french did? They never took from us our lands, indeed they were in common with us – they planted where they pleased and they cut wood where they pleased and so did we – but now if a poor Indian attempts to take a little bark from a tree to cover him from the rain, up comes a white man and threatens to shoot him, claiming the tree as his own."[58]

The multifaceted crises of the villages bred nativism, but like Neolin and Pontiac, Tecumseh and his brother Tenskwatawa were paradoxical nativists. They are only comprehensible on the middle ground. In a sense, they were the most powerful Algonquian response to Benjamin Lincoln's musings about the sons of Ishmael; they were the answer to the American combination of Jefferson's imperial benevolence and backcountry Indian hating. In rejecting an American vision of the future that promised them only alternative routes to obliteration, they invented a traditional past of their fathers. But because both brothers had grown up in the complex and intimate European and Algonquian world of the *pays d'en haut*, their traditions rested on an intermingling of existing Algonquian and white ways. They were the

[57] Council held at Cahokia, Apr. 11, 1812, Ninian Edwards Papers, Chicago Historical Society.
[58] Harrison to Secretary of War, July 5, 1809, Esarey (ed.), *Harrison Messages*, 353–54.

final and most intriguing cultural and political creations of a *pays d'en haut.*

Contemporary American observers and later scholars have, as R. David Edmunds and Gregory Dowd note, overemphasized the uniqueness of both men, particularly that of Tecumseh. Tenskwatawa emerged as a visionary when the Algonquian and white villages of the backcountry teemed with visionaries and God seemed to scatter revelations across the land with abandon. And Tecumseh, for all his ability and audacity, essentially sought the same political ends as the Indian confederations of the 1790s, while his vision of the world of the villages in many ways mirrored that of the early republicans. Even his extension of the confederation into the South only followed the efforts of other Shawnee emissaries.[59]

The influence of Tecumseh and of Tenskwatawa flowed out of the vision that came to Tenskwatawa in the White River country in early 1805 while the villages were full of sickness and drunkenness. Lalawethika was a drunkard, a poor and ineffective shaman, a triplet among people who regarded multiple births as unlucky, a failure in a family noted for its warriors. He was a Kispoko Shawnee, one of the few who remained in the *pays d'en haut,* for most had migrated across the Mississippi. The vision came while Lalawethika sat smoking his pipe at his fire. He fell backward and lay as if dead. When he awakened, he had a story of death, heaven, and resurrection. Christianity clearly inspired the story. Lalawethika glimpsed heaven and hell. He witnessed sinners atoning for their sins in fiery torture. The visionary on awakening vowed to renounce liquor and changed his name to Tenskwatawa, "the Open Door."[60]

For nearby Moravians, Tenskwatawa and his message initially seemed little different from other visionaries and their messages in the villages in the White River country. Elements later incorporated into the Prophet's vision had already appeared. An "old Indian woman" had a vision blaming the decline of game on the Indians' imitation of whites. "You are to live again as you lived before the white people came into this land." The Moravians themselves had to confront memories of Neolin when a "number of heathen" urged them to paint their doctrine of heaven, hell, sins, and so forth on a deerskin so that they could remember it better. "They said that an Indian

---

[59] Several recent studies of Tecumseh and Tenskwatawa have eliminated the need for any detailed retelling of the brothers' lives. R. David Edmunds has rightfully removed Tenskwatawa from the shadow of his brother, Edmunds, *The Shawnee Prophet.* Edmunds, *Tecumseh,* and Gregory Dowd, "Paths of Resistance: American Indian Religion and the Quest for Unity, 1745–1815" (Ph.D. diss., Princeton University, 1986), 2:537ff. have de-emphasized Tecumseh's distinctiveness.

[60] I have followed Edmunds's account of Tenskwatawa's background. The vision is a blend of various accounts, most of which date considerably after the vision itself, Edmunds, *Shawnee Prophet,* 28–33. For a good analysis of the Prophet's appeal, see Dowd, "Paths of Resistance," 2:597–600.

had once had a vision and had then pictured everything on a skin, and that
many Indians had seen and believed that it was the truth." In the spring of
1805, Tenskwatawa's own vision seemed less influential than that of a
second Indian woman, "the teacher," who had had a vision forbidding "all
evil, fornication, stealing, murder and the like." This prophetess took over
supervision of the annual Delaware Big House ceremony. The Indians
believed her but were "unable to give up what she forbids." As late as
January 1806, Tenskwatawa still had a formidable rival in an ex-Moravian
woman named Beade (who may have been "the teacher"), who claimed to
have seen God himself and also an angel. She originally assumed a role later
identified with Tenskwatawa: the identifier of witches. Even after the
Prophet had overshadowed other prophets along the White River, other
influential teachers – Main Poc of the Potawatomis, Handsome Lake of the
Senecas, and the Prophet's own associate, Trout of the Ottawas – competed
with him for influence or complemented his own message.[61]

These other prophets and visionaries obviously affected the Shawnee
prophet but so, too, did religious ideas and religious upheavals among the
whites. In 1802, word had reached the White River region that whites along
the Miami and Ohio rivers were falling over and "lay as if dead for 2 or 3
hours." When they regained consciousness, they repented of their former
sinful lives. When similar phenomena became apparent among the Indians,
the Shakers, at least, were willing to view it as an identical outpouring of the
Holy Spirit.[62]

The connection between the Prophet and the Shakers was a tenuous but
intriguing one. After Tenskwatawa moved to Greenville, the Shakers sought
him out and, despite the Catholic influence they detected in his practice of
confession, the Shakers became convinced that the "Lord is in this place."
Thereafter, the Prophet maintained sporadic contact with the Shakers. As
late as 1810, the Prophet claimed "to follow the Shaker principles in
everything but the vow of celebacy [sic]," and a leader of the Shakers assured
Harrison that he believed the Prophet "to be under the same divine
inspiration as himself." Harrison thought this "by no means improbable."
The Prophet assured Harrison in 1808 that he only aspired "to introduce

[61] Gipson, *Moravian Mission*, Nov. 7, 1803, 252; Aug. 21, 1804, 308., May 14, 1805, 355. For
Beade, see *ibid.*, Feb. 13, 1805, 333–34; Jan. 25, 1806, 402–3; Oct. 25, 1805, 383. See also
Kluge to Loiskel, *ibid.*, Apr. 28, 1805, 531. For other references to female prophets, see
Shane's Statement, 1821, Tecumseh Papers 12YY 18, Draper Mss. For Main Poc, see
Thomas Forsyth, Main Poque, Tecumseh Papers, Draper Mss. 8YY57. Main Poc had great
influence among the Potawatomis, Sauks, Chippewas, Ottawas, Fox, and Kickapoos. For
Handsome Lake, see Anthony Wallace, *The Death and Rebirth of the Seneca* (New York:
Vintage, 1972). Handsome Lake attempted to expand his teachings westward, William Kirk
to Daniel Drake, May 10, 1807, Tecumseh Papers 3YY, Draper Mss.
[62] Gipson, *Moravian Mission*, July 14, 1802, 176.

This print, captioned "An Indian and his Squaw," is from an 1810 travel account. The rags the man is wearing and the bottle that he is holding are signs of the social conditions against which Tecumseh and his brother Tenskwatawa reacted. (National Archives of Canada/C−14488)

among the Indians, those good principles of religion which the white people profess." The Prophet remained familiar enough with whites to gain prior knowledge of the 1806 eclipse of the sun. He predicted it, claimed to have caused it, and used it as a demonstration of his power.[63]

Tenskwatawa constructed a social and theological response to the conditions of the border villages. He did this on the most obvious level by providing a social program: a ban on drinking, a reduction of dependence on trade, a prohibition of skin hunting, an end to cohabitation of women with whites, and a promotion of monogamous marriage among the Shawnees. But this social program rested on an explanation of the nature of the relation between Americans and Algonquians and between whites and Indians.[64]

The language used by Tenskwatawa, by his brother Tecumseh, and by his associate Trout was one of differences. They differentiated Algonquians from Americans with a language coded to emphasize gender differences and the distinctions between wild and tame, old and new, and master and slave. The initial coding emphasized an Indian way versus a white way; Indians were to whites as "wild" was to "tame." Such coding made Tenskwatawa's vision merge smoothly with the ongoing discourse of the White River villages.

By the early nineteenth century, the dichotomy of separate Indian and white ways established by a common Great Spirit, or Master of Life, was at least half a century old. It had become the stock response to attempts at Christian conversion. Buckongahelas had repeatedly reiterated the need for his people to keep the customs and ceremonies his ancestors had "received from God." The Moravian teaching was only for white people; "you yourselves see that we have another skin." The middle ground depended on Indian-white distinctions, but it also depended on the porousness of the boundaries between Indian and white. Buckongahelas's arguments had evolved as part of the very religious and cultural syncretism they seemed to

---

[63] For early contacts, see Richard McNemar, *The Kentucky Revival or a Short History of the Later Extraordinary Outpouring of the Spirit of God in the Western States of America . . .* (New York: Edward Jenkins, 1846; repr. New York: AMS Press 1974), 123–32. Also see J. P. MacLean, "Shaker Mission to the Shawnee Indians," *Ohio Archaeological and Historical Publications* 11 (1903): 215–29. For Prophet quotation, see Prophet to Harrison, Aug. 1, 1808, in Esarey (ed.), *Harrison Messages*, 300. For eclipse, see Shane's Statement, 1821, Tecumseh Papers 12 YY18, Draper Mss.; Edmunds, *Shawnee Prophet*, 48. For Shakers, Harrison to Secretary of War, May 15, 1810, Esarey (ed.), *Harrison Messages*, 421–22.

[64] For social program, see Substance of a Talk . . . by Le Maigouis, May 4, 1807, MG 19, F. 16, PAC.; Thomas Forsyth's "An Account of the Manners and Customs of the Sauk and Fox Nations of Indians . . . ," in Emma Helen Blair (ed.), *The Indian Tribes of the Upper Mississippi Valley and Region of the Great Lakes*, 2 vols. (Cleveland: Arthur H. Clark, 1912), 2:276–79. Forsyth's "Account" is a letter to William Clark, Dec. 23, 1812. See also Edmunds, *Shawnee Prophet*, 34–41.

reject. By the early nineteenth century, this syncretism was in many ways traditional in the *pays d'en haut*.[65]

Tenskwatawa sought to create firmer boundaries, and in this he paralleled those Americans busy reinventing Indians as alien and other. Tenskwatawa forged his boundaries by reverting to the orginal formulation of Indian-white differences in the *pays d'en haut*. He, and Trout after him, made the Americans – but not the British, French, or Spanish – other-than-human persons. In Algonquian cosmology, the Great Serpent represented potentially evil powers, and Algonquians connected the Great Serpent with the sea. Tenskwatawa had Americans come from the sea; they were the spawn of the Great Serpent. Whites had orginally entered the *pays d'en haut* as manitous; Tenskwatawa, in effect, made them devils. Just as Indian haters envisioned Algonquians as devil worshipers and "red devils," so Americans had become children of the Great Serpent.[66]

Connected in Algonquian thinking with differences between Indian and white – coded in terms of skin color – was a second set of differences: will versus tame. In rejecting conversion, Indians spoke of not being "tamed." In this discourse, conversion made Indians "tame," and once "tamed," Indians could be slaughtered by whites in the same way domestic livestock was. This had, as Buckongahelas reminded the Moravians, actually happened at Gnaddenhutten.[67]

Alongonquian visionaries amplified the analogies between Christian and tame and Indian and wild into codes of conduct. Thus the unnamed woman visionary of 1803 identified the loss of wild animals with the inappropriate Indian adoption of tame animals. To restore the wild, Indians had to break connections with the tame. To restore deer, cattle must be killed. Warriors expressed their hostility to the Moravians by shooting "our best hog before our eyes." Tenskwatawa ordered Indians to kill their cattle.[68]

The next step in this logic of differences was to argue that Americans sought to reduce Indian men to the status of women. This language of

[65] For Buckongahelas, see Gipson, *Moravian Mission*, Sept. 4, 1803, 256. Also see *ibid.*, Sept. 3, 1805, 377; July 4, 1806, 437–38; Autobiography of Abraham Luckenbach, *ibid.*, 616. See Substance of a Talk . . . by Le Maigouis, May 4, 1807, MG 19, F. 16, PAC.

[66] In the earliest accounts of the Prophet's vision, the Americans are symbolized by a crab emerging from the sea at Boston, Gipson, *Moravian Mission*, Dec. 6, 1805, 392–93. See Edmunds, *Shawnee Prophet*, 28–41. For Trout, see Substance of a Talk . . . by Le Maigouis, May 4, 1807, MG 19, F. 16, PAC.

[67] For tame, slaughter at Gnaddenhutten, Gipson, *Moravian Mission*, Sept. 4, 1803, 256. Also see *ibid.*, Nov. 25, 1801, 131. For won't be tamed, see *ibid.*, Apr. 5, 1802, 155.

[68] Gipson, *Moravian Mission*, Nov. 24, 1803, 262. For hog, see *ibid.*, July 3, 1805, 364. For Prophet, see *ibid.*, Dec. 3, 1805, 392. This logically extended, too, to dietary restrictions emphasizing Indian and white foods, see Substance of a Talk . . . by Le Maigouis, May 4, 1807, MG 19, F. 16, PAC.

emasculation carried a quite particular meaning. Because William Kirk, the American agent to the Shawnees under Black Hoof, was a Quaker – a man who rejected war – the Prophet argued that by sending him, "it was evident that the President intended making women of the Indians." Making women of them in this sense was the equivalent of the Iroquois putting the petticoat on the Delawares, making them men who had no say in war and were not to be warriors. The Prophet's response was to urge the Indians to unite in order to be "respected by the President as men." The Prophet, too, logically emphasized visible signs of maleness. Algonquians were to readopt older hair styles, plucking their heads and leaving only scalp locks. But a more important innovation of his was the stressing of a gender system that emphasized the subordination of Indian women to Indian men. The status of Algonquian warriors as masters and men would be visible in how they treated Algonquian women. It is notable that the women who dominated the initial visionary outbreak largely vanished after 1806. They yielded influence to Tenskwatawa, Main Poc, and Trout.[69]

Tenskwatawa coupled this subordination of women with a rejection of their role as cultural intermediaries. He denounced intermarriage in no uncertain terms: "All Indian women who were living with White Men was to be brought home to their friends and relatives, and their children to be left with their Fathers, so that nations might become genuine Indian." Women, in many ways the most influential creators of the middle ground, were, in effect, to withdraw from it.[70]

Finally, and most surprisingly, given the emphasis on return to ancestral ways, both the Prophet and Trout emphasized young over old. The Prophet told the Sauks and Fox that "medicine" or power that "had been good in its time, had lost its efficacy; . . . it had become vitiated with age." The world, as Trout taught, "is broken and leans down and as it declines the [Chippewas] will fall off & die." The followers of the Prophet along the White River in

---

[69] For quotation, see Wells to Secretary of War, Apr. 20, 1808, Carter (ed.), *Territorial Papers*, 7:560. This gender emphasis, as well as the other differences, appears particularly clearly in Thomas Forsyth's account of the Prophet's teachings, "An Account of the Manners and Customs of the Sauk and Fox," in Blair, *Indian Tribes*, 2:276–79. See also Shane's Statement, 1821, Tecumseh Papers 12YY 8–12, Draper Mss. It should also be pointed out that Trout and the Prophet both partially condemned the violence toward women then apparently common in Algonquian villages, see Substance of a Talk . . . by Le Maigouis, May 4, 1807, MG 19, F. 16, PAC. In what is an admittedly embroidered and distorted version of Tecumseh's speech, but which probably transmits the substance of his rhetoric, he is quoted as accusing the Americans of making "women of our warriors, and harlots of our women." John Francis Hamtramck Claiborne, *Mississippi as a Province, Territory, and State* (Jackson, Miss.: Power and Barkside, 1880; repr. LSU, 1964) 1:317. Whites reported that Tecumseh scorned "everything that looked like effeminacy of manners," Draper's note of communication with John Johnston, Tecumseh Papers 11YY, Draper Mss.

[70] For intermarriage, see Edmunds, *The Shawnee Prophet*, 39.

1806 believed: "We have now found something new.... The old no longer has any weight because the old people no longer have anything to say. The young people now rule."[71]

This ideological and theological structure did not arise full blown from the Prophet's first vision; it evolved and changed in response to changing conditions and challenges. Because the Prophet sought to implement it in political and social life, Tenskwatawa's teachings involved a constant testing against competing formulations and actual experience. Actual decisions about what was Indian and what was white, what was wild and what was tame, what was male and what was female became difficult and compromised in practice. Thus, because the only domestic animals the northern Ottawa, Cree, and Ojibwa hunters possessed were dogs, the Prophet's message, to the dismay and disillusionment of these northern hunters, became: "Kill your dogs." Farther south, the Prophet's message mandated the slaughter of cattle but did not touch the horses that had become integral to the hunt. Indeed, warriors rode horses to slaughter hogs.[72]

An important compromise involved the Prophet's and Trout's attitudes toward agriculture. Eventually Tenskwatawa and Tecumseh adopted a strict gender division of labor. Women, not men, grew crops; but initially, during the subsistence crisis caused by the lack of game, the Prophet and Trout had thought differently: "You must plant corn for yourselves, for your women and for your children, and when you do it you are to help each other," Trout had told the Ottawas and Ojibwas around Michilimackinac in 1807. In 1808, a follower of the Prophet's understood his message to mean that men should "work and make corn" and that they were not "ashamed to work and make corn for our women and children." The Prophet himself endorsed these sentiments.[73]

---

[71] For quotation on medicine, see *Narrative of an Expedition to the Source of St. Peter's River, Lake Winnepeeke, & Lake of the Woods . . . Performed in the Year 1823* (Philadelphia: H. C. Carey & I Lea, 1824) 1:223–24. For similar emphasis on new medicines, see Radin Notes, Winnebago Informant, APS Freeman guide, no. 3857, Radin, Shawnee Prophet, American Philosophical Society; Substance of a Talk . . . by Le Maigouis, May 4, 1807, MG 19, F. 16, PAC. For White River, see Gipson, *Moravian Mission*, Mar. 10, 1806, 411–12. The young still had an obligation to care for the aged, Shane's Statement, 1821, Tecumseh Papers 12YY 8–12, Draper Mss.

[72] For horses cause confusion, Prophet doesn't condemn horses, see Gipson, *Moravian Mission*, Dec. 3, 1805, 392. For hogs and horses, see *ibid.*, July 3, 1805, 364. For Prophet and dogs, see James (ed.), *Tanner Narrative*, 125, 155–58.

[73] Substance of a Talk . . . by Le Maigouis, May 4, 1807, MG 19, F. 16, PAC. Drake thought Tecumseh and his brother opposed white agricultural implements, Drake's Notebooks 1:25, Tecumseh Papers, Draper Mss.; Prophet to Harrison, June 24, 1808, in Esarey (ed.), *Harrison Messages*, 295; Prophet to Harrison, Aug. 1, 1808, *ibid.*, 300. In 1816, the Prophet rejected any Indian adoption of American agricultural methods and gender roles, Speeches in Council of the Shawawnee Chiefs Yealabahca and the Prophet, 1–4, 1816, Cass Papers, Clements Library.

Between 1805 and 1809, despite widespread suspicion among the Americans that the Prophet was a British agent, the main focus of his reforms was internal, and his enemies were the chiefs of the border villages rather than the Americans. The Prophet entered into village politics as a witch-hunter. Earlier prophets had also hunted witches; and one of the Prophet's contemporaries, the Seneca prophet Handsome Lake, hunted witches among the Iroquois. In a winter of want, sickness, and death, it was logical for the villagers to suspect witches were at work. It was not customary, however, for chiefs to be numbered among the witches. Although the Prophet verified that the chiefs were witches, young Delaware warriors, angry at land sales, murders by whites, and diminishing game, had already accused them. The Prophet, by confirming their suspicions, sided with the young against the old and became the enemy of chiefs, a position he would maintain through the War of 1812. Not all chiefs of the interior villages were automatically hostile to the Prophet, but most chiefs of the border villages seemed to have glimpsed their own potential fates in that of Tetapuska.[74]

Established as an accuser of chiefs, a champion of the young against the old, the Prophet became what the French had earlier called a republican. He established first at Greenville and later at Tippecanoe (or Prophetstown) a series of multitribal villages under the leadership of himself and his brother Tecumseh. John Johnston, who succeeded William Wells as Indian agent at Fort Wayne, dismissed these villages as being populated by "all the vagabond Indians in the country." They remained largely, but not entirely, outside the network of American alliance chiefs. The only American chief among them was Blue Jacket, the Shawnee war leader, who apparently sought to use the Prophet's appeal to buttress his own standing against Black Hoof and the chiefs of Wapakoneta.[75]

Blue Jacket's association with the Prophet and Tecumseh put the brothers in touch with a continuing, if weak, movement by the Shawnees to breathe life into the nearly dead embers of the confederation council fire at Brownstown (or Big Rock). In 1806, however, hope for a resurrection of the confederation seemed forlorn. Blue Jacket tried in 1801 to bring the fire to

---

[74] Edmunds, *The Shawnee Prophet*, gives a good account of the witch-hunting episodes, 42–48. For rise of witch hunting among the Delawares, see Gipson, *Moravian Mission*. The chiefs themselves condemned the first victims, two old women, one Mingo and one Nantikoke, *ibid.*, Oct. 19, 1802, 194–95. For accusations of chiefs, see *ibid.*, May 24, 1805, 358; July 3, 1805, 365; Mar. 12, 1806, 412; March 17, 1806, 415–16. Apr. 9–10, 1806, 420. For young people, see March 10, 1806, 411; Apr. 9–10, 1806, 420. For sickness and sorcery, see Apr. 9, 1802, 156; June 7–8, 1805, 360, (Shawnees) June 19–20, 1805, 362. See also Shane's Statement, 1821, Tecumseh papers, 12YY14–18, Draper Mss.

  Roundhead, a Wyandot war leader, joined the Prophet in his opposition to Black Hoof, Joseph Vance to Draper, n.d., Tecumseh Papers, 2YY, Draper Mss. Proceedings of Council Held at Springfield, June 24–25, 1807, Frontier Wars, 5U183–84, Draper Mss.

[75] For Blue Jacket, see *Virginia Argus*, Sept. 6, 1806, Tecumseh Papers, 3YY, Draper Mss; Johnston to Drake, n.d., Tecumseh Papers, 11YY, Draper Mss.

life by restoring an alliance between the Brownstown allies, the Cherokees, and the Sauks and Fox. He had failed, but Tecumseh and Tenskwatawa found in Blue Jacket a knowledgeable confederation chief who still dreamed of a restored Algonquian alliance supported by the British.[76]

The villages of the Maumee and the Wabash and those of Detroit and Sandusky that had once been the main strength for the council fire at Brownstown were, however, by the early nineteenth century unpromising sources of resistance to the Americans. Racked by liquor, disease, and famine, they were dominated by American chiefs such as Little Turtle, Tarhe of the Wyandots, and Black Hoof of the Shawnees. Tenskwatawa and his teachings only sharpened the divisions in these villages, and he and Tecumseh sought not to unify them but to draw off their own adherents into republican villages.

The main source of resistance to the Americans – and the one that Tecumseh would tap – was not at Brownstown; it lay in the villages of Illinois, Michigan, and Wisconsin. Here direct pressures from American settlers were intially weak, but there were other sources of resentment. Kickapoos, Sauks and Fox, Chippewas, Winnebagos, Menominees, and western Potawatomis all witnessed the encroachments of the Americans elsewhere. The Louisiana Purchase, the movement of Americans up the Mississippi, the purchase of southern Illinois from the Kaskaskias, the creation of new American forts – all aroused their fears. Contact between these groups and the Americans led to murders, and the unavenged dead tormented their kinspeople. And because most of these groups had not signed the Treaty of Greenville or made cessions to the United States, their chiefs initially received no annuities and therefore did not serve as a buffer against the anger of the young men. Finally, they continued to be provisioned by British traders, no friends to the United States and eager to confirm the Indians' worst fears. When American demands for land did begin, Indians from the Saginaw Chippewas, to the Potawatomis around Chicago, to the Winnebagos and Sauks near the Mississippi became even more anti-American.[77]

---

[76] Blue Jacket kept up his contacts with the British, although he depended on U.S. annuities to maintain his influence, McKee to Claus, Aug. 15, 1800, Claus Papers, 8:117, PAC.

  The Brownstown (or Big Rock) Council Fire incorporated the Shawnees, Wyandots (and Hurons), the Detroit Ottawas, and Chippewas, and most likely the Potawatomis. There all matters of importance among themselves and between them and the British were to be decided. Ironside to Claus, June 11, 1801, Dept. Supt. General's Office, IA, RG 10, PAC. For Blue Jacket's attempts to expand this council fire and restore confederation, see Ironside to Claus, June 12, 1801, Dept. Supt. General's Office, v. 26, IA, RG 10, PAC; Ironside to Selby, June 15, 1801, Claus Papers 8:150, PAC.

[77] For attitudes of western groups, see Johnston to Drake, Sept. 24, 1840, Tecumseh Papers 11YY, Draper Mss.; Edmunds, The Shawnee Prophet, 78. For an excellent description of the villages of people west of Michilimackinac to the Mississippi and south to Peoria, see Hays to Edwards, May 31, 1812, Ninian Edwards Collection, Chicago Historical Society.

The origin of the confederation the Americans would confront in the War of 1812 lay neither in the old council fire at Brownstown, nor in British machinations, nor in the original efforts of Tecumseh. Instead, these were tributaries to a movement that began in the north and west and predated Tenskwatawa's vision. An alliance against the Osages west of the Mississippi produced the core of anti-American resistance. In June 1805, a delegation of Sauks, Fox, northern Ottawas, and Potawatomis came to British head-quarters at Amherstburg. The Sauk chief who acted as speaker explained that they had come to consult their father over a message from the Sioux who, sending a war pipe, had asked the Sauks and their allies to halt their wars with the Osages across the Mississippi and confront the "new white nation now encroaching on our Lands and wishing to be considered as our father." The Sioux went on to use the old confederation language of a common dish and spoon to symbolize their holding the land in common, and compared the happiness of those people living under the British to the insecurity of those living under the Americans.[78]

Accompanying this war pipe was a pipe of peace sent to the British by the village chiefs of the Sioux. The Sioux claimed a confederation of ten nations that they wished to unite with the British alliance. This confederation already included the Sauks and Fox, some Chippewas and Ottawas, the Kickapoos, and the Potawatomis of Chicago, where the warriors "have taken charge of the affairs of our nation and we must abide by the determination of the war chiefs." Against the "White Devil with his mouth wide open ready to take possession of our lands by any means," these westerly villages were ready to act together. By the next year, the Americans feared war with the Kickapoos and Sauks, but the British declined to give a decisive answer to this invitation to alliance. For now, they urged peace with the United States. These western villagers reiterated their desire for British aid in 1806, and nearly annually thereafter, only to be put off and urged to maintain the peace. Even when warfare between the Sioux and the western Algonquians resumed, the western villages remained hostile to the Americans.[79]

---

[78] Meeting of Sauks, Foxes, northern Ottawas and Potawatomis held at Amherstburg, June 8, 1805, Sir John Johnson Correspondence, Supt. General's Office, v. 10, IA, RG 10, PAC; Secretary of War to Harrison, June 20, 1805, National Archives, WD, SO, LS, IA, B:56. By 1806 the United States was worried about hostilities with these western Indians, Secretary of War to Harrison and Hull, June 11, 1806, National Archives, WD, SO, LS, IA, B:233; Secretary of War to Johnston, Feb. 18, 1811, NA, WD, SO, LS, IA, C:64.

[79] Meeting of Sauks, Foxes, northern Ottawas and Potawatomis held at Amherstburg, June 8, 1805, Sir John Johnson Correspondence, Supt. General's Office, v. 10, IA, RG 10, PAC. For alliance, see Claus to Green, July 24, 1805, Supt. General's Office, v. 10, IA, RG 10, PAC. A Sioux attack on the Sauks apparently ended, at least temporarily, their connection with this confederation, Wells to Secretary of War, Apr. 20, 1808, Carter (ed.), *Territorial Papers*, 7:559.

For the fear of war, see Harrison to Jefferson, July 5, 1806, Esarey (ed.), *Harrison Messages*,

The Prophet tapped rather than created this hostility. As his message spread north across the Great Lakes and west into the prairies, it reached many who were already organizing to resist the Americans. Indeed, it is likely that the increasingly political bent of the Prophet's message in 1807 and 1808 came from the Chippewas, Sauks and Fox, Potawatomis, and others who visited him at Greenville and Prophetstown. His first reference to halting separate cessions of land came in 1808. He predicted that by fall "every nation from the west" would unite with him and cessions would cease. When Wells warned of possible hostilities, he cited the Prophet's calling on the western villagers – Sauks, Fox, Iowas, Winnebagos, and Menominees – and his reliance on Main Poc, the western Potawatomi war chief and shaman, to secure him aid. But the Prophet himself undermined the unity he anticipated. His failure to procure sufficient supplies for the people living at and visiting Tippecanoe led to famine, and famine brought disease. More than 160 Ottawas and Chippewas from Arbre Croche and other Michigan villages died at Prophetstown. The dead included the important Ottawa chief Little King, and the survivors accused the Prophet of being a fraud at best and a witch at worst. In April 1809, a small Ottawa and Chippewa war party, testing the Prophet's claim that the Master of Life would kill anyone who violated the peace of his village, murdered a woman and a child there. They boasted of the act, and nothing happened to them.[80]

The Prophet, already embroiled with the American chiefs who surrounded him and the Americans who feared him, now faced a war with northern villagers previously sympathetic to his message. But by 1809, he could look to the British for aid. Village conflicts once more merged with larger imperial conflicts, for by now war threatened between the United States and Great Britain. With the British attack on the American ship *Chesapeake* in June 1807, the United States and Great Britain had nearly gone to war. Thereafter, each sought Indian aid, or at least neutrality, in a conflict both expected. What happened in the villages once more mattered a great deal to imperial fathers. Although the British did not initially comprehend the strained relations between the Prophet and the Shawnee chiefs, they abandoned their charge that the Prophet was a French agent and became assiduous in courting his favor.[81]

---

195. For requests for answer and aid, see Claus to Grant, July 30, 1806, Lt. Governor's Office, Upper Canada, v. 1, IA, RG 10, PAC.

80 Edmunds, *The Shawnee Prophet*, 74–78. For death of Little Otter, see Elliott to?, May 19, 1809, Lt. Governor's Office, UC 1790–1816, v. 3, IA, RG 10, PAC. For murder, see Harrison to Secretary of War, 26 Apr. 1809, Esarey (ed.), *Harrison Messages*, 342–43, also May 3, 1809, *ibid.*, 345. For western villages, see Wells to Secretary of War, 6 Mar. 1808, Carter (ed.), *Territorial Papers*, 7:531. For quotation on western nations, see Wells to Secretary of War, *ibid.*, 7:558–60.

81 For visits of Sauks, Fox, Chippewas, Kickapoos, see Information had of Letourneau ... 21 May 1807, McKee Papers, MG 19 F 16, PAC. Note, too, the emphasis on land sales. Main

Gradually after 1808, first as the Prophet's agent and then as the leader of an Indian confederation, Tecumseh eclipsed his brother as the dominant Algonquian figure in the *pays d'en haut*. A man too often seen as unique and inexplicable, he was instead the culmination of the complicated village and imperial politics of the middle ground. In him the various strands of the politics of the *pays d'en haut* came together. He was a republican who sought to attract warriors from many groups to intertribal villages. He disavowed the chiefs; indeed, he threatened to execute them for betraying their people and selling the land. He was in this sense subversive, an underminer of village politics. He also, however, sought to restore a confederation that was a league of villages. He sought to attach the western villages to the old Brownstown confederation, which the British began to reinvigorate in 1808. The Wyandots entrusted him with the huge belt with which the British asked the Brownstown council to communicate to the west. And in 1810, Tecumseh and his brother persuaded the Wyandots to bring the great belt of the old confederation on to Prophetstown. Nor was Tecumseh's eventual attempt to unite the northern and southern Indians unique to him. It was an old Shawnee ambition, and as recently as 1808, Blackbeard, a Shawnee chief, had gone south "to feel the pulse" of the Cherokees and determine their stance in case of war. Tecumseh explained all this to Harrison with an irony derived from the middle ground: "The White people were unnecessarily alarmed at his [Tecumseh's] measures – that they really meant nothing but peace – the U. States had set him the example by forming a strict union amongst all the fires that compose their confederacy."[82]

Poc became an important ally of the Prophet during this period, Edmunds, *The Shawnee Prophet*, 63–65. For hostility of American chiefs, see Wells to Secretary of War, Apr. 20, 1808, Carter (ed.), *Territorial Papers*, 7:558–60.

For Prophet as French agent, see Johnson to Craig, Nov. 1807, Supt. General's Office, v. 11, John Johnson Corespondence, IA, RG 10, PAC. For strategy and solicitation, see Instructions to William Claus, Jan. 29, 1808, Supt. General's Office, v. 11; IA, RG 10; Claus to Lt. Governor Gore, Feb. 27, 1808, Claus Papers 9:177, PAC. Craig to Gore, May 11, 1808, Lt. Governors Office, UC. 1796–1816, v. 2, IA, RG 10, PAC.

For solicitation of other Shawnee chiefs – Captain Johnny, Blackbeard, and the Buffalo – see Claus to Selby, March 25, 1808, Claus Papers 9:184, PAC. For recognize rivalry with Prophet, see Claus to Selby, May 3, 1808, Claus Papers 9:192. PAC; Claus Diary, July 1–9, 1808, Claus Papers 9:207–10, PAC. See also Horsman, *Matthew Elliott*, 157–91. For Americans, see Jefferson to Chiefs of the Ottaways, Chippeways, Poutewattamies, Wiantos & Senecas of Sandusky, National Archives, Apr. 22, 1808, WD, SO, LS, IA, B:369; Wiandotts, Ottawas, Chippeways, Poutewatamies & Shawanese, Jan. 1809, National Archives, WD, SO, LS, IA, B:410.

82 For British and Brownstown Confederation, see Lt. Gov. Gore's Speech to Western Confederation, July 11, 1808, Supt. General's Office, v. 11, IA, RG 10, PAC. Gore to Craig, July 27, 1808, Supt. General's Office, v. 10, IA, RG 10, PAC. Tecumseh carried a belt from the Brownstown confederation west, Elliott to?, May 19, 1809, Lt. Governor's Office, UC 1790–1816, v. 3, IA, RG 10, PAC.

In 1810, the bulk of the warriors at Prophetstown were Kickapoos, Winnebagos, Potawatomis, and Shawnees, with some Chippewas and Ottawas, Harrison to Secretary of

Gradually and grudgingly, Tecumseh became a British-alliance chief. He had not forgotten the treachery of the British who had shut the gates of Fort Miami against Algonquian warriors after the Battle of Fallen Timbers. But out of necessity he once more allied himself to British soldiers. He wore a British uniform and, far more willingly, demanded that his warriors adopt European conventions in regard to the treatment of prisoners.[83]

His meteoric rise to power after 1809 came at the expense of the chiefs. In the Treaties of Fort Wayne and Vincennes, the Wabash and Delaware chiefs had made yet another cession to Harrison. The Wyandots simultaneously found their village sites threatened by the Americans, and they were unable to get satisfaction for people murdered by whites. Tecumseh and his brother responded by resurrecting the old confederation doctrine of the common ownership of land, of the *pays d'en haut* as a bowl with one spoon. He threatened the village chiefs with death for their cessions, and as far away as the Winnebago land, villages put aside their chiefs and let warriors and war chiefs govern affairs. When the Brownstown council met in 1810, the chiefs vowed to make no more cessions. And in a distant echo of 1806, Leatherlips, a Wyandot chief who opposed the Prophet, met his death as a witch.[84]

War, Apr. 25, 1810, Esarey (ed.), *Harrison Messages*, 417. For belt of confederation, see Harrison to Secretary of War, June 14, 1810, *ibid.*, 423–24. For his most famous statement against the chiefs, see Tecumseh's Speech to Governor Harrison, Aug. 20, 1810, Esarey (ed.), *Harrison's Messages*, 465–66.

For south, see Gore to Craig, July 27, 1808, Supt. General's Office, v. 10, IA, RG 10, PAC; Black Fox's Speech to Black Beard, March 26, 1809, McKee Papers, MG 19, F 10, PAC. For quotation on U.S., see Harrison to Secretary of War, Aug. 6, 1811, Esarey (ed.), *Harrison's Messages*, 541.

83 For Fort Miami, Gore to Craig, July 27, 1808, Supt. General's Office, v. 10, IA, RG 10, PAC.

84 For these cessions, see Journal of the Proceedings at the Indian Treaty at Fort Wayne and Vincennes, Sept. 1 to Oct. 27, 1809, Esarey (ed.), *Harrison's Messages*, 362–78. For chiefs and land, see Tecumseh's Speech to Governor Harrison, Aug. 20, 1810, *ibid.*, 465–66. Harrison to Secretary of War, Aug. 22, 1810, *ibid.*, 459–63. Harrison to Secretary of War, July 4, 1810, *ibid.*, 438–40. For Winnebagos, see Harrison to Secretary of War, Aug. 28, 1810, *ibid.*, 470–71; Elliott to?, July 11(?), 1811, Deputy Supt.'s Office, v. 27, IA, RG 10, PAC; Speech of Tehkumthai...Nov. 15, 1810, Deputy Supt.'s Office, v. 27, IA RG 10, PAC; Speech of Little Chief, Aug. 16, 1811, Ninian Edwards Papers, Chicago Historical Society. For Brownstown, see Harrison to Secretary of War, Dec. 24, 1810, *ibid.*, 497–500. Hull's Speech to the Different Nations, Sept. 3, 1810, Cass Papers, Clements Library. For Wyandots, land, see Jefferson to Ottoways, Chippeways, Poutewatomies, Wiandots and Shawanese, c. Jan. 1809, National Archives, WD, SO, LS, IA, B:418.; Speech of the principle chief of the Wiandots...30 Sept. 1809 (*sic*), Cass Papers, Clements Library. Wyandots to Governor Hull, n.d., Cass Papers, Clements Library; Harrison to Secretary of War, June 14, 1810, Esarey (ed.), *Harrison Messages*, 422–26. Heckewelder provides a distorted account of the death of Leatherlips. Tarhe was an enemy, not an agent, of the Prophet, Heckewelder, *History*, 298–99. The Americans resisted any attempts to strip the chiefs of their power to cede lands, Secretary of War to Hull, Dec. 5, 1810, NA, WD, SO, LS, IA C:53. Edmunds offers an excellent summary of Tecumseh's and the Prophet's activities, *Shawnee Prophet*, 67–93.

By 1810, the Algonquians and the British were following separate, but converging, trajectories leading to war with the Americans; the British fear was that the Indians would come into conflict with the Long Knives prematurely. This, despite the efforts of Tecumseh, is what happened when Harrison marched against Tippecanoe while Tecumseh was absent in the South. Harrison's victory at Tippecanoe came with significant losses and was, in the end, less of a defeat for the Indians than for Tenskwatawa, who had tested his supernatural powers against an American army and lost. The Americans supposed to be dead or dying from his magic fought back and, although they took heavy casualties, repelled the Algonquian attack. Tenskwatawa blamed the failure of his power on the menstruation of his wife. Unclean, she had polluted his medicine and sapped his strength. Only fear of the absent Tecumseh kept Tenskwatawa's life from being taken by angry warriors. Tenskwatawa's influence declined markedly after Tippecanoe. Tecumseh, seeking to rebuild his confederation's strength, placated the Americans, but he also strengthened his connections with the British through the Wyandot emissary Isadore Chene, a *métis* chief the Americans thought "more of a Frenchman than an Indian." To the west, the Potawatomis launched raids against the frontier. Potawatomi raids and Tecumseh's rebuilt confederacy both merged into a British alliance in the War of 1812.[85]

Briefly in 1812 and 1813, as in the closing days of the Revolution, the British and the Algonquians resurrected an alliance on the middle ground. Tecumseh struck the British general Isaac Brock as an extraordinary character: "A more sagacious or a more gallant Warrior does not I believe exist. He was the admiration of every one who conversed with him." For a time the imperial strategy for the defense of western Canada was a joint British-Algonquian strategy. But Brock died at Niagara, the two sieges of Fort Meigs failed, Perry cut the British supply lines, and Tecumseh watched the Algonquian goal of blocking American expansion yield to the British goal

---

[85] By June 1810, Harrison was contemplating a preemptive strike on the Prophet, Harrison to Secretary of War, June 14, 1810, Esarey (ed.), *Harrison Messages*, 422–26. By the next year he was convinced of hostilities, Harrison to Secretary of War, June 19, 1811, *ibid.*, 518–19; Harrison to Clark, June 19, 1811, Ninian Edwards Papers, Chicago Historical Society. Harrison acted with the clear authority and support of the president who thought the Prophet could be attacked and a general war avoided, Secretary of War, July 21, 1811, NA, WD, SO, LS, IA, C:90; Secretary of War to Harrison, Sept. 18, 1811, NA, WD, SO, LS, IA, C:112. For Tippecanoe and aftermath, see Edmunds, *The Shawnee Prophet*, 94–142. For Indian militance, see Elliott to Claus, July 9, 1810, Deputy Supt.'s Office, v. 27, IA, RG 10, PAC.; Elliott to Claus, June 10, 1810, Deputy Supt.'s Office, v. 27, IA, RG 10, PAC; Horsman, *Matthew Elliott*, 179–80.

For Prophet's failure, see Snelling to Harrison, Nov. 20, 1811, Esarey (ed.), *Harrison Messages*, 643–46; Edmund, *The Shawnee Prophet*, 115. On Chene, see Stickney to Hull, May 25, 1812, Esarey, *Harrison Messages*, 54.

of defending Canada. Tecumseh could in the end match only his eloquence against British incompetence, control of supplies, and larger imperial goals. The middle ground demanded a more effective balance than that.[86]

It would be an exaggeration to say the middle ground died in battle with Tecumseh at Malden. It died in bits and pieces, but with the death of Tecumseh, its attempt to rally failed. The imperial contest over the *pays d'en haut* ended with the War of 1812, and politically the consequence of Indians faded. They could no longer pose a major threat or be a major asset to an empire or a republic, and even their economic consequence declined with the fur trade. Tecumseh's death was a merciful one. He would not live to see the years of exile and the legacy of defeat and domination.[87]

---

[86] Brock to Lord Liverpool, 29 Aug. 1812, William Wood (ed.), *Select British Documents of the Canadian War of 1812*, 3 vols. (Toronto: Champlain Society, 1920), 1:508.
[87] For the final days of Tecumseh and the defeat of the British and the Indians, see John Sugden, *Tecumseh's Last Stand* (Norman: University of Oklahoma Press, 1985).

Epilogue: Assimilation and otherness

In different ways, both Anglo Americans and Algonquians subverted the middle ground in the nineteenth century. The compromises intrinsic in the middle ground yielded to stark choices between assimilation and otherness. Americans made Tecumseh and Tenskwatawa into symbols of the alternatives. Tecumseh, the paradoxical nativist who had resisted the Americans, became the Indian who was virtually white. He had, as his first American biographer put it, risen "above the prejudices and customs of his people."[1]

The remaking of Tecumseh and his assimilation into the mythology of Anglo-American society took its most enduring and revealing form in the Rebecca Galloway story. In that legend, Tecumseh, dark and black-haired, falls in love with the blond, blue-eyed Rebecca. She reads to him from the Bible and from Shakespeare and tells him of world history. Tecumseh learns of Moses, Hamlet, and Alexander the Great – figures to whom his Anglo-American opponents will later compare him. Tecumseh asks Rebecca to marry him, and she accepts, but only on the condition that he give up his life as an Indian and adopt her people's "mode of life and dress." He sadly refuses. They never meet again.

The Galloway story – still retold each summer as part of a tourist pageant at Chillicothe, Ohio – "explains" Tecumseh by explaining how a man of such vision, such virtue, such overarching abilities, and such keen intelligence arose among "savages." He was a Moses; he was an Alexander; and, in the end, he was a Hamlet, dying to avenge not only his father, killed at Point Pleasant, but his race. Americans named their towns and their children after him. And they were not wrong to see parts of themselves in him. In life, a British major, John Richardson, called him "a savage such as civilization herself might not blush to acknowledge as her child," thus recognizing unwittingly and backhandedly the common world that produced him. But in the American adulation of Tecumseh, this common world disappeared. Tecumseh became a miracle, a figure of genius who arose among savages.

---

[1] For an excellent overview of the Tecumseh mythology, see R. David Edmunds, *Tecumseh and the Quest for Indian Leadership* (Boston: Little, Brown, 1984), 216–25. For quotation, see Benjamin Drake, *Life of Tecumseh* (New York: Arno Press, 1969), 226.

His inspiration, received at the feet of Rebecca Galloway, came from European traditions. When the eminent ethnologist James Mooney sought to convey his talents, he compared his eloquence to Henry Clay's and his logic to Daniel Webster's. The middle ground that explained Tecumseh disappeared; culturally cannibalizing him for the same reasons that Algonquians ate the hearts of their admired enemies, Americans absorbed Tecumseh. And once they had assimilated him, the world that produced him ceased to matter.

Tenskwatawa embodied the fate of what remained of the middle ground. Tenskwatawa became the ultimate other, the alien savage. At the height of Tenskwatawa's influence, Jefferson regarded him as more rogue than fool, but by the 1820s Lewis Cass thought him "the dupe of his own feelings. . . . His conduct was certainly incompatible with any rational policy." Tecumseh died and was assimilated. Tenskwatawa lived to confront his otherness.

Tenskwatawa, despite his origins in the common world of the *pays d'en haut*, despite the Shaker and other Christian influences on his teaching, and despite his own early attempts at accommodation, had cultivated otherness. He had worked to disengage the white and Indian societies; he had tried to restrict the sway of the common world. He appears, however, to have had no inkling of how exotic and alien the Americans would make him. In seeking to escape his exile in Canada after the War of 1812, Tenskwatawa opened negotiations with Lewis Cass. Cass cultivated Tenskwatawa in order to make him an agent of removal, a policy based on the premise that whites and Indians could not coexist alongside each other until Indians were ready to be assimilated fully into American society. Tenskwatawa became an advocate of removal. He did so for his own reasons, seeking in the tradition of the middle ground to use whites to enhance his own standing against his old rival Black Hoof, who opposed removal.[2]

For nearly two centuries, negotiations and conversations such as those that took place between Tenskwatawa, Cass, and Cass's young private secretary, Charles Trowbridge, had taken place on the middle ground. But now, although the Americans treated the Prophet courteously, he had become for them an exotic. In 1824, Tenskwatawa sat down with Charles Trowbridge, who also served as the assistant secretary of the Indian Department, to record Shawnee "traditions." Trowbridge was not really interested in talking to the aged and one-eyed Shawnee. He was interested in examining him, getting information from him, in recording an already nearly vanished past. He, not Tenskawatawa, would determine what in-

[2] For Jefferson, see quotation in Drake, *Tecumseh*, 219. For Cass quotation, see Vernon Kinietz and Erminie W. Voegelin (eds.), *Shawnese Traditions: C. C. Trowbridge's Account, Occasional Contributions from the Museum of Anthropology of the University of Michigan*, no. 9 (Ann Arbor: University of Michigan Press, 1939), xvi.

formation was necessary and meaningful. He used a standard list of questions sent to Indian superintendents across the country. He quizzed
Tenskwatawa on Shawnee kinship, government, and customs. Tenskwatawa
spontaneously tried to break through the American's often odd inquiries
(Are there animals the Shawnees never eat? Have any actions been fought in
canoes? Do Shawnees ever visit one another to converse?) and tell stories.
He constructed the stories from traditional Shawnee elements, but the
stories were very much creations of the teller, reflecting not the timeless
Shawnee understanding that Trowbridge sought but Tenskwatawa's own
understanding of the Shawnee experiences and their current condition.[3]

An old, one-eyed man, rejected as a witch by the majority of his own
people, who were themselves now scattered and broken, told the stories
to a curious but uncomprehending white man. Many of the tales that
Tenskwatawa told, not surprisingly, were filled with figures whose experience imaged those of Tecumseh and Tenskwatawa. The images were not
simple – indeed, from one tale to another, the images reversed themselves –
but this makes them all the more compelling. For these two men were not
simple. The brothers were both exiles from the Shawnees and leaders of the
Shawnees, saviors of the Shawnees and killers of the Shawnees. They were
remembered, respectively, as a hero and as a witch.[4]

Two stories in particular evoked not only Tenskwatawa and Tecumseh
but also an attempt to get at the meaning of the dramatic changes that
followed the Revolution. The first was "Pakilawa," or "Thrown Away," a
tale of abandonment and return. Abandoned by his father, other relatives,
and his people, Pakilawa, a small boy, had to survive in a deserted village.
Only his youngest sister, who hid fire for him, and his spirit guardian,
Brother Dog, took pity on him. But with their aid, and using the castaway
debris of the village, the child grew into a strong hunter within a year. He
returned to the village of the people who had abandoned him. Failing to
recognize him and ignorant of his spirit guardian, they mocked his weapons

---

[3] James Clifton points this out in his excellent afterword to *Star Woman and Other Shawnee Tales*
(Lanham, Md.: University Press of America, 1984), 63–68. A summary of Tenskwatawa's
answers to Cass's list of questions is in Kinietz and Voegelin (eds.), *Shawnese Traditions*,
1–59. For the list of questions that Trowbridge worked from, see C. A. Weslager, *The
Delaware Indian Westward Migration with the Texts of Two Manuscripts (1821–22) Responding to
General Lewis Cass's Inquiries About Lenape Culture and Language* (Wallingford, Pa.: Middle
Atlantic Press, 1978), 89–191. For Trowbridge, see Vernon Kinietz (ed.), *Meearmeear
Traditions: Occasional Contributions from the Museum of Anthropology of the University of
Michigan*, no. 7 (Ann Arbor: University of Michigan Press, 1938), Kinietz (ed.), *Meearmeear
Traditions*, ix–x.
[4] For Shawnee memories of Tenskwatawa and Tecumseh, see Kinietz and Voegelin (eds.),
Shawnese Traditions, xi–xii. For modern Shawnees, see James H. Howard, *Shawnee!: The
Ceremonialism of a Native American Indian Tribe and Its Cultural Background* (Athens: Ohio
University Press, 1981), 198.

(which had been their weapons) until they discovered the mound of meat and skins he had obtained. He had been successful where they had failed. Although his father attempted to welcome him, Pakilawa acknowledged only his sister as his relation. With his guardian's aid, Pakilawa became a successful war leader, and his father, grieving over his crime and Pakilawa's rejection of him, resigned his office as hokima, or chief, to Pakilawa. The warriors, however, insisted on Pakilawa's status as a war leader. And so Pakilawa did "an uncommon thing," and assumed both offices.[5]

In the second story, "Hamotaleniwa Maneto," Tenskwatawa reversed the basic elements of the Pakilawa tale. Here again the hero is a child, the boy Pthe?kwa, but he lives with his grandmother and uncle. The family is threatened by a one-eyed cannibal monster and his dog, who take their victims to an island where they are lost to their kin and people. The cannibal monster forces his prisoners to hunt game that they cannot possibly find, and, as they fail, they become the game. The monster devours them. Only Pthe?kwa, the hero, with the aid of a spirit helper, a wren, and a unique weapon, can kill game. He not only saves his uncle and the other prisoners but revives the victims of the cannibals. They become a clan, that is, relatives who follow him.

Of all the tales he could have told to a white man, Tenskwatawa told stories of men isolated from, or abandoned by, their people who return triumphant, of people threatened and redeemed, of one-eyed monsters who serve as distorted reflections of the one-eyed teller of the tale himself. For in the Pakilawa tale the hero's plight and triumph reflect Tecumseh's and Tenskwatawa's own numerous "desertions" by parents; by the Kispoko, their own Shawnee division whose members migrated across the Mississippi; by the bulk of the remaining Shawnees, who deserted the cause of resistance to the Americans in 1795. But the hero remains divinely sanctioned, for the boy and the guardian dog resemble not just Tecumseh and Tenskwatawa but also Haapochkilaweetha, the grandson of the female creator of the Shawnee world, who is always accompanied by his dog. The tale communicates on another level, too. For the larger desertion is not that of Tecumseh and Tenskwatawa but that of the Algonquians by their British father, who left them alone to struggle against the Americans. Faced with the resurgent Tecumseh, this father, too, resigned his leadership to him, and Tecumseh became both a war leader and a civil leader.

In the second tale, resolution is also achieved but at the price, in a sense, of Tenskwatawa himself. The cannibal monster, with his one eye, evokes the

---

[5] The story is given in James Clifton, *Star Woman*. I thank George Cornell for pointing out the correspondence between the boy and Tenskwatawa and Tecumseh. To a Shawnee, the motif of a boy and his dog would immediately have been associated with the grandson of the female creator, Papoothkwe, and his dog.

one-eyed Tenskwatawa. The imagery of the monster and his dog reverses the conventional image of the creator's grandson and his dog. Tenskwatawa becomes, in effect, another figure who exists in Shawnee mythology, the twin of Haapochkilaweetha, his evil brother. The one-eyed monster, the devourer of his own people, the evil twin, is particularly apt because many Americans believed, incorrectly, that Tenskwatawa was the twin of Tecumseh. If Tenskwatawa was a witch, then his elimination was necessary for the Shawnees to survive, just as the cannibal monster's elimination is necessary. His elimination comes at the hand of Pthe?kwa, who, like Haapochkilaweetha, lives with his grandmother, and like Haapochkilaweetha he ignores her warnings. But Pthe?kwa possesses powers associated with Kokomthena, or Our Grandmother, the Creator. The food he cooks, for example, expands so as to be virtually inexhaustible.[6]

Insofar as they embody sacred elements, the Prophet's tales thus stand in relation to his life as dreams stood in relation to the lives of warriors. When John Heckewelder asked old Delaware warriors how they accomplished their deeds, the warriors "uniformly answered that as they knew beforehand [that is, from dreams and visions] what they could do, they did it of course." So, in the same sense, the Prophet, Tenskwatawa, knew that his tales, mirroring as they did the stories of creation, had a truth of their own, a truth mirrored in his life and in his brother's life.[7]

But Tenskwatawa's stories are also revealing and moving on another level. They were told to whites, and the teller, Tenskwatawa, had become an exotic. He was no longer a figure familiar to whites, although whites had lived among Indians for nearly two centuries and were, in multiple senses of the word, their relatives. Instead, Tenskwatawa had reverted to a *sauvage*. Trowbridge was studying him, preserving him and his people against the day they would disappear. From creators of the middle ground, from people who strove to maintain the necessary understanding of a common world, the Algonquians had become objects of study in a world of white learning. That Tenskwatawa tried to break through Trowbridge's methodical and relentless search for isolated facts in order to tell stories that communicated meaning is not surprising. That he failed is not surprising either.

Stories and dreams had lost most of their power. It was a decline Tenskwatawa and those who had come before him had at once opposed and

---

[6] See James H. Howard, *Shawnee!*, 166. Kokomthena is also known as the Cloud Woman. Kokomthena became the most prominent Shawnee deity early in the nineteenth century. She appears to have replaced a male creator, Howard, *Shawnee!*, 166–70. Howard says that the modern Shawnees make Tenskwatawa the equivalent of the evil twin, 198.

Pthe?kwa is Paapooøkwaki, or Cloud Woman, see C. F. Voegelin, *The Shawnee Female Deity*, Yale University Publications in Anthropology, no. 10 (repr., New Haven: Human Relations Area Files Press, 1970). The figure "?" in Pthe?kwa signifies a glottal stop.

[7] Heckewelder, *History*, 246.

helped precipitate. For Algonquians, history had long been the realm in which dreams and myths took on tangible forms. But history – because Europeans had appeared and because the middle ground existed – was also the realm in which dreams had to be tested against both contingent events and the competing conceptions of people to whom dreams did not matter.[8]

On the middle ground, the landscape of the *pays d'en haut* had long ceased to be just a dreamscape where dreams took physical shape. As the eighteenth century waned, the *pays d'en haut* had increasingly become a place where dreams failed to materialize at all. Algonquians continued to dream, but it was as if they dreamed of the dead – people who never returned. Now they dreamed of once-familiar animals and places, but those animals and places remained trapped in their dreams. In many villages, dreaming of beaver or dreaming of deer eventually could not yield material beaver or deer, because beaver and deer were disappearing from large sections of the *pays d'en haut* by the early nineteenth century. They had vanished both at the hands of white hunters and at the hands of Algonquian hunters themselves, who killed them for their skins and left their rotting carcasses to the wolves.

Once there had been a complicated world that could be both dreamscape and landscape, that contained both masters of the game and the fur trade, prophets and missionaries, villages like Detroit and villages like Tippecanoe. This world, pulled forward by Europeans and Indians in tandem, vanished from most of what had been the *pays d'en haut*. The middle ground itself withered and died. The Americans arrived and dictated. Tenskwatawa was left to sit and relate jumbled and isolated facts in answer to a white man's odd questions although, but a short time before, those facts had been part of a common world shared with white men. The French savant Volney, so unlike the French habitants and traders, had prefigured this world when he had compiled his vocabularies and collected his facts about Algonquian life. He had concluded: "These men are in the state of wild animals, which cannot be tamed after they have reached a mature age." Volney had announced the return of the *sauvage*. Once Tenskwatawa had been a human being whom whites had spoken to, listened to, argued with, and feared. He was now but an object of study. When Tenskwatawa tried to break through, to tell his stories as if the middle ground survived, Trowbridge dutifully recorded them, filed them away, and forgot them. He forwarded the questionnaire to Washington, where its data were sorted and compiled.[9]

[8] For significance of dreams as "revelations from God," see Zeisberger, *History*, 140.
[9] Volney, *A View of the Soil and Climate*, 377.

Index